CW00801371

To George Martin
with best wishes
for good listening
Leo Beranek
Jan 23, '01

Concert and Opera Halls

How They Sound

Concert and Opera Halls

How They Sound

Leo Beranek

Published for the
Acoustical Society of America
through the
American Institute of Physics

Acoustical Society of America
500 Sunnyside Boulevard
Woodbury, NY 11797-2999

Library of Congress Cataloging-in-Publication Data
Beranek, Leo Leroy, 1914–
Concert and opera halls: how they sound / Leo L. Beranek.
p. cm.
Includes bibliographical references and indexes.
ISBN 1-56396-530-5
1. Architectural acoustics. 2. Music-halls. 3. Theaters. I. Title.
NA2800.B39 1996 95-35793
725' .81--dc20 CIP

10 9 8 7 6 5 4 3 2 1

CONTENTS

Preface

Concert and Opera Halls: How They Sound is dedicated to all who love "good music," whether they perform or listen, or participate in its creation. Compiling this book has been a labor of love for me. It has entailed years of work to assemble the architectural, scientific, and musical attributes of the 76 concert and opera halls that I have studied in 22 countries. The results of my efforts are discussed here in text, illustrative charts, photographs, and drawings.

Questions that the musical aficionado invariably ask are: How do all these concert halls compare? Which of them are among the world's best? Is it possible to rank them for acoustical quality? Why do so many old halls remain popular while some newer ones have already undergone extensive renovation? In this book I have sought answers to these questions.

The early chapters of the book propose a common language that should enable the acoustical, musical, and lay worlds to converse with each other in the same vocabulary. The heart of the book portrays the characteristics of 66 concert halls and 10 opera houses. In order to rank order these halls, two procedures were devised to permit their comparison. In the first test, a group of conductors, music critics, and sound engineers that I interviewed provided a base of informed opinion. The categories of quality that were deduced were comparable to the responses made to a written questionnaire mailed to a different group of musicians and music critics as reported in Appendix 3.

The remaining chapters address the interests of architects and acousticians and deal in greater detail with the 76 halls studied. For the professional acoustician, a detailed tabulation of computer-based measurements on 80 halls is presented in Appendix 4.

Throughout this book my goal has been to enlarge our understanding of the acoustical attributes that a hall needs in order to meet today's high standards of acoustics, comfort, and originality—without resort to obvious mimicking of older successes, the dream of every architect.

Quite frankly, musical acoustics still calls upon art as well as science. The science lies in applying to the design of new halls the known acoustical attributes derived from measures on existing halls; and the art lies in judging and applying those acoustical attributes that are still unmeasurable. Knowing that the conclusions reached here will be revised and reshaped over time, I offer them as milestones on the road to a fuller understanding of a very complex subject.

CREDITS AND ACKNOWLEDGMENTS

It gives me great pleasure to acknowledge the assistance I have received from conductors, composers, musicians, orchestra and opera directors, hall managers, architects, acousticians, and musical friends, numbering in the hundreds. All have contributed to the contents of this book.

I am particularly indebted to the many colleagues who supplied me with the bulk of the acoustical data: Takayuki Hidaka, Toshiyuki Okano, and Norita Nishihara of the Takenaka Research and Development Institute of Chiba, Japan; Michael Barron of Bath University, England; John S. Bradley of the Acoustics Laboratory of the National Research Council of Ottawa, Canada; and Anders C. Gade of the Technical University of Denmark. Much of the work by Bradley and Gade received support from the Concert Hall Research Group, a USA-based consortium of acoustical practitioners. A valued contribution is Appendix 3 by Fergus R. Fricke of the University of Sydney, Australia, which contains the hall rank-orderings resulting from the written and mailed questionnaire.

To two men, Richard Shnider and the late Wilfred Malmlund, I am beholden for the drawings of the 76 halls in Chapter 6. Malmlund executed 36 of them for inclusion in *Music, Acoustics, and Architecture* (Beranek, Wiley, 1962). Richard Shnider rendered the drawings for the 40 additional halls in this book and made modifications as needed to the older drawings. Laura Selvitella prepared the figures in the other chapters.

Geraldine Stevens applied her consummate editorial talents to making the first five chapters, which are especially directed to the musical world, an understandable version of my original manuscript.

Finally I wish to thank my wife, Gabriella, for her patience while I sat at my 1992 PC computer pounding out seemingly endless correspondence and drafts of chapters—80 hours a week for three years.

Leo Beranek
975 Memorial Drive, Suite 804
Cambridge, MA 02138

◇1◇

Acoustics and Music

ACOUSTICS AND COMPOSITION

Music is sound or a combination of sounds that varies continuously or discontinuously with time, usually rhythmically, changing in pitch, timbre, and loudness in such a way as to communicate something to listeners in its own terms. The composition and performance of music are arts.

Acoustics, taken in the broadest sense, is the science of sound. Resonance, frequency (pitch), amplitude, wave reflections and delay times—these are some of the things about which acousticians ask questions and formulate answers. In the sense that acoustics is referred to in this book, it is defined as those attributes of a space that affect the production, transmission, and perception of music or speech.

The art of music and the science of sound must fuse if criteria are to be established for the design of halls in which music is to be played, since the experience of music can never be divorced from the acoustics of the space in which it is performed. Depending on how the hall affects the sounds they hear, the musicians play or sing differently, both consciously and unconsciously, adapting the performance to the acoustics. The auditorium transfers the music to the listeners, preserving the musical qualities of timbre, pitch, clarity, balance and dynamic range; the hall must contribute fullness of tone, loudness, spaciousness, envelopment, intimacy, clarity and a wide range of crescendo and decrescendo. A superior space enhances the music in some ways, without detracting from it in others.

One objective of this book is to define criteria for the design of halls to house the presentation of music. A first step in this quest has been to interview musicians, music critics and critical concert-goers on what constitutes good acoustics; in other words, which halls do they prefer and which do they find of inferior quality. As expected, musicians and experienced listeners expressed a preference for performing and hearing the works of J. S. Bach and his predecessors in small halls with relatively low reverberation times, and the richly orchestrated symphonic compositions of the late nineteenth and early twentieth centuries in larger, relatively reverberant halls.

This agreement bolsters the view that many musical compositions seem to have been written for performance in particular musical settings. Thursten Dart, the musicologist wrote [*The Interpretation of Music*, Hutchinson's University Library, Hutchinson House, London, pp. 56–57 (1954)]:

> But even a superficial study shows that early composers were very aware of the effect on their music of the surroundings in which it was to be performed, and that they deliberately shaped their music accordingly. Musical acoustics may be roughly divided into "resonant," "room," and "outdoor." Plainsong is resonant music; so is the harmonic style of Léonin and Pérotin....Pérotin's music, in fact is perfectly adapted to the acoustics of the highly resonant cathedral (Notre Dame, Paris) for which it was written....Gabrieli's music for brass consort is resonant, written for the Cathedral of St. Mark's; music for brass consort by Hassler or Matthew Lock is open-air music, using quite a different style from the same composers' music for stringed instruments, designed to be played indoors. Purcell distinguished in style between the music he wrote for Westminster Abbey and the music he wrote for the Chapel Royal; both styles differ from that of his theatre music, written for performance in completely "dead" surroundings. The forms used by Mozart and Haydn in their chamber and orchestral music are identical; but the details of style (counterpoint, ornamentation, rhythm, the layout of chords and the rate at which harmonies change) will vary according to whether they are writing room-music, concert-music or street-music.

Such a list could be extended indefinitely, though it is doubtful whether the list would include all the composers of the present day.

Richard Wagner composed and orchestrated his operas from the *Ring* onward while imagining how they would sound in the auditory conditions of the Bayreuth Festspielhaus. Frederic Spotts (*Bayreuth*, Yale University Press, 1994, pp. 5, 11) relates in detail the linkage of the acoustics of the Festspielhaus to Wagner's composing—parts of which I shall quote or paraphrase here.

> "The *Ring* and *Parsifal* are Bayreuth's particular specialities. The Festspielhaus was built for the *Ring*, while *Parsifal* was scored with its

acoustics in mind. And nowhere else are the two works given in such ideal conditions." The novelty is the covered pit. "The forward cowling was originally intended to shield the auditorium from reflected light from the pit while the rear overhang was added in 1882 for acoustical purposes [see the discussion of the Bayreuth Festspielhaus in Chapter 6]. The effect is...to create a sound that is fully blended and balanced. Because the low frequencies escape from the pit more readily than high ones, the orchestral sound is exceptionally dark and silky." Wagner was able "...to create the type of sound and the constant, subtle shifting of instrumental colour and the balance between voice and orchestra that he desired." Moreover, the subdued orchestra did not override the singers, thus making his productions more dramatic than the usual operas. Wagner even said,

> " '...after creating the invisible orchestra, I would now like to invent the invisible theatre,'—adding with sardonic wit, 'and the inaudible orchestra.' "

An example of considerable interest is provided by Daniel Pinkham:

> Music that I have composed for King's Chapel in Boston is in a style which might sound muddy when performed in a reverberant concert hall but which sounds at its best in this rather dry environment, which transmits the details of each line with crystalline clarity while still providing a useful blend for the various lines.
>
> In writing scores for moving pictures and TV, which are to be performed in acoustically dead recording studios, this approach must be carried even further, since any persistence of sound must be deliberately written into the music. When I was preparing my *Easter Cantata for Chorus, Brass and Percussion,* the rehearsals were held in Jordan Hall, Boston, which is fairly live. For the actual performance in a TV studio, I found that the only way to cope with the dead acoustics was to permit the percussion instruments to ring as long as they would, and this gave to the *whole sound* the impression of adequate reverberation. As a result of this experience, I have written my *Concertante No. 3 for Organ and Percussion Orchestra* so that the after-ring of the percussion following each phrase is deliberately carried over into the beginning of the next phrase; in a dead hall this will compensate for the lack of reverberation, while in a live hall it may either enhance the reverberant sound of the room or the percussion ring may be curtailed at the will of the performers to minimize confusion. On the other hand, I

> have found great difficulty, even with highly experienced musicians in performing in a live hall some music which had originally been written for the dead acoustics of the TV studio.

Some composers appear not to be fully aware of the interrelation between acoustics and their music. For example, a writer who composes at the piano in his studio may fail to imagine adequately the acoustics of the hall and may indicate metronomic markings that, while appropriate in his dead studio, are so fast as to be impossible to perform in a reverberant hall. Boris Goldowsky, pianist and conductor, stated [High Fidelity, Vol. 11, p. 28 (April 1961)]:

> Verdi, for instance, could hardly have brought a metronome to an actual performance of La Traviata and estimated the tempo while the opera was in progress. He undoubtedly arrived at his metronomic markings by playing the score at home on the piano, probably singing the vocal lines to himself, with the result that ... the home performance—ignoring the acoustics of the hall, the natural gravitational pull of the orchestra, and the effort of a professional singer to project the voice with full intensity—was considerably faster than the real thing.... Verdi's indication of 108 to the dotted quarter for "Non sapete quale affeto" is impossible. Now, the opening of [Beethoven's] Hammerklavier Sonata is noted 138 to the half note, which is so unmanageable you think it must have been marked by a superman or a madman. But, when you hum it, it seems exactly right.

Clearly there is a strong relation between the composition and the performance of music on one hand and the acoustics of the halls in which it is played on the other. Let us look deeper into the historical styles of music and the acoustics best suited to them.

At the outset, it is apparent that many early composers were constrained in their choice of musical material by the acoustics available to them for performance. It is certainly not a coincidence that Gregorian chant sounds best in acoustics similar to those of the medieval cathedrals in which it was originally performed—where the reverberation time may be as long as 5 to 10 sec.[1] For example, as Thurston Dart pointed out, the composer Giovanni Gabrieli, who was organist of St. Mark's Basilica at the turn of the seventeenth century, wrote chordal music in slow tempo for antiphonal choirs and assemblies of brass or wind instruments, music particularly well suited to the

[1]*In lay terms, reverberation time is the number of seconds it takes for a loud sound in a room to die to inaudibility after its source is abruptly turned off.*

acoustics of a large reverberant church. It can be argued that between 1600 and 1900 there was a relation between architecture and music in Europe, and that the music of each of the stylistic periods—Renaissance, Baroque, Classical, and Romantic—coincided with a contemporary acoustical environment sympathetic to its performance (Forsyth, 1985). Indeed, only since 1900 and the advent of radio, recordings, television, and a variety of available concert halls and opera houses, has the composer had no clearly defined acoustics peculiar to his own time for which to write!

Organ music is somewhat different. It can hardly be assigned to "different periods" of composition, since a similar form is common to the work of all great organ composers. Nearly all such music benefits from the flattery of a long reverberation period.

Baroque period

The term Baroque is a convenient designation for the style of contrapuntal music written between 1600 and approximately 1750, and best exemplified by Bach and Handel in the north of Europe and Correlli and Vivaldi in Italy. These hundred and fifty years witnessed the evolution of music from an unaccompanied choral song to a more highly rhythmic, harmonic-thematic balance, where voice and instrument frequently combined in concert, and the parts were not all of equal melodic interest. Another aspect of Baroque music is the spacing of instrumental colors; each movement confined to a fixed palette, the variety occurred only from one movement to another. In spite of differences in the music written by hundreds of composers scattered over much of Europe, it is possible to speak of a Baroque style for the purposes of acoustical analysis.

A conspicuous characteristic of the late Baroque period is several independent melodic lines, played or sung simultaneously, the combination emphasizing the equal importance of several voices rather than a single accompanied solo melody. The independence of the melodic lines may be heightened by being given to instruments of contrasting timbre. The sound is light, clear, and transparent. In Baroque music the detail is important and no portion of the sound should mask another.

Leonard Bernstein said in his *The Joy of Music* [Simon and Schuster, New York, pp. 232–233 (1959)]:

> Counterpoint *is* melody, only accompanied by one or more additional melodies, running along at the same time....The art of counterpoint fixes rules for making two or more melodic lines go well together....this music is difficult for us to listen to. But it's only a question of our having been

> spoiled by the music we hear most of the time, music which emphasizes harmony instead of counterpoint. In other words, we are used to hearing melody on top, with chords supporting it underneath like pillars—melody and harmony, a tune and its accompaniment....But [in Bach's time and earlier] people used to listen to music differently. The ear was conditioned to hear *lines*, simultaneous melodic lines rather than chords. That was the natural way of music, strange though it seems to us. Counterpoint came before harmony which is a comparatively recent phenomenon.

What can we say about the acoustical environment for the performance of secular music in Bach's time? Baroque orchestral music was usually performed in relatively small rooms with hard, reflecting walls, the rectangular ballroom of a palace, for instance, which had considerable intimacy and, when occupied, a reverberation time longer than that of a conventional living room, yet low—under 1.5 sec.

Concerts were given either in music rooms or in small theaters like the Altesresidenz Theater in Munich, which was opened in 1753. In such a room the music sounded intimate because of the many nearby sound-reflecting surfaces, and when an audience was present the reverberation time was short. Thus music played there had high definition and low fullness of tone.

The Baroque composer was familiar with these acoustical environments, and the music he wrote was scaled to them. Even today, we prefer to listen to this highly articulated music in a small room, acoustically intimate, with fairly low reverberation time.

Baroque sacred music is more difficult to relate to its environment than secular music. Most of the important churches of the eighteenth century were very large and highly reverberant, and the musical forms of earlier times, such as the plainchant, continued to be heard in them. On the other hand, a large body of the sacred music of this period was written for performance in private royal or ducal chapels with low reverberation times that make possible the brisk tempos of Bach's early fugues. Also the many converted and newly built Lutheran churches, in which the congregation occupied galleries as well as the main floor, and for which Bach composed many of his choral works, had a moderate reverberation—considerably less than that of the medieval cathedral. Hope Bagenal, architectural acoustician of England, wrote,

> The reducing of reverberation in Lutheran churches by the inserted galleries, thus enabling string parts to be heard and distinguished and allowing a brisk tempo, was the most important single fact in the history of music because it lead directly to the *St. Matthew Passion* and the *B-Minor Mass.*

Bach wrote some of his church music for this type of church. While he was cantor of the Thomaskirche in Leipzig (a church about which a great deal is known) he wrote many of his large works, including the *B-Minor Mass* and the *St. Matthew Passion*. From available lithographs, and from descriptions of the tapestries, altars, and other art works, we can estimate the acoustical qualities of the Thomaskirche. With a full congregation, the reverberation time must have been about 1.6 sec at mid-frequencies and, when it was partly filled, a little over 2 sec. The Thomaskirche was rebuilt during the nineteenth century with a higher ceiling. Today it has a reverberation time at mid-frequencies with full audience of about 1.9 sec [L. Keibs and W. Kuhl, "Zur Akustik der Thomaskirche in Leipzig," *Acustica*, Vol. 9, pp. 365–370 (No. 5, 1959)]. The original reverberation time of 1.6 sec is short for a church—a dry environment for ecclesiastical organ and choral music, as we would call it today.

Classical period

From 1750 until perhaps 1820 European audiences enjoyed music written in the style called "Classical." This was the period of the great symphonies of Haydn, Mozart, and Beethoven. In the eighteenth century, music was still commissioned by the court and the church, but a wider secular appeal now gave a new impetus to the composer. Publishers of music, entrepreneurs, and purveyors of public entertainment all increased the composer's area of influence and imposed changing demands upon him.

The most important development in the Classical period, from an acoustical point of view, was the appearance of the Classical symphony and sonata. These musical forms tied into a single unit, a number of independent musical ideas, some of them related, some contrasting. The way in which the ideas were put together—the structure of the music—sometimes became even more important than the musical material itself. Characteristic of the Classical period is a diminished contrapuntal emphasis, following the operatic idea of accompanied melody rather than the interweaving of equal parts that characterizes a Brandenburg Concerto. The strings carried the main part of the melodic material, but as the woodwind passages became more prominent, they also grew in importance. Larger movements were emphasized by bringing in the full orchestra.

The first real concert halls were built in the last half of the eighteenth century, and they showed the influence of the court halls. For example, the Holywell Music Room in Oxford, England, which was completed in 1748 and has recently been restored, seats about 300 persons. When it is fully occupied its reverberation time is about 1.5 sec at mid-frequencies. The Altes Gewandhaus, which stood in Leipzig from 1780 until it was razed in 1894, seated about 400 persons and, when fully occupied, had a reverberation time of not more than 1.3 sec at mid-frequencies. The rectangular-shaped Redoutensaal of Vienna, which stood in Beethoven's time, seated an audience of about 400 people and had reverberation time, with full audience, of about 1.4 sec at mid-frequencies.

By the end of the eighteenth century, public concerts became more popular, owing mainly to historical and sociological developments but perhaps also to the new musical style of the Classical period. Throughout the eighteenth century, concerts had been performed in London and Paris, but it was not until the turn of the century that concert music began to appear as public entertainment in Leipzig, Berlin, Vienna, Stockholm, and elsewhere. Significantly, twelve of Haydn's symphonies were composed between 1791 and 1795 especially for Salomon's series of concerts at the Hanover Square Room in London.

The gradual rise in popularity of orchestral concerts led, toward the middle of the nineteenth century, to the construction of the first large halls specifically designed for concerts. These halls also had longer reverberation times. For example, the old Boston Music Hall, which opened in 1863, seated 2,400 persons and had a reverberation time of over 1.8 sec, with full audience. The longer reverberation times of the best of these large concert halls added to their fullness of tone and, hence, to the dramatic value of the music, while at the same time the clarity necessary for music written in the classical style was preserved by their narrow rectangular shapes.

Today the preferred reverberation times for music of the Classical period appear to be in the range of 1.6 to 1.8 sec, which is reasonably consistent with the acoustics of the Leipzig, Oxford, and Vienna halls of that time. Beethoven's symphonies, particularly his later ones, showed the immense scope of his imagination—he wrote almost as though he anticipated the large reverberant halls that would be built in the next half-century.

Romantic period

By the last years of Beethoven's life the emphasis in music had changed from elegant formal structure to the personal and emotional expression that is characteristic of the Romantic period. For the next hundred years, a succession of composers—from Schubert and Mendelssohn, through Brahms, Wagner, Tchaikovsky, Richard Strauss,

Ravel, and Debussy—created a body of music that, together with the Classical symphonies make up the preponderant part of today's orchestral repertoire. From Haydn onward, each generation of composers increased the size and tone color of the orchestra and experimented with the expressive possibilities of controlled definition. The music no longer required the listeners to separate out each sound they heard to the same extent as did Baroque and Classical music: in some compositions a single melody might be supported by complex orchestral harmonies; sometimes a number of melodies are interwoven, their details only partly discernible in the general impression of the sound; and in some musical passages no melody seems to emerge, only an outpouring of sound, perhaps rhythmic or dramatic, often expressive or emotional.

The music of the Romantic period thrives in an acoustical environment that provides high fullness of tone and low definition. Conductors and musicians confirm the experience of recording engineers that these qualities are achieved with a relatively long reverberation time, perhaps 1.9 to 2.1 sec, and a small ratio of direct-to-reverberant sound.

Composers of this period sometimes wrote with a specific concert hall in mind. Wagner composed *Parsifal* expressly for his Festspielhaus in Bayreuth, Germany; Berlioz composed his *Requiem* for Les Invalides in Paris; and so on. In the last half of the nineteenth century, halls built specifically for the performance of concert music reflected the desires of the composers for acoustics with high fullness of tone. The Grosser Musikvereinssaal in Vienna, for example, which was completed in 1870, has a reverberation at mid-frequencies of about 2 sec when the hall is fully occupied. The hall is small enough for loud orchestral effects to sound very loud; its narrowness, emphasizing the early sound, lends significant definition to the music. The Concertgebouw of Amsterdam, which was completed in 1887, also has a reverberation time of 2.0 sec at mid-frequencies, but as it is wider it emphasizes the direct sound less; therefore, the music played in it emerges with less clarity and more fullness of tone. The Concertgebouw has excellent acoustics for music of the late Romantic period.

Twentieth century

Since the 1880's, concert-going has grown into an established European and American custom, and more recently a Japanese custom. Attending concerts was very popular in the United States in the 1920's; the radio and the economic depression displaced concert-going during the next two decades, but again since the end of World War II concerts have become increasingly popular. Most impressive is the surge of interest in classical music in Japan. Its capital, Tokyo, is speeding toward becoming the capital of concert-hall music in the world, as evidenced by the inclusion of descriptions of six Japanese halls in this book, the large number of Japanese symphony orchestras, music conservatories, and public patronage of its concerts.

The concert music of the twentieth century is extremely varied. Many contemporary composers have written for large orchestras along lines similar to those developed in the second half of the nineteenth century, though with the addition of new harmonies, new instruments, and new effects. In some of the other works there is evidence of a return to the smaller, clearer sound of earlier periods, which requires smaller instrumental combinations, some calling for instruments directly patterned on the instruments of an earlier day. And more innovators yearly, experimenting with sounds from sources other than conventional instruments, have resorted to the electronics laboratory, the tape machine, and the computer, to furnish the components of a new music or at least a novel sound.

To be suitable to the needs of modern concert music, a hall must accommodate a great variety of styles. Music of the transparent, "intellectual" type wants a hall with relatively high definition, of the kind required for Bach. Modern halls have been built that fulfill this requirement—with reverberation times, when occupied, of the order of 1.4 sec at mid-frequencies and with high definition. They are usually referred to as "hi-fi" halls. Modern music of a more passionate or sentimental quality sounds best in a hall with high fullness of tone and low definition. But the real answer to the need for a concert hall to accommodate a spread in music style is variable acoustics—which has been attempted in several halls studied here. In the USA, Dallas's McDermott Concert Hall in the Meyerson Symphony Center is the most striking example of an acoustic that can be varied over a wide range. Following on its heals are the attempts to make concert-hall acoustics variable by electronic means—an art and craft that is slowly gaining in acceptance.

Perhaps in time, music will seldom be performed in a concert hall at all, as multiple-channel recordings and wide-screen television with "surround" sound supplant the live concert. If that time comes, reverberation could be varied from one part of the composition to another, electronically, by the listener. Is it conceivable that even the musician would be eliminated; the concert hall would pass from the scene, along with the symphony orchestra, the concert-goer, the usher, and the ticket taker. The computer, the CD disk or its successor—and the Internet—would then rule supreme!

European (non-Wagnerian) opera

The European opera house has been the most stable home for music ever designed. From at least 1700 on, the horseshoe-shaped theater has been built, with rings of boxes one atop the other, and capped by a gallery of low-priced seats. The form reached its perfection in the Teatro alla Scala, the well-loved La Scala of Milan, which was completed in 1778. The horseshoe design has been copied in nearly every important city in Europe. So ubiquitous is the circular, tiered opera house that composers of opera have been able to write with only one kind of acoustics in mind.

Opera imposes different acoustical requirements from those for orchestral concerts. The vocal part must be considered as some form of communication not unlike speech. To preserve the libretto's intelligibility, especially at the tongue-twisting musical speeds of Mozart and Rossini, the reverberation time must be relatively short, so that successive syllables will not be masked by the reverberation of the immediately preceding sounds.

Except for the works of Wagner, European opera fits well into halls with acoustics suitable to the concert and chamber music of the Baroque period, that is to say, halls with high definition and relatively low fullness of tone. Many opera houses fulfill these requirements—La Scala, Le Fenice in Venice, San Carlo in Naples, Paris Opera Garnier, Royal Opera in London, Staatsoper in Vienna and Academy of Music in Philadelphia. In these houses the voices of the singers are projected to the audience with clarity and sufficient loudness, and the orchestra sounds clean and undistorted. Balance between the orchestra and the singers is assisted by the acoustical design as well as by the conductor's control of the orchestra.

In Europe, opera is nearly always performed in a language intelligible to the audience, and most European opera-goers stress the importance of understanding the words. In America—and perhaps soon to be in Japan—this is not true. Opera is seldom sung in the local language and opera-goers often have to look up (or down) at translations in order to understand the libretto. Erich Leinsdorf said of American opera-goers, "People come to an opera house to hear the music. Most of them either do not understand the language in which the opera is sung, or they have come so often to the opera that they follow the drama even if it is poorly articulated or masked by reverberation. In my opinion the music alone should govern the reverberation for an opera house." It appears, therefore, that opera elsewhere can be performed in houses with longer reverberation times than those of Europe. An example of such a house is the Metropolitan

Opera House in New York where the reverberation time at mid-frequencies, with full audience is about 1.7 sec.

Wagnerian opera

Wagner broke with the tradition of Baroque-like opera and evolved a style that was wholly personal, yet within the traditions of the Romantic period. From his pen flowed some of the most unusual and stirring of operas, "musical dramas" as he called them. Wagner's rich Romantic music is best supported by high fullness of tone and low definition.

In an effort to achieve the perfect acoustical environment for his musical style, Wagner designed his own opera house—the Festspielhaus at Bayreuth, Germany—a house that combines a relatively long reverberation, 1.6 sec at mid-frequencies, fully occupied, with a thoroughly blended orchestral tone. Although a very large orchestra (100 to 130 pieces) is used, proper balance is maintained between singers and orchestra by means of a sunken and covered pit, which also imparts a mysterious quality to the music.

Wagner's orchestral passages, with their relatively low speed, sound best in a hall with a long reverberation time, approximately 2 sec at mid-frequencies; but in order for the libretto to be intelligible the reverberation time needs to be somewhat shorter, in the vicinity of the 1.6 sec found in Bayreuth, or perhaps as high as 1.8 sec if the ratio of early to reverberant sound is high.

ACOUSTICS AND THE PERFORMERS

In addition to its direct effects on the music, the acoustics of the space in which music is presented can also affect music indirectly by influencing the way in which it is performed. Most musicians are sensitive to the sound of their music in a hall and automatically adjust their performance accordingly. Isaac Stern has said:

> Reverberation is of great help to a violinist. As he goes from one note to another the previous note perseveres and he has the feeling that each note is surrounded by strength. When this happens, the violinist does not feel that his playing is bare or "naked"—there is a friendly aura surrounding each note. You want to hear clearly in a hall, but there should also be this desirable blending of the sound. If each successive note blends into the previous sound, it gives the violinist sound to work with. The resulting effect is very flattering. It is like walking with jet-assisted take-off.

Music for the organ is a special problem. Since the organ has no sustaining pedal, the tone stops very soon after a key is released. The performer can, with considerable effort, make partial compensation by his technique to achieve some fullness of tone, but technique alone cannot really substitute for reverberation. E. Power Biggs wrote:

> An organist will take all the reverberation time he is given, and then ask for a bit more, for ample reverberation is part of organ music itself. Many of Bach's organ works are designed actually to exploit reverberation. Consider the pause that follows the ornamented proclamation that opens the famous *Toccata in D minor*. Obviously, this is for the enjoyment of the notes as they remain suspended in air. In harmonic structure, Mendelssohn's organ music is tailored to ample acoustics, for the composer played frequently in the great spaces of St. Paul's Cathedral in London. Franck's organ music, like that of Bach, frequently contains alternation of sound and silence, and depends for its effect on a continuing trajectory of tone.
>
> Some organ music, the Hindemith Sonatas, many chorale preludes and shorter pieces, are enjoyable in any acoustical surroundings. Yet it must be added that certain French music [of this century] depends so completely on a long period of reverberation that, no matter how well played, in acoustically dead surroundings it falls apart into disconnected fragments. In general, a reverberation period of at least two seconds, and preferably more, is best for the organ and organ music.

Pianists appear to be satisfied with less reverberant spaces than other instrumentalists. One rarely hears a pianist complain of a short reverberation time with the same dissatisfaction as a violinist, probably because, when chordal change is slow, the pianist has a sustaining pedal that can prolong notes. With the sustaining pedal, pianists can also blend successive tones played at fast tempos. Too "dead" a hall prevents them from hearing what is played; a hall that is too live renders the music muddy. Because there is a technique for merging a tone with its successor, and because the piano is itself loud and reverberant, the pianist depends more on the performance than on the hall to create the desired effects.

Most conductors are well aware of the effects that a hall may impart to the character of a performance. Conducting in an unfamiliar hall has an element of uncertainty about it. Rehearsal in an empty hall does not give the orchestra a sense of how the music will sound in a full hall. For these reasons a visiting orchestra often is at a disadvantage in a single engagement when compared with a resident orchestra that has learned to adjust its performance to the peculiarities of a hall. And as history has amply demonstrated, the full potentialities of a new concert hall are seldom realized in its initial concerts.

Leopold Stokowski wrote me:

> My experience has been that every concert hall in the world has different acoustical qualities and, as a concert hall is really an instrument for the sound of music, the differences of each hall must be taken care of during rehearsals and concerts. Also, the differences of an empty hall and a full hall must be considered. All this becomes very difficult when one is on tour visiting new cities, performing in a new hall where sometimes one does not have an opportunity for rehearsal. Many considerations must be kept in mind, but one of the most important is reverberation in the low, medium, and high frequencies—in other words, over the whole tonal range. By keeping these considerations in mind, the clarity of the music in performance will enable the public to understand and receive the message that all great music contains.

All conductors have their own musical style, a set of musical traits, that characterize them as surely as the styles of painters—Rembrandt, Van Gogh, Picasso, Sheeler—characterize them. A conductor's style is evident in the handling of any orchestra, and in the playing of any composer's works in any hall. But to achieve an individual style, conductors must vary their technique to conform to the various acoustics of different halls. One conductor said to me, "I not only seat the orchestra differently according to the hall in which I play, but I handle the musicians differently."

In the 1930's when Leopold Stokowski was conducting the Philadelphia Orchestra and Serge Koussevitzky the Boston Symphony Orchestra, some students of acoustics at Harvard University attempted to single out differences in their conducting techniques that apparently had been adopted to achieve their individual musical styles in the acoustics of their respective halls.

Leopold Stokowski was known for his emphasis on orchestral color—bar to bar and phrase to phrase—as well as on a long, rich, flowing melodic line. The Academy of Music in Philadelphia, in which he was the resident conductor from 1912 until 1936, has dry, clear, warm acoustics that lend high definition and rather low fullness of tone to compositions performed in it. It is a copy of the European horseshoe opera house, and was specifically planned for grand opera. In achieving his musical style in this hall, the Harvard study suggested, Stokowski had developed an orchestral technique that rounded and prolonged the attack and release of each tone, tended to blend successive notes, and gave the performance a flowing, silky tone. He required his violinists to practice free bowing to assure smooth orchestral texture. The violas, cellos, and basses were encouraged to produce a smooth, rich foundation to the full ensemble. Stokowski experimented with novel arrangements of the orchestra on the stage and with the dimensions and materials of the orchestra enclosure. Recording and radio engineers came to know him as the conductor most concerned with his acoustical surroundings. Stokowski's special style was clearly apparent when he conducted in other halls, but perhaps not to the same degree as in the Academy of Music, since he would not have had as much time to adapt the technique of his musicians to a novel acoustical environment.

Serge Koussevitzky's primary emphasis was also on orchestral color. But his style was more easily achieved in the lively acoustics of Symphony Hall—a hall with a relatively long reverberation that imparts fullness of tone to any composition played in it. The Harvard acoustics group observed that Koussevitzky made his attacks and releases more abrupt than Stokowski's, and he depended on the hall to enhance the fullness of tone. The bowing techniques of the cellos and basses were not so critical, since the reverberation of Symphony Hall elongates and rounds the tones. Koussevitzky's violin tone—ringing, brilliant, and loud—was easy to achieve in the acoustics of Symphony Hall, so much so that even slight imprecisions could go unnoticed—something that Koussevitzky would not have tolerated if they had been perceptible. He too loved to build up a dramatic conclusion to an allegro finale, an effect particularly suited to the acoustics of Symphony Hall.

Stokowski and Koussevitzky were themselves well aware of the different acoustics of their two halls. Each of them developed his technique to achieve his greatest perfection in his own hall and then strongly preferred that hall to all others. Koussevitzky is known to have said, "The Academy of Music is good, but not nearly as good as Symphony Hall." And Stokowski said, "Symphony Hall has good but not outstanding sound. The Academy of Music is the best concert hall in America. It has natural clear sound."

Audiences also sensed the differences that had developed in those two men's techniques. When the Philadelphia Orchestra visited Boston, there were comments about the "over-smooth, too-silky tone." In Philadelphia, the tone of the visiting Boston Symphony Orchestra was described as "crisp, too clearly molded, and sometimes slightly imprecise." Both reactions are eminently understandable. The result was that many years ago the two orchestras ceased visiting each other's hall—the reason given then was that the halls were unable to sell enough seats in either city.

LISTENERS' PREFERENCES

From the interviews I have conducted and from the experience of the recording industry, it seems clear that today's listeners still prefer particular kinds of acoustical spaces for the performance of music of particular styles. We may well ask whether the halls available when each style of music was composed had characteristics compatible with the acoustical preferences of today's audiences for listening to the same music. But this only raises the question: are the preferences of today's listeners a consequence of their listening experience, or does each style of music in fact require its own kind of acoustics?

The composer, the conductor, and the performers are engaged in a complex interplay with their particular acoustical environments. But audiences too have an important role in determining the kinds of music that are acceptable in their times and consequently the types of concert halls that will be built in their communities.

Paul Henry Lang, an American musicologist, wrote in the magazine High Fidelity (August, 1961, pp. 26–28) on "The Bach Renascence:"

> It is generally accepted that Bach was totally forgotten until Mendelssohn discovered the *St. Matthew Passion* and performed it in 1829....To understand whether Bach's music was properly appreciated by the rank and file of musicians [from 1700 to 1850], however, requires a glance at the historical situation.
>
> As late as Mozart's time, musical life evolved around contemporary art. The public wanted new music and was scarcely aware of the existence of music even one generation back, except, of course, such traditional church music as Gregorian chant and Lutheran hymn. The indifference, even hostility, of today's audiences towards contemporary music was unknown to our forebears. Indeed, when Mozart prepared a few works of Handel and Bach for performance, such a return to music a couple of generations earlier than that favored by the prevailing taste was unheard of....Bach was never a modern musician; when his colossal works were being composed, the style had already begun to change and by the time he reached the *Art*

> *of Fugue* and *Musical Offering* he had been left behind—there were few active musicians who could comprehend this art....
>
> With the spread of public concerts and the growth of audiences, a gradual estrangement of the public from contemporary music took place....By the opening of our century neither really old nor really new music was relished or even generally known.

Thus, we are returned to our original question: is it simply from habit that today's audiences prefer to hear music of earlier periods in acoustical environments similar to those in which they were first played? Or does each musical style in fact actually have a preferred acoustical environment?

An investigation of how the acoustical preferences of today's listeners vary with the style of the music was carried out by W. Kuhl, of the Technical Broadcasting Institute in Nuremburg, Germany. Kuhl presented 28 short excerpts of symphonic music, recorded in 20 different acoustical environments, to over 100 musicians and sound engineers. The music included samples of various styles, and the rooms varied in both size and degree of occupancy, and thus in reverberation time and clarity. Their cubic volumes varied between 70,000 and 500,000 ft^3 (1,980 and 14,160 m^3); acoustical measurements were made for all conditions of occupancy.

The musical excerpts, each about 2.5 min long, were identified to the listeners only by number. Each listener was asked to pay attention to all of the audible acoustical properties of each room; the reverberation, the recognizability of individual instrumental groups in tutti passages, the precision of the attack, and the attack tone. The listeners were asked to pay as little attention as possible to musical interpretation and minor technical defects. Each person recorded his judgment of the suitability of the room used during the recording for each sample of music by indicating "good" or "bad," and whether the reverberation time was "too short," "satisfactory," or "too long." For the recognizability of instrument groups and for quality of attack tone, he was asked to record "good" or "bad." In all about 13,000 judgments were made on these questions.

The reverberation times preferred by the musicians and sound engineers for the various styles of music are as follows:

for a symphony in Classical style (Mozart's *Jupiter*), about 1.5 sec;
for a symphony in Romantic style (Brahms' *Fourth*), 2.1 sec;
for a sample of modern music (Stravinsky's *Le Sacre du Printemps*), a little longer than 1.5 sec.

These preferred reverberation times appeared to be independent of the cubic volumes of the rooms, and the spread of the judgments was not large. [This study was described by W. Kuhl in his article, "Uber Versuche zur Ermittlung der Gunstigsten Nachhallzeit Grosser Musikstudios," *Acustica*, Vol. 4, pp. 618–634 (1954).]

For Romantic style music, the results of Kuhl's tests agree closely with our current thought. But for music of Classical style, today's audiences seem to prefer a longer reverberation time, 1.7 or 1.8 sec. Music composed in the last 30 years cannot be categorized. According to the composition, it could fall in any of the types mentioned above.

Some musicologists believe that each age has its own way of listening to music. It would appear that young people have different preferences from their parents and grandparents—a difference confirmed by the ubiquity of popular and Western music on recordings. Perhaps we cannot expect to derive the same experience from the music of an earlier time as its contemporaries did. Certainly, most twentieth-century concert-hall music has to be listened to in a manner and with an attitude far different from that demanded by any music that Bach, for example, would have known.

The different styles of interpretation that have become associated with differently proportioned halls may lead people who habitually listen to music in a certain hall to come to expect the musical style consonant with that hall, and this expectation may bias their attitudes toward other styles and other halls. It has been suggested that listening to recordings in non-reverberant living rooms, even with reverberation artificially introduced, may accustom us to demand music with high definition and low fullness of tone. But acoustical practice belies this. Because of ease and low cost of travel, committees in communities where halls are being planned sample acoustical environments in many cities, both in their own country and in others. Almost invariably, they seek to emulate the sound in a hall that would also have pleased audiences of half a century ago.

DIGITAL PROCESSING

Digital sound processing is opening cost-effective ways of providing variable acoustics or corrective acoustics in existing concert halls. And in time it may even enable the construction of lower-ceilinged rooms that mimic the sound of famous halls of any size or even that of cathedrals. Although digital sound processing has found widespread use in small auditoriums and studios, it has yet to be tried in a new concert hall for a city housing a major symphony orchestra. This author makes no recommendation.

Sample paragraphs from the sales literature of a sound studio describing its product reads:

> XX can improve the acoustic quality of virtually any space without architectural alteration. It generates time-variant lateral energy that is perceived by the listener as reflections from side walls, and other reflective surfaces. These reflections contribute to the rich sound and lush reverberant decay heard in good concert halls. The diffuse field of ambience and reverberation that XX creates envelopes the audience, and greatly enhances the enjoyment of listening in every seat in the house.
>
> For residences, the acoustical ambiance for a single listener in a designated spot in a living room, is described as: "The *Ambience* and *Reverberation* modes transform the listening room into a new acoustic space....The *Ambience* modes generate the side and rear reflection patterns of both idealized rooms and concert halls. The modes for larger spaces add the true depth and realism of a concert hall to classical and popular music, while the modes for smaller spaces are ideal for jazz and rock....The *Reverberation* modes are similar, but place more emphasis on rich, dense reverberant decay than on early reflections. They are especially good for simulating large, highly reverberant spaces such as churches, stadiums, and cathedrals."

With this ambitious promise, we conjecture the concert hall of the twenty-first century.

⬦2⬦

Seeking a Common Language for Musicians and Acousticians

Music and acoustics grew up independent of each other, and it is no surprise that they developed quite different vocabularies to describe their various concepts. Both vocabularies grew in the usual fashion of language—common words borrowed from the dictionary and shaped to a new purpose, and new words coined to fill a need which have over time grown into respected technical terms.

Because many of the linguistic needs of acoustics and music overlap, communication between the two professions is hampered by the lack of a common language with which to discuss their common interests. Although this problem is not likely to be resolved soon, the gap is not as wide today as it was fifty years ago.

A third language that hinders easy communication between science and the arts is the aesthetic diction of the music critic. The primary function of music critics is not to explicate either the acoustics or the music, but rather to describe their impressions of the composition and its performance. The critics use a subjective language that is rarely amenable to close definition but is arbitrary and evanescent. Since words can only approximate the response of listeners to their musical experience, the critics continually change and refine their vocabulary to weed out the words that no longer carry the impact of their impressions. Thus when music critics describe their reactions to a new concert hall with such words as overbearing, shattering, shimmering, or ravishing, we are without a rule by which to translate the words into specific acoustic recommendation. Because the music critic is a perceptive, experienced music listener, however, both the musician and the acoustician do well to tune their ears to critic's reactions.

In the years since I wrote my earlier book on *Music, Acoustics, and Architecture* (1962), a common language has been growing, however slowly. Not every musician is familiar with all the terms, nor do all acousticians agree with the definitions that I am suggesting. But since I need a consistent language in which to express myself, I offer the following terms as the best compromise between the interviews I have conducted with musicians and music critics and the scientific jargon that is current in the study of acoustics.

To begin with, the word resonance needs discussion. The physical scientist generally uses "resonance" to mean the large-amplitude vibration that occurs when a body is excited at one of its natural modes of vibration by an external source of sound or vibration having the same frequency as that of the natural mode. For example, the air column inside the resonator beneath a bar of a xylophone vibrates vigorously, that is, resonates, if the frequency of a natural mode of vibration of the air column is equaled by the frequency of vibration of the bar.

The musician often uses resonance to describe the addition of any acoustical after-ring to a musical tone combined with an augmentation of its loudness. Thus the musician speaks of the resonance of a violin—even though the frequency of the vibrating string may not coincide with a resonance frequency, a natural mode of vibration, of the violin body. Even without resonance in its acoustical meaning, the violin body augments the loudness of a string because it has a larger radiating surface than the string itself. And the string has its own after-ring, which might be interpreted, erroneously of course, as the after-ring of the violin body.

In speaking of a room, the musician may also interchange the acousticians' terms resonance and reverberation. The acoustician uses the word reverberation to designate the audible decay of sound in a room. Since music sounds louder when played in a reverberant room than in a dead room, a musician may speak of the room as resonant.

This book distinguishes between acoustic "resonance" in its scientific sense and the other acoustical concepts "augmentation of loudness" and "reverberation."

DEFINITIONS OF SELECTED TERMS

The eighteen terms defined herein should be usable and understandable by both the musical and the acoustical arbiters. Although other attributes could undoubtedly be named, and various of the eighteen could probably be discussed either in combination with others or subdivided even more finely, the present eighteen should cover all the important aspects of music performed in a closed space.

Intimacy or presence

A hall that is small has visual intimacy. A hall is said to have "acoustical intimacy" if music played in it gives the impression of being played in a small hall. In the special language of the recording and broadcasting industry, an intimate hall has "presence."

Reverberation or liveness

"Reverberation" refers to sound that persists in a room after a tone is suddenly stopped. " Reverberation time" is the number of seconds it takes for a loud tone to decay to inaudibility after being stopped. A hall that is reverberant is called a "live" hall. A room with a short reverberation time is called "dead" or "dry."

"Liveness" is related primarily to the reverberation times at the middle and high frequencies, those above about 350 Hz. A hall can sound live and still be deficient in bass. If a room is sufficiently reverberant at low frequencies, it is said to sound "warm."

Spaciousness: apparent source width (ASW)

A concert hall is said to have one of the attributes of "spaciousness" if the music performed in it appears to the listener to emanate from a source wider than the visual width of the actual source. This attribute is called "apparent source width" (abbreviated, ASW).

Spaciousness: listener envelopment (LEV)

Envelopment, the second component of spaciousness, as used here describes a listener's impression of the strength and directions from which the reverberant sound seems to arrive. "Listener envelopment" (abbreviated LEV) is judged highest when the reverberant sound seems to arrive at a person's ears equally from all directions—forward, overhead, and behind.

Clarity

"Clarity" is the degree to which the discrete sounds in a musical performance stand apart from one another. Clarity depends critically on musical factors and the skill and intention of the performers, but it is also closely related to the acoustics of the room.

Warmth

"Warmth" in music is defined as liveness of the bass, or fullness of the bass tones (between 75 and 350 Hz), relative to that of the mid-frequency tones (350 to 1,400

Hz). Musicians sometimes describe as "dark" a hall that has too strong a bass, or whose high frequencies are greatly attenuated. An example is the sound that reaches the listener from the partly covered pit of the Festspielhaus in Bayreuth, Germany.

Loudness

"Loudness" hardly needs definition. Clearly, a sound emitted in a concert hall seating 1,000 listeners would be louder than that in a hall seating 3,000 to 5,000 persons if both halls had the same reverberation time. Music also sounds louder in a highly reverberant hall than in a dead hall, even though both may be of the same size.

Acoustic glare

If the side walls of a hall or the surfaces of hanging panels are flat and smooth and are positioned to produce early sound reflections, the sound from them may take on a brittle or hard or harsh quality, analogous to optical glare. "Acoustical glare" can be prevented by adding fine-scale irregularities to these surfaces or by curving them. In the eighteenth and nineteenth centuries, fine-scale irregularities on sound-reflecting surfaces were provided by baroque carvings or plaster ornamentation.

Brilliance

A bright, clear, ringing sound, rich in harmonics, is called "brilliant." In a brilliant sound the treble frequencies are prominent and decay slowly. This means that the high frequencies are diminished only by the natural absorption of the sound in the air itself. The sound may become overly brilliant if electronic amplification is improperly used.

Balance

Good "balance" entails both the balance between sections of the orchestra and balance between orchestra and vocal or instrumental soloists. Some of the ingredients that combine to give good balance are acoustical and others are musical. Balance is impaired if the stage enclosure or some other surface near the players overemphasizes certain sections of the orchestra or fails to support the soloists adequately. Beyond that, balance is in the hands of the musicians, their seating, and the conductor's control of the players.

In an opera house, balance between singers and orchestra is achieved by the stage design, the early reflective surfaces provided near the stage, the pit design, and, again, the conductor's control of the orchestra.

Blend

"Blend" is defined as a mixing of the sounds from the various instruments of the orchestra so that the listener finds them harmonious. Blend depends partly on the placement of the orchestra, which should be spread neither too wide nor too deep. Blend also depends heavily on the design of the sound-reflecting surfaces close to the stage, such as those of a stage enclosure.

Ensemble

"Ensemble" refers to the ability of the performers to play in unison, to initiate and release their notes simultaneously so that the many voices sound as one. Orchestral ensemble depends on the ability of the musicians to hear their fellow performers. The sound-reflecting surfaces near the performers should carry the sound from the players on one part of the stage to those on other parts.

Immediacy of response (attack)

From the musician's standpoint, a hall should give the performers the feeling that it responds immediately to a note. "Immediacy of response" is related to the manner in which the first reflections from surfaces in the hall arrive back at the musician's ears. If the reflections occur too long after the note is sounded, they will be heard as an echo; if reflections are heard only from the nearby surrounding stage walls of the stage around him, the musician will fail to sense the acoustics of the hall altogether.

Texture

"Texture" is the subjective impression the listeners derive from the patterns in which the sequence of early sound reflections arrive at their ears. In an excellent hall those reflections that arrive soon after the direct sound follow in a more-or-less uniform sequence. In other halls there may be a considerable interval between the first and following reflections. Good texture requires a large number of early reflections, uniformly but not precisely spaced apart, and with no single reflection dominating the others.

Freedom from echo

"Echo" describes a delayed reflection sufficiently loud to annoy the musicians on stage or the listeners in the hall. Ceiling surfaces that are very high or that focus sound into one part of the hall may create echoes. They may also result from a long, high, curved rear wall whose focal point is near the front of the audience or on the stage. Echoes are more likely to be obtrusive in halls with short reverberation times.

Dynamic range and background noise level

"Dynamic range" is the spread of sound levels over which music can be heard in a hall. This range extends from the low level of background noise produced by the audience or the air-handling system to the loudest levels produced by the performers. All extraneous sources of noise—including traffic and aircraft noise—are distracting and must be avoided.

Extraneous effects on tonal quality

"Tonal quality" is beauty of tone. Like a fine instrument, a concert hall can have fine tonal quality. Tonal quality can be marred in a number of ways, for example, by a rattle in a metallic surface, or metal bars in the front of an organ that resonate in unison with certain musical notes. Sometimes there is a special kind of distortion—some aspect of the hall may add a rasping sound to the orchestral music. Fine-scale irregularities on plane reflecting surfaces are often necessary to alleviate this type of distortion.

Another extraneous sound effect, heard at certain seats, in even some of the best halls is caused by a "shift of source." A particular sound-reflecting surface may focus a large amount of sound toward one part of the audience, and the listeners there will hear the sound as emanating from that surface rather than as coming directly from the orchestra.

Uniformity of sound

Another requisite of a good hall is "uniformity of sound." The quality of a hall suffers if part of the audience is subjected to inferior sound, for example, under a deep overhanging balcony, or at the sides of the front of the hall, or if in certain locations reflections produce echoes, or muddiness, or lack of clarity.

Musicians sometimes speak of "dead spots"—where the music is not as clear or as live as it is in other parts of the hall. Acousticians usually use that term only in reference to locations where the music is especially weak.

◇3◇

Acoustics and Musical Qualities

This chapter examines in greater depth the acoustical attributes of concert halls and depicts the ways in which they interrelate with the music performed in them. The first section distinguishes between direct sound, early sound, and reverberant sound. The second section concerns how musical factors and acoustical attributes affect vertical and horizontal definition of the music. Figures 3.2 and 3.3 illustrate the ways that the sounds of fast and slow music are altered by different acoustical conditions. The final section discusses the important acoustical attributes, intimacy, spaciousness, timbre, and tone color.

BASIC ASPECTS OF SOUND IN HALLS

Direct sound

Suppose you are seated close to the stage of an outdoor stadium or in a sound-deadened room where there is no echo or reverberation. When a performer near you plays a tone, you hear the tone precisely as the instrument has produced it. The build-up of the tone, its loudness, and the termination that you hear are exactly characteristic of the instrument and the player. The tones of wind instruments cease almost immediately after the excitation is stopped. The tones of stringed instruments persist a little longer because of the vibrations of the strings and the wood. The sounds from drums and freely vibrating piano or harp strings may persist considerably longer unless damped by the player. In any case, the sound that reaches you is only the direct sound. There is no enclosed space, hence, no surfaces to provide reflections that would follow the direct sound.

In a concert hall or opera house, the sound that first reaches the listener before any reflections arrive from the walls and ceiling is called the "direct sound."

Early sound, early sound decay, and reverberation time

EARLY SOUND: The sound transmitted from an orchestra is radiated in all directions and travels through the air at about 1,128 ft (344 m) per sec and within 1 or 2 sec is reflected many times over from the different surfaces of the space. To understand the effect of the acoustical attributes of a hall on the music, we must consider the reflections as divided into two time intervals. First, the "early sound," defined as the direct sound and those reflections that take place within 80/1,000 of a sec (80 msec) after the arrival of the direct sound. Second, the reverberant sound that is created by the many reflections that occur subsequently.

These reflections come from the side walls, the ceiling overhead, and the walls of the stage enclosure. If they arrive at the listener's position from side walls, that is, from lateral directions, they appear to broaden the source and thus increase the apparent source width (ASW). An increase in ASW lends quality to the music heard in a concert hall. Lateral reflections are easy to achieve at listeners' positions in the center of the main floor of a narrow hall with parallel side walls. But in a fan-shaped hall they are directed to the rear seats only, unless special sound-reflecting panels are attached to the walls (see Fig. 3.1). Many of the famous old halls, such as those in Boston, Vienna and Amsterdam, are "shoebox" in shape, which means parallel side walls and horizontal ceiling.

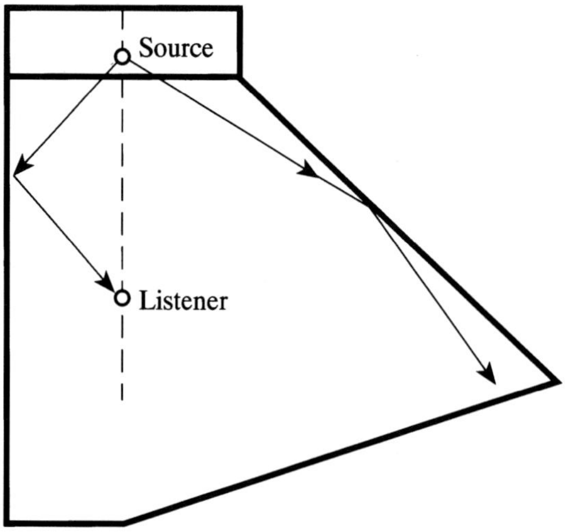

Figure 3.1. The left half of the sketch shows how a rectangular hall reflects early sound from a source on the stage laterally to the audience on the main floor. The right side shows how a fan-shaped hall reflects sound to the far corners of a hall, so that early reflections may arrive at main floor listeners only from the ceiling, thus depriving those listeners of early lateral reflections.

REVERBERATION TIME RT: Each time the traveling sound wave bounces back from a room surface, its strength is weakened by the "sound absorption" of that surface. Thus the sound created by the succession of reflections dies down with time and is said to "decay." The time in seconds that it takes for a loud sound to decay 60 dB, that is, to decay to inaudibility after being cut off, is called the "reverberation time" (RT). RT is usually determined separately at a number of frequencies, such as, 125, 250, 500, 1,000, 2,000, and 4,000 Hz.

EARLY DECAY TIME EDT: To add to our baggage of new terms, the first 10 dB of the sound decay after a source is cut off is called "early decay time" (EDT), not to be confused with "early sound." EDT becomes very important when intercomparing the acoustical quality of halls.

Loudness

Loudness is a function of the energy in a sound divided by the number of people who must share it. The energy is also decreased by the absorption caused by the people, furnishings, and materials. Loudness at a particular listener's ears is also divided into two parts, early and reverberant. "Loudness of the early sound" is determined by the energy of the sound that comes directly from the source, plus the energy received from the early reflections in the next 80 msec. "Loudness of the reverberant sound" is defined as the total sound energy that reaches the listener in the period following 80 msec after the arrival of the direct sound.

INTERRELATIONS BETWEEN ACOUSTICAL ATTRIBUTES AND MUSIC

Fullness of tone and liveness

In a concert hall, when a tone is sounded and is then suddenly turned off, the reverberation is heard for about 1.5 to 2.2 sec. Two aspects of reverberation combine to increase the "fullness of tone" of an instrument or ensemble at a particular listener's position. The first is the length of the reverberation time (RT), and particularly the length of the early part of the sound decay (EDT). The term "liveness" is related to RT alone. The second ingredient of "fullness of tone" is the ratio of the loudness of the "reverberant sound" to that of the "early sound."

Reverberation is not in itself desirable or undesirable; it is one of the components available to the composer (and the performer) for producing a musical effect and as such is actually a part of the music. Some styles of music depend on the tying together of successive tones to produce their overall effect. Many early choral compositions, particularly plainchant, were written to be performed in reverberant cathedrals and require considerable fullness of tone. When these compositions are performed in an acoustically dead environment, they suffer from want of body and lose much of their power. Early composers of organ music often wrote pauses into the music to emphasize the after-ring of the church.

When a hall is designed to guide the sound from the performers directly to the audience, most of the energy produced by the instruments reaches the listeners almost simultaneously with the direct sound, and the tone will lack fullness. If the sound of the music rises freely into the upper reaches of the room, the energy in the early sound will be reduced and the energy in the reverberant sound increased. The interior shaping of the surfaces and the inclusion of special sound-reflecting panels can be combined to control the proportions of these two factors, and, thus, the degree of fullness.

Definition or clarity

When a musician speaks of "definition" or "clarity," he means the degree to which the individual sounds in a musical performance stand apart from one another. Definition depends critically on musical factors and the skill and intention of the performers, but it is also closely tied to the acoustics of the room. There are two kinds of definition: horizontal, which applies to tones played in succession, and vertical, in which tones are played simultaneously.

"Horizontal definition" refers to the degree to which sounds that follow one another stand apart. The composer can specify certain musical factors that determine the horizontal definition—such as tempo, repetition of tones in a phrase, and the relative loudness of successive tones. The performer can vary the horizontal definition by the manner chosen to phrase a passage.

The acoustical factors that affect horizontal definition are the length of the reverberation time and the ratio of the loudness of the early sound to that of the reverberant sound—the same two factors that determine fullness of tone, but in inverse relation. That is to say, an increase in horizontal definition goes hand in hand with a decrease in fullness of tone.

"Vertical definition" refers to the degree to which sounds that occur simultaneously are heard separately. Vertical definition depends on the score, the performer, the acoustics of the room, and the auditory acuteness of the listener. The composer specifies the vertical definition by choosing simultaneous tones and their relation to the tones surrounding them (whether the composition is hymnlike, chordal, contrapuntal, or simply an accompanied melody), and his choice of instruments on which they are played. Performers can alter the vertical definition by varying the dynamics of their simultaneous sounds and through the precision of their ensemble.

Vertical definition is also responsive to such acoustical factors as balance among the sounds of the various instruments as they reach the audience, the degree of blending of the tones of the different instruments in the stage enclosure, the relative response of the hall at low, middle, and high frequencies, and, once again, the ratio of the energy in the early sound to that in the reverberant sound.

Definition, both horizontal and vertical, results from a complex of factors, both musical and acoustical—a certain piece of music, played in a certain way, in a certain environment. The degree of definition that the composer intended is necessary in order for the music to be communicated faithfully to the audience. Gregorian chant—with its slow melodic lines that build and recede gradually, is performed with little horizontal definition; it is usually sung in a room with a very long reverberation time and a high ratio of reverberant to early sound energy. Bach's *Toccata in D Minor* for organ needs a reverberation time of at least 3 sec in order for the full sonorities to be realized. At the other end of the spectrum, a piano concerto by Mozart—with its rapid solo passages and the delicate interplay of piano and different orchestral voices—needs considerable horizontal and vertical definition. It should be performed in a room with a relatively short reverberation time and a large ratio of early to reverberant sound energy. Mozart, after listening to a performance of *Die Zauberflote* from various locations in the hall and backstage, wrote in October 1791:

> By the way, you have no idea how charming the music sounds when you hear it from a box close to the orchestra—it sounds much better than from the gallery.

Mozart knew what later generations have confirmed, that his style of music sounds best where the ratio of the early to reverberant energy is large (e.g., at a box near the orchestra where the direct sound is stronger).

Speed of music relative to fullness of tone and definition (clarity)

Fullness of tone and definition or clarity are both related to the speed with which music is played. The chart of Fig. 3.2 shows the effect on music played slowly and music played rapidly of two different reverberation times and various ratios of the loudnesses of early to reverberant sound.

In (a) and (b) the individual tones of both the slow and fast music stand out distinctly, and the full extent of their attack and decay is discernible, because the reverberation time is very short and the ratio of early to reverberant sound energy is very large. In other words, there is negligible fullness of tone. Note that the rapid decay of

	Acoustical Conditions		Notes Played Slowly	
	Reverberation Time	Ratio of Loudness of Early Sound to Reverberant Sound	Music-Acoustic Results	Definition and Fullness of Tone
Tones of Identical Loudness	Short	Large	(a) 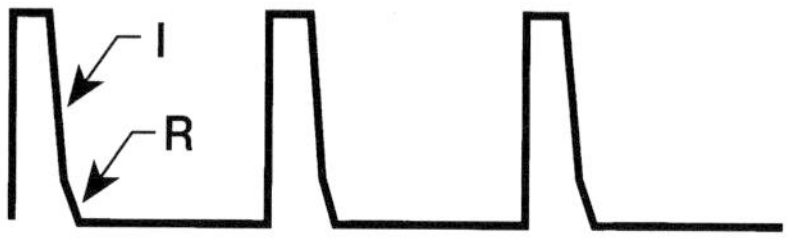	High definition Negligible fullness of tone
	Long	Medium	(c) 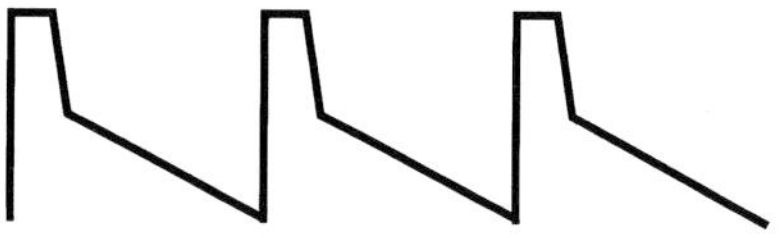	High definition Some fullness of tone
	Long	Small	(e) 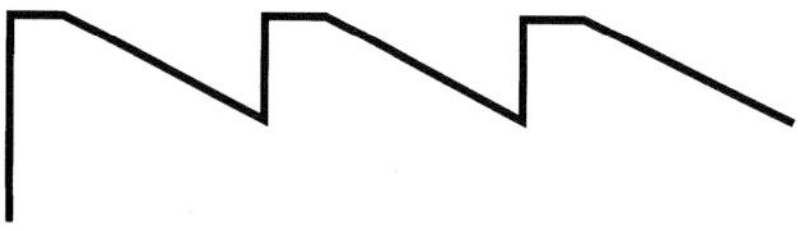	Medium definition High fullness of tone
Tones of Different Loudness	Long	Medium	(g) 	High definition Some fullness of tone
	Long	Small	(i) 	Low definition High fullness of tone

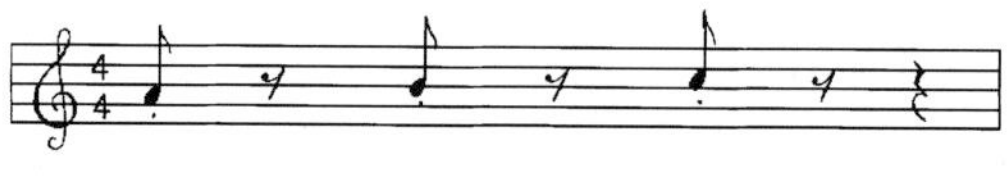

the instrumental sound *I* is followed by the slower decay of the room sound *R*, because the reverberant sound arrives at a listener's ears after the early sound.

In (c) we see the effect on slow music of a long reverberation time and a medium ratio of early to reverberant sound energy. The full extent of the attack and part of the natural decay of the sound are heard before the reverberation takes over. A certain amount of the natural decay of the instrumental tone is buried in the reverberation.

In (d), because of the closer spacing of the tones in the fast music, both part of the attack and part of the natural decay of the tone are buried in the reverberation. The reverberation adds fullness to the tone, although the definition is still high.

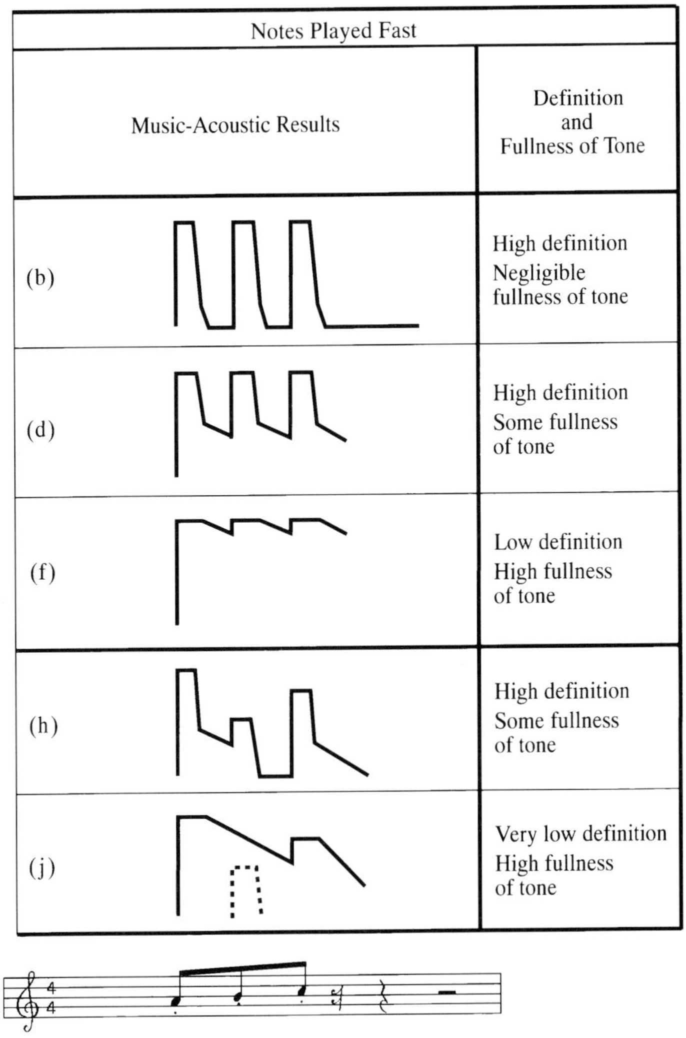

Figure 3.2. Chart illustrating the interrelations among speed of music, reverberation time, and ratio of loudness of early sound to that of reverberant sound, and the music itself (tempos are identical). *I* is the decay of the instrumental sound and *R* is the decay of the room sound.

In (e) the length of the reverberation time is the same as in (c), but the ratio of the loudness of early sound to reverberant sound is small. Here, part of the attack and all of the natural instrumental decay of sound are obscured by the reverberation. The tones are bonded, one to another, so that no one sound stands out clearly. When the speed of the music is increased, in (f), each tone is still observable, but most of the natural attack and the decay of the instrument are buried in the reverberation. The music is almost continuous. Definition is sacrificed to fullness of tone and there is no possibility of a staccato sound.

Let us see how successive tones of different loudnesses fare in these rooms (lower graphs). When the music is played slowly and the ratio of the loudness of early to reverberant sound is fairly large, as in (g), each tone is heard clearly. With the faster speed (h) definition is sacrificed, but the tones are still distinct. In (i) , where the ratio of the loudness of the early to reverberant sound is small, the weakest tone (in the middle) is barely audible in the reverberation "tail" of the preceding tone. Finally, in (j), when the music is fast, the weakest tone is lost completely in the tail of reverberation of the preceding tone; the definition is very low, and the fullness of the tone is great.

The interplay of speed of music, definition, and fullness of tone illustrated in Fig. 3.2 is characteristic of music performed in concert halls. With a mental picture of the acoustical environment in which the piece is likely to be played, the composer may be able to create a composition with a particular degree of definition and fullness of tone in mind. The performer must then select a tempo and phrasing that seem to fulfill the composer's intent. And if the performance is presented in an acoustically appropriate hall, the audience is rewarded with music that follows the composer's conception accurately.

IMPORTANT INDICATORS OF ACOUSTICAL QUALITY

Intimacy

Acoustical "intimacy" suggests to the listener the size of the space in which it is performed. Different styles of music sound best in a hall with the appropriate degree of acoustical intimacy. It is not necessary that the room have a particular size, but only that it *sound* as though the size is appropriate. Acoustical intimacy is largely determined by the initial-time-delay gap—the difference in time of arrival of the direct sound and the first reflected sound—but also in part by the loudness of the overall sound since the listener assumes that a performance sounds louder in a small room than in a large one.

The initial-time-delay gap is illustrated in Fig. 3.3 which pictures the direct sound *D* traveling from a violin *V* on the stage to a listener *L*. If, for Hall No. 1, *D* equals 80 ft (24.4 m) the sound will take about 7/100 of a sec, or 70 msec, to reach the listener. The first reflection occurs from a side wall and, as drawn here, will travel a distance of 108 ft (32.9 m), taking 95 msec to reach the listener. Thus the initial-time-delay gap for that listener would be 25 msec. In Hall No. 2 the ITDG would be 73 msec. In the best halls for today's symphonic repertoire, the initial-time-delay gap for a listener seated in the center of the main floor usually lies between 15 and 30 msec.

In every period composers have written chamber music to be played by small groups of instruments in small rooms. Between 1700 and 1900 most orchestral music was written for larger groups who performed in the larger but quite narrow concert halls of Europe, such as the Grosser Musikvereinssaal of Vienna. Opera is usually per-

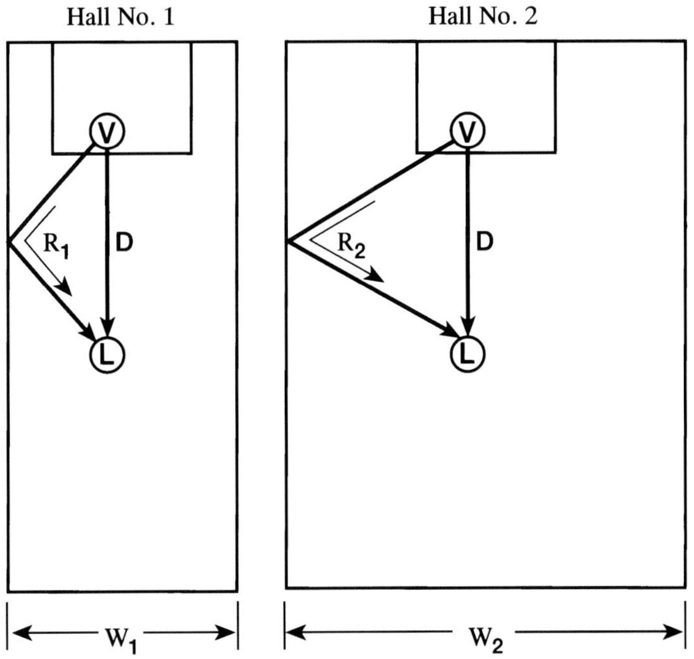

Figure 3.3. Drawings showing the effect of hall width *W* on the difference between the length *D* and the length R_1 or R_2. The direct sound travels path *D* from the violinist *V* to the listener *L*. The reflected sound travels path *R*. The distance $(R_2 - D)$ in Hall No. 2 is longer than $(R_1 - D)$ in Hall No. 1. The ceilings of the two halls are assumed to be so high that reflections from the ceilings occur later than the reflections (as shown) from the side walls.

formed in relatively small horseshoe-shaped opera houses like La Scala in Milan or the Staatsoper in Vienna. Beginning in the sixteenth century composers have written choral and liturgical music for performance in both large cathedrals and smaller, less reverberant churches or chapels. These varied settings confirm that the composer conceives of each musical work with a particular degree of intimacy in mind. If the work is performed in a hall whose intimacy is not scaled to it, the listener is quickly aware of the inappropriateness of the acoustic environment. The organist E. Power Biggs once said, "The listener immediately senses something wrong when he hears one of the organ works, such as those by Bach, played in a small college auditorium."

Since chamber music has for almost three centuries been written for performance in rooms of similar acoustical characteristics—intimacy and high definition, imparting relatively low fullness of tone—little need be said about the acoustical design of such rooms. The following discussion concerns the acoustics of concert halls and opera houses seating more than 1,500 persons, with occasional references to the acoustics of churches and cathedrals.

Spaciousness

A recent addition to the indicators of acoustical quality is the two-pronged attribute of spaciousness, composed of apparent source width (ASW) of the early sound and listener envelopment (LEV) by the reverberant sound. ASW is a major indicator of acoustical quality in concert halls.

Apparent source width (ASW): the larger the better

At this writing, the best measure of ASW at mid-frequencies appears to be a quantity called "interaural cross-correlation coefficient" ($IACC_E$), where the subscript *E* indicates that only the early sound is considered in the calculation. This calculation measures the degree of dissimilarity of the musical sounds that reach the two ears. The less similar they are, the lower the value of $IACC_E$ and the greater the value of ASW. ASW is also increased by the level of the music at low frequencies, usually rated in decibels and designated G_{low}.

Measurements have been performed in some of the world's best concert halls to set a standard for the desirable values of $IACC_E$ and *G*, and these are discussed in later chapters entitled, "Spaciousness" and "Loudness."

Listener envelopment (LEV)

The reverberant sound that reaches the listener after 80 msec is most pleasant if the listener hears it coming from all directions. In Symphony Hall, Boston, a listener on the main floor hears the reverberation as filling the entire space above, ahead, and behind. By contrast, a listener seated in a steeply raked balcony will hear the reverberation as coming primarily from the front. At this writing, listener envelopment can best be estimated by visual inspection of the hall—including whether the sound has the freedom to surround the listener, and the degree of irregularities and ornamentation on side wall and ceiling surfaces and on balcony fronts.

Timbre, tone color, and bass warmth

"Timbre" is the quality of sound that distinguishes one instrument from another or one voice from another. "Tone color" describes balance between the strengths of low, middle, and high frequencies, and balance between sections of the orchestra. It is affected by the acoustic environment in which the music is produced. If a hall either amplifies or absorbs the treble sound, either brittleness or a muffled quality may mar the music. If the surfaces of the walls or ceiling or seats absorb the low frequencies, the full orchestra may sound deficient in basses or cellos. If the stage enclosure or the main ceiling directs certain sounds toward some parts of the hall only and not toward others, the tone color will be affected differentially.

One facet of concert hall acoustics that has a clearly observable effect on orchestral timbre occurs when the length of the RT at low frequencies is either too long or too short compared to the RT at middle frequencies. This ratio is directly related to the musical attribute called "warmth." A hall lacks warmth when the reverberation times are lower at low frequencies than at mid-frequencies, i.e., a low bass ratio BR. *But that measurement is meaningful only when the hall is fully occupied, because people absorb the high frequencies more than the low frequencies.*

Summary of the musical qualities affected by acoustics

Figure 3.4 summarizes the interrelations between the musical qualities heard in a concert hall and the acoustical factors that affect those qualities. This chart, together with the definitions of this and the preceding chapter cover the known interrelations

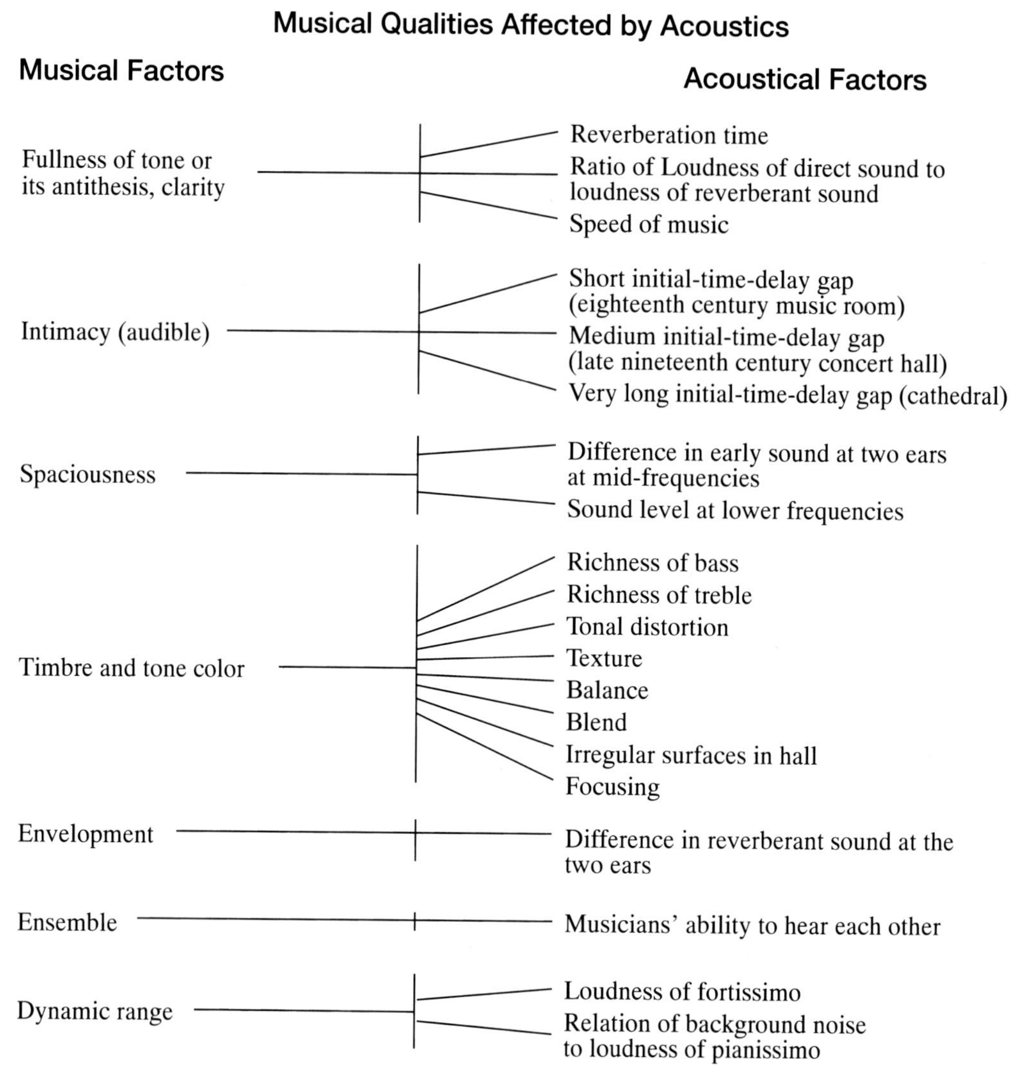

Figure 3.4. Chart showing the interrelations between the audible factors of music and the acoustical factors of the halls in which the music is performed.

between acoustics and the quality of music performed in a concert hall. Much of the information is also applicable to opera houses, but there are sufficient differences to require a separate discussion (see Chapter 16).

4

Laboratory Determined Psychoacoustic Parameters

In the 1962 edition of *Music, Acoustics, and Architecture* the subjective parameters of intimacy, reverberance, warmth, loudness, and envelopment (diffusion) were identified from interviews I carried out with conductors, musicians, and music critics. These musical descriptors could be related to the physical measurements of the acoustical attributes: intimacy with initial-time-delay gap (ITDG); reverberance with reverberation time (RT); warmth with the ratio of RT at low frequencies to those at mid-frequencies called "bass ratio" (BR); loudness with the level of the sound in the hall (G). In addition, a subjective parameter now called "listener envelopment" (LEV) was associated with an acoustical attribute, then called "diffusion," which was assigned a value from visual inspection of the amount of large and small irregularities in the surfaces of the side walls, ceiling, and balcony fronts in a concert hall.

Measured values of RT and BR for 47 concert halls were supplied to the author by acousticians in Europe and North America. The other quantities were calculated from architectural drawings or, in the case of diffusion, visually from photographs.

Similar to the presentation in Chapter 6 of this book, subjective rank-orderings of those 47 halls into five categories of acoustical quality were also made from the interviews.

For the halls contained in each of the subjective categories, an average value of each of the measured acoustical attributes was determined. For example, for the six halls in Category A+ (excellent) the average RT was 1.9 sec; for Category A (very good), 1.7 sec; and so forth. These average values were used to derive computational scales that could be used to convert the physical data for each hall into a single number whose magnitude correlated well with the subjective rank orderings. For example, a maximum of 15 rating points was assigned to an RT of 1.9 sec. For 1.7 sec, the rating points decreased to 11 and for 1.5 sec to 7.

To evaluate the overall quality of a hall, each measured acoustical attribute was given rating points using these scales, and the sum became a single number that would represent the probable subjective ranking of the hall. The halls in the A+ subjective category had calculated ratings of 90 to 100 and those in the fifth subjective category (C) had rating values of 50 to 59.

Although the computational method for rank-ordering the halls used in *Music, Acoustics, and Architecture* gave results that agreed with the rank-orders obtained from the interviews, a recently discovered attribute guided us to great improvement in the designing and evaluation of halls.

That new factor, discovered and developed by A. H. Marshall, calls for increasing the sound energy in the *lateral* reflections from side walls that arrive at a listener's position in the first 50 to 80 msec after the arrival of the direct sound (Marshall 1967, 1968, and 1979). That subjective parameter is now called "apparent source width" (ASW). It is related most closely to binaural measurements made in a hall, using a dummy head with microphones for ears, and a computational method called "interaural cross-correlation coefficient" (IACC) that derives its basis from the outputs of the two microphones.

The Beranek book of 1962 and the 1967 and 1968 papers of Marshall aroused considerable activity in the acoustical community. Because many new concert halls were being planned throughout the world, there was considerable pressure to update our understanding of concert hall acoustics. Intensive research projects have been pursued at university and government laboratories in several countries. The results of these psychoacoustic studies are summarized in this chapter and more extensive reviews are available in the literature [Cremer, Mueller, and Schultz, 1982; Beranek (review paper), 1992; and Barron, 1993].

PSYCHOACOUSTIC STUDIES

Two German universities instituted programs in the early 1970's to determine a set of acoustical parameters for concert halls that would be statistically independent of each other and would, in combination, correlate highly with subjective judgments of acoustical quality.

Goettingen studies

In Goettingen University an investigation was performed in several stages. First, stereophonic tapes of the reprise and coda of the finale of Mozart's Jupiter Symphony were recorded by the BBC orchestra in an anechoic environment (completely dead acoustically, so that no effects of a hall were on the tape). In each of 25 *unoccupied* European concert halls, these tapes were played over two non-directional loudspeakers, 15 ft (5 m) apart, placed on the stage. A dummy head with microphones at each ear was located in the center of each hall to record stereophonically the sound of the orchestral music as it would be heard by a listener in the unoccupied hall. These sound recordings were then played back in an anechoic room over stereophonic loudspeakers to 13 university students.

The acoustical attributes described in the Beranek's 1962 book—RT, EDT, *G*, and the new attribute IACC, plus C_{50} (see below) were measured in each of the 25 halls.

The students were presented with a recording from each of two different halls, played one after the other, and they were asked whether they had a preference for one, or the other, or no preference. A mathematical "factor analysis" was used to determine which acoustical attributes (determined from the physical measurements made in the 25 halls) influenced most the subjective judgments of the 13 student subjects.

The subjects found three acoustical attributes dominant (Schroeder *et al.*, 1974): (1) the difference in the sound at the two ears as measured by IACC; (2) the RT, but only if it was significantly lower than 2.0 sec, which is the value considered optimum for music of the late Classical and the Romantic periods; and (3) the clarity, as measured by the ratio of the energy in the early sound to the energy in the reverberant sound, determined from the recordings in the first 50 msec, starting from and including the direct sound, and designated as "clarity factor" (C_{50}).

Loudness was held constant during the subjective comparisons, and neither it nor the initial-time-delay gaps of the different halls covered a large enough range of values to enter into the findings.

Berlin studies

At the Technical University in Berlin the procedure differed in three respects. (1) Instead of recorded music, the Berlin Philharmonic Orchestra played a number of bars from three symphonies in six unoccupied halls; (2) the binaural recordings from the dummy head were played back to the subjects through headphones; and (3) the subjects were asked to rate their impression of the acoustics of each sample by placing marks along the lengths of 19 scales, whose end points were labeled: loud...quiet, dry...reverberant, unclear...clear, emphasized bass...bass not emphasized, appealing...unappealing. Subsequently, each scale was given a length of 10 and therefore a value assigned to each mark.

The following acoustical attributes were isolated by factor analysis (Cremer, Mueller, and Schultz, 1982): (1) strength of the source *G* (which was related to the loudness and reverberation scales); (2) clarity C_{80} (total energy to 80 msec and related to the unclear-clear scale); and (3) timbre of the sound (defined as similar to "warmth BR"and related to the emphasized bass scale).

An interesting result in the Berlin judgments was that the 40 test subjects seemed to divide into two groups, one more responsive to the strength of the sound (*G*) and the other to clarity (C_{80}). The first group found the sound more appealing when the loudness of the music was greater and the second group found it more pleasing when the music was clearer. The results indicated that RT was not relevant unless it contributed to loudness or measured 1.7 sec or less.

Marshall and Barron's studies

Marshall (1967–1968) examined the effect of cross-sectional shapes of concert halls on the energy and time distribution of early sound reflections. He hypothesized that the preferences for narrow rectangular halls over wide rectangular halls seemed to lie in the fact that more and stronger *lateral* reflections reached the listener's ears.

Marshall later concluded (1979) that lateral reflections give a listener the subjective impression of being enveloped by the sound, and that this feeling of envelopment, which is now called "spatial impression" grows with the sound level. The sensation of spatial impression is described as the difference between feeling wholly or partly surrounded by the sound and feeling outside the sound, observing it as through a window. He proposed, as a measure, the ratio of the energy in the lateral reflections alone to the total energy. Barron joined Marshall (1981) to confirm these findings and to extend their scope.

Two different measures have been applied to compare the effects of the lateral reflections: (1) the ratio of the output of a figure-eight directional microphone (which automatically eliminates any sound energy coming to the measurement position whether directly, or from the ceiling, or from an overhead reflector) to that arriving from all directions in the first 80 msec *after* arrival of the direct sound. This measured quantity is called "lateral fraction" (LF); and (2) determination of IACC from the outputs of two microphones placed at the ears of a person or a dummy head. Recently, Hidaka, Beranek, and Okano (1995) have shown that IACC is a more accurate measure of that aspect of spaciousness in which Marshall was interested.

Ando's studies

Ando (1985), using the Goettingen facilities, exposed young listeners to electronically created sound fields, using several different symphonic compositions of different tempos. The acoustical fields in his experiment simulated those in concert halls, and included the direct sound, a number of reflected sounds from various directions at various strengths, and reverberations with various RTs. Using the experimental method of paired comparisons, Ando found from the subjective responses four orthogonal (statistically different) subjective parameters important to judgments of acoustical quality: (1) loudness (measured by G); (2) intimacy (measured by the initial-time-delay gap t_I); (3) reverberance (measured by RT) ; and (4) the difference in the sound at the two ears (measured by IACC). Ando also devised a rating system that combined the four acoustical attributes into a single rating number, but it has yet to find general use in concert hall design because of its complexity.

Ando's data show that listeners prefer a relatively short initial-time-delay gap for lively music, about 30 msec in length. Also they prefer a relatively short initial-time-delay gap, again about 30 msec, if there is sufficient energy in the subsequent reverberant sound field. Ando also suggests that there is "an overall preference of the listeners ... to hear sound fields containing more acoustic information in the [early-reflection] spatial domain." These results agree with the 1962 findings of Beranek, although Ando's rating system is quite different and Beranek's preferred initial-time-delay gaps were a little shorter. Ando also found that some listeners like less reverberation and some like more clarity.

Yamamoto and Suzuki study

Yamamoto and Suzuki (1976) employed a duplicate of the Goettingen system as Ando had used it. They produced electronically synthesized sound fields that were reproduced in an anechoic chamber, and subjects were asked to make their preferences. Their judgments correlated extremely well with customary acoustical measurements, e.g., at a central seat in a hall (1) clarity correlated with the ratio of early sound energy to late sound energy C_{50}; (2) loudness correlated with sound level G; and (3) spaciousness correlated with the ratio of the energy arriving from the back of the hall to that arriving from the front. The authors seemed not to be concerned with the importance of lateral reflections or the initial-time-delay gap.

Kimura and Sekiguchi study

Kimura and Sekiguchi (1976) made the same type of recordings as the Goettingen group in 13 Japanese halls. Playback was through earphones. The quantities judged were loudness, quantity and quality of reverberation, spatial impression, brilliance, definition, proximity, and overall preference. Their results indicated that the preferences could be explained primarily by the mean width of the hall and its cubic volume.

Multi-institutional study

Five scientific groups, four from Japan and one from Germany, joined together to perform an acoustic survey of fifteen auditoriums in Europe and five in Japan between 1986 and 1989 (Tachibana *et al.*, 1989). Subjective listening tests were conducted in an anechoic chamber in which the listener faced two loudspeakers. The listening sound levels were held constant. In all, 88 subjects participated, each of whom was asked to indicate a preference for one of a pair of sound fields presented (7 halls, 2 musical motifs). Surprisingly, the test results showed no significant preferences among the seven halls when the data from all the subjects were averaged. When the subjects' preferences were separated into two groups, one group preferred three halls that the other group placed last. The authors state, "We acousticians should (by listening) evaluate each attribute of auditory events perceived in a concert hall (loudness, reverberance, spaciousness and timbre)."

Barron's listening experiments

Barron (1988) conducted listening experiments using subjects drawn from a group of 27 expert listeners, most of whom were acoustical consultants. They attended concerts in 11 British halls and they all changed seats during intermission. The subjects recorded their judgments on questionnaires (Fig. 4.1). The subjects' "overall impressions" correlated most closely with the questionnaire's scales of reverberance, envelopment, and intimacy. There were high correlations between reverberance and envelopment, and between envelopment and intimacy, but a low correlation between reverberance and intimacy. But the scales with the highest significance were bass balance and reverberance (occupied halls).

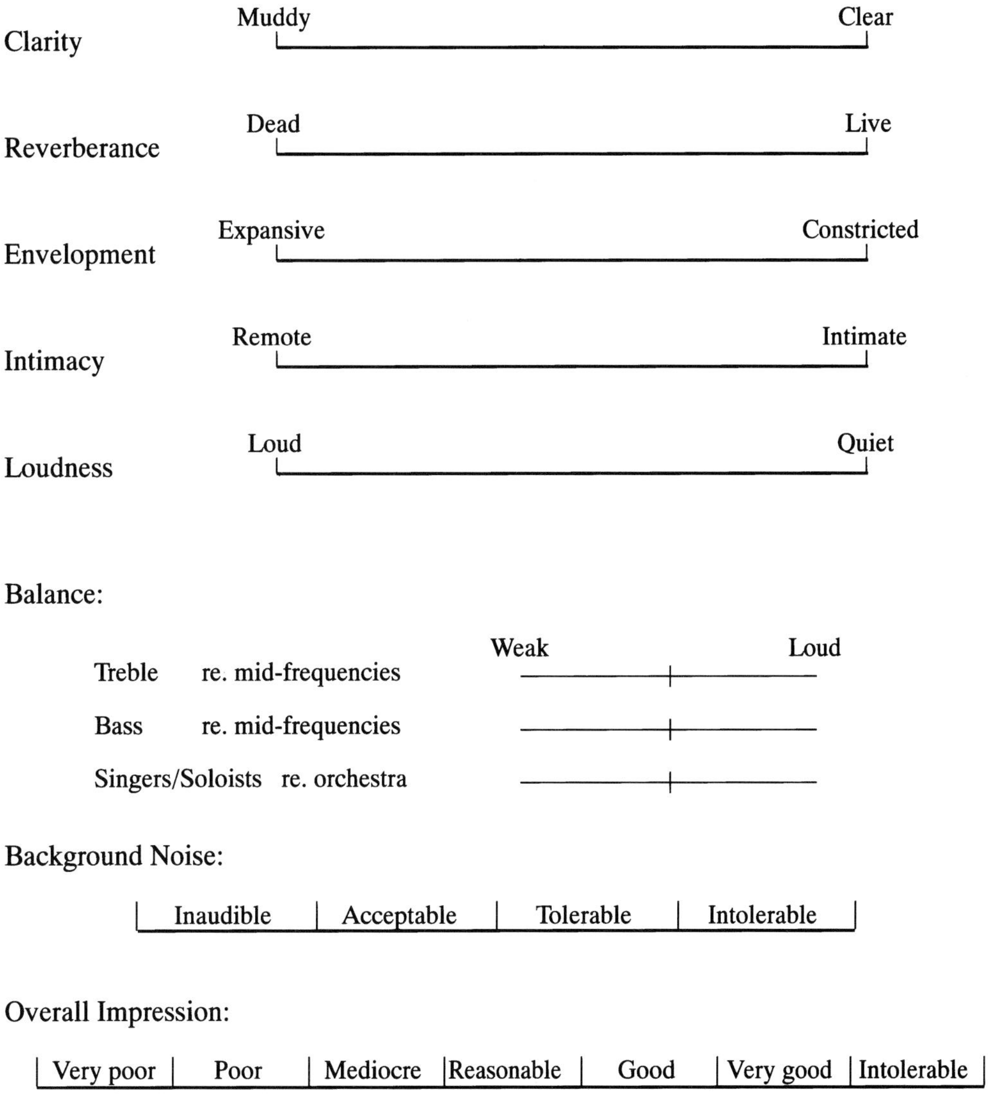

Figure 4.1. Subjective questionnaire used by Barron (1988).

The listeners appeared to be divided into two groups, those who preferred intimacy and those who preferred reverberance. Also, these two groups seemed to judge envelopment differently, one group associating it with reverberance and the other with intimacy. This may be a matter of semantics because the instruction given to the subjects for envelopment was, "envelopment refers to the spatial aspect of the perceived sound, the degree to which the listener feels surrounded by the sound." This instruction would seem to relate to LEV, but since ASW was not included in the definition, it is reasonable that those who preferred intimacy would be sensitive to ASW and those who preferred reverberance would be sensitive to LEV.

Gade studies

Gade (1985, 1989a, and 1991) made objective measurements in 35 unoccupied European concert halls in an effort to learn whether the various measured acoustical factors were orthogonal, i.e., statistically independent, and whether some acoustical or architectural measurements could be found to correlate with subjective judgments.

By factor analysis Gade determined that RT, EDT, and C_{80} are highly correlated with each other and hence, are tautological. Sound level (G) and the lateral energy fraction (LF) are orthogonal to each other and to attributes just discussed. Gade did not mention the initial-time-delay gap (ITDG) or the bass ratio BR, and did not measure IACC. He also made measurements on concert stages that showed the degree to which the sound a musician's instrument emits is reflected both to him and to neighboring musicians (early energy, 20–100 msec, ST1).

Gade concluded that cubic volume, RT, and the mean width of the hall are the main factors governing most aspects of overall room acoustics as heard by the audience. In particular, he found that the lateral fraction (LF) (see Marshall and Barron above) correlates highly with mean hall width measured between the side walls (provided a fan-shaped hall is not too wide).

Vian and Pelorsen finding

Vian and Pelorsen (1991) measured RT, EDT, C_{80}, and G in both an opera house with a cubic volume of 742,000 ft^3 (21,000 m^3) and a small chamber music hall with about one-tenth the cubic volume. Those measured quantities were found to be nearly identical in the two halls, though it was obvious that the halls sounded very different. They observe, "New [physical] criteria or meaningful combinations of criteria have to be determined in order to describe better all the [subjective] dimensions of an acoustical situation." It is possible that, since ITDG and IACC would be very different for these two halls, they may be the "new" criteria.

CONSENSUS ACOUSTICAL PARAMETERS

The psychoacoustic laboratory studies presented here have been of immense value. They have identified an expanded set of acoustical attributes that can be measured in a concert hall or opera house and that correlate in varying degrees with the acoustical quality of the rooms. More attributes may be identified in the coming years, and some of these concepts may not survive, but the progress in understanding concert hall and opera house acoustics in the years since *Music, Acoustics, and Architecture* was published in 1962 has been significant.

Acoustical attributes that are now agreed upon as important are shown in Table 4.1. All measurements, except ITDG, are made as a function of frequency, always at multiples of 125 Hz up to 4 kHz. ITDG is usually determined from architectural drawings at a main-floor position about halfway between the most protruding balcony front and the front of the stage.

Table 4.1. Acoustical attributes derived from laboratory psychoacoustic and acoustic experiments. Although different variations of the attributes are found in the literature of the past 30 years, those listed here appear to be the current consensus. The mathematical formula for each quantity is given in Appendix 2. The word "early" means in the first 80 msec after arrival of the direct sound.

Acoustical Attribute	Symbol
For loudness:	
Strength of the arriving energy at mid-frequencies	G_{mid}
For reverberance:	
Reverberation time, occupied	RT
Early decay time, unoccupied and, if possible, occupied	EDT
For clarity:	
Early reflected energy to late reverberant energy ratio, unoccupied	C_{80}
For spaciousness:	
Inter-aural cross-correlation coefficient, early, unoccupied,	$\mathrm{IACC}_{E(\mathrm{arly})}$
Strength of arriving energy at low frequencies	G_{low}
Lateral Fraction, early, unoccupied	$\mathrm{LF}_{E(\mathrm{arly})}$
For envelopment:	
Inter-aural cross-correlation coefficient, late, unoccupied	$\mathrm{IACC}_{L(\mathrm{ate})}$
Visual inspection of surface irregularities	
For intimacy:	
Initial-time-delay gap, from tapes preferrably	ITDG, or
or from drawings	t_I
For warmth:	
Bass ratio, occupied	BR
Stage support:	
Early energy, between 20 and 100 msec. Hall unoccupied with source and micro-phone onstage separated by one meter.	ST1

The customary source of sound used in concert halls for determining these attributes is a dodecahedron omni-directional loudspeaker, with sufficient frequency range to permit impulse measurements at the usual six frequencies. Measurements are generally made at between 8 and 20 seats in a hall, for each of three positions of the loudspeaker on the stage, if time permits. No positions are closer than 3 m from the front of the stage. An average of the data is made of all seat and source combinations to obtain whole-hall values.

It would be desirable if all measurements could be made with the hall fully occupied and an orchestra on stage. But it is unlikely that either management or the audience would willingly lend themselves to such an experiment unless it were to become much less intrusive. Measurements of RT can sometimes be obtained non-intrusively in an occupied hall from digital tape recordings made during a concert, provided the musical composition chosen contains stop chords for the full orchestra. However, the measurement can be distorted by the reverberation time of the tympani if it is contained in the stop chord, making consultation with the musical score necessary.

Finally, not all the parameters listed in Table 4.1 are statistically independent of each other, that is to say, not all are orthogonal. In the later chapters an attempt is made to reduce the number in this list and to establish a procedure for combining them so that we can compare (1) a rank ordering of halls by that computational method with (2) subjective judgments of their acoustical quality.

COMMENTS

To a significant extent, the psychoacoustic studies discussed above have demonstrated a close relation between acoustical qualities, both measured and judged. However, laboratory tests often have a common problem. Those experimenters have mainly used as subjects university students who may not be representative of the audiences at symphony concerts or operas. Instructions given to subjects might be interpreted differently by sophisticated concert-goers than by students who habitually hear their music from radios or record players—many of whom probably listen to popular music only. In these days in which pop music is played at decibel levels rarely reached in concert, it is hard to know how they react in comparing two recorded binaural symphonic compositions. Are they listening to the presence or absence of high or low frequencies? Or to the relative loudnesses of the pieces? Or to some difference that has yet to be quantified? The discussions of the experiments in the literature do not make it clear how the subjects were instructed or what they actually listen for.

In one recent psychoacoustic test, where recording engineers were used as subjects, their judgment of the most important acoustical attribute of concert hall music was "brilliance," the presence of strong high frequencies. This could be a direct result of the subjects' experience with high-fidelity sound systems, where strong high-frequency response is usually an important indication of a good sound-reproducing system. We might also ask; are the headphones and loudspeakers faithfully reproducing the concert hall experience? Some studies have shown that subjective judgments may be different when the music is presented to the subjects on headphones rather than by loudspeakers. Finally, can simulated concert halls, and unoccupied concert halls with a single loudspeaker radiating the music, come even close to representing the music that is heard from a spread-out orchestra on stage performing before a full audience?

In Chapters 8 through 15 the modern measurements listed in Table 4.1 and made in concert halls and opera houses are compared with the subjective judgments obtained in the interviews presented in Chapter 6.

◇5◇

World Concert Halls Ranked According to Acoustical Quality

SUBJECTIVE EVALUATION OF CONCERT HALLS

The psychoacoustic studies reported in Chapter 4 have given rise to a different and exhaustive way to evaluate the acoustics of a group of halls. The ideal method would differ from the Goettingen and Berlin studies in that the basic material would be obtained only in occupied halls. It is common knowledge that the acoustics of a new concert hall cannot be judged reliably until the hall is filled for the opening concert. Appraising the acoustics of an unoccupied hall can mislead the listener since many acoustical parameters change with the degree of occupancy, viz: reverberance, strength of the bass as well as of the higher frequencies, warmth, clarity, and even the way the orchestra plays.

Proposed method for evaluation

In the proposed method, several persons or dummy heads on torsos would be seated in each concert hall during several regular concerts. Each head would be provided with two tiny microphones placed at the entrance to the ear canals. Binaural recordings would be made from the outputs of these microphones during the concerts so that a variety of music from the contemporary symphonic repertoire could be sampled. Ideally binaural recordings would be made in 20 or more halls, carefully chosen to represent a range of acoustics that would yield a range of acoustical attributes.

The recordings could then be presented binaurally to listening subjects in a laboratory environment. The subjects chosen would be limited to professional musicians, music critics, and classical music aficionados. They would register their judgments of quality either by choosing one member of a paired comparison in the manner of the Goettingen study or by category scales as in the Berlin study.

Such an experiment would require skilled musical subjects and engineering time and would perhaps be deemed prohibitively expensive. In addition, perfecting this method to present recorded music that was effectively equivalent to music heard in halls might turn out to be excessively difficult and time consuming.

Judging acoustical quality

Are good acoustics reducible to a single scale? Can musical listeners be expected to agree on what constitutes good acoustics? Are there "good" and "bad" acoustics, or is acoustics a mere matter of taste? It is hard to believe that acoustics could stand alone as the one factor in the world lacking in degrees of quality.

The need for skilled subjects is underscored by McAdams (1982) who has written, "We may never have the ability to predict the experience of a listener since a lot of what is perceived by an actively attentive listener ultimately depends on what the listener brings to the music..." Who best fulfills this requirement?

Certainly musicians provide a first source for reliable judgments, particularly orchestral conductors who elicit and listen to music in a variety of venues. A second valuable source is the music critic, particularly those who travel widely, both abroad and in their own environs. Most are skilled listeners, and many have learned to associate the acoustics of a hall with musical quality. But few skilled musicians or critics are acquainted with a large number of halls. Thus, they may need to be joined by other music lovers who travel extensively and attend symphonic concerts in many countries.

The interview preliminaries

In the absence of the time and resources required for the elaborate experiment just described, and in the firm belief that judgments of acoustical quality must be made on occupied halls, I chose to extend the interviews carried out for my 1962 book to include halls constructed in the years since those earlier studies.

Many of the conductors and music critics who were selected for interviews were first contacted by mail. My letters explained that for the book I was writing I needed their appraisals of concert halls with which they were acquainted. A surprising number of them responded positively.

In order to make acquaintance with music centers near each of them, I arranged trips to obtain both the interviews and the chance to hear symphonic music by acclaimed orchestras playing in their accustomed halls. In the process I traveled to England, Continental Europe, Japan, China, Australia, New Zealand, and from end to end of the Americas. Opportunities for additional interviews occurred when traveling orchestras visited Boston or when I traveled to hear them elsewhere.

Fewer of the music critics were interviewed, though some responded by mail. In addition, I have conferred with acoustical consultants and concert-goers from many countries.

The names of the 44 persons interviewed for the earlier study are listed in Beranek (1962). After that date I ceased asking for permission to quote them by name because I found many of them were guarded in their statements. For example, during the pre-1962 interviews, I heard nothing but praise for one hall by one conductor and for another by a second conductor. I knew that these halls were not highly regarded by many and subsequently they have been dropped for concert purposes. Only later did I learn that the advocates had each had a commercial relation with the hall he praised.

I continue mindful of the admonition of two music critics who warned me that "all knowledge of a musical phenomenon must arise from experiencing it, and judgments can only be communicated to those who have also experienced it." I have listened to music in all but four of the halls described in the next chapter. In a few halls I have attended upward of 20 musical performances, and in all halls I have made a point of listening in at least two different positions, one before and the other after intermission.

The interview procedure

The interviews were conducted one-by-one. Whenever possible, I showed them pictures of 10 to 20 halls that I thought they might know. After they had commented on those they knew, I asked them to comment on any other halls that came to mind. Finally, I asked them to rank order all the halls they knew well. Their rank orders contributed substantially to the assignment to categories of the concert halls studied. Some examples of comments elicited from conductors that appeared in Beranek (1962) are still pertinent:

> Bruno Walter, [one of the most respected conductors of his time], said about Vienna's Grosser Musikvereinssaal, "It is certainly the finest in the world. It has beauty of sound and power. It sounds good either empty or full which is not the case for a number of halls.... I consider it better than

> Carnegie. Boston is very fine, more live than Carnegie. I like the Concertgebouw; it is really a live hall."
>
> Herbert von Karajan, whom I interviewed in the Green Room of the Vienna Staatsoper, compared Boston Symphony Hall with the Grosser Musikvereinssaal, "The sound in the Musikvereinssaal is so full that the technical attack of instruments—bows and lips—gets lost. The Boston hall is superb acoustically. For much music, it is even better than the Vienna hall because of its slightly lower reverberation time."
>
> Pierre Monteux said of the Amsterdam Concertgebouw, "The Concertgebouw has marvelous acoustics. It is probably one of the best in the world....The Musikvereinssaal too is very good. I find Carnegie a little dead with audience. Symphony Hall I like very, very much, and Tanglewood is also extremely good."
>
> [In reference to British halls] Sir John Barbirolli wrote, "I would be inclined to rate the acoustics of the Liverpool Philharmonic Hall as 'fair' rather than 'good' owing to its dryness of sound, though it is not unpleasant. It shares some of the properties of the Royal Festival Hall in its clarity and inclination to dryness, but I rate it higher in tone quality."
>
> George Szell observed, "The Musikvereinssaal in Vienna and Symphony Hall in Boston are excellent halls—the reverberation times in them are about right."
>
> Fritz Reiner said, "The Musikvereinssaal is just right acoustically. Boston has one of the world's best halls. Carnegie is not as reverberant as it might be."

Other quotations appear in Chapters 8 and 9 of this book and in the writeups of the halls in Chapter 6.[1]

No one of those interviewed was acquainted with more than one-third of the 76 concert halls and opera houses chosen for the study. From these overlapping responses I felt justified to make an overall rank order. I am well aware that the combination of their remarks and my interpretation does not constitute a scientific canvass of expert

[1] *Quotes from interviews can be found in Chapter 6 in the descriptions for halls Nos. 3–6, 9,19, 25–28, 32, 33, 35, 37, 47, 51, 55, 56, 58, 59, 69, 73, and 74.*

opinions. But the only other technique available, would have been to use written questionnaires. It is my experience and that of many pollsters that only a small percentage of busy people take the time to complete and return questionnaires. Also, written questions and answers preclude the ferreting out of the basis for their judgments, as well as the opportunity to quiz the responders in more depth. Nevertheless, an excellent study, based on a self-administered questionnaire, is presented in Appendix 3.

THE HALLS

The 66 concert halls investigated are listed in Table 5.1, along with some of their acoustical and physical attributes. Of these, 13 were not assigned to a category because insufficient discussion precluded their inclusion. In addition, the 10 opera houses of

TABLE 5.1. Basic material for the studies of subsequent chapters, including the size and seating capacity of 66 concert halls, and for each, RT, EDT, and various dimensional ratios. Definitions of terms are given in Appendix 1 and formulas in Appendix 2. Opera houses are listed in Table 16.1, Chapter 16.

	No. of Seats	Cubic Volume cu m	RT Occ. sec	EDT Unocc. sec	EDT/RT	V/S_T m	V/N cu m	N/S_T 1/sq m
Amsterdam, Concertgebouw	2,037	18,780	2.0	2.6	1.3	14.6	9.20	1.60
Baltimore, Meyerhoff Hall*	2,467	21,520	2.0	2.3	1.2	12.9	8.72	1.48
Basel, Stadt-Casino	1,448	10,500	1.8	2.2	1.2	11.8	7.25	1.63
Berlin, Kammermusiksaal	1,138	11,000	1.7	2.1	1.2	12.1	9.66	1.25
Berlin, Konzerthaus (Schauspiel)	1,575	15,000	2.05	2.4	1.2	13.6	9.53	1.43
Berlin, Philharmonie	2,335	21,000	1.95	2.1	1.1	13.5	9.00	1.42
Birmingham, Symphony Hall	2,211	25,000	1.85	2.0	1.1	15.6	11.30	1.38
Bloomington, Indiana. Univ. Aud.	3,760	26,900	1.4	-	-	10.2	7.20	1.42
Bonn, Beethovenhalle	1,407	15,730	1.65	-	-	11.9	11.20	1.06
Boston, Symphony Hall	2,625	18,750	1.85	2.4	1.3	12.3	7.14	1.72
Bristol, Colston Hall	2,121	13,450	1.7	1.85	1.1	11.7	6.34	1.85
Brussels, Palais des Beaux-Arts	2,150	12,520	1.4	-	-	8.4	5.83	1.44
Budapest, Pátria Hall	1,750	13,400	1.7	-	-	9.3	7.66	1.21
Buffalo, Kleinhans Music Hall*	2,839	18,240	1.3	1.6	1.2	8.5	6.42	1.32
Caracas, Aula Magna	2,660	24,920	1.3	-	-	11.9	9.37	1.27
Cardiff, Wales, St. David's Hall	1,952	22,000	1.95	2.1	1.1	15.8	11.20	1.41
Chicago, Orchestra Hall*	2,582	18,000	1.25	-	-	9.7	7.00	1.39
Christchurch, N. Z., Town Hall	2,662	20,500	2.1	2.0	1.0	12.7	7.70	1.65
Cleveland, Severance Hall	2,101	15,690	1.5	1.7	1.1	11.2	7.50	1.49
Copenhagen, Radiohuset, Studio 1	1,081	11,900	1.5	2.0	1.3	11.8	11.00	1.07
Copenhagen, Tivoli Koncertsal	1,789	12,740	1.3	-	-	9.6	7.10	1.35
Costa Mesa, Segerstrom Hall	2,903	27,800	1.6	2.2	1.4	14.2	9.58	1.48

TABLE 5.1. *Continued*

	No. of Seats	Cubic Volume cu m	RT Occ. sec	EDT Unocc. sec	EDT/RT	V/S_T m	V/N cu m	N/S_T 1/sq m
Dallas, McDermott/Meyerson Hall	2,065	23,900	2.8	1.9	0.7	16.4	11.60	1.41
Edinburgh, Usher Hall	2,547	15,700	1.5	2.1	1.4	10.8	6.16	1.75
Edmonton, Alberta Jubilee Hall	2,678	21,500	1.4	1.4	1.0	10.0	8.00	1.25
Glasgow, Royal Concert Hall	2,459	22,700	1.75	1.7	1.0	14.3	9.23	1.55
Gothenburg, Konserthus	1,286	11,900	1.65	1.75	1.1	14.2	9.25	1.54
Helsinki, Kulttuuritalo	1,500	10,025	1.05	-	-	9.0	6.70	1.34
Jerusalem, Binyanei Ha'Oomah	3,142	24,700	1.75	1.85	1.1	10.3	7.90	1.30
Leipzig, Gewandhaus	1,900	21,000	2.0	-	-	15.2	11.00	1.38
Lenox, Seiji Ozawa Hall	1,180	11,610	1.7	-	-	12.3	9.83	1.25
Lenox, Tanglewood Music Shed	5,121	42,480	1.9	3.3	1.7	13.9	8.29	1.68
Liverpool, Philharmonic Hall*	1,824	13,560	1.5	1.8	1.2	9.5	7.43	1.28
London, Barbican Concert Hall*	2,026	17,750	1.75	1.9	1.1	11.9	8.76	1.36
London, Royal Albert Hall	5,080	86,650	2.4	2.6	1.1	23.5	17.00	1.38
London, Royal Festival Hall**	2,901	21,950	1.5	1.7	1.1	10.2	7.56	1.35
Manchester, Free Trade Hall	2,351	15,430	1.6	1.7	1.1	9.9	6.60	1.50
Mexico City, Salla Nezahualcoyotl	2,376	30,640	1.95	-	-	15.7	12.90	1.22
Minneapolis, Minn. Orch. Hall	2,450	18,975	1.85	-	-	10.7	7.74	1.38
Montreal, Salle Wilfrid-Pelletier*	2,982	26,500	1.65	1.9	1.2	13.7	8.90	1.54
Munich, Herkulessalle	1,287	13,590	1.8	-	-	16.1	10.60	1.52
Munich, Philharmonie Am Gasteig	2,487	29,700	1.95	2.1	1.1	15.9	12.40	1.28
New York, Avery Fisher Hall	2,742	20,400	1.75	1.95	1.1	12.1	7.44	1.63
New York, Carnegie Hall	2,804	24,270	1.8	-	-	13.3	8.65	1.54
Osaka, Symphony Hall	1,702	17,800	1.8	2.1	1.2	11.7	10.50	1.11
Paris, Salle Pléyel	2,386	15,500	1.5	1.8	1.2	11.9	6.50	1.83
Rochester, Eastman Theatre	3,347	25,500	1.65	-	-	11.5	7.62	1.51
Rotterdam, De Doelen Concert Hall	2,242	24,070	2.05	2.3	1.1	14.2	10.7	1.33
Salt Lake, Utah, Symphony Hall	2,812	19,500	1.7	2.1	1.2	10.3	6.93	1.49
Salzburg, Festspielhaus	2,158	15,500	1.5	1.85	1.2	9.9	7.20	1.38
San Francisco, Davies Hall*	2,743	24,070	1.85	2.15	1.2	13.0	8.78	1.48
Stuttgart, Liederhalle	2,000	16,000	1.6	2.1	1.3	10.4	8.00	1.30
Sydney Opera House, Concert Hall	2,679	24,600	2.2	2.2	1.0	14.0	9.18	1.53
Taipei, Concert Hall Auditorium	2,074	16,700	2.0	-	-	10.9	8.00	1.36
Tel Aviv, Fredric Mann Auditorium	2,715	21,240	1.55	1.7	1.1	11.0	6.76	1.63
Tokyo, Bunka Kaikan, Ueno	2,327	17,300	1.5	1.85	1.2	11.2	7.40	1.51
Tokyo, Hamarikyu Asahi	552	5,800	1.7	1.8	1.1	11.4	10.50	1.09
Tokyo, Metropolitan Art Space	2,017	25,000	2.15	2.55	1.2	16.5	12.40	1.33
Tokyo, NHK Hall	3,677	25,200	1.7	-	-	12.5	6.85	1.82
Tokyo, Orchard Hall, Bunkamura	2,150	20,500	1.8	-	-	13.4	9.53	1.41
Tokyo, Suntory Hall	2,006	21,000	2.0	2.45	1.2	13.1	10.50	1.25
Toronto, Roy Thompson Hall	2,812	28,300	1.8	1.9	1.1	14.9	10.06	1.48
Vienna, Musikvereinssaal	1,680	15,000	2.0	3.0	1.5	13.4	8.93	1.50
Washington, Kennedy Concert Hall	2,759	19,300	1.85	1.75	0.9	12.0	7.00	1.71
Worcester, Mechanics Hall	1,343	10,760	1.55	2.15	1.4	12.5	8.01	1.56
Zurich, Grosser Tonhallesaal	1,546	11,400	2.05	3.1	1.5	11.2	7.37	1.52
Average	2,311	20,432	1.7	2.1	1.2	12.6	8.88	1.43

*Before renovations either recently completed, underway, or in planning, designed to improve the acoustics.

**Assisted resonance turned on.

Chapter 6 are dealt with in Chapter 16. Based on the interviews, the remaining 53 concert halls are assigned to six categories—A+, A, B+, B, C+, and C. See Table 5.2.

THE SIX CATEGORIES

The six categories of Table 5.2 are defined in this section. As is inevitable in category scales, some halls fall near the border lines between categories, but it is unlikely that any hall would be judged more than one category higher or lower.

Category A+— "Superior"

The three concert halls in this category were nearly unanimously rated as the best in the world, whether because of their age and the eminence of the performances in them throughout their history, or because of some ideal confluence of their acoustical attributes, or both. All were built by 1900.

Category A— "Excellent"

The six concert halls in this category received few negative comments, although there were differences of preferences, with some discussants wishing for greater clarity in a hall and others for less, and so on. Only three of the halls were built before World War II. Again, it is possible that other rating procedures might find several other halls belonging in this category. The independent study reported in Appendix 3, using a self-administered questionnaire, has produced some differences that are discussed in the following section on the Fricke–Haan study.

Category B+— "Good to excellent"

The 35 concert halls that are assignable to Category B+ received mixed judgments. Halls were sometimes called excellent (Category A) by some raters and C+ (fair to good) by others. Other raters simply said they could not assign them to the A category.

Category B+ raised special problems. In discussions of the rankings with the managements of some halls—though science might have been served by specifying the halls—their commercial concerns would have threatened my getting some of the data

TABLE 5.2. Assigment of 53 Concert halls in subjective categories of acoustical quality. RT and EDT are averages at 500 and 1,000 Hz. Within categories halls are not rank ordered. Listings are alphabetical.

CITY AND NAME OF HALL	RT Occ. sec	EDT Unocc.	BR Occ.	No. of Seats	Cubic Vol. cu m
Category A+ "Superior":					
Amsterdam, Concertgebouw	2.0	2.6	1.08	2,037	18,780
Boston, Symphony Hall	1.85	2.4	1.03	2,625	18,750
Vienna, Gr. Musikvereinssaal	2.0	3.0	1.11	1,680	15,000
Category A "Excellent":					
Basel, Stadt-Casino	1.8	2.2	1.17	1,448	10,500
Berlin, Konzerthaus (Schauspielhaus)	2.05	2.4	1.23	1,575	15,000
Cardiff, Wales, St. David's Hall	1.95	2.1	0.96	1,952	22,000
New York, Carnegie Hall	1.8	-	1.14	2,804	24,270
Tokyo, Hamarikyu Asahi	1.7	1.8	0.94	552	5,800
Zurich, Grosser Tonhallesaal	2.05	3.1	1.23	1,546	11,400
Average of Categories A+ & A:	**1.9**	**2.45**	**1.10**	**1,802**	**15,722**
Median of Categories A+ & A:	**1.95**	**2.4**	**1.11**	**1,680**	**15,000**
Category B+ "Good to Excellent":					
Number of halls:	**35**				
Average volume:				**19,200 m³ (680,000 ft³)**	
Average seat count:				**2,320**	
Average BR			**1.08**		
Average EDT		**2.0 sec**			
Average RT:	**1.7 sec**				
Category B "Good":					
Chicago, Orchestra Hall*	1.25	-	1.15	2,582	18,000
Edmonton, Alberta Jubilee Hall	1.4	1.4	0.99	2,678	21,500
Montreal, Salle Wilfrid-Pelletier*	1.65	1.9	1.21	2,982	26,500
San Francisco, Davies Hall*	1.85	2.15	1.11	2,743	24,070
Tel Aviv, Mann Auditorium	1.55	1.7	0.98	2,715	21,240
Category C+ "Fair to Good":					
Bloomington, Univ. Auditorium	1.4	-	1.12	3,760	26,900
Buffalo, Kleinhans Music Hall*	1.3	1.6	1.28	2,839	18,240
London, Barbican Concert Hall*	1.75	1.9	1.07	2,026	17,750
Average of Categories B & C+:	**1.5**	**1.8**	**1.12**	**2,791**	**21,422**
Median of Categories B & C+:	**1.5**	**1.8**	**1.14**	**2,729**	**21,370**
Category C "Fair":					
London, Royal Albert Hall	2.4	2.6	1.13	5,080	86,650

*Before renovations either recently completed, underway or in planning to improve acoustics.

of Chapter 6 and Appendix 4. With reluctance I have not identified these 35 halls by name in the succeeding analyses.[2] This B+ group is composed of good to excellent halls, most of which serve as home bases for superior orchestras. Their local reputations are almost always excellent.

[2]*Identification of these halls may be requested on a confidential basis by research workers.*

Category B—"Good"

Almost all the raters found the five concert halls in this category below those in the category above. However, several halls need special explanations.

All the data on the Davies Hall, San Francisco, including the interviews and the acoustical measurements of Appendix 4, were in place *before* completion in 1992 of major renovations designed to improve the acoustics. Thus, the ranking in Table 5.2 is based on the configuration of the hall as it was originally built. However, the drawings and photographs of Davies Hall, No. 18 in Chapter 6, show its present configuration, including renovations.

The Board of Trustees of Chicago's Orchestra Hall, are planning to make major renovations for improvement of the acoustics before the end of this decade, which will raise the roof and ceiling and deepen the stage. The Edmonton and Tel Aviv halls were completed in 1957, and the state of the art at that time allowed deficiencies in several acoustical attributes. Finally, revisions are under consideration for the Montreal hall.

Category C+—"Fair to good"

The three concert halls in this category received low ratings. The Buffalo hall, also constructed during a period of little acoustical guidance (1940), has a number of deficiencies. The Bloomington University Auditorium is a general- purpose hall of very large size, and is deficient in the major acoustical attributes for concert halls. It ranks better as an opera house. Renovations are also in process for London's Barbican Hall to improve its acoustics. Barron (1993) finds little to recommend it—lack of bass, short reverberation time, little early reflected energy, and lack of excitement.

Category C—"Fair"

Only one hall falls in this category, the Royal Albert Hall in London. This rating is based on the suitability of its acoustics for the entire symphonic repertoire. But for some kinds of music the Royal Albert perhaps deserves a higher rating than "fair." I quote Barron (1993), who has had experience with the history and acoustics of this hall:

> In spite of its problems and its immense size, more than twice the volume of any other auditorium considered here, the Royal Albert Hall manages annually to house London's vibrant "Prom" concerts during eight weeks

> between July and September. In 1985, for instance, the average attendance at 60 concerts was nearly 4,000 per concert—a remarkable achievement. This success owes little to the acoustics but is likely to be affected by the peculiar power of the arena form. This power to stimulate a strong sense of the shared experience has not escaped the notice of many organizations....It is regularly used for large-scale performances, an ideal location for such spectaculars as Tchaikovsky's *1812 Overture.* In this and grand choral works the space really comes alive, but at the smaller scale the impact can be dull.

The 53 halls listed in the six categories are tabulated in Table 5.2. No halls are rank ordered within the categories. The halls are listed alphabetically by city.

Most conductors and music critics familiar with 10 or more halls, called the same three halls, Amsterdam, Boston, and Vienna "excellent" or "the best in the world." They are rated here as A+—"superior." At the other end of the scale, several halls, among them London's Barbican and Albert halls, were called "fair" or "poor" in the interviews. I have rated them C+ and C, respectively, "fair to good" and "fair."

It has also come to my attention that several have recently had, or are expected to have, major renovations to improve their acoustics. Consequently some interviews and categories no longer match. They will be dealt with in detail as they occur in Chapter 6.

THE FRICKE–HAAN STUDY

Professor Fergus R. Fricke and his doctoral student Chan H. Haan at the University of Sydney, Australia, asked musicians and music critics to evaluate the acoustics of halls using a self-administered questionnaire. Because their survey was designed, in part, to serve as a comparison with the evaluations of acoustical quality to appear in this book, Professor Fricke, at my invitation, prepared Appendix 3 so that direct comparisons can be made. Except for one orchestral conductor, the musicians and music critics who responded to Fricke's questionnaire were completely different from those interviewed for the rankings in this chapter.

In Group (A+, A) Fricke lists eleven halls. Table 5.3 lists nine although there were several borderline cases where my personal judgment was used. Perhaps, my Group (A+, A) could be increased by two or three more. The two lists will be discussed further in Chapter 15.

TABLE 5.3. Beranek's list of Group (A+, A) halls based on interviews.

Group (A+, A) Halls
Amsterdam, Concertgebouw
Basel, Stadt-Casino
Berlin Konzerthaus (Schauspielhaus)
Boston, Symphony Hall
Cardiff, Wales, St. David's Hall
New York, Carnegie Hall
Tokyo, Hamarikyu Asahi*
Vienna, Gr. Musikvereinssaal
Zurich, Grosser Tonhallesaal

* Because of the small size of this hall and the small stage area, this hall is not designed for full symphony orchestras. It is included as an example of successful design of a chamber-music hall.

It is my opinion that Chicago does not belong in Category A because of the planned, extensive renovations to improve its acoustics that are to be executed by 1997. The Berlin (Philharmonie), Chicago, and Cleveland halls are the homes of three of the world's renowned orchestras and that fact may have influenced some judgments of the halls' acoustical rankings. Further, the music critics in Fricke's study were from the USA and they would be likely to expand the vote count for American halls.

Except for the few exceptions noted, both surveys placed the same halls in Category B+, "good to excellent."

COMMENTS

The category orderings in Table 5.2, like all subjective assessments, are difficult to make, and possibly even to justify. In regard to the rank orderings, I understand and value the opinions and judgments of those who read this book and who may have had different experiences, different impressions, and who might express different rank orderings based on the concerts they have heard and where they have sat in the hall. The reader is hereby invited to share with the author any opinions garnished during concerts of unusual music or in spaces these halls or in halls not included here.

The categories of Table 5.2 and Appendix 3 will be used to evaluate the objective rating scheme of Chapter 15.

Acoustical data measured by recognized laboratories around the world are tabulated for these halls and for opera houses in Appendix 4. The next chapter presents descriptions, photographs, drawings, and architectural data on 66 concert halls and 10 opera houses.

Finally, I wish to emphasize that the interviews were carried out and the rank orderings were made before the modern acoustical data of Appendix 4 were collected from the many acousticians credited. Hence, the extent to which the physical data and the subjective ratings agree has been awaited by me with intense interest and will be covered in Chapter 15.

◇6◇

THE SEVENTY-SIX HALLS

POCHEÉ CODE FOR ARCHITECTURAL DRAWINGS OF CHAPTER 6

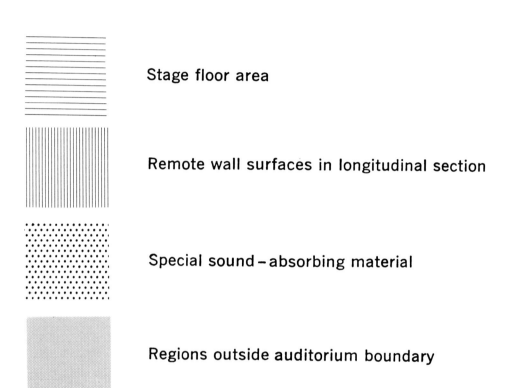

Stage floor area

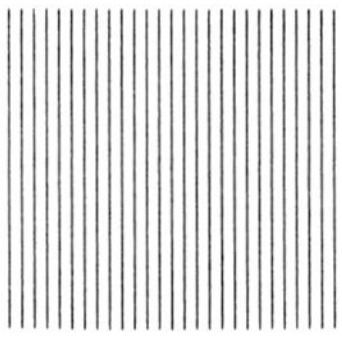

Remote wall surfaces in longitudinal section

Special sound-absorbing material

Regions outside auditorium boundary

USA

1

Baltimore
Joseph Meyerhoff Symphony Hall

The Joseph Meyerhoff Symphony Hall was completed in 1982. Seating 2,467, it takes its place among America's important halls as the home of the Baltimore Symphony Orchestra. Built only for concert use, it is a beautiful building, with unique shape, panorama of glass and brick, and grand staircases. Commanding one's attention inside the hall are the sweeping curved balcony fronts and 18 adjustable, fiberglass, sound reflecting and diffusing disks above and slightly forward of the stage. There are no flat walls, no ninety-degree angles, instead at each level there are curved randomly shaped "bumps" that reflect and diffuse the sound field. The ceiling is covered with 52 convex disks that emulate the coffered ceilings of classical halls.

Three acoustical features have been added since the hall's opening, designed to improve communication on stage and to reflect more sound energy to the front main floor seats. In regard to the first, Meyerhoff's Executive Director wrote in 1991, "We have been very happy with the acoustics of the Meyerhoff, but musicians are always striving to improve their environment. They have had some difficulty hearing each other on stage, and there have been some early reflections strong enough to be distracting to both the musicians and the conductor. A series of panels called QRD Diffusors[R] have been set up around the perimeter of the stage. These panels have had a very dramatic and positive effect of clearing up the sound on stage. I believe they have also rendered the sound in the auditorium somewhat clearer, with no serious loss of warmth." The musicians report improved ensemble playing.

The diffusers, as installed, are shown by two of the following photographs taken in 1993. The principle of a QRD diffuser is analogous to that of a light diffuser. If a flashlight beam is incident on a mirror at a certain angle, it will reflect off the mirror away from the flashlight at the same angle. Similarly, for a sound wave reflecting off a flat plaster surface the angle of incidence and the angle of reflection are the same. To diffuse a light wave so that the reflections go in all directions, even back toward the source, the surface of the mirror must be frosted. In acoustics, diffusion is accomplished by large and small irregularities on the sides of the stage, the walls, balcony, and ceiling.

Baltimore, Joseph Meyerhoff Symphony Hall

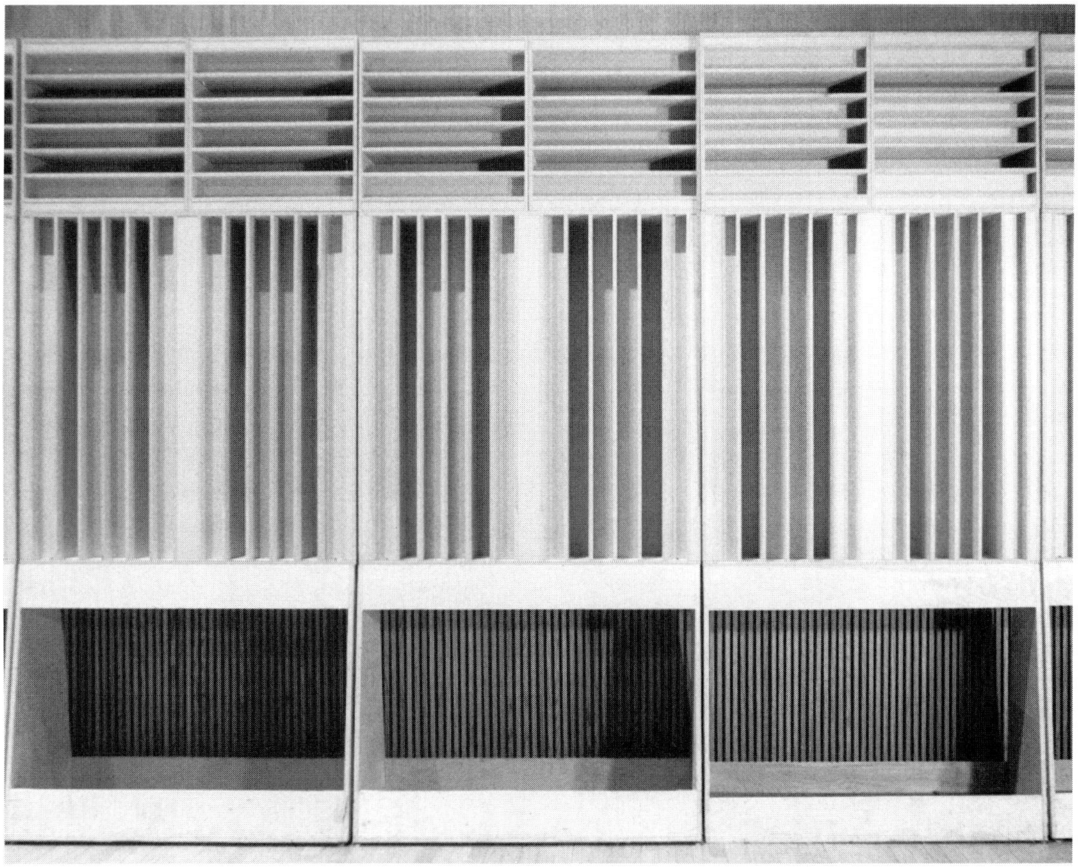

The diffusers on the stage of Meyerhoff are built in three parts (see photographs). The middle section is 8.3 ft (2.53 m) high and 3.6 ft (1.09 m) wide and diffuses the sound laterally; the upper element is 3.6 ft^2 and diffuses the sound upward and downward. The cross section of a 3.6 ft wide unit is comprised of longitudinal slots of varying depths, the overall depth in Meyerhoff being 8.5 in. (see the drawing; the pattern shown repeats itself). The properties of QRD diffusers are discussed further in Chapter 10.

A second addition to the stage acoustics were four Lucite reflecting panels, each 2 ft high and 3.6 ft long, located at the tops of the four diffuser units on either side. Each is sloped about 30° from vertical. They are designed to preserve more of the sound energy on stage and to combine direct reflections with diffuse reflections, and to assist members to better hear each other, which benefits ensemble playing.

The third addition was to extend the diffusing "tubes," located near the upper part of the wall at the back of the stage, over the entire width of the back wall and into the spaces on either side before the first box.

The reverberation time in Meyerhoff is 2.0 sec, fully occupied, which is optimum. The ratio of early sound energy (within 80 ms) to later reverberant sound energy is a little larger than in Boston Symphony Hall (BSH), and the strength of lateral reflections is lower. This means a little less spaciousness and greater clarity of the sound. The hall-average strength of the sound at mid-frequencies is about 0.6 dB lower than in BSH and the hall-average low-frequency sound level is about 0.7 dB higher. Also the bass ratio is higher in Baltimore so that the low-frequency sound is excellent.

QRD® DIFFUSOR

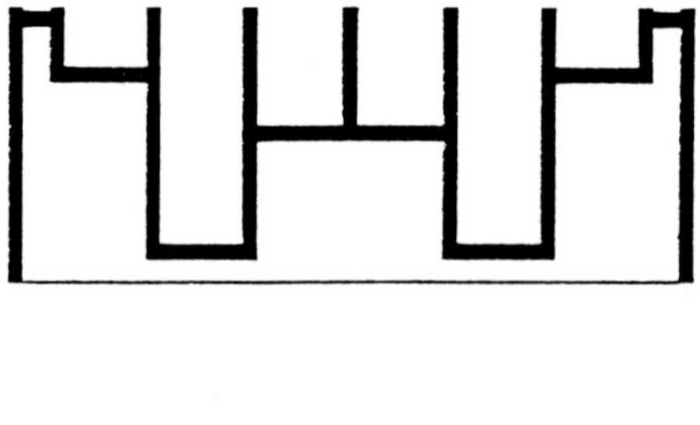

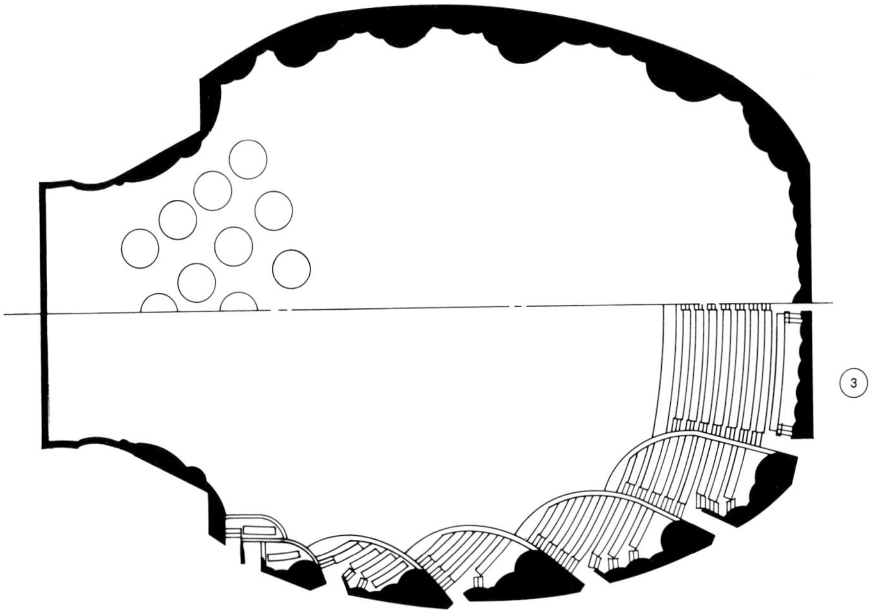

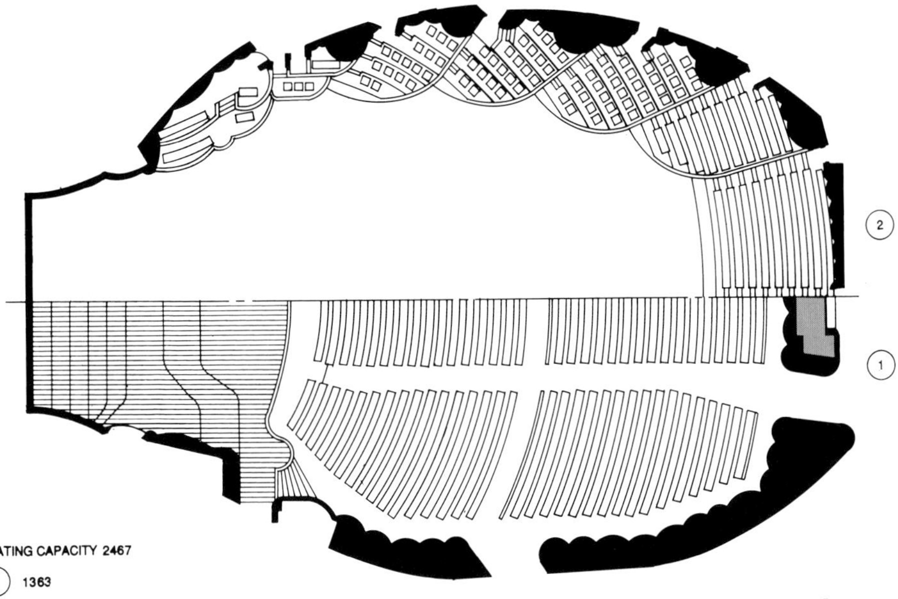

SEATING CAPACITY 2467

1 1363

2 564

3 540

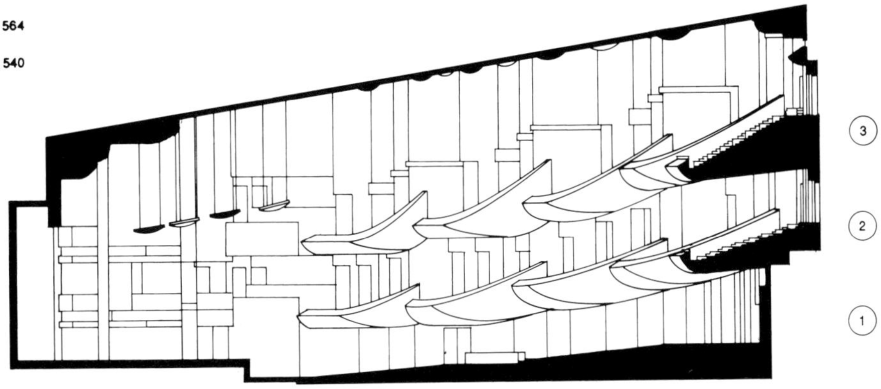

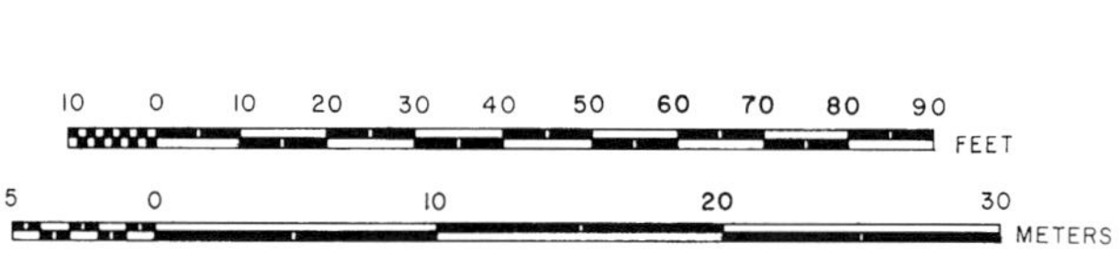

Architectural and structural details

Uses: concerts, recitals, and conferences. *Ceiling:* plaster over concrete planks. *Walls:* plaster over concrete block; plaster on balcony faces. *Sound diffusion:* on the upper walls of the stage with an area of 5 ft (1.52 m) × 46 ft (14 m); 52 convex panels on the ceiling, *Quadratic residue diffusers:* located on side walls of the stage, see the text and photographs. *Floors:* cast in place concrete slab. *Carpets:* on aisles of main floor and balconies—0.33 in. directly affixed to concrete. *Stage enclosure:* side walls concrete block, plastered, with wood veneer; ceiling, seventeen, 7 ft (2.2 m) diameter convex disks, adjustable height, 27–32 ft (8.2–9.75 m) above stage level; back wall—steel frame, solid plaster with wood veneer—can move back 9 ft (2.74 m) adding 380 ft^2 (36 m^2) to the stage. *Stage floor:* wood, tongue-and-groove over planks. *Stage height:* 39 in.(1 m) above floor level at first row of seats. *Seating:* backrest is 3/8 in. molded plywood; front of the backrest and the seat top are upholstered, porous fabric over open-cell foam; seat bottom is perforated; seat arms are wooden.

Architect: Pietro Belluschi, Inc. Associate architect: Jung/Brannen Associates, Inc. *Acoustical consultant:* Bolt Beranek and Newman, Inc.: *Photographs:* main hall: Richard S. Mandelkorn; courtesy of Jung/Brannen. *Stage:* Max G. Bennet; courtesy of Baltimore Symphony Orchestra.

*Technical details**

Concerts

V = 760,000 ft^3 (21,524 m^3)	S_a = 12,870 ft^2 (1,196 m^2)	S_A = 16,000 ft^2 (1,486 m^2)
S_o = 2,000 ft^2 (186 m^2)	S_T = 18,000 ft^2 (1672 m^2)	N = 2,467
H = 59 ft (18 m)	W = 96 ft (29.3 m)	L = 116 ft (35.4 m)
D = 123 ft (37.5 m)	V/S_T = 42.2 ft (12.9 m)	V/S_A = 47.5 ft (14.5 m)
V/N = 308 ft^3 (8.72 m^3)	S_A/N = 6.48 ft^2 (0.60 m^2)	H/W = 0.61
L/W = 1.21	t_I = 13 msec	

**The terminology is explained in Appendix 1.*

USA
2

Bloomington
Indiana University Auditorium

The Indiana University Auditorium is an extremely large hall. Not only does it contain 3,760 seats, but it is also very wide, with an impressive vaulted ceiling, and grilled penetrations on the two side walls. Close inspection reveals large areas of sound-absorbing material on the ceiling and side walls. The auditorium has a large stagehouse with a conventional proscenium opening. The rear of the hall can be closed off by a great curtain, which reduces the number of seats to 1,200. The Metropolitan Opera Company of New York performed many times in the Auditorium before it discontinued touring. The hall is used for all types of musical events as well as a variety of university functions.

The reverberation time in the Auditorium is short for orchestral music but excellent for opera, 1.4 sec with full occupancy. In operatic productions the singing voice projects well, and the balance between the singers and the pit orchestra is satisfactory in most locations in the hall. At the sides of the front half of the main floor the singing voice drops in level, and the instruments at the end of the pit nearer the listener become too loud. In the pit the brass and percussion tend to dominate the strings.

Throughout most of the hall one hears little reverberation. Near the front and on the stage there is a special kind of liveness due to reflections from the rear wall of the main floor, the balcony front, the solid surfaces projecting back from the edges of the large grilles on the side walls, and the lighting coves in the ceiling. Singers say that the Auditorium supports their voices well. Conductors in the pit report that the ensemble is satisfactory and the orchestra easy to control. The low ceiling provides adequate short-time-delay reflections on the main floor, with the result that the hall sounds more like one that seats half the audience. Previous poor listening conditions in the seats deep under the overhang of the balcony have been improved with a time-delayed, under-balcony, fill-in loudspeaker system.

For orchestral music the intimacy rating is low, but the bass ratio is optimal. Concert music is lacking in liveness and, in most of the hall, is not sufficiently loud, but the music is projected faithfully.

Bloomington, Indiana University Auditorium

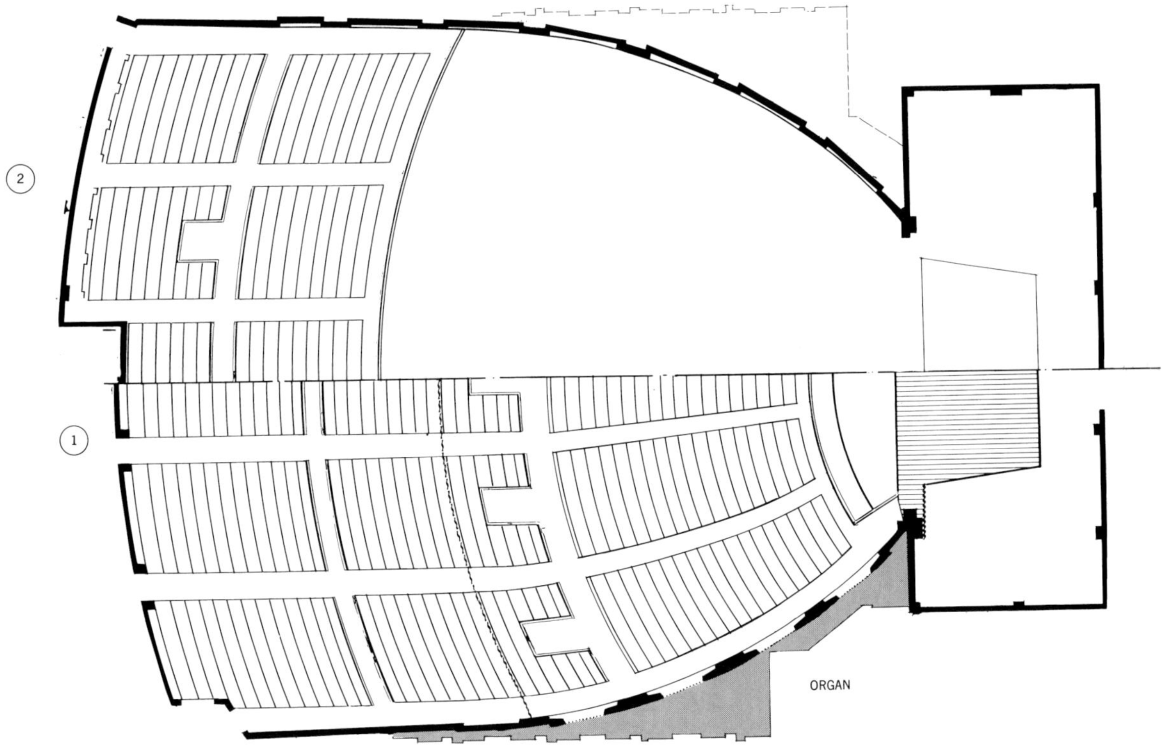

SEATING CAPACITY 3760

(1) 2592

(2) 1168

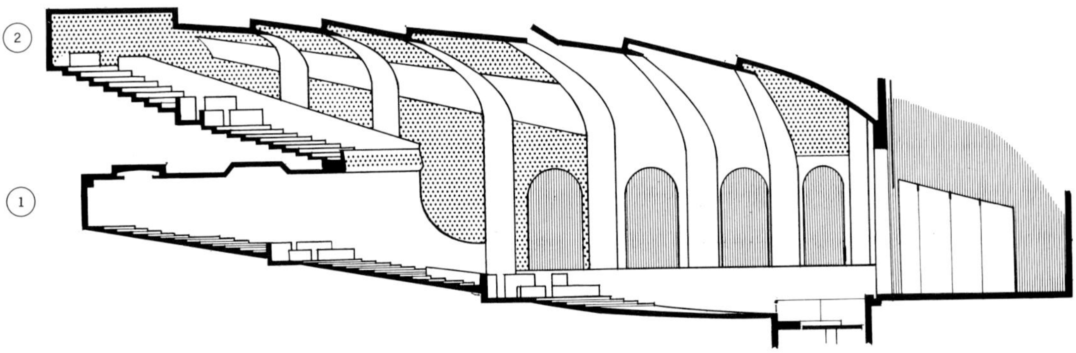

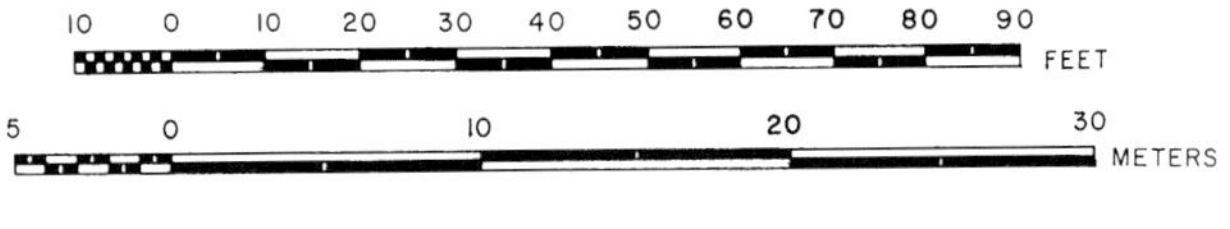

Architectural and structural details

Uses: music, drama, dance, lectures, and student assemblies. *Ceiling and side walls:* plaster on metal lath or masonry. *Floors:* concrete. *Stage floor:* wood. *Pit:* concrete and wood sides; an upholstered hanging is used on the rail when the pit is enlarged for full orchestra. *Stage height:* 42 in. (107 cm). *Orchestra enclosure:* fiberglass on light framing; openings in the ceiling for border lights. *Carpets:* on all aisles. *Absorptive material:* all ceiling sections except the second and third sections from the front are covered with perforated cane acoustic tile; two-thirds of the side walls are covered with another porous material called "Spongeacoustic;" the organ pipes are located on the left side behind and in front of three grilles; the other grilles in the hall cover sound-absorbing material; almost the only hard surfaces on the side walls are below the dado. *Seating:* seats are fully upholstered.

Architect: A. M. Strauss. *Associated architect:* Eggers and Higgins. *Photographs:* courtesy of University of Indiana and Musical America. *Drawings:* courtesy of L. L. Davis.

*Technical details**

Concerts

V = 950,000 ft³ (26,900 m³)	S_a = 20,200 ft² (1877 m²)	S_A = 26,240 ft² (2438 m²)
S_o = 2,000 ft² (186 m²)	S_T = 28,240 ft² (2,624 m²)	N = 3,760
H = 45 ft (13.7 m)	W = 129 ft (39.3 m)	L = 173 ft (52.7 m)
D = 177 ft (54 m)	V/S_T = 33.6 ft (10.2 m)	V/S_A = 36.2 ft (11 m)
V/N = 253 ft³ (7.2 m³)	S_A/N = 6.98 ft² (0.65 m²)	H/W = 0.35
L/W = 1.34	t_I = 40 msec	

Opera

V = 902,000 ft³ (25,545 m³)	S_a = 19,800 ft² (1,915 m²)	S_A = 25,740 ft² (2,391 m²)
S_p = 1,652 ft² (153.5 m²)	S_o (pit) = 878 ft² (81.6 m²)	S_T = 28,270 ft² (2,626 m²)
N = 3,718	V/S_T = 31.9 ft (9.72 m)	V/S_A = 35 ft (10.7 m)
V/N = 243 ft³ (6.9 m³)	S_A/N = 6.92 ft² (0.64 m²)	t_I = 40 msec

**The terminology is explained in Appendix 1.*

USA
3

Boston
Symphony Hall

Symphony Hall, built in 1900, is rectangular in shape with a high, horizontal, coffered ceiling and two wrap-around balconies. On entering the hall, one encounters two strong architectural features: the stage with its back wall devoted to a row of gilded organ pipes, and the upper walls with their niches, in front of which stand replicas of Greek and Roman statues. The combination of shades of gray and cream paint, gilded balcony fronts, red-plush balcony rails, black leather seats, and red carpets would place this hall architecturally in the middle of the nineteenth century, although it was built fifty years later. In some ways it resembles the Vienna Grosser Musikvereinssaal; nevertheless it is different, primarily because it seats 2,625 people compared with 1,680 for the Vereinssaal. During May and June each year, tables are installed on the main floor for "pops" concerts and the capacity is reduced to 2,369.

The sound in Symphony Hall is clear, live, warm, brilliant, and loud, without being overly loud. The hall responds immediately to an orchestra's efforts. The orchestral tone is balanced, and the ensemble is excellent.

Interviewed in 1961, conductors Walter, von Karajan, Bouldt, Munsch, Bernstein, and Leinsdorf agreed it is the "most noble of American concert halls." They, and other conductors, ranked it as one of the three best in the world, with such encomiums as: "one of the world's greatest halls," "when this hall is fully occupied the sound is just right-divine," "an excellent hall, there is none better."

There are a few negative features in Symphony Hall, as there are in every hall. The seats in rear corners under the overhangs of the balconies are shielded from the reverberant sound of the upper hall, and the reflected sound that reaches these seats from the soffits of the side balconies is somewhat unnatural. In the centers of the side balconies, echoes from the corners of the rear wall can be heard when staccato forte trumpet notes are played. Both these blemishes involve very few seats.

In my experience, only the Grosser Musikvereinssaal in Vienna, the Concertgebouw in Amsterdam, the Konzerthaus in Berlin, and the Tonhalle in Zurich have the same growth of crescendo and quality of reverberation as Symphony Hall. It is a rewarding experience to listen to music there.

Boston, Symphony Hall

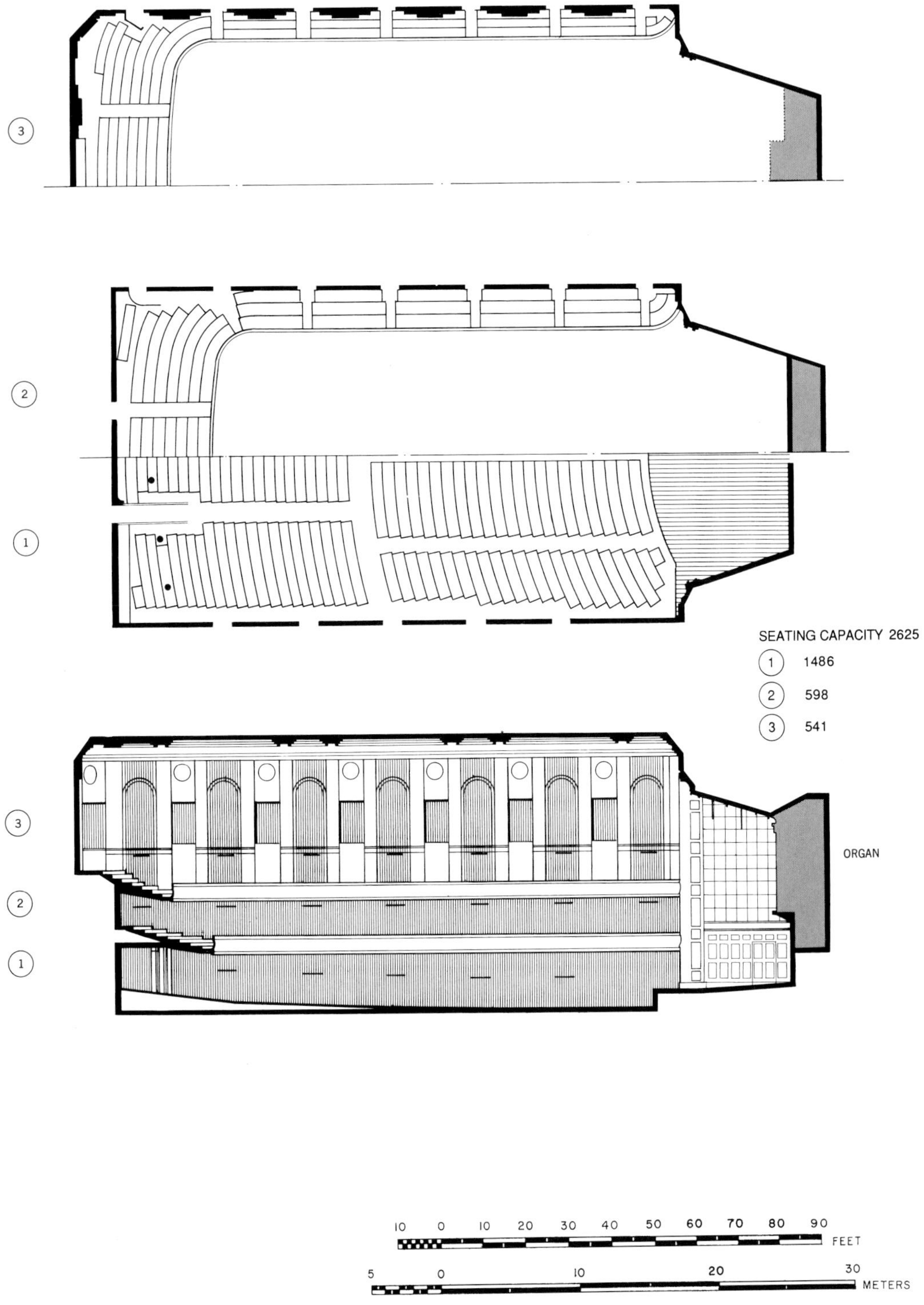
3
2
1
SEATING CAPACITY 2625
1 1486
2 598
3 541
3
2
1
ORGAN
10 0 10 20 30 40 50 60 70 80 90
FEET
5 0 10 20 30
METERS

Architectural and structural details

Uses: mostly orchestra and soloists. *Ceiling:* 3/4 in. plaster on metal screen. *Walls:* 30% plaster on metal lath, 50% plaster on masonry backing, 20% is 1/2 in. to 1 in. (2.5 cm) thick wood, including the stage walls; balcony fronts are an open-pattern cast iron. *Floors:* the base floor is flat concrete with parkett wood affixed; during the winter concert season, a sloping floor is installed (see the drawing) constructed of 3/4 in. (1.9 cm) boards on 4 × 4 in. (10 cm) framing members, supported on angle irons; the airspace varies from zero at the front to 5 ft (1.52 m) at the rear; the balcony floors are wood supported above the concrete base. *Carpets:* on main aisles downstairs, with no underpad. *Stage enclosure:* most of the enclosure, including the ceiling, is wood paneling in sections about 3 ft^2 (0.91 m^2) and 1/2 in. thick, held in frames 1 in. thick and 6 in. (15.2 cm) wide; from the stage floor up to a height of about 14 ft (4.3 m), the paneling is about 1 in. thick. *Stage floor:* part of the stage, starting 23 ft (7 m) from the rear, permanently slopes upward, reaching a height of about 5 in. (12.7 cm) at the rear; all the stage is 1.5 in. wooden planks over a large air space with 3/4 in. flooring on top. *Stage height:* 54 in. (137 cm) above floor level at first row of seats. *Seating:* the front and rear of the backrests and the top of the seat-bottoms are leather over hair; the underseats and the arms are made of solid wood.

Architect: McKim, Mead and White. *Acoustical consultant:* Wallace C. Sabine. *References:* H. E. Johnson, *Symphony Hall, Boston,* Little, Brown and Company, Boston, 1950; L. Beranek, "An Acoustician's Tour of BSH," J. Audio Eng. Soc., **36** (Nov. 1988).

*Technical details**

V = 662,000 ft^3 (18,750 m^3)	S_a = 11,360 ft^2 (1,056 m^2)	S_A = 14,750 ft^2 (1,370 m^2)
S_o = 1,635 ft^2 (152 m^2)	S_T = 16,385 ft^2 (1,522 m^2)	N = 2,625
H = 61 ft (18.6 m)	W = 75 ft (22.9 m)	L = 128 ft (39 m)
D = 133 ft (40.5 m)	V/S_T = 40.4 ft (12.3 m)	V/S_A = 44.9 ft (13.7 m)
S_A/N = 5.62 ft^2 (0.52 m^2)	V/N = 252 ft^3 (7.14 m^3)	H/W = 0.81
L/W = 1.71	t_I = 15 msec	

**The terminology is explained in Appendix 1.*

USA

4

Buffalo

Kleinhans Music Hall

One of the architectural gems of America is the Kleinhans Music Hall in Buffalo, which was dedicated in 1940. Well-proportioned lines and a primavera wood interior give an immediate feeling of intimacy, warmth, and comfort. The Kleinhans Hall, which has 2,839 seats, is one of only a half-dozen important halls for music built between 1900 and 1950. The centerline profile of Kleinhans is typical of many halls built from 1940 to 1960. The seats are luxuriously upholstered and widely spaced. The balcony is enormous, yet it leaves one with the feeling of intimate space. Buffalo audiences are proud of the hall and most find no fault with its acoustical qualities.

A local professor of physics, after making an acoustical study, was reported in the Buffalo *Evening News, May 16, 1941,* as saying, "The overall deadness of the Kleinhans Music Hall and the extra deadness at the low and the very high frequencies usually are noticed even more by the performers than the audience....[It is] more objectionable to single performers than to large groups such as a large orchestra."

I have on several occasions attended concerts in the Kleinhans Music Hall. The hall unquestionably lacks liveness, but contrary to the newspaper report, the brilliance of the string tone is excellent, particularly on the main floor, and the sound is warm with rich full bass. In certain parts of the main floor, the sound takes on a reverberant character. This sound can be classified as "stage liveness" rather than "hall liveness." In general, music comes through clearly and faithfully, but with a lack of the desirable support from room reverberation. This lack of support also means that the sound is not as loud as it is in Symphony Hall, Boston, for example, nor are the fortissimos as impressive. For speech and for highly articulated music, this hall is excellent. Plans are underway (1994) to reduce the background (air-conditioning noise) to a current-day standard.

Izler Solomon said, "I conducted there for many years. The acoustics are good, perhaps not quite as good on the stage as on the main floor of the auditorium." Nine musicians who are familiar with this hall mentioned its deadness. A concert violinist said that on stage the sound is quite good. He feels a sense of immediacy and support.

Buffalo, Kleinhans Music Hall

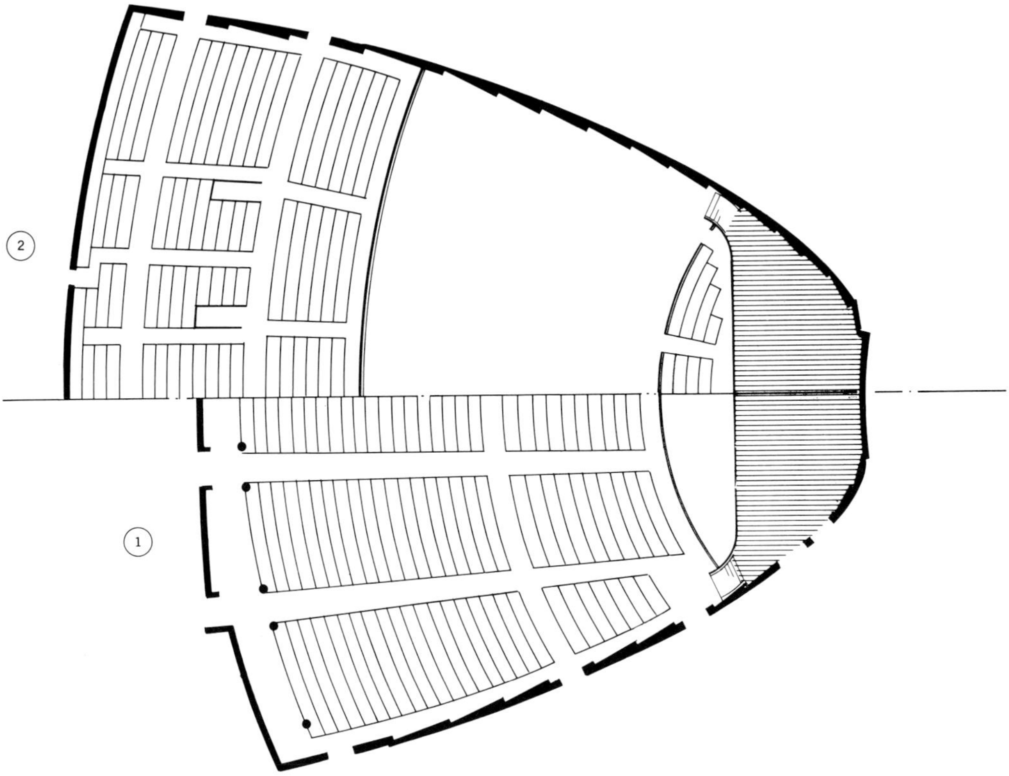

SEATING CAPACITY 2839

(1) 1575

(2) 1264

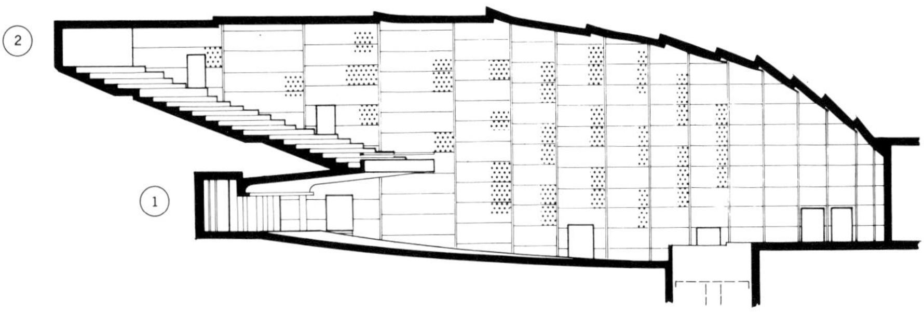

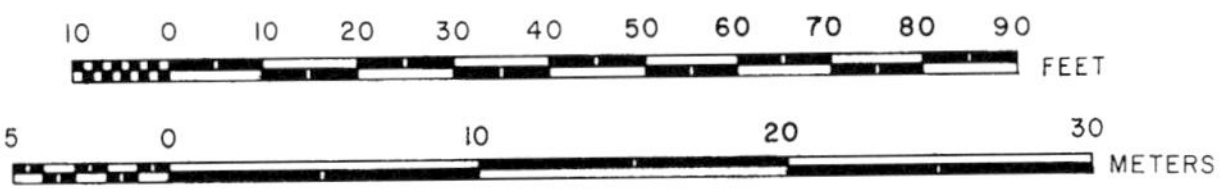

Architectural and structural details

Uses: orchestra, soloists, glee club, and lectures. *Ceiling:* 0.75 in. (2 cm) painted plaster. *Side walls:* 0.75 in. plaster on metal lath on which is pasted a linen cloth over which is cemented 0.06 in. (0.16 cm) flexible wooden sheets. *Rear walls:* 0.75 in. plaster on metal lath on which is cemented a heavy woven monk's cloth. *Floors:* concrete. *Carpet:* the main floor seating area and aisles are fully carpeted. *Stage enclosure:* the orchestra enclosure is permanent and is made of 0.75 in. (2 cm) plywood irregularly supported on 2 × 2 in. (5 × 5 cm) furring strips held, in turn, by a hollow-tile structure. Lighting coves overhead open to a high attic and permit air to filter out. *Stage floor:* 1.1 in. (2.8 cm) wooden planks on 0.75 in. subfloor over a large airspace. *Stage height:* 42 in. (107 cm). *Added absorbing material:* on each wall are located ten vertical strips of thin, perforated asbestos, backed in places by patches of sound-absorbing material. *Seating:* the rear of the backrest is plywood; the front of the backrest and the top of the seat are upholstered in hard-weave cloth; the seat-bottoms are unperforated metal; the armrests are wooden.

Architect: Eliel Saarinen and F. J. and W. A. Kidd. *Acoustical consultants:* C. C. Potwin and J. P. Maxfield *Photographs:* courtesy of Kleinhans Music Hall Management, Inc. *References:* J. P. Maxfield and C. C. Potwin, "A modern concept of acoustical design," pp. 48–55 and "Planning functionally for good acoustics," pp. 390–395, J. Acous. Soc. Am. **11** (1940).

*Technical details**

V = 644,000 ft^3 (18,240 m^3)	S_a = 17,000 ft^2 (1,580 m^2)	S_A = 21,000 ft^2 (1,951 m^2)
S_o = 2,200 ft^2 (205 m^2)	S_T = 23,200 ft^2 (2,156 m^2)	N =2,839
H = 44 ft (13.4 m)	W = 129 ft (39.3 m)	L = 123 ft (37.5 m)
D = 144 ft (43.9 m)	V/S_T = 27.8 ft (8.5 m)	V/S_A = 30.7 ft (9.35 m)
V/N = 227 ft^3 (6.42 m^3)	S_A/N = 7.4 ft^2 (0.69 m^2)	H/W = 0.34
L/W = 0.95	t_I = 32 msec	

**The terminology is explained in Appendix 1.*

USA
5
Chicago
Orchestra Hall

This oddly shaped hall was primarily the design of Chicago's musical giant, Theodore Thomas, who conducted the Chicago Symphony Orchestra from 1891 until 1905. Its acoustics, when fully occupied, are much less reverberant than the classical rectangular halls of Europe, but are clear and well balanced. This was a result that Thomas yearned for, and he was overjoyed to leave the Auditorium, happy to throw off the "deadly mishmash of sound where his passion was for clarity and sweet reasonableness." So wrote Charles Edward Russell (*The American Orchestra and Theodore Thomas*, Doubleday, Page and Company, Garden City, NY, 1927, pp. 292–301). Let us read on:

> But the public was fond of the Auditorium, which was a beautiful place, admirably adapted to spectacles, operas, and public meetings....If the Chicago public was ever to reach that stage of musical perception and development he had hoped for it, he must have a hall where he could show veritable effects....He announced that other quarters must be had for the orchestra or he would leave it.
>
> Daniel H. Burnham was the architect....he put into practice every suggestion that Mr. Thomas had made. The exceptions were small and unimportant....The hall was dedicated on December 14, 1904....About the building. It was so different from the Auditorium; everything sounded so strange in it....The orchestra in the Auditorium and the orchestra in the new orchestral hall were different machines. The new hall had hardly a third of the depth of the old and its acoustics were so perfect that the slightest whisper on the stage was audible at the back of the upper gallery. For thirteen years the orchestra had been accustomed to play so it could make itself heard in the great hollow of the Auditorium....[In Orchestra Hall] the sound was so clear that problems of technique and blend, not noticed before, appeared. Thomas felt that with adequate trial in a short time all the apparent harshness of the orchestra in its new quarters would be smoothed away. Thomas [probably] felt that Chicago...might have known that he would not stumble at the summit and crisis of his art....[But, nevertheless,] the cry arose that after all the labor and sacrifice the new hall was a failure...a part of the press used it industriously.

Mrs. Theodore Thomas wrote, after Mr. Thomas's death on January 4, 1905 (ibid., pp. 110–111):

> But unfortunately an adverse criticism of the new hall appeared, which he feared would injure its reputation unless immediately counteracted, and this made him feel, all too keenly, the necessity of adjusting the orchestra to its new surroundings in the shortest possible time, in order that the fine acoustics which he knew the hall possessed, *and with which he was perfectly satisfied*, might be made apparent to the world also, without delay.

Through the years, many attempts have been made to increase the reverberance of the hall—the most recent was by opening the ceiling acoustically, using a perforated metal screen in place of part of the plaster, so that the cubic volume of the hall was enlarged by the size of the attic. At the same time all ventilation ducts were removed from the attic and all surfaces hardened so as not to absorb sound. This treatment would have been effective, except at the same time the wooden seats of the balconies were replaced by upholstered seats which left the hall approximately with its original reverberance. An adverse effect of the addition of upholstered seats was to render the hall unsuitable for recording.

In 1990, the plaster dividers between the boxes shown in the photograph were cut down and replaced with acoustically transparent perforated metal panels. This has significantly improved the sound at the seats at the rear of the boxes. A further improvement in the sound in the boxes and in the hall in general was made in 1994, by creating closets at the rear of the boxes to contain the winter fur coats that were always hung on the open walls. To prevent echoes from the new doors to these closets, QRD diffusers (see Chapter 10) were installed on their faces.

There have always been differences of opinion as to where the best sound in Orchestra Hall exits. Most listeners agree that the front of the balcony is best. Robert Marsh of the Chicago *Sun-Times* reported that, "Towards the rear center of the main floor there are about 100 seats in which the sound equals the best in this country. Under the balcony on the main floor, the sound is pretty dreadful." Roger Detmer of the *Chicago American* said during an interview: "In my opinion, the best seats are on the main floor, between rows K and N, center. Other people maintain that the sound is better in the front balcony."

I have attended many concerts in Orchestra Hall and have found that the acoustics are dry but in most of the exposed seats, the sound is in good balance. In my opinion, the best seats are in the first three rows of the lower balcony and toward the rear of the upper balcony. As might be expected, the excellence of the Chicago Symphony Orchestra, certainly during the tenure of Maestro George Solti, has enabled their adjustment to these unique acoustics and together they achieved a proper bass-string balance. The brass never have to force. The ensemble of the orchestra is usually good, although the stage is wide and shallow, and the players complain about the difficulty of hearing sections on opposite ends of the stage.

There is now active talk about renovating Orchestra Hall to bring its acoustics in conformance with those of the world's better halls. The proposed steps, slated for completion in 1997, would entail several major changes. First, the roof would be demolished and replaced by a new roof about 20 ft (6 m) higher. The stage would be made about 10 ft (3 m) deeper and its front would be narrowed by about 18 ft (5.5 m). A choir/audience gallery would surround the orchestra. The seats would be replaced with ones less sound absorptive and would be made more comfortable. With those changes, the projected reverberation time, fully occupied, would be increased from its present value of about 1.2 sec to 1.8 sec or more.

This venerable hall has been a warm spot in Chicago's life and appears to bring out the best in the city's splendid orchestra. The projected changes should give the patrons of the hall a renewed appreciation of the orchestra's greatness.

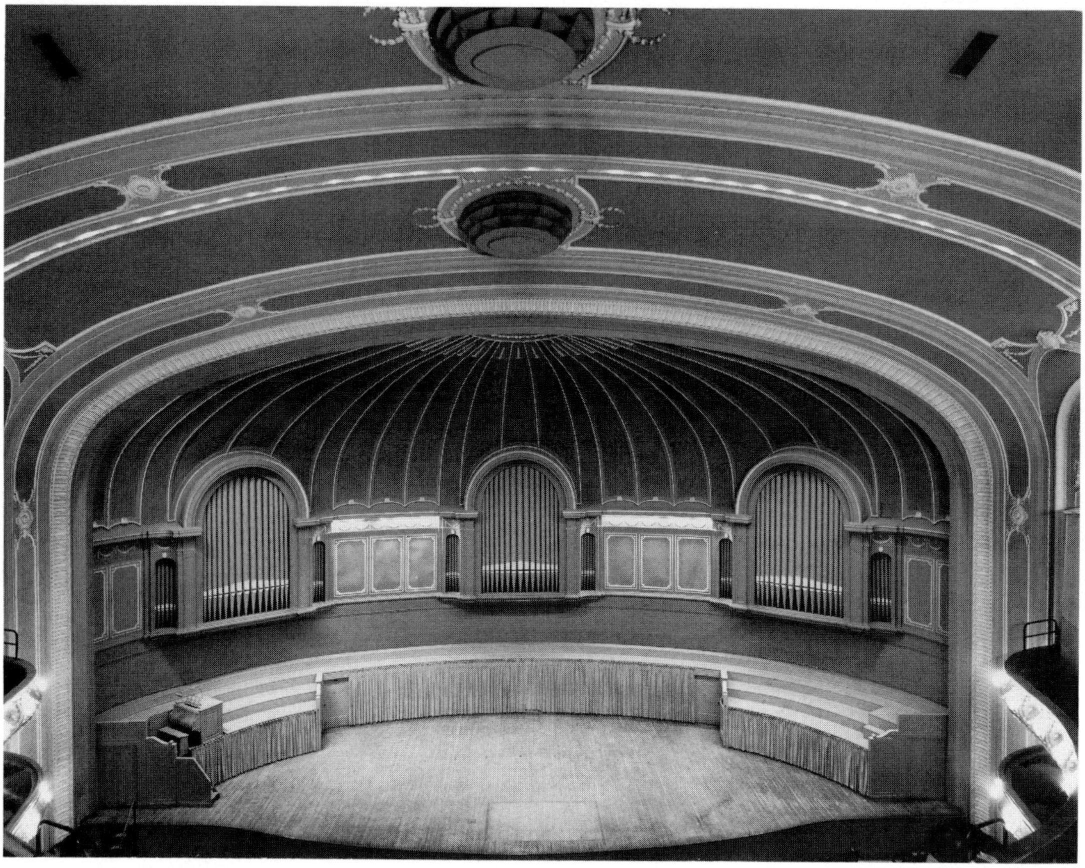

CHICAGO, ORCHESTRA HALL

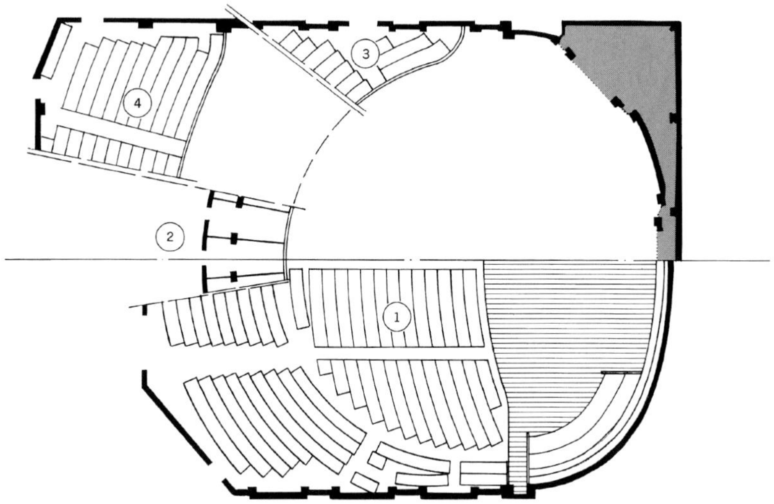

SEATING CAPACITY 2582

- (1) 1001
- (2) 138
- (3) 929
- (4) 514

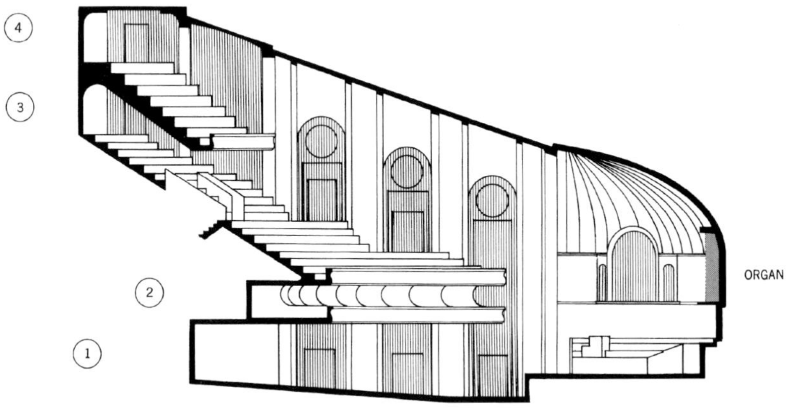

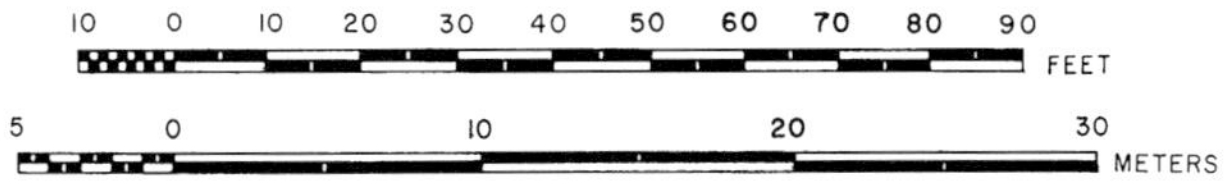

Architectural and structural details

Uses: orchestra, chamber music, soloists, lectures. *Construction changes since the drawings and photographs were made:* the attic space (not shown) couples acoustically to the main hall space, its cubic volume is included in the volume given in the table below; the stage was extended about 3 ft (0.9 m) giving it a centerline depth of about 39 ft (12 m). *Hall ceiling:* comprised of both plaster bands and perforated metal bands; plaster bands are 1 in. (2.5 cm) plaster on metal lath; metal bands are 16 gauge aluminum with 0.078 in. (2 mm) holes 0.125 in. (0.32 cm) on centers. *Added absorptive material:* some thin felt on rear walls to control echo. *Walls:* 1 in. (2.5 cm) plaster on wire lath. *Balcony fronts:* fibrous plaster, 1/2 in. (1.2 cm) thick. *Seating steps:* concrete. *Floors:* concrete. *Carpet:* on all aisles except upper balcony. *Stage floor:* wood on concrete. *Stage height:* 43 in. (109 cm). *Stage ceiling:* two layers of 1 in. (2.5 cm) hard board set in a step pattern to follow the curve of the half dome; hung below is a 16 gauge aluminum panel perforated as in the hall ceiling. *Seating:* Molded plywood back and unperforated plywood seat bottom; front of seat back is a cushion only 0.25 in. (0.6 cm) thick; seat cushions are 5 in. (cm) thick on main floor and 1 in. (2.5 cm) thick in the top balcony; armrests are wooden.

Architect: D. H. Burnham. *Acoustical consultant for attic revisions:* Bolt Beranek and Newman, Inc. *Consultants since 1981:* Kirkegaard & Associates. *Photographs:* courtesy of Shaw, Metz and Associates. *Reference:* L. Kirkegaard, D. Kirkegaard and D. Eplee, "Acoustics metamorphoses of Orchestra Hall, Chicago," Proceedings of W. C. Sabine Symposium, 7 June 1994, available from the Acoustical Society of America, Woodbury, NY 11797.

*Technical details**

V = 636,000 ft^3 (18,000 m^3)	S_a = 14,000 ft^2 (1,290 m^2)	S_A = 18,000 ft^2 (1,672 m^2)
S_o = 2,000 ft^2 (186 m^2)	S_T = 20,000 ft^2 (1,858 m^2)	N = 2,582
H = 59 ft (18 m)	W = 94 ft (28.7 m)	L = 84 ft (25.6 m)
D = 113 ft (34.5 m)	V/S_T = 31.8 ft (9.7 m)	V/S_A = 35.3 ft (10.8 m)
V/N = 246 ft^3 (7.0 m^3)	S_A/N = 7 ft^2 (0.65 m^2)	H/W = 0.63
L/W = 0.89	t_I = 36 msec	

**The terminology is explained in Appendix 1.*

USA
6

Cleveland
Severance Hall

Severance Hall is a handsome classical building, located in the University Circle area of Cleveland. Completed in 1931, Severance Hall was designed during the period when some American acousticians adhered to the philosophy expressed by F. R. Watson in his book *Acoustics of Buildings* (Wiley, New York, 1923), namely, provide a stage with reflecting surfaces so that performers can hear each other, and line the hall with acoustical material and draperies to create listening conditions comparable with outdoor conditions.

In 1958, as part of a program of rehabilitation, most of the draperies and carpets were removed, and a better stage enclosure was installed. The reverberation time of the hall increased noticeably. Certainly, the hall, with only 2,101 seats, is favorable to the production of good music—having assisted two famous conductors, George Szell and Christoph von Dohnanyi to bring the Cleveland Orchestra world acclaim as equal to the best of today's symphonic orchestras.

Several outside conductors have stated that the acoustics are very good. Robert Marsh (1961) of the Chicago *Sun Times* said, "For me, Severance Hall now has just about the right reverberation period. I don't like terribly reverberant halls. The sound in Severance is very uniform. There is a little damping under the balcony overhang. The sound is so beautifully integrated as it comes through the proscenium that, even if you are sitting far over on the left-hand side, you get just as good a sense of presence from the basses and cellos as you do from the violins that are much closer to you. Severance is not an extremely bright hall, although one does not have any feeling of loss of high frequency."

I have listened to only one symphonic concert in Severance and from my seat in the center main floor the balance between instrumental sections, the ratios of early-to-late sound energy, and the strength of the bass were excellent. The sound was clear and the loudness seemed right. Certainly, the ensemble was excellent. While, for works of the Romantic period, one might prefer a higher mid-frequency reverberation time than 1.5 sec, the fullness of the sound is just right for music of the classical period, which I heard that night.

CLEVELAND, SEVERANCE HALL

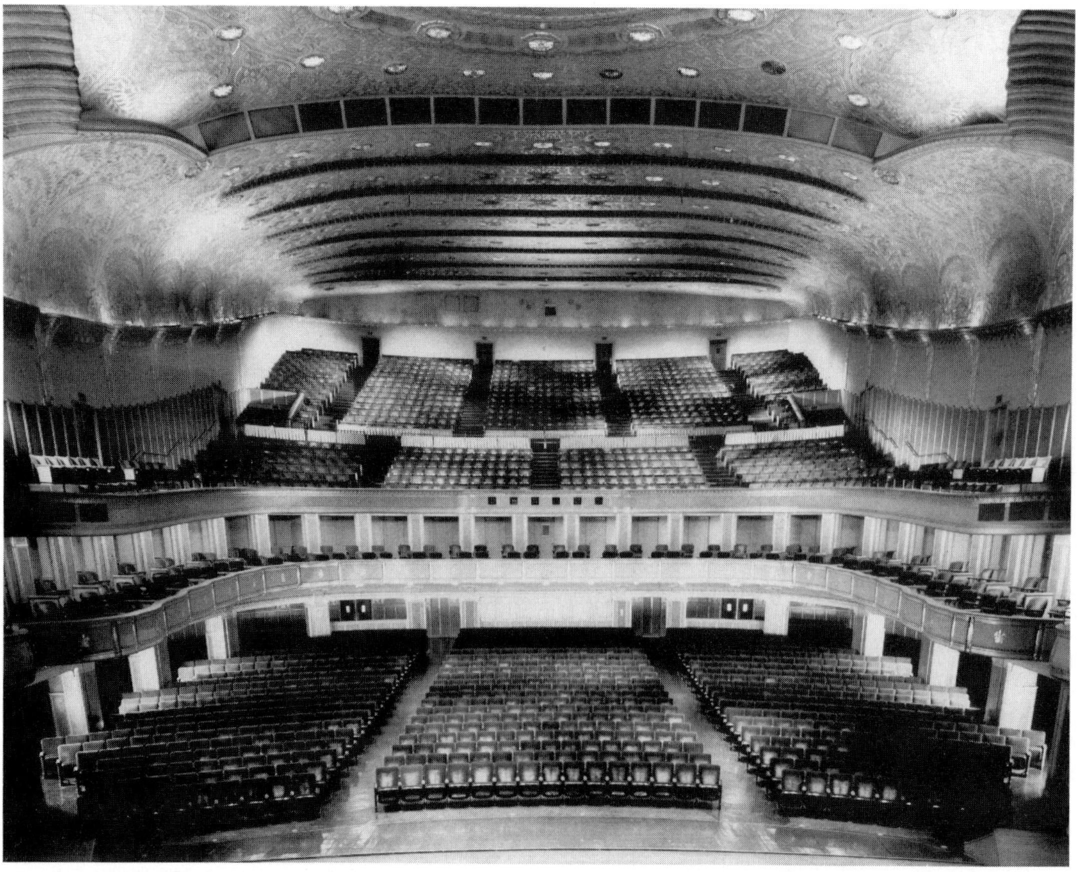

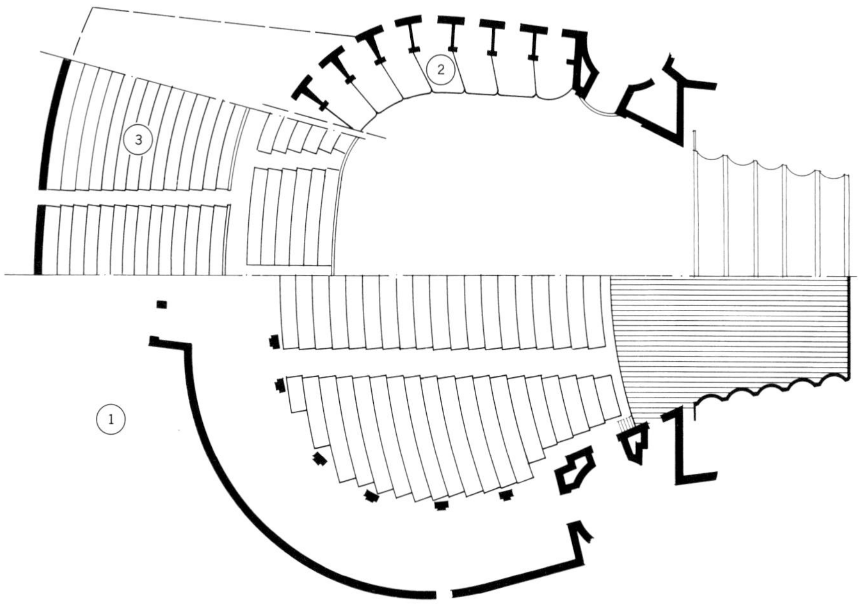

SEATING CAPACITY 2101

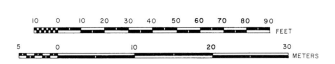

(1) 967

(2) 196

(3) 938

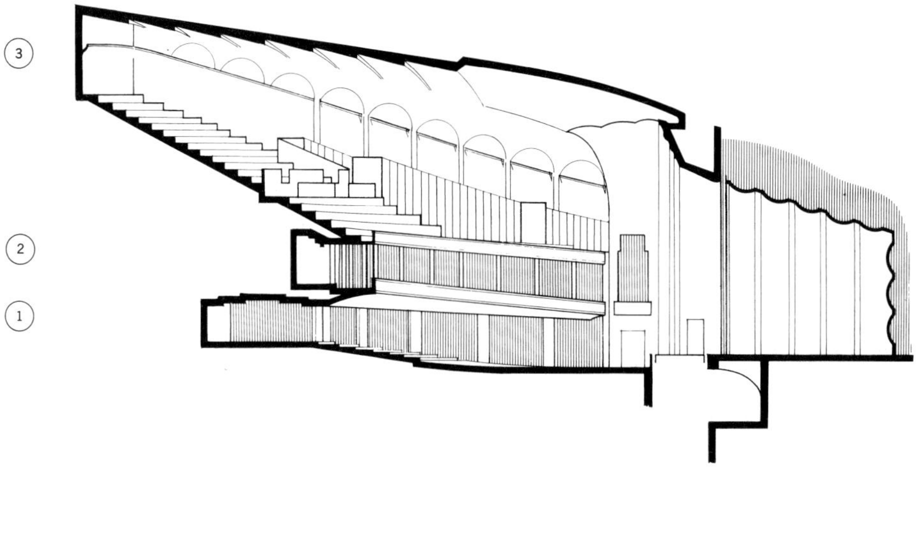

Architectural and structural details

Uses: symphonic music, chamber music, and recitals. *Ceiling:* plaster on wire lath. *Walls:* plaster, except for doors and space dividers. *Floors:* concrete covered with vinyl tile. *Carpet:* none. *Stage floor:* wood over airspace. *Stage height:* 27 in. (69 cm). *Seating:* front of backrests, top of seat-bottoms, and armrests are upholstered; rear of backrests are plywood and bottom of seats are perforated metal. *Orchestra enclosure:* surface on interior of stage is 1/8 in. (0.3 cm) plywood glued to 0.77 in. (1.8 cm) softwood core, on the back of which another layer of 0.25 in. (0.64 cm) plywood is attached; the lower 9 ft (2.74 m) of the plywood sections (above the stage floor) are filled with sand, approximately 5 in. (12.7 cm) thick.

Architect: Walter and Weeks. *Acoustical Consultant:* Dayton C. Miller. *Photographs:* courtesy of Cleveland Orchestra. *References:* R. S. Shankland and E. A. Flynn, Jour. Acoust. Soc. of Amer., **31**, 866–871 (1959); H. J. Ormestad, R. S. Shankland, and A. H. Benade, Jour. Acoust. Soc. of Amer., **32**, 371–375 (1960).

*Technical details**

V = 554,000 ft^3 (15,690 m^3)	S_a = 10,000 ft^2 (930 m^2)	S_A = 13,000 ft^2 (1,208 m^2)
S_o = 2,000 ft^2 (186 m^2)	S_T = 15,000 ft^2 (1,394 m^2)	N = 2,101
H = 55 ft (16.8 m)	W = 90 ft (27.4 m)	L = 108 ft (32.9 m)
D = 135 ft (41.2 m)	V/S_T = 36.9 ft (11.2 m)	V/S_A = 42.6 ft (13 m)
V/N = 264 ft^3 (7.5 m^3)	S_A/N = 6.2 ft^2 (0.57 m^2)	H/W = 0.61
L/W = 1.2	t_I = 20 msec	

**The terminology is explained in Appendix 1.*

USA
7

Costa Mesa, California
Orange County Performing Arts Center, Segerstrom Hall

Opened in 1986, Segerstrom Hall, seating 2,903 for full orchestra, is a multi-use auditorium. The acoustical design called for early, laterally reflected sound to all seating areas. These reflections are produced by walls created at the edges of four seating trays; by large tilted panels that float within the volume near the front of the hall; and by tilted rear walls. The tilted front panels are pleated (so-called quadratic residue diffusers, QRD, discussed in Chapter 10), designed to spread a sequence of early sound reflections to each listener. They also decrease the intensity of overtones relative to fundamental tones, which gives the music a warm, mellow characteristic, and eliminates acoustic "glare" common to reflections from large smooth surfaces. All seats share the same reverberant sound field which is determined by the outer walls of the auditorium, including the volume behind the floating panels. The reverberation time can be shortened for rehearsals or speech events by curtains that are drawn out in varying lengths from suspended housings distributed throughout the ceiling area and from behind the large panel reflectors. At the stage end, the proscenium opening is high, chosen to make the performing orchestra part of the room, while its width is dictated by the owner's request for a stage area of 2,400 ft^2 (223 m^2) for normal symphony, increasing to 3,060 ft^2 (284 m^2) for choral works or decreasing to 500 ft^2 (46 m^2) for soloists. The orchestra enclosure is only 15 ft (4.6 m) deep, so that about half the players are in front of the curtain line. To provide them with cross-stage communication, three removable reflecting panels are located overhead.

The measured acoustical data show that the hall has met the design objectives of achieving sufficient early laterally reflected sound energy, an optimum early decay time (2.2 sec, unoccupied), and excellent sound levels over the audience area. Segerstrom Hall differs from the classical halls in that the ratio of early sound energy compared to later reverberant energy is higher and the later reverberation time is shorter—1.6 sec like that of Cleveland. In the upper two trays, the later reverberant sound is not heard as surrounding the listener, as in a conventional rectangular hall, but rather is heard as a broadening of the source, a satisfactory result.

Costa Mesa, California, Orange County Performing Arts Center, Segerstrom Hall

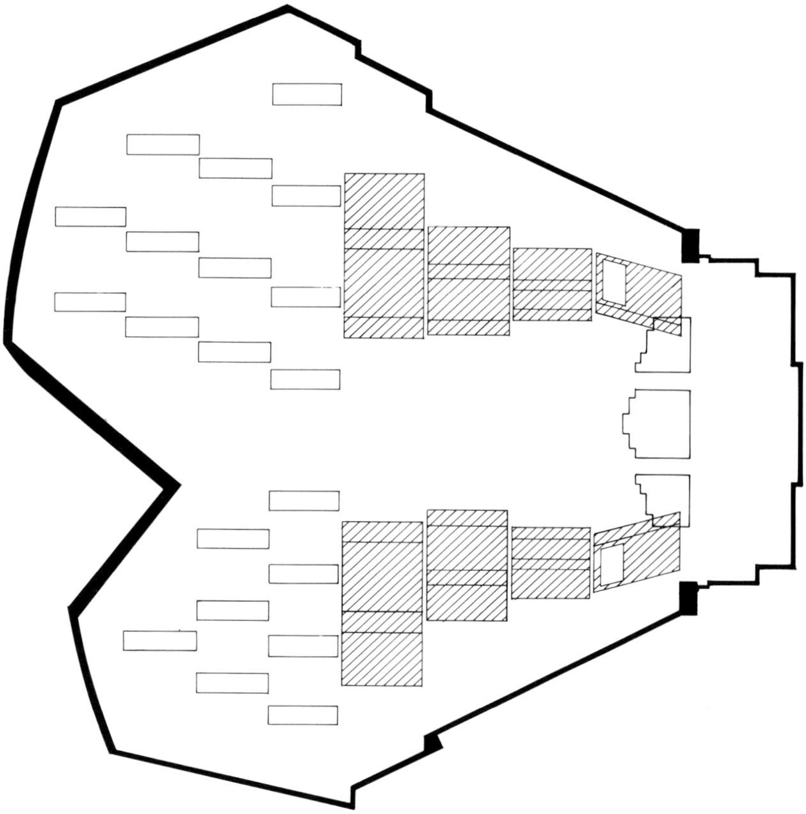

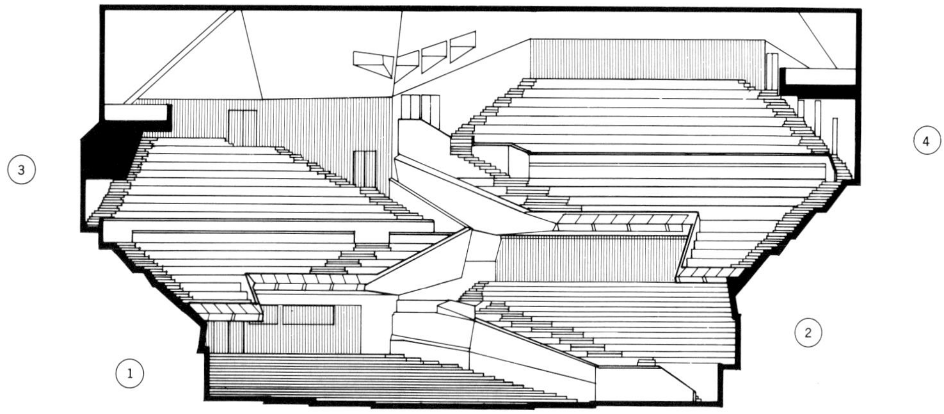

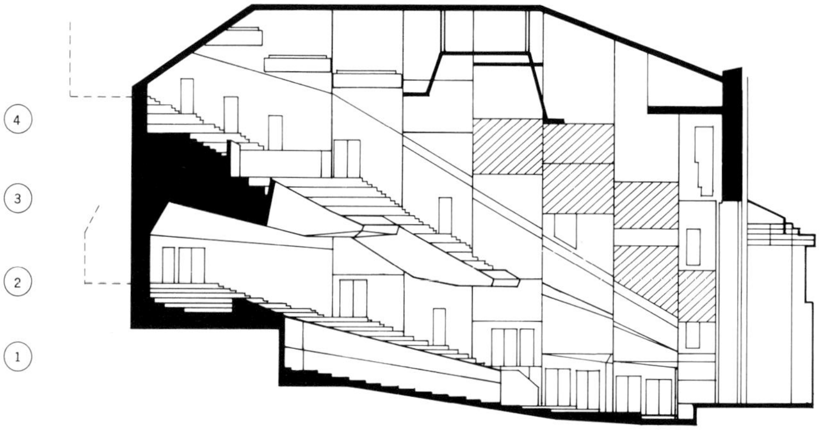

CENTERLINE SECTION

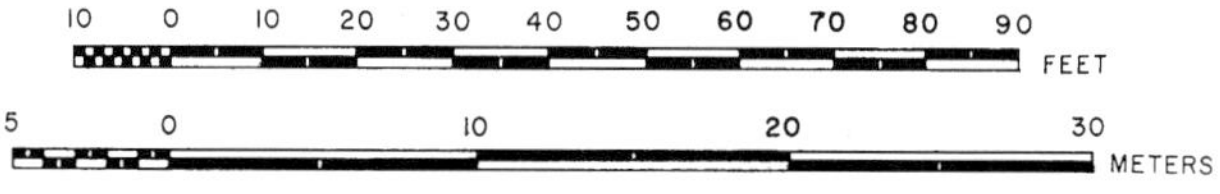

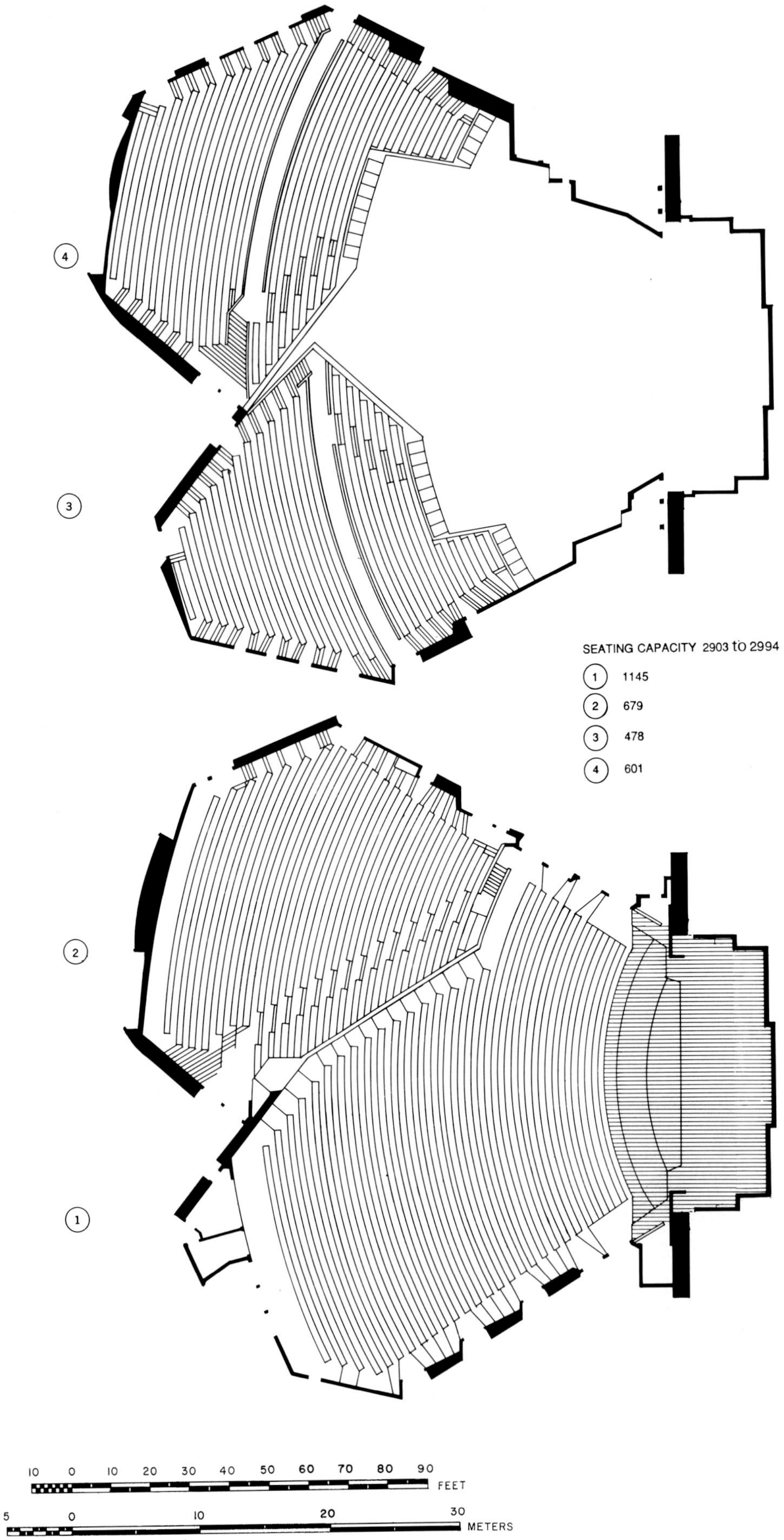

4
3
SEATING CAPACITY 2903 to 2994
1 1145
2 679
3 478
4 601
2
1
10 0 10 20 30 40 50 60 70 80 90 FEET
5 0 10 20 30 METERS

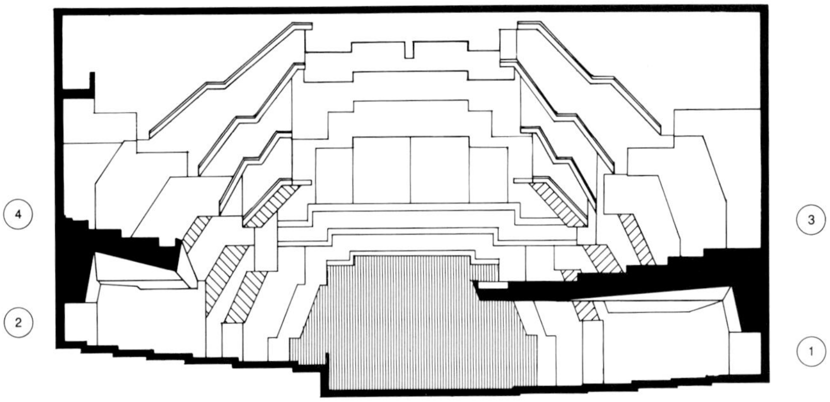

TRANSVERSE SECTION AT CENTER

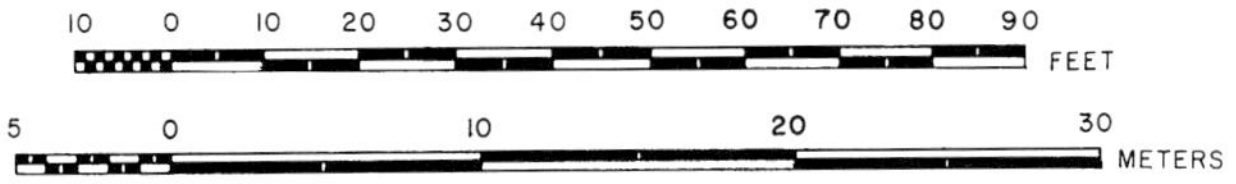

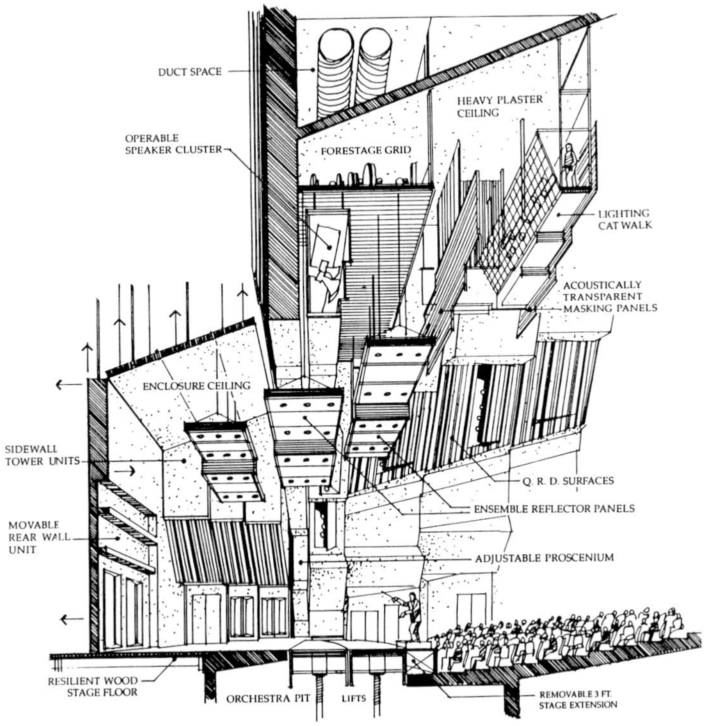

Architectural and structural details

Uses: about 25% each for classical music, musicals, and dance; remainder divided among opera, pops, and rentals. *Ceiling:* 2 in. (5 cm) high-density plaster; under-balcony soffits 1 in. (2.5 cm) plaster. *Walls:* 2 in. high density plaster; balcony faces and surfaces between trays, same. *Sound diffusers:* located in back corners of each seating area, chevron in shape, made of 3/4 in. (1.9 cm) wood; each about 70 ft^2 (6.5 m^2) in area; depth 1 to 8 in. (20 cm); and open at perimeter. *Quadratic residue diffusers:* Twelve in number. Constructed of 0.5 in. (1.25 cm) plywood, totaling 1,550 ft^2 (144 m^2); design frequency near 500 Hz based on prime number. *Floors:* Dense concrete. Vinyl tile cemented to concrete in seating areas. *Variable elements:* Proscenium opening variable between 68 and 52 ft horizontally and 42 to 32 ft vertically; variable part, 1 in. plywood. *Carpets:* 1/3 in. directly affixed to concrete, totaling about 3,630 ft^2 (340 m^2). *Stage enclosure:* (see sketch) each side formed by three tall rolling towers; backwall section and the three ceiling sections are flown by rigging, all comprised of 3/4 in. plywood laminated to 1/2 in. plywood; for large choral works, a 12 ft (3.7 m) insert increases the performing area; between lower and upper portions of the sidewalls, an intermediate 10 ft (3 m) length, 20 degrees from vertical, is built in.; these sloped surfaces have a single period QRD attached to them; chevron diffusers are attached to the lower vertical surfaces on the tower portions and are arrayed across the entire back wall of the enclosure; three large reflecting panels above the players, each about 50 ft (15 m) wide and 9 ft (2.74 m) deep at heights (from downstage to upstage) of 33 ft, 30 ft, and 28 ft (10 m, 9.25 m, and 8.5 m) above stage level. *Stage floor:* extends into auditorium on two pit lifts plus a 3 ft. extension; fixed floor is comprised of 3/4 in. particle board on 1 in. x 4 in. (10 cm) tongue-and-groove subfloor, supported on 2 in. x 3 in. strips, 10 in. (25 cm) on centers—strips are separated from the flat concrete surface below by 3/8 in. (1 cm) neoprene pads. *Stage height:* 40 in. (1.02 m) above floor level at first row of seats. *Seating:* The backrest is 3/8 in. molded plywood. The front of the backrest and the seat top are upholstered. The seat bottom is unperforated. Seat arms are wooden.

Architect: Charles Lawrence. *Associate architects:* Caudill–Rowlett–Scott and The Blurock Partnership. *Acoustical consultants:* Joint Venture: Paoletti/Lewitz Associates, Jerald R. Hyde and Marshall/Day Associates. *Photographs:* courtesy of J. R. Hyde. *Stage sketch:* John von Szeliski.

References: D. Paoletti and J. R. Hyde, "An Acoustical Preview of OCPAC," p. 23, Sound & Video Contractor, (July 15, 1985); J. R. Hyde and J. von Szeliski, "Acoustics and Theater Design: Exploring New Design Requirements for Large Multi-Purpose Theaters," 12th International Congress on Acoustics, Vancouver, Canada (August 1986); A. H. Marshall and J. R. Hyde, "Some Practical Considerations in the Use of Quadratic Residue Diffusing Surfaces," Tenth International Congress on Acoustics, Sydney, Australia, (1980); J. R. Hyde, "Segerstrom Hall in Orange County—Design, Measurements and Results After a Year of Operation," *Proceedings of Institute of Acoustics*, **10**, 155 (1988).

*Technical details**

V = 981,800 ft^3 (27,800 m^3)	S_a = 16,190 ft^2 (1,504 m^2)	S_A = 18,750 ft^2 (1,742 m^2)
S_o = 2,400 ft^2 (223 m^2)	S_T = 21,150 ft^2 (1,965 m^2)	N = 2,903 for concerts and 2,994 for recitals and theater
H = 80 ft (24.4 m)	W = 136 ft (41.5 m)	L = 119 ft (36.2 m)
D = 144 ft (44 m)	V/S_T = 46.4 ft (14.2 m)	V/S_A = 60.6 ft (18.5 m)
V/N = 338 ft^3 (9.58 m^3)	S_A/N = 6.46 ft^2 (0.6 m^2)	H/W = 0.59
L/W = 0.88	t_I = 31 msec	

**The terminology is explained in Appendix 1.*

USA

8

Dallas
Eugene McDermott Concert Hall in Morton H. Meyerson Symphony Center

The McDermott Hall in the Meyerson Symphony Center is a classical rectangular hall in the front two-thirds and a classical opera house in the remainder. Entrance is via circular, beige, Italian marble stairs that lead one into an asymmetrical lobby that surrounds the hall like an eighteenth century glass ball-gown. The concert hall, seating 2,065, is in direct contrast—an intimate, warm room in soft red and dark wood tones trimmed with bronze. On the occasion of its opening in 1989, a *New York Times* critic wrote, "One of the handsomest new rooms in which to hear music anywhere".

Acoustically, the unusual feature of the Meyerson is the 254,000 ft^3 (7,200 m^3) of partially coupled reverberation space wrapped around the perimeter of the hall above the highest audience level and concealed by an open-weave cloth. The chamber is opened and closed by 74, 4 in. (10 cm) thick, hinged, concrete doors, motor operated by remote control. With them, the length of the reverberation time can be varied. And, the four-part canopy can be raised to give the sound energy greater access to the chamber for large scale works, or lowered for more intimate chamber and recital music.

During my two-concert, five-seats visit to the hall the canopy was raised high enough that its surface was parallel to the vision of auditors in the highest rows. It was obvious that the reverberation chamber doors, at least part of them, were open. The fidelity of tone, orchestral balance, and intimacy were excellent, nearly everywhere. The spaciousness and the fullness of the sound was best on the main floor and in the seats in the curved rear one-third. On the sides the orchestra was less well balanced, one side or the other dominating over the cello in the Shostakovich, Concerto No. 1. The effect of the chamber was hard to evaluate. Its presence was not obvious in all the seats, except after sudden-stop chords, when it seemed to reverberate for about 3.0 sec. In the running music, the early reverberation time sounded like 2.0 sec. Critical reviews have been very favorable. The new sound of the Meyerson/McDermott, plenty of clarity with simultaneous lengthy reverberance, promises a new direction for acoustical design.

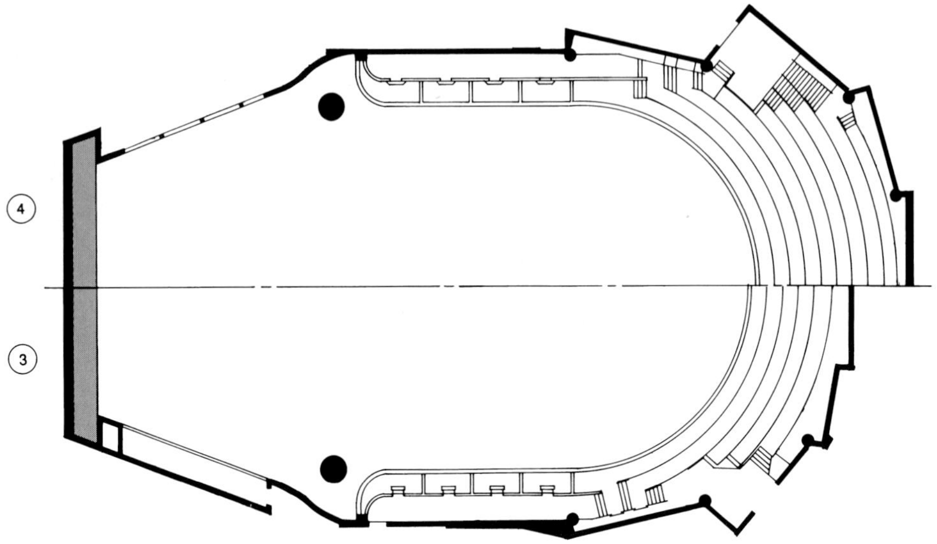

SEATING CAPACITY 2065

1 966

2 353

3 305

4 441

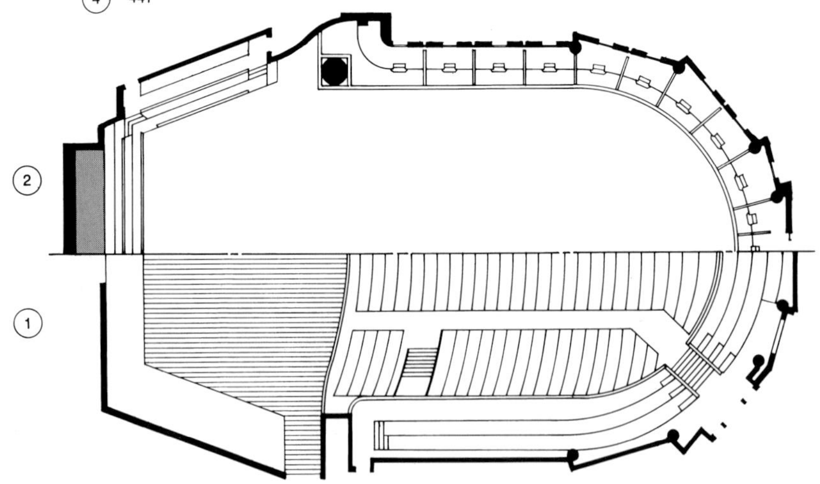

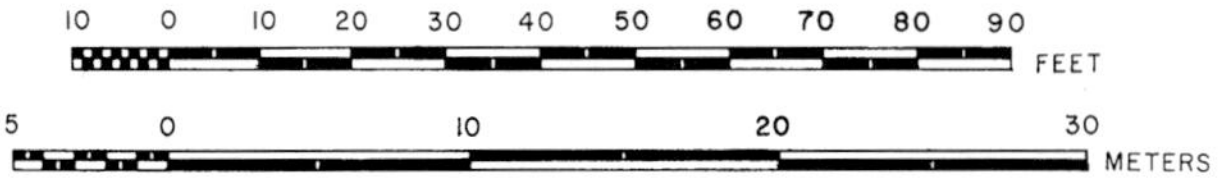

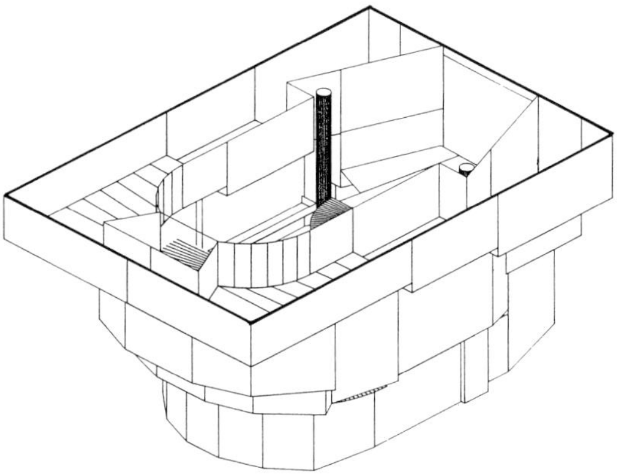

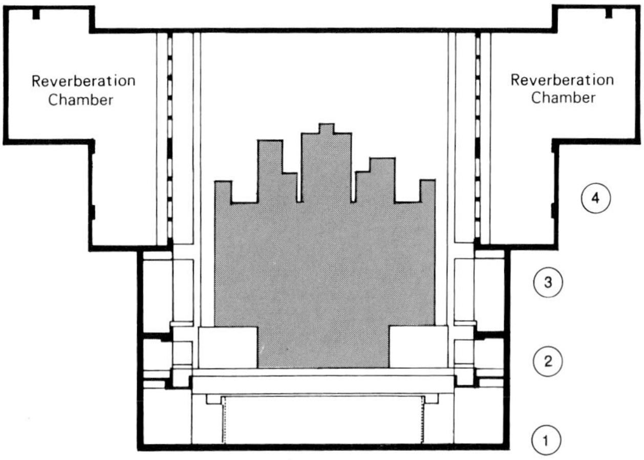
Reverberation Chamber
Reverberation Chamber
4
3
2
1

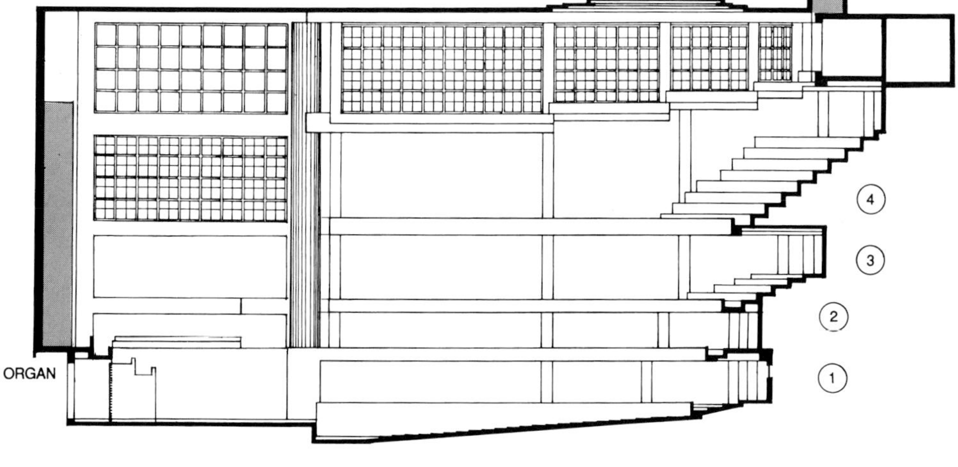
ORGAN
4
3
2
1

10 0 10 20 30 40 50 60 70 80 90
FEET
5 0 10 20 30
METERS

Dallas, Eugene McDermott Concert Hall
in Morton H. Meyerson Symphony Center

Architectural and structural details

Uses: symphonic and chamber orchestras, recitals, and soloists. *Ceiling:* 5.5 in. (14 cm) concrete with plaster skim coat. *Overstage canopy:* 6 in. (15 cm) laminated wood, 4,000 ft^2 (372 m^2), over orchestra and front of audience; normal height 36–50 ft (11–15 m). *Walls:* thin wood veneer on 0.5 in. (1.5 cm) particle board bonded by adhesive and plaster to 10 in. (25 cm) masonry, some areas of limestone; center canopy has 0.06 in. (0.16 cm) layer of felt to suppress acoustic glare. *Balcony fronts:* 2.0 in. (5 cm) plaster, on upper two fronts, added thin wood veneer. *Variable absorption:* motor-operated curtains in storage pockets for covering 6,190 ft^2 (575 m^2) of walls; in each pocket, one set of curtains is single-layer thin fabric, the other is multi-layer, tightly woven, heavy velour. *Floor:* Terrazzo or painted concrete; no carpet. *Stage floor:* 0.5 in. (1.5 cm) tongue-and-groove wood on wood boards on joists. Floor beneath cellos and double basses has 2 in. (5 cm) wood over 3 ft (0.9 m) airspace. *Stage walls:* Lower 14 ft (4.3 m) is 2 in. (5 cm) wood doors that are selectively opened to expose a 12 ft (3.7 m) deep airspace behind instruments. *Reverberant chamber:* 254,000 ft^3 (7,200 m^3), containing 4,844 ft^2 (450 m^2) of variable sound absorption. *Stage height:* 42 in. (1.38 m). *Seating:* molded plywood back and unperforated plywood bottom; upholstered seatback and seat with porous fabric over polyvinyl foam cushion; armrests wood.

Architect: Pei Cobb Freed & Partners. *Acoustical consultant:* ARTEC Consultants, Inc. *Theater consultant:* ARTEC Consultants, Inc. *Photographs:* courtesy of Pei Cobb Freed & Partners.

*Technical details**

V = 844,000 ft^3 (23,900 m^3) (doors closed)

S_a = 10,550 ft^2 (980 m^2)	S_A = 12,500 ft^2 (1,161 m^2)	S_o = 2,691 ft^2 (250 m^2)
S_C = 527 ft^2 (49 m^2)	S_T = 15,718 ft^2 (1,460 m^2)	N = 2,065
H = 86 ft (26.2 m)	W = 84 ft (25.6 m)	L = 101 ft (30.8 m)
D = 133 ft (40.5 m)	V/S_T = 53.7 ft (16.4 m)	V/S_A = 67.5 ft (20.6 m)
V/N = 409 ft^3 (11.6 m^3)	S_A/N = 6.05 ft^2 (0.56 m^2)	H/W = 1.02
L/W = 1.2	t_I = 21 msec	

**The terminology is explained in Appendix 1.*

USA

9

Lenox, Massachusetts

Tanglewood, Serge Koussevitzky Music Shed

Tanglewood, where the Boston Symphony Orchestra's Koussevitzky Music Shed is located, is an incredibly beautiful estate in the Berkshire Hills of Massachusetts. The Music Shed at Tanglewood boasts a unique position among concert halls. It is the only place that houses a very large audience, 5,121 listeners, under acoustical conditions that rival the best in America. And an additional 10,000 people seated on the lawns outside can enjoy the music that issues from the partly open sides of the Shed and a superior sound amplification system. Even though the sides of the Shed are open to a height of about 15 ft (4.6 m), the reverberation behaves like that in a regular auditorium.

The Shed began its life using an inadequate stage enclosure that was moved indoors from a tent in 1938. The combination of a high reverberation time, and no surfaces for projecting the sound from the stage, led to a "muddy" acoustical environment. The sound lacked definition and the balance between early and late sound energy was poor. In 1954, the Trustees engaged Bolt Beranek and Newman to undertake a study to improve the acoustical quality. Working from 1958 with the architect, a new orchestra enclosure, acoustic canopy and rear-wall sound diffusing surface were designed and the whole was dedicated in 1959.

The 50 percent-open, low ceiling, comprising 26 non-planar triangular panels, varying in width from 7 to 26 ft (2.1 to 7.9 m), reflects about half of the early sound energy down onto the audience, arriving shortly after the direct sound, thus giving music the quality heard in classical rectangular halls. And, the upper volume of the hall receives sufficient energy to maintain an optimum ratio of early sound energy to later reverberant sound energy at the listeners' ears. On-stage, the enclosure/canopy also contributes to excellent sectional balance and ease of ensemble playing.

Isaac Stern said after the 1959 season, "The new orchestra enclosure in the Tanglewood Music Shed is one of the most fantastically successful efforts to create brilliant, ringing sound with wonderful definition, despite the enormous size of this hall. It is particularly successful in providing an equal sound value wherever one sits.

On stage there is a wonderfully live quality, and yet complete clarity for balancing with a large orchestra."

At the end of the summer season of 1959, Charles Munch, then the Music Director of the Boston Symphony Orchestra, wrote, "The new canopy has solved all the old problems of disproportion among the various elements of the orchestra. The greatest benefit has come to the strings and especially the violins which now can be heard in the Shed with as much brilliance and clarity as in the best concert halls."

Pierre Monteux said in 1959, "What has been done is absolutely marvelous. Last year I could not hear the violins. This year the sound is marvelous."

Owning a summer home nearby, Eugene Ormandy, then Music Director of the Philadelphia Orchestra said (1962), "This year and also a year ago I sat in boxes at the center of the Shed and was amazed at the fine quality of the sound. The acoustical enclosure is wonderful. The brass is somewhat predominant in the large orchestra, though the conductor should be able to control it."

The acoustics of the completed hall corroborated our predictions. The Shed's canopy and enclosure were the first application of the results of a six-year program of studies. The low ceiling over the stage and front part of the audience (almost 50% open) produces the necessary short-time-delay reflections in the hall, yet leaves the upper volume of the hall available for reverberation. In addition, the canopy contributes to excellent sectional balance for a large orchestra and improved clarity inside the shed.

Measurements of reflected sound from this type of panel array, in the laboratory, are in agreement with mathematical theory, which shows that lateral diffraction from the edges of the panels maintain an uniform energy flow even down to very low frequencies. This energy flow seems mostly to come from direct ahead because measurements in the *unoccupied* Shed reveal low values for lateral reflection LF and (1– $IACC_{E3}$). But this apparent deficiency is more than made up for by the strength of the bass. The bass ratio BR is 1.45, far greater than Boston's 1.03.

It has been suggested that the optimum reverberation time, 1.9 sec at mid-frequencies, fully occupied, and the BR so enhance the effectiveness of this type of canopy that lateral reflections are not necessary to give a feeling of spaciousness. No confirming experiments have been performed to show that the favorable values of these two acoustical attributes are necessary to make this type of canopy work.

Lenox, Massachusetts, Tanglewood, Serge Koussevitzky Music Shed

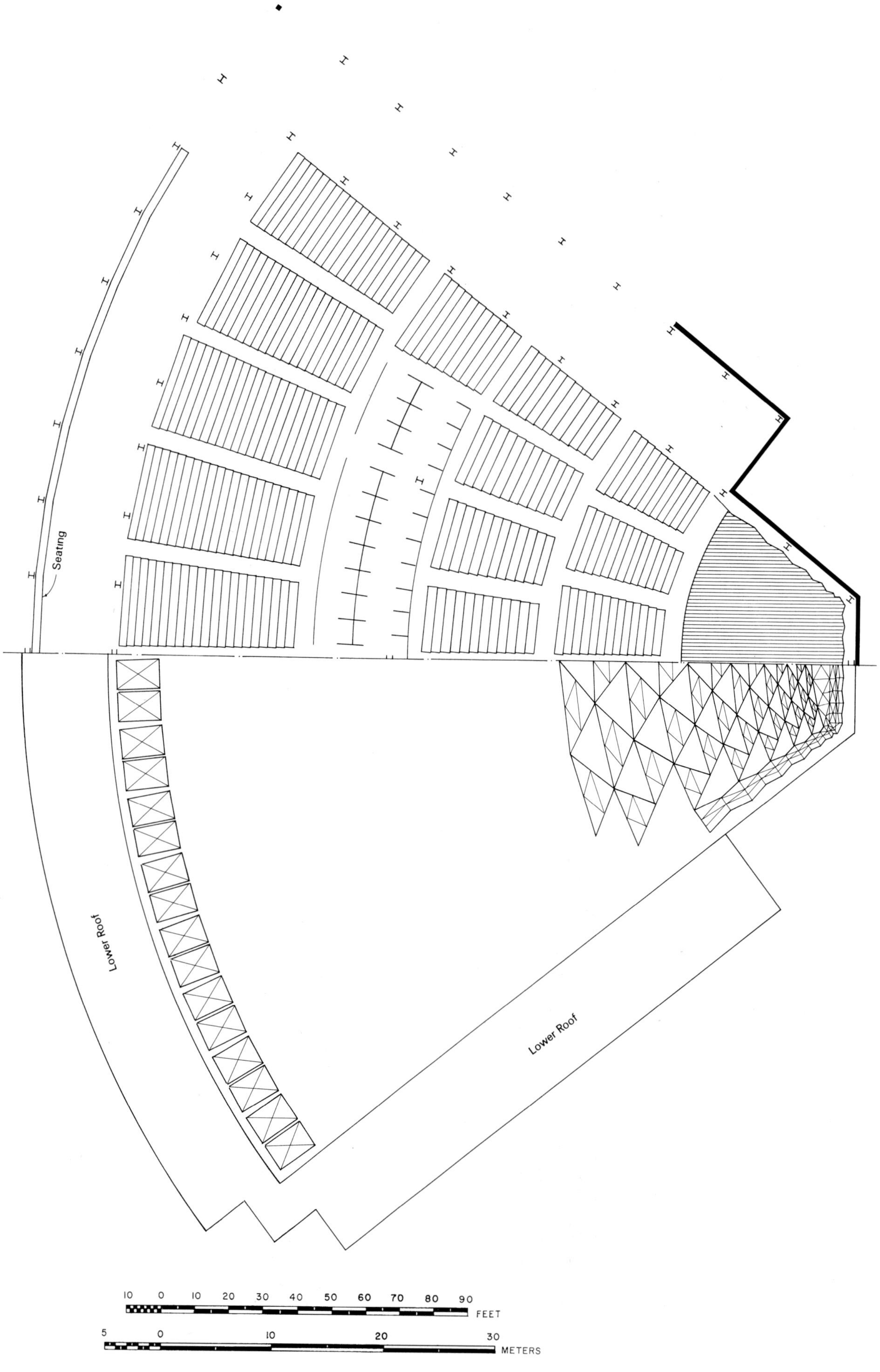

Seating
Lower Roof
Lower Roof
10 0 10 20 30 40 50 60 70 80 90
FEET
5 0 10 20 30
METERS

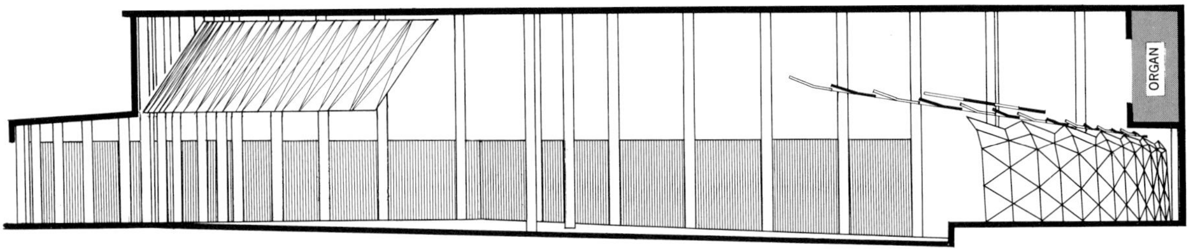

SEATING CAPACITY 5121

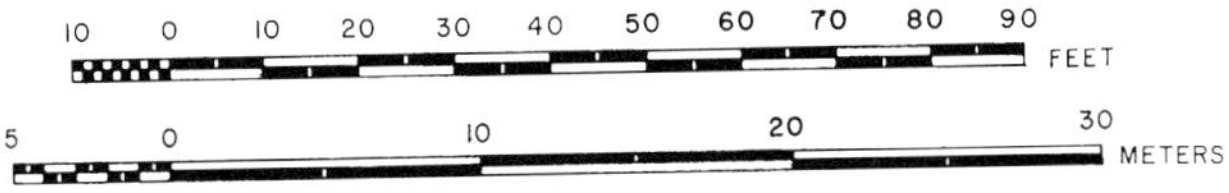

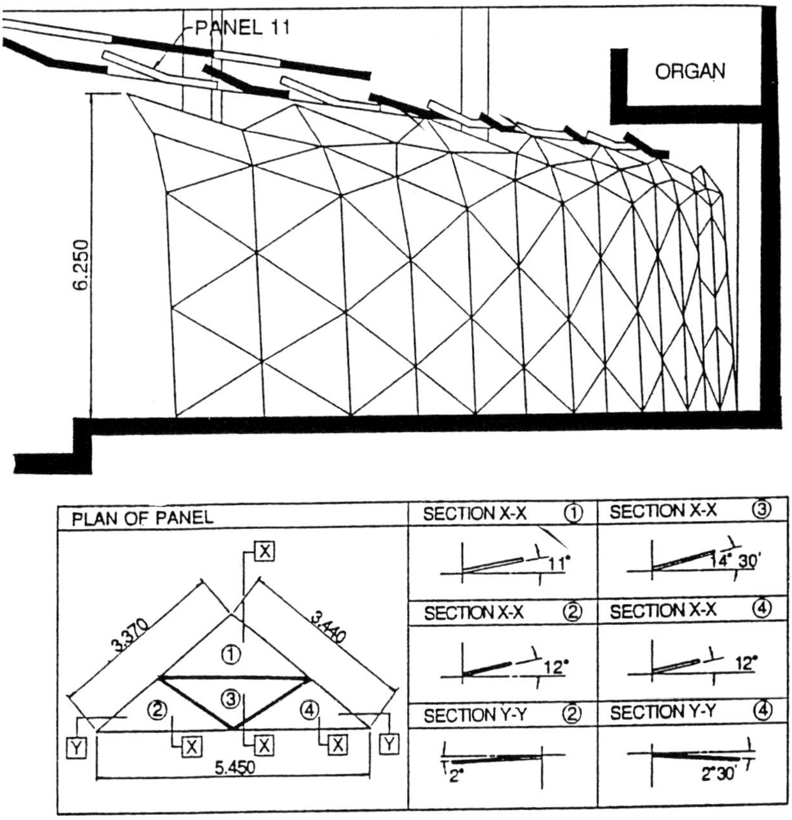

DETAIL OF PANEL 11

Architectural and structural details

Uses: symphony orchestra, chamber orchestra, and choral music. *Ceiling:* 2 in. (5 cm) wooden planks. *Side and rear walls:* closed part of walls is 0.75 in. (1.9 cm) painted fiberboard; large area open to outdoors during concert season. *Floors:* packed, treated dirt. *Stage enclosure:* 0.4 to 0.6 in. (1 to 1.5 cm) plywood with modulations in shape and randomly and heavily braced. *Canopy:* suspended by steel cables from the roof, consisting of a series of non-planar triangular plywood panels 0.4 to 0.6 in. thick, heavily framed, connected tip-to-tip (see the drawings). *Stage floor:* 1.25 in. (3.2 cm) wood over large airspace. *Stage height:* 33 in. (84 cm). *Sound absorbing materials:* none. *Seating:* all wooden with metal arms, no cushions.

Original architect: Joseph Franz, engineer (1938), from preliminary design of Eliel Saarinen. In 1937, Saarinen consented to the use of his original drawings with such changes as were necessitated by the financial resources of the Berkshire Festival Corporation. *Renovation architect:* Eero Saarinen and Associates (1959). *Acoustical consultant:* Bolt Beranek and Newman, now Acentech. *Photographs:* courtesy of Boston Symphony Orchestra. *References:* F. R. Johnson, L. L. Beranek, R. B. Newman, R. H. Bolt, and D. L. Klepper, "Orchestra Enclosure and Canopy for the Tanglewood Music Shed," *Jour. Acoust. Soc. of Amer.*, **33**, 475–481 (April 1961).

*Technical details**

V = 1,500,000 ft^3 (42,480 m^3)	S_a = 24,000 ft^2 (2,200 m^2)	S_A = 30,800 ft^2 (2,861 m^2)
S_o = 2,200 ft^2 (204 m^2)	S_T = 33,000 ft^2 (3,065 m^2)	N = 5,121
H = 44 ft (13.4 m)	W = 200 ft (61 m)	L = 167 ft (50.9 m)
D = 163 ft (49.7 m)	V/S_T = 45.5 ft (13.9) m	V/S_A = 48.7 ft (14.8 m)
V/N = 293 ft^3 (8.29 m^3)	S_A/N = 6.01 ft^2 (0.56 m^2)	H/W = 0.22
L/W = 0.835	t_I = 19 msec	

**The terminology is explained in Appendix 1.*

USA
10

Lenox, Massachusetts
Seiji Ozawa Hall

The Seiji Ozawa hall opened July 7, 1994 with four conductors, two symphony orchestras, and a three hour program that ended with the audience singing Randall Thompson's *Alleluia.* Modeled after Vienna's Grosser Musikvereinssaal, Ozawa Hall is a somewhat smaller "shoebox" seating 1,180 vs 1,680. The hall is beautiful inside, with stucco walls painted a warm, off-white. The two tiers of balconies are faced with railings and gridded fronts in teak wood. The loge boxes, with the railings, become the most important architectural element when filled with people. Even the backrests of the seats pick up this gridded pattern. The ceiling is made of pre-cast coffers and the side walls are irregular to provide good sound diffusion.

The musicians sit on risers modeled so that they can see each other and be seen by the audience. High up, there are clerestory windows. Unusual, are high narrow windows above and behind the stage, northerly directed, that give one partial views of the sky changing evenings from sunset to twilight to night.

The hall had to meet one other requirement, an audience seated outside on the lawn. Located in a natural shallow bowl, the rear wall can be completely opened, bringing the concert to outdoor audiences as large as 2,000, with sound augmented by an excellent sound system.

The very thick concrete walls, doors, windows, and ceiling, preserve the bass like that in no other hall, giving the music a rich sound and emphasizing the tones of the lower strings. The reverberation time, fully occupied with rear wall open, is 1.7 sec at mid frequencies. At the lower frequencies, the reverberation is 2.2 sec and the bass ratio equals 1.32, which accounts for the warmth and richness of the bass sound. Being narrow and with plenty of surfaces for reflecting sound laterally to the audience, the subjective acoustical parameter called "spaciousness" also exceeds that in any larger hall, including that in its Vienna mentor. It contrasts with the nearby 5,000 seat Koussevitzky Music Shed, with greater loudness and a feeling of listening in a small group. Edward Rothstein, music critic of the *New York Times,* said, "[It] is precisely what a concert hall should be: a resonant, warm space that comes to life with sound."

Lenox, Massachusetts, Seiji Ozawa Hall

3

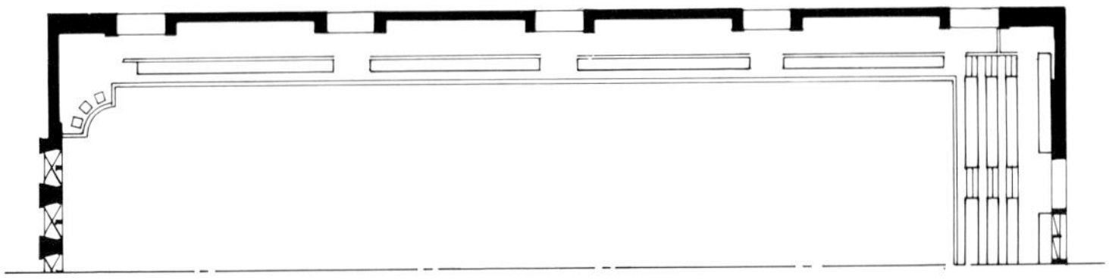

2

1

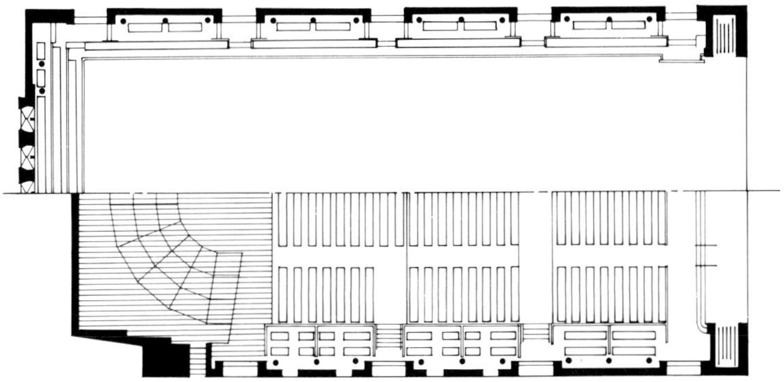

SEATING CAPACITY 1180

1 692

2 268

3 220

3

2

1

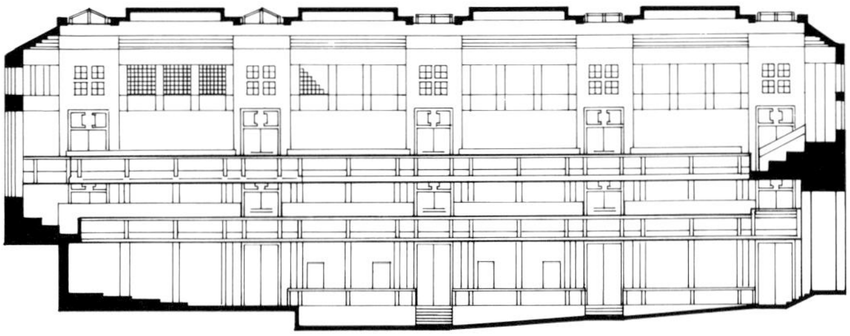

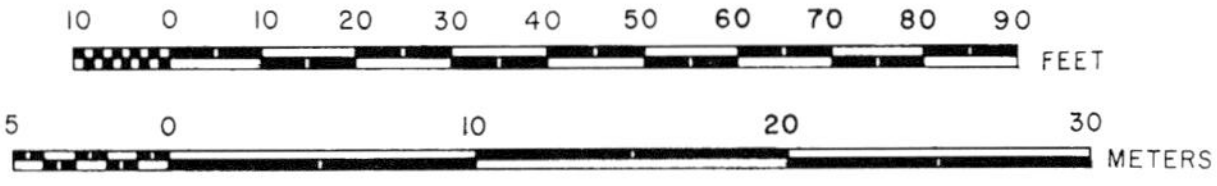

Architectural and structural details

Uses: rehearsals, performances, and recording. *Ceiling:* 35 pre-cast concrete panels weighing 27,000 lbs (12,200 kg) each. *Main side walls:* 12 in. (30 cm) grout-filled concrete blocks with stucco covering. *Balcony fronts:* lower part irregular to provide early lateral reflections; upper part open gridded wood. *Stage ceiling:* none; overhung slightly by balconies. *Stage side walls:* removable wooden panels; on stage right and canted concrete block walls, behind wood trimed skrim fabric panels on stage left. *Stage floor:* tongue-and-groove maple wood strips glued to canvas and floated on bed of plastic and 1.12 in. (2.8 cm) plywood to approximate the looseness of classic, aged, tongue-and-grooved stage floors and to prevent off-season buckling. *Stage height:* 42 in. (106 cm). *Audience floor:* wooden tongue-and-groove boards affixed to 3.25 in.(8.26 cm) tongue-and-groove timber planking. *Carpet:* none. *Sound absorption:* Six large panels, 6 in. (15 cm) thick can be lowered by steps from the ceiling over the stage and absorbing curtains along the upper sidewalls can be dropped to reduce the empty reverberation time (with closed rear wall) down by 0.4 to 0.6 sec to the desired recording reverberation time. *Seating:* seat back, open slatted; seat pans covered with thin cushions; structure, backrest and armrests, solid wood.

Architect: William Rawn Associates, Architects, Inc. *Acoustical consultant:* Kirkegaard & Associates. *Photographs:* Steve Rosenthal.

*Technical details**

V = 410,000 ft^3 (11,610 m^3)	S_a = 5,340 ft^2 (496 m^2)	S_A = 7,955 ft^2 (739 m^2)
S_o = 2,175 ft^2 (202 m^2)	S_T = 10,130 ft^2 (941 m^2)	N = 1,180
H = 49 ft (14.9 m)	W = 68 ft (20.7 m)	L = 94 ft (28.6 m)
D = 94 ft (28.6 m)	V/S_T = 40.5 ft (12.3 m)	V/S_A = 51.5 ft (15.7 m)
V/N = 347 ft^3 (9.83 m^3)	S_A/N =6.74ft^3 (0.63m^2)	H/W = 0.72
L/W = 1.38	t_I = 23 msec	

* *The terminology is explained in Appendix 1.*

USA
11
Minneapolis
Minnesota Orchestra Association Orchestra Hall

Orchestra Hall opened in October 1974. Designed primarily for The Minnesota's Symphony Orchestra, which turned 90 in 1993, it seats 2,450. The concert hall, one of two components in the complex, is made of concrete, brick, and oak. In the tradition of Vienna's Grosser Musikvereinssaal and Boston's Symphony Hall, it is basically rectangular shaped, but with three wrap-around balconies and a much less exposed wall above the top balcony. Missing also are the gilded or white statues of its famous predecessors.

Orchestra Hall must be seen to be believed. As one approaches, the exposed pipes come into view, blue on the exterior and yellow, green, and blue in the lobby. Inside the concert hall, a newcomer is awe stricken by the playful cube-like shapes that cover the entire ceiling and the rear wall of the stage. In direct contrast is the militaristic formality of the balcony fronts and the stage side walls. These intriguing rectangular boxes are made of plaster and are randomly oriented to create a diffuse sound field—one in which the reverberant energy is uniform throughout the hall, giving the music a pleasant singing tone.

The balconies seat only 938 people, with movable cushioned chairs arranged in boxes along the sides and theater-style seats in the rear. Their shallowness assures the ticket buyer that no under-balcony dead spots exist. Great efforts were made to eliminate outside noises. The hall is separated by a 1 in. (2.5 cm) airspace from the structure which surrounds it on three sides. Adjacent to the entry doors on the three sides is a "ring corridor," with carpeted walls and floors designed to combat the noise of air-handling equipment, transformers, and office noises. This second part of the building also contains rehearsal space, artistic and administrative offices, and the lobby.

Orchestra Hall's usable stage area is 2,174 ft^2 (202 m^2). The hall is sufficiently narrow—no central aisle is needed. A state-of-the-art sound system renders it usable for pops concerts, popular artists, seminars, and school functions. During the month of June, for Pops, the seating configuration on the main floor is converted into terraced levels with tables and chairs, reducing the hall's capacity to 1,838.

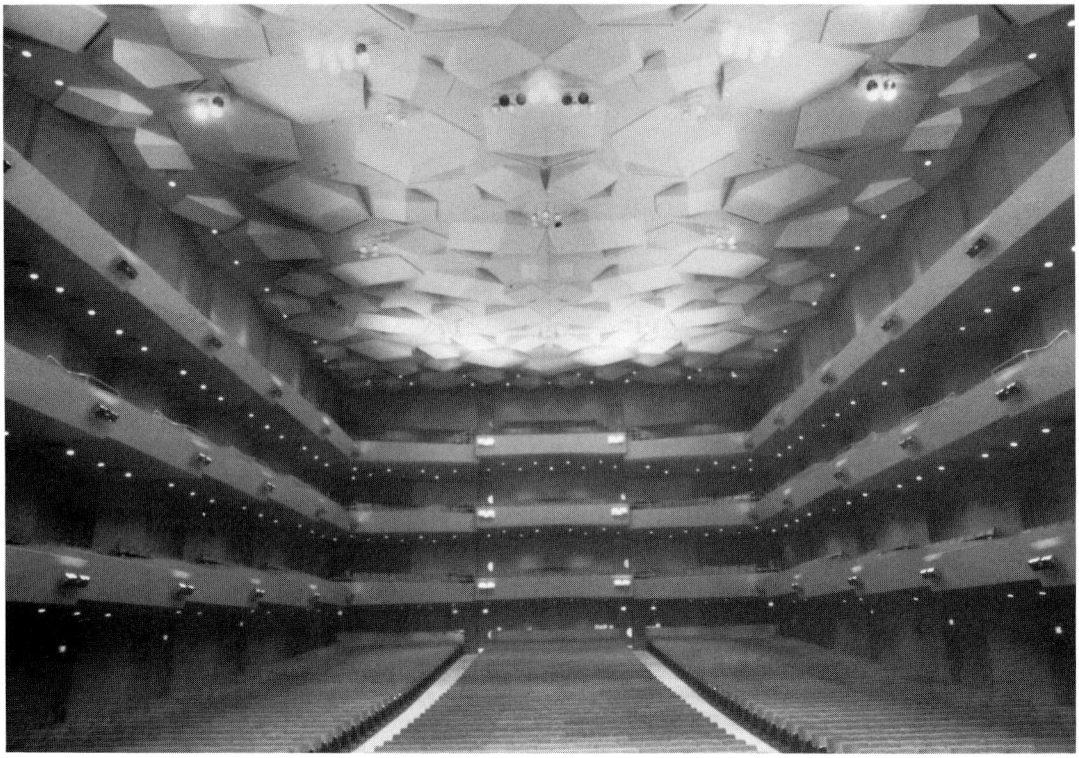

Minneapolis, Minnesota Orchestra Association Orchestra Hall

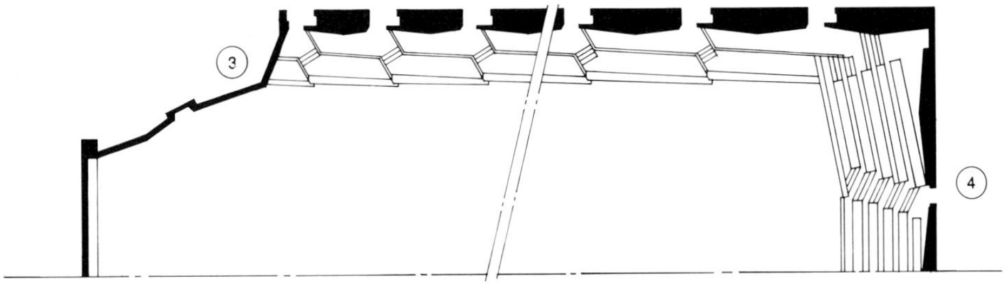

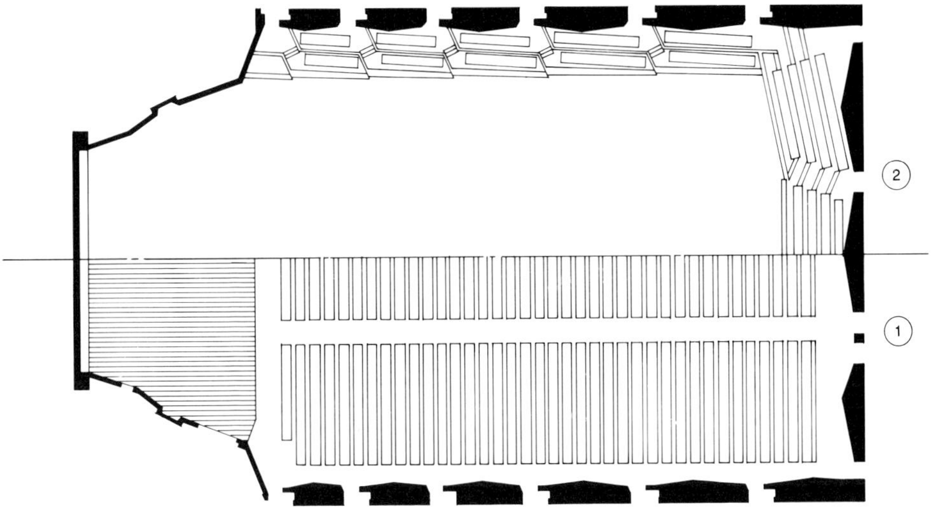

SEATING CAPACITY 2450

(1)	1512
(2)	317
(3)	300
(4)	321

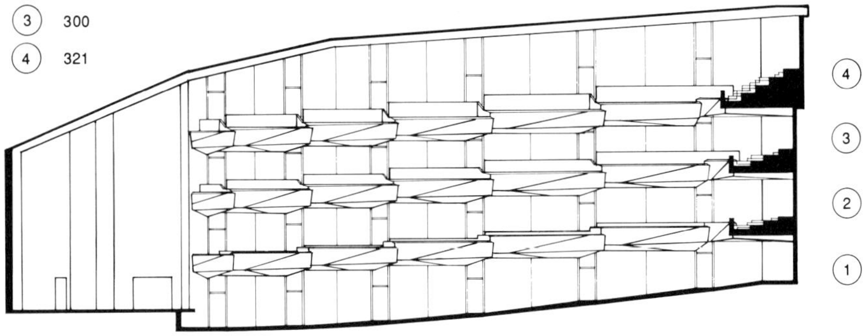

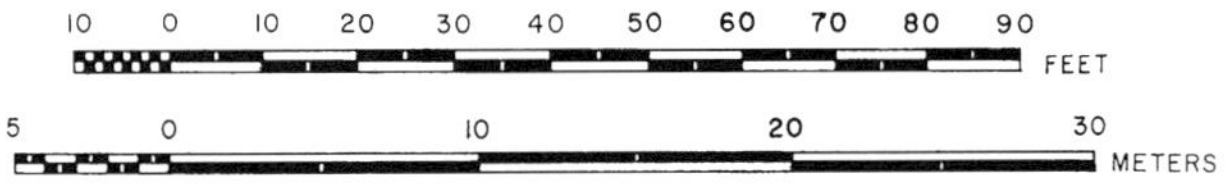

Architectural and structural details

Uses: mostly orchestra, soloists, and popular artists. *Ceiling:* plaster on wire lath. *Walls:* side walls are hardwood on concrete block. Balcony wall is plaster on wire lath. *Floors:* the base floor is flat concrete with parquet wood affixed; during the winter concert season, a sloping floor is installed (see the drawing). *Carpets:* on main aisles downstairs, with no underpad. *Stage enclosure:* most of the enclosure, including the ceiling, is thick wood. *Stage floor:* 1.5 in. (3.8 cm) wooden planks over a large air space with 3/4 in. (1.9 cm) flooring on top. *Stage height:* 46 in. (117 cm) above floor level at first row of seats. *Seating:* the rear of the backrest is 0.5 in. (1.25 cm) molded plywood. The front of the backrest and the top of the seat-bottom is upholstered over a polyurethane cushion. The underseat is unperforated. The arms are wooden.

Architect: Hammel Green and Abrahamson. *Associate architect for design:* Hardy Holzman Pfeiffer Associates. *Acoustical consultant:* Cyril M. Harris. *Photographs:* Tom W. McElin and Banbury Studios.

*Technical details**

V = 670,000 ft^3 (18,975 m^3)	S_a = 16,942 ft^2 (1,266 m^2)	S_A = 16,942 ft^2 (1,574 m^2)
S_o = 2,185 ft^2 (203 m^2)	S_T = 19,127 ft^2 (1,777 m^2)	N = 2,450
H = 54 ft (16.5 m)	W = 94 ft (28.6 m)	L = 125 ft (38.1 m)
D = 134 ft (40.8m)	V/S_T = 35 ft (10.7 m)	V/S_A =39.5 ft (12 m)
V/N = 273 ft^3 (7.74 m^3)	S_A/N = 6.92 ft^2 (0.64 m^2)	H/W = 0.57
L/W = 1.33	t_I = 33 msec	

**The terminology is explained in Appendix 1.*

USA

12

New York
Avery Fisher Hall

Avery Fisher Hall is the successor to Philharmonic Hall, although the exterior and the lobbies to the building have remained unchanged. The original hall was opened in 1962 and suffered such criticism that a series of renovations were performed over the next several years. Then, through the generosity of Avery Fisher, a complete reconstruction was made, including relocating the balconies, lowering the ceiling somewhat, adding irregularities to all surfaces, installing a new stage enclosure, changing the contour of the main floor (beneath the seats) and selecting new seats. Also, the decor is completely different. The new hall is a classical rectangular shoebox, like Boston Symphony Hall, but its drawings more resemble those of Salt Lake and Minneapolis.

The reconstructed hall opened in 1976. It seats 2,742 persons. On entering the hall, three elements command one's attention. First, the sound reflectors on the walls and ceiling of the stage enclosure. Then, the side balconies, resembling boxes, each with a gold-leaf-covered, cylindrical front. And, third, the ceiling with "waves" colored almost like the ocean. The change in acoustics was welcome, and the music critics, immediately after the reopening, placed Avery Fisher Hall on an approximate par with Carnegie Hall.

The stage is large for a regular concert hall, 2,230 ft^2 (207 m^2) in area, 81,000 ft^3 (2,295 m^3) in volume and 41 ft (12.5 m) in depth. It was augmented in 1992 by the addition of two tiers of rounded sound diffusers on the side walls (see the photograph) and two diffusing elements in the ceiling. The published purpose was to reflect sound back to the musicians so that they could hear themselves and their colleagues better. The result has apparently been satisfactory.

Acoustically, the reverberation time (occupied) is lower than that in Boston Symphony Hall (1.75 compared to 1.85 sec), and the ratio of the reverberation times at low to those at middle frequencies is appreciably less in Avery Fisher (0.93) than in Boston (1.03). There are still some complaints about bass weakness, as is borne out by the acoustical data just quoted, but the many changes have strengthened the bass in the early sound significantly over its 1962 predecessor.

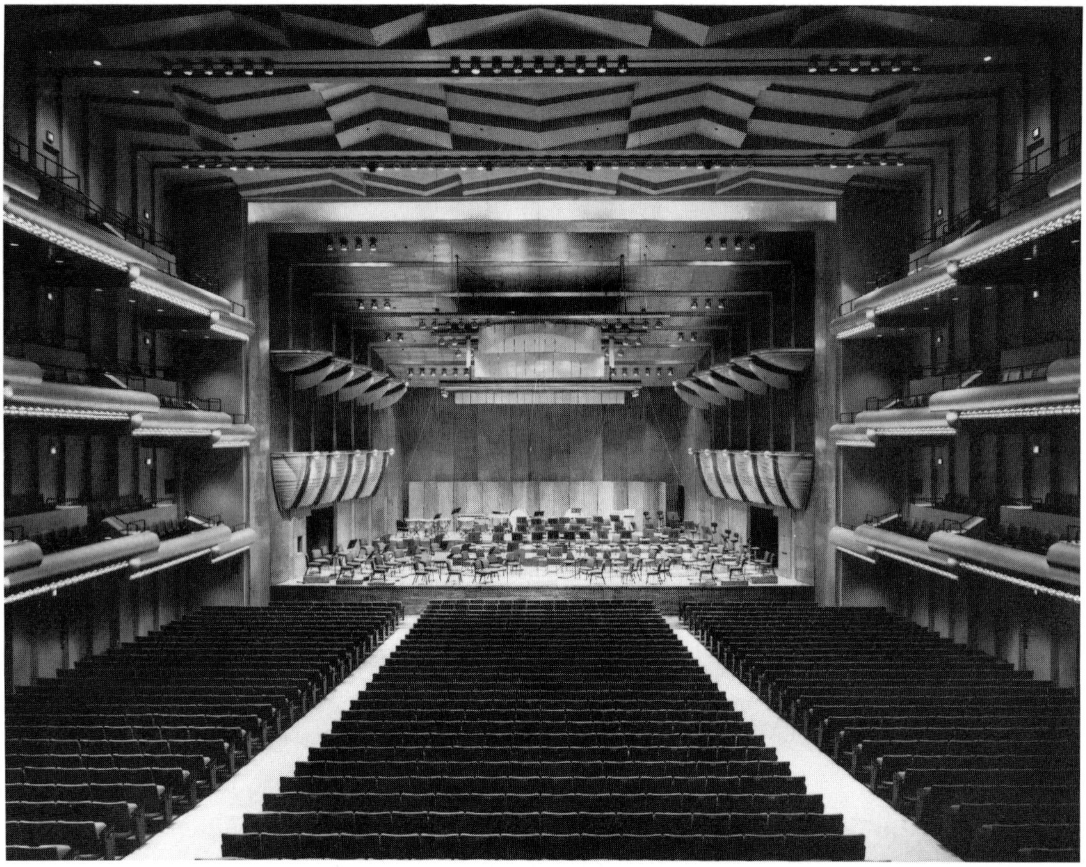

New York, Avery Fisher Hall

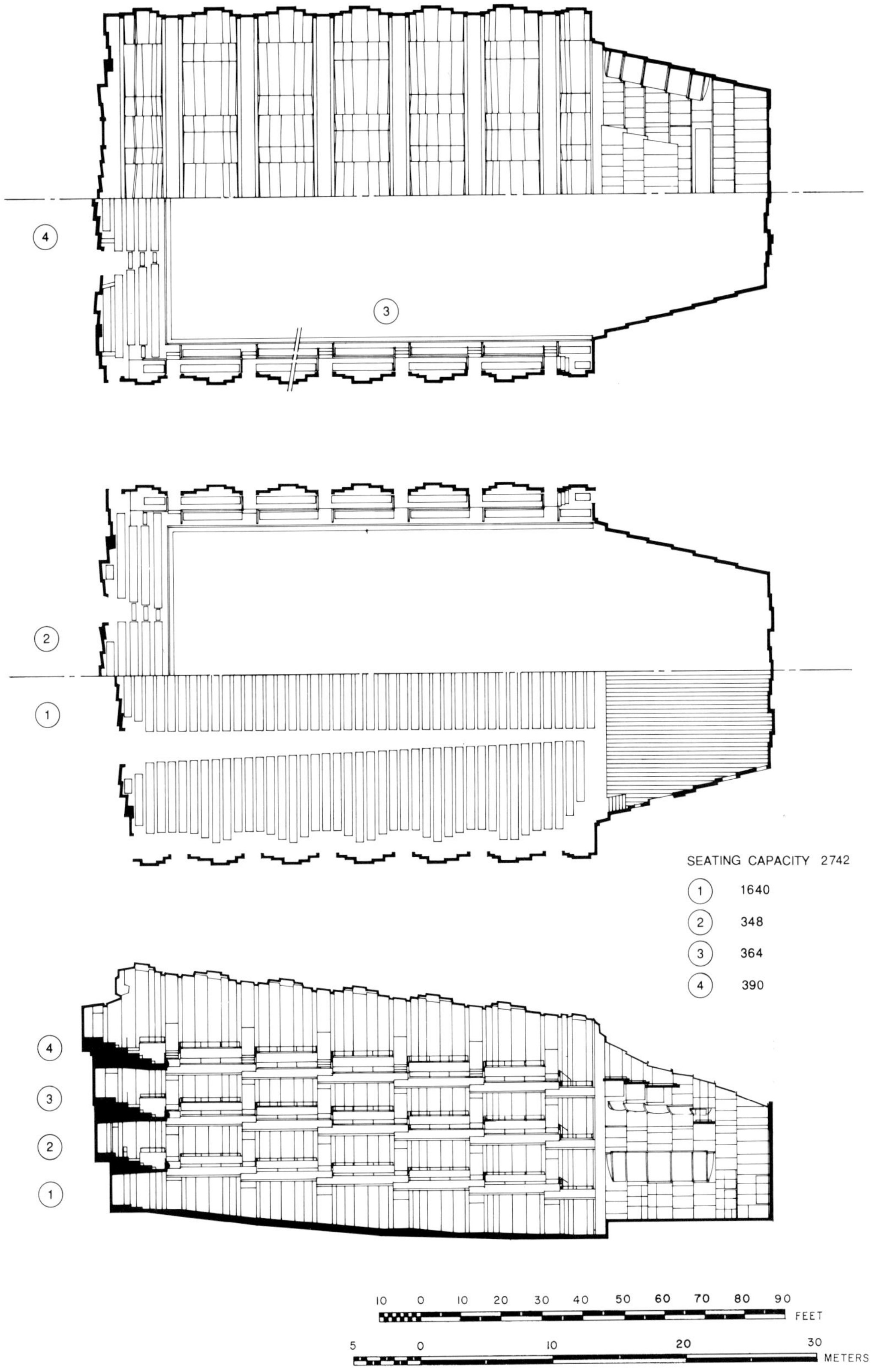
4
3
2
1
SEATING CAPACITY 2742
1 1640
2 348
3 364
4 390
4
3
2
1
10 0 10 20 30 40 50 60 70 80 90
FEET
5 0 10 20 30
METERS

Architectural and structural details

Uses: concerts, primarily. *Ceiling:* 1.5 in. (3.8 cm) plaster on metal lath. *Main and balcony side walls:* 0.75 in. (1.9 cm) painted plywood panel over minimum 1 in. (2.5 cm) compressed fiberglass (varies with angle of wall) screwed to grounds attached to 6 in. (15 cm) concrete block. *Balcony fronts:* gold-leaf surface on 1 in. plaster. *Stage ceiling:* 0.75 in. (1.9 cm) natural-faced wooden plywood over which was poured 4 in. (cm) layered plaster ceiling. *Stage sidewalls:* 0.75 in. (2 cm) natural wooden plywood over 0.75 in. compressed fiberglass screwed to 10 in. (10 cm) concrete blocks. *Stage floor:* 0.6 in. (1.5 cm) tongue-and-groove oak wood strips over 0.75 in. plywood on 2 × 4 in. (5 × 10 cm) sleepers over original 3 in. (7.5 cm) wooden planks. *Stage height:* 42 in. (106 cm). *Audience floor:* to give the floor a new slope a new concrete floor was poured; 1.62 in. (4.1 cm) sleepers were laid on the floor; a 0.5 in. [1.25 cm plywood subfloor was attached and the finish flooring is 0.6 in. (1.5 cm)] oak wood boards. *Carpet:* thin, on aisles. *Added sound absorption:* none. *Seating:* seatback, molded plywood; tops of seats, and fronts of the backrests are upholstered with vinyl cushion, porous cloth covering; underseat unperforated metal; armrests, wooden.

Architects: for building exterior (1962), Harrison and Abramovitz; for concert hall (1976), Philip Johnson/John Burgee Architects; stage modifications (1992), John Burgee Architects. *Acoustical consultants:* for the hall (1976), Cyril M. Harris; for the stage modification (1992), ARTEC Consultants Inc. *Photographs:* Sandor Acs and Norman McGrath.

*Technical details**

V = 720,300 ft^3 (20,400 m^3)	S_a = 1,189 ft^2 (1,189 m^2)	S_A = 15,930 ft^2 (1,480 m^2)
S_o = 2,180 ft^2 (203 m^2)	S_T = 18,110 ft^2 (1,683 m^2)	N = 2,742
H = 55 ft (16.8 m)	W = 85 ft (25.9 m)	L = 126 ft (38.4 m)
D = 135 ft (41.2 m)	V/S_T = 39.8 ft (12.1 m)	V/S_A = 42.2 ft (13.8 m)
V/N = 262 ft^3 (7.44 m^3)	S_A/N = 5.81 ft^2 (0.54 m^2)	H/W = 0.65
L/W = 1.5	t_I = 30 msec	

* *The terminology is explained in Appendix 1.*

USA

13

New York
Carnegie Hall

"The Finest Music of All Comes to Carnegie Hall." This couplet, which was heard on American radios in the heyday of broadcasting, was literally true. Any concert artist or symphony orchestra that aspired to world-wide fame appeared in Carnegie Hall sooner or later. When plans were revealed in 1960 to demolish this famous structure to make room for an office building, musicians and music lovers rose to its defense, and pushed through legislation that made it possible for the City of New York to buy Carnegie Hall and lease it to a non-profit association to operate. Under the leadership of Isaac Stern, Carnegie Hall is flourishing today.

Carnegie Hall is basically a rectangular hall with strongly curved balcony fronts, making it partially resemble a horse-shoe opera house. It seats 2,804 persons, 1,012 on the main floor and 837 in the top balcony. The first and second tiers above the main floor are configured as boxes with movable chairs.

The forward end of Carnegie Hall was renovated in 1986. As the lower photo shows, prior to 1986 at the proscenium a masking curtain made of lightweight fabric was hung, behind which was an operable theatrical curtain. Even when pulled, the theatrical curtain remained visible on either side of the stage. The masking curtain terminated nearly halfway between the high point of the proscenium and the stage. Behind it, above the players, were two sound reflecting panels made of painted canvas stretched over frames, tilted 20°, each 8 ft (2.4 m) deep and extending laterally, short of either side wall, by about 6 ft (1.8 m). Covering either side wall of the stage were thin nylon draperies. In addition, on each side near the procenium, were three folding thin-plywood screens, each 9 ft (2.7 m) high by 8 ft (2.44 m) wide.

The sound of an orchestra playing on that stage was "mellow." The instruments at the rear of the orchestra were neither as loud nor as penetrating as in classic rectangular halls. This "Carnegie sound" was well accepted. It had the atypical characteristic that its acoustics remained in the background.

In the renovation of 1986, this whole kludge was wiped out and the stage was returned to its 1891 condition. The visual result was spectacular. But, sad to say there was a significant change in the orchestral sound. The brass and percussion strode forth

New York, Carnegie Hall

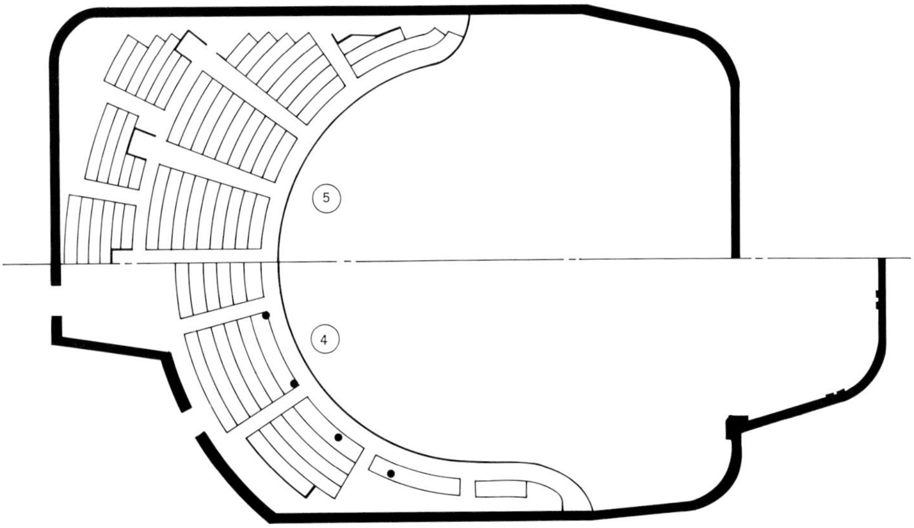

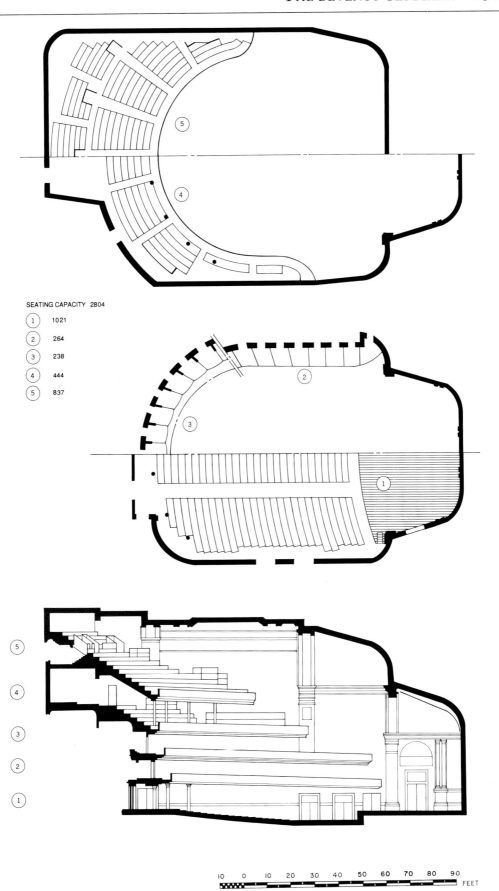

SEATING CAPACITY 2804

1	1021
2	264
3	238
4	444
5	837

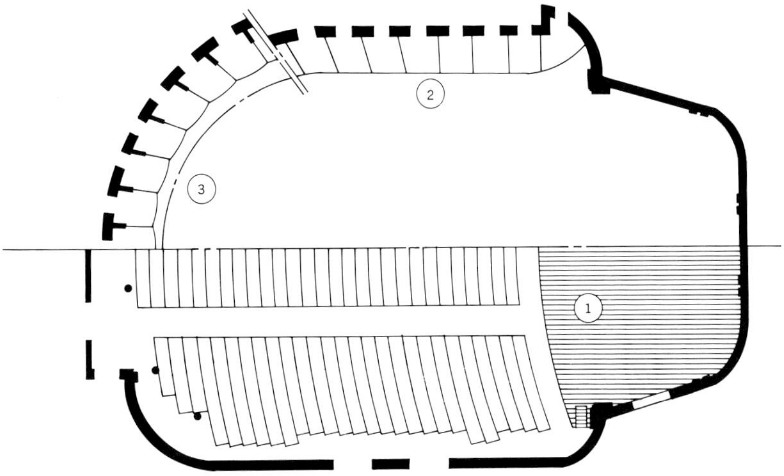

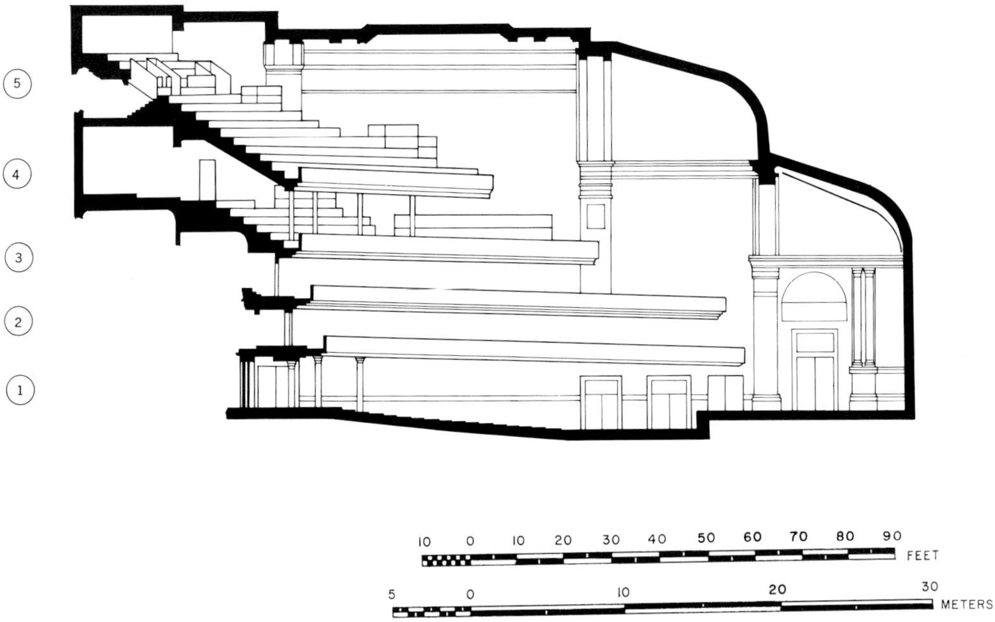

in full volume. The mellow tone ceased to exist. The reflected sound took on a "hard" texture. The audience at the front of the main floor was troubled by echoes from the rear wall of that floor and from the rear stage wall. On stage, the musicians were troubled by focused ceiling echoes and by the same echoes as the audience. Those time-delayed reflections exceeded the direct sound heard from one section to another, and made ensemble playing difficult. Something had to be done.

In 1989, novel and effective renovations were instituted. The shape of the stage ceiling was altered and a thin layer of sound absorbing material was applied to it. In the three square panels on the back wall of the stage, felt was attached in thicknesses varying from 1/4 to1/2 in. (see the upper photograph). In the small rectangle and the semicircular decoration above each side-stage door, more felt was applied. During concerts, chevron-shaped reflectors, 4 ft (1.2 m) high, are placed on the left and right front edges of the stage to reduce main-side-wall reflections and to help the players who sit on the stage outside the proscenium. Finally, to eliminate the high frequency components of the reflections from the rear wall of the main floor, scientifically designed acoustic panels, "quadratic residue diffusers QRD," 6 in. (15 cm) deep, 5.8 ft (1.7 m) high, and about 28 ft (8.53 m) long (in three sections), were installed just below the soffitt of the balcony above. They act to spread the high and middle frequency sound energy sideways, which improves spaciousness on the main floor, eliminates the echo from the lower rear wall, and masks the echoes from the box levels. As discussed in Chapter 10, the spreading of energy at high frequencies is a desirable feature whether achieved by technically designed diffusing surfaces or the elaborate ornamentation of the older shoebox halls.

These changes appear to have produced acceptable results but of different character from Carnegie's state before 1986, about which conductors interviewed in 1961 agreed, "Carnegie Hall is very good, better than Philadelphia's Academy of Music, ranking only below Boston Symphony Hall." Those who responded to questionnaires sent by Fricke (Appendix 3) rated the "new" Carnegie "Excellent."

Architectural and structural details

Uses: mostly orchestra, soloists, and chorus. *Ceiling:* 1 in. (2.5 cm) plaster on metal screen, 5% open for ventilation. *Walls:* 0.75 in. (1.9 cm) plaster on metal screen with small airspace between the plaster and the solid backing; beneath the first tier of boxes, the walls are plaster on solid backing; balcony fronts are plaster. *Floors:* wood flooring on sleepers over concrete. *Carpets:* in the aisles on main floor and upper two tiers (3 and 4); carpet in the boxes. *Stage enclosure:* walls of the stage are mostly plaster on masonry, but a few areas are plaster on metal lath; stage ceiling is vaulted, plaster resiliently suspended free of wall surfaces (other details in the text). *Stage floor:* prior to 1995, the construction was wood on sleepers over concrete. In mid-1995, the concrete was removed, opening a large airspace underneath. *Stage height:* 48 in. (122 cm) above floor level at first row of seats. *Seating:* Irwin PAC chair with high-impedance mohair upholstery, perforated metal pans.

Architect: William B. Tuthill; for the 1986 and 1989 revisions, James Polshek. *Acoustical consultants:* for 1986 renovation, Abraham Melzer; for 1989 renovation, Kirkegaard & Associates. *Photographs:* lower photograph courtesy of Carnegie Hall in 1962; upper photograph, Michelle V. Agins/New York Times (1991).

*Technical details**

V = 857,000^3 (24,270 m^3)	S_a = 12,300 ft^2 (1,145 m^2)	S_A = 17,220 ft^2 (1,600 m^2)
S_o = 2,440 ft^2 (227 m^2)	S_T = 19,660 ft^2 (1,826 m^2)	N = 2,804
H = 78 ft (23.8 m)	W = 85 ft (25.9 m)	L = 108 ft (32.9 m)
D = 147 ft (44.8 m)	V/S_T = 43.6 ft (13.3 m)	V/S_A = 59.8 ft (15.2 m)
V/N = 306 ft^3 (8.65 m^3)	S_A/N = 5.71 ft^2 (0.53 m^2)	H/W = 0.92
L/W = 1.27	t_I = 23 msec	

**The terminology is explained in Appendix 1.*

USA
14

New York
Metropolitan Opera House

In September 1966, the new Metropolitan Opera House opened with all the pomp and circumstance that a devoted New York opera public could muster. The renowned Metropolitan Opera Association regularly features on its roster some of the world's finest singers. Its pit orchestra is among the best in this country. Its tradition has been carefully nurtured by a proud New York society and by the nationwide audience devoted to its Saturday afternoon broadcasts.

Its 3,816 seats make the "Met" one of the largest houses in the world used exclusively for opera. Its shape is not like Milan's horseshoe La Scala, traditionally used as a model for most opera houses, though there are resemblances. The seating is on five tiers, plus a balcony, and the fronts of the tiers are flattened to make the viewing distance from the stage as short as possible. Its volume of 873,000 ft^3 (24,724 m^3) is more than double that of La Scala making it necessary that the singers have strong voices—more than twice the vocal power. Its reverberation time, fully occupied, at mid-frequencies, is about 1.7 sec, higher than that in any other opera house, but which aids in augmenting the loudness of the singer's voices.

The Met's stage is probably the most highly mechanized in the world. Scenes can float up from below on seven hydraulic lifts which occupy a 60 × 60 ft (18 × 18 m) area. Scenes can glide in from two side stages on large motorized wagons and from backstage, which also boasts a 57-ft-diameter (17.4 m) turntable. Scenes and people can pop up through traps in the lifts. The front-stage curtains and all hanging-scenery battens are motorized. The extensive controls for these and the lighting are awesome.

The acousticians wisely tailored the box fronts and the tall flat areas to either side of the proscenium to create the necessary early, lateral, sound reflections that give the voices breadth and intimacy. The acoustics are benefited by the large apron on the stage which reflects the voices of the singers into the upper four tiers and the balcony. The sound is distributed reasonably equally to all seats throughout the house except those in the upper tiers nearest to the proscenium.

New York, Metropolitan Opera House

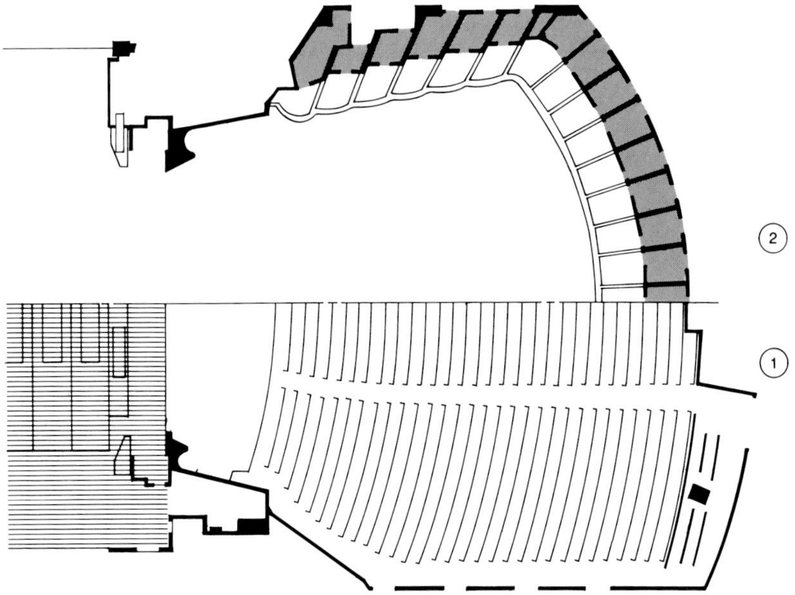

SEATING CAPACITY 3816

(1)	1583
(2)	232
(3)	454
(4)	454
(5)	442
(6)	651

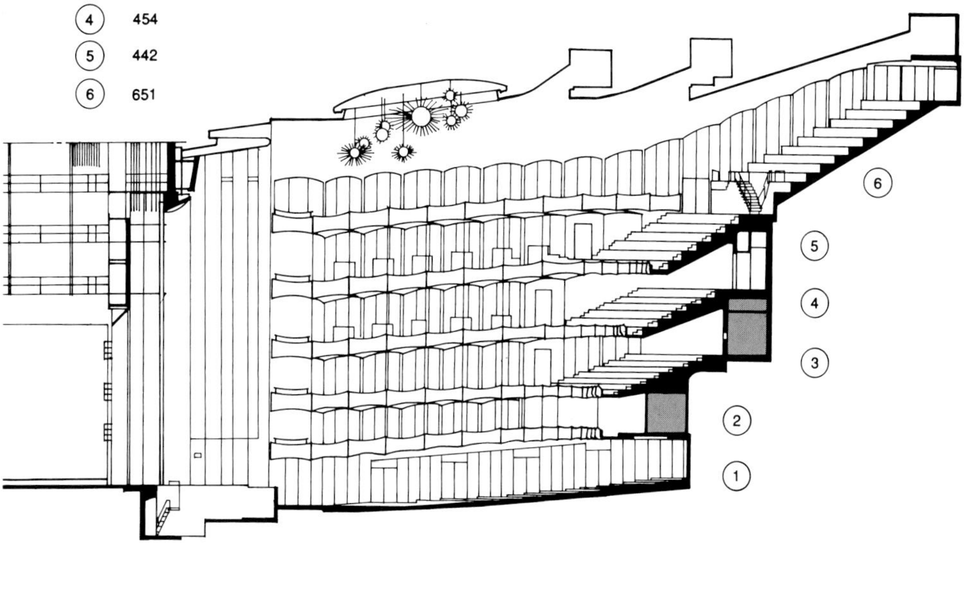

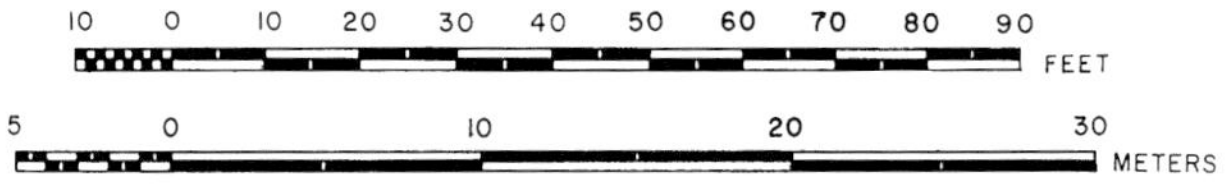

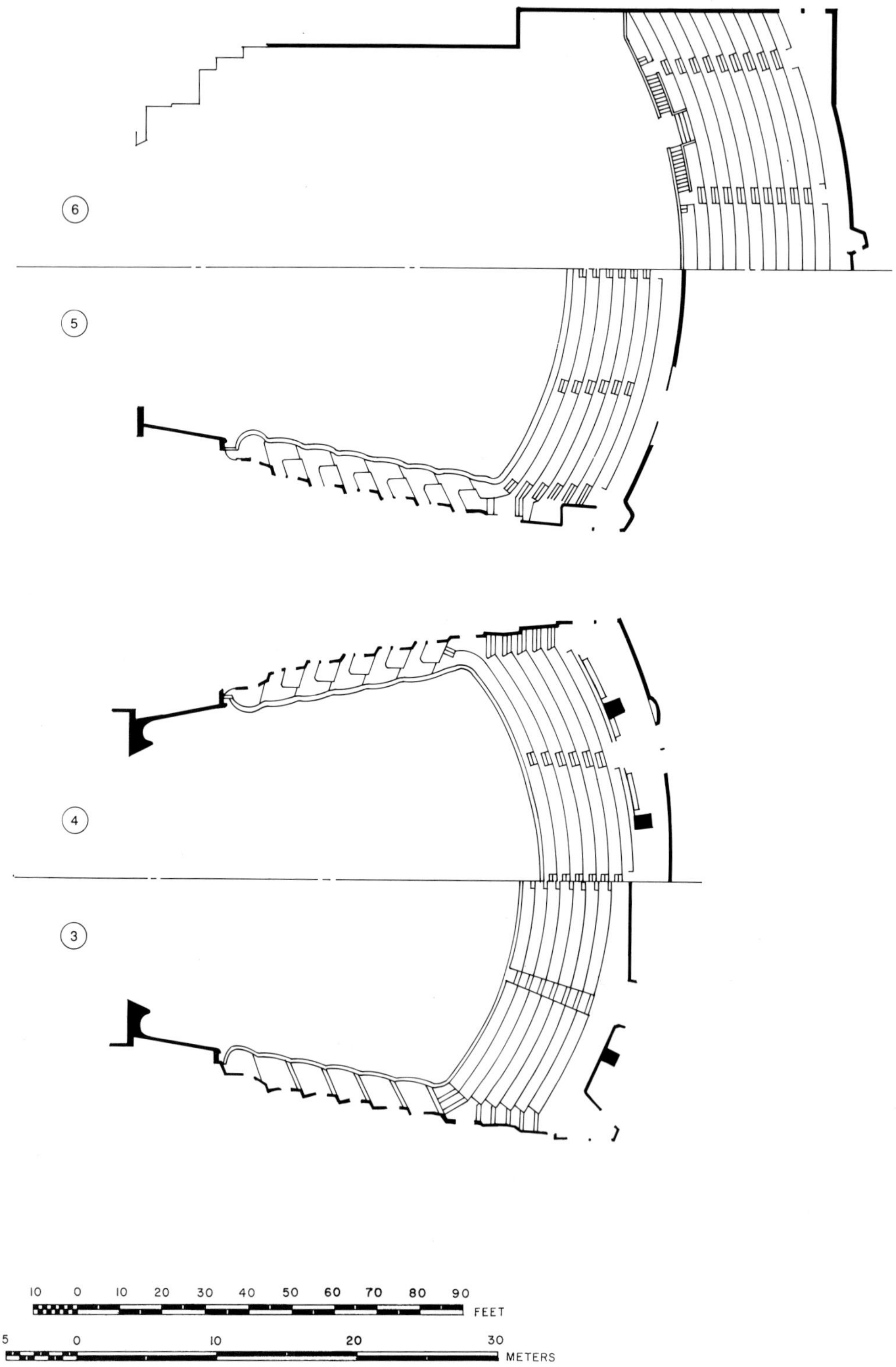
6
5
4
3
10 0 10 20 30 40 50 60 70 80 90
FEET
5 0 10 20 30
METERS

Architectural and structural details

Uses: opera. *Ceiling:* plaster, covered with 4,000 rolls of 23 carat gold leaf. *Walls:* plaster, some areas covered with 27,000 ft^2 (2,500 m^2) of burgundy velour, some painted and some with wood paneling. *Floors:* Solid. *Carpets:* 18,000 ft^2 (1,670 m^2). *Pit:* floor is made of 2.5 in. (6.4 cm) wooden planks; the pit walls are of 0.75 in. (1.9 cm) wood. *Stage height:* 48 in. (122 cm) above floor level at first row of seats. *Seating:* fully upholstered, except underseats are solid; seats range in width from 19 to 23 in. (48 to 58 cm) to conform to "three-row vision" sequence. *Proscenium curtain:* Gold patterned silk damask, tableau drape, 9,000 ft^2 (836 m^2). *Proscenium opening:* 54 ft (16.5 m) square.

Architect: Wallace K. Harrison of Harrison and Abramovitz. *Acoustical consultants:* V. Lassen Jordan and Cyril M. Harris. *References:* Plans and details, John Pennino, archivist office of the Metropolitan Opera Association. *Photographs:* Metropolitan Opera Archives and United Press International Photo.

*Technical details**

Opera

V = 873,000 ft^3 (24,724 m^3)	S_a = 20,600 ft^2 (1,914 m^2)	S_A = 24,350 ft^2 (2,262 m^2)
S_o (pit) = 1,420 ft^2 (132 m^2)	S_T = 25,770 ft^2 (2,394 m^2)	N =3,816 plus ~200 standees
H = 82 ft (25 m)	W = 110 ft (33.5 m)	L = 130 ft (39.6 m)
D = 184 ft (56.1 m)	V/S_T = 33.8 ft (10.3 m)	V/S_A = 35.8 ft (10.9 m)
V/N = 229 ft^3 (6.48 m^3)	S_A/N = 6.38 ft^2 (0.59 m^2)	H/W = 0.745
L/W = 1.18	t_I = 34 msec	

**The terminology is explained in Appendix 1.*

USA

15

Philadelphia Academy of Music

Except for the Teatro alla Scala in Milan, after which it was modeled, the Academy of Music is the oldest hall in this book. In the middle of the nineteenth century, there were no symphony orchestras to speak of in this country, but grand opera was immensely popular and enjoyed unique prestige both in Europe and in New York. The Academy was built for the express purpose of bringing this art to Philadelphia. Acoustically, it is unquestionably the finest opera house in the United States, and the most beautiful, and will be tabulated in this book only for this purpose.

Venerated for nearly a century and a half of concerts and operas, beautiful and intimate, this hall and the world renowned Philadelphia Orchestra mean to America the best in music.

With a cubic volume only 40 percent greater than that of the Vienna Staatsoper, the Academy nevertheless holds 70 percent more people. Each of its 2,827 (for opera) seats is allotted only 5.5 ft^2 (0.5 m^2), including aisles, as compared to 7.5 ft^2 (0.7 m^2) in Vienna in the 1955 reconstruction. For symphonic music, the biggest criticism of the Academy of Music is its low reverberation time. Measured in 1992, fully occupied, at mid-frequencies, it is 1.2 sec, comparable to La Scala's 1.2 and Vienna's 1.3, but well below the 1.85 sec of Boston's Symphony Hall.

The orchestra enclosure is comprised of twelve rolling "towers" (see the drawing), four on each side and four at the rear. Each has three convex sections, designed to diffuse the sound on the stage for better inter-player communication. The ceiling is made of three flat, sloped sections, as shown in the drawing.

Every conductor and music critic interviewed in 1960 said that the Academy was excellent for opera, but for symphonic music, "somewhat dry," "sound too small," "not very live." My own judgment, listening to concerts many times, is that the orchestral sounds are balanced, clear, and beautiful. Basses and cellos are strong. There is a feeling of intimacy, both visually and musically. But there is no audible reverberation and the sound does not envelope one as in rectangular orchestral halls. It does not seem right in this book to compare it with the world's great concert halls.

PHILADELPHIA, ACADEMY OF MUSIC

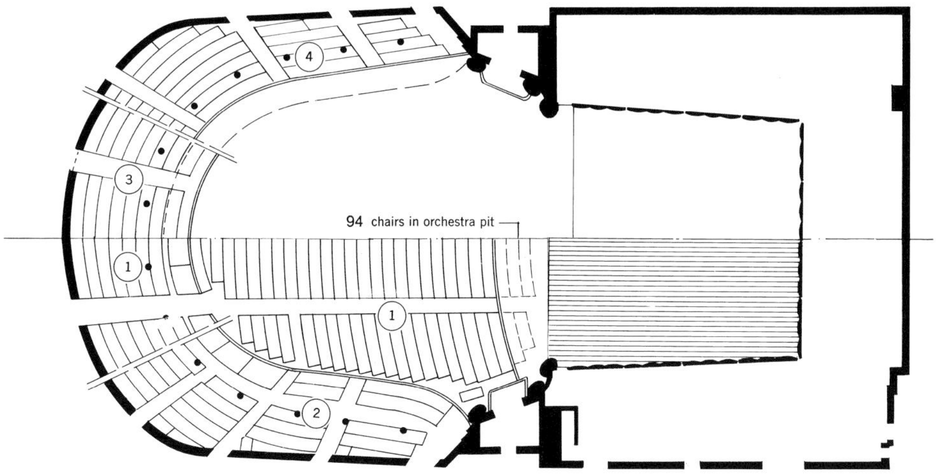

SEATING CAPACITY 2827 to 2921

(1) Concerts 1307; Small pit 1213; Large pit 1147	
(2)	524
(3)	561
(4)	529

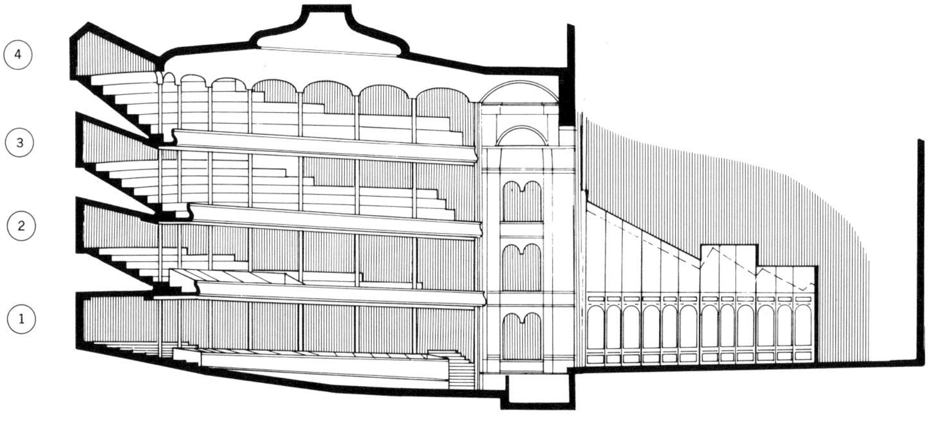

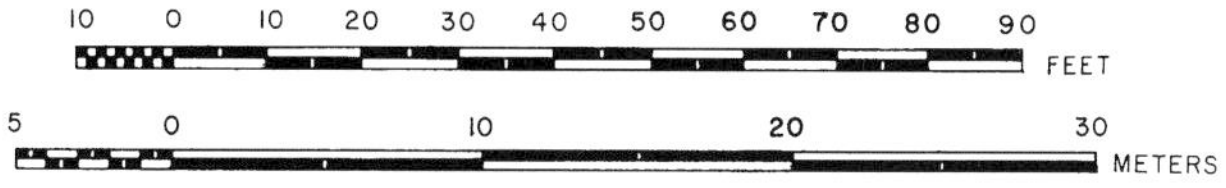

Architectural and structural details

Uses: opera, orchestra, chorus, chamber orchestra, and soloists. *Ceiling:* 0.75 in. (1.9 cm) plaster on wood lath on flat surfaces; plaster on metal wire screen on curved surfaces. *Walls:* pine-wood boards, 0.4 × 3 in. (1 × 7.6 cm), nailed to wooden framing and covered with heavy burlap glued in place; with the passage of time the boards have shrunk and separated; behind the boards, the air space is about 1 in. (2.5 cm) widening to as much as 1 ft (30 cm) near doors. *Floors:* two layers of 0.4 in. (1 cm) boards on joists. *Carpets:* 3 to 4 ft (0.9 to 1.2 m) wide on main aisles downstairs with underpad and in the first ring; no carpets in top two rings; carpets under seats in boxes (see 1 and 2 in the upper drawing). *Stage enclosure:* the side walls and ceiling are mostly 0.4 in. (1 cm) curved plywood panels with 0.4 in. battans for bracing and 1 in. (2.5 cm) ribs at edges. *Stage floor:* two layers of wood on joists. *Stage height:* 52 in. (132 cm). *Seating:* deep upholstering on top of seat bottoms and front of seat backs; underseat is unperforated metal; back side of seat back is plywood. Bench-type backs at the uppermost level with same type of seat bottom and with a cushion on the bench backs.

Architects: Napoleon E. H. C. Le Brun and Gustavus Runge. *Stage enclosure design:* Paul S. Veneklasen. *Credits:* drawings, seating, room, and stage enclosure details from Academy of Music. *Photographs:* Ed Wheeler.

*Technical details**

Opera

V = 533,000 ft^3 (15,100 m^3)	S_p = 2,401 ft^2 (223 m^2)	S_A = 15,700 ft^2 (1,460 m^2)
S_o (pit) = 640 ft^2 (59 m^2)	S_T = 18,740 ft^2 (1,740 m^2)	N = 2,827
V/S_T = 28.4 ft (8.7 m)	V/S_A = 33.9 ft (10.4 m)	S_A/N = 5.55 ft^2 (0.52 m^2)
H = 64 ft (19.5 m)	W = 58 ft (17.7 m)	L = 102 ft (31.1 m)
D = 118 ft (36 m)	H/W = 1.1	L/W = 1.76
t_I = 19 msec		

Concerts

V = 555,000 ft^3 (15,800 m^3)	S_a = 14,000 ft^2 (1,300 m^2)	S_A = 16,700 ft^2 (1,550 m^2)
S_o = 2,350 ft^2 (186 m^2)	S_T = 19,050 ft^2 (1,770 m^2)	N = 2,921
V/S_T = 29.1 ft (8.9 m)	V/S_A = 33.2 ft (10.1 m)	V/N = 190 ft^3 (5.38 m^3)
S_A/N = 5.72 ft^2 (0.53 m^2)		

The terminology is explained in Appendix 1.

USA
16
Rochester, New York
Eastman Theatre

New theaters in America no longer exhibit the expensive handwork that went into the Eastman Theatre. Built in 1923, it embodies fabrics, metals, and decorations of a quality found in the royal palaces of old. It contains 3,347 large comfortable seats. One is aware immediately on entering the hall of the high volume of nearly 900,000 cubic feet (25,488 m^3).

The high ceiling and wide, splayed side walls direct sound primarily to the rear of the hall. Before a major renovation (1972), regular concertgoers complained about a lack of clarity of the music, particularly on the main floor, which resulted from a very long initial-time-delay gap and a complete lack of early lateral sound reflections. This condition did and does not exist in the rear part of the upper balcony because lateral reflections naturally occur there, along with a shorter initial-time-delay gap.

The renovation was directed at improving the acoustics of the hall for concert music, which is presented regularly by the Minneapolis Symphony and the Eastman School orchestras. It primarily consisted of a new stage enclosure (shell) with a large storable canopy. The design of the orchestra enclosure and canopy was to reflect and project more sound outward through the proscenium. The canopy is shaped and located to send a higher percentage of acoustic energy from the instruments in the front third of the orchestra to the audience, particularly onto the previously neglected main floor area. The result is an increase in the ratio of the energy in the direct sound to that in the reverberant sound and the canopy provides a short initial-time-delay gap in that area. This change spells "clarity." The reverberation times were carefully not altered. Other objectives were restortion and preservation of the decorative features.

The Theatre is used for opera. With a full 85 piece pit orchestra, half of the musicians sit under the stage. This makes it difficult for them to hear what is happening on stage and to maintain proper balance among themselves. To a listener, the instruments back under the stage sound as though they were in another room. The recessed pit provides better balance between the louder instruments and singers, who may be less powerful than those at the NY Metropolitan Opera.

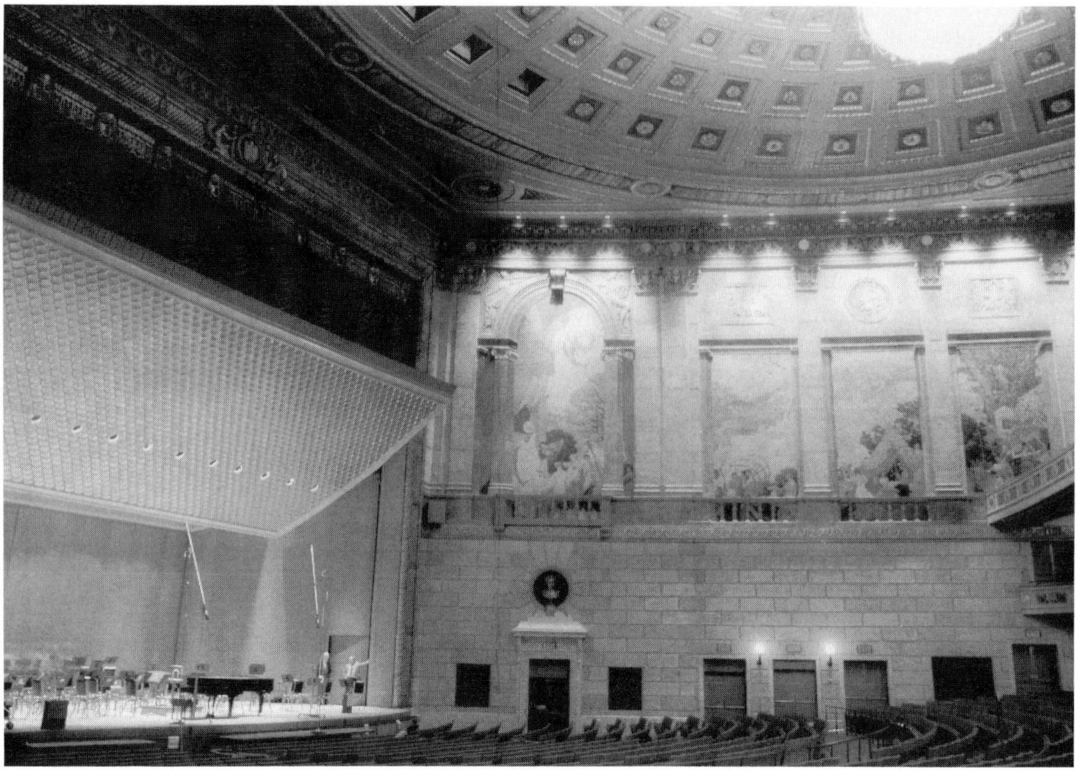

Rochester, New York, Eastman Theatre

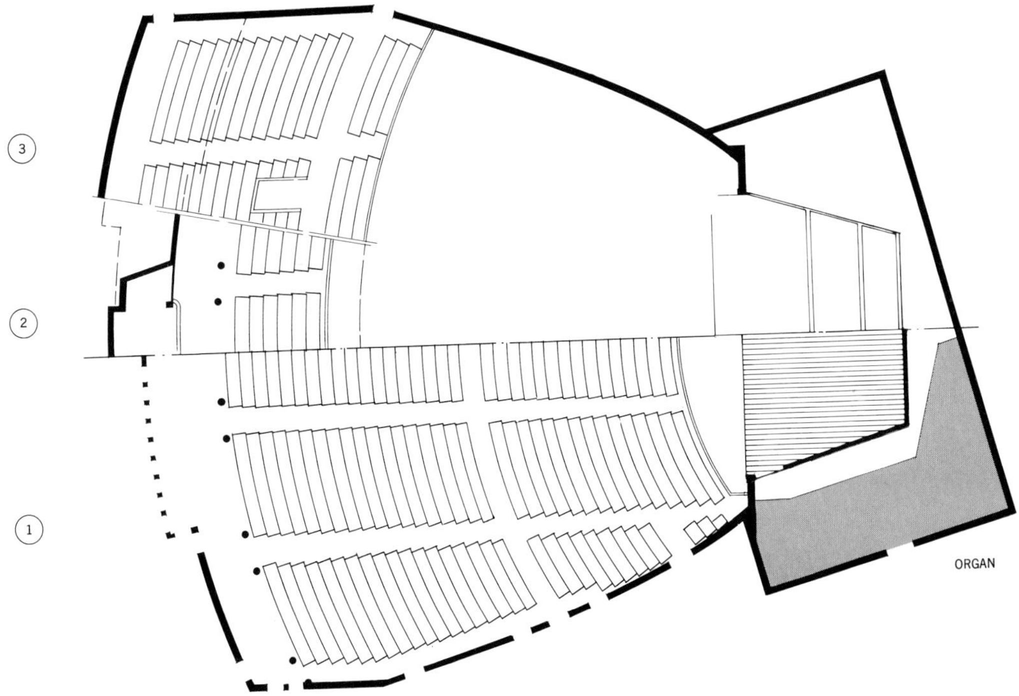

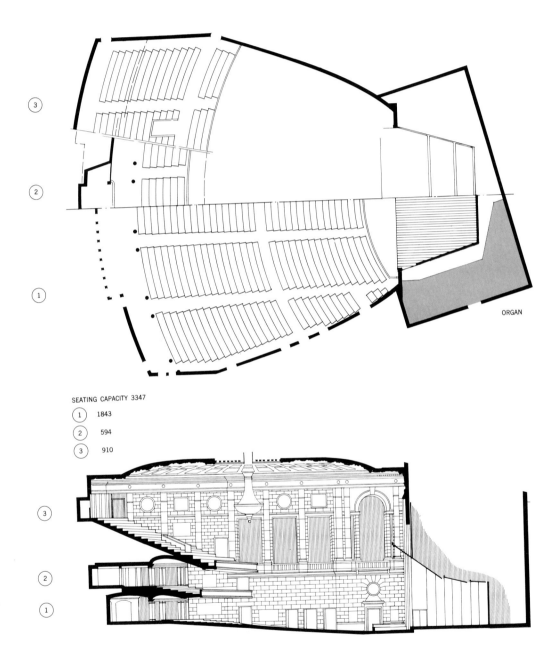

SEATING CAPACITY 3347

(1) 1843

(2) 594

(3) 910

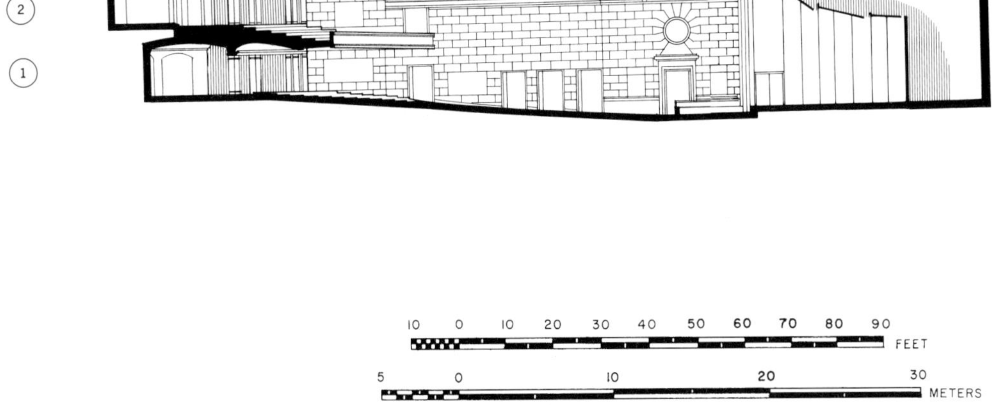

Architectural and structural details

Uses: general purpose. *Ceiling:* plaster. *Side walls:* plaster, approximately 50% covered with sound-absorbing materials that have been heavily painted. *Rear walls and balcony fronts:* covered with sound-absorbing materials, heavily painted. *Floors:* concrete. *Stage enclosure:* the sidewalls and ceiling are mostly curved plywood panels, 0.38 in. (1 cm) thick with random bracing and randomly spaced transverse ribs. *Stage floor:* wood on joists. *Stage height:* 42 in. (107 cm). *Carpets:* on all floors. *Seating:* fully upholstered both sides of backrest; underseat is solid. *Pit:* half-recessed under stage; the floor is of wood; the walls are concrete; the railing is asbestos board.

Architect: Gordon E. Kaelber. *Associate architect:* McKim, Mead and White. *Architect for 1972 renovation:* Thomas Ellerbe Associates. *Stage enclosure design (1972):* Paul S. Veneklasen. *Credits:* original drawings from the *American Architect*, February 1923. *Photographs:* lower photograph courtesy of Ansel Adams, Eastman Kodak Company (1962); upper photograph courtesy of Paul Veneklasen.

*Technical details**

Concerts

V = 900,000 ft^3 (25,500 m^3)	S_a = 17,000 ft^2 (1,580 m^2)	S_A = 21,750 ft^2 (1,907 m^2)
S_o = 2,200 ft^2 (204 m^2)	S_T = 23,950 ft^2 (2,225 m^2)	N = 3,347
H = 67 ft (20.4 m)	W = 120 ft (36.6 m)	L = 117 ft (35.7 m)
D = 142 ft (43.3 m)	V/S_T = 37.6 ft (11.5 m)	V/S_A = 41.3 ft (12.6 m)
V/N = 269 ft^3 (7.62 m^3)	S_A/N = 6.5 ft^2 (0.60 m^2)	H/W = 0.56
L/W = 0.97	t_I = 22 msec	

Opera

V = 846,500 ft^3 (23,970 m^3)	S_P = 2,752 ft^2 (256 m^2)	S_A = 21,750 ft^2 (1,907 m^2)
S_T = 25,270 ft^2 (2,348 m^2)	S_o (pit) = 770 ft^2 (71.5 m^2)	S_{OF} (pit) = 1,750 ft^2 (162.5 m^2)
N = 3,347	V/S_T = 33.6 ft (10.2 m)	V/S_A = 38.9 ft (11.9m)

**The terminology is explained in Appendix 1.*

USA
17

Salt Lake City
Abravanel Symphony Hall

Salt Lake City is proud of its Symphony Hall, home of the Utah Symphony Orchestra. Dedicated in 1979 with special honors to retiring Maestro Maurice Abravanel, its music director for 32 years, the hall is well situated. As one enters the site, on the left is a well attended garden. Just behind it is an outdoor amphitheater and sculpture court, both associated with Salt Lake's Community Art Center. The lobbies give concert-goers an uplifting experience and smiles everywhere give one a feeling of warmth and welcome.

The specification for the acoustics of the hall was that they should approach those of the highly accepted halls of the world. The architect, working closely with the acoustical consultant, decided on the classic "shoebox" shape, which has proven its quality in many venues. One must remark that, 2,812 seats, with 1,838 on the main floor, express optimism as to the possible number of subscribers in the Salt Lake City/Ogden, Utah, metropolitan area with a population of only 1.2 million. The metropolitan statistical areas of Chicago, 8.5 million, Washington, D.C., 6.8 million, and Boston, 5.5 million, support only one hall each and they seat between 2,759 and 2,582, with the smallest in Chicago. The width of Salt Lake's Symphony Hall is 90 ft (27 m) which contrasts with Boston's 75 ft (22.8 m), and, along with continental seating, tends to give a visitor a feeling of entering a vast room.

The hall has the proper features for providing good acoustics. The side and rear walls are made of randomly dimensioned oak panels and the plaster ceiling closely approximates the sound diffusing properties of the coffered ceilings of Boston and Vienna's halls. The rectangular shape provides early, lateral sound reflections which give a feeling of intimacy. Its reverberation time, with full audience, is about 1.7 sec, good for music of the Classical period and for a hall that must serve some other purposes than symphonic concerts. Compared to Boston, there are a few decibels weakness in the bass. There is no tonal harshness and the string and woodwind sounds are excellent. The bass/treble balance and the sectional balance are very good. The stage is large, 2,350 ft^2 (218 m^2), compared to Boston's 1,600 ft^2 (149 m^2), which may make ensemble playing more difficult.

Salt Lake City, Abravanel Symphony Hall

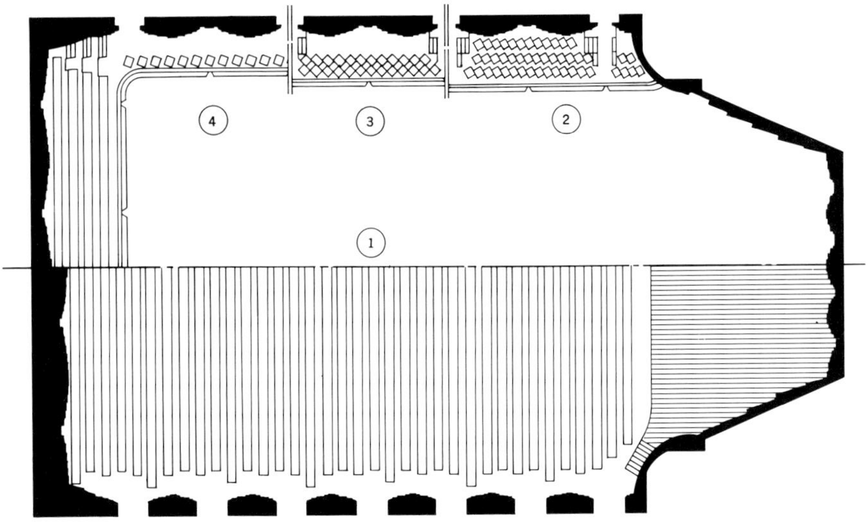

SEATING CAPACITY 2812

1	1838
2	405
3	305
4	264

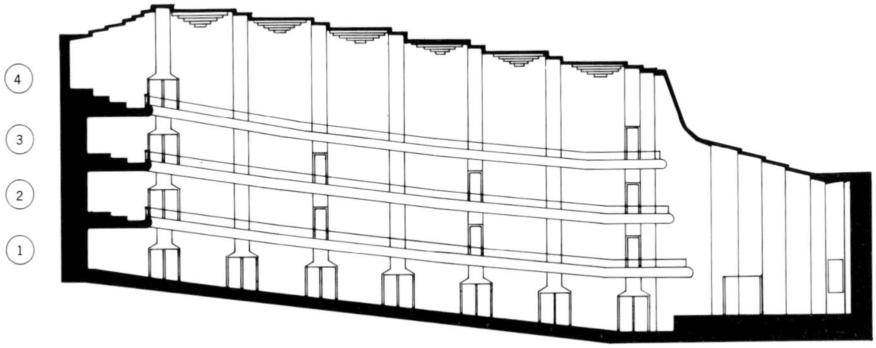

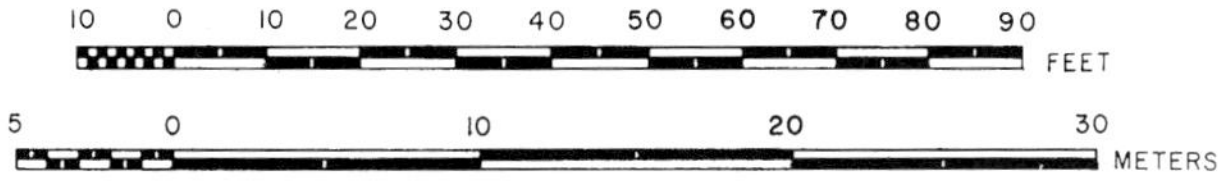

Architectural and structural details

Uses: music, 90%; speech, 10%. *Ceiling:* 1.5 in. (3.8 cm) hardrock plaster—all openings sealed with gaskets. *Walls:* side and rear walls, poured in place concrete with 0.75 in. (1.9 cm) plywood finish surface mounted on 0.75 in. furring strips, space between filled with fiberglass; balcony faces 1.5 in. hardrock plaster on furring strips on concrete structure. *Floors:* main and balcony floors: 0.75 in. tongue-and-groove oak wood on furring strips on main floor and on frames in balconies. *Carpet:* none. *Stage enclosure:* see Walls above. *Stage floor:* 0.75 in. tongue-and-groove oak boards on 0.75 in. plywood subfloor on sleepers. *Stage height:* 43 in. (109 cm). *Sound absorbing materials:* none. *Seating:* wooden seat back; front of seat back and seat bottom upholstered with sprayed, impervious fabric over polyvinyl foam; underseat, perforated metal; arms, wooden.

Architects: Fowler, Ferguson Kingston Ruben. *Acoustical consultant:* Cyril M. Harris. *Photographs:* Schoenfeld.

*Technical details**

V = 688,500 ft^3 (19,500 m^3)	S_a = 16,000 ft^2 (1,486 m^2)	S_A = 17,965 ft^2 (1,669 m^2)
S_o = 2,350 ft^2 (218 m^2)	S_T = 20,315 ft^2 (1,887 m^2)	N = 2,812
H = 54 ft (16.5 m)	W = 96 ft (29.3 m)	L = 124 ft (37.8 m)
D = 134 ft (40.85 m)	V/S_T = 33.9 ft (10.3 m)	V/S_A = 38.3 ft (11.7 m)
V/N = 245 ft^3 (6.93 m^3)	S_A/N = 6.39 ft^2 (0.59 m^2)	H/W = 0.56
L/W = 1.29	t_I =30 msec	

**The terminology is explained in Appendix 1.*

USA
18

San Francisco
Louise M. Davies Symphony Hall

Davies Symphony Hall, as opened in 1980, was approximately circular in plan and had a maximum width on the main floor of 100 ft (30 m), about 20 ft in excess of the best of the well liked, large, rectangular concert halls. Lower wall surfaces produced useful lateral reflections, but also generated echoes back to the stage. In addition, there was a rear wall echo. The hall's flat ceiling, 68 ft (17.7 m) above platform level caused an immense overhead cubic volume. The circular acrylic panels suspended above the players were sparse and helped their ensemble little.

A major remodeling of Davies Hall was undertaken during the summers of 1991 and 1992. The volume in the upper front part of the hall was reduced by building new side walls above the chorus seating—they are now 24 ft (7.3 m) closer to each other and shaped to direct sound energy to the main floor (see the photograph). A computer-controlled array of 59, 6 ft (1.83 m) square, convex, panels was hung at a height of 30–35 ft (9–10 m) above the stage and the first four rows of seats. These panels improve communication onstage and provide strong early reflections to the main floor and first balcony.

The walls around the platform are 1.5 ft (0.46 m) higher than before although the exposed wall area is less due to the height of the orchestra risers—2 ft (0.61 m) high at the sides and 3 ft (0.92 m) high at the rear. The side and corner walls of the stage surround are devoted to 8 in. deep quadratic residue diffusers QRDs (see Chapter 10) to further improve communication among the musicians. The entire rear wall of the main floor is covered with QRDs to eliminate echo. To reduce the width of the main floor to 84 ft at the front, the side walls were moved in and reshaped. Ten raised boxes were built on either side to improve sightlines and to provide early lateral reflections. The hall now seats an audience of 2,743.

The changes have worked. The sound is more intimate and clear and the bass response is greatly improved. These modifications signal the changes in acoustical design since 1975. At that date the importance of early lateral reflections was not yet proven; the theory of multiple hanging panels was in its infancy; and quadratic residue diffusers QRDs were not yet born.

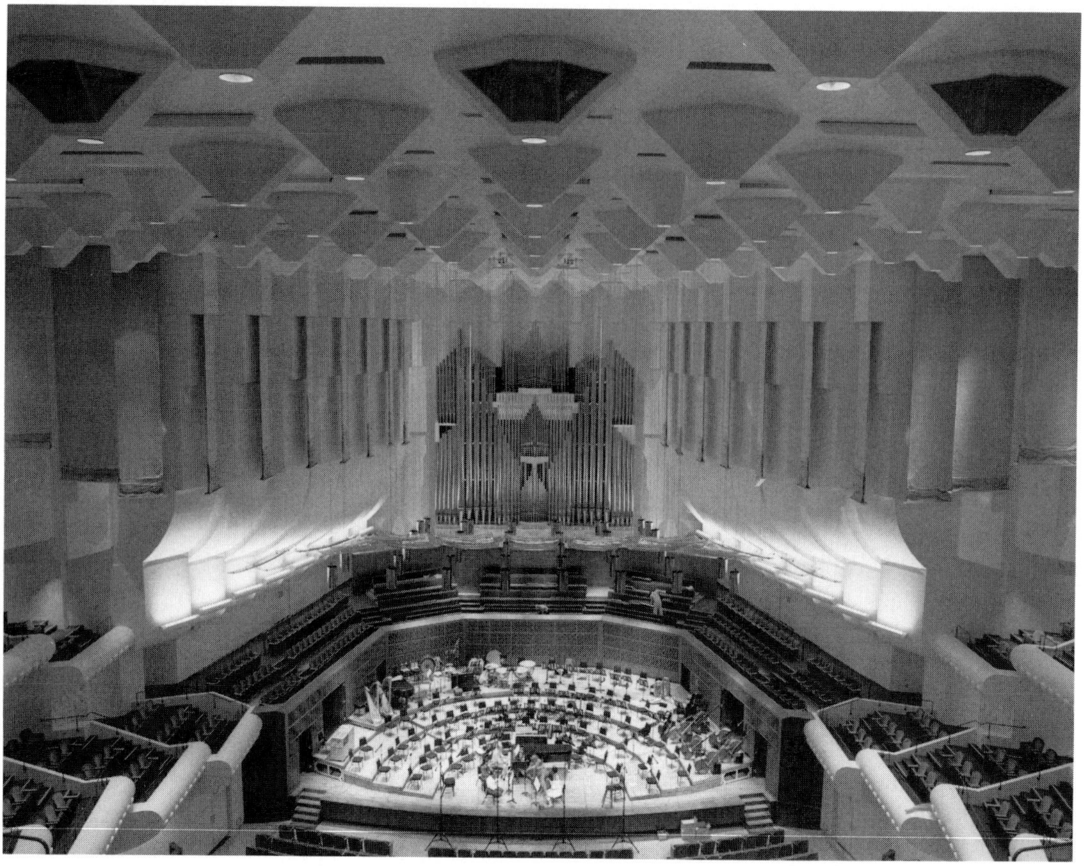

San Francisco, Louise M. Davies Symphony Hall

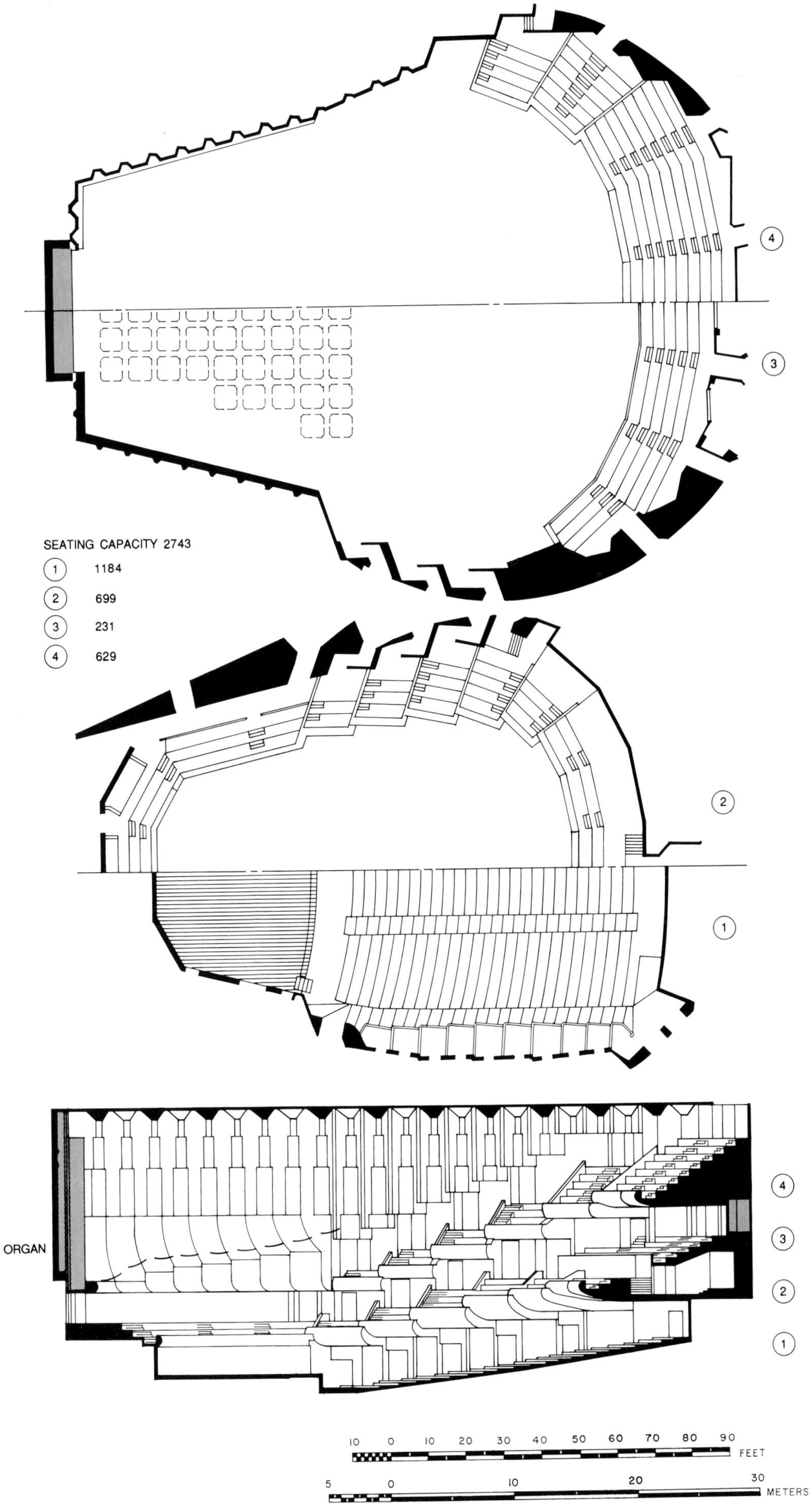

SEATING CAPACITY 2743
1 1184
2 699
3 231
4 629
4
3
2
1
ORGAN
4
3
2
1
10 0 10 20 30 40 50 60 70 80 90 FEET
5 0 10 20 30 METERS

Architectural and structural details

Uses: orchestral music and recitals. *Ceiling:* 6 in. (15 cm) concrete *Walls:* front, side, and rear walls are multi-faceted pre-cast concrete 4 in. (10 cm) thick. Above the sides of the stage, the new reflecting walls are glass fiber shells containing sand-packed steel tubes—the total weighing 40 lb/ft^2 (195 kg/m^2); balcony fronts and soffits are 2 in. (5 cm) plaster; box fronts, plaster on gypsum lath. *Floors:* parquet over wood over small airspace and concrete base. *Carpet:* in aisles only. *Stage enclosure:* (see the text). *Stage height:* 39 in. (99 cm). *Sound absorbing materials:* none, except QRD diffusers have an absorption coefficient of 0.1 to 0.25 over a wide band of frequencies. *Seating:* molded wooden seat back; lightly upholstered front of seat back; relatively thin seat cushion with porous fabric covering; underseat, unperforated wood—all designed to reduce low frequency sound absorption.

Architect: Skidmore Owings and Merrill. *Original acoustical consultant:* Bolt Beranek and Newman. *Acoustical consultant for revisions:* Kirkegaard and Associates. *Photographs:* Dennis Gearney. *References:* L. Kirkegaard, "Concert Acoustics: The Performers' Perspective." Paper presented at the 116th meeting of the Acoustical Society of America, Honolulu, 15 November, 1988.

*Technical details**

V = 850,000 ft^3 (24,070 m^3)	S_a =13,070 ft^2 (1,214 m^2)	S_A = 16,800 ft^2 (1,562 m^2)
S_o =2,155 ft^2 (200 m^2)	S_T = 19,955 ft^2 (1,762 m^2)	N = 2,743
H = 68 ft (20.7 m)	W = 92 ft (28 m)	L = 107 ft (32.6 m)
D = 127 ft (38.7 m)	V/S_T = 42.6 ft (13 m)	V/S_A = 50.6 ft (15.4 m)
V/N = 310 ft^3 (8.78 m^3)	S_A/N = 6.1 ft^2 (0.57 m^2)	H/W = 0.74
L/W = 1.16	t_I = 12 msec	

**The terminology is explained in Appendix 1.*

USA

19

San Francisco
War Memorial Opera House

The War Memorial Opera House surpasses many of the world's opera houses in beauty of exterior and lobbies. The hall itself is reminiscent of other theaters built in the United States in the early 1930's. Yet it has a dignity and beauty that exceed that of many contemporary halls, partly because the architect eschewed adornments and confined the design to simple lines, a high ceiling, and a majestic proscenium.

I have attended two performances, the world premier of *Blood Moon* by Norman Dello Joio, and *Nabucco* by Verdi. The long thin pit gave the conductor some trouble with ensemble, but the timbre was satisfactory throughout the house. The singers were easy to hear above the orchestra, although some may have forced their voices somewhat, probably because to them the hall looks huge. Most pleasant was the general liveness, greater than that of La Scala, or the Staatsoper in Vienna.

I had access to seats in four parts of the house during the two operas. In the front of the house (the 15th row near the left aisle of the main floor), the reverberation tended to interfere with intelligibility of opera sung in English. But the hard materials of the interior also gave warmth to the music, and a fullness of bass not found in many European houses. At the other seats the sound was very good.

The shallow dome presents no acoustical problem, because the very large chandelier beneath it effectively diffuses the sound. G. Albert Lansburgh, one of the architects for the San Francisco Opera, told me that the dome is treated with acoustic plaster. He said that there are good sight lines to all 3,252 seats.

Seven conductors who have had experience in the San Francisco Opera House were interviewed. Each rated it good from the positions of both the conductor and the listeners. Several of them remarked that the audience hears much better in the balcony than on the main floor.

As is true of all wide halls with high ceilings, the initial-time-delay gap is somewhat too long for the listeners in the forward part of the main floor. The ceiling supplies these first reflections to the fronts of the balconies and the side walls supply their first reflections to the rear of the balconies. Still, for its size and the comfort of its seating, this house is acoustically quite satisfactory.

San Francisco, War Memorial Opera House

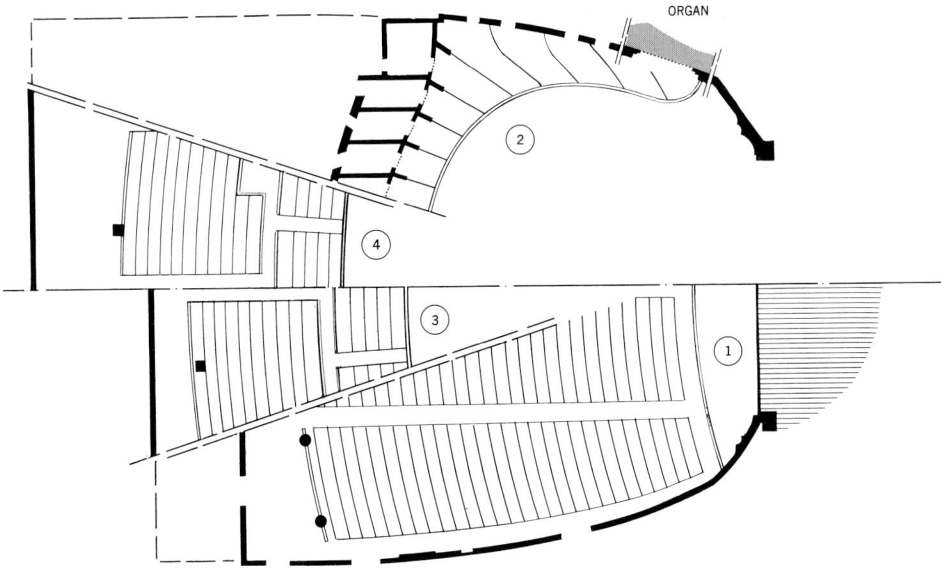

SEATING CAPACITY 3252

(1) 1300

(2) 192

(3) 852

(4) 908 + 300 standees

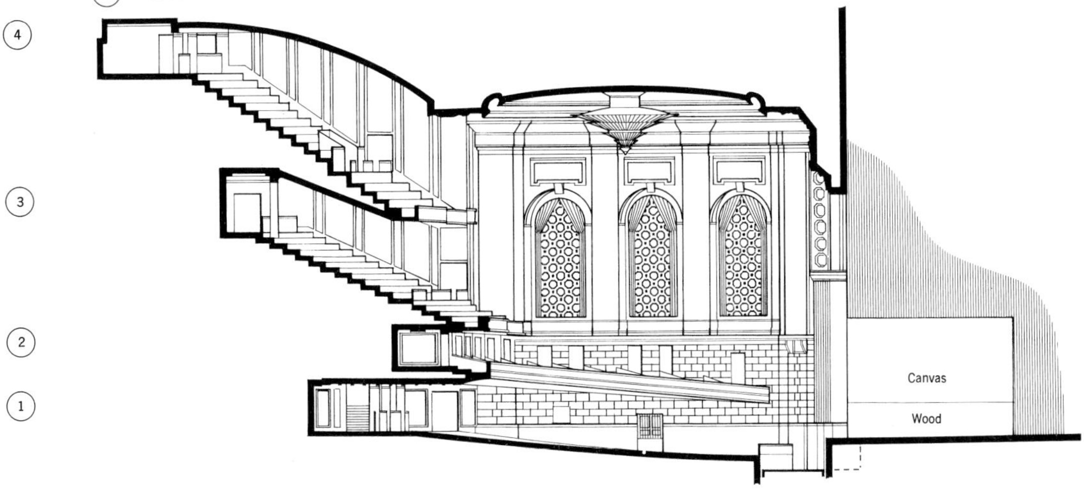

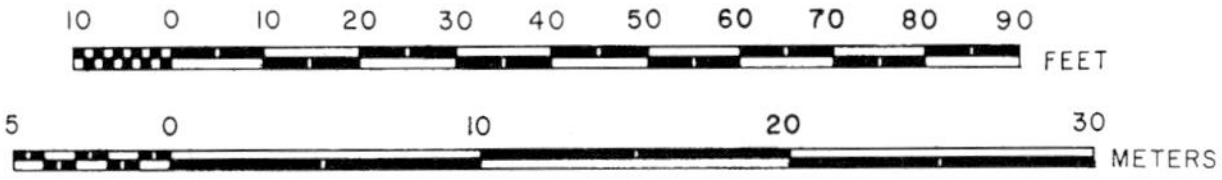

Architectural and structural details

Uses: opera, general purpose. *Ceiling:* plaster except for center domed section which architect says is acoustic plaster. *Walls:* plaster with some wood trim. *Floors:* entire floor area carpeted except in upper part of top balcony where carpet is only in aisles. *Stage:* wood over air space. *Pit:* wooden floor on elevator; wooden rear and front walls with 1 ft (30 cm) of velvet covering over an open railing. *Stage height:* 40 in. (102 cm) above floor level at first row of seats. *Added absorptive materials:* velvet draperies, about 1 ft (2.5 cm) high above rails of cross aisles. *Seating:* main floor, fully upholstered with four holes 1 in. (2.5 cm) in diameter in underseat; balcony, but with hard backs. *Orchestra enclosure:* canvas throughout except that 1/4 in. plywood covers the bottom part of the walls extending upward 10 ft (3 m) from the floor.

Architect: Arthur Brown, Jr. *Collaborating architect:* G. Albert Lansburgh. *References:* B. J. S. Cahill, "The San Francisco War Memorial Group." *The Architect and Engineer*, **111**, 11–44, 59 (November 1932); *Photographs:* courtesy of *Musical America* and *Opera News*. Details verified by the author during a visit and by management (1993).

*Technical details**

Opera

V = 738,600 ft^3 (20,900 m^3)	S_a = 16,500 ft^2 (1,518 m^2)	S_A = 21,240 ft^2 (1,973 m^2)
S_o (pit) = 760 ft^2 (70.6 m^2)	S_p = 2,500 ft^2 (232 m^2)	S_T = 24,500 ft^2 (2,276 m^2)
N = 3,252	H = 73 ft (22.2 m)	W = 104 ft (31.7 m)
L = 120 ft (36.6 m)	D = 122 (37.2 m)	V/S_T = 30.1 ft (9.19 m)
V/S_A = 34.8 ft (10.6 m)	V/N = 227 ft^3 (6.43 m^3)	S_A/N = 6.53 ft^2 (0.61 m^2)
H/W = 0.70	L/W = 1.15	t_I = 51 msec

**The terminology is explained in Appendix 1.*

USA

20

Washington, D.C.
John F. Kennedy Center for the Performing Arts
Opera House

The John F. Kennedy Center for the Performing Arts was opened in 1971 at a site along the Potomac River upstream from the Lincoln Memorial. It fills a cultural need in this city of politicians, diplomats, civil servants, companies doing business with the Federal government, and lobbyists. The Center incorporates into a single building three auditoriums, the Eisenhower Theater, the Concert Hall, and the Opera House.

The size is unusual for the United States in that the House seats only 2,142 with the orchestra pit in use—56 percent of New York's Metropolitan Opera House and 66 percent of San Francisco's Opera House. For opera lovers and singers this is good. Because the roof height of the overall building was restricted, the conventional multi-ringed, horse-shoe style of House had to be eschewed. Instead it has a box tier and two balconies. The audience is as close to the stage as possible.

It was expected from the beginning that grand opera would not be a dominant use. Included are musicals, soloists, speaking functions, and ballet. As a house that emphasizes voice, the reverberation time is optimum, even a little higher than many of the famous opera houses in Europe, measuring 1.5 sec at mid-frequencies when the House is fully occupied (taken from recordings made during the performance of an opera), compared to their 1.1 to 1.45 sec.

The rear and side walls of the Opera House are formed by a series of contiguous convex-shaped cylindrical surfaces that run from floor to ceiling. Not being identical in size they provide diffusion of sound over a wider frequency range. Their average radius of curvature is 15 ft (4.6 m) and the cord length is 13 ft (4 m) and they vary in width. A short recess or doors separate one from another. The facias of the tiers are sub-divided into a series of convex panels which are bowed outward, each about 5.5 ft (1.67 m) across. The overall result is good sound diffusion at all frequencies which helps the quality of the reverberation. The center of the ceiling is a recessed circular area in which a sound-diffusing crystal chandelier hangs.

No acoustical adjustments had to be made in the hall after completion. Music critics have compared the House favorably with the Staatsoper in Vienna.

Washington, D.C., John F. Kennedy Center for the Performing Arts Opera House

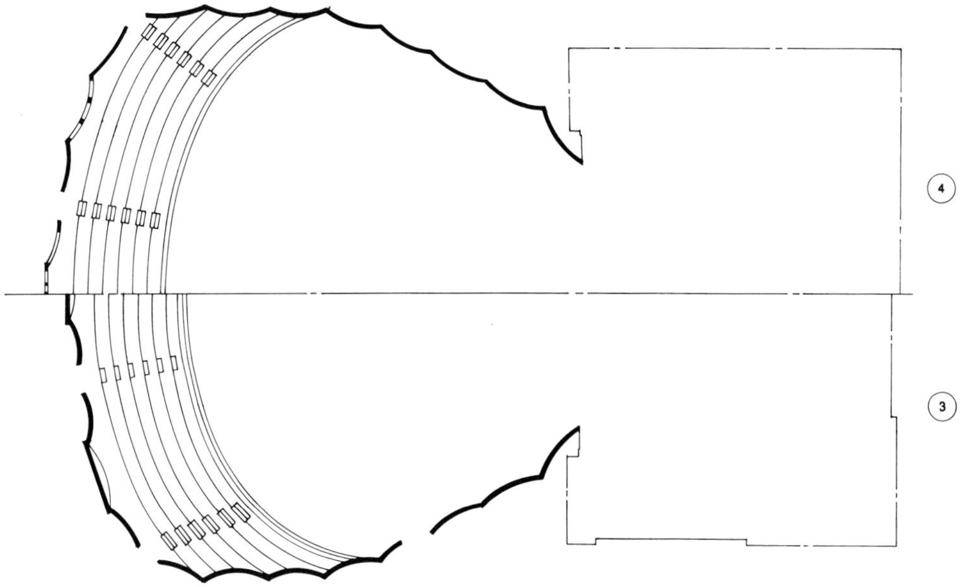

SEATING CAPACITY 2318 Concerts; 2142 Opera

1	1374 - 1198
2	108
3	434
4	402

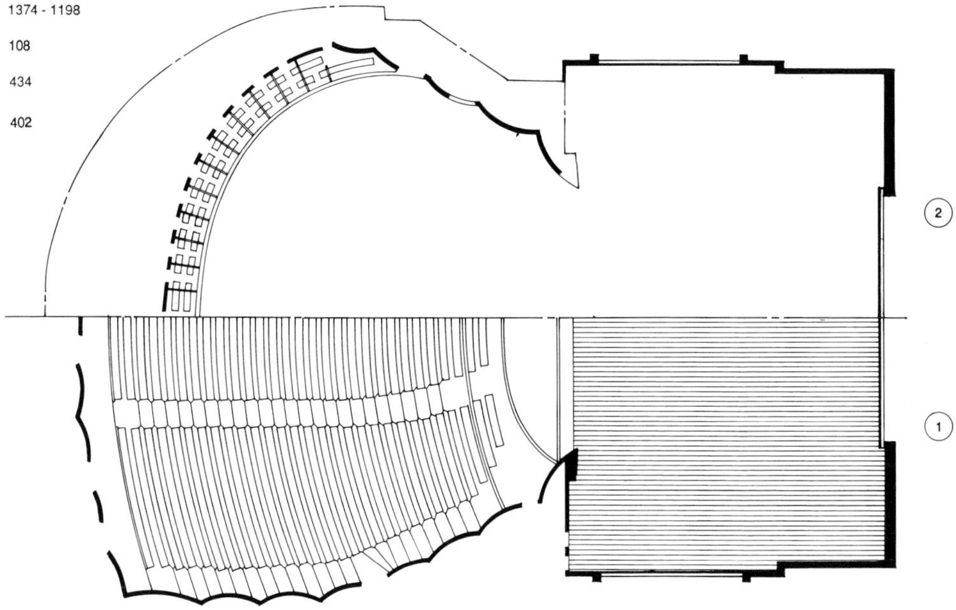

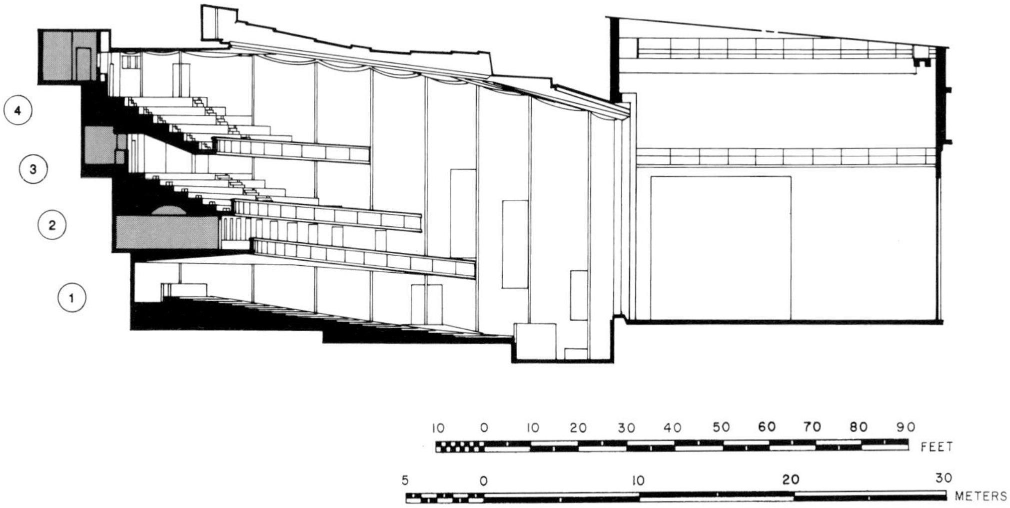

Architectural and structural details

Uses: opera, musicals, ballet, and speaking functions. *Ceiling:* 1 in. (2.5 cm) (minimum) plaster on metal lath; under-balcony soffits 1 in. plaster. *Walls:* 1 in. plaster (see the text) on metal lath separated by 1 in. airspace from 6 in. (15 cm) solid block; rear walls are molded 0.75 in. wood paneling, fixed, with 1 in. airspace to solid block; balcony and box tier facias, 0.75 in. (1.9 cm) plaster on metal lath. *Floors:* dense concrete. *Carpets:* floors fully covered with thin carpet. *Stage height:* 40 in. (102 cm) above floor level at first row of seats. *Seating:* backrest, seat bottom, and armrests fully upholstered.

Architect: Edward Durell Stone. *Acoustical consultant:* Cyril M. Harris. *Photographs:* Carol Pratt. *Reference:* Cyril M. Harris, "Acoustical Design of the John F. Kennedy Center for the Performing Arts," Journal of the Acoustical Society of America, **51**, pp 1113–1126 (1972).

*Technical details**

V = 460,000 ft^3 (13,027 m^3)	S_a = 12,196 ft^2 (1,133 m^2)	S_A = 13,875 ft^2 (1,289 m^2)
S_o = 1,173 ft^2 (109 m^2)	S_P = 2,120 ft^2 (197 m^2)	S_T = 17,168 ft^2 (1,595 m^2)
N_p (Opera) = 2,142	N_{NP} (no pit) = 2,318	H = 56 ft (17.1 m)
W = 104 ft (31.7 m)	L = 105 ft (32 m)	D = 115 ft (35.1 m)
V/S_T = 26.8 ft (8.17 m)	V/S_A = 33.2 ft (10.1 m)	V/N_P = 215 ft^3 (6.08 m^3)
V/N_{NP} = 198 ft^3 (5.62 m^3)	S_A/N_P = 6.48 ft^2 (0.602 m^2)	H/W = 0.54
L/W = 1.0	t_I = 38 msec	

**The terminology is explained in Appendix 1.*

USA
21

Worcester
Mechanics Hall

Opened in 1857, Mechanics Hall became known as one of the finest halls (as distinct from theater or opera house) in the United States. The *Worcester Daily Spy* reported, " ...the Hall is a perfect success, ...both for music and for speaking." In its heyday it attracted musical greats (Caruso, Paderewski, Rachmaninoff, Rubinstein) and distinguished lecturers (Thoreau, Emerson, Dickens, Mark Twain). After the great depression of the 1930's, the hall fell into disuse.

In 1977, Mechanics Hall opened again to its original beauty and excellent acoustics, restored by the Worcester County Mechanics Association under the watchful eye of the Society for the Preservation of New England Antiquities. Some further renovations followed in 1990. Seating 1,343 with a 1,080 ft^2 (100 m^2) stage, or 1,277 with a 1,400 ft^2 (130 m^2) stage, it is closest in all dimensions to the Stadt-Casino in Basel, Switzerland, which was built 19 years later. Today, it retains its original purpose as a multi-use auditorium for concerts, conventions, large receptions and dinners. Artists who have performed there recently include Yo Yo Ma, Itzhak Perlman, Jessye Norman, and many others. The hall boasts two concert series that bring in symphony orchestras and chamber groups from all over the world. It is used extensively for recording. The Hall's organ, built in 1864, was returned to its original condition by organ-builder Fritz Noack and was rededicated in 1982.

The Hall provides the intimacy and early lateral reflections common to a rectangular hall, being 80 ft (24.4 m) in width and 58 ft (17.7 m) between balcony faces. The distance from the farthest balcony seat to the stage is 98 ft (30 m), making it visually intimate. Surfaces for the diffusion of reflected sound are evident everywhere, from the coffered ceiling to the niches and pilasters on the walls. There are no sound absorbing materials, only thin carpets in the aisles. The reverberation time measured during intermission at a concert with full audience, but no orchestra on stage, is 1.6 sec at mid-frequencies, excellent for a multipurpose hall that normally does not present large orchestral groups. Its principal deficiency is the flat main floor which makes neck stretching necessary to view performances. Also, organ recitalists would prefer longer reverberation times, particularly at low frequencies.

Worcester, Mechanics Hall

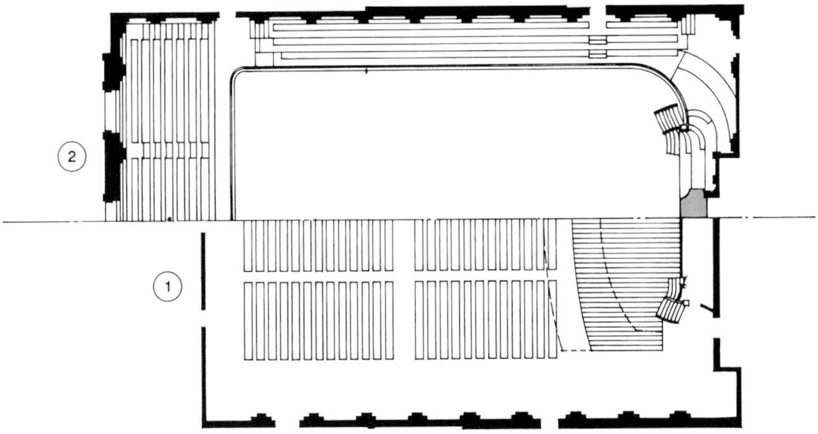

SEATING CAPACITY		SMALL GROUPS	SMALL ORCHESTRA	LARGE ORCHESTRA
Main floor	(1)	891	825	759
Balcony	(2)	518	518	518
		1409	1343	1277

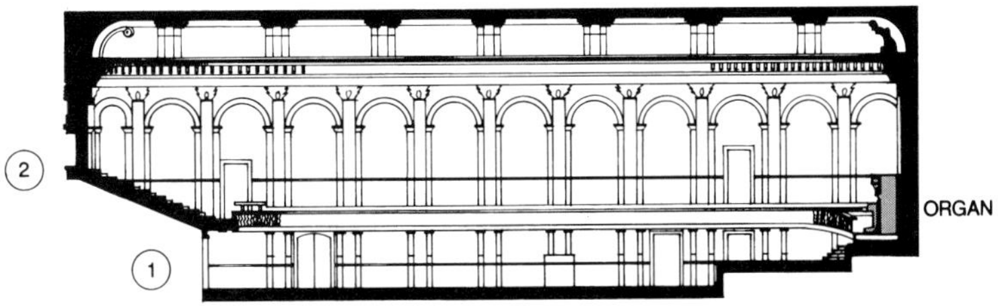

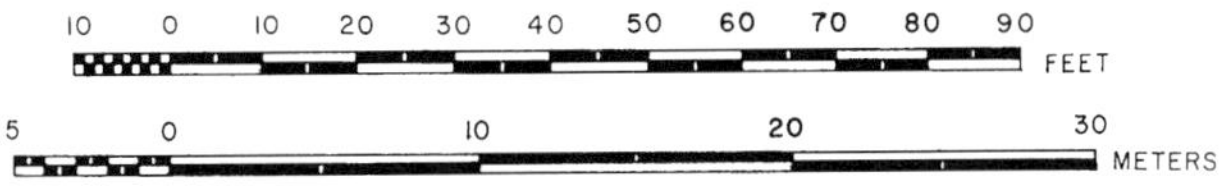

Architectural and structural details

Uses: music, speech, and social events. *Ceiling:* 1 in. (2.5 cm) plaster on wood lath; balcony soffits 0.6 in. (1.5 cm) gypsum board. *Walls:* 1 in. plaster on wood lath, balcony fronts wood, about 50% open. *Floors:* the finish is 0.6 in.(1.5 cm) red oak over 0.5 in.(1.25 cm) tongue-and-grove oak over two layers of 0.75 in. (1.9 cm) pine subflooring. *Carpets:* on aisles, with no underpad. *Stage floor:* 0.75 in. maple over two layers 0.6 in. wood chipboard over 1 in. wood boards over large airspace. *Stage height:* 31 in. (79 cm). *Seating:* main floor, moveable upholstered seat bottom and back on metal frame; balcony, molded plywood, upholstered seat top and front of seat back; all armrests wood.

Architect: original hall, Elbridge Boyden; 1970's renovation, Anderson Notter Finegold, Inc.; 1990's renovation, Lamoureux Pagano & Associates, Inc. *Acoustical consultant:* both renovations, Cavanaugh Tocci Associates, Inc. *Sound consultant:* David H. Kaye. *References:* W. J. Cavanaugh, "Preserving the Acoustics of Mechanics Hall: A Restoration Without Compromising Acoustical Integrity," *Technology & Conservation* (Fall 1980).

*Technical details**

Concert stage, small orchestra

V = 380,000 ft^3 (10,760 m^3)	S_a = 5,823 ft^2 (541 m^2)	S_A = 7,546 ft^2 (701 m^2)
S_o = 1,658 ft^2 (154 m^2)	S_T = 9,204 ft^2 (855 m^2)	N = 1,343
H = 41 ft (12.5 m)	W = 81 ft (24.7 m)	L = 89 ft (27.1 m)
D = 99 ft (30.2 m)	V/S_T = 41.3 ft (12.5 m)	V/S_A = 50.3 ft (15.4 m)
V/N = 283 ft^3 (8.01 m^3)	S_A/N = 5.61 ft^2 (0.52 m^2)	H/W_I = 0.51
L/W = 1.1	t_I = 28 msec	

**Terminology explained in Appendix 1.*

Argentina

22

Buenos Aires
Teatro Colón

The Teatro Colón is one the beautiful large opera houses of the world. With 2,487 seats, it is larger than most of the famous opera houses in Europe but smaller than the Metropolitan Opera House in New York. It has been very successful since its dedication in 1908.

Because of its size, the Colón is not as highly praised for opera as the Staatsoper in Vienna or La Scala in Milan. On the whole it is better than the New York Metropolitan Opera House, particularly on the main floor, partly because of its lower cubic volume and partly because it is narrower, providing a shorter initial-time-delay gap and greater laterally reflected sound energy to that area. One aspect of the house that pleases soloists is the well-defined reflections of adequate intensity back to the stage from the ceiling and the balcony faces, thus giving the performer a feeling of support from the house.

Regular opera-goers in Buenos Aires say that the best seats are in the top two galleries. It is only in those galleries that the violin tone (from the pit orchestra) comes through with its full quality, which is directly attributable to reflections from the main ceiling.

Depending on the depth of the floor of the pit below the edge of the pit railing, the sound of the pit orchestra is somewhat muffled on the main floor. When I attended several operas in the Colón, the depth of the pit was as much as 10 ft (3 m). The remote ceiling was of no help in sending early reflections to that audience location.

As a concert hall, the Teatro Colón is surprisingly satisfactory. To accommodate a full orchestra the pit is generally closed over and a rather shallow concert enclosure is used. The front side-surfaces of the boxes to either side of the stage and the fronts of boxes in the first ring reflect lateral energy to most of the main floor and, selectively, to the rings above. In the highest rings, the ceiling helps produce early reflections. The reverberation is higher than in the European opera houses, about 1.8 sec with full audience at mid-frequencies, the same as in Carnegie Hall in New York, and nearly ideal for symphonic music.

Buenos Aires, Teatro Colón

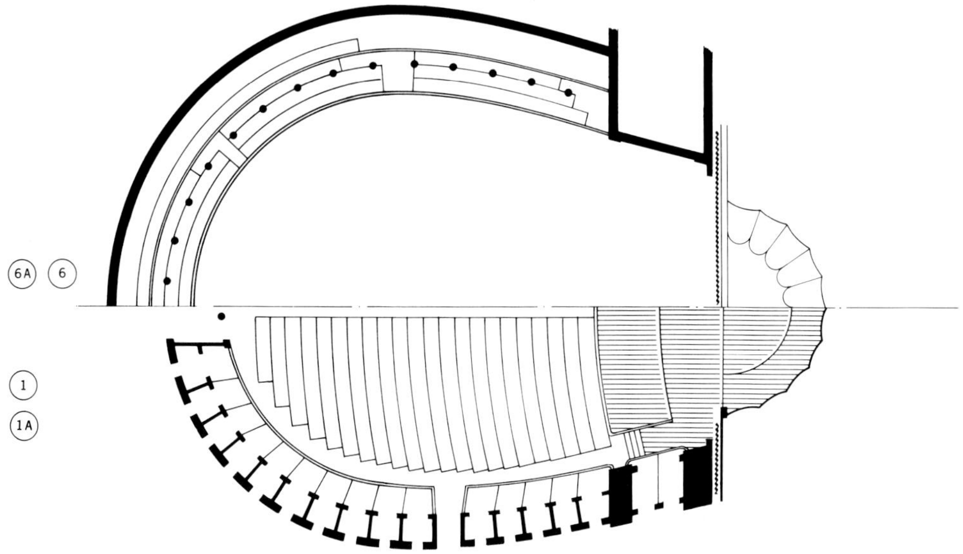

SEATING CAPACITY 2487

1	632
1A	236
2	252
3	252
4	319
5	372
6	346
6A	78 (paradise) + standees

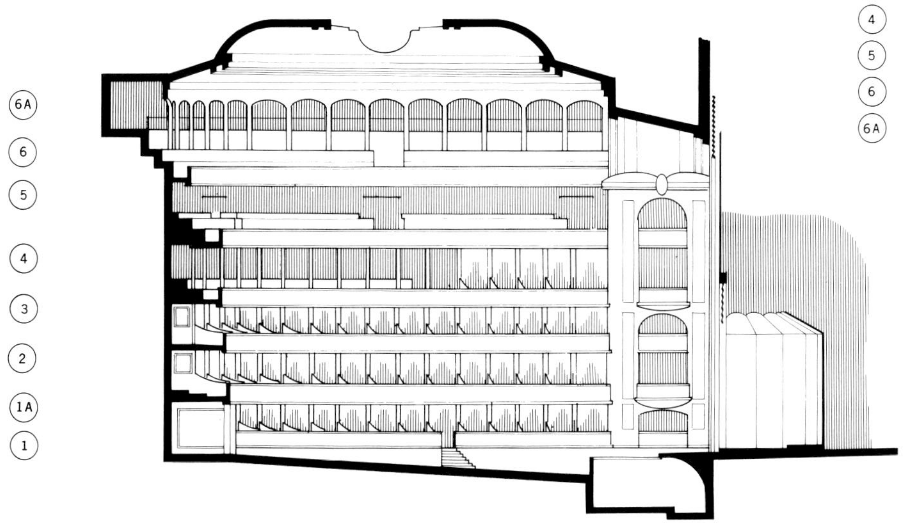

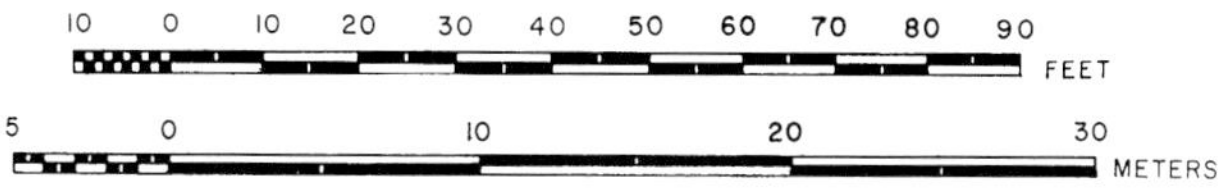

Architectural and structural details

Uses: opera, concerts, recitals, and conferences. *Ceiling:* plaster on metal lath. *Walls:* 1 in. (2.5 cm) plaster on wire lath, including balcony front. *Floors:* wood. *Carpet:* on all aisles except in upper two rings. *Stage floor:* wood over airspace; surface inclines at rate of 1 unit for each 100 units. *Orchestra pit:* floor and side walls made of wood. *Stage height:* 30 in. (76 cm). *Stage enclosure for concerts:* floor and side walls made of wood; pit is raised to form a forestage. *Seating:* Fully upholstered chairs, including rear of back rest and armrests.

Architect: Victor Meano. *Photographs:* Burri, Magnum. *Architects drawings:* made from the building in 1930, courtesy opera administration.

*Technical details**

Opera

V = 726,300 ft³ (20,570 m³)	S_a = 15,200 ft² (1,410 m²)	S_A = 19,000 ft² (538 m²)
S_o (pit) = 675 ft² (63 m²)	S_p = 3,402 ft² (316 m²)	S (pit floor) = 2,050 ft² (190 m²)
S_T = 23,077 ft² (2,144 m²)	N_{ST} = 2,787	N = 2,487
H = 87 ft (26.5 m)	W = 80 ft (24.4 m)	L = 113 ft (34.4 m)
D = 141 ft (43 m)	V/S_T = 31.5 ft (9.6 m)	V/S_A = 38.2 ft (11.6 m)
V/N_{ST} = 261 ft³ (7.39 m³)	S_A/N_{ST} = 6.8 ft² (0.63 m²)	H/W = 1.09
L/W = 1.4	t_I = 19 msec	

Concerts

V = 760,000 ft³ (21,524 m³)	S_a = 16,522 ft² (1,535 m²)	S_A = 19,000 ft² (1,765 m²)
S_o = 2,200 ft² (186 m²)	S_T = 21,200 ft² (1,970 m²)	N = 2,487
V/S_T = 35.8 ft (10.9 m)	V/S_A = 40 ft (12.2 m)	V/N = 306 ft³ (8.67 m³)
S_A/N = 7.64 ft² (0.71 m²)	t_I = 19 msec	

**The terminology is explained in Appendix 1.*

23

Sydney
Concert Hall of the Sydney Opera House

The concert hall of the Sydney Opera House was opened in 1973. Contained in one of the most spectacular buildings in the world, it seats 2,679 and is the home of Sydney Symphony Orchestra. The enormous circular ceiling, which rises up to 82 ft (25 m) above the stage and radiates out and down to form about two-thirds of the walls, is paneled with white birch plywood. The lower wall, boxes, and stage are paneled with hard brown wood, brush box. Both woods are Australian. Suspended from this center point are 21 giant acrylic rings, acoustic reflectors installed to give acoustic feedback to the orchestra and some early sound reflections to the audience immediately surrounding the stage.

The orchestra platform is placed in the front fourth of the hall, with 410 seats of the 2,696 total located to its rear and 158 seats in two boxes at the sides of the stage. The ten boxes, which take the place of side balconies, are unusual in that they are steeply sloped and seat from 50 to 79 each. The main audience area is steeply raked compared to the main floor of classical shoe-box halls. Behind this block are two elevated seating areas, even more steeply raked, which take the place of balconies—without overhang.

The large side walls that comprise the fronts of the boxes, are planned to give early sound reflections to at least half of this center area of seating. The upper seating receives early reflections from the bottoms and edges of the white birch ceiling.

The grand organ, designed and built by an Australian, Ronald Sharp, with 127 stops comprising 10,500 pipes, is said to be the largest tracker action organ in the world.

I attended a symphonic concert in the Concert Hall and was seated in the fourth side box from the rear. At that location there was not an abundance of early sound reflections. I had hoped to experience the acoustic conditions on the main floor, where the early reflections from the fronts of the side boxes certainly contribute much toward making the hall sound spacious and intimate. I was quite aware of the 2.0 sec reverberation time which was well suited to that night's symphonic compositions. Sydney can be proud of the Concert Hall because of its beauty and acoustics.

Sydney, Concert Hall of the Syndey Opera House

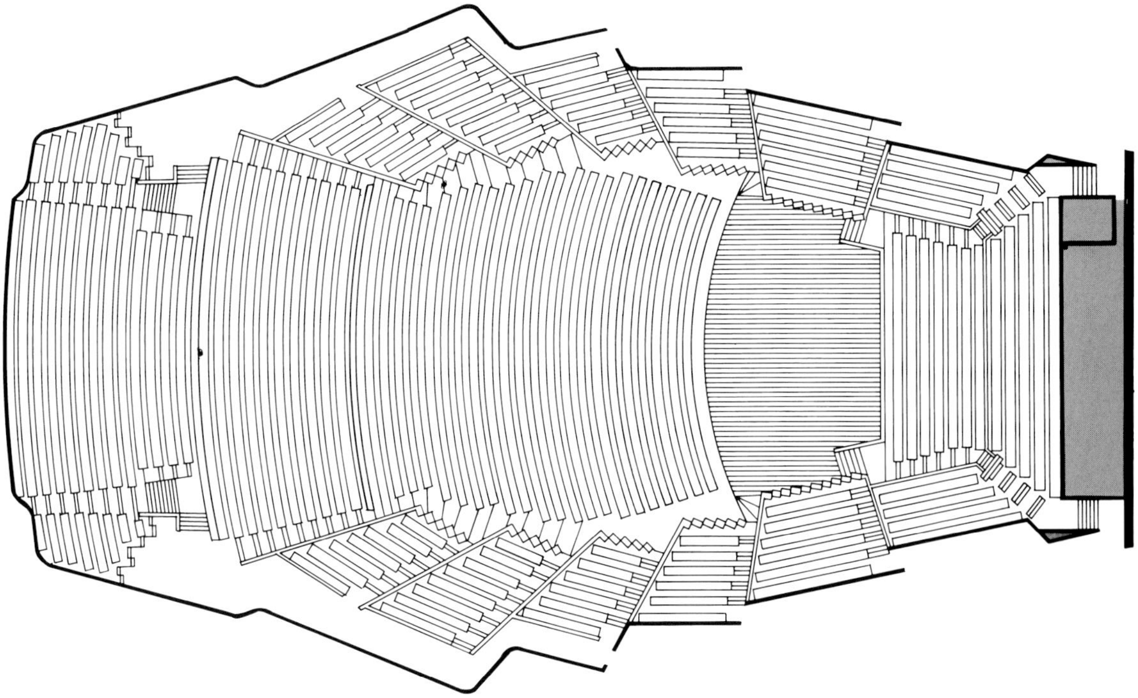

SEATING CAPACITY 2696

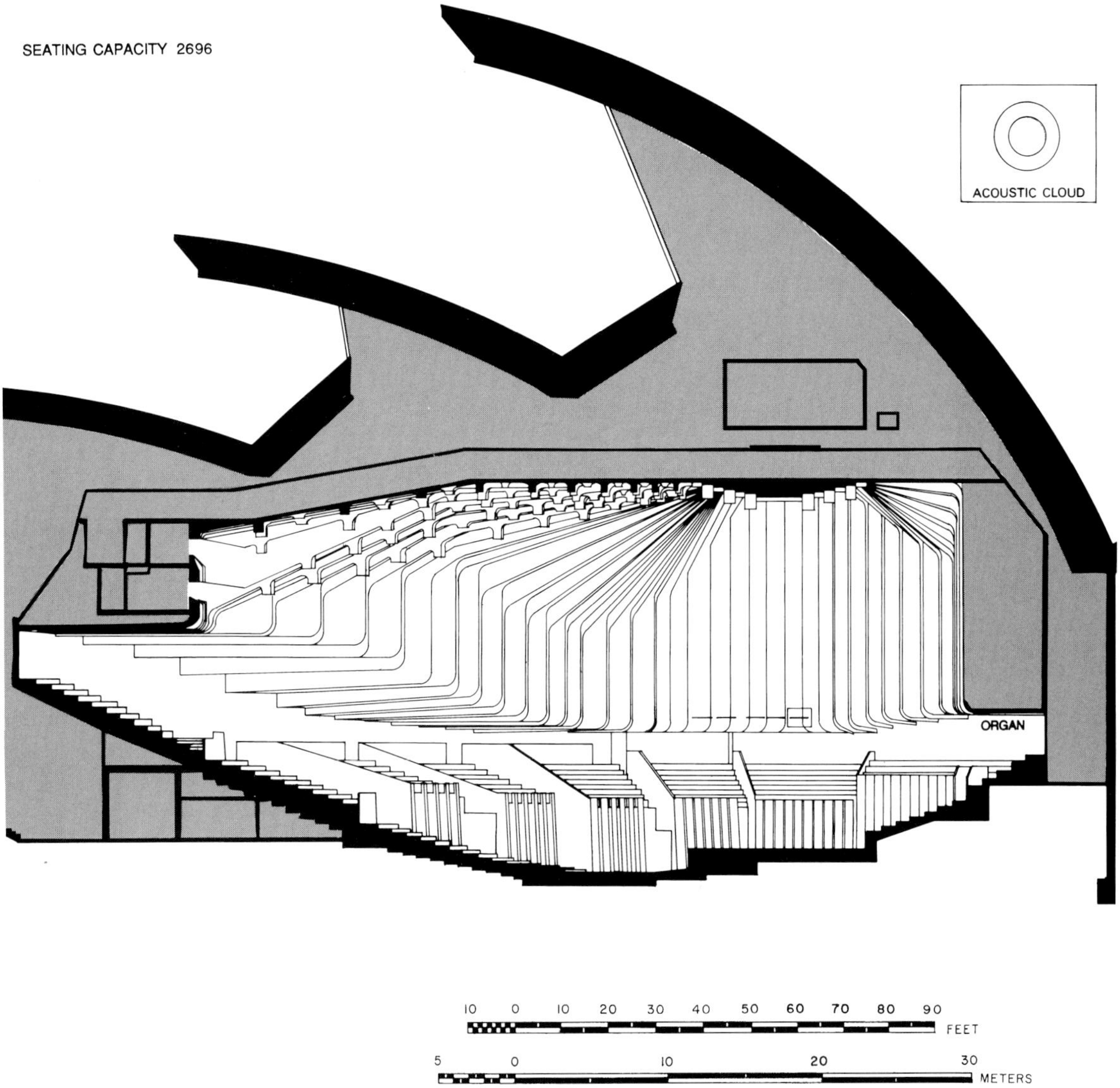

Architectural and structural details

[**Note: This hall was originally planned as an opera house, which accounts both for its name and the steeply raked seating.**] *Uses:* orchestra, chamber music, and soloists, 43%; drama and speech, 22%; school concerts, 16%; popular music, 9%. *Ceiling:* 0.5 in. (1.25 cm) plywood on 1 in. plasterboard backing, constituting 66% of normal side wall area. *Walls:* Lower 33% normal sidewall is 0.75 in.(1.9 cm) laminated wood. *Balcony faces:* Same as lower walls, with slight outward slope in the vertical direction and stepped to aid in diffusion of reflected waves. *Floors:* 1.25 in. (3.2 cm) laminated wood over 0.75 in. air return space. *Carpets:* None. *Stage enclosure:* Same as walls elsewhere. *Stage floor:* Same as floors elsewhere. *Stage height:* 50 in. at the apron. *Seating:* Backrest of 1/2 in. molded plywood; back cushion, wool-upholstered contoured polyurethane; armrests molded plywood; seat bottom similar to the backrest with cushion of same material. *Floating canopy:* 21 circular reflectors of clear acrylic and toroidal in section (see the sketch). Settings range from 27 to 35 ft (8.2 to 10.7 m) above stage level, with latter most common.

Initial Architect: Joern Utzon, responsible for the exterior design. *Principal Architect:* Peter Hall, responsible for the entire interior design and overall architectural management. *Acoustical consultant:* V. L. and N. V. Jordan. *References:* V. L. Jordan, "Acoustical Design Considerations of the Sydney Opera House," pp. 33–53 and Peter Hall, "The Design of the Concert Hall of the Sydney Opera House," pp. 54–69, Journal and Proceedings, Royal Society of New South Wales, **106**, 1973.

*Technical details**

V = 868,600 ft^3 (24,600 m^3)	S_a = 14,666 ft^2 (1,362 m^2)	S_A = 16,824 ft^2 (1,563 m^2)
S_o = 1,945 ft^2 (180.7 m^2)	S_T = 18,769 ft^2 (1,744 m^2)	N = 2,679
H = 55 ft (16.8 m)	W = 109 ft (33.2 m)	L = 104 ft (31.7 m)
D = 146 ft (44.5 m)	V/S_T = 46.3 ft (14.0 m)	V/S_A = 51.6 ft (15.7 m)
V/N = 324 ft^3 (9.18 m^3)	S_A/N = 6.24 ft^2 (0.58 m^2)	H/W = 0.50
L/W = 0.95	t_I=36 msec	

**The terminology is explained in Appendix 1.*

24

Salzburg Festspielhaus

The Salzburg Festspielhaus, with 2,158 seats, was opened July 26, 1960. In keeping with Salzburg tradition, it was both a musical and social occasion, attracting diplomats, industrialists, and artists. The Festspielhaus has a width of nearly 112 ft between the faces of the side balcony boxes. On the main floor the width approaches 124 ft! This hugeness, both visual and acoustical, must concern the patrons who regularly attend operas and concerts in Europe's small halls.

For opera, the sound in the balcony has generally been praised. On the main floor, some seats are not as good because of the outward sloping walls which means that lateral sound reflections are not extensive in the front part of the hall and sound reflected from the ceiling travels primarily to the rear of the hall and the balcony. The sound from the pit orchestra is also projected by the ceiling to the rear half of the main floor and by the side walls to the rear half of the main floor and to the boxes.

In 1979, to improve the sound for symphonic concerts, a new stage enclosure was installed (see the middle photo, not shown on the drawings). For aesthetic reasons, it was replaced by a second enclosure in 1993 (see the lower photo). With either, the musicians can hear each other better and the sound is projected to the front parts of the main floor with good results. Satisfaction with the acoustics has increased greatly.

The materials of the hall are excellent from an acoustical standpoint. The walls and ceiling are of vibration-damped plaster, on reeds. Since the plaster and wood panels on the side walls are over 1.5 in. (3.8 cm) thick, they do not absorb the lower registers of the orchestra. In the balcony the sound is warm, intimate, clear, and brilliant. The reverberation time at mid-frequencies, fully occupied, is 1.5 sec, ideal for most opera, but somewhat low for symphony music of the Romantic period.

The Festspielhaus takes its place among the more important halls of Europe because of the high quality of its musical performances. Great opera is produced by the Vienna Opera Company and orchestral music comes from the best European and overseas traveling orchestras.

Salzburg, Festspielhaus

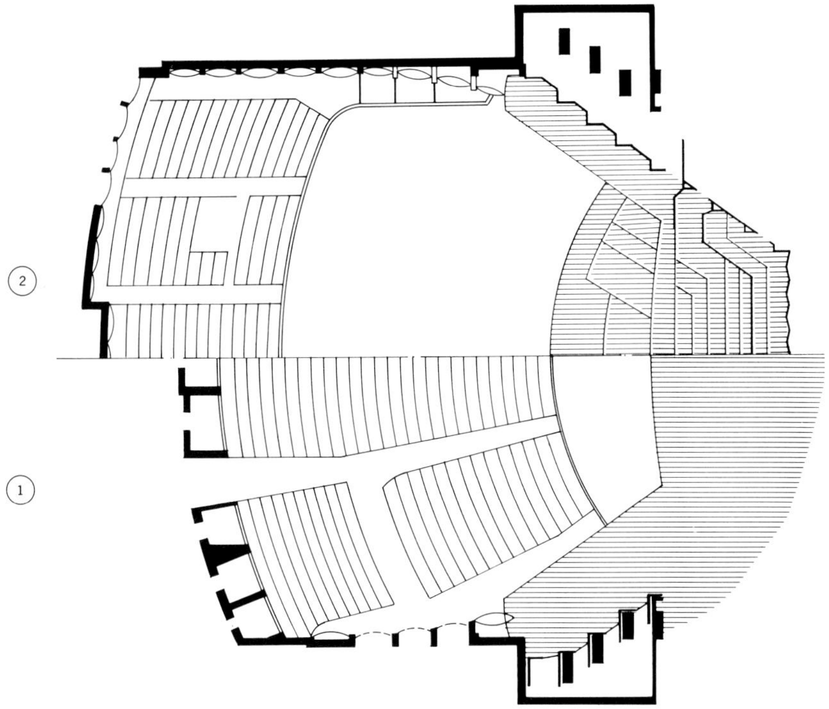

SEATING CAPACITY 2158

1	Main floor	1289
	Boxes	71
2	Balcony	762
	Boxes	36

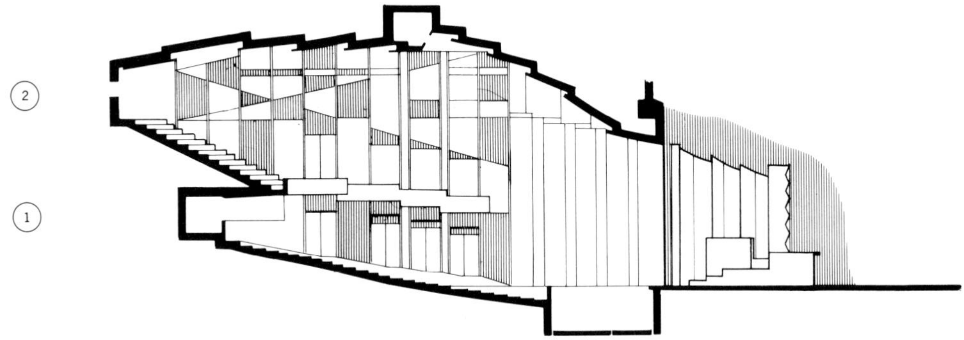

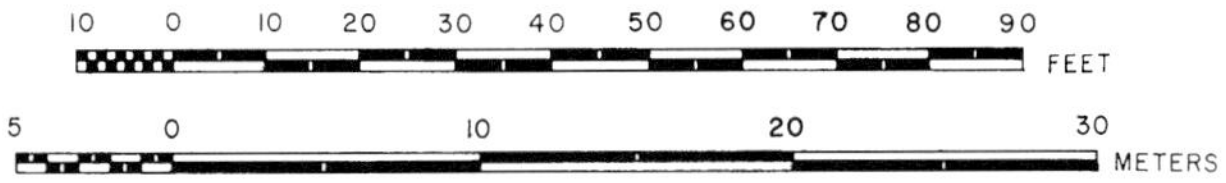

Architectural and structural details

Uses: opera, symphonic concerts, and drama. *Ceiling:* 1.5 to 2.0 in. (3.8 to 5 cm) plaster on reeds, painted. *Sidewalls:* concave-curved portions extend from floor to ceiling, also made of plaster on reeds with a thin, finish-wood layer; in front of the concave portions are convex trapezoidal or rectangular curved panels of irregular size, about 1.5 in. (3.8 cm) thick, made of three layers of wood-fiber sheets. *Rear walls:* above boxes, convex wooden panels about 6 ft (1.82 m) wide and bowed out 10 in. (25 cm) at the center. *Floors:* wood panels, supported above concrete structure by standards; the seat rows and steps of the aisles have cork linoleum cemented on the top of the panels. *Carpet:* on all aisles and in boxes, except in balcony. *Stage floor:* wood. *Stage height:* 35.5 in. (90 cm). *Orchestra pit:* 2 in. (5 cm) thick wood floor over deep airspace; walls are wooden wainscoting, some panels removable for possible addition of sound absorbing materials. *Seating:* molded plywood; top of the seatbottom and a portion of the armrest are upholstered.

Architect: Clemens Holzmeister. *Acoustical consultant:* G. A. Schwaiger. *Photographs:* upper, courtesy of the architect (1962); middle, Jens Rindel (1982); lower, Anrather Photo (1995).

*Technical details**

Concerts

V = 547,500 ft^3 (15,500 m^3)	S_a = 11,400 ft^2 (1,058 m^2)	S_A = 14,800 ft^2 (1,375 m^2)
S_o = 2,100 ft^2 (195 m^2)	S_T = 16,900 ft^2 (1,570 m^2)	N = 2,158
H = 47 ft (14.3 m)	W = 108 ft (32.9 m)	L = 97 ft (29.6 m)
D = 95 ft (29 m)	V/S_T = 32.4 ft (9.9 m)	V/S_A = 37 ft (11.3 m)
V/N = 254 ft^3 (7.2 m^3)	S_A/N = 6.9 ft^2 (0.30 m^2)	H/W = 0.44
L/W = 0.9	t_I = 27 msec	

Opera

V = 495,000 ft^3 (14,020 m$^{3)}$	S_a = 10,850 ft^2 (1,008 m^2)	S_A = 14,100 ft^2 (1,310 m^2)
S_o (pit opening) = 800 ft^2 (74.3 m^2)	S_o (pit floor) = 950 ft^2 (88.2 m^2)	N = 2,158
S_T = 17,000 ft^2 (1,580 m^2)	S_p = 2,100 ft^2 (195 m^2)	V/S_T = 29.1 ft (8.87 m)
V/S_A = 35.1 ft (10.7 m)	V/N = 229 ft^3 (6.5 m^3)	S_A/N = 6.53 ft^2 (0.61 m^2)

**The terminology is explained in Appendix 1.*

Austria

25

Vienna
Grosser Musikvereinssaal

The "Grosse Saal der Gesellschaft der Musikfreunde in Wien" opened in 1870. Without doubt, the pulse of any orchestra conductor quickens when he first conducts in this renowned hall. The Vienna Philharmonic, the parade of famous conductors, and the fine music played there make this the Mecca of the old halls of Europe.

The side walls are made irregular by over forty high windows, twenty doors above the balcony, and thirty-two tall, gilded buxom female statues beneath the balcony. Everywhere are gilt, ornamentation, and statuettes. Less than 15% of the interior surfaces is of wood. Wood is used only for the doors, for some paneling around the stage, and for trim. The other surfaces are plaster on brick or, on the ceiling and balcony fronts, plaster on wood lath.

The superior acoustics of the hall are due to its relatively small size (volume 530,000 ft^3 (15,000 m^3) and seats 1,680), its high ceiling with resulting long reverberation time (2.0 sec, fully occupied), the irregular interior surfaces, and the plaster interior. Any hall built with these characteristics would be an excellent hall, especially for symphonic music of the Romantic and Classical periods.

Nearly every conductor echoes Bruno Walter, "This is certainly the finest hall in the world. It has beauty of sound and power. The first time I conducted here was an unforgettable experience. I had not realized that music could be so beautiful." Herbert von Karajan, added, "The sound in this hall is very full. It is rich in bass and good for high strings. One shortcoming is that successive notes tend to merge into each other. There is too much difference in the sound for rehearsing and the sound with audience."

The Grosser Musikvereinssaal is similar acoustically to Symphony Hall in Boston. Most critical listeners agree that the clarity or definition is better than in the Amsterdam Concertgebouw. The sound in this hall is much louder than in Boston, and some feel that this is a disadvantage for a touring orchestra which may not be in the habit of restraining itself. Also, it is overly easy for the brass and percussion to dominate the strings. The string and woodwind tone are delicious and the sound is uniform throughout the hall.

Vienna, Grosser Musikvereinssaal

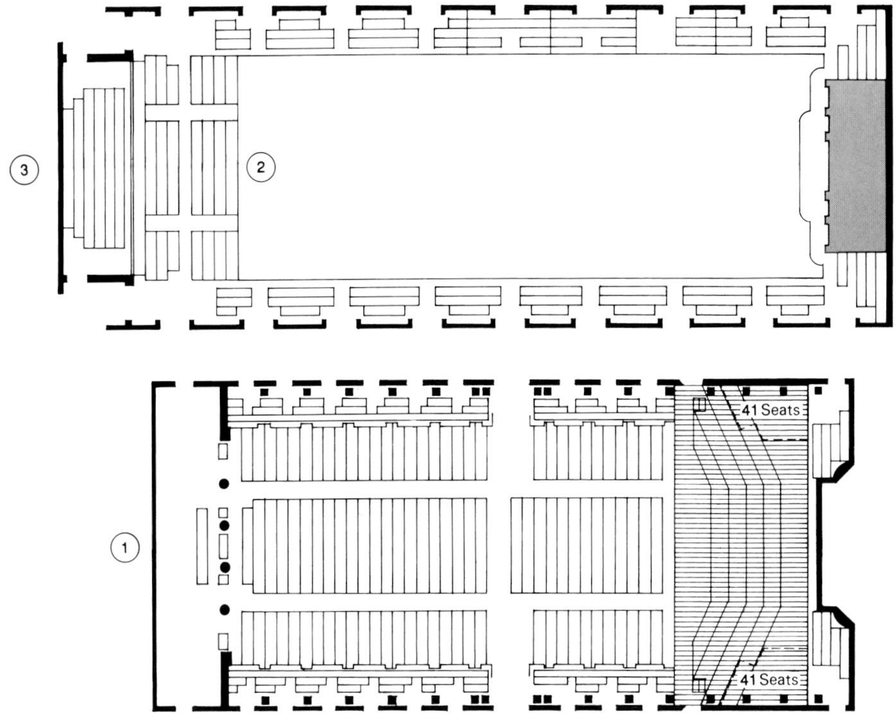

SEATING CAPACITY LARGE STAGE 1598, SMALL STAGE 1680

(1) LARGE STAGE 914, SMALL STAGE 1021

(2) 539

(3) 120

+ STANDEES

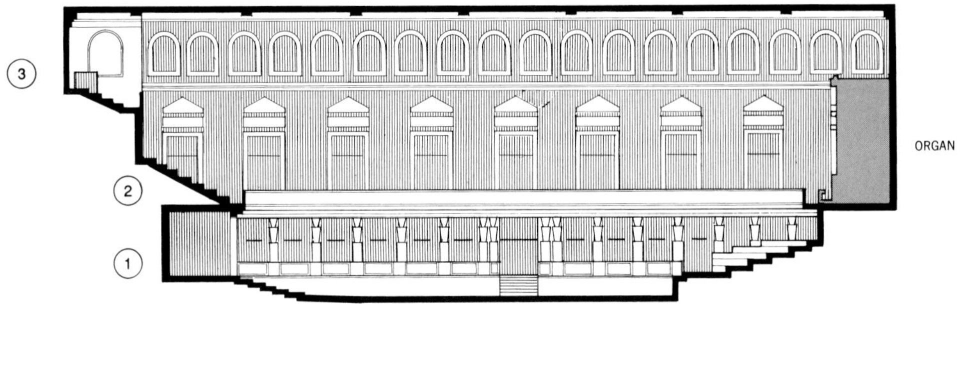

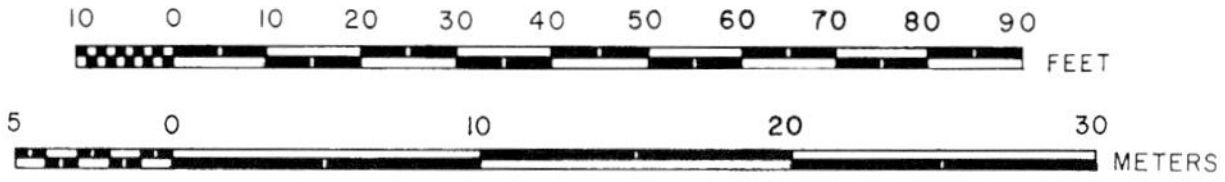

Architectural and structural details

Use: orchestra and soloists. *Ceiling:* plaster on spruce wood. *Side and rear walls:* plaster on brick, except around the stage, where walls are of wood; doors are of wood; balcony fronts are plaster on wood. *Floors:* wood. *Carpets:* none. *Stage floor:* wood risers over wood stage. *Stage height:* 39 in. (1 m) above floor level. *Added absorbing material:* 200 ft^2 (18.6 m^2) of draperies over front railing on side loges. *Seating:* wood structure on main floor and side balconies, except that tops of seat bottoms are upholstered with 4 in. (10 cm) of cushion covered by porous cloth; rear balcony seats, plywood.

Architect: Theophil Ritter von Hansen. *Photographs:* courtesy of Sekretariat, Gesellschaft der Musikfreunde in Wien.

*Technical details**

V = 530,000 ft^3 (15,000 m^3)	S_a = 6,350 ft^2 (690 m^2)	S_A = 10,280 ft^2 (955 m^2)
S_o = 1,754 ft^2 (163 m^2)	S_T = 12,030 ft^2 (1,118 m^2)	N = 1,680
H = 57 ft (17.4 m)	W = 65 ft (19.8 m)	L = 117 ft (35.7 m)
D = 132 ft (40.2 m)	V/S_T = 44 ft (13.4 m)	V/S_A = 51.5 ft (15.7 m)
V/N = 315 ft^3 (8.93 m^3)	S_A/N = 6.1 ft^2 (0.57 m^2)	H/W = 0.88
L/W = 1.8	t_I = 12 msec	

**The terminology is explained in Appendix 1.*

26

Vienna Staatsoper

The main hall of the Staatsoper is modern in design. Bombed during the war and rededicated in 1955, it has the same architectural shape as the original house of 1869 but without baroque decoration and gilded statues. There are three tiers of boxes, a central box for dignitaries, and two upper galleries. The interior is dominated by red velvet and red damask, and the decoration is mainly white with gold. There is a large torus-shaped crystal chandelier against the ceiling.

The conductors who know the Staatsoper are unanimous in their opinion that the house has good sound. Bruno Walter said (1960), "The Staatsoper is the most alive of all opera halls. It is much better than New York and better than La Scala. The orchestra does not overpower the singers."

The auditorium has 1,709 seats, compared to the New York Metropolitan Opera House, 3,816 seats, and San Francisco, 3,252 seats—indeed, a miniature. One year I attended four consecutive performances with the privilege of sitting in any part of the house. On the last evening I sat in the orchestra pit through an entire act. The sound is louder than in its American counterparts, largely because of the smaller cubic volume. On the main floor the sound is more intimate, beautifully clear and brilliant. Since it is only 64 ft (19.5 m) wide, the early lateral reflections are strong and the initial-time-delay gap is short, which accounts in large part for the superior sound.

The auditorium itself is not very live. The liveness heard during the performances I attended came primarily from the stagehouse, which is large, and quite reverberant. The canvas backdrop, the "cyclorama," is thick, heavily painted, and, hence, does not absorb high-frequency sounds.

At the ends of the pit, behind the brass (left) and percussion (right), there are small entrance chambers, open to the pit, the doors at the back of which are simply covered with red velvet. The double basses are lined up against the hard wall of the pit on the stage side, which increases their loudness.

I judge the sound of the Staatsoper excellent, and I rate the auditoriums of the Staatsoper and La Scala about equal, with the codicil that the live stagehouse gives the former an overall advantage, at least for the audience.

VIENNA, STAATSOPER

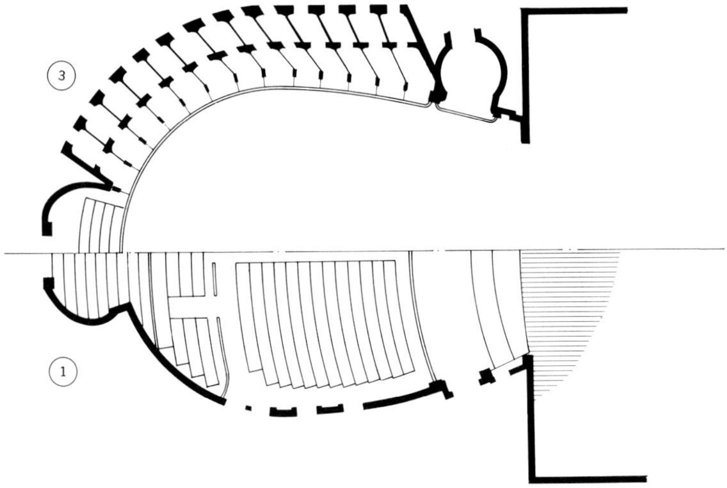

SEATING CAPACITY 1709

(1) 488+2 wheelchairs

(2) 148

(3) 220

(4) 166

(5) 309

(6) 342

(7) 567 standees (all levels)

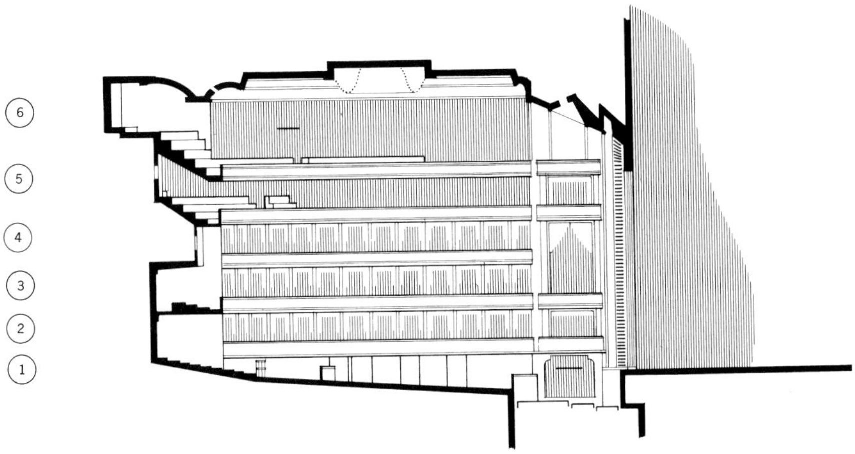

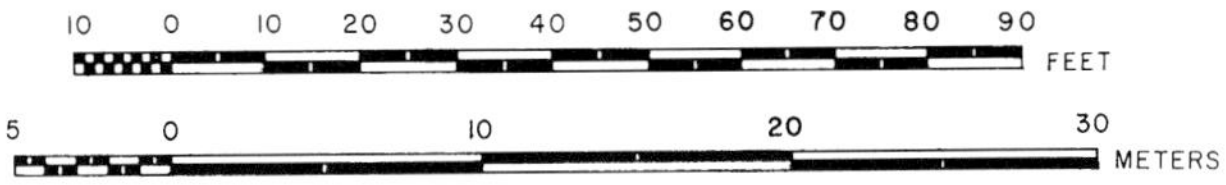

Architectural and structural details

Uses: opera. *Ceiling:* plaster. *Walls:* in the top galleries, the walls are covered with damask behind Plexiglas to prevent damage by standees; faces of the rings are of wood; in the balcony beneath the gallery, the walls are of damask over plywood with 0.25 in. (0.64 cm) airspace between them; in the boxes the walls are of tightly stretched damask on wood. On main floor, walls are 0.5 in. (1.3 cm) wood. *Floors:* In the gallery and balcony, the floors are PVC linoleum over concrete; the main floor is of wood with carpet in the aisles; the main-floor standing room is of wood. *Pit:* on the pit floor are 3 in. (7.6 cm) wooden planks; the pit walls are of 0.75 in. (1.9 cm) wood; there are small rooms at the end of each pit, with velvet on the doors behind. *Stage height:* 41 in. (104 cm) above floor level at the first row of seats. *Seating:* the boxes have simple chairs with upholstered seats; on the main floor the seats are of solid wood except that the front of the backrests and the top of the seat-bottoms are covered with 1 in. (2.5 cm) upholstering.

Architect: August Siccard von Siccardsburg and Eduard van der Nuell. *Architect for reconstruction:* Erich Boltenstern. *References:* plans, details, and photographs courtesy of the management of the Staatsoper. *Acoustical consultant for reconstuction:* G. Schwaiger.

*Technical details**

Opera

V = 376,600 ft^3 (10,665 m^3)	S_a = 10,000 ft^2 (930 m^2)	S_A = 12,850 ft^2 (1,194 m^2)
S_o (pit) = 1,150 ft^2 (106.8 m^2)	S_p = 1,720 ft^2	S_T = 15,720 ft^2 (1,460 m^2)
N = 1,709	H = 62 ft (18.9 m)	W = 60 ft (18.3 m)
L = 98 ft (29.9 m)	D = 111 ft (33.8 m)	S_T = 24 ft (7.3 m)
V/S_A = 9.3 ft (8.9 m)	V/N = 220 ft^3 (6.24 m^3)	S_A/N = 7.75 ft^2 (0.72 m^2)
H/W = 1.03	L/W = 1.63	t_I = 15 msec

*The terminology is explained in Appendix 1.

27

Brussels
Palais des Beaux-Arts

The Palais des Beaux-Arts ranks as one of the better concert halls with both conductors and listeners. The hall opened in 1929 and has 2,150 seats. All the surfaces are painted an old ivory, relieved only by dark balcony railings and horizontal gold stripes. The coves in the ceiling, designed to permit recessing of the lights, sweep around in flowing curves and tie the hall together aesthetically.

I attended symphonic concerts in the Palais des Beaux-Arts, first in 1961, following close upon a week of listening to music in the Royal Festival Hall in London. I sat in the first row of the rise of seats at the rear of the main floor, off the center line. The rich full bass and the quality of the violin tone were stunning in contrast to the Festival Hall. The quality of the bass is largely due to the construction of the walls, plaster on brick, and of the ceiling, plaster on metal lath. There was an abundance of early lateral reflections, and I was only 60 ft (18 m) from the stage. Briefly, I sat in the front row of the main floor and the sound was not as good. On my second visit in 1988, I sat in the fourth row of the first balcony, near the centerline. The orchestra seemed much louder than at the other position. The trumpets and tympani were often too loud, perhaps because of the unfamiliarity of the Boston Symphony Orchestra with this hall, or, perhaps, because the ceiling may focus that part of the orchestra to this particular seating region.

F. Winckel (*Der Monat*, February 1957, p. 77) reports that he sent a letter to a number of European conductors asking them to name their favorite hall anywhere in the world. The answers mentioned the Palais about as often as the Grosser Musikvereinssaal in Vienna, or Symphony Hall in Boston, or the Concertgebouw in Amsterdam. My own evidence, obtained recently by questioning informally a number of well-known musicians, is that the hall has a very good reputation from their standpoint and that of regular concert-goers. However it is not as live as the three halls just mentioned, it does not have the singing tone of the classical rectangular halls and is not as highly regarded for music of the Romantic Period as for that of the classical period.

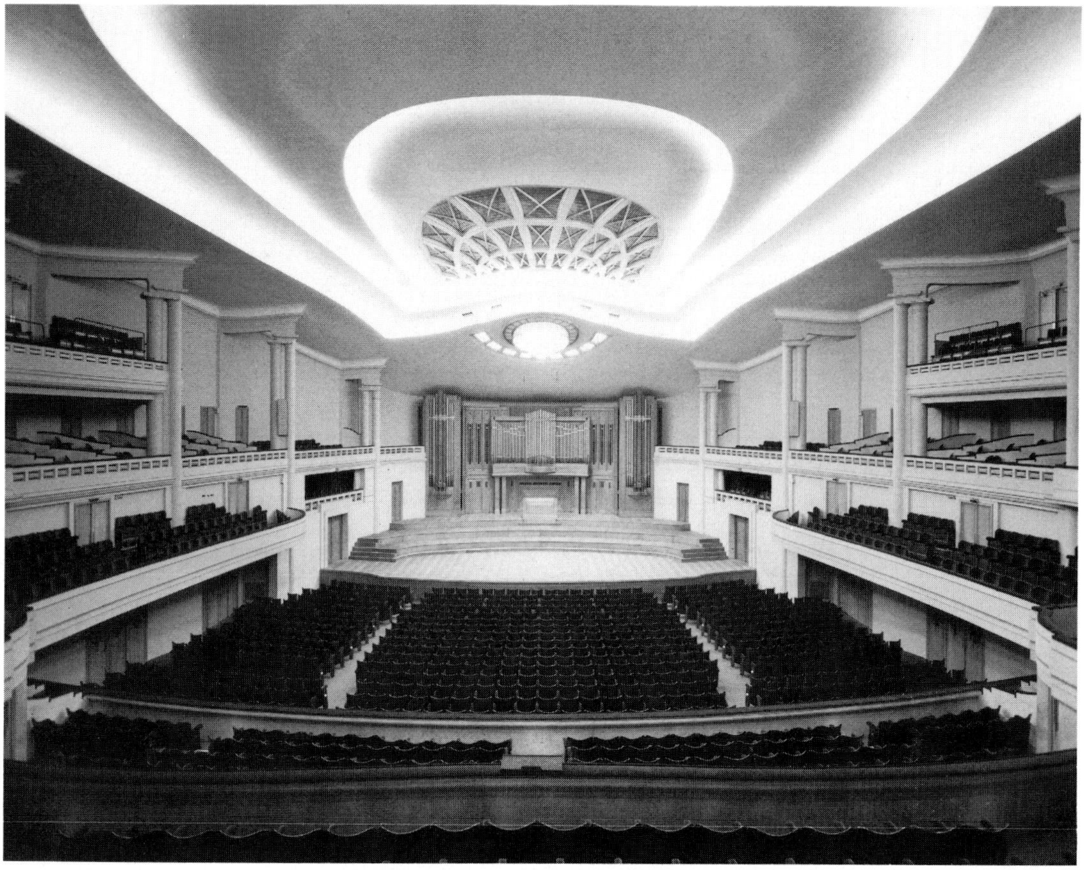

Brussels, Palais des Beaux-Arts

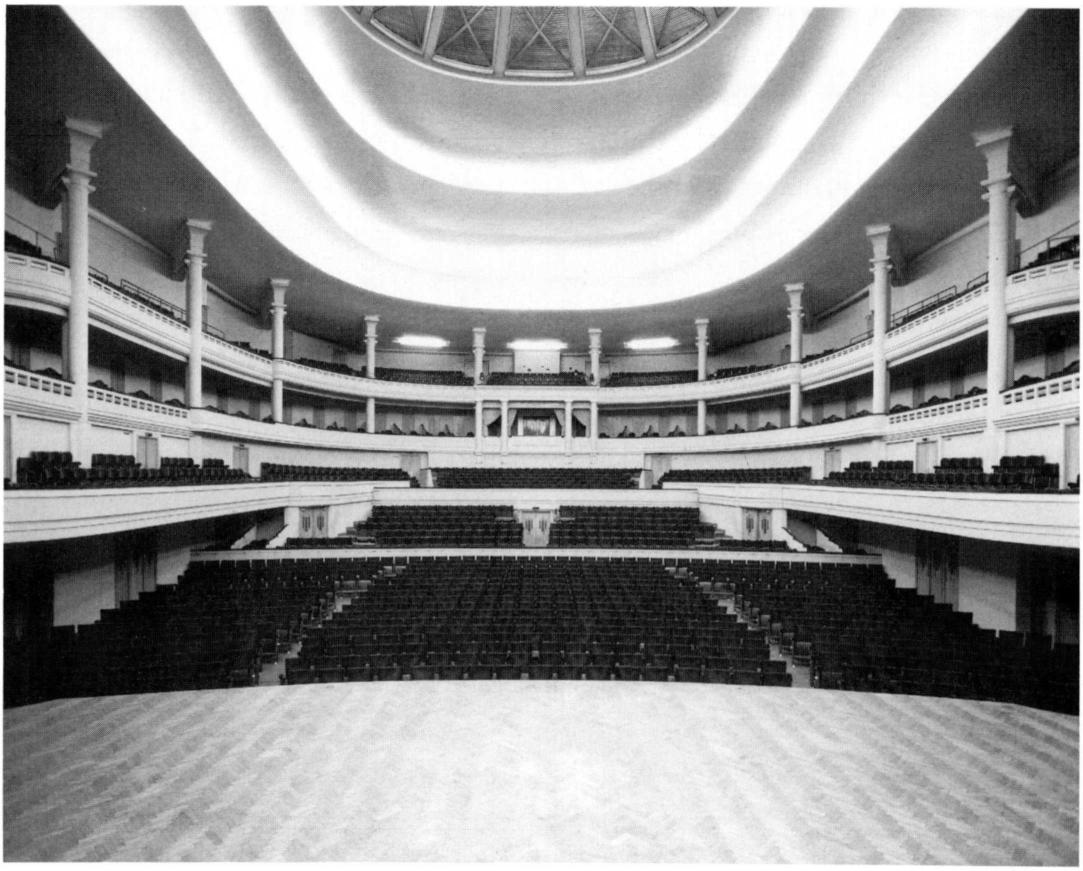

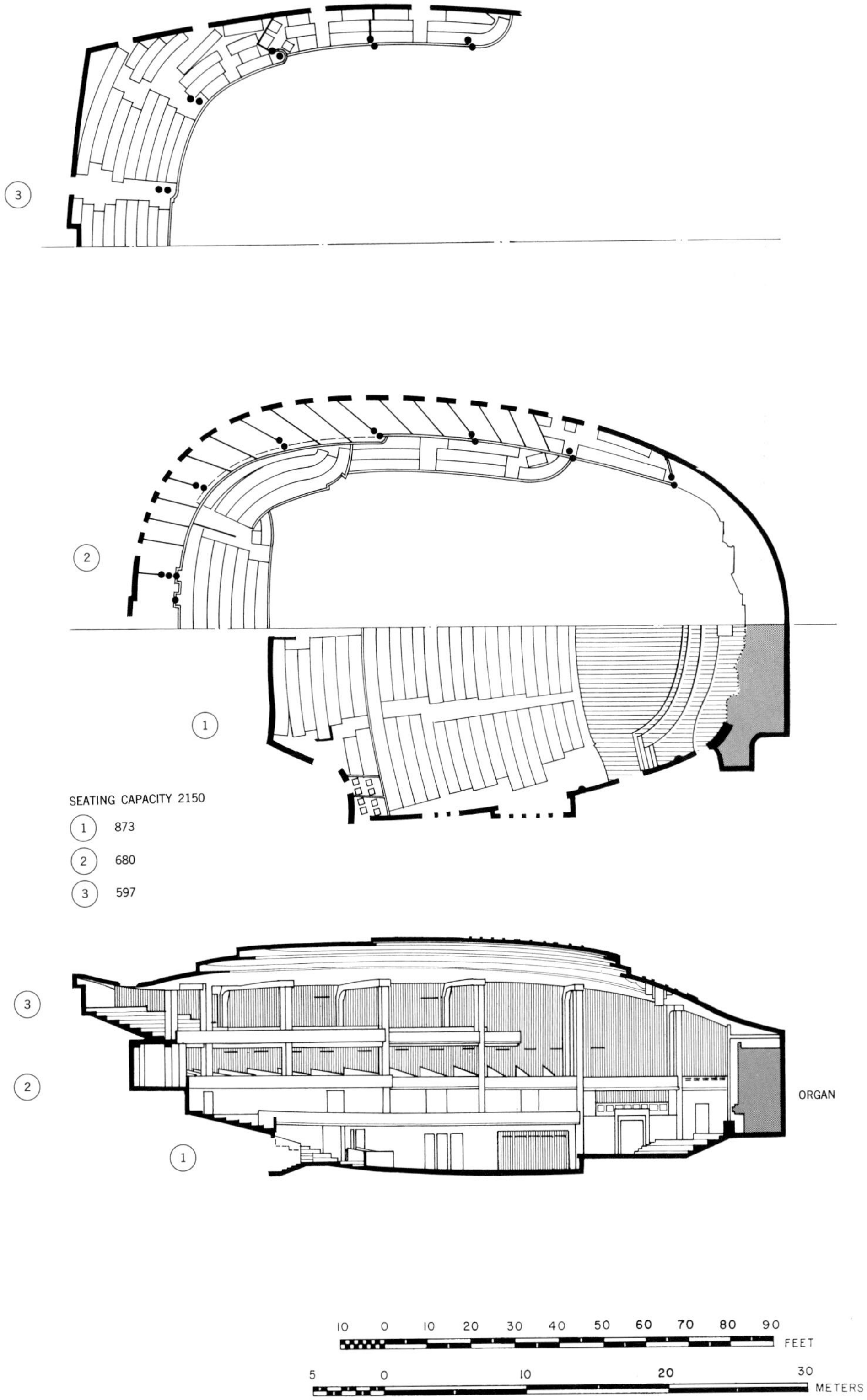
3
2
1
SEATING CAPACITY 2150
1 873
2 680
3 597
3
2
ORGAN
1
10 0 10 20 30 40 50 60 70 80 90
FEET
5 0 10 20 30
METERS

Architectural and structural details

Uses: orchestra, motion pictures, theater, ballet, and conferences. *Ceiling:* 75% is plaster on metal lath, 20% is thick glass on heavy metal frames, and 5% is lighting fixtures. *Rear and side walls:* plaster on brick, painted; columns are plaster on concrete. *Floors:* on main floor, pine wood on 3 in. (7.6 cm) wooden sleepers resting on concrete; on upper floors, wood cemented directly to concrete. *Stage floor:* wood parquet on wood boards, supported by concrete posts and wooden beams; the air space beneath varies between 4 in. (10 cm) and 5 ft (1.5 m). *Stage height:* 36.5 in. (93 cm). *Carpets:* on main floor, in boxes and in balconies. *Seating:* front of backrest and top of seat-bottom are upholstered.

Architect: Baron Victor Horta. *Credits:* drawings, plans, photographs, and details courtesy of Director General of the hall.

*Technical details**

V = 442,000 ft^3 (12,520 m^3)	S_a = 11,000 ft^2 (1,020 m^2)	S_A = 14,000 ft^2 (1,300 m^2)
S_o = 2,000 ft^2 (186 m^2)	S_T = 16,000 ft^2 (1,486 m^2)	N = 2,150
V/S_T = 27.6 ft (8.42 m)	V/S_A = 31.6 ft (9.6 m)	V/N = 206 ft^3 (5.83 m^3)
S_A/N = 6.51 ft^2 (0.60 m^2)	H = 96 ft (29.3 m)	W = 76 ft (23.2 m)
L = 102 ft (31.1 m)	D = 117 ft (35.7 m)	H/W = 1.26
L/W = 1.34	t_I = 23 msec	

**The terminology is explained in Appendix 1.*

28

Edmonton
Northern Alberta Jubilee Auditorium

Architecturally, the Northern Alberta Jubilee Auditorium resembles the Kleinhans Music Hall in Buffalo. It has a low ceiling, is fan-shaped, and has an audience size customary to that period. The French walnut interior is very attractive, creating a sense of splendor to which the unbroken lines of the inward-leaning side walls contribute.

The Jubilee Auditorium, seating 2,678 was dedicated in 1957 and has been the home of the Edmonton Symphony Orchestra since. A prededication concert was held to which a group of musicians and acousticians was invited. That is the only concert that I have attended in that hall.

The musicians on stage at the test concert felt that the sound was not vital, not live enough. They agreed that energy in the low frequencies was seriously lacking. They all found the definition or clarity good to excellent. Of the professional musicians and acousticians in the audience, 86% thought the Auditorium equal to London's Royal Festival Hall (before electronic assisted resonance was added). Some of the acousticians found the reverberation time, 1.4 sec, satisfactory, more found it too low. Most of them thought the low-frequency response weak and the violins somewhat lacking in brilliance. All of them said the plastic orchestra shell, used temporarily during the test concert, was harmful to the warmth of the music. That shell has been replaced by a demountable wooden one.

Geoffrey Waddington, then director of music of the Canadian Broadcasting Company, said: "This hall is quite dead, with a pronounced lack of low frequencies." Arnold Walter, then on the faculty of music at the University of Toronto, said, "The sound is never vital—not bright enough. Low frequencies are definitely lacking."

My own comments recorded at the time were in part: "Reverberation is a very satisfying and wonderful thing. However, one can get pleasure out of a hall that does not take such an active part in the performance. The reverberation time at low frequencies in this hall is certainly short compared to that for the middle registers. The hall is excellent for speech."

Edmonton, Northern Alberta Jubilee Auditorium

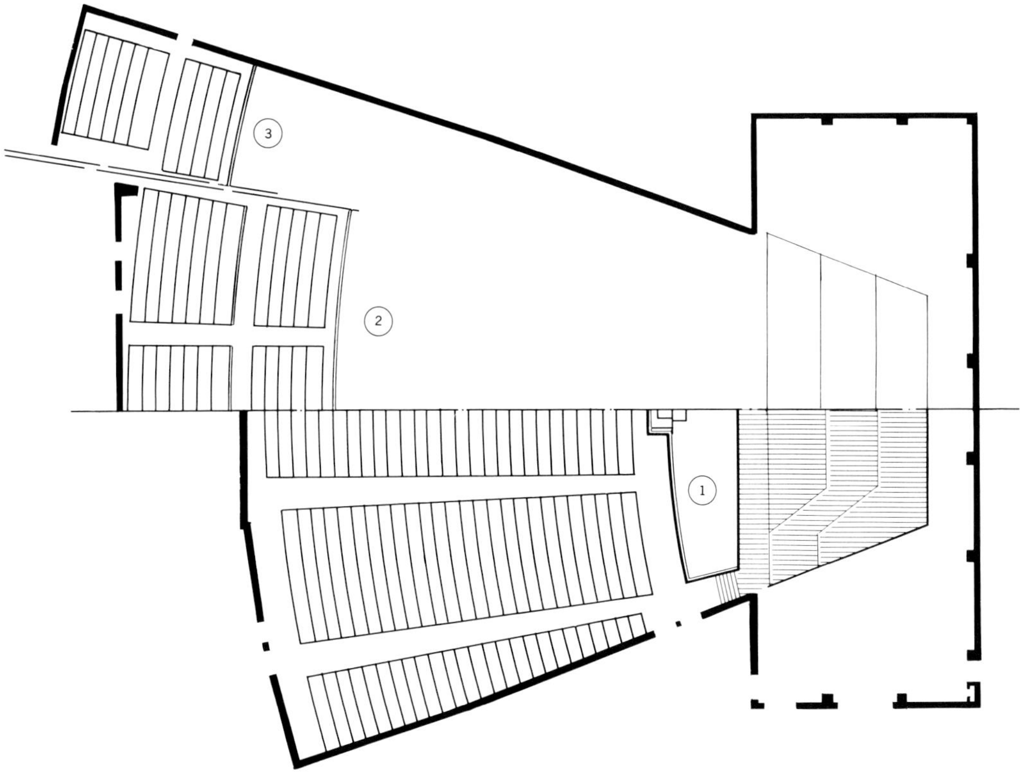

SEATING CAPACITY 2678

(1) 1252

(2) 790

(3) 636

Architectural and structural details

Uses: all purpose; home of the Edmonton Symphony Orchestra. *Ceiling:* 2 in. (5 cm) of gypsum plaster on metal lath supported from the main structure. *Side walls:* 2 × 4 ft (61 × 132 cm) panels of French walnut plywood, 0.25 in. (0.63 cm) thick, glued to 1.5 × 1.5 in. (3.8 × 3.8 cm) frames mounted 1.5 in. from wall on 0.75 in. (1.9 cm) wood furring and 0.75 in. wedges; half of the plywood panels have glass fiber batts fastened against the backs of them. *Rear walls:* carpet over plywood with a small amount of diffusion obtained with 145 outward projecting panels. *Floors:* plastic tile on concrete. *Carpet:* latex-sealed carpet with underpad in aisles. *Stage enclosure:* four-sided demountable, made of 0.5 in. (2.54 cm) plywood attached to a light aluminum framework. *Stage floor:* varnished pine boards; under orchestra, hollow wooden risers. *Stage height:* 42 in.(107 cm). *Seating:* top of seat-bottoms, front of backrest, and arms are upholstered in polyvinyl cushion covered with a densely woven fabric; the underseat is solid.

Architect: Architectural Branch of the Provincial Department of Public Works of Alberta, Ronald Clarke, chief architect. Arnold B. Steinbrecher, project architect, and G. A. Jellinek, senior architect. *Acoustical consultants:* Research Council of Alberta, T. D. Northwood and E. J. Stevens. *Photographs:* courtesy of the architect. *References:* T. D. Northwood and E. J. Stevens, "Acoustical Design of the Alberta Jubilee Auditiria" Jour. Acoust. Soc. Amer. **30**, 507–516 (1958).

*Technical details**

V = 759,000 ft^3 (21,500 m^3)	S_a = 16,150 ft^2 (1,500 m^2)	S_A = 21,000 ft^2 (1,951 m^2)
S_o = 2,000 ft^2 (186 m^2)	S_T = 23,000 ft^2 (2,137 m^2)	N = 2,678
H = 52 ft (15.8 m)	W = 114 ft (34.8 m)	L = 131 ft (40 m)
D = 158 ft (48.2 m)	V/S_T = 33 ft (10 m)	V/S_A = 36.1 ft (11 m)
V/N = 283 ft^3 (8.0 m^3)	S_A/N = 7.84 ft^2 (0.73 m^2)	H/W = 0.46
L/W = 1.15	t_I = 31 msec	

**The terminology is explained in Appendix 1.*

Montreal
Salle Wilfrid-Pelletier

Located in Place des Arts, Canada's largest center for the arts, the Wilfrid-Pelletier Hall is the jewel in the city's crown. Opened in 1963 with a gala concert by the Montreal Symphony Orchestra, it has served well since. It underwent some renovation in 1993. Seating 2,982, with a pit for 70 musicians by removing 78 seats, the W-P Hall accommodates concerts, ballet, opera, musical comedies, and variety shows. More down-to-earth than its cousin, the Roy Thompson Hall in Toronto, it has a proscenium and a stage house of large proportions. For concerts, a stage enclosure is erected on stage, shown in the drawings. A sound system is used for non-orchestral events.

As a concert hall, it has not been without criticism. The principal objections are that the orchestral sound is not sufficiently loud on the main floor and the hall lacks intimacy. Studies have been made by several acoustical consultants with some preliminary comments: First, the ceiling of the shell is too high and the rear wall is too wide. Too much sound is trapped on the stage and the music lacks clarity. Second, there are no surfaces at or near the sides of the procenium to reflect lateral sound energy onto the main floor. Laterally reflected sound energy would give the audience a feeling of intimacy and of being enveloped by the sound. Third, the semi-open ceiling does not reflect enough sound energy to the main floor seating sections.

One acoustician reports that an experiment showed that when the back wall of the orchestra enclosure was brought forward toward the audience so that the front half of the orchestra sat over the pit, the music sounded louder, fuller, and more intimate on the main floor. If this shift were accompanied by adding reflecting surfaces on either side of the pit location and if others of proper shape were located in the space below or above the ceiling, the loudness of the orchestral sound in the audience areas would increase further and the listeners would feel more enveloped by the sound. The musicians would also sense better the acoustics of the hall. Finally, if modifications to the lower side walls and the doors were made, lateral reflections could be increased further and thus add to the feeling of spaciousness and envelopment. These *suggestions* would need to be subjected to investigation in a model both for refinement and to make certain of a suitable solution.

Montreal, Salle Wilfrid-Pelletier

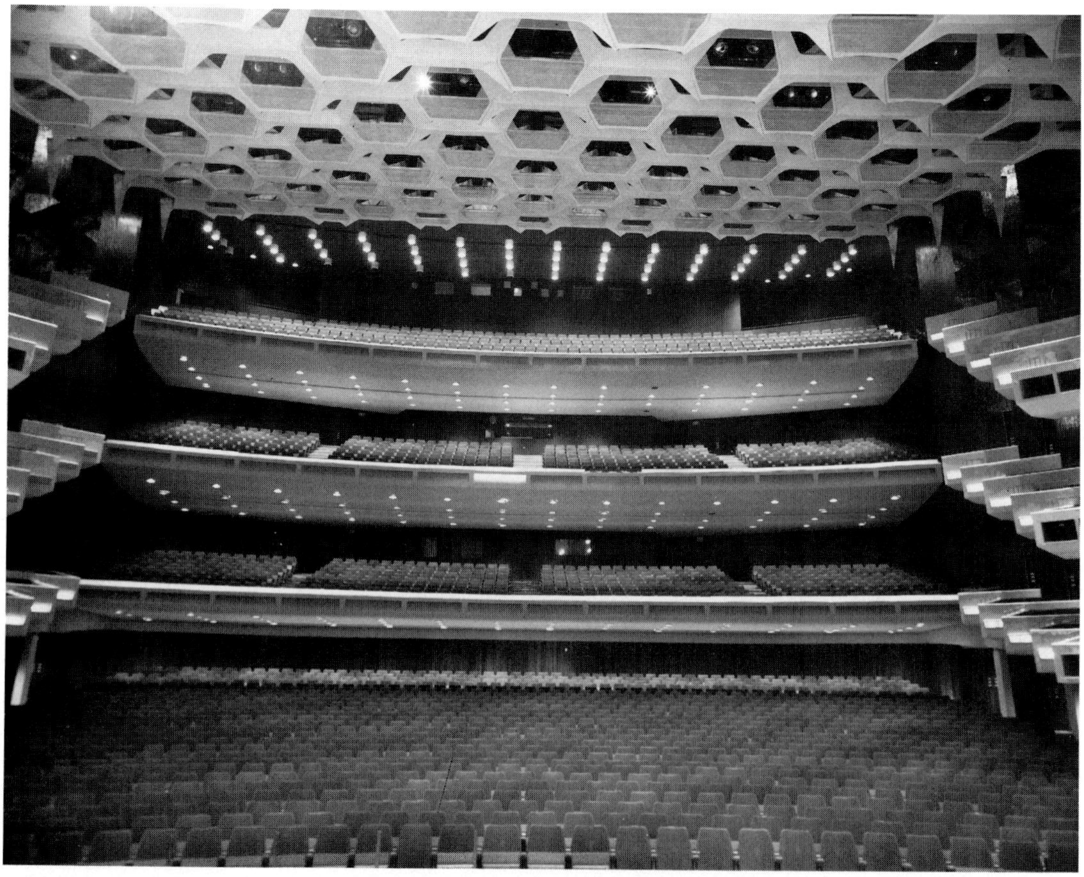

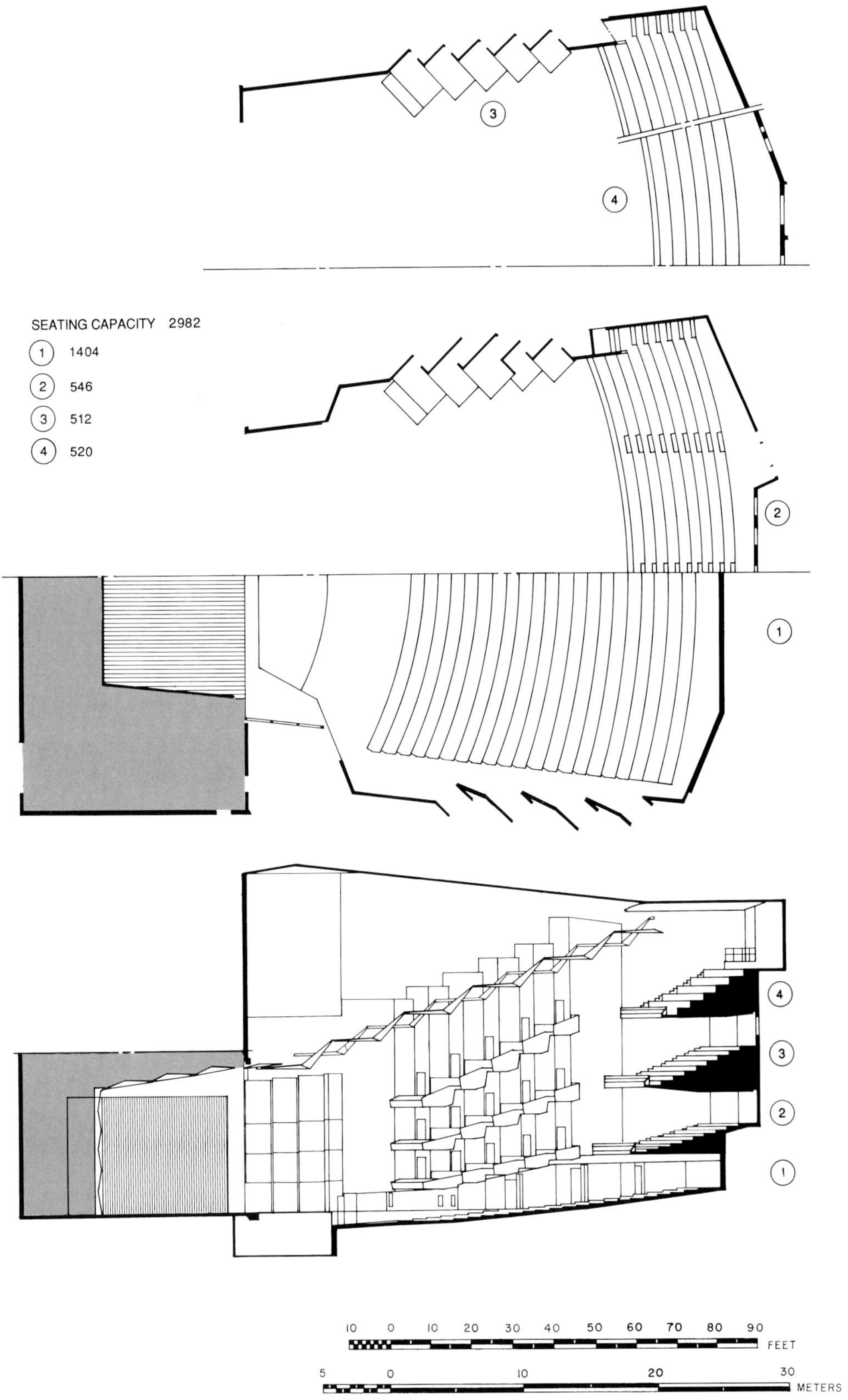
SEATING CAPACITY 2982
1 1404
2 546
3 512
4 520
1
2
3
4
4
3
2
1
10 0 10 20 30 40 50 60 70 80 90
FEET
5 0 10 20 30
METERS

Architectural and structural details

Uses: multipurpose, including classical music. *Ceiling:* heavy plaster beneath which is hung precast plaster lattice. *Walls:* plaster over concrete block; balcony faces molded plaster. *Floors:* parquet on concrete, except all boxes are carpeted. *Stage enclosure:* 2 in. (5 cm) panels, each about 4 ft by 6.5 ft (1.22 by 2 m) made into irregular, off-center, shallow pyramids supported on frames. *Stage floor:* tongue and groove wood over timber. *Stage height:* 36 in. (91 cm) above floor level. *Seating:* Upholstered top of seat-bottom and front of seat back; underseat molded plywood; rear of seat back moulded plywood; arms upholstered.

Architect: Affleck, Desbarats, Dimakopoulos, Lebensold, Michaud and Sise. *Acoustical Consultant:* Bolt Beranek and Newman. *Photographs:* Studio Lausanne and Panda Associates.

*Technical details**

V = 936,000 ft^3 (26,500 m^3)	S_a = 16,684 ft^2 (1,550 m^2)	S_A = 19,020 ft^2 (1,767 m^2)
S_o = 1,850 ft^2 (172 m^2)	S_T = 20,870 ft^2 (1,939 m^2)	N = 2,982
H = 77 ft (23.5 m)	W = 108 ft (32.9 m)	L = 123 ft (37.5 m)
D = 135 ft (41.2 m)	V/S_T = 44.8 ft (13.7 m)	V/S_A = 49.2 ft (15 m)
V/N = 314 ft^3 (8.9 m^3)	S_A/N = 6.38 ft^2 (0.59 m^2)	H/W = 0.71
L/W = 1.14	t_I = 20 msec	

**The terminology is explained in Appendix 1.*

CANADA

30

Toronto
Roy Thompson Hall

Roy Thompson Hall is a semi-surround, non-proscenium hall, with only a small percentage of the audience to the sides and behind the orchestra. Seating 2,812 persons, it ranks as one of the larger concert halls, but the distance from the stage to the farthest seat is only 130 ft (40 m).

Entering the hall is a breathtaking experience. It appears circular, with a huge wheel seemingly supporting the ceiling, the periphery of which is surrounded by a forest of stalactites, called banners, all brilliantly colored and illuminated. During concerts, this luxurious, steel-spoked chandelier is darkened and spotlights illuminate the stage.

The stalactites serve an acoustical purpose. They are circular tubes, containing cylindrical sound-absorbing units that can be lowered in three steps to add up to 12,000 ft^2 (1,100 m^2) of exposed soft material for the purpose of reducing the reverberation time to suit the composition being played or to provide the best environment for other uses. The reverberation time, in the fully occupied condition is 1.8 sec, and can be reduced to 1.4 sec by the banners. Acoustically, many of the necessary early sound reflections are provided by an array of sixteen hung, convex, acrylic reflectors, each 7 ft (2.1 m) in diameter hung 25 to 30 ft above the stage and over the front of the audience. These reflectors aid on-stage communication and establish instrumental balance and, in the audience areas, clarity of sound.

The height of the stage side walls, 10.5 ft (3.2 m) including the curved balcony railing, are planned to created cross-stage reflections. The balcony facia are a source of early lateral reflections to the audience. In 1987, tilted sound reflectors were installed around the side walls to increase the number of early lateral reflections. The measured lateral reflected sound energy is comparable to that in other well accepted halls. The average level of the sound in Roy Thompson Hall is about 1 dB less than that in Boston Symphony Hall, but is equal to that of a number of well accepted halls. The measured early sound energy compared to the later reverberant sound energy indicates greater clarity of the orchestral music than that in the classical rectangular halls.

Toronto, Roy Thompson Hall

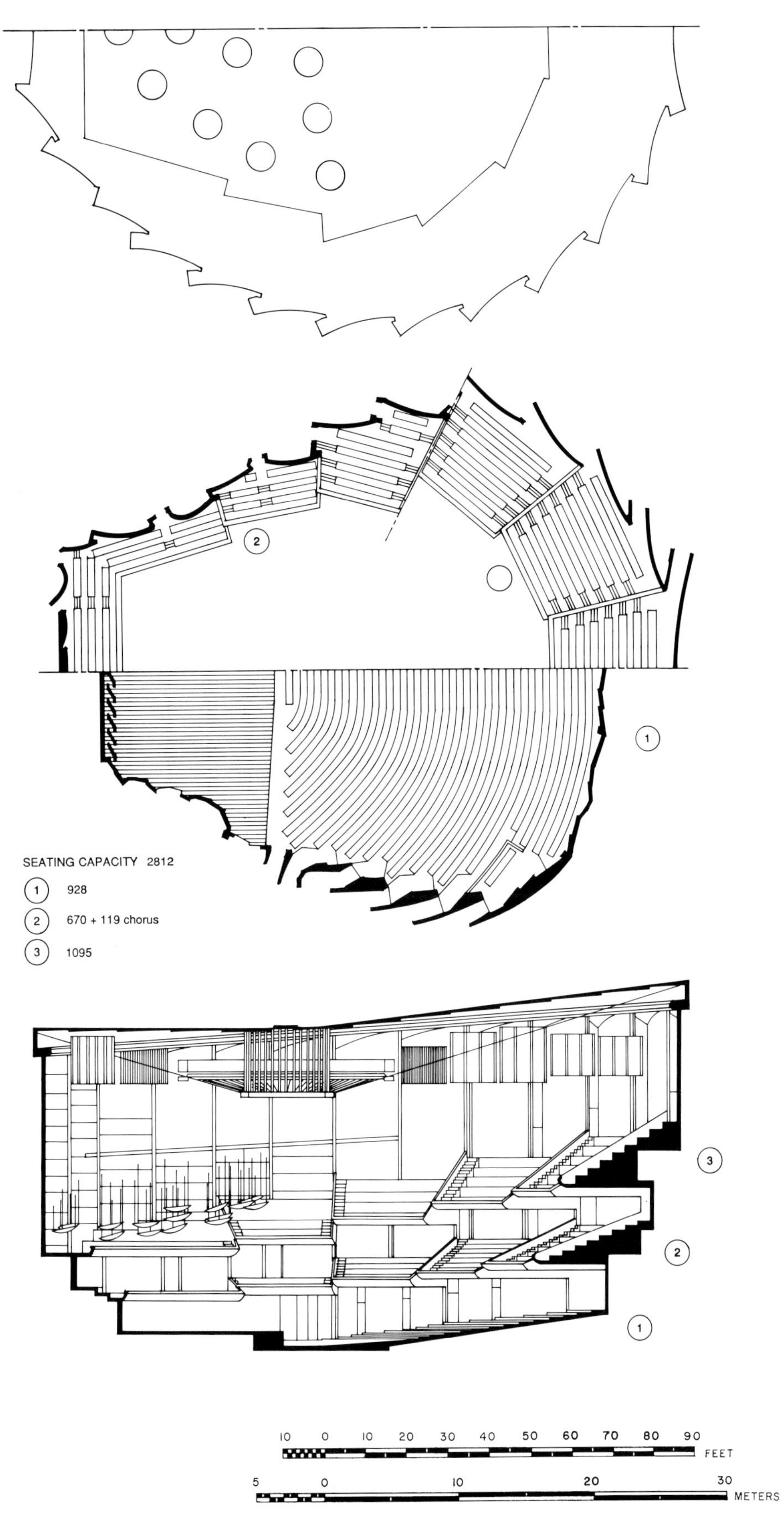
SEATING CAPACITY 2812
1 928
2 670 + 119 chorus
3 1095
10 0 10 20 30 40 50 60 70 80 90
FEET
5 0 10 20 30
METERS

Architectural and structural details

Use: primarily concert, recitals, choral events, and organ. *Ceiling:* convex precast sections tilted variously. *Main sidewalls*: 6 in. (15 cm) poured-in-place and precast concrete, substantially segmented to avoid echoes; at upper levels, envelope consists of 26 vertical convex sections. *Sound absorption:* provided on a variable basis by banners (see text). *Stage floor:* wooden strips on wooden subbase on sleepers over airspace. *Stage height:* 39 in. (1 m). *Audience floor and aisles:* carpet on concrete. *Seating:* seatback, molded plywood; tops of seats and fronts of the backrests upholstered with vinyl cushion, porous cloth covering; underseat perforated wood; armrests, wooden.

Architect: Arthur Erickson and Mathers & Haldenby Associated Architects. *Acoustical Consultant:* Bolt Beranek and Newman. *Photographs:* Fiona Spalding-Smith. *References:* "Award of Excellence," The Canadian Architect Yearbook, from Canadian Architect, December 1977, 5 pages.

*Technical details**

V = 1,000,000 ft^3 (28,300 m^3)	S_a = 15,080 ft^2 (1,401 m^2)	S_A = 18,100 ft^2 (1,681 m^2)
S_o = 2,390 ft^2 (222 m^2)	S_T = 20,490 ft^2 (1,903 m^2)	N = 2,812
H = 76 ft (23.2 m)	W = 102 ft (31.1 m)	L = 89 ft (27.1 m)
D = 108 ft (32.9 m)	V/S_T = 48.8 ft (14.9 m)	V/S_A = 55.2 ft (16.8 m)
V/N = 356 ft^3 (10.1 m^3)	S_A/N = 6.44 ft^2 (0.60 m^2)	H/W = 0.74
L/W = 0.87	t_I = 35 msec	

**The terminology is explained in Appendix 1.*

DENMARK

31

Copenhagen
Radiohuset, Studio 1

The Radiohuset is the home of the Danish Radio Symphony Orchestra. The stage and the great organ dominate the room, and the audience area is small, seating 1,081, compared to that in a conventional concert hall. Opened in 1945, the cylindrical ceiling, low over the stage, has caused on-stage dissatisfaction among the orchestra players and has resulted in two major revisions. In the most recent renovation, completed in 1989, a canopy of acrylic panels was hung over the stage, a number of sloped large reflecting panels (see the photograph) were attached to the stage side walls and a new floor, more favorable to bass and cellos, was installed along with hydraulic risers on stage. These recent changes have improved communication among the orchestra members and have provided more intimate sound to the audience than when the hall was without panels. The hall is also better acoustically for recordings. The reverberation time, 1.5 sec, fully occupied, is on the low side, the optimum in a hall for symphonic music and of this size is about 1.7 sec.

The object of the acrylic panels is to improve communication on stage, ease of orchestral timing, better balance, and blend. The size and number of panels for the Radiohuset followed studies by J. H. Rindel (1990). He found that a large number of smaller panels, each slightly curved as compared to larger ones used elsewhere, give a more uniform reflection of the entire range of frequencies. The open area in the panel array should be about 50%. Installed in Studio 1 are 61 panels, each 5.9 × 2.62 ft (1.8 × 0.8 m), 0.3 in.(0.8 cm) thick and slightly curved.

In the ceiling of the Radiohuset, there are low-frequency sound absorbing Helmholtz-type resonators, 105 of which are (currently, 1994) tuned to absorb sound at 98 Hz and 45 at 64 Hz. Their purpose is to remove low-frequency standing waves between the floor and the curved ceiling. Because of the small volume of the hall, 420,000 ft^3 (11,900 m^3), the sound of a full symphony is loud, which helps create a feeling to the listener of being enveloped by the sound field and adds spaciousness to the orchestral music. The reports are that the 1989 changes have been well accepted by the orchestra. Reviews by music critics are mixed, some saying that the sound is much the same as before the stage renovations.

Copenhagen, Radiohuset, Studio 1

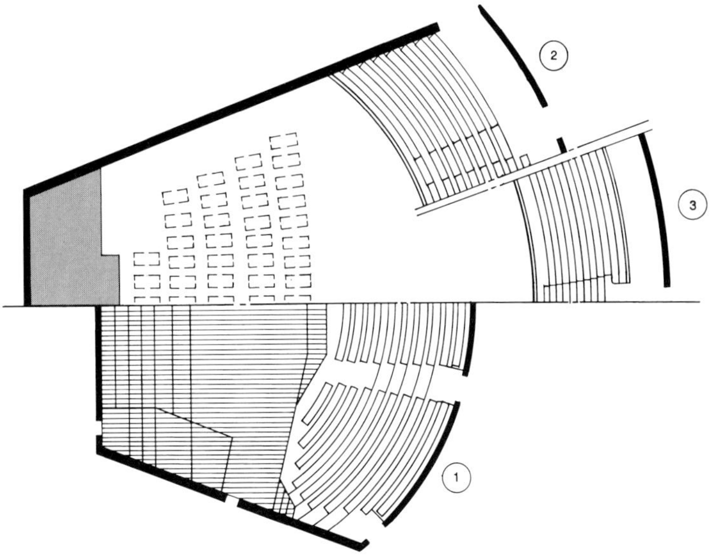

SEATING CAPACITY 1081

1 368

2 375

3 338

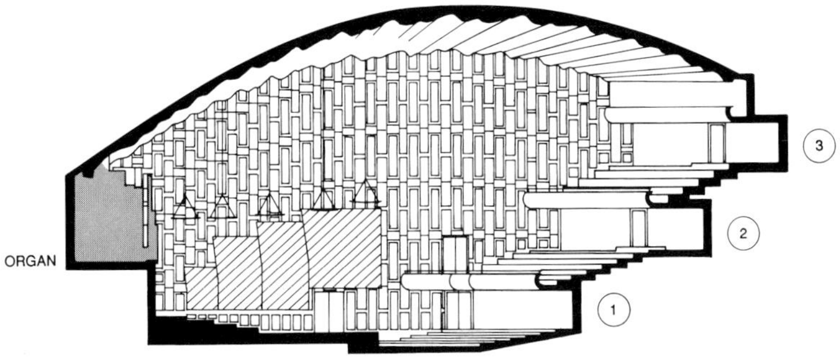

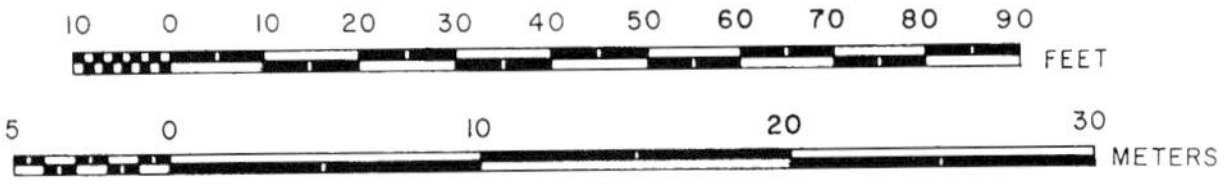

Architectural and structural details

Uses: concerts, broadcasting, recordings, and recitals. *Ceiling:* 3 in. (8 cm) concrete roof, covered by 1 in. (2.5 cm) tongue-and-grooved wood strips (no airspace) beneath; under balconies, 0.5 in. wood panels partly with shallow airspace behind. See the text for resonators in ceiling. *Suspended stage panels:* (see the text). *Side walls:* 0.83 in. (2.1 cm) wood with either 1 in. or 4 in. (2.5 or 10 cm) deep airspace, about 50% each. *Rearwalls:* on main floor and 1st balcony, 0.12 in. (0.3 cm), 25% perforated, wooden panels behind which is 1 in. to 4 in. airspace partly filled with mineral wool; on 2nd balcony, 0.5 in. wood panels with airspace. *Audience floor:* parquet in asphalt over concrete. Sound reflectors on stage side walls: 0.5 in. plywood boxes, shaped, faced with 0.5 in. semicircular vertical strips, spaced 2.5 in. (6.2 cm) apart. *Rear wall of stage:* 22% perforated thin plywood panel in front of thin perforated steel plate, which can be slid with a handle for matching two sets of holes to provide sound absorption if needed; 4 in. (10 cm) mineral wool is cemented to back of steel plate and the panel is tilted forward slightly. *Stage floor:* 0.9 in. (2.2 cm) parquet on joists spread apart 16 in. (40 cm), over 14 in. (36 cm) airspace; rear part divided into 26 hydraulic risers. *Stage height:* 27.5 in. (70 cm). *Seating:* upholstered in leather, underseat unperforated.

Architect: Vilhelm Lauritzen. *Acoustical Consultant:* Jordan Akustik. *Research:* A. C. Gade and J. H. Rindel from The Acoustics Laboratory, Technical University of Denmark. *Reference:* N. V. Jordan, J. H. Rindel & A. C. Gade, "The New Orchestra Platform in the Danish Radio Concert Hall." Proceedings of Nordic Acoustical Meeting, Lulea, Sweden, 1990.

*Technical details**

V = 420,000 ft³ (11,900 m³)	S_a = 6,512 ft² (605 m²)	S_A = 7,761 ft² (721 m²)
S_o = 3,100 ft² (288 m²)	S_T = 10,860 ft² (1009 m²)	N = 1,081
H = 58 ft (17.7 m)	W = 110 ft (33.5 m)	L = 61 ft (18.6 m)
D = 75 ft (22.9 m)	V/S_T = 38.7 ft (11.8 m)	V/S_A = 54.1 ft (116.5 m)
V/N = 388 ft³ (11 m³)	S_A/N = 7.2 ft² (0.67 m²)	H/W = 0.53
L/W = 0.55	t_I = 29 msec	

**The terminology is explained in Appendix 1.*

Denmark

32

Copenhagen
Tivoli Koncertsal

In keeping with the spirit of the Tivoli entertainment park in Copenhagen, this concert hall, which opened in 1956 with 1,789 seats, is cheerful and intimate. Fan-shaped, with a small balcony that extends down the sides, this little theater seems particularly suited to drama and musical comedy. It is the home of the Zealand Symphony Orchestra.

For orchestral concerts the reverberation time is short, about 1.3 sec, fully occupied. But because it is narrow, the Tivoli Koncertsal overcomes some of the difficulties of halls like the Kleinhans Hall in Buffalo and the Alberta Jubilee Halls in Canada, which also have reverberation times of 1.5 sec or less. Music played in the Tivoli Concert Hall is intimate and warm.

The hall has not undergone any internal changes since its opening, the chairs have only had a change of fabric. The glass facades have been changed to heavier sound isolating glass after a noisy roller-coaster was placed nearby in the early 1980s. The hall is considered too small in volume for the full size orchestras of today, and the small orchestra enclosure also reduces the essential lateral energy content for the listeners. The hall is at its best with chamber music and soloist performances.

Four of the music critics interviewed had heard concerts at Tivoli. One said, "This is a good little hall, quite homogeneous acoustically. I had the impression of its being a very bright, yet respectably warm, hall." No one of the other three music critics was quite as enthusiastic about the sound. The short reverberation time may well have underlay their apathy.

Two conductors spoke favorably, but briefly, about the acoustics: Eugene Ormandy (1960) commented, "Very good sound. Of course, music always sounds good in small halls."

And Tauno Hannikainen (1960) said, "It is quite different from other halls, but the sound is good."

Copenhagen, Tivoli Koncertsal

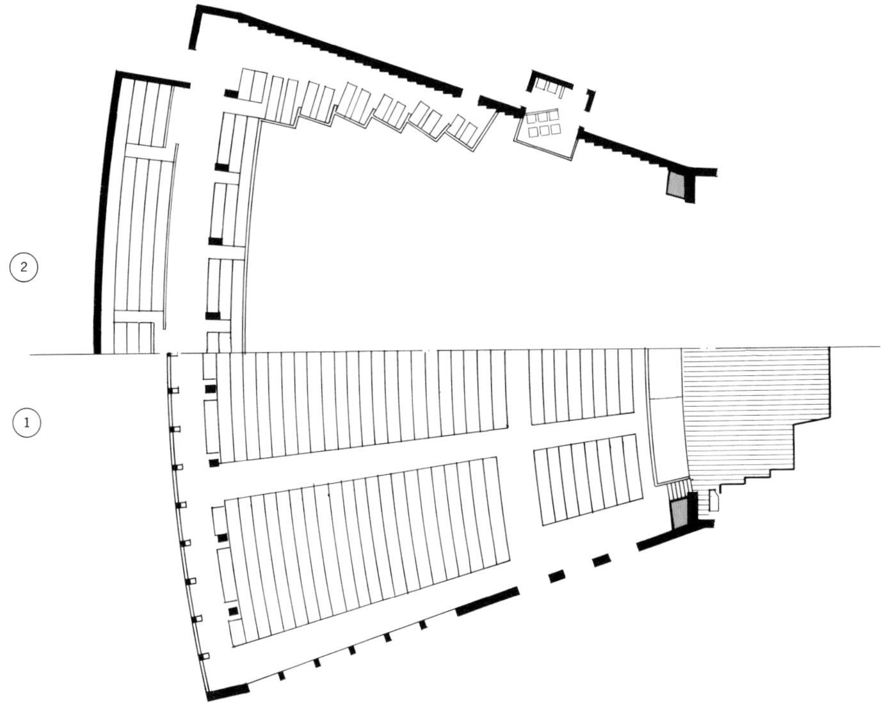

SEATING CAPACITY 1789

(1) 1316

(2) 467 + 6 in Royal box

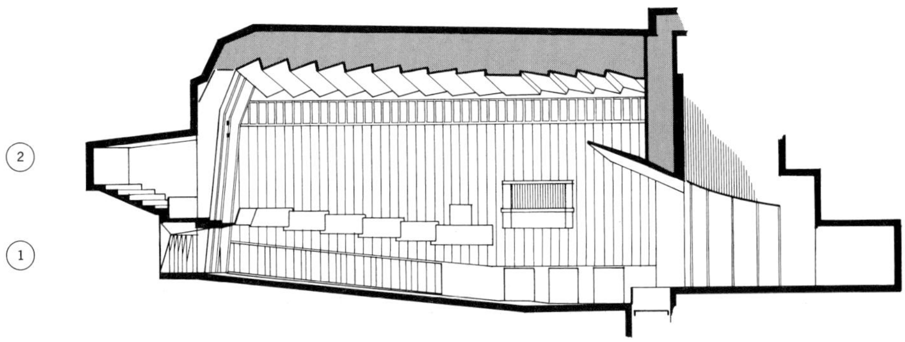

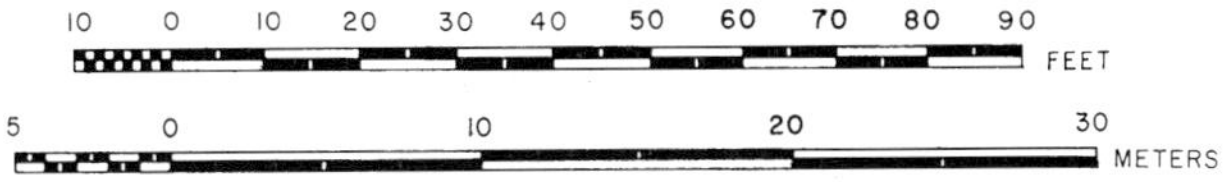

Architectural and structural details

Uses: orchestra, 35%; chamber music and soloists, 20%; general entertainment, 30%; theater and meetings, 15%. *Ceiling:* gypsum with a surface covering of fiberboard. *Side Walls:* 0.6 in. (1.5 cm) wood panels with airspace behind; the side wall panels are mounted in sections parallel to the main axis of the hall. *Rear walls:* main floor is inclined glass; upper level is wood panels and plaster on concrete. *Floors:* asphalt tile on concrete and air-conditioning outlets built into the risers. *Stage enclosure:* 0.6 in. wood panels; ceiling is wood panels, turned vertical when stage is used for theatricals. *Stage floor:* wood on risers. *Stage height:* 38 in. (97 cm). *Seating*: upholstered on both sides of backrest and top of seat-bottom. Underseat is perforated.

Architect: Fritz Schlegel and Hans Hansen. *Acoustical consultant:* Jordan Akustik. *References:* private communication and photographs courtesy of V. L. and N. V. Jordan.

*Technical details**

Concerts

V = 450,000 ft^3 (12,740 m^3)	S_a = 10,635 ft^2 (988 m^2)	S_A = 12,230 ft^2 (1,136 m^2)
S_o = 2,100 ft^2 (195 m^2)	S_T = 14,330 ft^2 (1,331 m^2)	N = 1,789
H = 45 ft (13.7 m)	W = 109 ft (33.2 m)	L = 106 ft (32.3 m)
D = 113 ft (34.4 m)	V/S_T = 31 ft (9.6 m)	V/S_A = 36.8 ft (11.2 m)
V/N = 252 ft^3 (7.1 m^3)	S_A/N = 6.8 ft^2 (0.63 m^2)	H/W = 0.41
L/W = 0.97	t_I = 16 msec	

**The terminology is explained in Appendix 1.*

33

Helsinki Kulttuuritalo

Helsinki's Kulttuuritalo is visually exciting both inside and out. It is used for concerts, meetings, and congresses. Opened in 1957, it seats 1,500 persons, and has a reverberation time at mid-frequencies, occupied, of 1.05 sec, much lower than that of any other concert hall in this book. Because the shape of its ceiling provides the essential short initial-time-delay gaps, and the one reflecting side wall provides some lateral reflections, this hall sounds much better than its low reverberation time and the wide fan shape of its plan would suggest.

A small orchestra of the Helsinki Broadcasting Company was rehearsing during my visit to the Kulttuuritalo in 1961. I had an opportunity to talk with Tauno Hannikainen, then Director of the Helsinki City Symphony Orchestra, during the rehearsal. In his opinion, at that time, this was the best concert hall in Helsinki; the musicians hear each other well and there is good contact with the audience. According to Hannikainen, a piano sounded better here than anywhere else in Finland; the upper registers are strong and clear, and the acoustics do not change appreciably when an audience is added.

In my opinion, this hall, at least as I heard it without an audience, is very good; the definition is excellent, and the music has adequate bass. The distribution of the sound through the hall is uniform. However, with an audience and a reverberation time of 1.05 sec, the hall may be somewhat dead.

David Oistrakh, the (late) violinist, said, "It is wonderfully easy and pleasant to play in this hall, which has excellent acoustics. The sound is initiated and grows easily, freely and naturally. The color and dynamics of the performance are fully preserved." This remark is made even though violinists generally are more favorably inclined toward higher reverberation times.

A new hall now exists in Helsinki. The Kulttuuritalo Hall is included here because it is a small hall, non-rectangular, with a short reverberation time, that receives good reports.

Helsinki, Kulttuuritalo

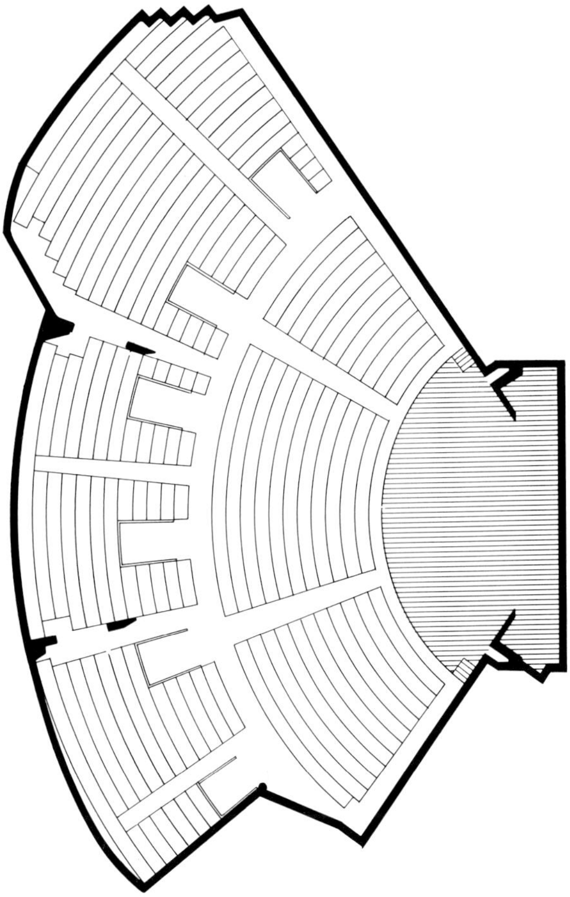

SEATING CAPACITY 1500

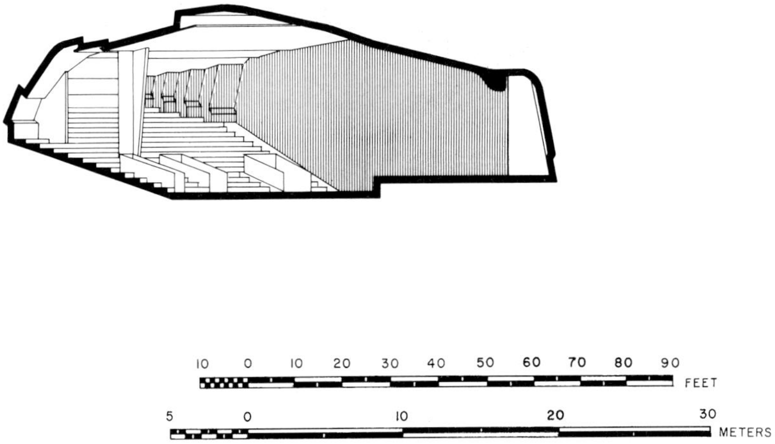

Architectural and structural details

Uses: orchestra, general music, meetings, and congresses. *Ceiling:* 1 to 1.5 in. (2.5 to 3.8 cm) plaster on concrete. *Side walls:* partly concrete with wood strips in front for sound diffusion; partly 0.8 in. (2 cm) wood panels with about 6 in. (15 cm) airspace behind. *Rear Wall:* partly 0.8 in. (2 cm) wood reflectors; partly concrete. *Floors:* on the main floor, 0.8 in. (2 cm) flooring over 2 in. (5 cm) air space; in stadium, concrete with linoleum. *Carpet:* none. *Stage enclosure:* 1 in. (2.5 cm) wood plastered, slightly slanted, and with cylindrical diffusers; ceiling 1 in. wood, plastered. *Stage floor:* 1.75 in. (4.5 cm) wood over about 30 in. (76 cm) airspace. *Stage height:* 34.5 in. (88 cm). *Seating:* tops of seat-bottoms and fronts of backrests upholstered; underseats perforated plywood.

Architect: Alvar Alto. *Acoustical consultant:* Paavo Arni. *Photographs:* Kuvatyo Oy.

*Technical details**

V = 354,000 ft³ (10,025 m³)	S_a = 9,254 ft² (860 m²)	S_A = 10,180 ft² (946 m²)
S_o = 1,790 ft² (166 m²)	S_T = 11,970 ft² (1,112 m²)	N = 1,500
V/S_T = 29.6 ft (9 m)	V/S_A = 34.8 ft (10.6 m)	V/N = 236 ft³ (6.7 m³)
S_A/N = 6.79 ft² (0.63 m²)	H = 31 ft (9.45 m)	W = 151 ft (46 m)
L = 78 ft (23.8 m)	D = 108 ft (32.9 m)	H/W = 0.2
L/W = 0.52	t_I = 26 msec	

**The terminology is explained in Appendix 1.*

FRANCE

34

Paris
Opéra Bastille

The Opéra Bastille opened in July 1989, thirty years after its conception. Seating an audience of 2,700 it is larger than all but a few opera houses in the world, three of the biggest being those in Milan (2,289), Buenos Aires (2,487), and New York (3,816). The architect rejected the multi-ringed house made so popular by the Teatro Alla Scala of Milan, inaugurated in 1778, and instead chose a two-balcony design, with moderate overhangs, to fulfill the government requirement that all spectators have a full frontal view of the stage.

The acoustical consultants provided the various parts of the audience with necessary early lateral sound reflections, including two-dimensional sound diffusing surfaces to the sides and above the proscenium, and on the front side walls and curved box fronts that spread the incident sound over large areas. The reverberation time, fully occupied, at mid-frequencies is 1.55 sec, less than the Buenos Aires Opera Colón (1.7), but well above the 1.3 sec average for the best known European houses, and for the Paris Opéra Garnier with a RT of 1.1 sec.

As usual in large halls, the sound is better in the balcony, particularly the rear part of the second balcony, than on the main floor center because of the higher density of early lateral reflections farther back. But excellent sound is heard on the main floor, the central area seats excepted. The reverberation is heard in all parts of the house, but more in the rear part. The measured early sound energy compared to the later reverberant energy is nearly optimum for opera, indicating clarity of the singing voice.

Those who criticize the house, say that the bass sound is weaker than desired. Some players say that communication among the orchestral sections in the pit is not ideal and that ensemble playing is difficult. But, the acoustical contact among musicians can be improved by the arrangement of the orchestra, and by making use of the full flexibility of the pit whose width, depth, and overhangs can be changed.

Paris, a city of opera lovers, needs two opera houses. The Opéra Garnier, with its plush interior, gold trimmings, and great heritage will always be loved by many. But the new House will satisfy another group who wish a different ambience and a more reverberant space. And the income from another 570 seats is significant.

Paris, Opéra Bastille

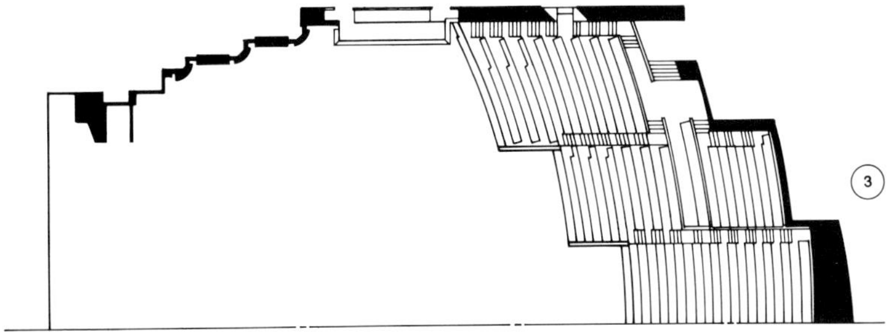

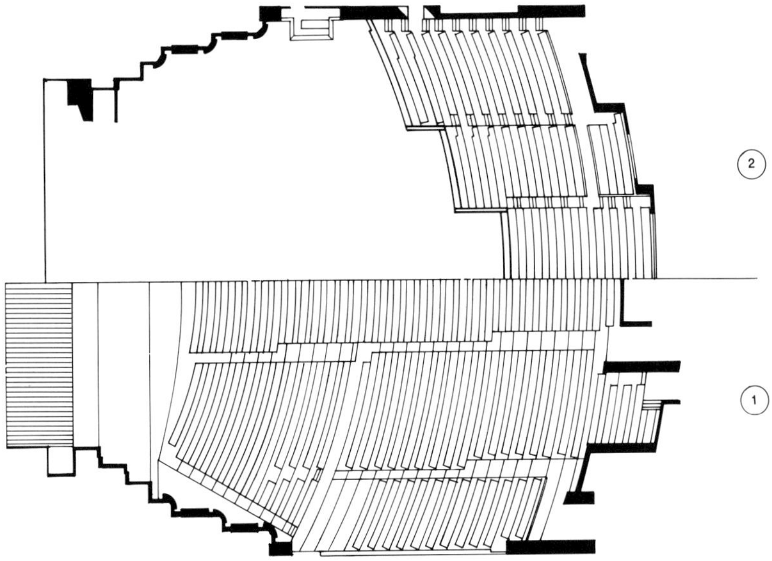

SEATING CAPACITY 2700

(1) 1545

(2) 460

(3) 695

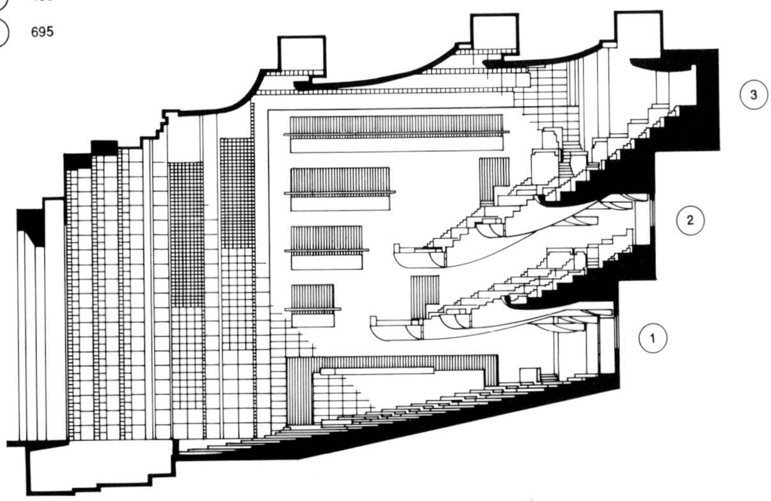

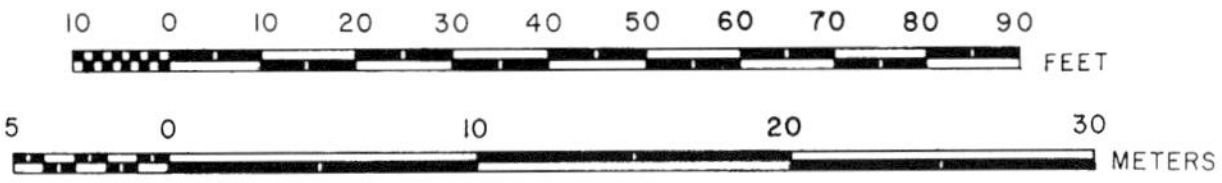

Architectural and structural details

Uses: opera, 90%; symphonic concert, 10%. *Ceiling:* clamped glass tiles, 1/4 in. (6 mm) thick. *Walls:* side and rear walls, granite 1.2 in. (3 cm) thick, fastened to concrete wall by hooks, over an air gap filled with mineral wool 1 to 2 in. (2.5 to 5 cm) deep; two-dimensional QRD diffuser (see Chapter 10) used for fixed part of the vertical proscenium area and on the front side walls. *Movable proscenium:* diffusing wood structures hidden behind highly transparent perforated metal sheet. *Floors:* wood cemented to concrete below seats; stone tiles in the aisles of the main floor; carpet (no underpad) in the aisles of the balconies. *Sound absorbing materials:* none except glass ceiling planned for low frequency absorption. *Pit:* size is variable, all surfaces are wood 0.8 in. (2 cm) for pit walls, 2 in. (5 cm) air slots in floor. *Seating:* rear of seatback is wood; upperside seat-bottom is upholstered with polyurethane foam and covered with porous velvet fabric; underside, perforated wood.

Architect: Carlos Ott. *Acoustical consultants:* Mueller-BBM. *Associated acoustical consultants:* Centre Scientifique et Technique des Salles. *Reference:* Bruno Suner, "Ott à L'Opéra Bastille," L'Architecture D'Aujourd'Hu. *Photographs:* courtesy of Opéra Bastille.

Technical details*

V = 741,500 ft³ (21,000 m³)	S_a =13,650 ft² (1,268 m²)	S_A = 16,382 ft² (1,522 m²)
S_o (pit) = 2,000 ft² (186 m²)	S_P = 2,600 (242)	S_T = 21,000 ft² (1,951)
N = 2,700	H = 70 ft (21.3 m)	W = 106 ft (16.2 m)
L = 123 ft (31.1 m)	D = 148 ft (39 m)	V/S_T = 35.3 ft (10.8 m)
V/S_A = 45.3 ft (13.8 m)	S_A/N = 6.1 ft² (0.56 m²)	V/N = 275 ft³ (7.8 m³)
H/W = 0.66	L/W = 1.16	t_I = 41 msec

**The terminology is explained in Appendix 1.*

France

35

Paris
Opéra Garnier

This famous opera house, which opened in 1875, was designed by the architect Charles Garnier. Garnier pursued diligently the elusive factors of good acoustics, but in his book, *The Grand Opera in Paris*, he confesses that he finally trusted to luck, "like the acrobat who closes his eyes and clings to the ropes of an ascending balloon," "Eh bien!" he concludes, "Je suis arrivé!"

The Opéra Garnier has very good acoustics—not the finest but very good. Garnier said, "The credit is not mine. I merely wear the marks of honor." He continues, "It is not my fault that acoustics and I can never come to an understanding. I gave myself great pains to master this bizarre science, but after fifteen years of labor, I found myself hardly in advance of where I stood on the first day....I had read diligently in my books, and conferred industriously with philosophers—nowhere did I find a positive rule of action to guide me; on the contrary, nothing but contradictory statements. For long months, I studied, questioned everything, but after this travail, finally I made this discovery. A room to have good acoustics must be either long or broad, high or low, of wood or stone, round or square, and so forth."

The baroque interior of the Opéra Garnier combines tan-gold plaster "carvings" and gold trim with burgundy-red plush upholstery and box linings. The allegorical paintings on the ceiling, beneath which hangs a grand chandelier, place this theater in an age of elegance far removed from the frugal reconstruction of La Scala or the almost chaste interior of the Vienna Staatsoper. On the main floor, there are only 21 closely spaced rows, the last 8 of which are elevated above those in front. The architectural effect of this raised area is to foreshorten the main floor and give the hall an intimate appearance.

The reason for the good acoustics is the room's small size. The audience area is 11,000 ft^2 (1,020 m^2) with 2,131 seats. Eighty-six of the seats fold down into the aisles during performances. The reverberation time is very low, the orchestra is said to dominate the singers, and the best seats in the house are in the front rows of the upper two rings, opposite the stage. Herbert von Karajan said (1960), "The acoustics of the Paris Opera House are wonderful."

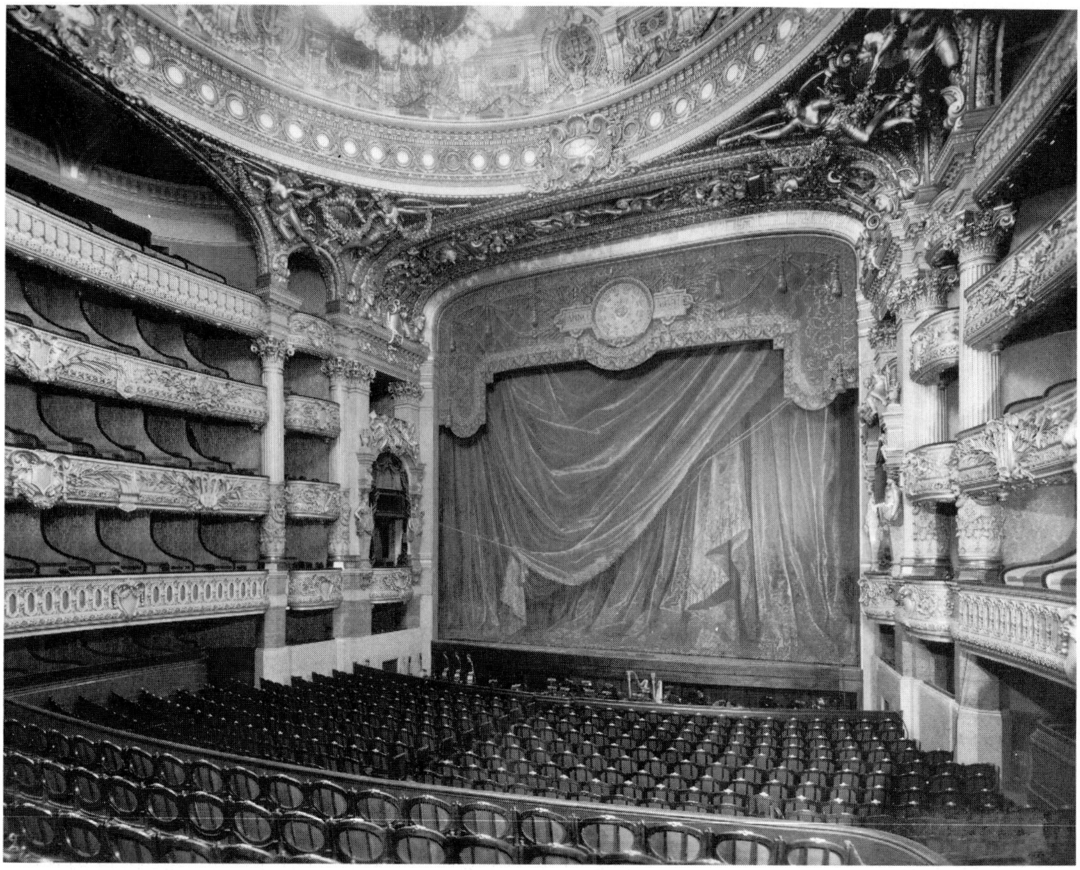

Paris, Opéra Garnier

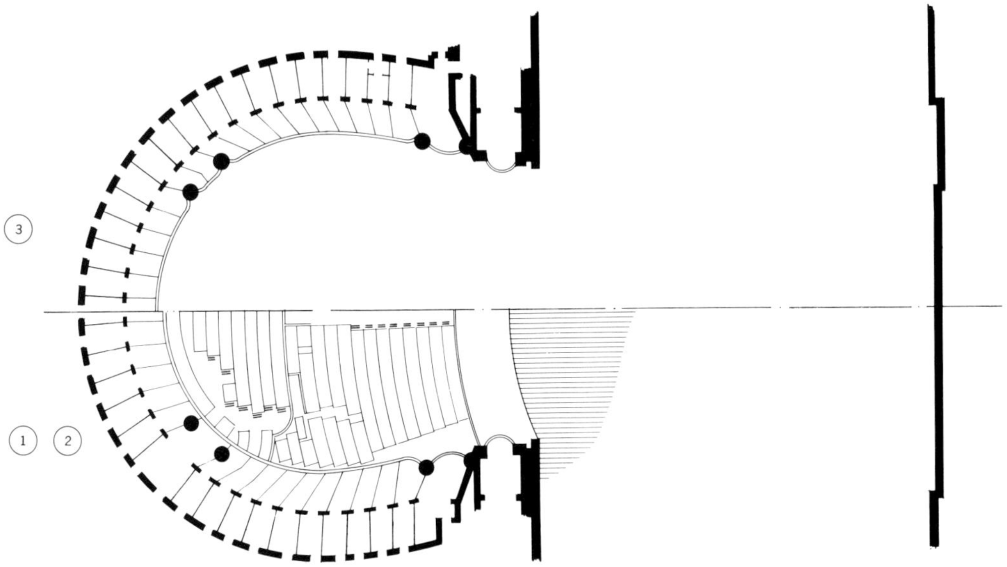

SEATING CAPACITY 2131

1	787
2	246
3	242
4	268
5	588 + stan

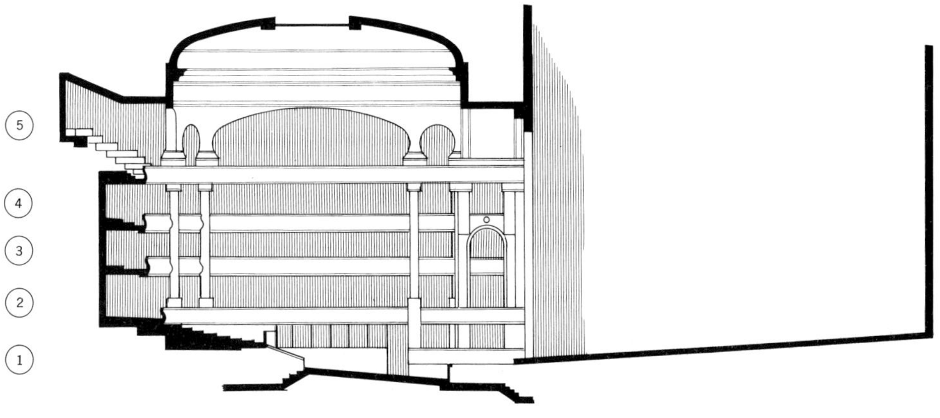

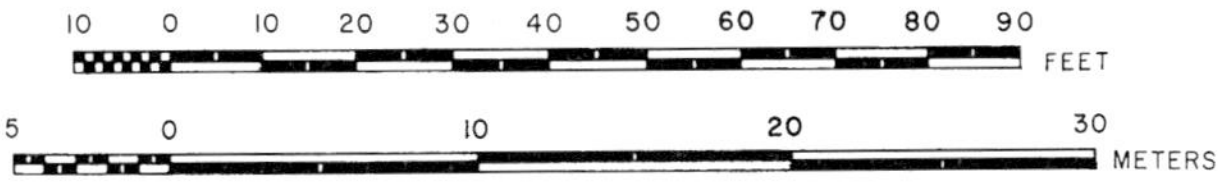

Architectural and structural details

Uses: opera and ballet. *Ceiling:* dome is 0.10 in. (2.5 mm) steel; above the top level (amphitheater) the ceiling is plaster; ceilings of the boxes are stretched damask cloth 1 in. away from the plaster. *Walls:* all visible surfaces (faces of the rings, columns, capitals, and so forth) are plaster; the dividers between boxes are 0.5 in. (1.25 cm) wood covered with damask; inside and top of the balcony railing are covered with plush; rear of boxes are separated from cloak room by velour curtains; walls at the rear of the amphitheater are of plaster. The front of the rail dividing the main floor is of wood; rear is lined with carpet. *Floors:* wood throughout the house. *Carpets:* main floor and all boxes fully carpeted; no carpet in amphitheater. Note: cyclorama on stage is of aluminum with canvas facing. *Orchestra pit:* floor is of wood over airspace; side walls are of solid wood. *Stage height:* 26 in. (66 cm) above floor level at first row of seats. *Seating:* main floor seats are fully upholstered on all surfaces except for wood trim; boxes have upholstered chairs; in amphitheater the seat-bottoms are fully upholstered, backrests are of open wood.

Architect: Charles Garnier. *References:* plans, details, and photographs courtesy of the management of the Opéra Garnier.

*Technical details**

Opera

V = 352,000 ft^3 (10,000 m^3)	S_a = 9,700 ft^2 (900 m^2)	S_A = 12,120 ft^2 (1,126 m^2)
S_o (pit) = 840 ft^2 (78 m^2)	S_P = 2,632 ft^2 (244 m^2)	S_T = 15,600 ft^2 (1,448 m^2)
N = 2,131	N_T = 2,231	H = 68 ft (20.7 m)
W = 62 ft (18.9 m)	L = 91 ft (27.7 m)	D = 106 ft (32.3 m)
V/S_T = 22.7 ft (6.9 m)	V/S_A = 29 ft (8.87 m)	V/N = 165 ft^3 (4.68 m^3)
S_A/N = 5.75 ft^2 (0.53 m^2)	H/W = 1.1	L/W = 1.47
t_I = 17 msec		

**The terminology is explained in Appendix 1.*

France

36

Paris
Salle Pléyel

Salle Pléyel, Paris' principal concert hall, was finished in 1927. The architect believed that once-reflected sound largely sets acoustical quality. But, the parabolic shape that he chose primarily reflected sound to the rear of the hall, although he tilted the side walls inward slightly to bring some sound to the audience areas. No attention was paid to reverberation time. A fire in 1928 did major damage. The redesign seemed influenced by the American consultant, F. R. Watson, who published, "Design the auditorium so that for listening the sound will be comparable to outdoor conditions." Upholstered seats were installed and sound absorbing materials were applied to all surfaces surrounding the balconies. The entire floor was carpeted. Some changes were made in 1981, mainly stage extension, the addition of stage ceiling reflectors, more stage ventilation, and removal of considerable sound absorbing material.

In 1994, extensive changes were made to increase the energy in the lateral sound reflections and to distribute them more evenly over the floor by the use of large MLS sound-diffusing reflectors spaced out from the side walls. Changes were made in the stage ceiling to improve communication among the musicians. The balcony fronts were made more irregular and small amount of sound absorbing material was added to the rear wall above the second balcony to reduce echoes heard primarily on stage. These changes are on the accompanying drawings, but not in the main-hall photographs. In 1996, changes are planned to increase the reverberation times.

The hall seats 2,386 and the unoccupied reverberation time at mid-frequencies is 2.0 sec. Fully occupied it is 1.6 sec, below the optimum of about 1.9 sec. Except for 860 ft^2 (80 m^2) near the proscenium of the stage, the ceiling is covered with a hanging array of wooden strips, 2 in. (5 cm) wide separated by 3 inches of space and located about 6.5 ft (2 m) (average) below the hard ceiling. Orchestral balance is adjusted by mechanical platforms, adjustable ceiling reflectors and tilting back-stage prismatic reflectors.

Paris music critics, in 1994, have generally stated that the string sound is clearer and the orchestral balance is better; the woodwinds are softened and clearer; and, overall, the orchestral tone is richer and less "frontal."

Paris, Salle Pléyel

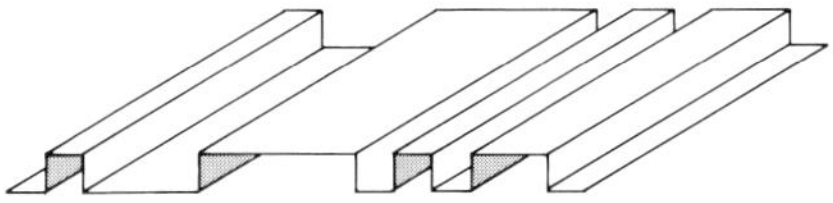

reflector, diffuser panel

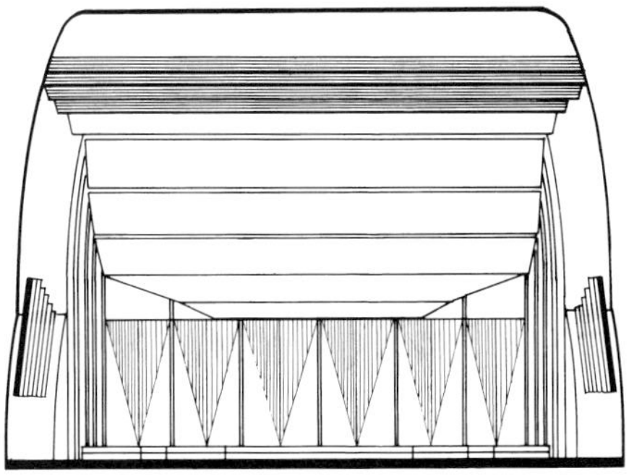

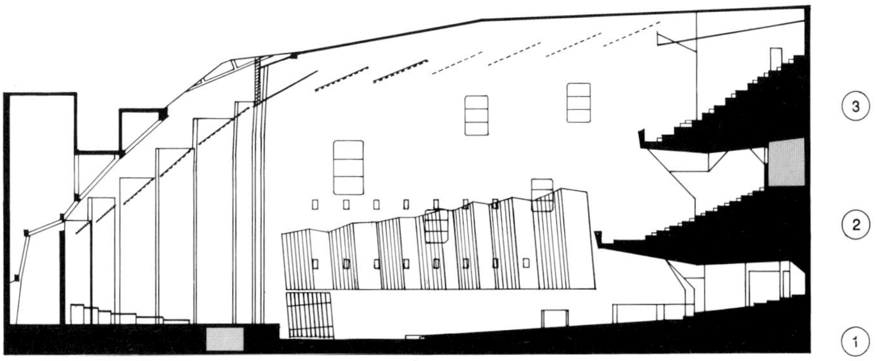

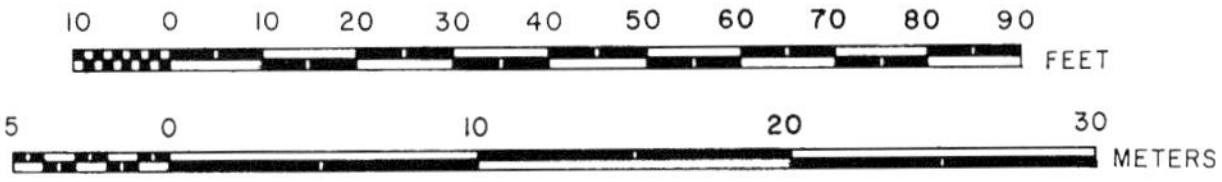

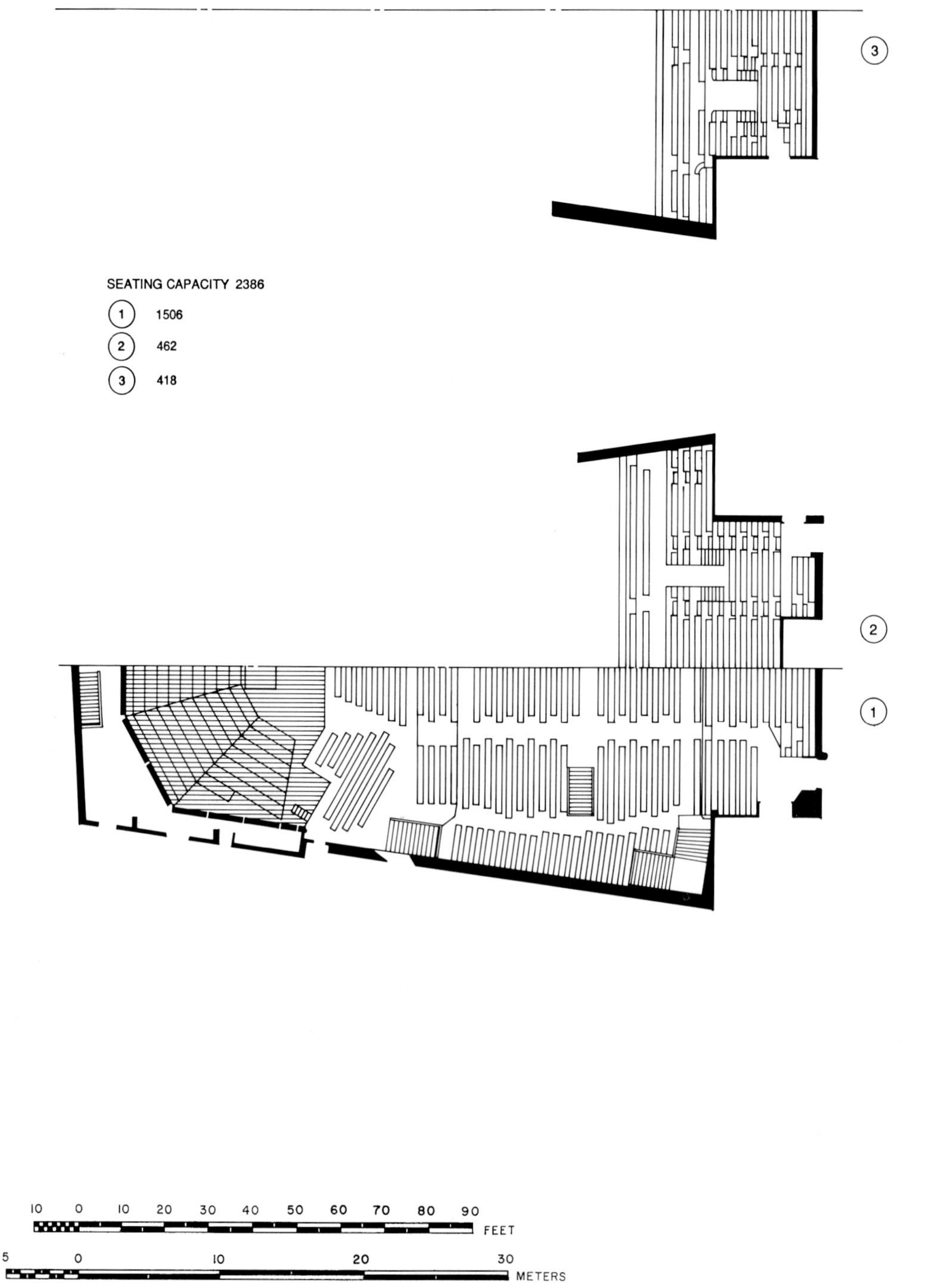
3
SEATING CAPACITY 2386
1 1506
2 462
3 418
2
1
10 0 10 20 30 40 50 60 70 80 90 FEET
5 0 10 20 30 METERS

Architectural and structural details

Uses: music and recitals, 80%; speech and others, 20%. *Ceiling:* brick, lightly plastered, beneath which, except for 860 ft² (80 m²) at the front, is hung a saw-tooth wooden-slat structure, each slat 2 in. (5 cm) wide, spaced 3 in. (7.5 cm) apart. *Walls:* sidewalls are heavy brick, plastered and painted to which are attached wide-band MLS acoustic diffusers, 13 to 16 ft (4 to 5 m) high, tilted at the same angle as the sidewalls; 50% of rear walls and walls under the balconies are light-weight gypsum boards with air spaces of variable thickness. *Floors:* wooden, including balconies. *Stage enclosure:* movable wooden panels, varnished, 1 in.(2.5 cm) thick. Panels forming the stage back wall are large and prism shaped (see the photograph). The curtain shown on the drawing at the top of the proscenium can be lowered, but generally is not. *Stage height:* 3 ft (1 m). *Sound absorbing materials:* some above rear of orchestra; also above second balcony on rear wall there is a wooden panel with 2 in. (5 cm) foam in front; gypsum panels on the rear walls below the two balconies absorb low frequencies. *Seating:* molded wooden seat back, upholstered front of seat back and top of seat-bottom with porous velour; underseat, unperforated wood.

Original architect and engineer: Gustave Lyon. *Renovation architect, 1994:* M. De Portzampare. *Acoustical consultant, 1994:* Albert Yaying Xu. *Photographs:* Paul Maurer.

*Technical details**

V = 547,000 ft³ (15,500 m³)	S_a = 8,396 ft² (780 m²)	S_A = 11,390 ft² (1,058 m²)
S_o = 2,605 ft² (242 m²)	S_T = 13,995 ft² (1,300 m²)	N = 2,386
H = 61 ft (18.6 m)	W = 84 ft (25.6 m)	L = 100 ft (30.5 m)
D = 120 ft (36.6 m)	V/S_T = 39.1 ft (11.9 m)	V/S_A = 48 ft (14.6 m)
V/N = 229 ft³ (6.5 m³)	S_A/N = 4.77 ft² (0.44 m²)	H/W = 0.73
L/W = 1.19	t_I = 35 msec	

**The terminology is explained in Appendix 1.*

Germany

37

Bayreuth Festspielhaus

The Festspielhaus in Bayreuth is probably the world's most unusual opera house. Its design is unique; it was conceived by the composer Richard Wagner to satisfy his own image of how an opera house should look and sound; and it responds well only to the music of its master and best to *Der Ring Des Nibelungen* and *Parsifal.*

In 1876, Wagner's dream of a building for his operas solidified into reality. Not only does the sunken pit (shown in the drawings) project under the stage, but the conductor and the strings are under a solid wooden cover. Their music radiates outward from a slot over the middle of the orchestra which extends from one end of the pit to the other. The whole orchestra is out of sight and the musicians can play, unseen, in their shirtsleeves!

The seating area of the audience is fan-shaped, but the side walls of the theater are parallel. To fill in the progressively wider space between the walls and the seats toward the front of the hall, a series of seven piers is employed, each one penetrating deeper into the hall than the one behind it and each capped by a column that extends to capitals just beneath the ceiling. Although the ceiling is flat (I walked on it), one has the impression that it rises from the back toward the front, like a great awning stretched over a Greek amphitheater.

The average height of the ceiling above the sloping floor of the Festspielhaus is great, with the result that the reverberation time is long. It is 1.55 sec at middle frequencies when the theater is fully occupied, which is especially favorable to Romantic Wagnerian music.

The sunken-pit design is the center of endless controversy. One purpose of the sunken pit is to give greater balance between the singers and the orchestra. But this was not the only feature Wagner had in mind. He desired the unusual and dramatic effect of a "mystical abyss." He expected to create acoustically a mysterious sound, emanating from an invisible orchestra, with a modified, somewhat uncanny timbre. One can easily conclude that the overriding purpose of the Bayreuth pit was to emphasize the drama, rather than to preserve the vocal-orchestral balance.

Most conductors love to perform in the Bayreuth pit. Every note can be heard at the podium. The orchestra can "let out the throttle" and not drown out the singers.

They feel that, because the blending of the sound takes place in the pit, it merges in the form intended by the composer.

Joseph Wechsberg's description of his experience in the August 18, 1956, issue of *The New Yorker* is the most colorful I have read:

> Then there was silence, and out of the darkness came a sustained E flat—so low that I couldn't distinguish exactly when the silence ended and sound began. Nor could I be sure where the sound came from; it might have come from the sides of the auditorium, or the rear, or the ceiling. It was just there. Slowly the orchestra began to play melodic passages, barely audible at first and gradually increasing in volume until the auditorium was filled with music—the music of the water of the Rhine. When the curtain parted, the whole stage seemed filled with water—blue-green waves, ebbing and flowing in precise synchronization with the music. The Rhine Maidens appeared from behind a rock, pretty, slim and wearing golden one-piece bathing suits, the music rose and fell back to the pianissimo; and Woglinde started her "Weia! Waga!" It took me a moment to realize that there were no props and no stage set; the whole scene—rock and all—were created by means of projected film and light. The music, the singing, the waters, and the lights blended perfectly. Although the brass dominated, it did not sound brassy, as it often does in the large orchestra Wagner calls for. By accident or design, the strings, particularly the first violins, were somewhat subdued....I was under a spell....

Some conductors have suggested that the cover over the violins be removed. Herbert von Karajan told me that he tried this experiment. He removed the cover, but he found that, with the rest of the orchestra buried beneath the stage the result was not satisfactory and the cover was replaced. At another time a perforated hood was tried. It was said to have given good results, but when objections were raised by one of the conductors, the old hood was re-installed.

In some productions, almost no teaser curtains are used and there is a minimum of hanging scenery. Also, a heavy, sound-reflecting cyclorama canvas ordinarily surrounds the acting area. As a result, the stage-house reverberation can be long; although the singers' voices project well into the house when the full undraped height of the proscenium is employed. The stage is lower than the audience, and thus the forestage is important as a sound reflector.

The interior finish is largely of plaster, either on brick or on wood lath. The ceiling combines wood and plaster. The horizontal ceiling contributes short-time-delay reflections at most seats. The projecting wings on the sides of the hall give a desirable mixing of the sound in the house. The Festspielhaus is small—it seats only 1,800 persons—and thus its size alone favors its acoustical quality.

Bayreuth, Festspielhaus

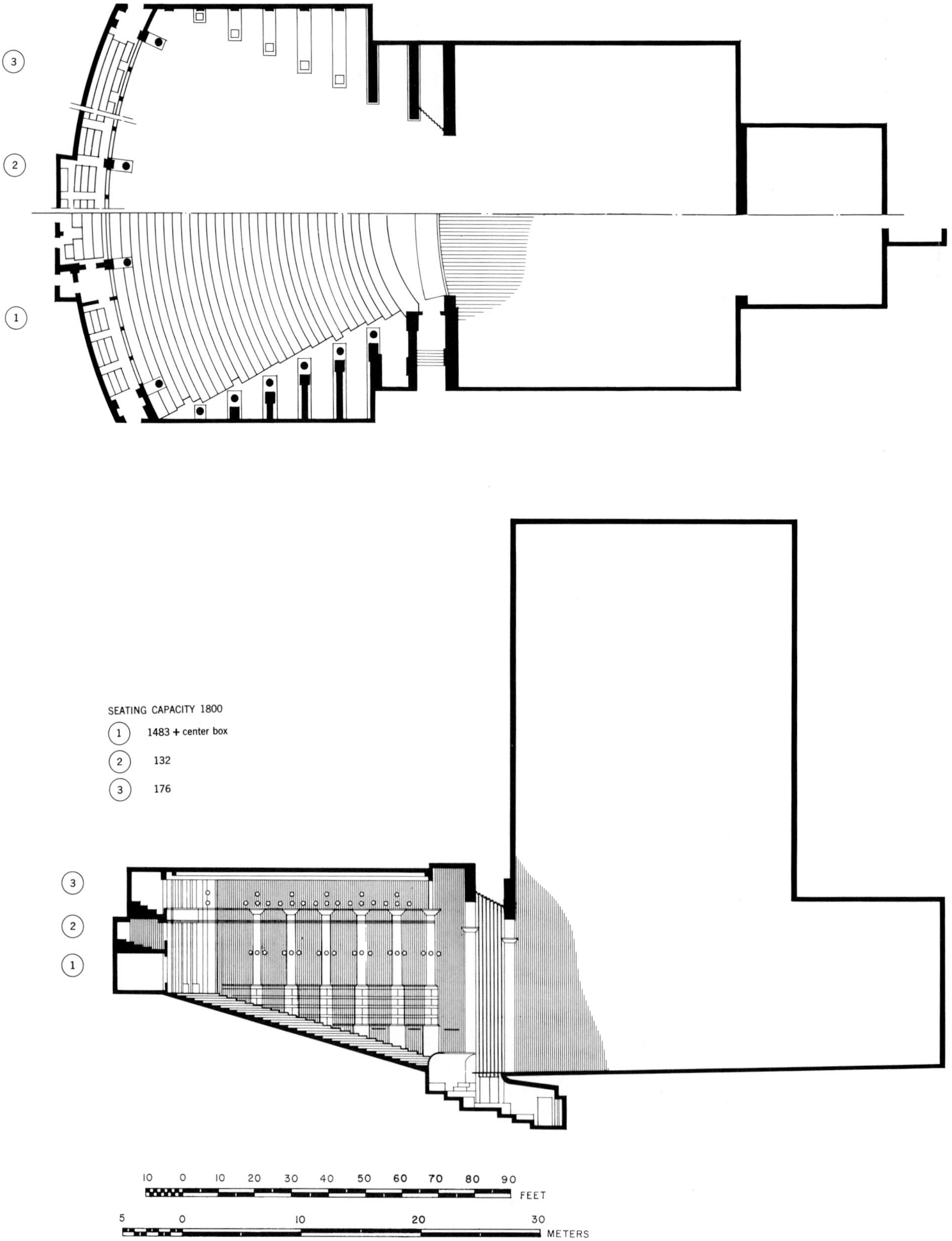
3
2
1
SEATING CAPACITY 1800
1 1483 + center box
2 132
3 176
3
2
1
10 0 10 20 30 40 50 60 70 80 90 FEET
5 0 10 20 30 METERS

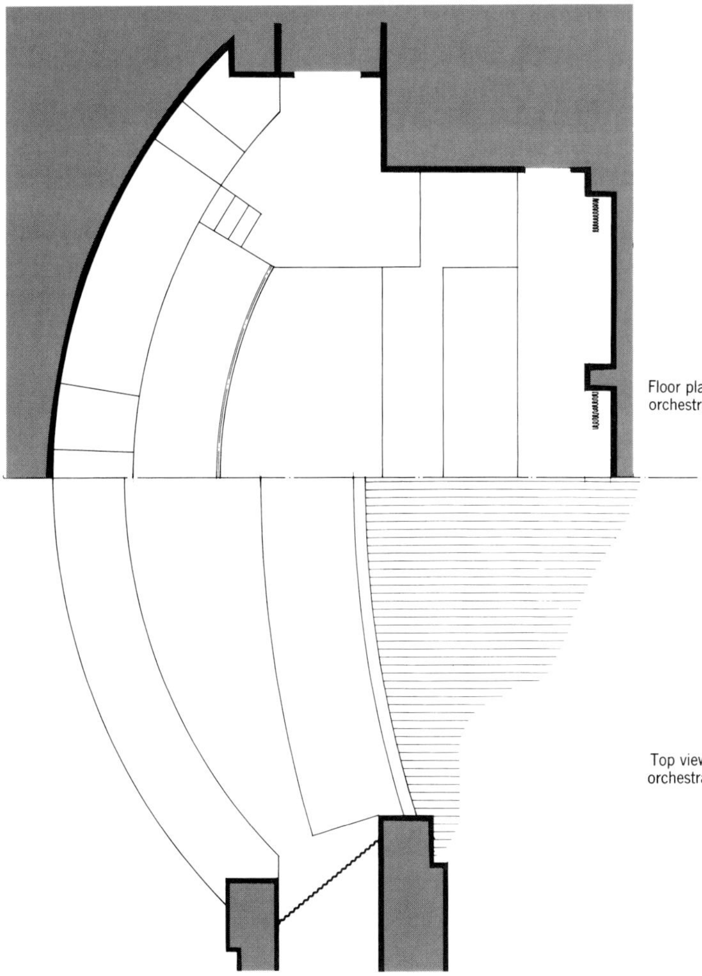

Floor plan of orchestra pit

Top view of orchestra pit

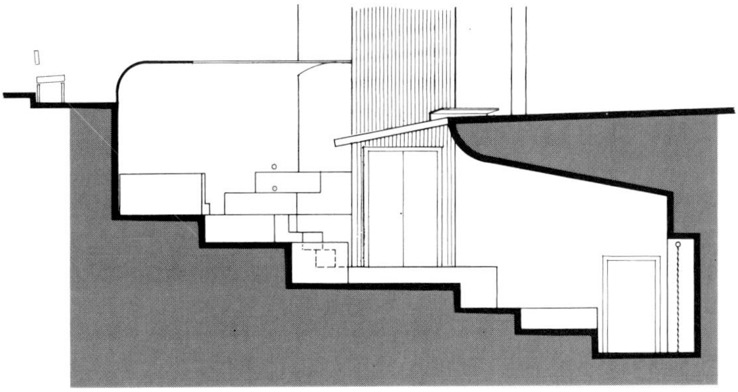

Cross section

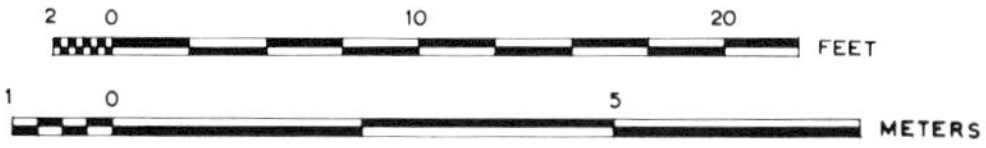

Architectural and structural details

Uses: Wagner opera. *Ceiling:* 0.5 in. (1.25 cm) plaster on reeds over 0.5 in. wood; wooden carvings used as decorations. *Rear and side walls:* plaster on brick or wood lath; the round columns and part of their capitals are of thick wood; the wing nearest the stage is closed off with corrugated asbestos sheet. *Seating:* seats wood with cane bottoms.

Architect: Otto Brueckwald. *Credits:* drawings from Edwin O. Sachs, Modern Opera Houses and Theatres, Vol I., London, B. T. Batsford, 1896–1897. Seating count from a box-office plan and other details, courtesy of Secretary. *Photographs:* Lauterwasser, Uberlingen/Bodensee. *Other:* pit drawings were developed from measurements by the author during the visit.

*Technical details**

V = 364,000 ft³ (10,308 m³)	S_a = 8,125 ft² (755 m²)	S_A = 9,100 ft² (845 m²)
S_o (pit) = 371 ft² (34.5 m²)	S_P = 1,640 ft² (152 m²)	S_T = 11,111 ft² (1,032 m²)
N = 1,800	V/S_T = 32.8 ft (10 m)	V/S_A = 40 ft (12.2 m)
V/N = 202 ft³ (5.72 m³)	S_A/N = 5.1 ft² (0.47 m²)	H = 42 ft (12.8 m)
W = 109 ft (33.2 m)	L = 106 ft (32.3 m)	D = 111 ft (33.8 m)
H/W = 0.385	L/W = 0.97	t_I = 14 msec

**The terminology is explained in Appendix 1.*

38

Berlin

Kammermusiksaal der Philharmonie

The Kammermusiksaal follows the concept of "Music in the Center" that was the design premise of the neighboring Philharmonie Konzertsaal. Seating about 1,138, it was completed in 1987 and embodies features consistent with the new multi-media age. The reverberation time is about 1.8 sec at mid-frequencies, occupied. The stage in the center of the hall is surrounded by two tiers of circular seating areas. The lower tier, seating 419 listeners, plus 40 on stage, is symmetrical and to that audience it constitutes an intimate hall suited to the traditional musical repertoire of soloists or groups up to the size of a chamber orchestra. The side walls around the stage are tilted to provide cross reflections that help the performers hear each other. The parapet surrounding the first tier was made larger than normal to attain greater strength of early lateral sound reflections for the audience. Above the stage at a height of about 30 ft (9 m) hang nine multi-sided sound reflectors in a circular arrangement, that provide early reflections to the players and to those seated in the lower tier.

The upper tier with 619 seats is asymmetrical and the architect describes the relation of the symmetry to asymmetry in the design of the room as corresponding to a dialog between the traditional and the future. The convex, tent-shaped ceiling provides early reflections to the listeners in the upper tier. Again, sound diffusion is provided by 95 pyramidal diffusing elements in the ceiling which do not also serve, as in the main hall, as sound-absorbing resonators. All walls are shaped to diffuse sound and are positioned to prevent echoes.

Three elevated sections, containing 101 seats can be used for special musical presentations, such as required by the music of Giovanni Gabrieli and Claudio Monteverdi, or by modern works. Special rooms, with operable windows, are provided around the periphery for multi-media and broadcasting controls.

Loudspeakers are located in the center and around the edges of the convex tent ceiling and at various places outdoors, thus permitting unusual sound effects associated with such music as that of composer Luigi Nono.

Berlin, Kammermusiksaal der Philaharmonie

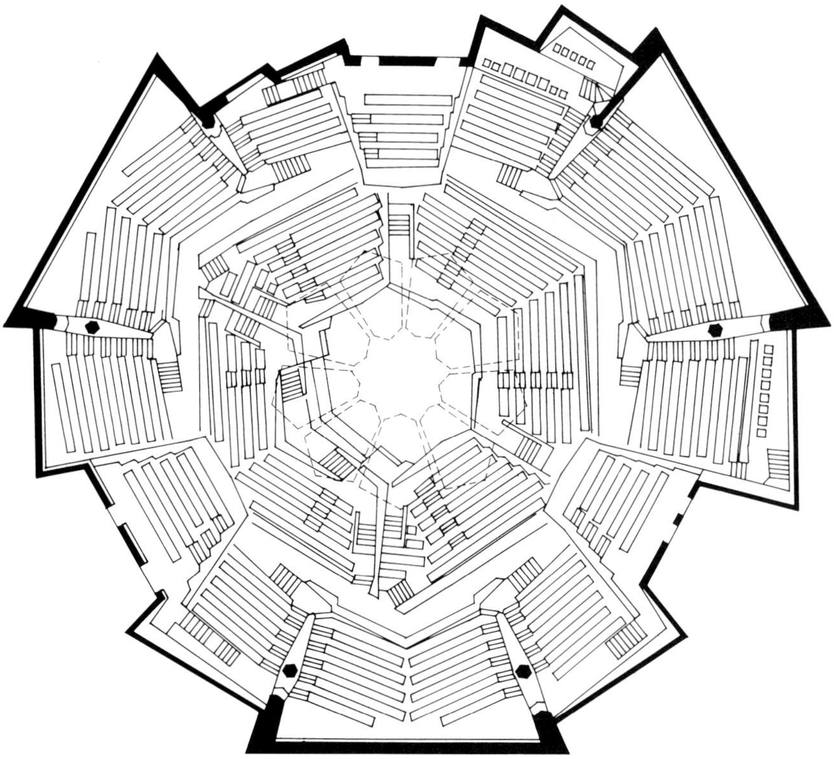

SEATING CAPACITY 1138

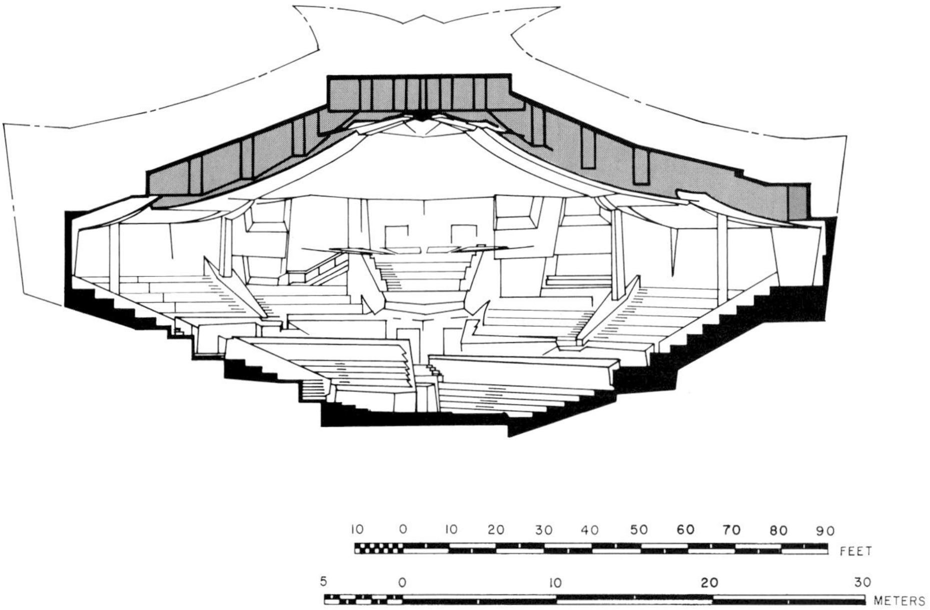

Architectural and structural details

Uses: chamber groups, soloists, and dance. *Ceiling:* three layers—the roof, an intermediate plate and the actual ceiling, which is 1.2 in. (3 cm) plaster on metal lath. *Suspended over-stage panels:* 9 multi-sided polyester panels, each about 90 ft^2 (8.4 m^2) in area, with equal airspace between and variable in height, 26–40 ft (8–12 m) above the stage. *Sound diffusing units:* 95 pyramidal-shaped, sound-diffusing units are located in the ceiling. *Side walls:* part of side walls are thin wood over airspace to control low-frequency reverberation. The parapets are faced with Jurassic limestone plaster. *Stage floor:* wooden floor on planks over airspace. *Audience floor:* oak parquet cemented to precast slabs which cover the air-handling plenum. *Seating:* seatback, molded veneered plywood, the upper part bent vertical so that maximum sound reflection occurs when occupied; cushion on front of seat back does not extend to top; seat-bottom is upholstered on top and the underside is covered with cloth only and is perforated; armrests are upholstered.

Architect: Edgar Wisniewski. *Acoustical consultant:* Lothar Cremer with Thomas Fuetterer. *Photographs:* courtesy of the architect and M. Barron. *References:* E. Wisniewski, *Die Berliner Philharmonie und ihr Kammermusiksaal Der Konzertsaal als Zentralraum*, Gebr. Mann Verlag (1993).

*Technical details**

V = 388,400 ft^3 (11,000 m^3)	S_a = 6,650 ft^2 (618 m^2)	S_A = 8,720 ft^2 (810 m^2)
S_o = 840 ft^2 (78.2 m^2)	S_C = 204 ft^2 (19 m^2)	S_T = 9,764 ft^2 (907 m^2)
N = 1,138	H = 37 ft (11.3 m)	W = 159 ft (48.5 m)
L = 60 ft (18.3 m)	D = 62 ft (18.9 m)	V/S_T = 39.8 ft (12.1 m)
V/S_A = 44.5 ft (13.6 m)	V/N = 341 ft^3 (9.66 m^3)	S_A/N = 7.7 ft^2 (0.71 m^2)
H/W = 0.23	L/W = 0.38	t_I = 20 msec

* *The terminology is explained in Appendix 1.*

39

Berlin

Konzerthaus Berlin (formerly, Schauspielhaus)

The old Schauspielhaus, opened in 1821, was totally destroyed in World War II. Restored to the original design of architect Karl Friedrich Schinkel and recently renamed Konzerthaus Berlin, it takes its place among the most architecturally distinguished halls in the world. Every detail inside, the gorgeous parquetry floor, the pictorial coffered ceiling, the white walls with illuminated sculptures, the balcony fronts with gold ornamentation, the stainless steel organ pipes, and the crystal chandeliers presage an extraordinary experience.

The hall, including the choir rows, seats between 1,507 and 1,677, depending on the size of stage. Sound diffusing surfaces are everywhere. To promote clarity-enhancing early reflections to the audience, the side walls of the stage were made as high as possible. To enable the players to hear each other better, the upper part of the wall, beneath the balustrade and molding around the stage are tilted inward.

The reverberation time, with audience, is now 2.0 sec at mid-frequencies, rising to 2.2 sec at low frequencies. Although, before opening, only about 20% of a judgment group thought the reverberation too large, afterwards there were reservations. The reverberation then, to many, was overwhelming, the time rising to 2.7 sec at low frequencies. Corrective steps took the form of a large number of sound absorbing resonators placed in the ceiling and tuned to reduce the low frequency reverberation. Even now, for a hall this size, the optimum reverberation time at all frequencies is usually considered to be 0.1 to 0.2 sec lower.

Seated on the main floor, the listener is immersed in the reverberant sound from all directions. Although there are no special surfaces directing the early sound reflections onto the audience, the ratio of early reflected sound energy to later reverberant energy is about the same, i.e., the same clarity, as in other rectangular halls (e.g., Vienna and Boston). The tonal and loudness balances among instruments are excellent. The hall is loud both because of its smaller size (about 60% of the number of seats that are in the Boston hall) and the high reverberation times. For music of the Classical and Romantic periods the acoustics equal the best in the world.

Berlin, Konzerthaus Berlin (formerly, Schauspielhaus)

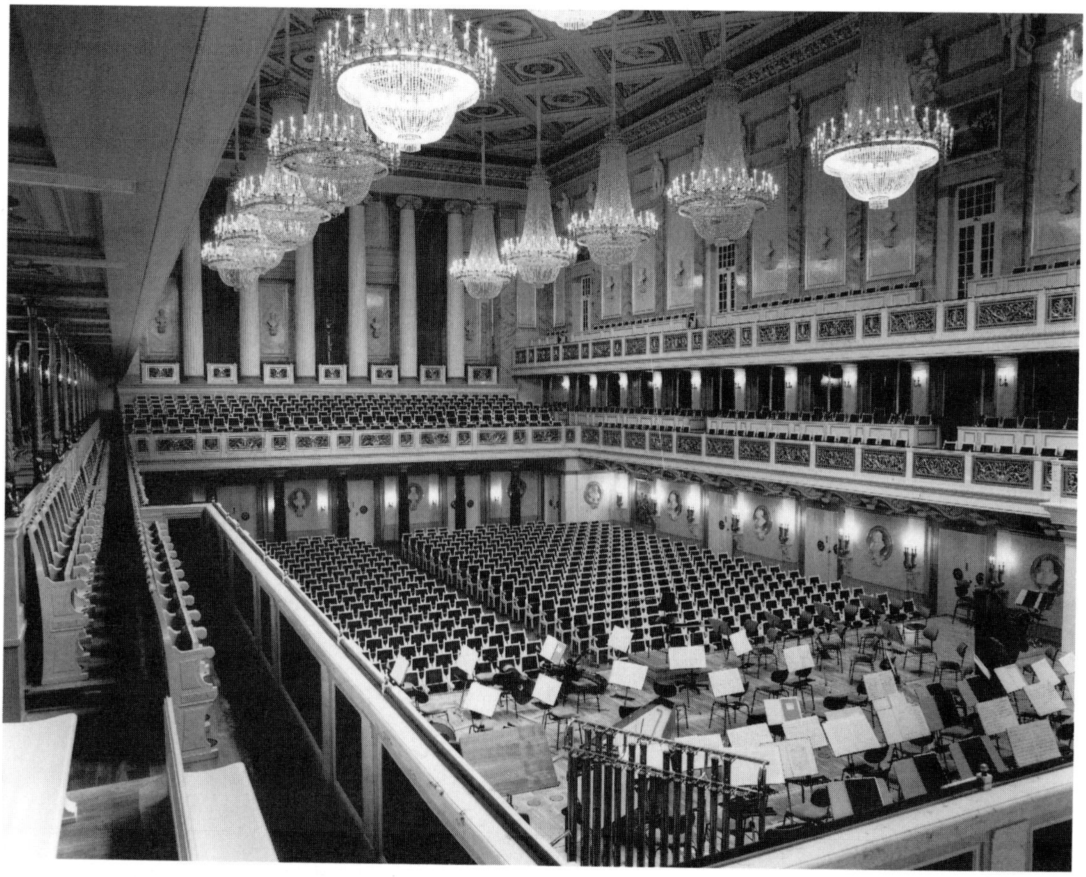

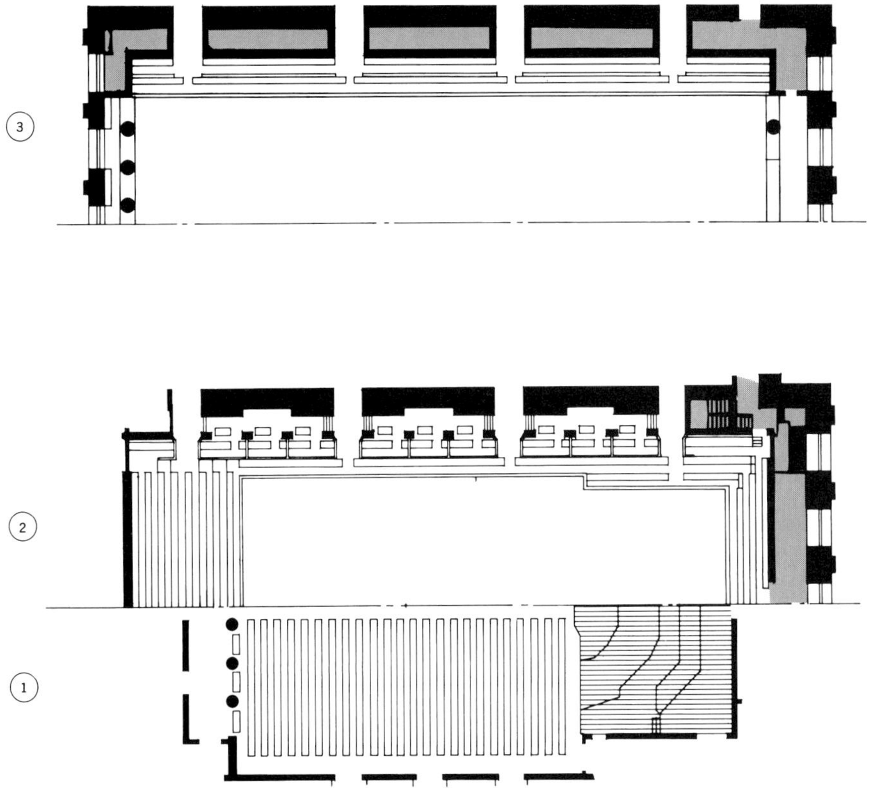

SEATING CAPACITY WITH CHOIR:

NORMAL ORCHESTRA, 22 ROWS, 1575
LARGE ORCHESTRA, 20 ROWS, 1507
SMALL ORCHESTRA, 25 ROWS, 1677

(1) 768 + CHOIR 116
(2) 481
(3) 210

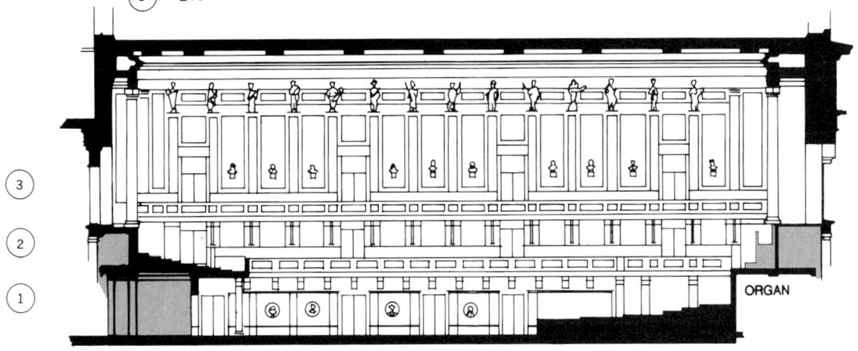

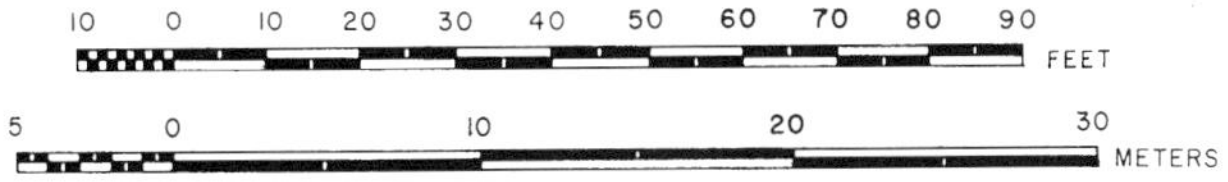

Architectural and structural details

Uses: classical music. *Ceiling:* plaster. *Walls:* plaster over concrete block; balcony faces, plaster. *Resonators:* Helmholtz type resonators, tuned from 130 Hz to 300 Hz. installed in the ceiling at the slot just above the upper side wall molding. *Floors:* parquet on concrete. *Stage enclosure:* side walls, plaster; no overhead reflectors. *Stage floor:* tongue-and-groove wood over timber 3 in. (8 cm) thick; risers adding 51 to 59 in. (1.3 to 1.5 m). *Stage height:* variable from 31 in. (0.8 m) to 95 in. (2.5 m) above floor level. *Seating:* wood chairs, upholstered seat-bottom and lightly upholstered backrest.

Architect: Architekten-kollektivs: Prasser. *Acoustical consultants:* Wolfgang Fasold, Ulrich Lehmann, Hans-Peter Tennhardt, Helgo Winkler. *References:* W. Fasold, U. Lehmann, H. Tennhardt and H. Winkler, "Akustische Massnahmen im Schauspielhaus, Berlin," Bauforschung, Baupraxis, Vol. **181**, 20 pages (1986). W. Fasold and U. Stephenson, "Gute Akustik von Auditorien, Planung Mittels Rechnersimulation und Modellmesstechnik," Bauphysik, **15**, 20–49 (1993). L. Beranek, "Concert Hall Acoustics—1992," J. Acoust. Soc. Am. **92**, 1–39 (1992). *Photographs:* Jens Huebner.

*Technical details**

V = 530,000 ft^3 (15,000 m^3)	S_a = 8,440 ft^2 (784 m^2)	S_A = 10,150 ft^2 (943 m^2)
S_o = 1,700 ft^2 (158 m^2)	S_T = 11,850 ft^2 (1,101 m^2)	N = 1,575
H = 58 ft (17.7 m)	W = 68 ft (20.7 m)	L = 79 ft (24.1 m)
D = 84 ft (25.6 m)	V/S_T = 44.7 ft (13.6 m)	V/S_A = 52.2 ft (15.9 m)
V/N = 336 ft^3 (9.53 m^3)	S_A/N = 6.4 ft^2 (0.60 m^2)	H/W = 0.85
L/W = 1.16	t_I = 25 msec	

**The terminology is explained in Appendix 1.*

40

Berlin

Berlin Philharmonie

"Music in the Center" was the overriding postulate of architect Hans Scharoun. He felt that the normal placement of the orchestra at one end of a hall prevents audience and musicians from communicating freely and intensely. The result is a most dramatic room, dedicated in 1963, with 250 of the 2,215 seats directly behind the orchestra and about 300 on either side. In addition, there are about 120 places on stage and spaces for 44 handicaps. No listener is more than 100 ft (30 m) away from the stage, compared to 133 ft in Boston Symphony Hall (seating 2,612).

Philharmonie Hall has become one of the models of successful acoustical designs, pioneering the concept of the "vineyard" style hall. The acoustical consultant agreed on the advantage of breaking the audience into blocks, so that the first row in each block receives unimpeded direct sound. The seats in many of the blocks receive early lateral reflections from the side walls that surround them, including the wall behind. The fronts of the terraced blocks provide early reflections for both the musicians and the audience seated in the middle of the hall. Additional early reflections are provided to the orchestra and audience by ten large suspended panels hung above the stage. The seats in the upper blocks receive additional early reflections from the convex, tent-shaped ceiling.

In the audience sections in front of the orchestra, the sound is beautiful, clear, balanced, and with a liveness that completely surrounds one. The principal disadvantage is that those seated to the rear, or near rear, of the stage hear a different sound: the trumpets and trombones radiate forward, and the French horns backward. Troubling is the sound from piano and singers, a large part of whose upper registers are projected forward. Fortunately, the visual impression of viewing the conductor face-on favorably shapes one's judgment of the acoustics. The mid-frequency reverberation time, fully occupied, is 1.9 sec. Extraordinary attention was paid to absorption of the lower frequencies "to balance," said the acoustical consultant, "the absorption of the high frequencies by clothing and upholstered seats." This was a little overdone. The bass is controllable by adjusting the 136 pyramid-shaped low-frequency resonators in the ceiling.

Berlin, Berlin Philharmonie

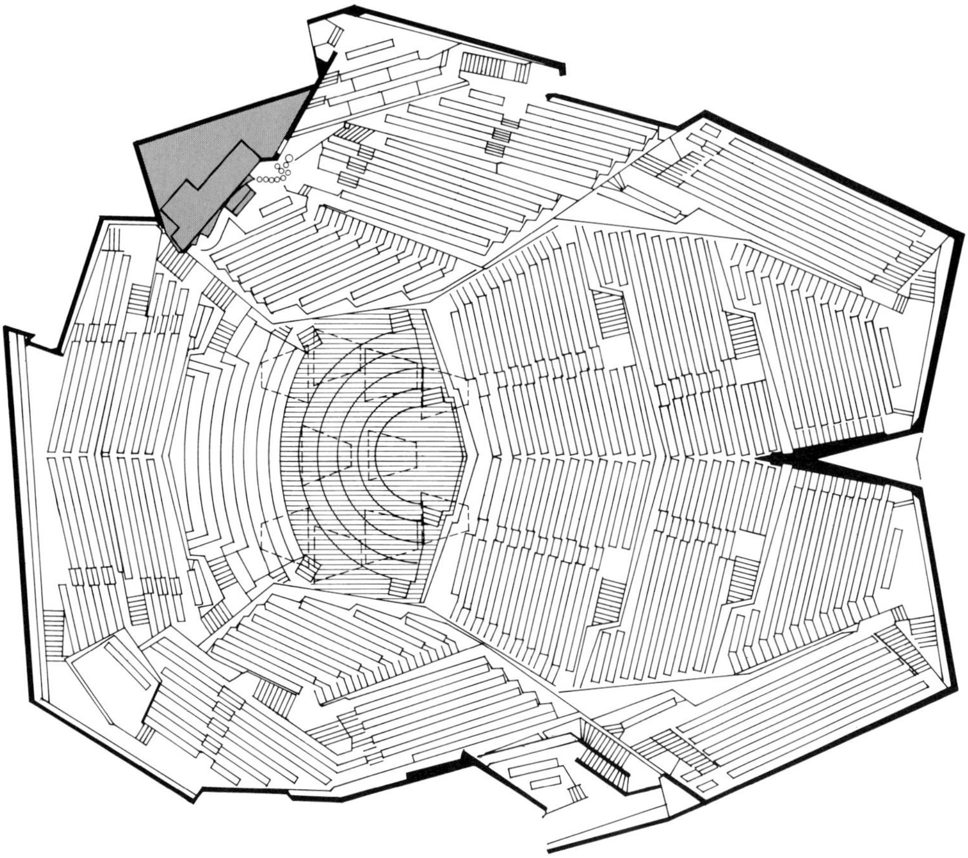

SEATING CAPACITY 2218 + 120 chorus

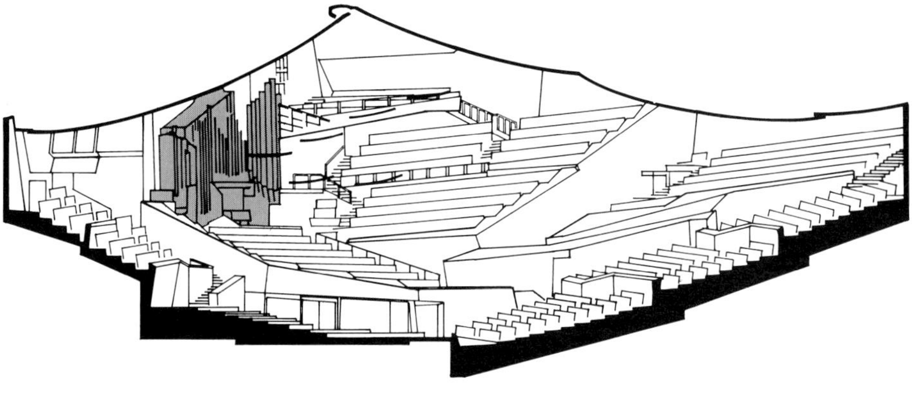

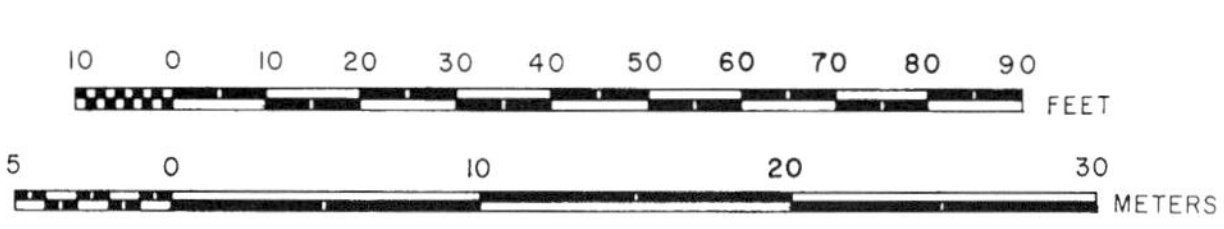

Architectural and structural details

Uses: concerts, primarily. *Ceiling:* three layers—roof, intermediate plate and actual ceiling (1.2 in., 3 cm, up to 4 cm at center) chalk-gypsum plaster on expanded metal, suspended by vibration-isolated metal rods from walkways. *Suspended stage panels:* 10 trapezoidal polyester panels, each 81 ft² (7.5 m²) in area, 50% open space between, variable in height 32–40 ft (10–12 m) above the stage. *Ceiling sound absorbing units:* 136 pyramidal-shaped, combination sound-diffusing, low-frequency Helmholtz-resonator type absorbing units are located there. *Side walls:* part of sidewalls are thin wood over airspace. The parapets are faced with Jurassic limestone plaster. *Stage side walls:* arranged to reflect sound back to the musicians. *Stage floor:* Wooden floor on planks over airspace. *Stage height:* 30 in. (76 cm). *Audience floor:* oak parquet in asphalt base over precast slabs which cover the air-handling plenum. *Seating:* seatback, molded veneered plywood, the upper part bent vertical (see the photograph) so that maximum sound reflection occurs when occupied; cushion on front of seatback does not extend to top; seat-bottom is upholstered on top and the underside is covered with cloth only and is perforated; armrests are wooden, not upholstered.

Architect: Hans Scharoun. *Acoustical consultant:* Lothar Cremer with Joachim Nutsch. *References:* L. Cremer, "Die raum- und bauakustischen Massnahmen beim Wiederaufbau der Berliner Philharmonie," Die Schalltechnik, 57, 1–11 (1964). R. S. Lanier, "Acoustics In-the-round at the Berlin Philharmonic," Architectural Forum, **120**, 99–105 (1964). E. Wisniewski, *Die Berliner Philharmonie und ihr Kammermusiksaal. Der Konzertsaal als Zentralraum,* Gebr. Mann Verlag (1993). Peter B. Jones, *Hans Scharoun*, Phaidon, London (1995). *Photographs:* Foto R. Friedrich.

*Technical details**

V = 741,300 ft³ (21,000 m³)	S_a = 11,380 ft² (1,057 m²)	S_A = 14,900 ft² (1,385 m²)
S_o = 1857 ft² (1,72.5 m²)	S_T = 16,765 ft² (1,558 m²)	N = 2,215 + 120 on stage
H = 42 ft (12.8 m)	W = 140 ft (42.7 m)	L = 95 ft (29 m)
D = 98 ft (30 m)	V/S_T = 42.2 ft (13.5 m)	V/S_A = 49.8 ft (15.2 m)
V/N = 317 ft³ (9 m³)	S_A/N = 6.72 ft² (0.62 m²)	H/W = 0.3
L/W = 0.68	t_I = 21 msec	

* *The terminology is explained in Appendix 1.*

41

Bonn
Beethovenhalle

The Beethovenhalle project in Bonn is one of the impressive cultural centers that have been built in Germany since World War II. Separated from the Rhine by a narrow mall on one side, and backed by ample parking space at the rear, the hall is well situated. Viewed from an airplane, its striped molded roof suggests a lively whale at play. Its lobbies are typical of contemporary architecture in Germany, a little aseptic but relieved by colorful murals. The Beethoven Halle opened in 1959 and after a 1983 fire was rebuilt identically.

The architecture of the interior takes the visitor by surprise. The main floor, which contains 1,030 seats, is flat, and the hall may be used for banquets, dances, or exhibitions. An asymmetrical balcony seats 377 listeners. On entering, one's eyes are immediately carried to the ceiling, which looks like a many-tufted yellow bedspread, held by an upward pull of gravity against a domed ceiling. From the ceiling down, the interior of the hall suggests the classic struggle between architecture and acoustics; the architect wants a majestic domed ceiling, and the acoustician, faced with the difficult acoustics usual to domes, must find a means of scattering the sound. The busy side walls also show the studied influence of acoustical considerations.

The 1,760 acoustical elements on the ceiling are designed not only to scatter the sound impinging on them but also to absorb sound in the region of 125 Hz. Low-frequency sound absorption is always debatable. Musicians and music critics express a preference for a rich, string bass—such as results from a room finished in heavy plaster. Yet the possible focusing of the dome, especially at the lower frequencies, had to be combated. The Beethoven Hall has a satisfactory bass response, although not as strong as before the fire.

The only change in the hall after the fire was the replacement of the upholstering on the seats with a thicker polyvinyl padding, which has reduced the reverberation time a small amount, particularly the bass.

Bonn, Beethovenhalle

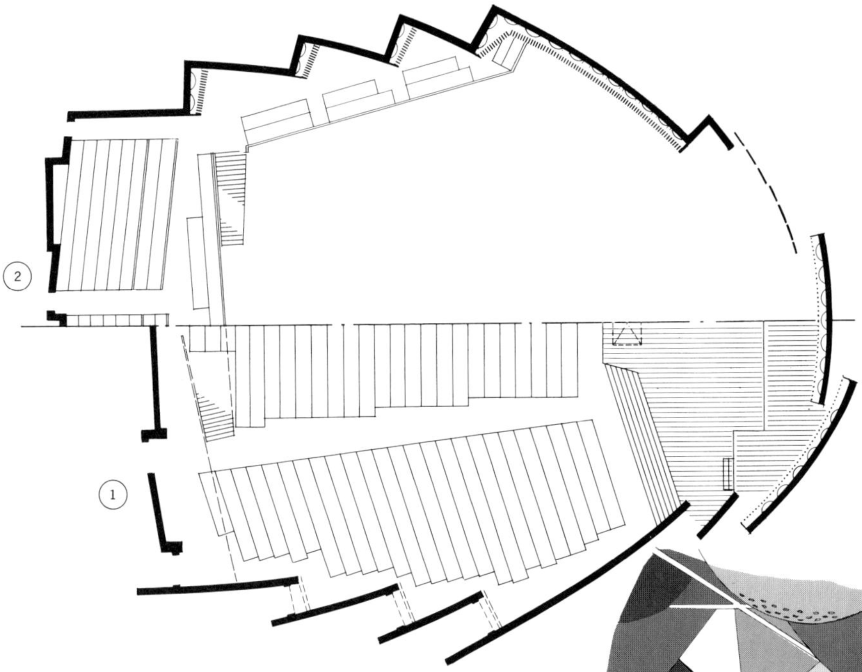

SEATING CAPACITY 1407

(1) 1030

(2) 377

Perspective ceiling detail
looking up

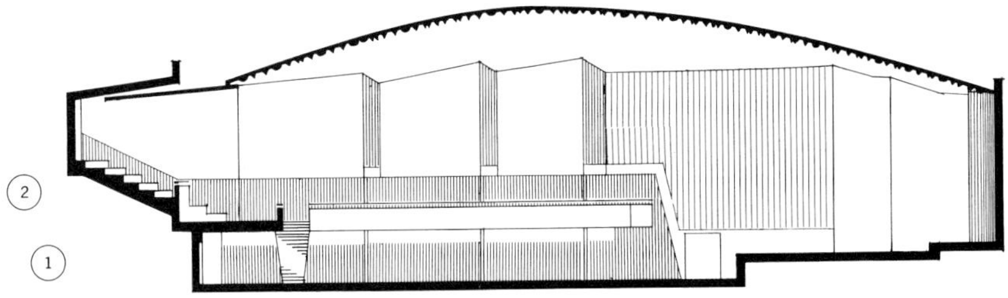

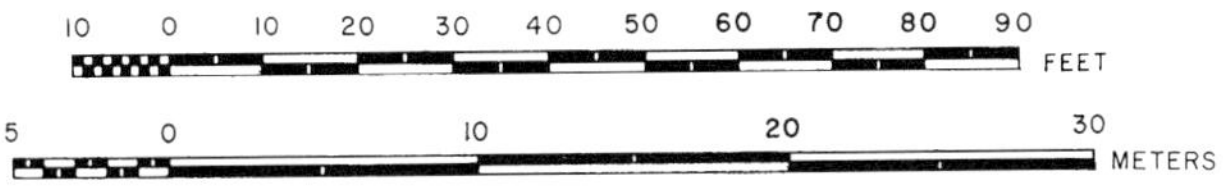

Architectural and structural details

Uses: concerts, meetings, and social events. *Ceiling:* beneath the concrete roof of the hall is hung a rhombic (egg crate) grid of 1 in. (2.5 cm) reinforced-gypsum sheets. Inside each unit a "sound scatterer" is placed, of one of three shapes, made from a gypsum-vermiculite mixture, 0.3 in. (0.8 cm) thick; each of these 1,760 scatters, with a height of 1 ft (30 cm) [the total area covered being 12,000 ft² (1,115 m²)], is either a double pyramid, a spherical segment, or a cylindrical segment obliquely cut on both sides with the curvature facing downward; to absorb low-frequency sound around 125 Hz, each spherical segment has on its low part 250 holes, 0.25 in. (0.6 cm), spaced about 1.2 in. (3 cm) apart; inside spherical segments is a 1 in. (2.5 cm) layer of rock wool; the ratio of spherical segments to double pyramids to cylindrical segments is 6:5:1. *Side walls:* the large area of wall on either side of the hall and the four small areas of wall facing the stage on either side above the balcony are built as follows: an acoustically transparent grid of vertical slats covers some vertically oriented cylindrical diffusers, each with a chord of 3 ft (1 m) separated from each other by 1 or 2 ft. Some damped resonators tuned to 250 Hz are located between each pair of the cylinders; the four sections of wall above the balcony on either side of the hall that face the audience are 0.75 in. (1.9 cm) wooden panels over air spaces that vary between 0.4 in. (1 cm) and 3.5 in. (9 cm) deep; behind half the panels there are 2 in. (5 cm) glass fiber blankets; the lower walls are of plaster. *Floor:* oak parquet. *Stage floor:* wood over airspace. *Stage height:* 43.5 in. (110 cm). *Seats:* the tops of the seat-bottoms and the fronts of the seat backs are thickly upholstered.

Architect: Siegfried Wolske. *Acoustical consultants:* Erwin Meyer and Heinrich Kuttruff. *Photographs:* courtesy of the architect. *Reference: Deutsche Bauzeitung,* **65**, 59–75 (February 1960). E. Meyer and H. Kuttruff, in a letter to the editor of *Acustica,* **9**, 465–468 (1959).

*Technical details**

Concert

V = 555,340 ft² (15,728 m²)	S_a = 9,300 ft² (864 m²)	S_A = 12,000 ft² (1,115 m²)
S_o = 2,200 ft² (204 m²)	S_T = 14,200 ft² (1,320 m²)	N = 1,407
H = 40 ft (12.2 m)	W = 120 ft (36.6 m)	L = 114 ft (34.8 m)
D = 125 ft (38.1 m)	V/S_T = 39.1 ft (11.9 m)	V/S_A = 46.3 ft (14.1 m)
V/N = 395 ft³ (11.2 m³)	S_A/N = 8.5 ft² (0.79 m²)	H/W = 0.33
L/W = 0.95	t_I = 27 msec	

The terminology is explained in Appendix 1.

42

Leipzig Gewandhaus

The predecessor to the Gewandhaus was the "Neues" Gewandhaus, completed in 1884 and destroyed in World War II. It was preceded by the "Altes" Gewandhaus which spanned the period from 1781 to 1894. Those older Gewandhauses were both famous, the 1781 one because of its excellent orchestra and small size (400 seats) and the "Neues" because of its great orchestra and famed acoustics (1,560 seats). Faced with the repute of those "shoebox"-type halls, the architect had courage to strike out in a contemporary direction.

Opened in 1981, the Gewandhaus is a striking building, located in the city center on the Augustus-Platz. At night the lights of the splendid foyer glisten and enliven the grand plaza. The concert hall's interior is dramatic in a very different sense than that of Berlin's Konzerthaus. The art that shows everywhere in the Konzerthaus is missing completely in the Gewandhaus. One is impressed instead by the white balcony fronts that contrast with the red upholstering, the assemblage of acoustical sound-diffusing boxes on the darkened side walls and the majestic pipe organ in the front of the hall. With the audience size of 1,900, the architect choose to make the hall fan/rhombic-shaped and to locate the platform about one-fourth of the room length from the front wall. The audience is seated on all sides of the stage. With this plan, the farthest auditor is only about 110 ft (33.5 m) from the front of the stage, compared to Boston Symphony Hall's 133 ft (40.5 m).

Much of the audience in a typical fan-shaped hall will receive too little early reflected sound energy unless special acoustical additions are made to the wall surfaces. An extreme example of such treatment are the very large sloping panels found in the Town Hall in Christchurch, New Zealand. In the Gewandhaus the solutions were to employ a large number of sound-reflecting tilted surfaces on the side walls (see the photograph and drawing) and to tilt the balcony fronts at various angles in the hall to direct early sound energy to the listeners. Around the stage the balcony fronts that form the upper wall are tilted inward to provide cross-reflections for the musicians which make ensemble playing easier. The shaped ceiling supplies early sound reflections to most of the audience in hall. The curved panels over the stage return early reflected sound energy to the musicians and to the audience sitting near the stage. The reverberation time is about 2.0 sec at mid-frequencies with full occupancy, and has almost the same value at all frequencies below 1,400 Hz. The low frequency absorption that reduces the reverberation time somewhat more than expected may be caused by the large number of openings in the ceiling for air conditioning, lights, loudspeakers, and lines. Also, the heavily upholstered seats absorb low frequencies.

With full audience, this listener was surprised to sense that the early sound energy predominates over the later reverberant sound energy. Only in fortissimo passages and after musical stops did the reverberation seem to take an active part in the music. The high walls surrounding the stage seem to shield the side walls from receiving a significant part of the sound energy, and the stage enclosure as a whole seems to direct a large part of the energy to the audience in the rear half of the hall. These factors would explain why more energy is not sent into the upper part of the hall where the reverberant sound is developed. On the side walls themselves, about 50% of the surfaces are directed to the upper part of the hall in an effort to strengthen the reverberation.

The tone quality is excellent and the orchestral balance is good, except in the seats on either side of the orchestra where the sections nearest the listener are louder.

A group of 50 subjects, chosen in equal number from music professionals, concert-goers, and acousticians, were asked to judge the hall's quality in the months before the hall opened. They listened to a range of symphonic compositions in five parts of the hall. All judged the loudness and clarity to be very good. About 20% felt that the room did not take an active enough part in shaping the sound and that the reverberation time was a little short. Strangely, about 5% felt that the reverberation time was a little long, which indicates the range of subjective judgements even from a selected group. About 40% said that the overall impression was less than perfect. But the unanimous response of the group as a whole was "sehr gut" or "gut" (very good or good). The general conclusion was that the acoustics of the hall had received high marks.

Leipzig, Gewandhaus

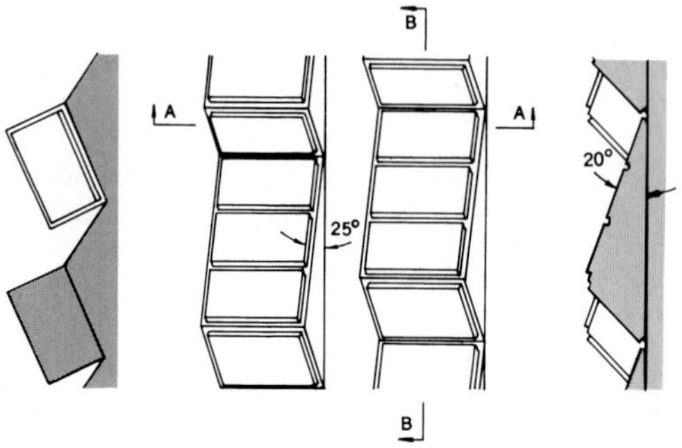

SECTION A-A   DETAIL OF SIDE WALL PANAL   SECTION B-B

SEATING CAPACITY 1900

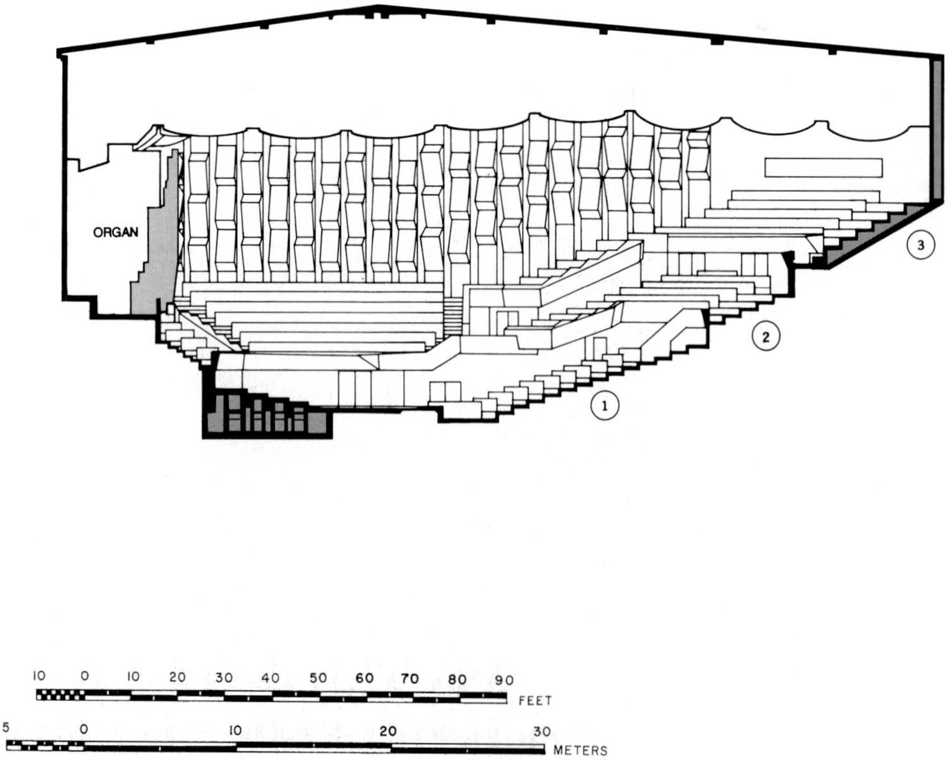

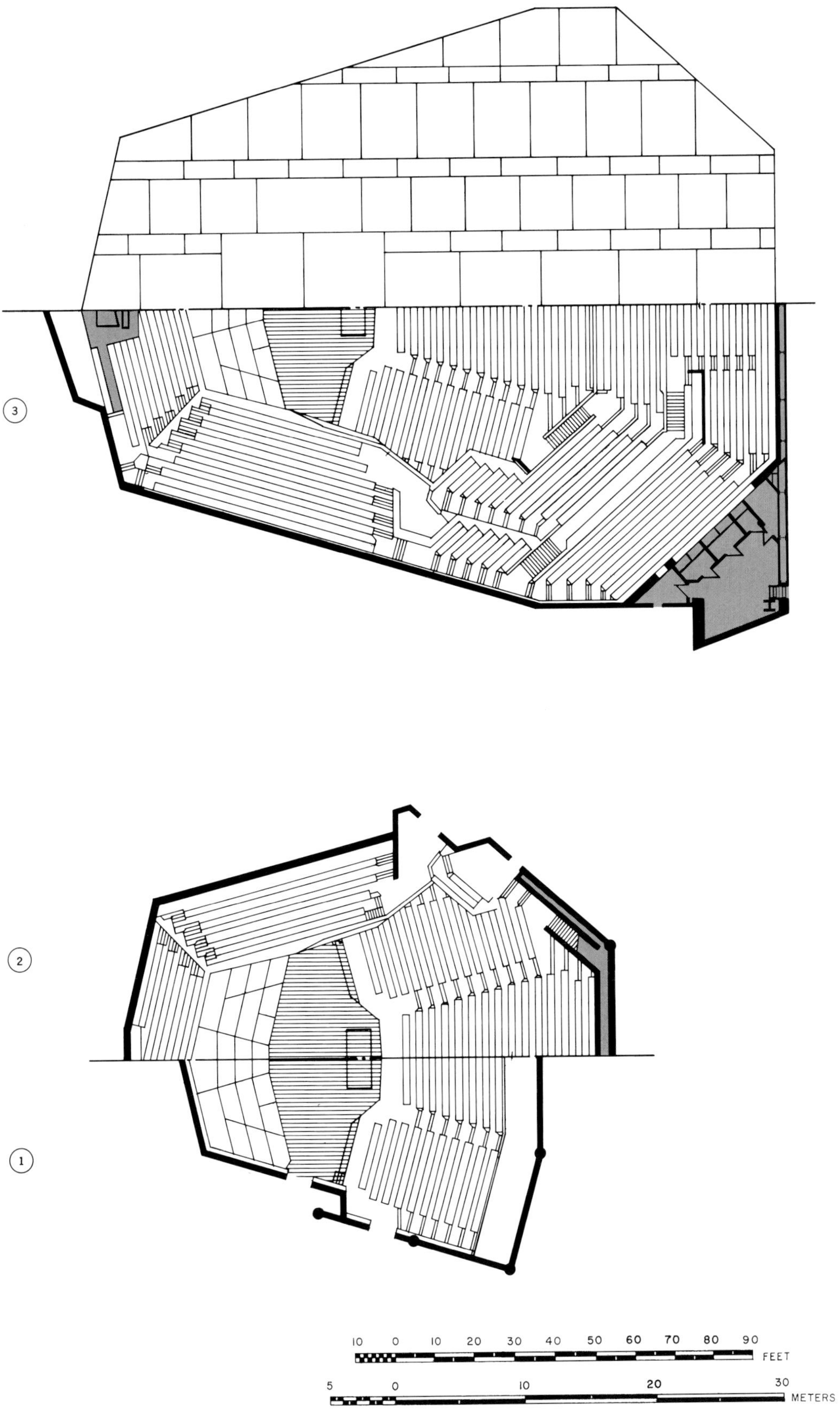
3
2
1
10 0 10 20 30 40 50 60 70 80 90
FEET
5 0 10 20 30
METERS

Architectural and structural details

Uses: classical music. *Ceiling:* at least 1.4 in. (3.5 cm) of gypsum board (8.2 lb/ft^2, 40 kg/m^2) formed as cylindrical sections, of several different lengths and widths (see the reflected ceiling plan), with a different radii of curvature of about 26 ft (8 m), oriented to direct reflections of sound energy to the various seating areas; larger panels are introduced over the podium to reflect more energy back to the musicians and to the seating areas near the stage; an unusually complex roof structure was used to eliminate noise. *Walls:* the walls around the platform and the side walls are 2 thicknesses of plywood, each 0.7 in. (1.8 cm) thick with a steel plate 0.12 in. (0.3 cm) thick cemented to the back; in the back parts of the side walls and the rear wall, the steel plates were eliminated, so that those areas resonate at a frequency of 63 to 110 Hz; a complex structure was used in the outer walls to eliminate noise. *Balcony fronts:* 1.1 in. (3 cm) artificial stone. *Floors:* parquet cemented to concrete base. *Stage floor:* 2 layers of wood, each 1.6 in. (4 cm) thick. *Stage height:* 27.5 in. (70 cm). *Seating:* Rear of seatback molded plywood; upholstering chosen to give same absorption unoccupied as occupied; the wood part of the seatbacks is higher, therefore larger, in the steeper raked audience sections.

Architect: Leipziger Architekten Gemeinschaft, Dr. Skoda & Partner. *Acoustical consultants:* (Same as *References*). *Photographs:* Foto Gert Mothes. *References:* W. Fasold, E. Kuestner, H. Tennhardt, and H. Winkler, "Akustische Massnahmen im Neuen Gewandhaus, Leipzig," Bauforschung, Baupraxis, Vol. **117**, 33 pages (1982). W. Fasold and U. Stephenson, *Gute Akustik von Auditorien*, Ernst & Sohn, Verlag, fur Architektur und technische Wissenschaften, Berlin (1993).

*Technical details**

V = 742,000 ft^3 (21,000 m^3)	S_a = 11,150 ft^2 (1,036 m^2)	S_A = 12,880 ft^2 (1,197 m^2)
S_o = 1,945 ft^2 (181 m^2)	S_T = 14,825 ft^2 (1,378 m^2)	N = 1,900
H = 65 ft (19.8 m)	W = 118 ft (36 m)	L = 106 ft (32.3 m)
D = 108 ft (32.9 m)	V/S_T = 50 ft (15.2 m)	V/S_A = 57.6 ft (17.6 m)
V/N = 390 ft^3 (11 m^3)	S_A/N = 6.78 ft^2 (0.63 m^2)	H/W = 0.55
L/W = 0.90	t_I = 27 msec	

**The terminology is explained in Appendix 1.*

GERMANY

43

Munich
Herkulessaal

Each distinguished hall has a unique appearance and personality. The flat floor, small area, large tapestries hanging high on the walls over a colonnade below give the Herkulessaal the appearance of a lecture room although it was designed specifically as a concert and festival hall. However, the long reverberation time, due to the high ceiling, renders the hall less than excellent for lectures. The quality of the overhead reverberation, which is usually so pleasant in a small rectangular hall, is marred to some extent by the hanging tapestries and the lack of upper side wall diffusion.

In 1953 the Herkulessaal, seating 1,287, was constructed with the same proportions and dimensions as the old throne room of the Royal Palace, which was destroyed during World War II. A feature of the reconstruction, no longer present today, was a canopy of twenty flat, transparent, plastic panels hung over the orchestra and the front section of the audience. Their purpose was to increase the strength of the direct sound in the rear seats of the main floor. Besides needing replacement owing to aging, they were not desired by the Bavarian Broadcasting Company because the sound at the microphones is cleaner without the extra reflections. Their removal has not caused any strong objections by the audience. In the photograph, taken in 1960, the plastic reflectors are barely visible. There are now some complaints by musicians of lack of balance among the sections of the orchestra.

As part of the construction, thirteen old Flemish gobelins, each with area of about 300 ft^2 (28 m^2), were hung on the upper side walls. These tapestries reduced the reverberation so much that three were removed. Now, because of wear owing to exposure, these have been taken out and put in museum storage. Perfect copies of them are being woven. In the meantime, curtains with nearly the same sound absorbing properties hang in their place. The reverberation time at frequencies near 250 Hz is shorter than it should be relative to the frequencies just above and just below, owing to the selective sound absorption in the ceiling caused by thin wood construction. Music critics say that the acoustics are "average," some adding that the sound is more distant when heard in the rear seats of the main floor and that the reverberation does not seem fully connected with the music.

Munich, Herkulessaal

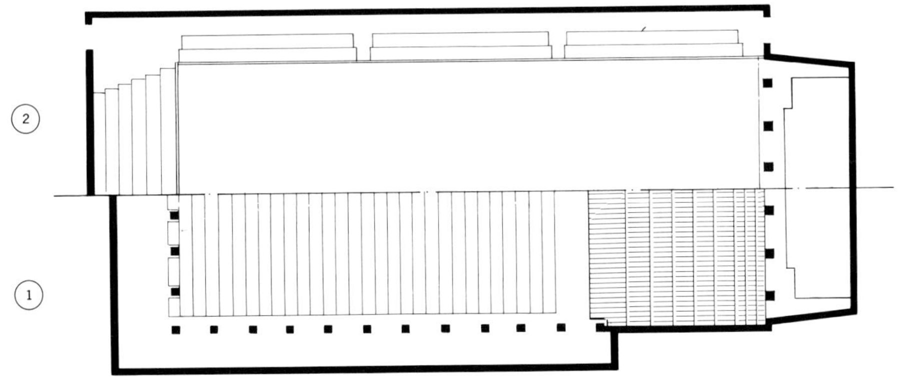

SEATING CAPACITY 1287

(1) 853

(2) 434

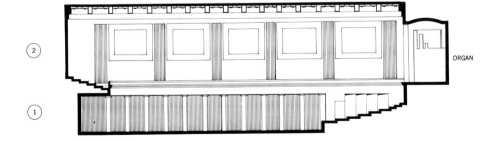

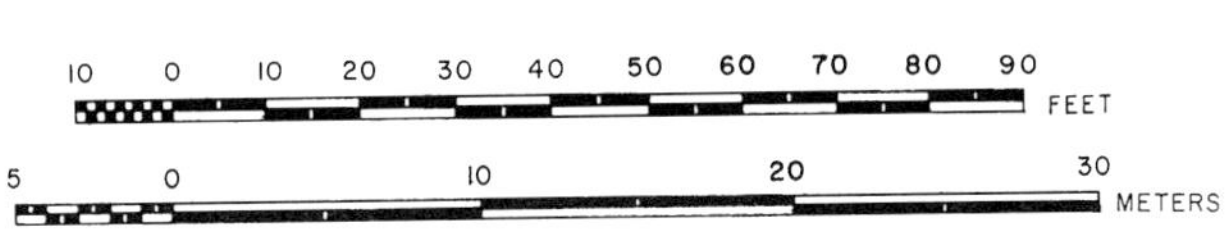

Architectural and structural details

Uses: orchestra, 60%; chamber music, 10%; chorus, 5%; soloists, 10%; other, 15%. *Ceiling:* 0.2 to 0.4 in. (0.5 to 1 cm) plywood, backed by rock wool over 4 to 10 in. (10 to 25 cm) airspace; laboratory tests indicate that the ceiling has the following absorption coefficients: 100 Hz, 0.25; 200 Hz, 0.33; 400 Hz, 0.22; 800 Hz, 0.12, and 1,600 Hz and above, about 0.035. *Side walls:* plaster on solid brick, except that 4,000 ft^2 (372 m^2) consist of 0.25 in. (0.64 cm) sheets of gypsum board separated by 2 in. (5 cm) from the solid wall behind. *Rear wall:* plastered brick; great doors are metal and plywood. *Added absorptive material:* 10 tapestries or heavy draperies hung on upper walls for architectural reasons. *Floors:* tile on concrete and tile on the wood of the risers. *Stage floor:* 2 in. (5 cm) wooden planks over airspace. *Stage height:* 40 in. (102 cm). *Seating:* upholstered on both sides of backrest and top of seat-bottom. Underseat is solid.

Architect: Rudolf Esterer. *Acoustical consultant:* L. Cremer. *Photographs:* courtesy of the management. *References:* L. Cremer, *Die Schalltechnik*, **13**, 1–10 (1953); L. Cremer, *Gravesaner Blatter*, Nos. **2/3**, pp. 10–33 (January 1956); E. Meyer and R. Thiele, *Acustica*, **6**, 425–444 (1956).

*Technical details**

Concert

V = 480,000 ft^3 (13,590 m^3)	S_a = 6,304 ft^2 (585.7 m^2)	S_A = 7,250 ft^2 (674 m^2)
S_o = 1,810 ft^2 (168 m^2)	S_T = 9,060 ft^2 (842 m^2)	N = 1,287
H = 51 ft (15.5 m)	W = 72 ft (22 m)	L = 105 ft (32 m)
D = 108 ft (32.9 m)	V/S_T = 53 ft (16.1 m)	V/S_A = 66.2 ft (20.2 m)
V/N = 373 ft^3 (10.6 m^3)	S_A/N = 5.63 ft^2 (0.52 m^2)	H/W = 0.71
L/W = 1.46	t_I = 24 msec	

The terminology is explained in Appendix 1.

44

Munich
Philharmonie am Gasteig

The Gasteig is a clear statement of Munich's desire to be a major cultural center in Germany. The name is taken from "gachen footpath" and its site is high enough to command vistas of the center of the city, the river Isar, the famous Deutsches science museum, and old residential sections. In planning for 14 years, it has five principal components, a concert hall, multipurpose theater, music conservatory, college, and library. The Philharmonie, which opened in November 1985, presents a whole new appearance in the world of concert halls. Finished in American red oak, with red seat upholstering, it is visually striking. The multitudinous acoustic panels, free-standing from the walls and ceiling, mean that every effort was made to realize good acoustics.

Seating 2,387, plus 100 chorus, it is 287 seats larger than the Berlin Phiharmonie and 587 seats larger than the Leipzig Gewandhaus. The great size, 1,050,000 ft^3 (29,800 m^3), necessary to achieve an occupied reverberation time of 1.95 sec at mid-frequencies, combined with the architects concept of two wings, brought special problems to the acoustical consultant. A fan-shaped plan and a rising ceiling, without embellishment, would mean that early sound reflections would not reach listeners in the front two-thirds of the hall. To solve this problem, free-standing, reflecting panels on the side walls and a suspended sound-reflecting ceiling, diffuse in cross-section, and a stepped audience area with intermediate reflecting walls (vineyards) were introduced to provide multiple reflections within the first 100 msec to each listener.

The sound is different in various seating areas; not bad anywhere, just of varying texture. In the exact center of the seating areas the music sounds as though played in a cathedral. When seated off the center line, especially in elevated levels, the sound is well-balanced, high quality, without giving the impression of a very large hall. The stage is very large, and often musical groups move toward the back wall for acoustical support, using the front and the elevated podium steps as reflecting surfaces. This is particularly helpful to soloists.

Since the hall's opening, plexiglass reflectors have been added above the stage to improve acoustical contact within the orchestra, details are unknown.

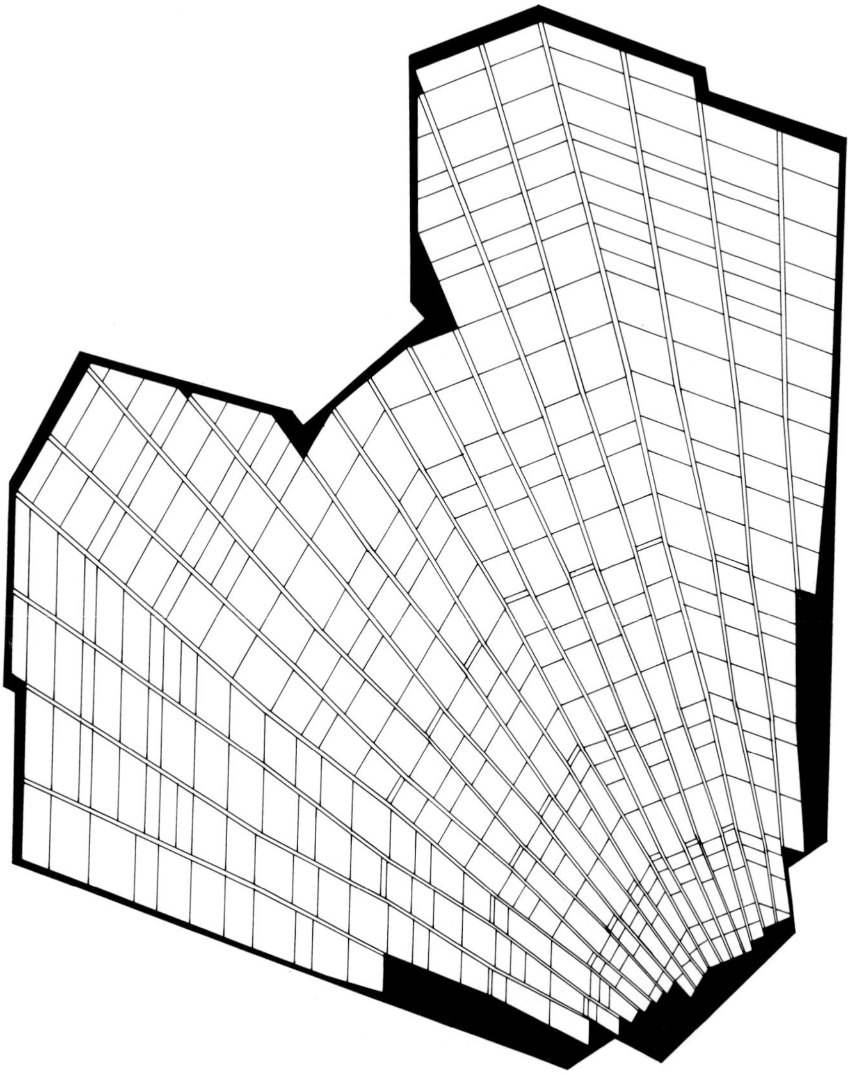

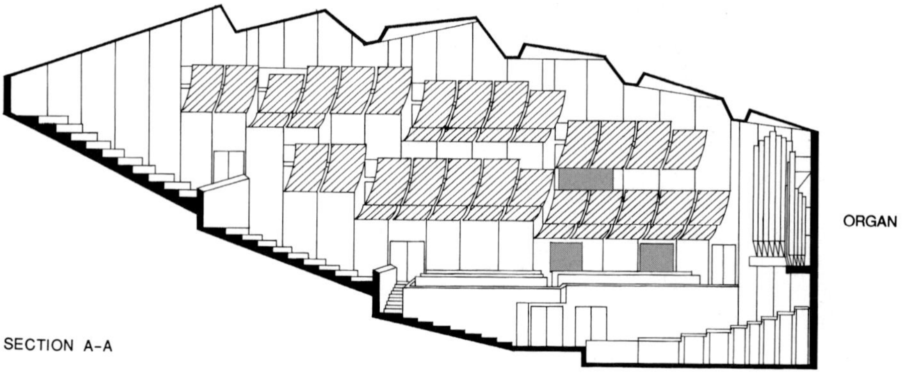

SECTION A-A

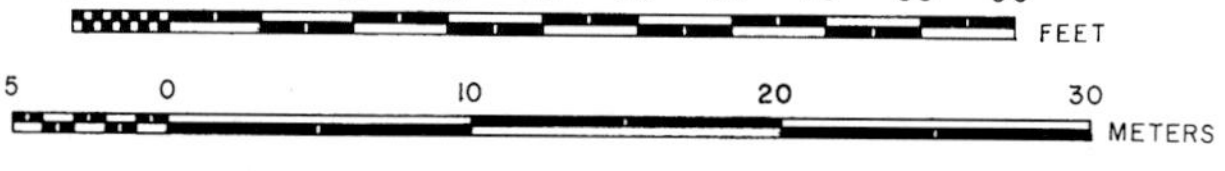

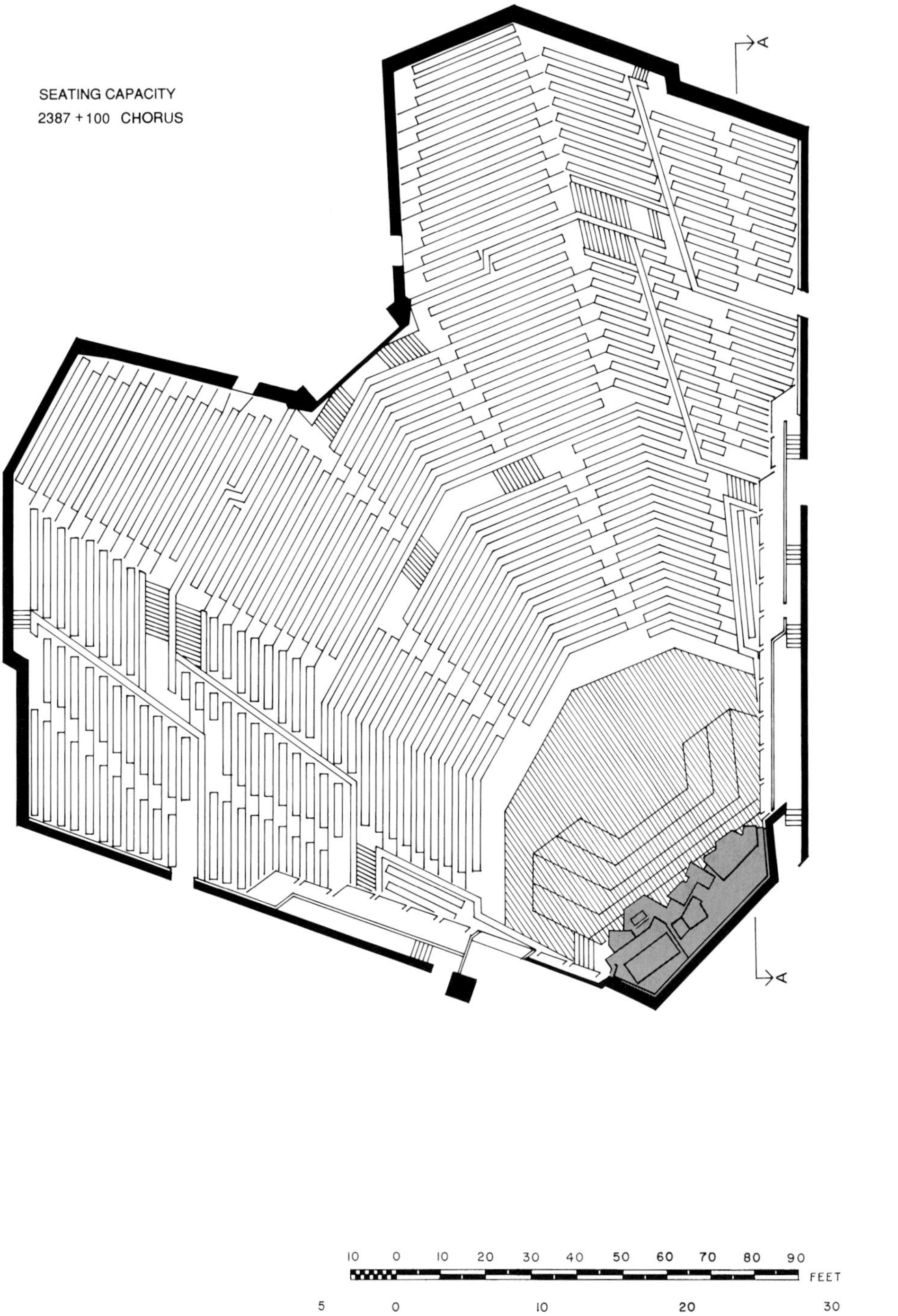
SEATING CAPACITY
2387 + 100 CHORUS
A
A
10 0 10 20 30 40 50 60 70 80 90
FEET
5 0 10 20 30
METERS

Munich, Philharmonie am Gasteig

Architectural and structural details

Uses: primarily classical music. *Ceiling:* wooden, with a uniform weight of 6 lb/ft^2 (30 kg/m^2); wooden suspended panels are hung from the ceiling (see the photographs); veneer of American red oak. *Walls:* concrete base with wooden particle-board lining weighing 2 to 10 lb/ft^2 (10 to 50 kg/m^2); veneer of American red oak. *Floors:* wood on prefabricated thin concrete plates. *Stage enclosure:* reflections from rear wall, some from low side walls, more from organ and hung plexiglass panels. *Stage floor:* wood on wooden joists. *Stage height:* 30 in. (75 cm). *Seating:* molded plywood backs, perforated wood underseats, upholstering on front of seat backs and on seat tops; arms are wood.

Architects: C. F. Raue, E. Rollenhagen, G. Lindemann, G. Grossmann. *Acoustical consultant:* Mueller-BBM. *Photographs:* Sigrid Neubert. *References:* H. A. Mueller, U. Opitz, G. Volberg, "Structureborne sound transmission from the tubes of a subway into a building for a concert hall." Proceedings of Internoise, **11**, 715–718 (1980). H. A. Mueller, U. Opitz, "Anweng der raumakustischen Modelltechniken bei der Planung des Konzertsaales der Muenchner Philharmonie," Buildungswerk des Verbandes Deutscher Tonmeister, 306–313 (1984). H. A. Mueller, U. Opitz, J. Reinhold, "Akustische Wirkung eines Raumes auf die ausfuehrenden Musiker," db Deutsche Bauzeitung, **123**, 69–81 (May 1989).

*Technical details**

V = 1,050,000 ft^3 (29,737 m^3)	S_a = 14,305 ft^2 (1,329 m^2)	S_A = 17,640 ft^2 (1,639 m^2)
S_o = 2,476 ft^2 (230 m^2)	S_T = 20,116 ft^2 (1,869 m^2)	N = 2,387 + 100 chorus
H = 48 ft (14.6 m)	W = 168 ft (51.2 m)	L = 134 ft (40.8 m)
D = 145 ft (44.2 m)	V/S_T = 52.2 ft (15.9 m)	V/S_A = 59.5 ft (18.1 m)
V/N = 440 ft^3 (12.4 m^3)	S_A/N = 7.39 ft^2 (0.69 m^2)	H/W = 0.29
L/W = 0.80	t_I = 29 msec	

**The terminology is explained in Appendix 1.*

Germany

45

Stuttgart
Liederhalle, Beethovensaal

Situated on one of Stuttgart's busiest streets, the Liederhalle contains four halls, two of which seat 2,000 persons—one general purpose and the other for concerts—and the other two seat 750 and 350 persons. Of these, the 750 seat hall is the most spectacular from the outside and the Beethovensaal from the inside. This concert hall has an unusual shape, like a grand piano, chosen for architectural and not acoustical reasons. The striking balcony rises like a grand staircase from the left side of the main floor, and with graceful line soars over the main floor seats and sweeps around the rear of the hall to the wall on the right-hand side.

A large, convex concrete wall, on which there is a mosaic of painted wooden pieces and gold threads, connects the left side of the stage to the rising portion of the balcony. The right-hand wall of the hall, which is finished in teak, is irregular with projecting boxes and control booths for radio and television broadcasting. All the other walls are of teak. The main floor is flat. The ceiling is interestingly contoured to provide sound diffusion and to give desirable short-time-delay sound reflections. Reflecting panels, hanging over the orchestra, direct the sound of the strings to the audience at the rear of the main floor to overcome the disadvantages of intervening heads between listeners and the stage.

The Beethovensaal was renovated in 1992. Measurements by the acoustical consultants show that the modernizing has not affected the acoustical conditions. The hall has about the same reverberation time (1.6 sec) as the Royal Festival Hall of London (with assisted resonance) but it is less reverberant than Symphony Hall in Boston (1.85 sec) and the Grosser Musikvereinssaal in Vienna (2.0 sec).

In general, visiting conductors have enjoyed this hall, saying that on the podium one can hear everything, even the smallest error in the performance. Some listeners speak of the hall as acoustically excellent. Others, say it is very good, but that it falls below the quality of the Vienna hall. In my one concert experience, I found the sound quite satisfactory. The sound in the balcony is excellent. In the rear half of the main floor, not under the balcony, I especially enjoyed the intimate, brilliant sound. I have not listened in the front half of the main floor.

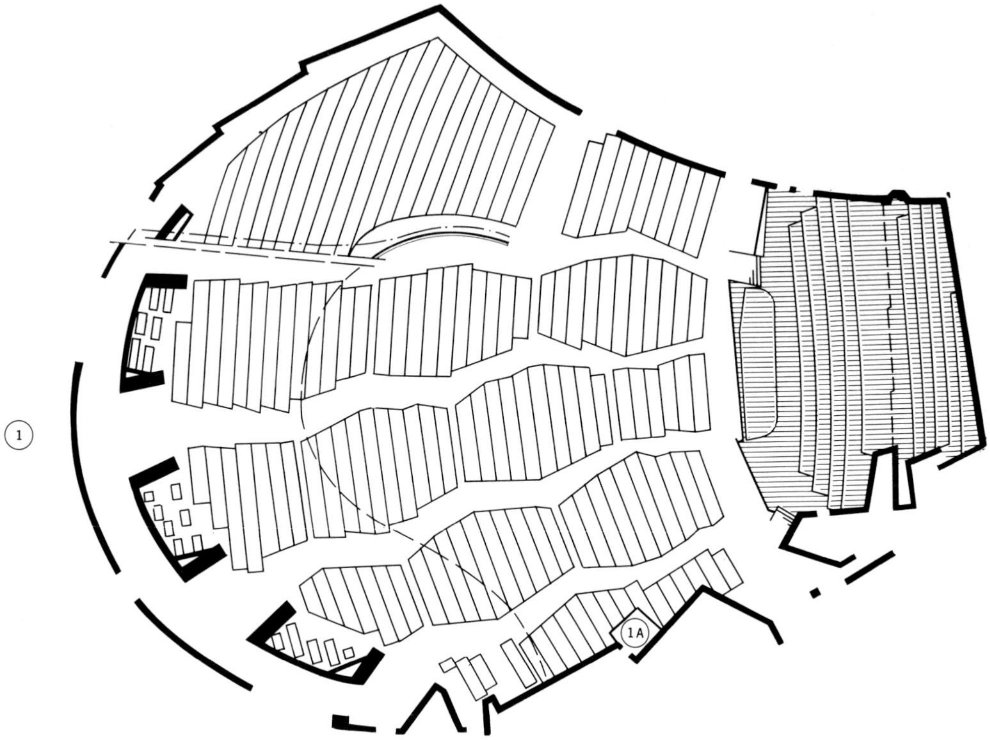

SEATING CAPACITY 2000

(1)	1175
(1A)	25
(2)	800

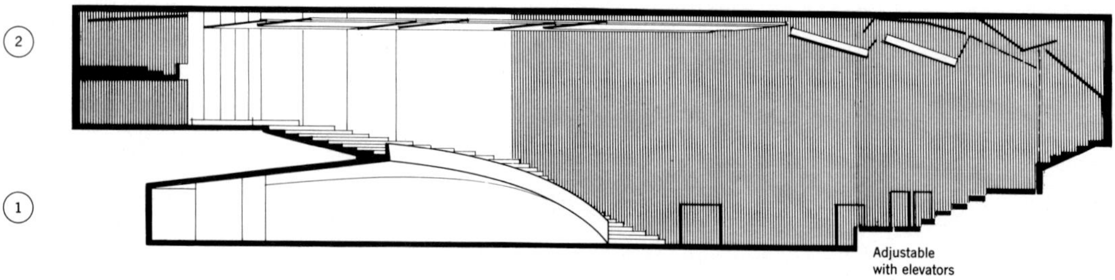

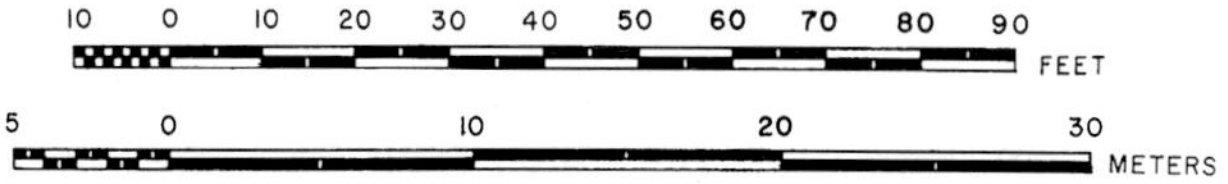

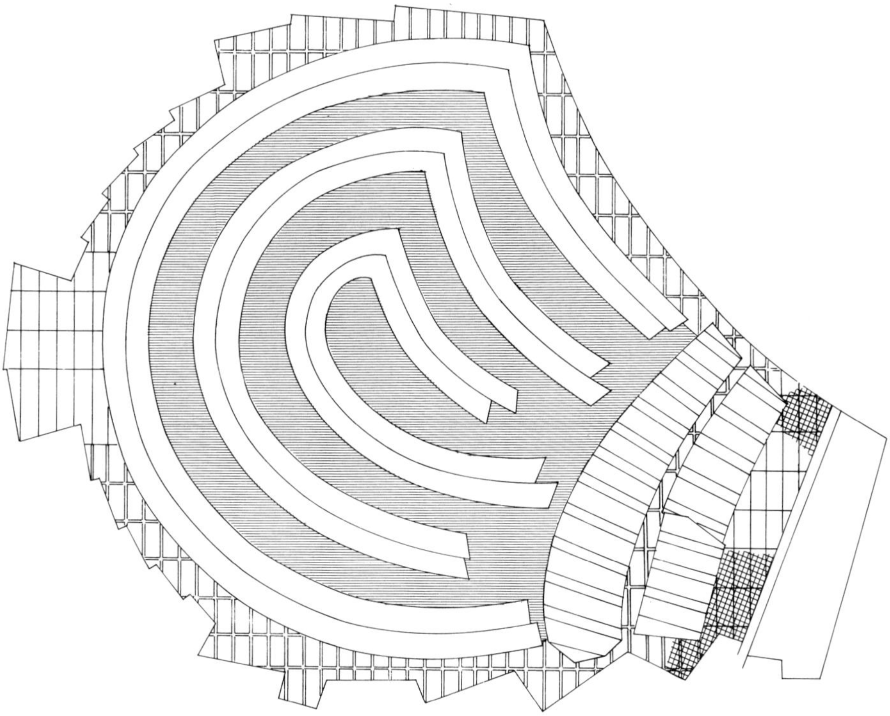

Reflected ceiling plan

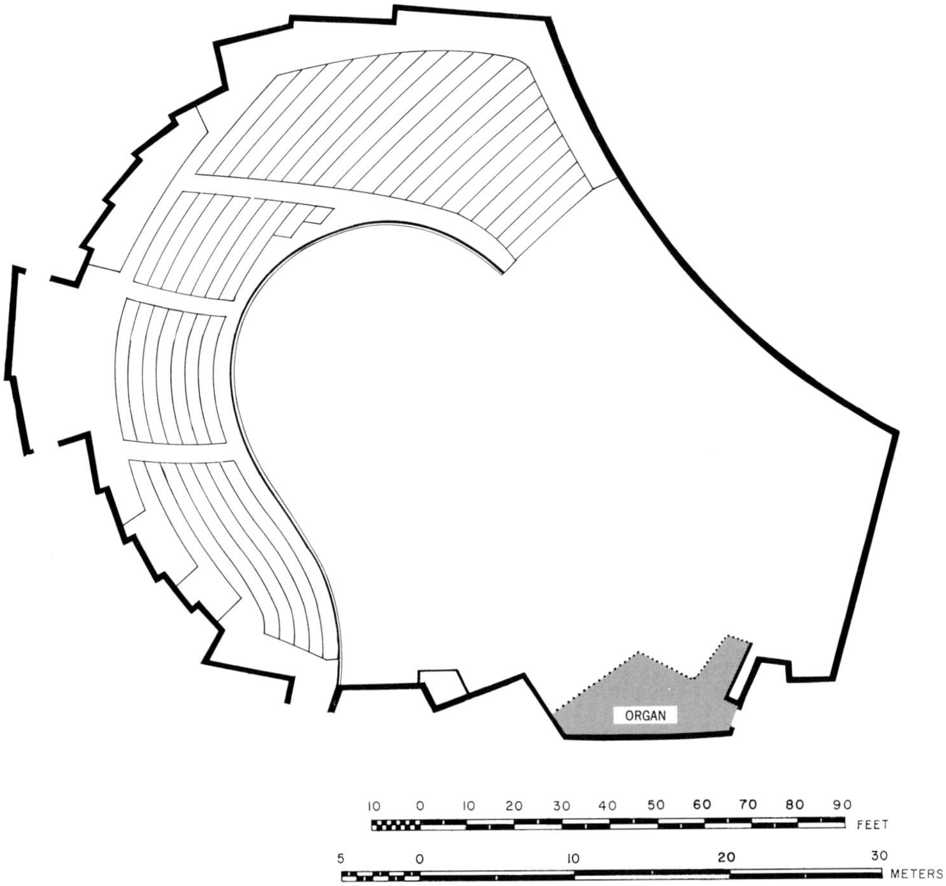

Stuttgart, Liederhall, Beethovensaal

Architectural and structural details

Uses: orchestra, organ, chamber, soloists, and general. *Ceiling:* gypsum plaster on metal lath except for a strip about 10 ft (3 m) near the walls, one-third of which is 0.62 in. (1.6 cm) fiberboard over airspace and two-thirds slotted fiberboard backed by layer of fiberglass. *Walls:* the left convex wall is concrete; other walls are plywood that varies from 0.38 in. (9.5 mm) to 0.88 in. (2.2 cm) thick over airspace 1 to 5 in. (2.5 to 12.7 cm) deep; some panels are slotted with fiberglass behind; the slotted panels and the thin panels are backed with a fiberboard egg-crate structure; these variations yield walls that absorb sound over a wide range of low frequencies. *Floors:* wood parquet; no carpet. *Stage enclosure:* largely 0.88 in. plywood; the organ is located behind closable "jalousies" on the right-hand side of the stage; splayed 0.88 in. (2.2 cm) plywood reflectors are hung over the orchestra and the front two rows of seating. *Stage floor:* 2 in. (5 cm) boards on elevators. *Stage height:* 49 in. (1.24 m). *Seating:* the front of the backrest and the top of the seat are upholstered; the underseats are solid; the armrests are upholstered in leather.

Architect: A. Abel and R. Gutbrod. *Acoustical consultants:* Lothar Cremer, Helmut Mueller and L. Keidel. *Photographs:* courtesy of the management. *References:* L. Cremer, L. Keidel, and H. Mueller, *Acustica*, **6**, 466–474 (1956). "Konserthaus Stuttgarter Liederhalle," Dr. Pollert Verlag, Stuttgart (1956).

*Technical details**

V = 565,000 ft^3 (16,000 m^3)	S_a = 10,800 ft^2 (1,000 m^2)	S_A = 14,000 ft^2 (1,300 m^2)
S_o = 1,900 ft^2 (176 m^2)	S_T = 16,500 ft^2 (1,533 m^2)	N = 2,000
H = 44 ft (13.4 m)	W = 119 ft (36.2 m)	L = 137 ft (41.8 m)
D = 134 ft (40.8 m)	V/S_T = 34.2 ft (10.4 m)	V/S_A = 40.36 ft (12.3 m)
V/N = 282.5 ft^3 (8.0 m^3)	S_A/N = 7.0 ft^2 (0.65 m^2)	H/W = 0.37
L/W = 1.15	t_I = 29 msec	

**The terminology is explained in Appendix 1.*

46

Birmingham Symphony Hall

The City of Birmingham has reestablished itself as a major European city through its Broad Street Development with a quality convention center and Symphony Hall which opened in 1991. Of no less an achievement has been the engagement of Simon Rattle as Principal Conductor and Artistic Advisor of the Birmingham Symphony Orchestra who has quickly raised it to world class level.

The entrance to the Hall is by way of a mall, a tall, fully glazed street, which is dominated on one side by Symphony Hall, with its curved walls and four cascading foyer levels that provide a dazzling spectacle of light and color at nighttime.

On entering the Hall through the doors near the rear, one is struck by the beautiful interior, with intimate warm soft red tones and generous use of wood, stainless steel, and granite. The Hall is a combination of a classical rectangular hall with the rear third curved and multi-tiered like an opera house. Seating 2,211, including the choir space behind the orchestra, it provides ample wall areas, not widely separated, for early, lateral reflections necessary to an intimate sound. The strong lines of the balconies that sweep to the front of the room, draw one's eyes to focus on the pipe organ. A special acoustical feature of the hall is the reverberation chamber. It is accessed by mechanized concrete doors that surround the organ and also are located on the upper side walls. These doors can be opened in any number to create variable reverberation that can be matched to the type of music or to other uses of the hall. To provide adjustability to the clarity of the sound a large wood canopy is provided over the orchestra and the front of the audience, which can be raised and lowered. The reverberation also can be reduced by a series of 3 in. deep sound-absorbing panels, mounted on rails, which can be moved in and out of the hall. The normal occupied mid-frequency reverberation time is 1.85 sec.

It is difficult for a one-time auditor to describe the acoustics of the hall, because of the great variability that can be provided in both the reverberation and the clarity, any combination of which might be in use during that visit. Critical reviews have mostly been ecstatic with one saying "not enough reverberance." Above all, Birmingham has received a musical boost of unimaginable force.

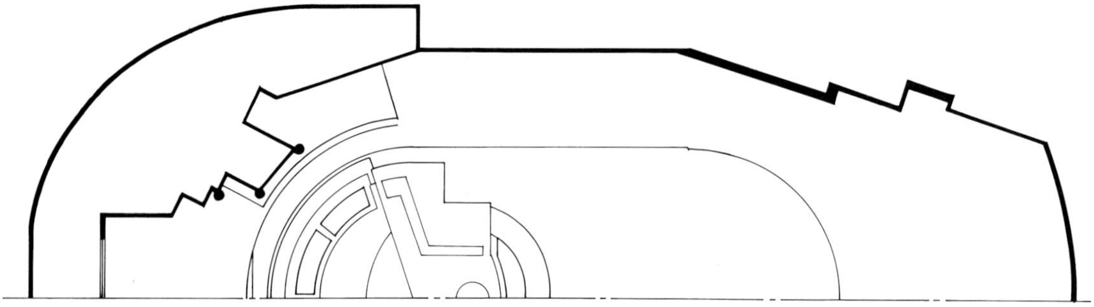

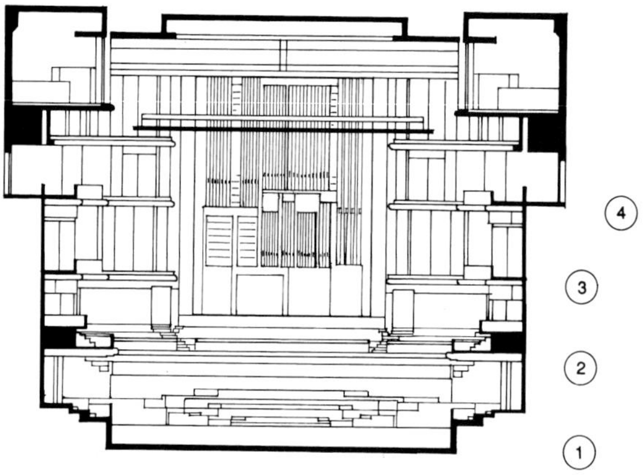
4
3
2
1

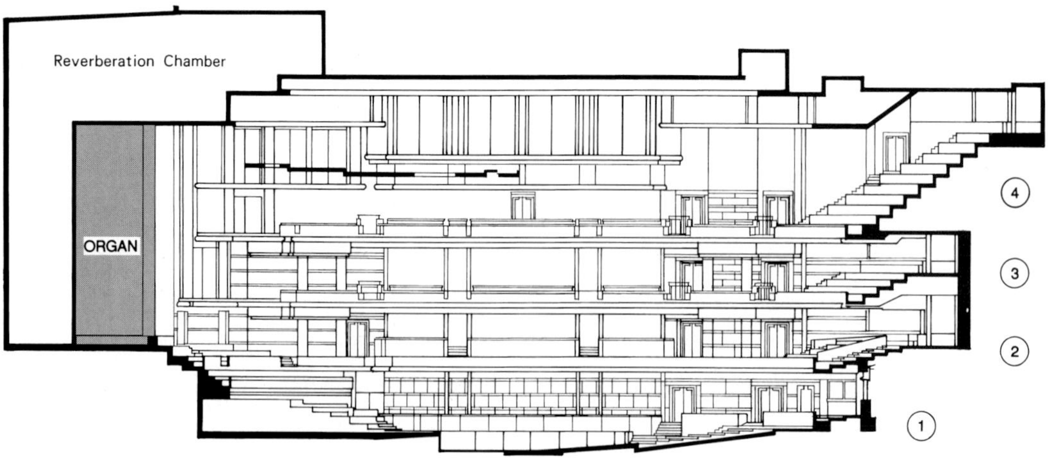
Reverberation Chamber
ORGAN
4
3
2
1

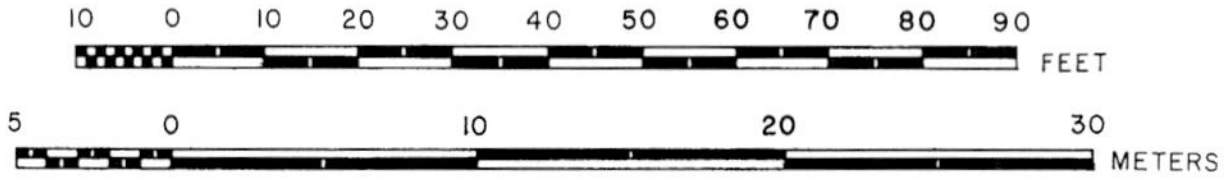
10 0 10 20 30 40 50 60 70 80 90
FEET
5 0 10 20 30
METERS

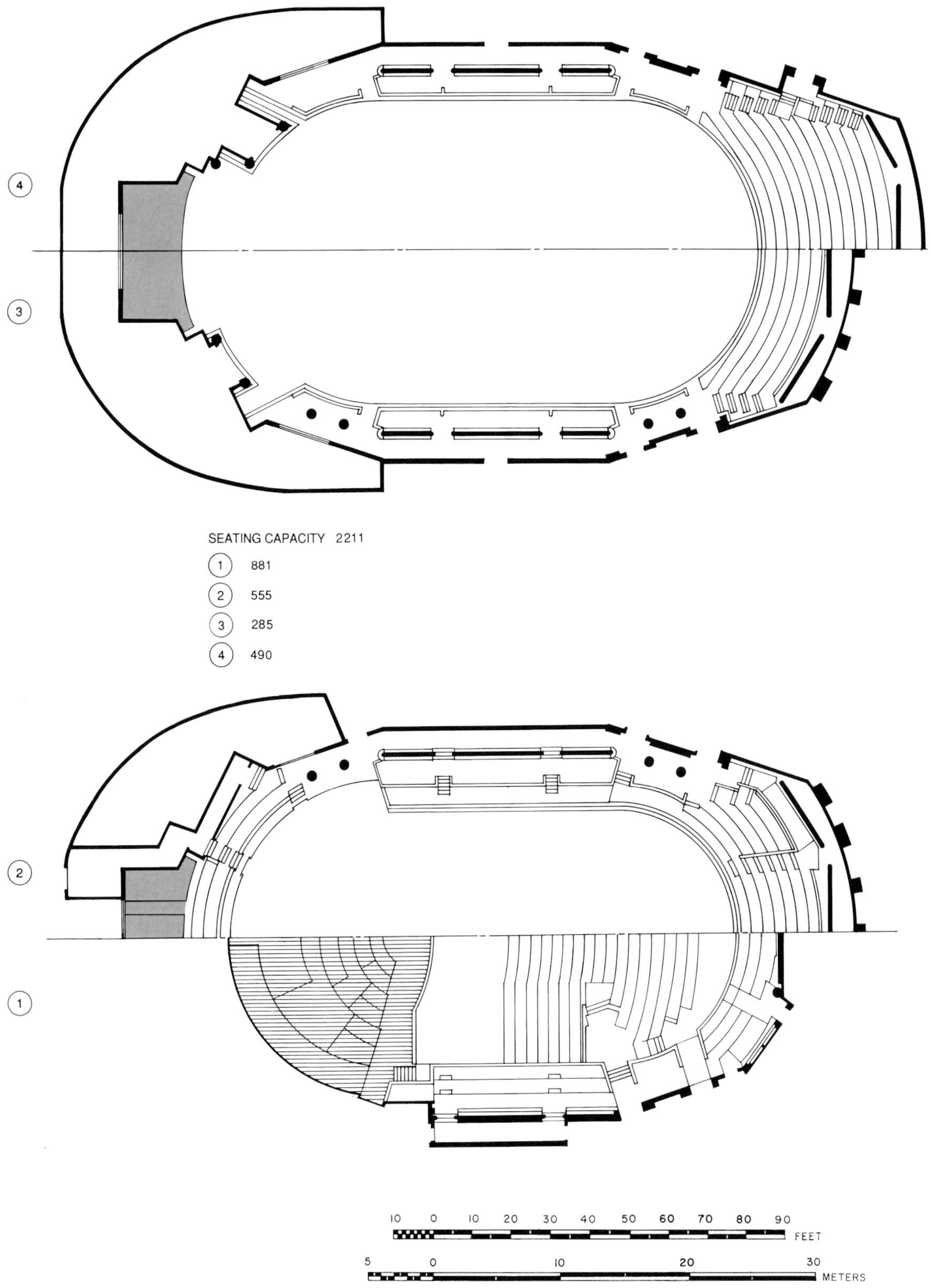

4
3
SEATING CAPACITY 2211
1 881
2 555
3 285
4 490
2
1
10 0 10 20 30 40 50 60 70 80 90
FEET
5 0 10 20 30
METERS

Birmingham, Symphony Hall

Architectural and structural details

Uses: symphonic and choral concerts, voice, instrumental, and organ recitals, conferences, and amplified popular music. *Ceiling:* precast concrete with plaster cover; balcony soffits, three layers of 2 in. (5 cm) plasterboard. *Overstage adjustable-height canopy:* 4.5 in. (11.4 cm) timber on steel frame, underside American Cherry paneling, area 2,900 ft^2 (270 m^2), plus small areas of 0.25 in. (0.64 cm) cork. The lowest regularly used height is 30 ft (9 m). *Walls:* hardwood veneered panels on battens infilled with sand/cement directly bonded to concrete structural walls, plus large areas of plaster on structural walls. *Terrace fronts at main floor level:* 0.75 to 1.5 in. (2 to 4 cm) granite. *Variable absorption:* top-hung, motor-operated, fabric covered panels of 3 in. (7.5 cm) mineral wool, hung on wood frames, totaling 2,050 ft^2 (625 m^2) area. *Floors:* 0.9 in. (2.2 cm) wood strip on 0.75 in. (1.9 cm) plywood on battens infilled with sand/cement screed over concrete base. *Carpet:* none. *Stage floor:* flat; for orchestra, risers are two steel-framed "wagons" on rubber-tired wheels, with top surfaces 0.9 in. (2.2 cm) wood strips on 0.75 in. (1.9 cm) plywood subfloor. *Stage walls:* a semi-circular enclosure formed by 13ft (4 m) high, 1.5 in. (3.8 cm) sliding wood doors; above the stage walls are plaster on 10 in. (25 cm) concrete masonry. *Reverberation chambers:* 369,000 ft^3 (10,300 m^3) hard-surfaced concrete and concrete block, containing operable two-layer velour drapes for variable sound absorption; openable by 20 remotely controlled doors of 6 in. (15 cm) concrete, totaling 2,100 ft^2 (195 m^2). *Stage height:* 47 in. (1.2 m). *Seating:* Molded plywood back and seat bottom; upholstered front of seat back and seat; armrests wood.

Architect: Percy Thomas Partnership. *Acoustical consultant:* ARTEC Consultants, Inc. *Theater consultant:* ARTEC Consultants, Inc. *Photographs:* Courtesy of the architect. *Reference:* "Inter-national Convention Centre Birmingham," *Architecture Today*, 17, April 1991.

*Technical details**

V = 883,000 ft^3 (25,000 m^3)	S_a = 11,100 ft^2 (1,031 m^2)	S_A = 14,210 ft^2 (1,320 m^2)
S_o = 3,000 ft^2 (279 m^2)	S_T = 17,210 ft^2 (1,599 m^2)	N = 2,211
H = 75 ft (22.9 m)	W = 90 ft (27.4 m)	L = 104 ft (31.7 m)
D = 132 ft (40.2 m)	V/S_T = 51.3 ft (15.6 m)	V/S_A = 62.1 ft (18.9 m)
V/N = 400 ft^3 (11.3 m^3)	S_A/N = 6.42 ft^2 (0.60 m^2)	H/W = 0.83
L/W = 1.15	t_I = 27 msec	

**The terminology is explained in Appendix 1.*

47

Bristol
Colston Hall

Colston Hall was dedicated on July 9, 1951, built within the walls of the previous Colston Hall that was destroyed by fire in 1945. The architect's concept combines the flowing lines of contemporary architecture with a straightforward and direct architectural style. The hall is rectangular having a large balcony with a deep overhang underneath, necessitated by the demand for a larger seating capacity.

The high ceiling and narrow width declare that the architect and his acoustical consultant wanted to provide a fairly long reverberation time, together with satisfactory acoustical intimacy. As we know now, this also provides early laterally reflected sound energy to the listeners on the main floor. A dominant architectural feature is the large suspended canopy over the concert platform which reflects the direct sound uniformly over the hall and enables the performers to hear their own instruments and other sections of the orchestra. Sound diffusion is provided by the sawtooth shape of the balcony faces and of the panels on the upper side walls of the front half of the balcony.

It is generally held among critical listeners that Colston Hall is the best of the 1951 series of halls built in Britain. Its modest size —it seats 2,121 including 182 choir —and narrow width are in its favor. It has a near optimum reverberation time of 1.7 sec, at mid-frequencies with full occupancy. There is a paucity of fine scale irregularities on the large plane reflecting surfaces, which tends to give the sound a slightly "edgy" quality, sometimes called "acoustic glare." Many prefer the balcony because there the orchestral balance and the brilliance of the strings are best. But everywhere, the hall has satisfactory liveness and a warm orchestral tone. The wall behind the orchestra acts as an amplifier which occasionally causes the timpani and brass to override the rest of the orchestra. The cello sound is particularly good.

My own evaluation is that the Hall is very good, almost excellent, exhibiting clarity, brilliance, warmth, and adequate liveness for Classical music. This is backed up by the opinions expressed during interviews of important conductors of the 1960's who generally agreed, "the sound is full and resonant and fully clear," "it is an excellent hall in every way."

BRISTOL, COLSTON HALL

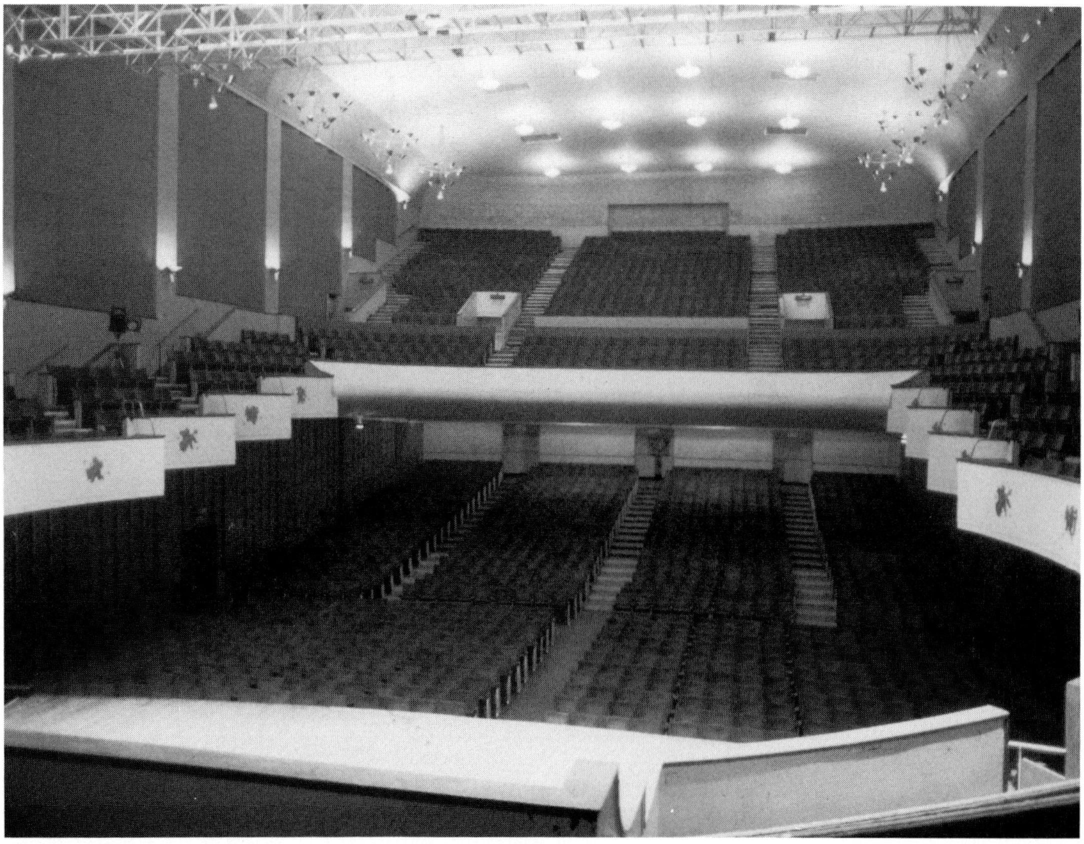

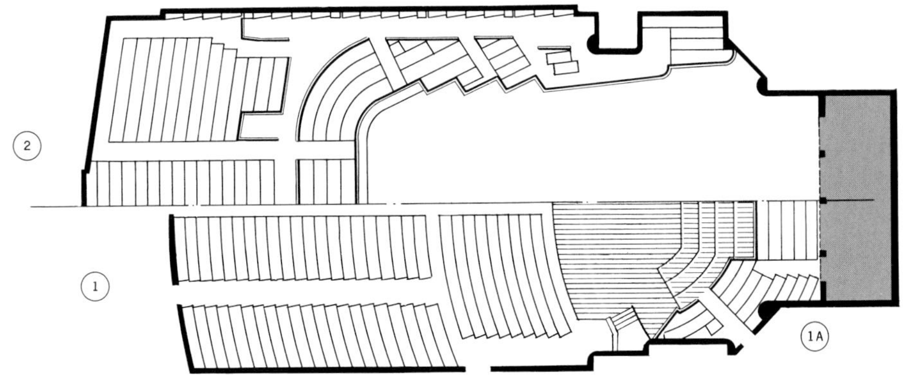

SEATING CAPACITY 2121

(1)	1048
(1A)	182
(2)	891

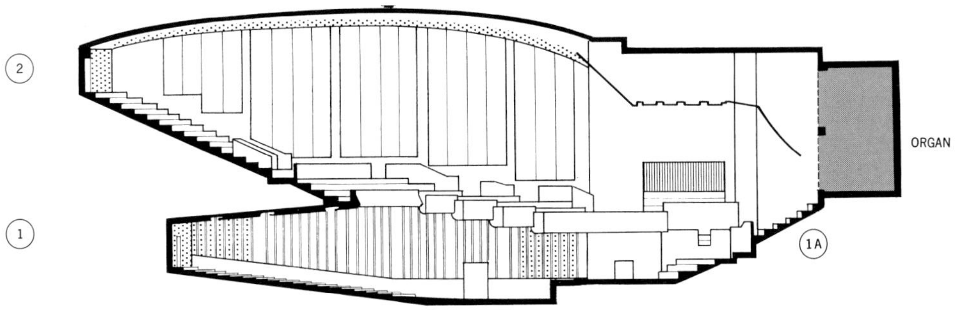

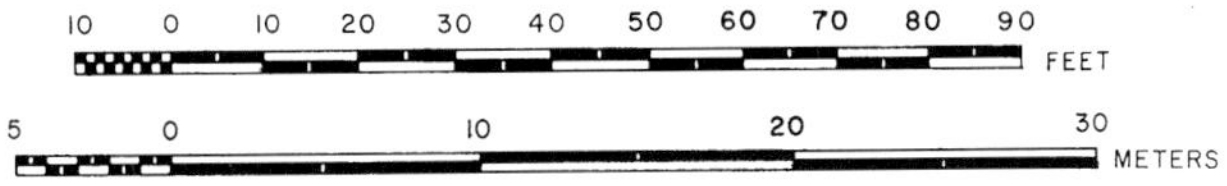

Architectural and structural details

Uses: classical concerts, popular music, and some sports. *Ceiling:* 0.75 in. (1.9 cm) plaster on metal lath backed with 1.5 in. (3.8 cm) vermiculite concrete; ceiling cornices formed with unplastered, curved, sound-absorbent wood-wool slab, 1,400 ft^2 (130 m^2). *Side walls:* most of upper side walls is plaster on metal lath; below the balcony, 260 ft^2 (24.2 m^2) is sound absorbent; the rest is curved 0.5 in. (1.25 cm) wood with 4 in. (10 cm) airspace behind. *Rear walls:* 0.9 in. (2.2 cm) perforated acoustic tiles on 1.5 in. (3.8 cm) wooden battens on brick walls. *Floors:* wood on battens on concrete in front of main floor; linoleum on concrete in raked sections; concrete in balcony. *Stage enclosure:* overhead reflector is plaster on metal lath; walls are plywood panels on furring on brickwork; large organ grille at rear, covered with curtain. *Stage floor:* 1.25 in. (3.2 cm) hardwood boards over deep airspace; choir (audience) area behind is wood on concrete; the percussion alcove is wood on concrete. *Stage height:* 42 in. (107 cm) *Sound absorbing materials:* none, except curtains in doorway. *Carpets:* none. *Seating:* molded wooden seat back, upholstered front of seat back and top of seat-bottom with porous velour; underseat, unperforated wood; choir seats partly upholstered in velour.

Architect: J. Nelson Meredith. *Acoustical Consultant:* Building Research Station (H. R. Humphreys, P. H. Parkin, and W. A. Allen.) *Photographs:* courtesy of Desmond Tripp, with permission of Bristol. *References:* P. H. Parkin, W. E. Scholes, and A. C. Derbyshire, *Acustica:* 2, 97–100 (1952). M. Barron, *Architectural Acoustics and Architectural Design,* E & FN Spon, Chapman & Hall, London and Paris (1993).

*Technical details**

V = 475,000 ft^3 (13,450 m^3)	S_a = 8,240 ft^2 (745 m^2)	S_A = 10,630 ft^2 (987 m^2)
S_o = 1,720 ft^2 (160 m^2)	S_T = 12,350 ft^2 (1,147 m^2)	N = 2,121
H = 58 ft (17.7 m)	W = 74 ft (22.6 m)	L = 90 ft (27.4 m)
D = 110 ft (33.5 m)	V/S_T = 38.5 ft (11.7 m)	V/S_A = 44.7 ft (13.6 m)
V/N = 224 ft^3 (6.34 m^3)	S_A/N = 5.01 ft^2 (0.47 m^2)	H/W = 0.78
L/W = 1.21	t_I = 21 msec	

**The terminology is explained in Appendix 1.*

48

Cardiff, Wales
St. David's Hall

Cardiff, the Welsh capital, has an exciting world-class concert hall. Opened in 1982, it is located in St. David's Centre, a major shopping area in the heart of the city. From the start, it was decided not to duplicate the classical shoebox hall, but rather to make it more "theatrical," involving the public more, with no one seated in excess of 125 ft (38 m) from the stage. There were other challenges. The building had to be shoehorned into the available ground space, and it was desired not to make it too high. These criteria were achieved by wrapping the audience around the stage, and by choosing its shape as an elongated hexagon, tapered in at the rear. Again, the vineyard style of the Berlin Philharmonie hall is suggested, with 16 tiers in all, each comparable in size to the orchestra. St. David's Hall seats 1,682 plus 270 choir, totaling 1,952.

Walls between tiers do not provide early reflections to listeners, as are found in Berlin and the Costa Mesa, California, halls, because they are parallel to the sight lines. A mid-frequency reverberation time of 2.0 sec, occupied, was achieved with full occupancy by incorporating the trusses for the roof and the ventilating system ducts into the room by an acoustically transparent ceiling. In St. David's Hall, a season of orchestral concerts is staged using the BBC National Orchestra of Wales and international/regional touring orchestras. For a Cardiff Festival of Music it contributes a broad based program and, in July, the Hall offers the Welsh Proms.

A subjective survey of eleven British concert halls (not including the recent halls, Birmingham and Glasgow) at public concerts by a group of mainly acoustical consultants seated throughout the halls, concluded that St. David's Hall was at or near the top in the characteristics of clarity, reverberance, intimacy, orchestral balance, and envelopment of the listener by the sound. Loudness was also optimum. Why? Even though the reverberation is high, there seems to be ample early sound energy reflections from the myriad of trusses, suspended ceilings, lighting grid, back-stage wall, and balcony fronts, as well as the ceiling in the upper levels, to achieve the desired qualities of clarity and intimacy. The judgment of good envelopment is surprising because of an apparent lack of surfaces to create early lateral reflections. Some believe that this may only be possible with a reverberation of 2 sec or more.

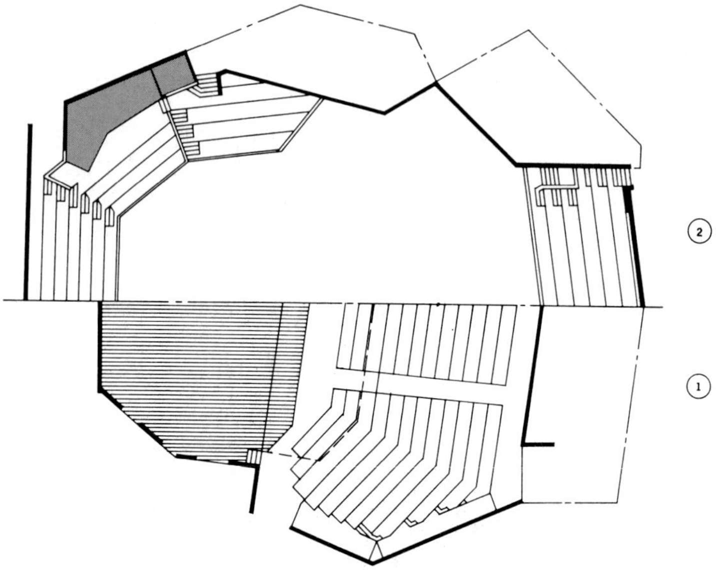

SEATING CAPACITY 1952

1	612
2	504
3	296
4	540

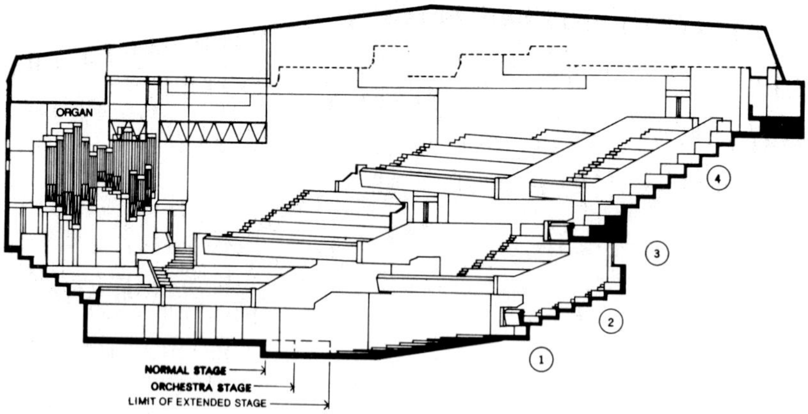

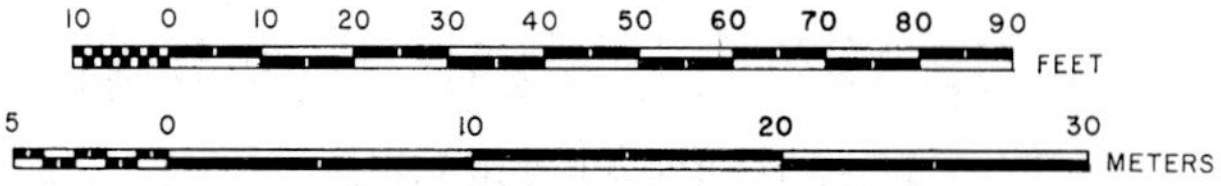

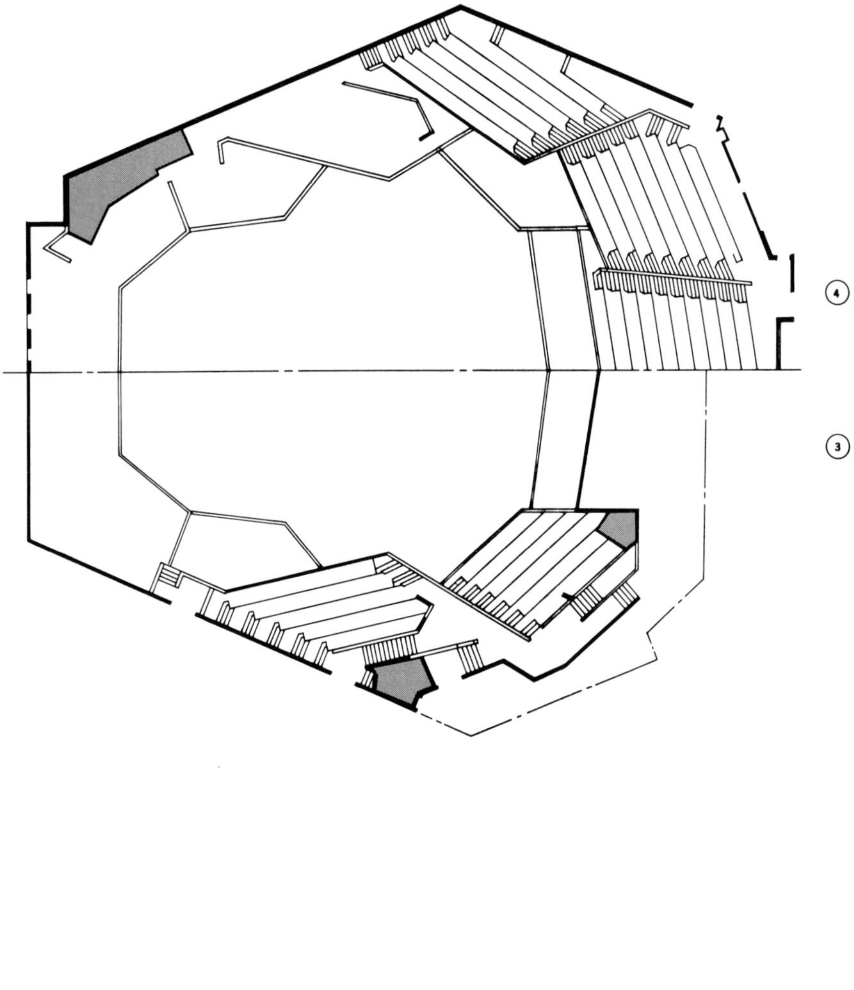
4
3

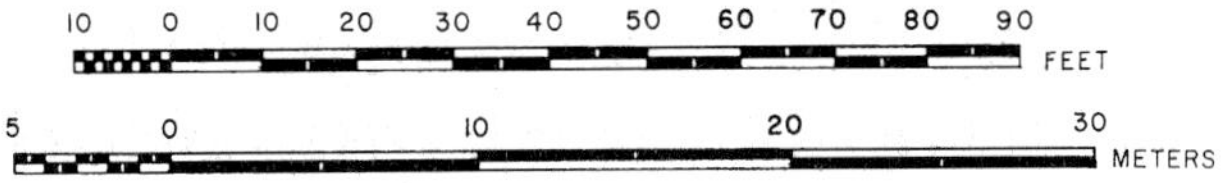
10 0 10 20 30 40 50 60 70 80 90
FEET
5 0 10 20 30
METERS

CARDIFF, WALES, ST. DAVID'S HALL

Architectural and structural details

Uses: (see the text). *Ceiling:* The roof is 8 in. (20 cm) precast foamed concrete slabs, sealed with paint. Open steel walkways with plywood flooring. Ventilation ducts are lined with sound absorbing material. *Suspended ceilings:* visual only, 4 in. by 4 in. (10 cm) open cells; a large suspended metal space frame incorporates stage lighting, loudspeakers, etc., and profiled plywood sound reflecting panels within the depth of the frame aimed at selected positions (see the photo). *Walls:* 8 in. (20 cm) brick with 0.5 in. (1.25 cm) plaster; behind choir seating, profiled panels with varying depths of painted plasterboard (see the photo); above suspended ceiling level, dense concrete block, surface sealed; rear wall around stage, plywood with ash veneer; balcony fronts, the same. *Main floors:* 0.75 in. (1.9 cm) wood over concrete ramp with 10 to 20 cm airspace beneath. Mushroom ventilation openings in floors. *Tier floors:* oak strips solidly imbedded in screed. *Carpets:* on perimeter aisles only. *Stage floor:* 0.75 in. (1.9 cm) oak screwed to 0.75 in. plywood, supported by joists on 0.2 in. resilient pads. *Stage height:* 32 in. (80 cm). *Seating:* seat backs and underseats, molded plywood. Upholstering on two surfaces.

Architect: Seymour Harris, Partnership. *Acoustical consultant:* Sandy Brown and Associates. *Photographs:* Gwyn Williams, courtesy of St. David's Hall. *References:* A. N. Burd, "St. David's Hall, Cardiff," Proc. Inst. of Acoustics and Electro-Acoustics meeting, Edinburgh, Sept. 1982. M. Barron, *Auditorium Acoustics and Architectural Design*, E & FN Spon (Chapman & Hall), pp. 173–181 (1993).

*Technical details**

V = 777,000 ft^3 (22,000 m^3)	S_a = 10,760 ft^2 (1,000 m^2)	S_A = 13,300 ft^2 (1,235 m^2)
S_o = 2,000 ft^2 (186 m^2)	S_T = 15,300 ft^2 (1,420 m^2)	N = 1,952
H = 59 ft (18 m)	W = 90 ft (27.4 m)	L = 90 ft (27.4 m)
D = 110 ft (33.5 m)	V/S_T = 50.7 ft (15.5 m)	V/S_A =58.4 ft (17.8 m)
V/N = 397 ft^3 (11.2 m^3)	S_A/N = 6.8 ft^2 (0.63 m^2)	H/W = 0.66
L/W = 1.0	t_I = 25 msec	

**The terminology is explained in Appendix 1.*

GREAT BRITAIN

49

Edinburgh
Usher Hall

On first entry to Usher Hall, the stage commands one's attention. Double columns painted ivory and trimmed in gold form the sides of the proscenium opening. The orchestra is seated as in a theater pit—extending far on either side of the conductor and shallow in depth. Behind the orchestra, on steeply raked platforms, are seats for 335 listeners. Above these seats the great organ cabinet rises to the ceiling in rich polished wood fronted by gold pipes. The hall seems small and the orchestra seems close to the listeners. Aside from the stage, only the two graceful lines of the balcony make an architectural impression.

Dedicated in 1914, Usher Hall seats 2,547 and has a reverberation time at mid-frequencies, fully occupied, of about 1.5 sec, which is well below the lower end of the optimum range of 1.8 to 2.0 sec for symphonic music. The hall is non-uniform acoustically.

The sound is best in the upper balcony. On the main floor, in back of about the fifth row, the sound is also quite good, although somewhat lower in level for a hall of this relatively small volume. The string tone comes through clearly, and the blend of orchestral tone is good. Also, the balance of the strings, woodwinds, brass, and percussion is satisfactory. Because the orchestra is spread so wide for its depth, cross echoes can be heard when a section at either end plays alone. The least satisfactory acoustics is in the center of the first balcony, where in most halls the sound is best. There the music lacks clarity and brilliance and the different orchestral sections do not blend well. There are insufficient short-time-delay reflections to give spaciousness to the tone. In the hall in general, the reverberation is not apparent.

In summary, Usher Hall has satisfactory acoustics on the main floor and in the upper balcony. It is not as good in the first balcony. The reverberation time at middle frequencies is short but the music is clear and the orchestral tone and sectional balance are good in most parts of the hall.

EDINBURGH, USHER HALL

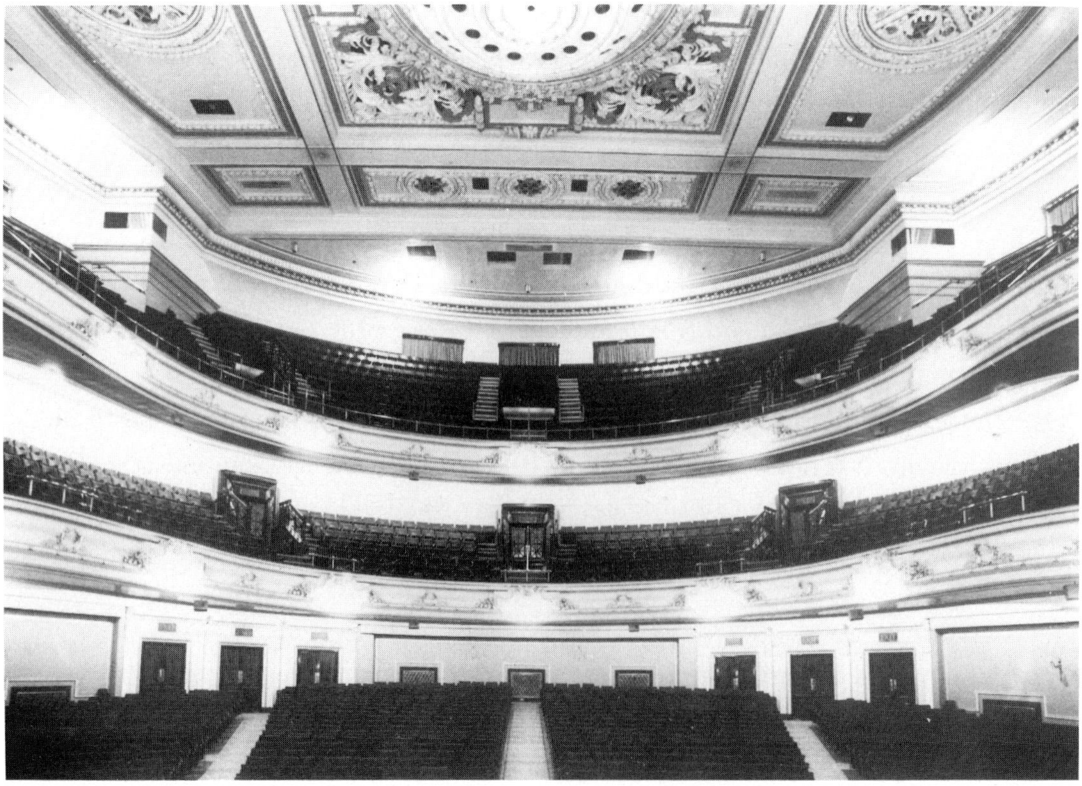

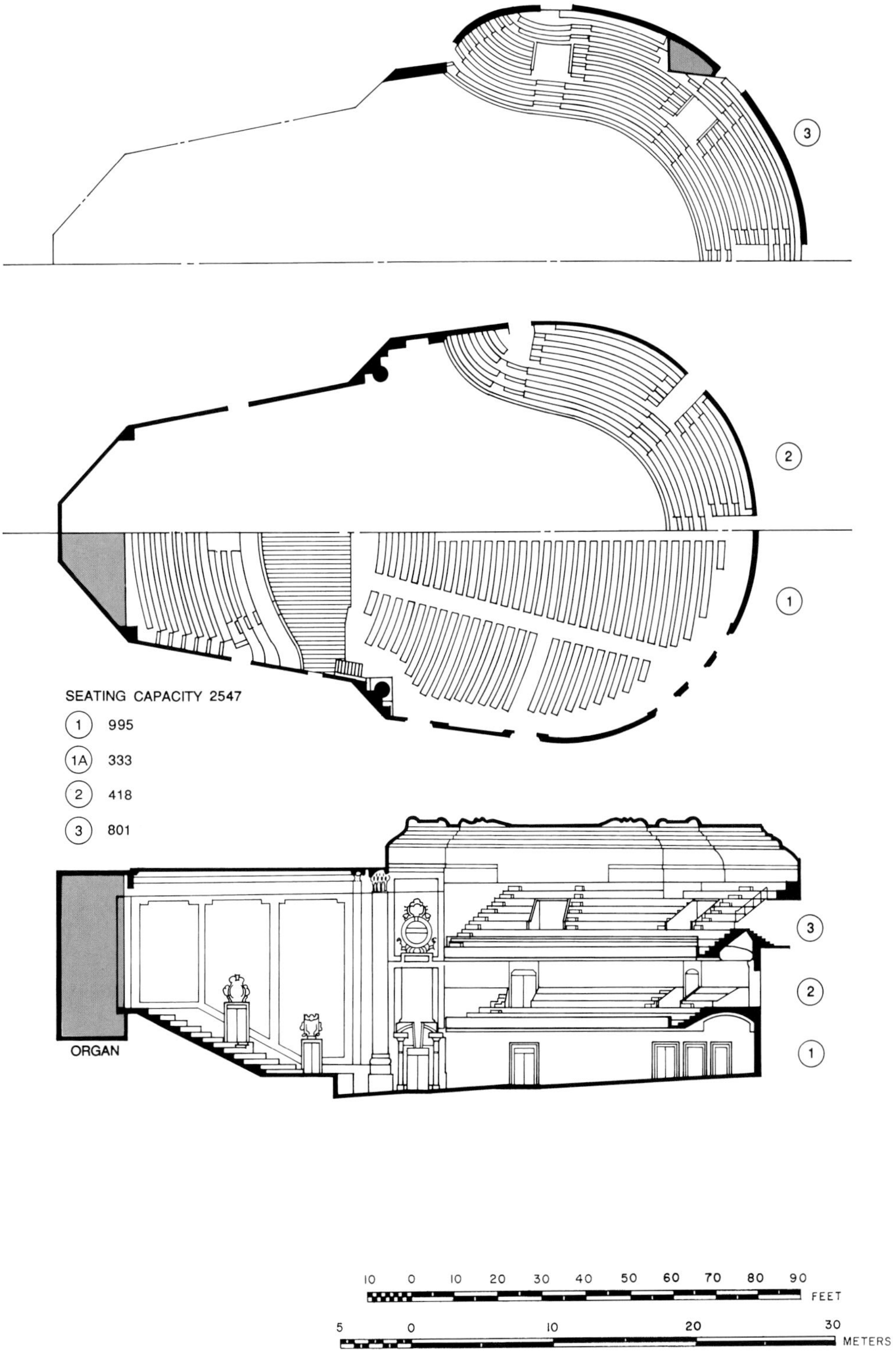
3
2
1
SEATING CAPACITY 2547
1 995
1A 333
2 418
3 801
ORGAN
3
2
1
10 0 10 20 30 40 50 60 70 80 90
FEET
5 0 10 20 30
METERS

Architectural and structural details

Uses: mostly orchestral and popular music. *Ceiling:* plaster on wood lath with thick plaster ornamentation; the main ceiling is ribbed, and the "rose" decorative panels are perforated. *Walls:* masonry finished with plaster on wood lath over batons with airspace behind. *Floors and carpets:* wood boards in the seating area on the main floor and in the first balcony; in the second balcony, there are wood boards under the seats and linoleum on boarding in the aisles; behind the orchestra there is carpet in the aisles and wood boards under the seats. *Stage enclosure:* plaster on wood lath. *Stage floor:* planks over large airspace with wood boxes for risers; the stage front is perforated for ventilation purposes. *Stage height:* 53 in. (135 cm) *Seating:* on the main floor and the first balcony, the top of the seat bottom is upholstered with a deep base; armrests are upholstered; plywood back is covered with the same fabric; underside is unperforated plywood; in the second balcony, the seats are lightly upholstered with solid backs; in the choir, the seats are of wood.

Architect: Stockdale Harrison and Sons, and H. H. Thomson. *Photographs:* courtesy of Michael Barron. *References:* T. Somerville and C. L. S. Gilford, Gravesaner Blatter, 3, No. 9 (1957). M. Barron, *Auditorium Acoustics and Architectural Design*, E & FN SPON, Chapman & Hall, London and New York. Details from Sandy Brown Associates and Michael Barron.

*Technical details**

V = 554,400 ft^3 (15,700 m^3)	S_a = 11,195 ft^2 (1,040 m^2)	S_A = 14,400 ft^2 (1,338 m^2)
S_o = 1,290 ft^2 (120 m^2)	S_T = 15,690 ft^2 (1,458 m^2)	N = 2,547
H = 56 ft (17 m)	W = 78 ft (23.8 m)	L = 100 ft (30.5 m)
D = 115 ft (35 m)	V/N = 218 ft^3 (6.16 m^3)	V/S_T = 35.3 ft (10.8 m)
V/S_A = 38.5 ft (11.7 m)	S_A/N = 5.65 ft^2 (0.525 m^2)	H/W = 0.72
L/W = 1.28	t_I = 33 msec	

**The terminology is explained in Appendix 1.*

GREAT BRITAIN

50

Glasgow, Scotland
Royal Concert Hall

The Glasgow Royal Concert Hall opened in 1990. It seats 2,195 plus 264 choir for full orchestra. The Royal Concert Hall replaces the well liked St. Andrew's Hall of 1877 which burned tragically in 1962. The plan of the hall is an elongated hexagon, resembling somewhat the plan of the De Doelen concert hall of Rotterdam. Besides the main floor, there is a terraced surround and a balcony with an elongated rear section. The Hall is partially multi-purpose; the first eleven rows can be removed and, with all stage sections on elevators, an extensive flat floor area is available for staging arena format productions. The extensive choir seating, peculiar to Great Britain, is also used for audience.

The stage, set up for full orchestra, has an area of about 2,260 ft^2 (210 m^2) which is much larger than Boston, but somewhat smaller than many modern stages. Although there is no visual canopy or hanging panels over the stage to provide cross-communication among the musicians, there are four panel structures for masking the lighting grids that reflect early sound energy back to the musicians and the front main-floor audience. Because the width of the hall is great at the highest level, eight large panel reflectors with QRD diffusers on the surfaces (see Chapter 10) are employed on each side to provide early reflections, particularly to the sides and lower-rear balcony seating areas. The QRD reflectors scatter the incident sound energy in various directions, so that the reflected sound has a mellow, pleasant texture.

The reverberation time measured with full audience at mid-frequencies is 1.75 sec. At 125 Hz it rises to 2 sec, giving the sound a warm patina. The ratio of early sound energy to later reverberant sound energy indicates clarity without emphasis on the reverberant sound. In the top balcony, the reverberation is more apparent because neither the reflecting panels nor other surfaces direct appreciable early sound energy there. The sound everywhere is clear, intimate, enveloping, and sufficiently loud. Overall, visually and acoustically, Glasgow can be proud of its excellent hall.

Glasgow, Scotland, Royal Concert Hall

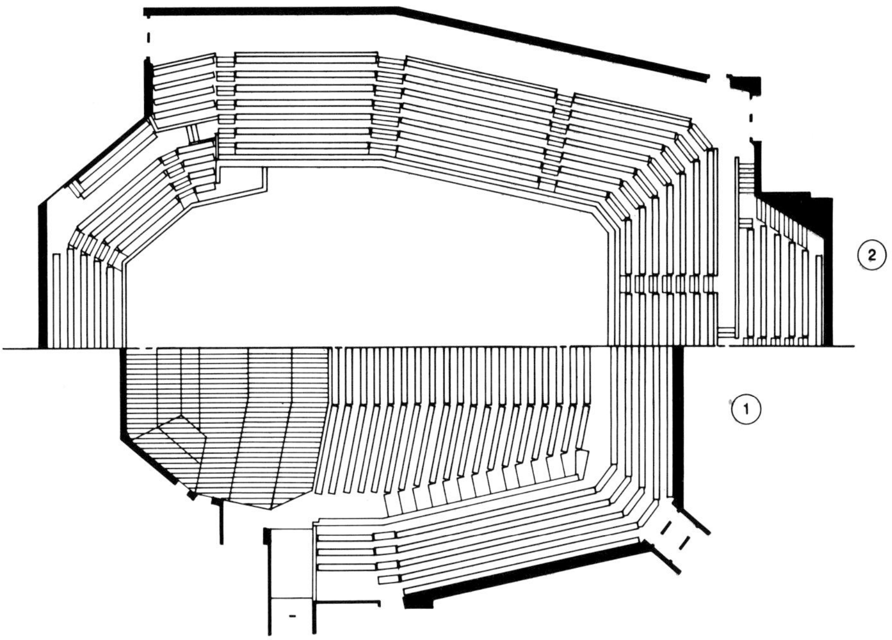

SEATING CAPACITY 2457

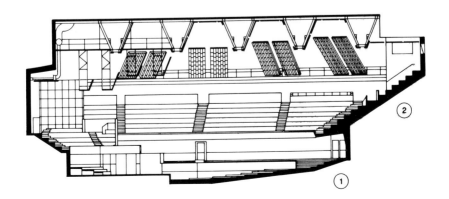

(1)	1160
(2)	1297

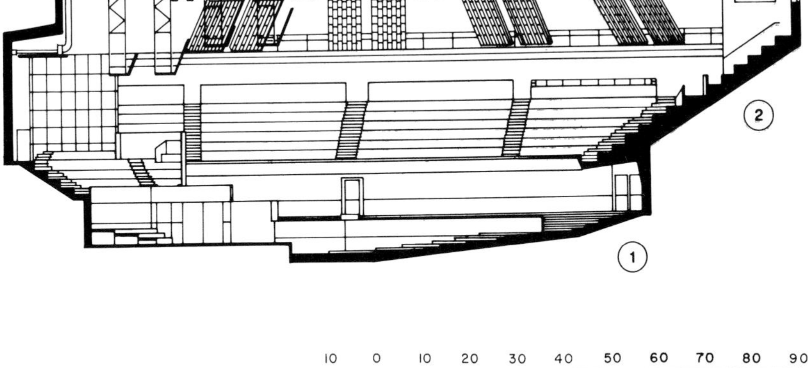

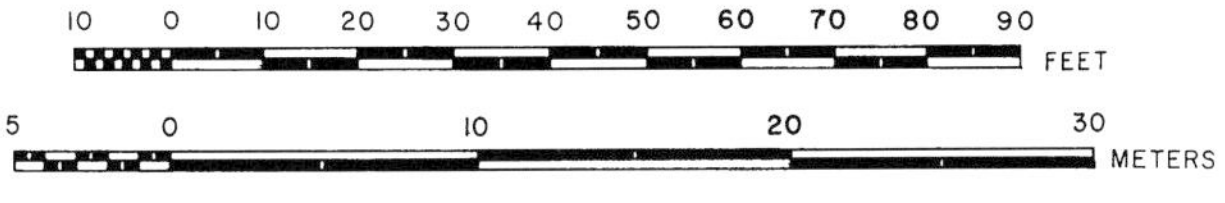

Architectural and structural details

Uses: events of all kinds, excluding opera and proscenium theater. *Ceiling:* described in 2 parts: spaces above QRD panels and roof trusses, 4 in. (10 cm) concrete deck, clad underside with ash veneered chipboard 0.7 in. (1.7 cm) thick, with 18 in. (45 cm) airspace above; ceiling panels above balcony and choir, same but 32 in. (80 cm) airspace above. *Ceiling of promenade above balcony:* plasterboard 1/2 in. (1.7 cm) thick. *Overstage reflecting panels:* (backward "L" shape on drawing) veneered chipboard as above. *Upper walls:* dense concrete, finished with painted slurry. *Walls above balcony:* same, with painted gypsum plaster finish. *Walls around main floor:* 0.8 in. (2 cm) thick wood over 1 ft (30 cm) airspace. *Balcony fronts:* fibrous plaster, 1/2 in. (1.5 cm) thick. *QRD reflectors:* fibrous plaster fixed to tubular frame. *Seating steps:* concrete. *Floors:* concrete. *Stage lifts:* 0.8 in. (2 cm) thick wood on 0.6 in.(1.8 cm) plywood on rubber pads on steel framing. *Carpet:* in aisles, thin, cemented to concrete slab; in promenade, carpet over underpad. *Stage height:* 39 in. (1 m). *Seating:* Molded plywood back and unperforated plywood seat bottom; upholstered front of seat back and seat with CMHR cushion covered by porous fabric; armrests upholstered.

Architect: Sir Leslie Martin and RMJM Scotland Ltd. *Acoustical consultant:* Fleming & Barron and Sandy Brown Associates. *Photographs:* courtesy of the Department of Architecture, City of Glasgow. *References:* M. Barron and A. N. Burd, "The Acoustics of Glasgow Royal Concert Hall." Proceedings of Institute of Acoustics, **14**, 21–29, Part 2 (1992), presented at Institute meeting in Birmingham, England, May 18–19, 1992.

*Technical details**

V = 810,540 ft^3 (22,700 m^3)	S_a = 11,560 ft^2 (1,074 m^2)	S_A = 14,700 ft^2 (1,365 m^2)
S_o = 2,346 ft^2 (218 m^2)	S_T = 17,046 ft^2 (1,584 m^2)	N = 2,459
H = 63 ft (19.2 m)	W = 108 ft (32.9 m)	L = 90 ft (27.8 m)
D = 111 ft (33.8 m)	V/S_T = 47.5 ft (14.3 m)	V/S_A = 55.2 ft (16.6 m)
V/N = 330 ft^3 (9.23 m^3)	S_A/N = 6.0 ft^2 (0.555 m^2)	H/W = 0.58
L/W = 0.83	t_I = 20 msec	

**The terminology is explained in Appendix 1.*

51

Liverpool Philharmonic Hall

Philharmonic Hall, pleasant, warm, and comfortable, opened in 1939. Its side walls and ceiling form a shell inside the basic construction, comprised of a series of sections, each about 15 ft (4.6 m) wide and extending down to the balcony and box levels. These sections, of decorated plaster, are arranged in echelon, with the front edge of each section rolled back to leave a recess for lighting. An audience of 140 is seated on a permanent stadium, semi-circular in shape, partially surrounding the orchestra. The exposed ends of this stadium, the wall behind it, and the semi-circular ring of boxes are finished in warm mahogany.

In 1960, I met with Gerald McDonald, then General Manager of the Royal Liverpool Philharmonic Society. He said, "From the point of view of artists performing in the hall, the fact that there are only 613 seats enclosed by a ring of most attractive boxes seating 128, with a further audience of 943 in the balcony, is an unusual and stimulating feature. Its relatively low reverberation time and beautiful well-defined tone make it uniquely favorable for Baroque and Classical music starting with Bach, for Modern music, and for any music that is cerebral in nature or requires refinement of definition." I fully agree with this perceptive analysis.

The conductors and music critics whom I interviewed spoke well of the hall. However, most remarked on its dryness of sound, caused by the relatively low reverberation time, 1.5 sec, particularly at low frequencies. The conductor rehearsing on stage that day said that he had tried every arrangement of the orchestra to strengthen the bass, but with no satisfaction.

I listened to Arriaga's *Symphony in D*, Beethoven's *Concerto No. 5 for Piano*, and Stravinsky's ballet music *Petrouchka* at a regular concert while moving among three seats. The music was clear, brilliant, and absolutely faithful. The piano sounded glorious. The violin pizzicato was absolutely true, as was the sound of each instrument. The blend and ensemble were excellent. However, the hall had little apparent reverberation and the basses and cellos were weak. On the main floor, the brass-percussion-strings balance was good. In the rear of the balcony, the brass and percussion tended to be overly loud.

Liverpool, Philharmonic Hall

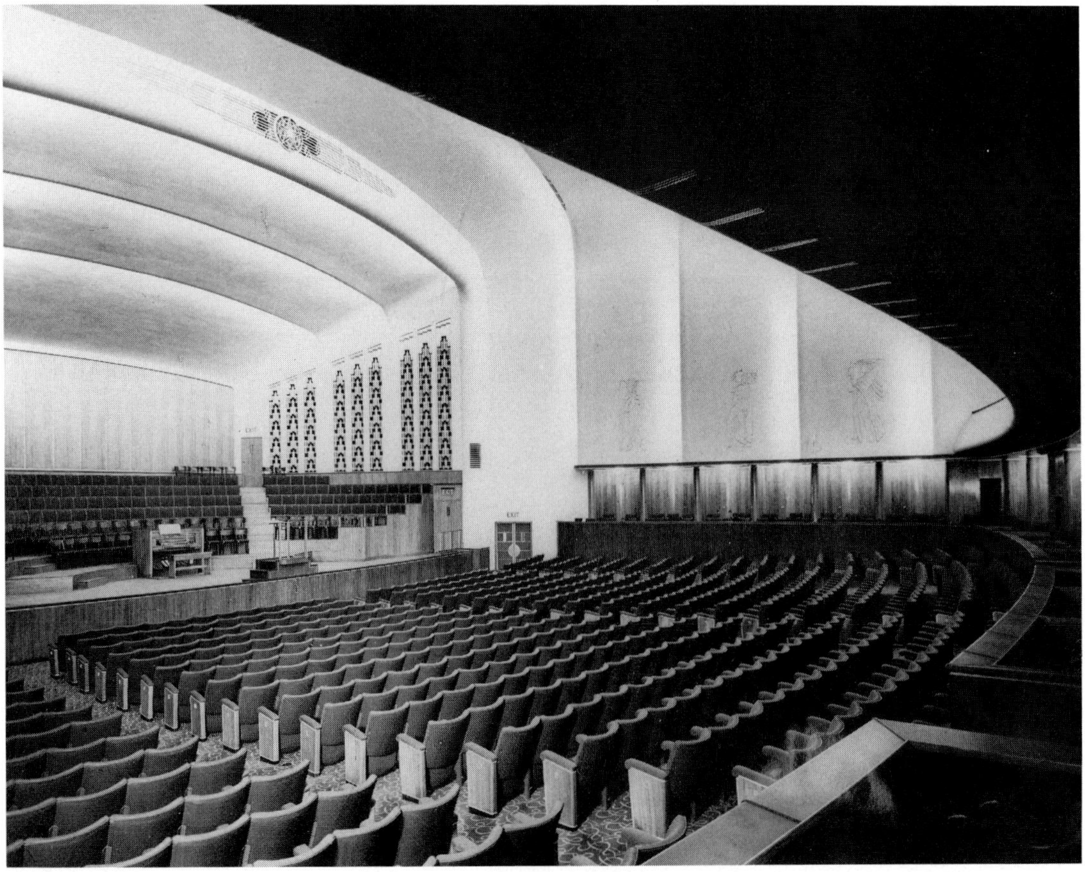

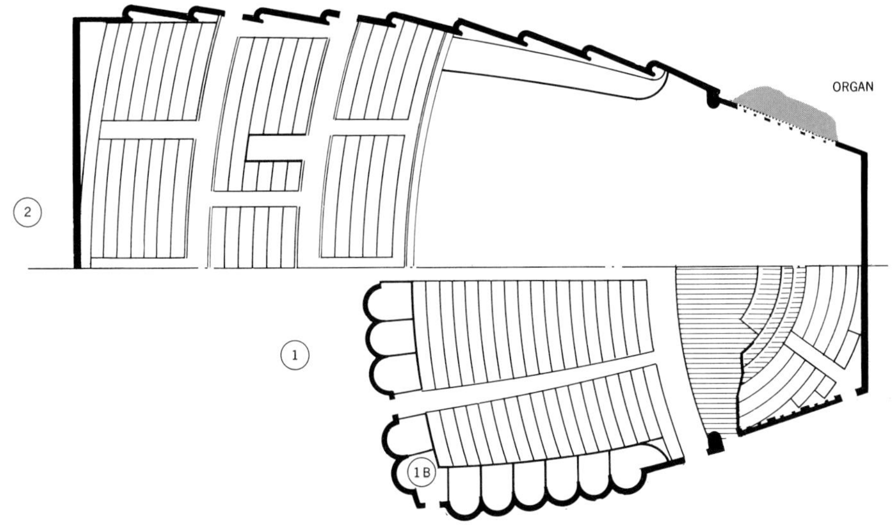

SEATING CAPACITY 1824

1	613
1A	140
1B	128
2	943

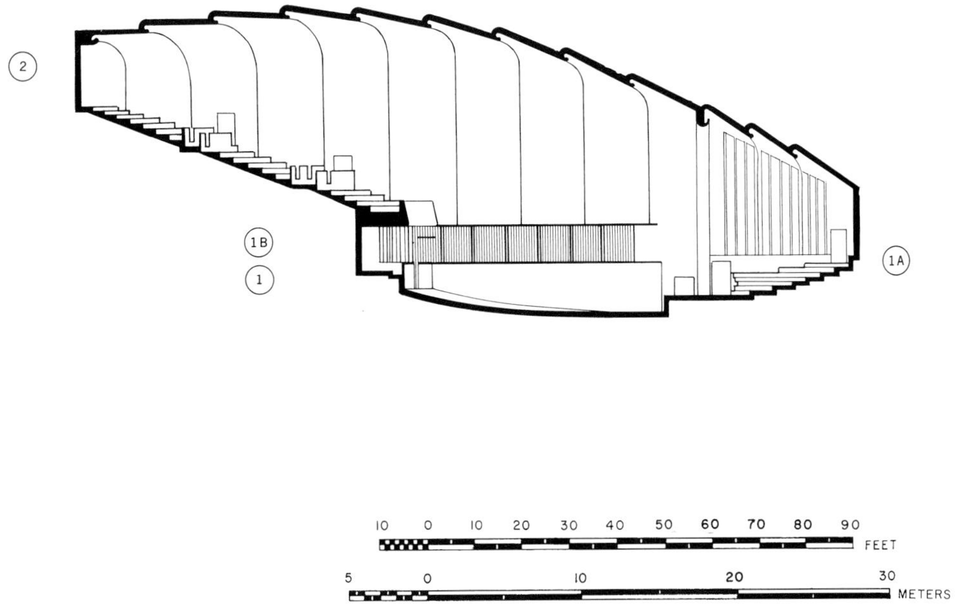

Architectural and structural details

Uses: half for symphonic music and half for speech. *Ceiling and side walls:* plaster on metal lath, divided above the boxes by lighting coves into 15 ft (4.6 m) sections; there are about 4,350 ft^2 (404 m^2) of wood paneling on the lower side walls; the boxes are of wood. *Rear upper walls:* rock wool batts covered with draperies. *Floors:* concrete. *Carpets:* all floors. *Stage enclosure:* the side walls are occupied by organ grilles; the back wall is paneled in wood. *Stage floor:* boards on joists over airspace. *Stage height:* 36 in. (91 cm) above floor level. *Seating:* both sides of the backrest and the seat are upholstered in tightly woven cloth.

Architect: Herbert J. Rowse. *Acoustical consultant:* Hope Bagenal. *Photographs:* courtesy of City of Liverpool. *References:* T. Somerville and C. L. S. Gilford, *Gravesaner Blatter*, **3**, No. 9, 1957. H. Parkin, W. E. Scholes, and A. G. Derbyshire, *Acustica*, **2**, 97–100 (1952). M. Barron, *Auditorium Acoustics and Architectural Design*, E & FN SPON, Chapman & Hall, New York and London (1993).

*Technical details**

V = 479,000 ft^3 (13,560 m^3)	S_a = 10,700 ft^2 (994 m^2)	S_A = 13,900 ft^2 (1,291 m^2)
S_o = 1,400 ft^2 (130 m^2)	S_T = 15,300 ft^2 (1,421 m^2)	N = 1,824
H = 46 ft (14 m)	W = 98 ft (30 m)	L = 94 ft (28.6 m)
D = 128 ft (39 m)	V/S_T = 31.3 ft (9.54 m)	V/S_A = 34.5 ft (10.5 m)
V/N = 263 ft^3 (7.43 m^3)	S_A/N = 7.62 ft^2 (0.71 m^2)	H/W = 0.47
L/W = 0.96	t_I = 25 msec	

**The terminology is explained in Appendix 1.*

Great Britain

52

London
Barbican Concert Hall

The Barbican Concert Hall is the home of the London Symphony Orchestra. It is located in the Barbican Centre, which also includes a theatre, two cinemas, and a school of music and drama. It is the largest center of its kind in Europe. The Concert Hall, seating 2,026, has three curved, raked seating tiers with no boxes. The interior is all wood, paneled in pine with a canopy above the stage The floor is end-cut wooden block.

The multi-segment over-stage reflector neither helps the musicians nor projects sound to the audience. Unusual are the deep transverse beams in the ceiling, necessitated by the hall's location below an outdoor plaza and the initial limited digging depth. The hall is very wide, 141 ft (43 m), and there are almost no surfaces appropriate to producing early lateral reflections.

The acoustics has received unsatisfactory reviews. The most serious stated deficiencies are lack of bass and delayed reflections from the side and angled rear walls, which are audible as echoes. Prior to 1994, the lack of bass was at least partly caused by the 0.39 in. (1 cm) plywood wall paneling on the walls and the unusual built-in seating. The large transverse beams and deep coffers prevent most of the ceiling from sending reflections of the sound to the upper tiers. A panel of British acousticians stated (before 1994 revisions) that, in addition to the short reverberation time and the lack of bass, there is generally a lack of excitement and a feeling that one is isolated from the performance because of the lack of early lateral reflections and the distraction of echoes.

Renovations of the summer of 1994 include backing the plywood wall panels to increase their thickness to 2.83 in. (7.2 cm). Felt, 0.125 in. (0.32 cm) thick, now covers the lower side walls to reduce the annoyance of the delayed reflections. The rear walls of the main floor and first balcony are covered with QRD diffusors (see Chapter 10). Future plans include narrowing the width of the main floor, installing a thick suspended ceiling at the bottom of the trusses, and replacing the ceiling of the stage with a better acoustical design to give support to the musicians and reflections to the audience.

London, Barbican Concert Hall

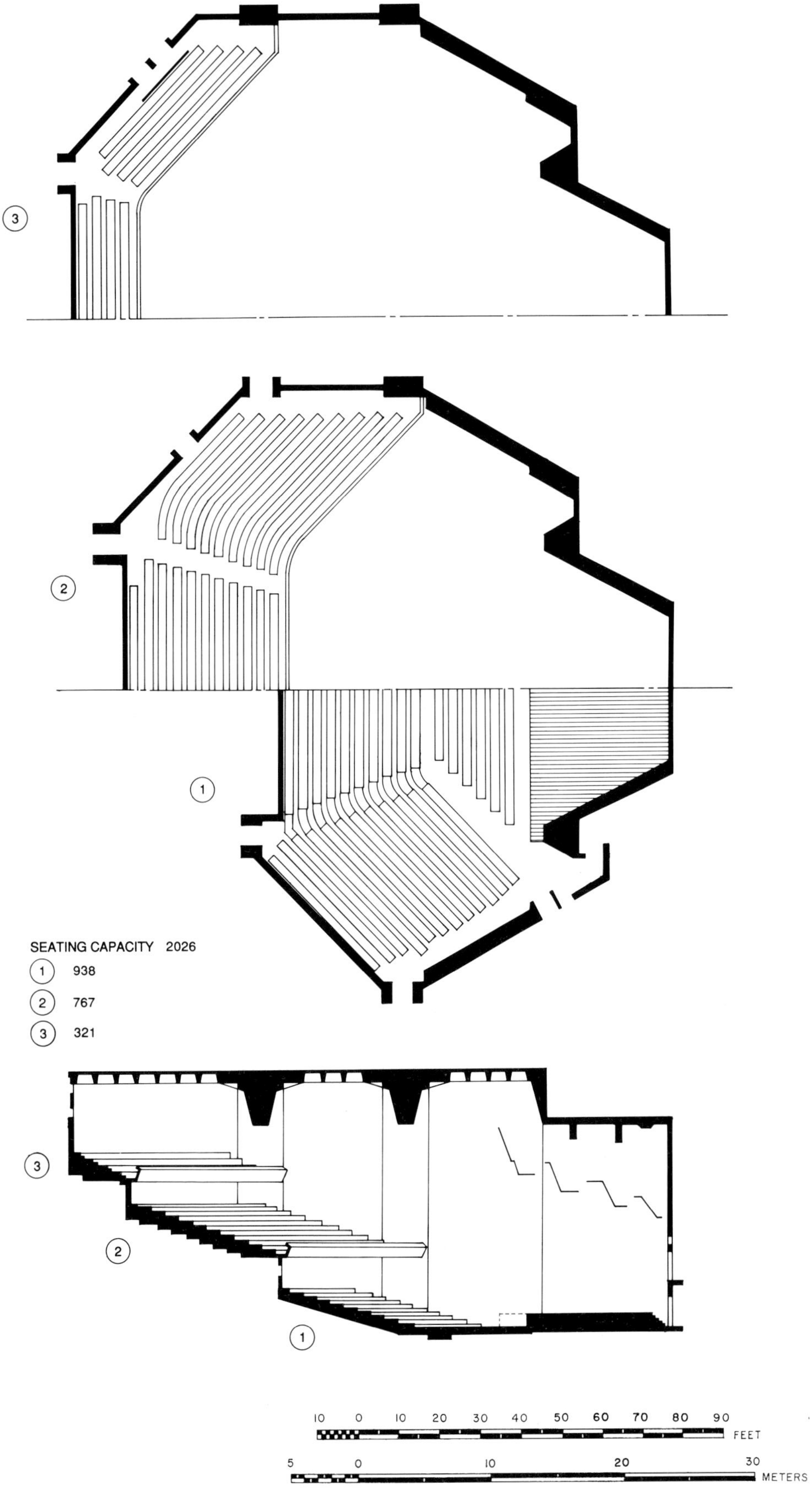
3
2
1
SEATING CAPACITY 2026
1 938
2 767
3 321
3
2
1
10 0 10 20 30 40 50 60 70 80 90
FEET
5 0 10 20 30
METERS

Architectural and structural details

Uses: symphonic music, chamber music, recitals, and some conferences. *Ceiling:* solid concrete. *Side walls:* upper side walls, 2.83 in. (7.2 cm) single-layer, plywood panels on frames; lower side walls are the same but covered with felt 0.125 in. (0.32 cm) thick; rear walls covered with diffusers like those in Carnegie Hall. *Floors:* end-grain, wood-block over concrete. *Added sound absorption:* lower side walls covered with thin 0.125 in. (0.32) felt; rear walls of main floor and first balcony covered with QRD diffusers which both diffuse the reflections and add some sound absorption. *Carpets:* none. *Stage enclosure:* timber with sculptured surface, with areas of panel absorption over concrete. *Stage canopy:* 0.5 in. (1.25 cm) plywood in non-acoustical-supporting configuration. *Stage floor:* partly wooden over airspace, four elevators with wood surface. *Stage height:* 3 ft (0.91 m) above floor level. *Seating:* top of seat bottom is upholstered, bottom is plywood; front side of backrest and armrests are heavily upholstered.

Consultant architects: Chamberlain, Powell & Bon. *Original acoustical consultant:* Hugh Creighton. *Acoustical consultant for 1994 revisions:* Kirkegaard and Associates. *Photographs:* courtesy of Michael Barron. *Reference:* Michael Barron, *Auditorium Acoustics and Architectural Design*, E & FN Spon and Chapman & Hall, London and New York (1993).

*Technical details**

V = 626,750 ft^3 (17,750 m^3)	S_a = 12,090 ft^2 (1,123 m^2)	S_A = 14,270 ft^2 (1,326 m^2)
S_o = 1,722 ft^2 (160 m^2)	S_T = 16,000 ft^2 (1,485 m^2)	N = 2,026
H = 47 ft (14.3 m)	W = 129 ft (39.3 m)	L = 90 ft (27.4 m)
D = 115 ft (35.1 m)	V/S_T = 39.2 ft (11.9 m)	V/S_A = 43.8 ft (13.4 m)
V/N = 309 ft^3 (8.76 m^3)	S_A/N = 7.04 ft^2 (0.65 m^2)	H/W = 0.36
L/W = 0.70	t_I = 27 msec	

**The terminology is explained in Appendix 1.*

GREAT BRITAIN

53

London
Royal Albert Hall

On Wednesday, March 29, 1871, Queen Victoria, on one of her rare public appearances after the death of the Prince Consort, appeared in the royal box of the newly completed Royal Albert Hall of Arts and Sciences, surrounded by members of the Royal Family, to participate in the official opening. The official record (see References, Clark, p. 58) relates: The "Prince of Wales ... began to read a welcoming address ... speaking distinctly in a clear voice that could be heard in all parts of the building; in many parts it could be heard twice, a curious echo bringing a repetition of one sentence as the next was begun." Thus began 100 years of experiments in an attempt to transform into a concert hall a space that is much too large ever to be fully successful for this purpose.

The Royal Albert Hall holds 5,080 persons seated plus about 1,000 standees. It is nearly elliptical in shape with a cubic volume of about 3,060,000 ft^3 (86,650 m^3), four times as great as the largest regular well-liked concert hall of the world. Its uses are many—pageants, lectures, exhibitions, choral presentations, symphony concerts, proms concerts, solo recitals, even athletic events. One of the buildings most famous features is the great pipe organ, installed in 1871, and rebuilt for a second official presentation in 1934. The Royal Albert Hall fulfills London's need for a hall with a large seating capacity.

The principal acoustical problems of the Royal Albert Hall, particularly before the 1970 additions, arise from its size. They are: (1) decrease in loudness of the direct and early sound emanating from the performers as it travels such large distances in the hall (consider a voice trying to fill nearly six times more cubic volume of air than there is in a typical European concert hall); and (2) echoes, owing to the return of very-long-delayed reflections from distant surfaces back to the front of the hall.

To alleviate the echoes, but further weakening the loudness of the sound, a large velarium of cloth weighing 1.25 tons (1,136 kg) was hung and remained until 1949. This velarium was raised and lowered from time to time in an effort to better the acoustics. In 1934, we read, "The echo persisted and there was even some suggestion that it had grown worse."

I take my next information on the Royal Albert Hall from M. Barron (see References, 1993, pp. 117–125). " ... it was only in 1968–1970 that the echo problem was finally suppressed by suspending 134 'flying saucer' diffusers at the level of the Gallery ceiling [see the photograph and sketch] ... Two aspects were also dealt with during this period....The reverberation time [that] was particularly long at mid-frequencies ... was rendered more uniform with frequency ... by placing absorbent which was most efficient at these frequencies on the upper side of the saucers...This location for absorbent is particularly apt because it increases the effect of the saucers by absorbing some remaining sound reflected from the dome. Another problem with a large space is maintaining sufficient early reflections when some seats are inevitably remote from useful surfaces. The reflections from the suspended saucers are very valuable at the upper seating levels. A reflector above the stage, as first used in 1941, has been retained to provide [early sound] reflections particularly to the [main floor] and [lower side] seating."

The measured occupied reverberation time (measurements by M. Barron in 1982) is 2.4 sec at mid-frequencies. This is not disastrous in a room this size. The more serious problem is the weakness of orchestral sound, partly because it is absorbed to some extent by the upper surfaces of the saucers, and partly because it has to be distributed over 5,080–6,000 heads, compared to 1,680 in Vienna's Grosser Musikvereinssaal. Perhaps, as electronic sound reinforcement becomes more common, the level can be increased by that means. The hall has been very successful in presenting popular (Pops or Proms) concerts—audiences of over 4,000 are common. It is also recognized that it is a most effective venue for large choral groups and for the presentation of such pieces as Tchaikovsky's *Overture 1812.*

I heard the *1812.* The great organ sounded out at the climax and the "cannon" boomed forth. The chimes clanged loudly through their part and, finally, in combination with the military fanfare theme, the *Russian Imperial Anthem* thundered forth. The general reverberation swelled with the increased vigor of the composition. Above all, the great organ sounded like the voice of Jupiter. The audience was left breathless and tingling. It is for these moments of ecstasy that Albert Hall continues to exist.

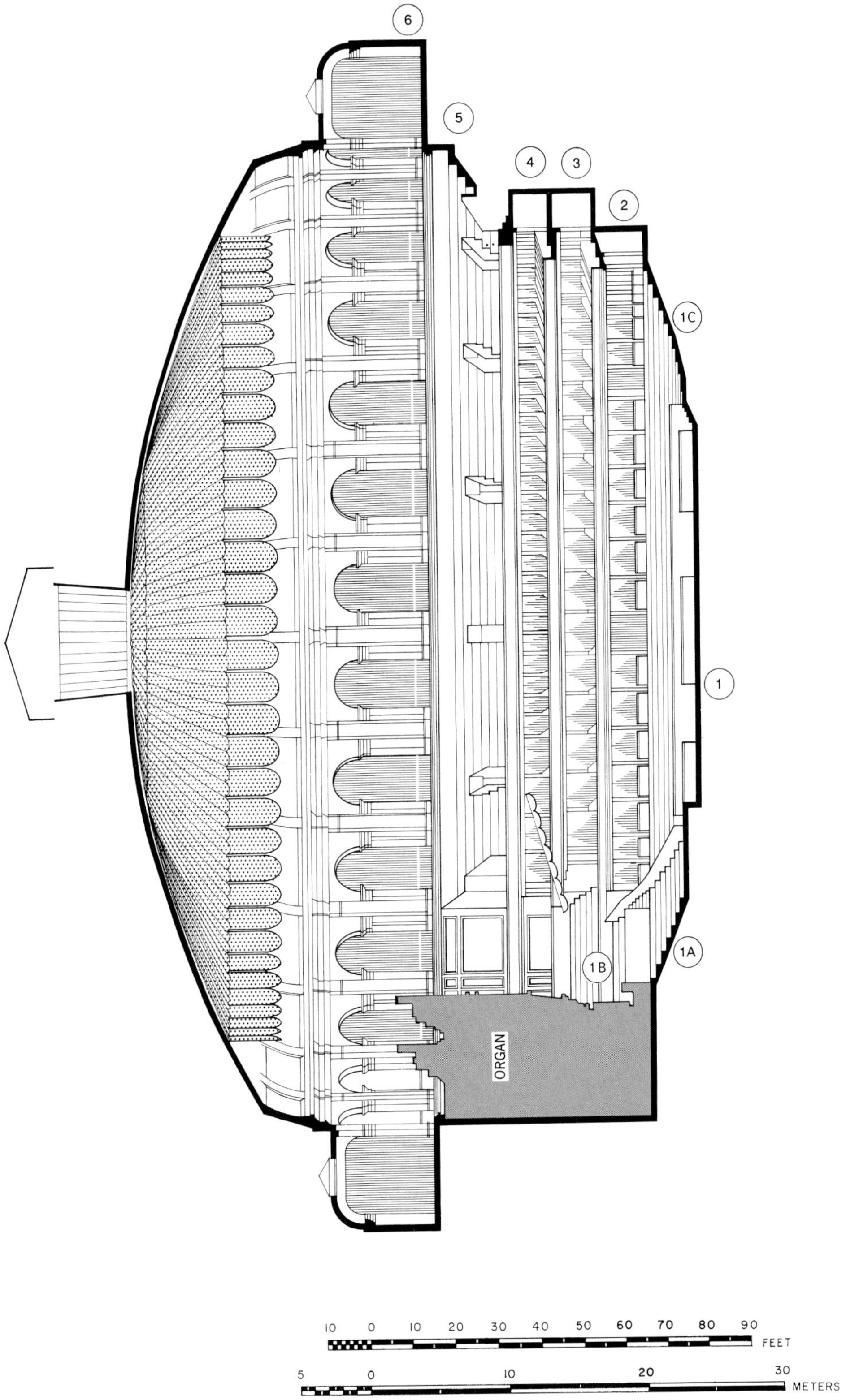
6
5
4
3
2
1C
1
1A
1B
ORGAN
10 0 10 20 30 40 50 60 70 80 90
FEET
5 0 10 20 30
METERS

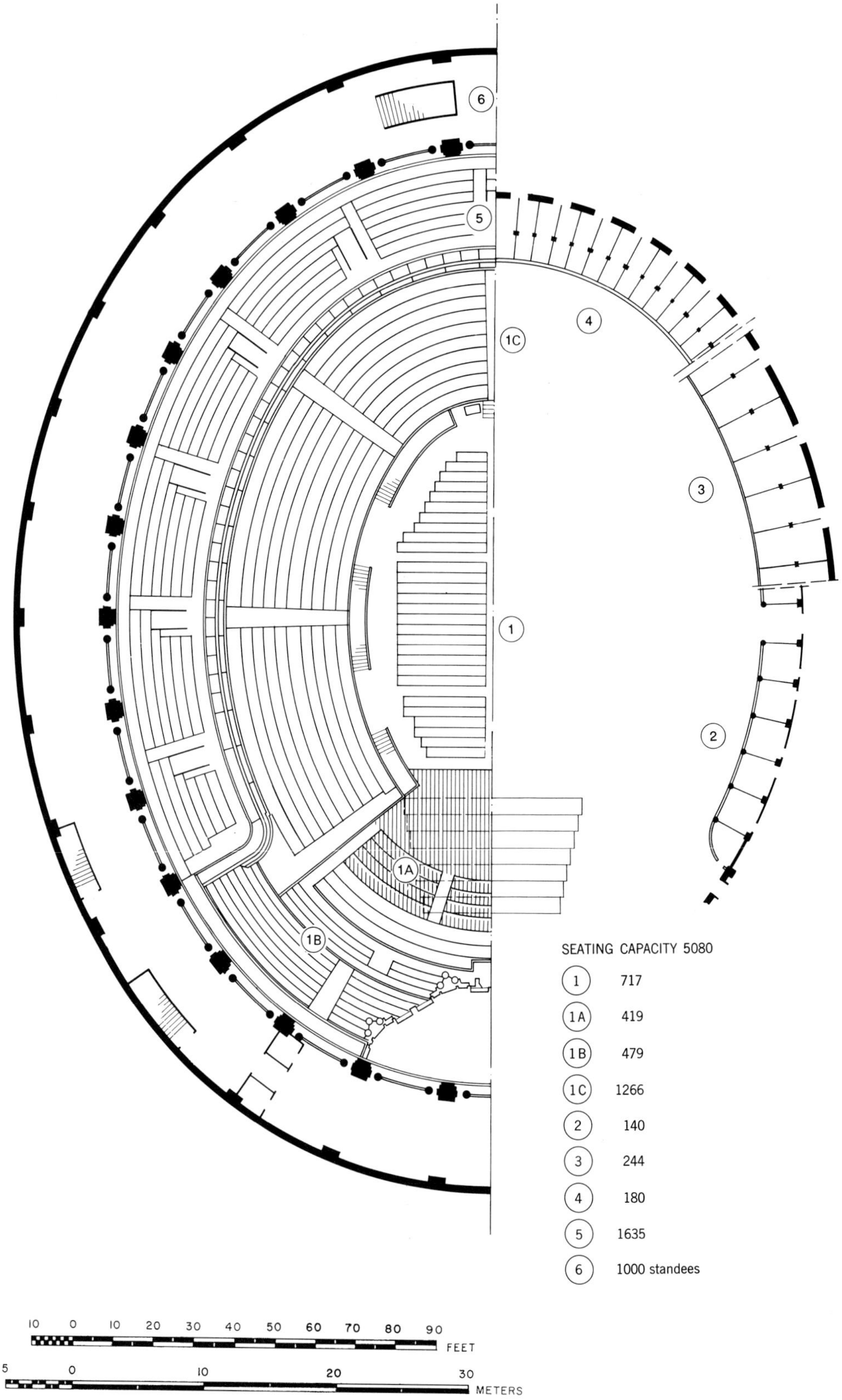
6
5
4
1C
3
1
2
1A
1B
SEATING CAPACITY 5080
1 717
1A 419
1B 479
1C 1266
2 140
3 244
4 180
5 1635
6 1000 standees
10 0 10 20 30 40 50 60 70 80 90
FEET
5 0 10 20 30
METERS

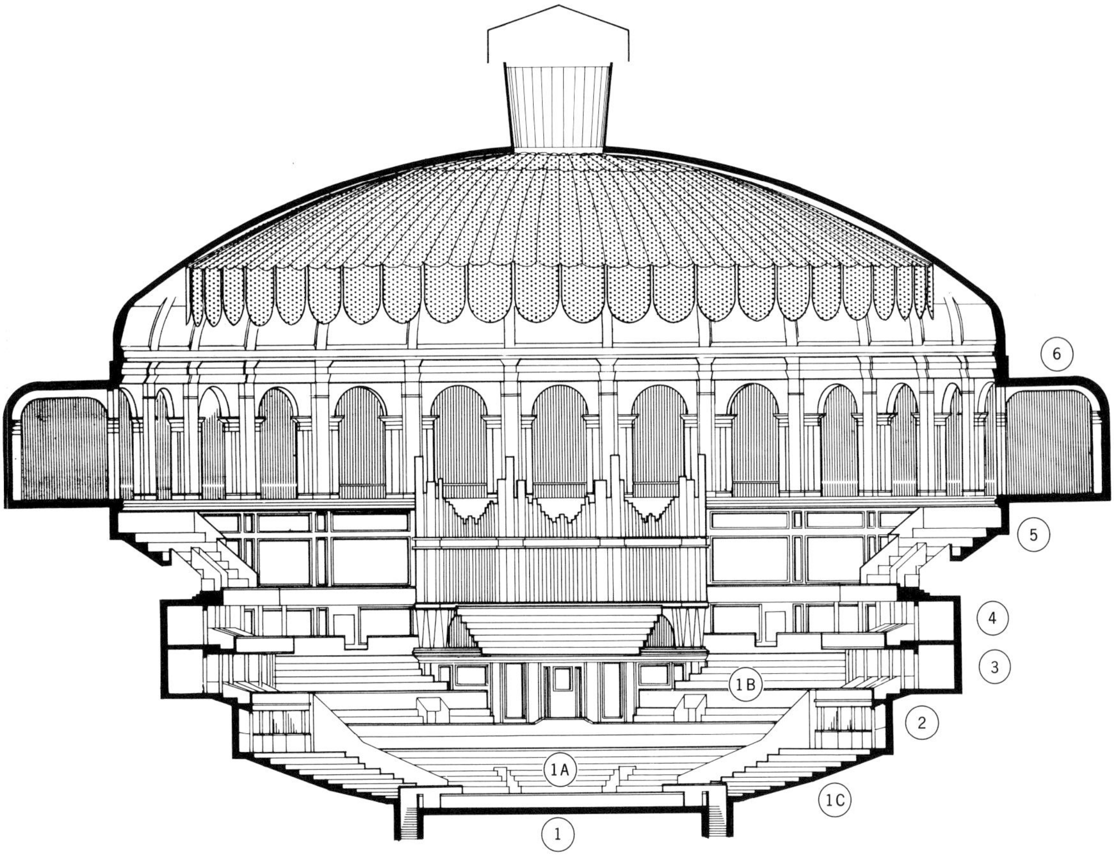
6
5
4
3
1B
2
1A
1C
1

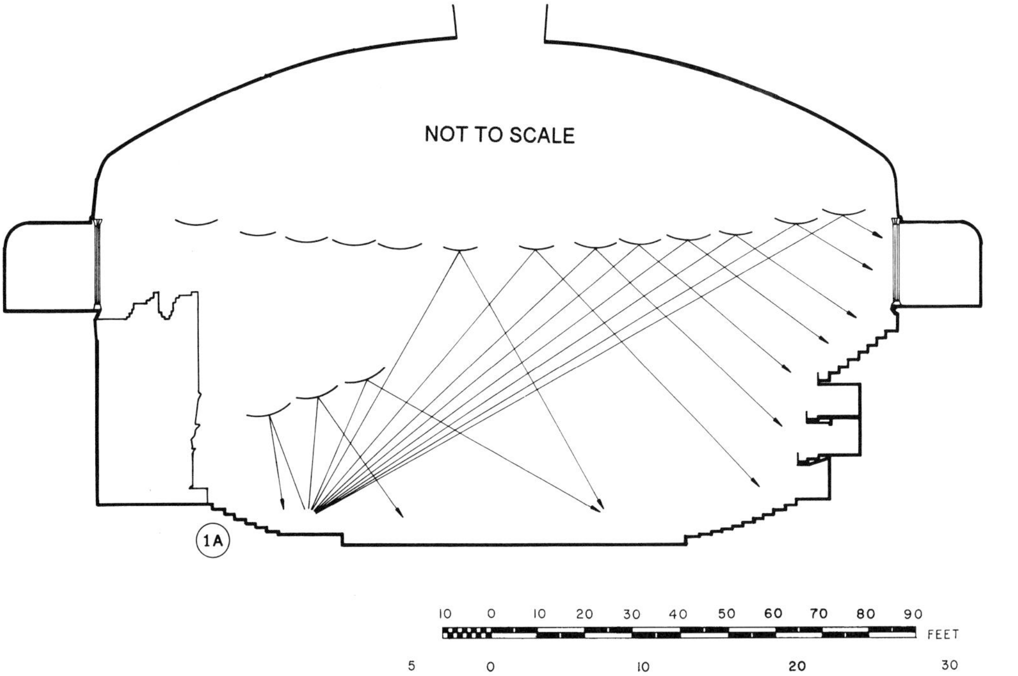
NOT TO SCALE
1A
10 0 10 20 30 40 50 60 70 80 90
FEET
5 0 10 20 30
METERS

LONDON, ROYAL ALBERT HALL

Architectural and structural details

Uses: general purpose. *Ceiling:* roof over balcony is of plaster directly on the structure; fluted inner dome with perforated inner skin backed by mineral wool, plus 134 hanging sound-diffusing reflectors—"flying saucers" which are glass reinforced plastic dishes with 1.5 in. (3.8 cm) glass fiber blanket on top. *Walls:* generally plastered, but the back of the boxes are of thin wood. *Floors:* arena floor is 1 in. (2.5 cm) on wooden joists over large airspace; balcony is of concrete; box floors are of wood. *Stage enclosure:* glass-reinforced canopy over orchestra. *Stage floor:* thick wood over airspace. *Stage height:* 40 in. (102 cm). *Carpets:* often used on arena floor. *Seating:* arena and main floor surrounding, tops of seats and fronts of backrests are upholstered with cloth covering—all other surfaces are of wood; boxes, loose occasional chairs upholstered the same as for arena; balcony, theater-type tip-up chairs upholstered in cloth; gallery, 300 wooden chairs for use in the standing areas.

Designers: Capt. Francis Fowke (who died during design in 1865) and Lt. Col. H. Y. D. Scott (who succeeded Fowke and continued as Director of Works under the supervision of a "Committee on Advice"). *References:* Ronald W. Clark, *The Royal Albert Hall*, Hamish Hamilton, London, 1958. M. Barron, *Auditorium Acoustics and Architectural Design*, FN SPON, Chapman & Hall, New York and London (1993). *Photographs:* courtesy of M. Barron and Royal Albert Hall.

*Technical details**

V = 3,060,000 ft^3 (86,650 m^3)	S_a = 29,000 ft^2 (2,700 m^2)	S_A = 37,800 ft^2 (3,512 m^2)
S_o = 1,900 ft^2 (176 m^2)	S_T = 39,700 ft^2 (3,688 m^2)	N = 5,080+1,000 standees
H = 118 ft (36 m)	W = 155 ft (47 m)	L = 146 ft (44.5 m)
D = 140 ft (42.7 m)	V/S_T = 77.1 ft (23.5 m)	V/S_A = 81 ft (24.7 m)
V/N = 602 ft^3 (17 m^3)	S_A/N = 7.44 ft^2 (0.69 m^2)	H/W = 0.76
L/W = 0.94	t_I = 15 msec	

**The terminology is explained in Appendix 1.*

54

London
Royal Festival Hall

The Royal Festival Hall, opened in 1951, is said to host more important musical events annually than any other large concert hall. The architecture is a triumph, a fascinating mosaic of stairways, carpets, lighting, and interior vistas. The approach up the stairs and through foyers is so cleverly made and so beautiful that it promises an evening of excitement. The designers have achieved beauty through proportion and color and admirably contrived lighting. Dominant features in the Hall itself are a large three-part canopy over the stage, projecting box fronts on the side walls, a large pipe organ, and a steeply raked main floor.

From 1900 to 1948 only a handful of large halls had been built in the world, and most of them before modern acoustical measuring equipment was available. Thus Festival Hall, seating 2,901, was the site for most of the experiments in concert hall acoustics in the first half of the twentieth century.

The general consensus by all types of listeners is that the hall is "too dry," not reverberant enough, particularly at low frequencies, and that the bass tone is weak. The primary cause was the lack of technical information on how much sound an audience absorbs when seated in modern theater chairs. The consultants used an absorbing indicator of 0.33 per person, compared to today's accepted 0.57 per person. The result: a reverberation time at 500 Hz of 1.5 sec, compared to the design goal of 2.2 sec. At the low frequencies the reduced reverberation time is also contributed to by the open area of the boxes, the light-weight ceiling, and other sound absorbing surfaces.

My analysis, backed by the interviews, is that the definition is excellent and the hall is very good for piano, chamber music, and modern music. The hall is not as effective for music of the late Classical and Romantic periods. The lack of bass (without electronic assistance) is the most serious problem.

The low reverberation times have led to the invention of an electronic, reverberation-enhancement system. Called "Assisted Resonance," it has increased the reverberation times, particularly at the lower frequencies. A number of music critics have responded favorably to the new "richness" of the sound. For many listeners, its effect is not enough to reverse the hall's reputation. Nevertheless, one can be excited by the clear sound in a large space, even without the fullness of tone of a Boston Symphony Hall.

We have all benefited from its presence and from its lessons. Above all, it illustrates that one hall cannot be all things to all compositions.

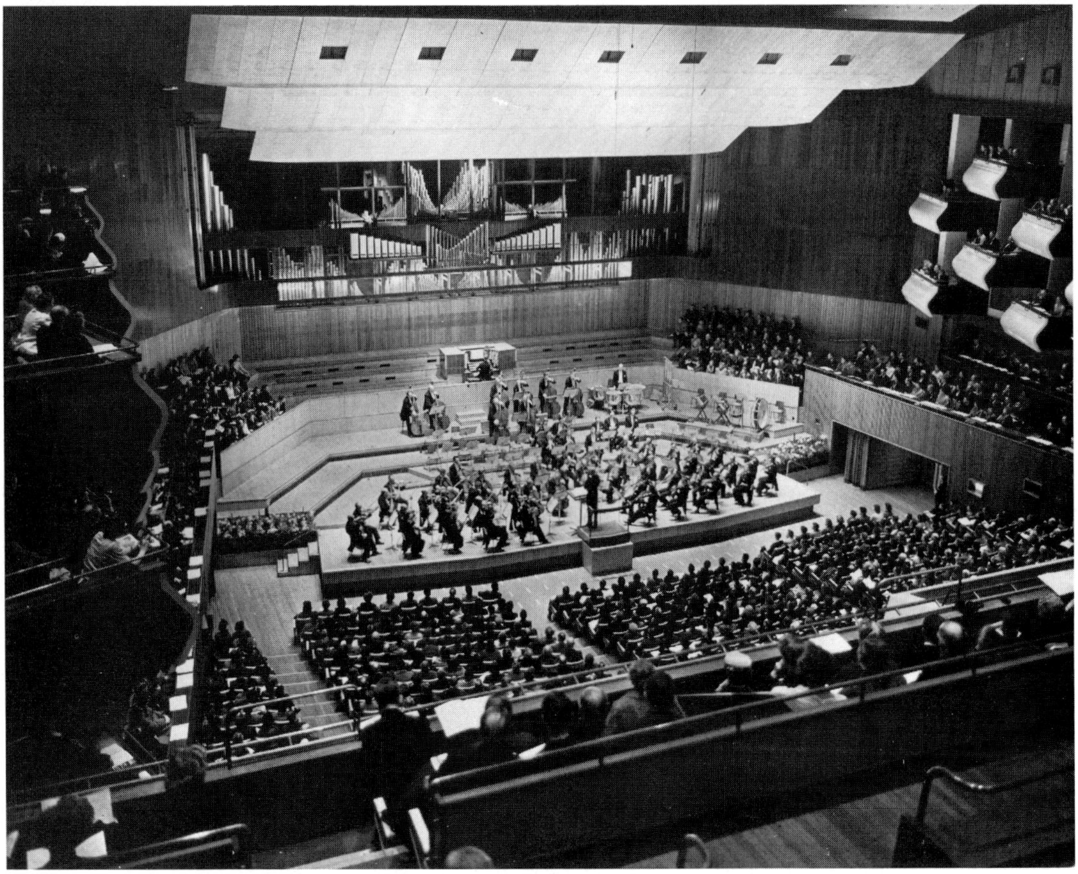

London, Royal Festival Hall

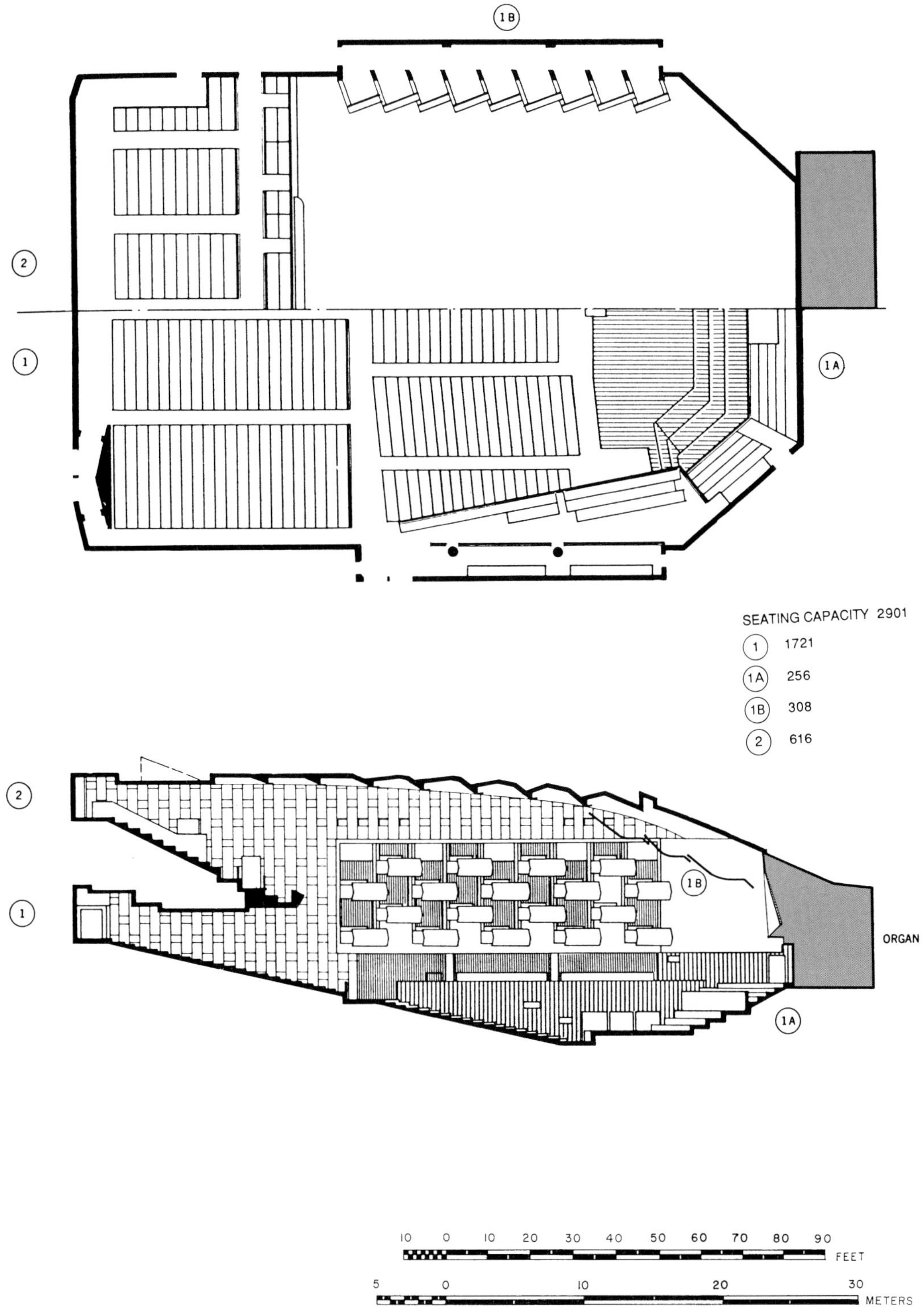
1B
2
1
1A
SEATING CAPACITY 2901
1 1721
1A 256
1B 308
2 616
2
1
1B
ORGAN
1A
10 0 10 20 30 40 50 60 70 80 90
FEET
5 0 10 20 30
METERS

Architectural and structural details

Uses: classical concerts, plus summer ballet season. *Ceiling:* 2 to 3 in. (5 to 7 cm) plaster, prefabricated with wood lath and rags for binding. *Side and rear walls:* 0.4 in. (1 cm) elm plywood with 3 to 4 in. (7 to 10 cm) airspace behind; the doors, the rears of the side balconies, and the rear walls are covered with leather, backed by rock wool with several inches of airspace behind; exposed wood wool, 2 in. (5 cm) thick is used in 33% of the cornice regions. *Floors:* principally thin, hard, compressed cork on concrete. *Carpets:* transverse aisles carpeted. *Stage floor:* wooden boards over airspace. *Stage height:* 30 in. (76 cm). *Sound absorbing materials:* see walls and ceiling. *Seating:* molded wooden seat back, upholstered front of seat back and top of seat bottom with porous fabric; underseat, perforated wood; choir seats partly upholstered in leather; armrests upholstered in leather.

Architect: London County Council Architects' Department, R. H. Mathews, J. L. Martin with E. Williams and P. M. Moro. *Acoustical consultant:* Hope Bagenal with Building Research Station (H. R. Humphreys, P. H. Parkin, and W. A. Allen). *Photographs:* courtesy of Royal Festival Hall. *References:* P. H. Parkin, W. A. Allen, H. J. Purkis, and W. E. Scholes, *Acustica*, **3**, 1–21 (1953); E. Meyer and R. Thiele, *Acustica*, **6**, 425–444 (1956). M. Barron, *Auditorium Acoustics and Architectural Design*, E & FN Spon, Chapman and Hall, New York and London (1993).

*Technical details**

V = 775,000 ft³ (21,950 m³)	S_a = 16,500 ft² (1,540 m²)	S_A = 21,230 ft² (1,972 m²)
S_o = 1,860 ft² (173 m²)	S_T = 23,090 ft² (2,145 m²)	N = 2,901 (with box seats)
H = 50 ft (15.2 m)	W = 106 ft (32.3 m)	L = 121 ft (36.8 m)
D = 126 ft (38.4 m)	V/S_T = 33.6 ft (10.2 m)	V/S_A = 36.5 ft (11.1 m)
V/N = 267 ft³ (7.56 m³)	S_A/N = 7.32 ft² (0.68 m²)	H/W = 0.47
L/W = 1.14	t_I = 34; 14 msec	

**The terminology is explained in Appendix 1.*

55

London
Royal Opera House

The Royal Opera House, Covent Garden, rebuilt in 1858 and seating 2,120, is one of the world's most important centers for opera. London profits from its long heritage and interest in producing all that is internationally good in opera, whether Italian, French, Austrian, German, English, Slavic, or other. It has presented the world's finest singers and has boasted of some celebrated music directors—Frederich Gye, Augustus Harris, Sir Thomas Beecham, and Bruno Walter. The Royal Opera House is a boon to artists because London appreciates opera and the house is small enough to be truly enjoyable.

The Royal Opera House differs from La Scala, which seats almost the same number, 2289, by having four instead of six rings and instead a large gallery. Those in the rear of the gallery are 130 ft (39.6 m) from the front of the stage compared to 105 ft (32 m) in La Scala.

Two British conductors said to me that the House has very good acoustics indeed. They remarked that it is not as brilliant in quality as La Scala, San Carlo in Naples, or the Teatro Colon in Buenos Aires, but it is very good, particularly in the boxes and upper parts of the house, and the sound in the pit is very pleasant.

Two of London's music critics agreed in saying that the house has the normally good acoustics of the traditionally round-shaped opera interior. They add that it has always been true that the best blend and clarity of tone is to be found in the upper tiers.

I have attended a number of operas there, the first time in 1958. The singing voice projects beautifully and the opera experience is good in all parts of the house. There is some deficiency in the bass tones, perhaps due to thin plywood barriers behind the seats at all levels of the house. The musical balance among the instrumental sections is, in general, satisfactory throughout the house, although on the main floor the violins are somewhat weak.

Taken all in all, I rate La Scala in Milan and the Staatsoper in Vienna as acoustically superior to the Royal Opera House. But it equals or betters the Paris houses and is distinctly better than New York's colossus.

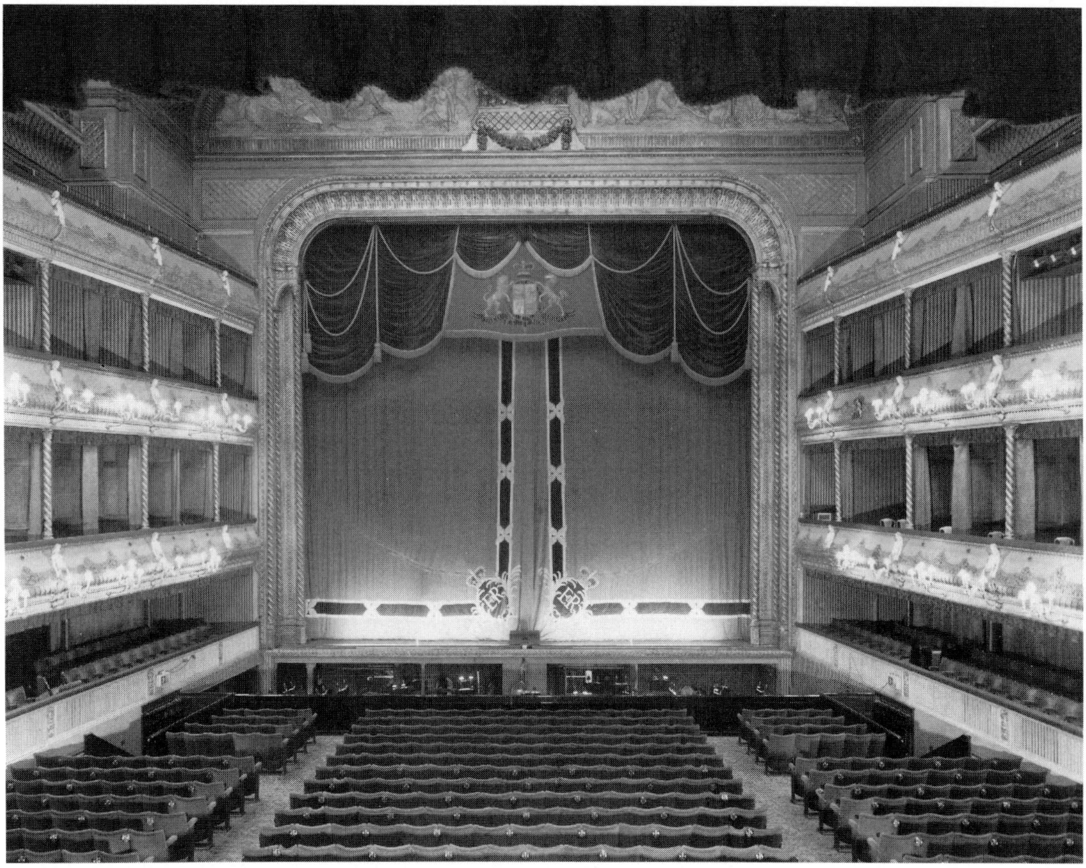

London, Royal Opera House

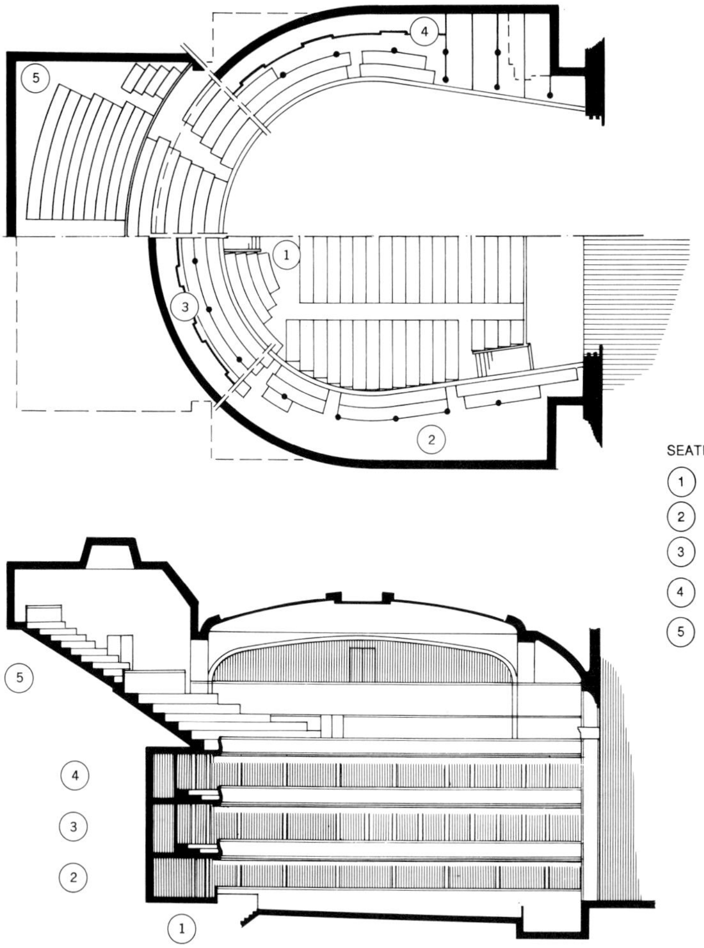

SEATING CAPACITY 2120

(1) 551

(2) 318 + 58 standies

(3) 214

(4) 221

(5) 816

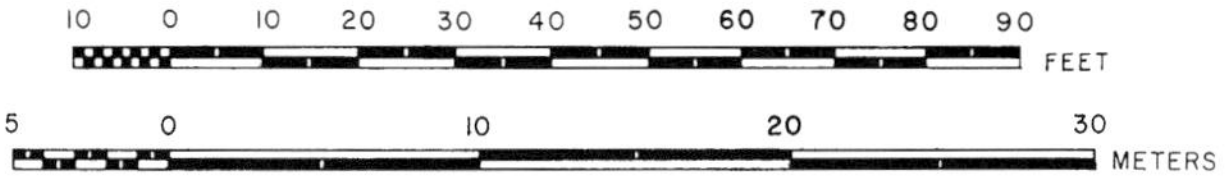

Archirtural and structural details

Uses: opera and ballet. *Ceiling:* plaster on 0.4 in. (1 cm) resin board. *Walls:* faces of all tiers are plaster on wood lath; rear of main floor and two lower tiers are thin plywood screens, wallpapered; gallery is plywood on battens. *Floors:* wood, all levels. *Pit:* hardwood floor over 18 in. (0.46 m) airspace; walls brick and papered; no sound-absorbing materials; rail is 2 in. (5 cm) solid teak. *Seating:* On main floor, two tiers and front balcony, the seat, backrest, and armrests are upholstered; rear of backrest, is cloth over wood; in upper gallery, continuous benches with moquette cloth over thin underpadding; in boxes, four upholstered chairs in each.

Architect: Edward Barry. *Photographs:* courtesy of British Travel Association. *References:* technical details courtesy Royal Opera House and W. A. Allen. M. Barron, *Auditorium Acoustics and Architectural Design*, E & FN SPON, Chapman & Hall, New York and London (1993).

*Technical details**

Opera

V = 432,500 ft^3 (12,250 m^3)	S_a = 11,720 ft^2 (1,090 m^2)	S_A = 14,630 ft^2 (1,360 m^2)
S_o (pit) = 670 ft^2 (62.2 m^2)	S_p = 1,880 ft^2 (175 m^2)	S_T = 17,180 ft^2 (1,600 m^2)
N = 2,120	H = 61 ft (18.6 m)	W = 80 ft (24.4 m)
L = 98 ft (29.9 m)	D = 130 ft (39.6 m)	V/S_T = 25.2 ft (7.67 m)
V/S_A = 29.5 ft (9 m)	S_A/N = 6.91 ft^2 (0.64 m^2)	V/N = 204 ft^3 (5.8 m^3)
H/W = 0.76	L/W = 1.2	t_I = 18 msec

**The terminology is explained in Appendix 1.*

56

Manchester
Free Trade Hall

The Free Trade Hall, one of the "Festival of Britain" halls, opened in 1951 along with London's Royal Festival and Bristol's Colston. The architect had to build within the boundaries of the facade, the only part of the building that remained after the bombings. A striking feature of the hall is the ceiling, with 35 octagonal indentations, each about 3 ft (1 m) deep. The inner sides of the coffers have seven or so steps, each of which is painted a different brilliant color—turquoise, red, yellow, green, and pink. The large panels between columns on the side walls are painted turquoise with a coat-of-arms in a small brown panel at the top of each. The dominant architectural feature at the front of the hall is the tremendous three-part canopy over the orchestra. Viewed from the stage, the 2,351 seat hall appears to be predominantly balconies.

Three conductors well familiar with the hall were enthusiastic, saying, "One of the most satisfactory acoustically in England. One experiences intimacy; the contact with the audience is quite remarkable for such a large hall." "The hall is comfortable to listen in and the sound satisfactory."

In my lone listening experience, the sound in the front part of the first balcony (opposite the stage) was most reverberant but lacked clarity, the piano was not at its best and the brass and percussion in the forte passages overpowered the strings. The least well liked parts of the hall, I am told, are those seats under the balcony overhangs. In the center of the main floor, the orchestral balance was much better and the basses, cellos, woodwinds, and piano were much clearer. The main overall-hall criticism is lack of reverberation, although 1.6 sec, occupied, is not unusual.

Barron (see references) writes, "But the surprise about the Free Trade Hall is that the disadvantaged seats do not sound worse. For instance at the rear of the [main floor] the acoustical response is better than the very unsatisfactory visual situation. One can even distinguish individual musical parts with some success there. The big compensation for the hall's acoustics may be related to [the feeling by a listener of] envelopment [by the sound field]." The reason, he says, is the reverse fan shape (in plan) at the rear of the main floor and each of the balconies, which provide important lateral reflections to the seating areas.

Manchester, Free Trade Hall

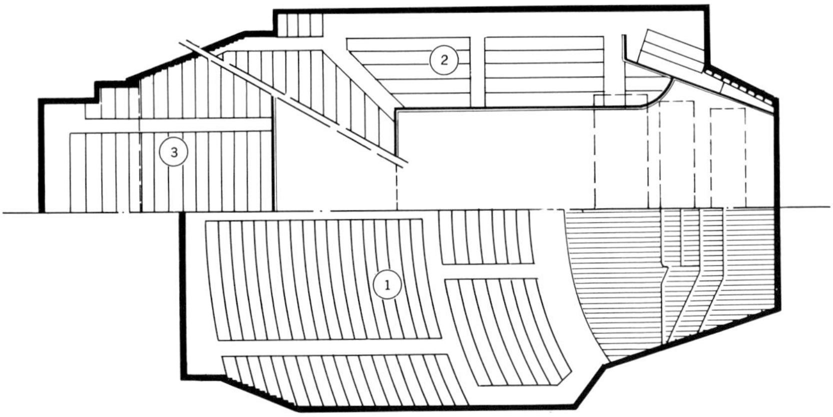

SEATING CAPACITY 2351

(1) 1076

(2) 865

(3) 410

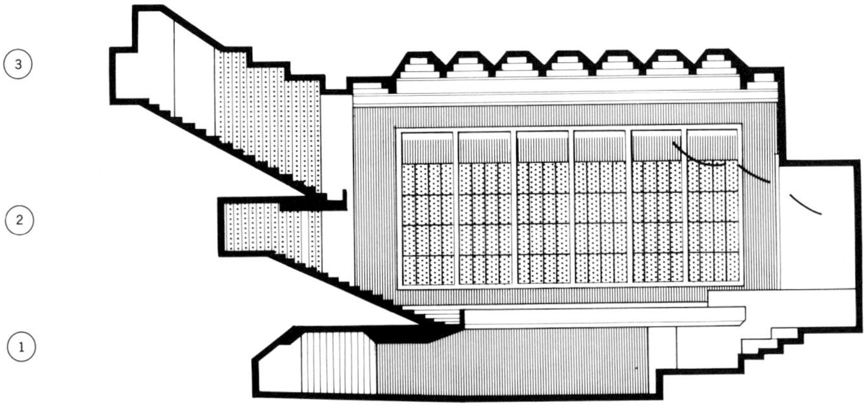

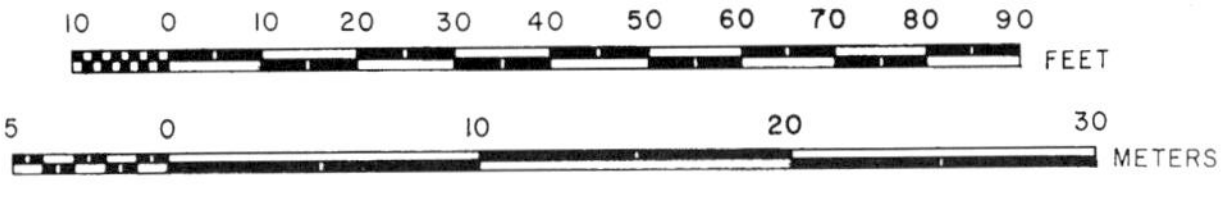

Architectural and structural details

Uses: classical concerts, popular music, meetings, and some sports. *Ceiling:* 3 ft (1 m) deep coffering of plaster. Side w*alls:* upper side walls are plaster on brick; main floor, wood panels, mainly flush on masonry; stepped section is over airspace; side walls in first balcony are 5% perforated hardboard panels (5,000 ft^2, 465 m^2) over 2 in. (5 cm) airspace filled with rock wool; wood panels on walls below the balcony. *Floors:* wood over some airspace; cork tile affixed at higher levels. *Stage enclosure:* rear stage wall and lower part of side walls are plywood on concrete and upper part of side walls are plaster on concrete. *Stage floor:* wood boards on wood framework with wood risers. *Stage height:* 60 in. (1.5 m). *Carpets:* none. *Seating:* fully upholstered.

Architect: Leonard C. Howett. *Acoustical consultant:* Hope Bagenal. *Photographs:* courtesy of Michael Barron. *References:* T. Somerville and C. L. S. Gilford, *Gravesaner Blatter*, **3**, No. 9 (1957); Michael Barron, *Auditorium Acoustics and Architectural Design*, E & FN Spon, London, Chapman & Hall, New York (1993).

*Technical details**

V = 545,000 ft^3 (15,430 m^3)	S_a = 11,380 ft^2 (1,057 m^2)	S_A = 14,800 ft^2 (1,375 m^2)
S_o = 1,940 ft^2 (100 m^2)	S_T = 16,740 ft^2 (1,555 m^2)	N = 2,351
H = 68 ft (20.7 m)	W = 80 ft (24.4 m)	L = 92 ft (28 m)
D = 122 ft (37.2 m)	V/S_T = 32.6 ft (9.92 m)	V/S_A = 36.8 ft (11.2 m)
V/N = 232 ft^3 (6.6 m^3)	S_A/N = 6.3 ft^2 (0.58 m^2)	H/W = 0.85
L/W = 1.15	t_I = 25 msec	

**The terminology is explained in Appendix 1.*

57

Budapest
Pátria Hall, Budapest Convention Centre

The Pátria Hall of the Convention Centre opened in 1985. A wide-fan-shaped room, it posed difficult acoustical problems. Nevertheless, with a seating capacity of 1,750 and a mid-frequency reverberation time of 1.6 sec, fully occupied, the hall has been selected as a concert venue by some of the world's orchestras on tour.

The acoustician's solution to the wide-fan plan was to design a system of reflecting plates for the side walls that directed sound to the upper rear part of the auditorium (space that contains the closed technical booths) so that it would be reflected across to the other side of the hall and back. This raised the reverberation time from a computed low of 1.3 sec to 1.6.

The necessary lateral reflections to the main floor of the hall are provided by the side walls and ceiling of the stage and additional early reflections by the suspended reflectors in the fore-part of the room. These stage reflectors, both on the sides and at the front edge, resemble fingers, with different slopes, that reflect sound energy both to the musicians and to the middle of the main-floor seating. As is the case in many halls, the best sound is to be heard in the front center of the balcony.

The stage has an area of 1,680 sq. ft^2 (156 m^2) and can be extended 3.9 ft (1.2 m) to accommodate a large orchestra and large chorus. For recitals or chamber music concerts chairs are placed on the stage for audience seating. Although the balcony overhang is large, the opening is also large and the front edge is shaped to reflect sound to the rear seats. Much of the floor is flat to accommodate convention and banquet activities.

The reflecting structures on the side walls and ceiling are 1.6 in. thick layered plates that do not absorb the low frequencies appreciably and the chairs on the main floor are not heavily upholstered. Therefore, the bass ratio (ratio of low to middle frequency reverberation times) and the low frequency strength level is high enough to contribute to the feeling of spaciousness in the hall.

One attendance at an all-Bartok concert in this hall by the Chicago Symphony Orchestra under Maestro George Solti was an experience to be remembered.

BUDAPEST, PÁTRIA HALL, BUDAPEST CONVENTION CENTRE

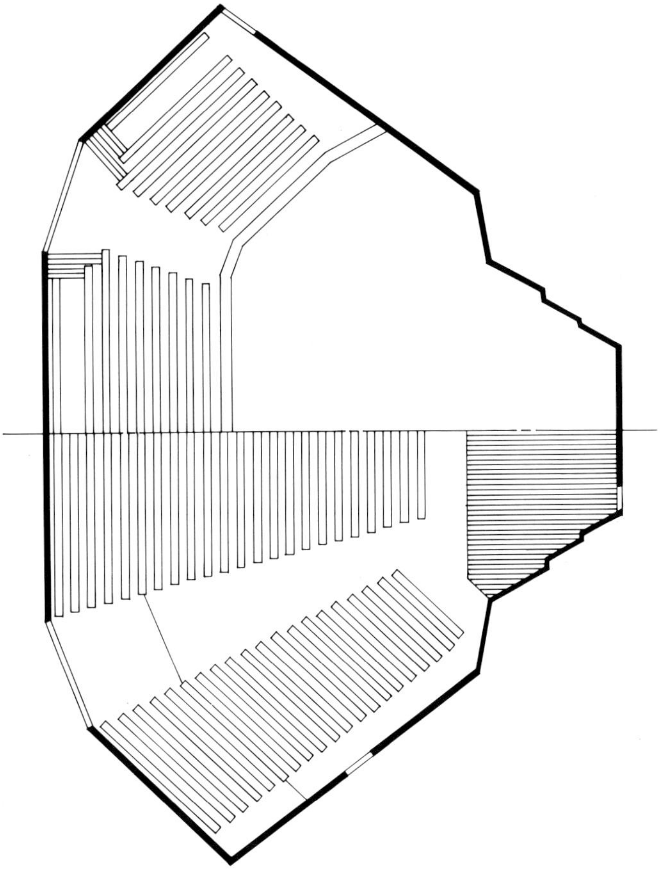

SEATING CAPACITY 1750

(1) 1212

(2) 538

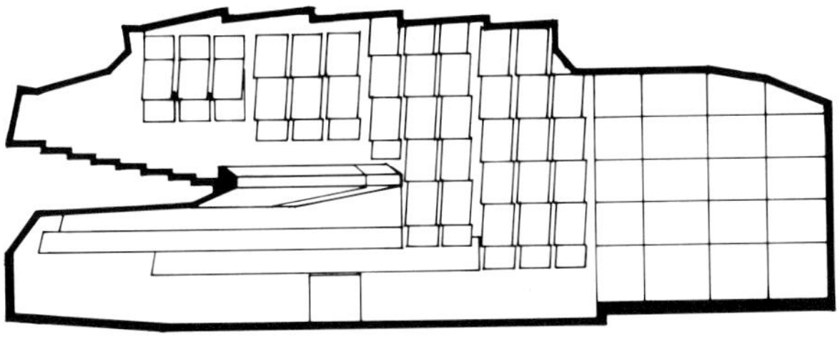

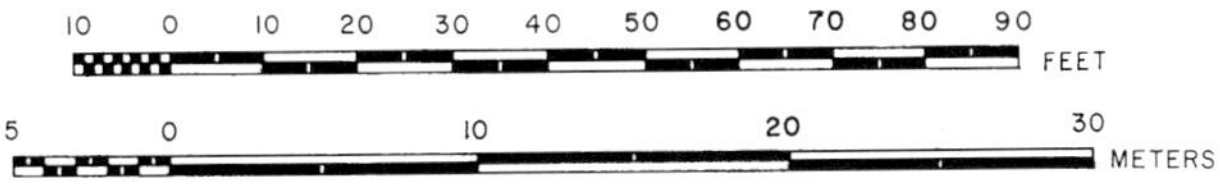

Architectural and structural details

Uses: concerts, chamber music, and recitals. *Ceiling:* thick plaster; hung panels are gypsum board, 1 in. (2.5 cm) thick. *Walls:* concrete covered by sound reflecting panels, 1.6 in. (4 cm) thick, suspended from steel tubing; the lowest part of the side walls are splayed concrete; rear walls behind seating, splayed plyboards, with low-frequency resonant absorbers. *Floors:* parquet cemented to solid concrete. *Carpet:* none. *Stage height:* 35 in. (0.90 m). *Seating:* plywood seat back, covered with stretched fabric; plywood underseat with polyvinyl cushion; backrest covered by porous fabric; armrests wooden.

Architect: J. Finta. *Acoustical consultants:* W. Fasold, B. Marx, H. Tennhardt, and H. Winkler. *Reference:* Fasold, Marx, Tennhardt, and Winkler, "Raumakustische Massnahmen im Budapester Kongresszentrum," Bauakademie der Deutschen Demokratischen Republik, Berlin 1986.

*Technical details**

V = 473,150 ft³ (13,400 m³)	S_a = 12,270 ft² (1,140 m²)	S_A = 13,840 ft² (1,286 m²)
S_o = 1,680 ft² (156 m²)	S_T = 15,520 ft² (1,442 m²)	N = 1,750
H = 43 ft (13.1 m)	W = 138 ft (42.1 m)	L = 86 ft (26.2 m)
D = 87 ft (26.5 m)	V/S_T = 30.5 ft (9.3 m)	V/S_A = 34.2 ft (10.4 m)
V/N = 270 ft³ (7.66 m³)	S_A/N = 7.9 ft² (0.73 m²)	H/W = 0.31
L/W = 0.62	t_I = 44 msec	

**The terminology is explained in Appendix 1.*

58

Jerusalem
Binyanei Ha'Oomah

The Jerusalem Congress Hall, containing 3,142 seats and opened in 1960, was designed initially for conventions. The shape of the hall, the balcony around the stage, and the inward sloping walls were fixed by that purpose. Construction was started in 1950, suspended for several years, and resumed with the purpose changed to include musical performances. Such modifications as could be made were then recommended by the acoustical consultant. The reverberation time was increased to 1.75 sec at mid-frequencies with full audience. The Binyanei Ha'Oomah has a ceiling higher than that of the Mann Auditorium in Tel Aviv. The hall is constructed of materials that preserve the warmth and liveness of the sound.

The overall architectural effect is one of simplicity and nobility. This design provides a handsome background for whatever event takes place on its stage. The rich wood interior is especially designed not to absorb the bass. When flooded with light, the white coffers overhead act to diffuse the light and provide uniform illumination to the seating areas.

The Binyanei Ha'Oomah received favorable comments from the conductors who have used it. Israeli Philharmonic Orchestra members prefer it to the Mann Auditorium, primarily because of its longer reverberation time.

A typical review of a performance by the Netherlands Kamerorkest:

> But as soon as the [chamber music] concert started, beauty of tone and the complete union of the 20 musicians into a single body made this concert one of the finest heard for some time. The sensitive acoustics allowed one to enjoy every phrase and every shade of dynamics employed in a highly polished presentation.

The hall's fan shape means that the spaciousness and intimacy are not ideal. Though it is not as good for concert performances as smaller rectangular concert halls (for example, the Grosser Musikvereinssaal in Vienna), Binyanei Ha'Oomah is superior for symphonic music to most of the larger multi-purpose halls built in its time. Its acoustics are satisfactory for lectures and conferences, many of which can be heard without an amplifying system, but a state of the art sound system is incorporated.

JERUSALEM, BINYANEI HA'OOMAH

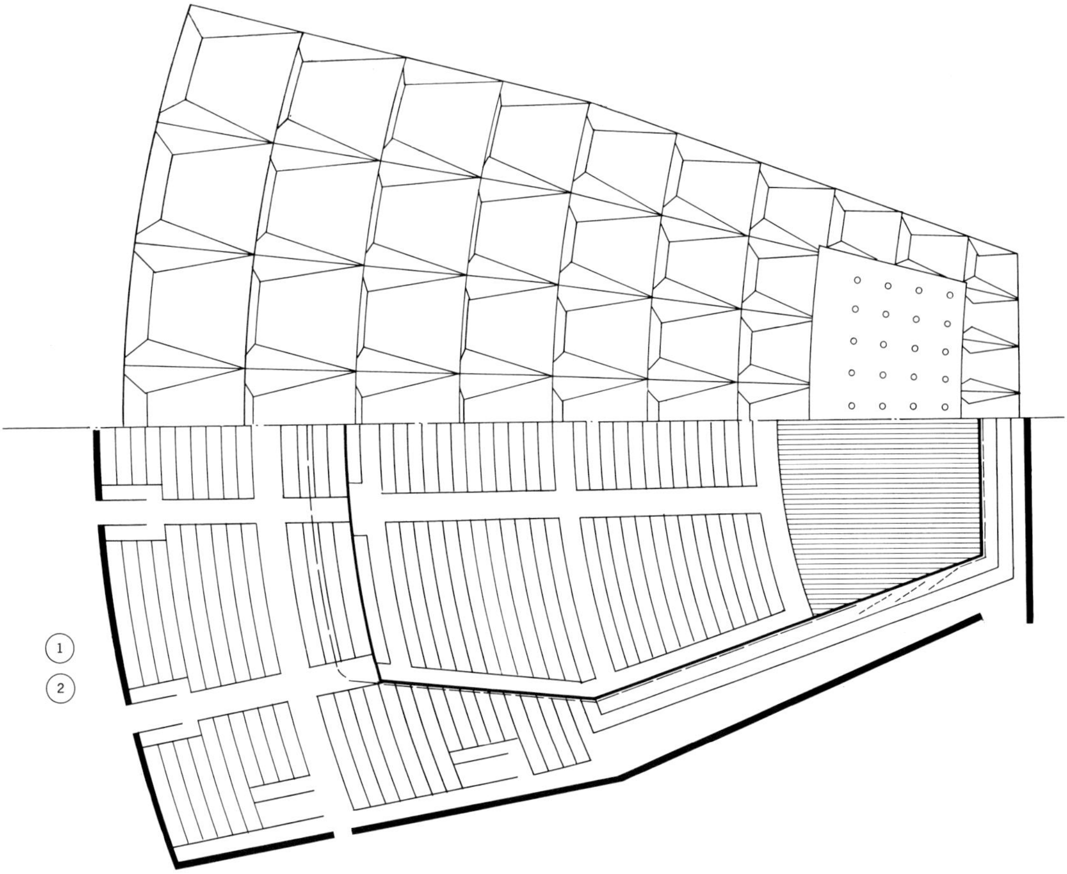

SEATING CAPACITY 3142

(1)	2103
(2)	1039

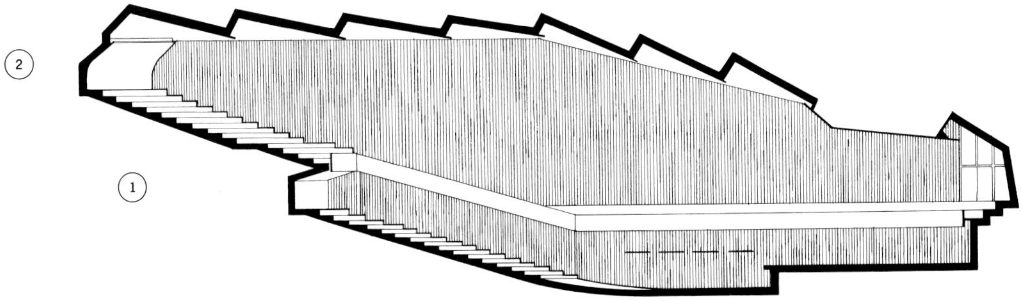

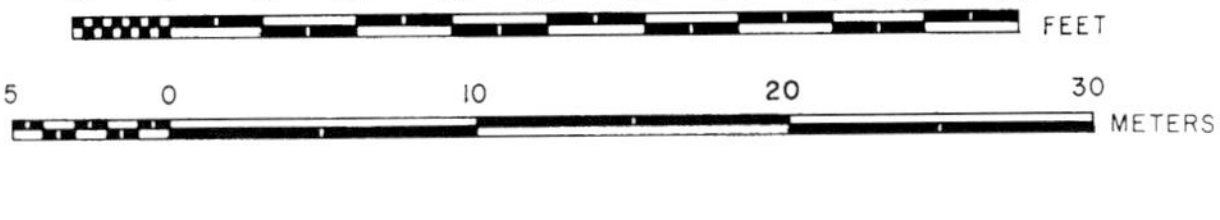

Archiectural and structural details

Uses: orchestra, general music, and meetings. *Ceiling:* prefabricated from 2 in. (5 cm) gypsum plasterboard. *Side walls:* 0.5 in. (1.25 cm) plywood affixed to 2-in. plaster. *Rear walls:* upper: 0.5 in. plywood over airspace; lower: 0.5 in. plywood on masonry. *Floors:* asphalt tiles on concrete. *Carpet:* none. *Stage enclosure:* ceiling: 0.5 in. plywood, fabricated into a movable canopy; back wall: 0.5 in. plywood on masonry; side walls: large plywood wooden doors, adjustable into sawtooth splays. *Stage floor:* heavy wood over air space. *Stage height:* 44 in. (112 cm). *Seating:* tops of seat-bottoms and fronts of backrests upholstered; underseats perforated with glass fiber blanket inside.

Architect: Rechter, Zarhy, Rechter. *Acoustical consultant:* Bolt Beranek and Newman. *Photographs:* courtesy of the architects. *References:* L. L. Beranek and D. L. Klepper, "The acoustics of the Binyanei Ha'Oomah Jerusalem Congress Hall," Jour. Acoust. Soc. Am. **33**, 1690–1698 (1961).

*Technical details**

V = 873,000 ft^3 (24,700 m^3)	S_a = 18,000 ft^2 (1,672 m^2)	S_A = 23,000 ft^2 (2,137 m^2)
S_o = 2,800 ft^2 (260 m^2)	S_T = 25,800 ft^2 (2,400 m^2)	N = 3,142
V/S_T = 33.8 ft (10.3 m)	V/S_A = 38 ft (11.6 m)	V/N = 278 ft^3 (7.9 m^3)
S_A/N = 7.32 ft^2 (0.68 m^2)	H = 45 ft (13.7 m)	W = 156 ft (47.6 m)
L = 122 ft (37.2 m)	D = 148 ft (45.1 m)	H/W = 0.29
L/W = 0.78	t_I = 26 msec	

**The terminology is explained in Appendix 1.*

ISRAEL

59

Tel Aviv
Fredric R. Mann Auditorium

The Fredric R. Mann Auditorium is a pleasant contemporary concert hall. The unusual arrangement of the seating reduces the apparent size of the hall, even for the viewer in the balcony. The pattern and lighting of the ceiling and the warm interior of wood give this hall a handsome yet relaxed appearance.

The design of the Mann Auditorium was begun in 1951 and the hall opened in 1957. On the advice of the late Serge Koussevitsky and the Israel Philharmonic Orchestra, the building committee and the architects wanted a hall that resembled Kleinhans Music Hall in Buffalo rather than one of the older rectangular halls.

It was planned that the reverberation time in the Mann hall should be about 1.9 sec, fully occupied, a number about halfway between the reverberation time in Boston Symphony Hall (then thought to be 2.3 sec, fully occupied) and that in Kleinhans Hall in Buffalo (then thought to be 1.5 sec). Unfortunately, the design preceded the author's findings in 1957 that the sound absorption of an audience must be calculated on the basis of the number of square meters that the chairs sit over and not on the number of people in them. The result, for a certain cubic volume, is that the reverberation time will be lower in the completed hall than that calculated. Nevertheless, the cubic volume per seat is greater than that of the Royal Festival Hall in London, at that time the most recently built large hall. The reverbertion time in the Mann hall measures 1.55 sec at mid-frequencies, fully occupied—about halfway between the correct reverberation times for Boston (1.85 sec) and Buffalo (1.3 sec).

A number of visiting conductors have been satisfied with the acoustics on stage. However, because of its low reverberation time, there have been complaints by the members of the Israel Philharmonic Orchectra and music critics. The Orchestra has stated, "Our main complaint is the lack of a certain sonority which we especially observe in the sound of our string body and which is particularly noticeable at the climaxes of the orchestral music."

These evaluations show that for a hall to be well received it must have adequate mid-frequency and strong low-frequency reverberation times as well as good stage communication.

Tel Aviv, Fredric R. Mann Auditorium

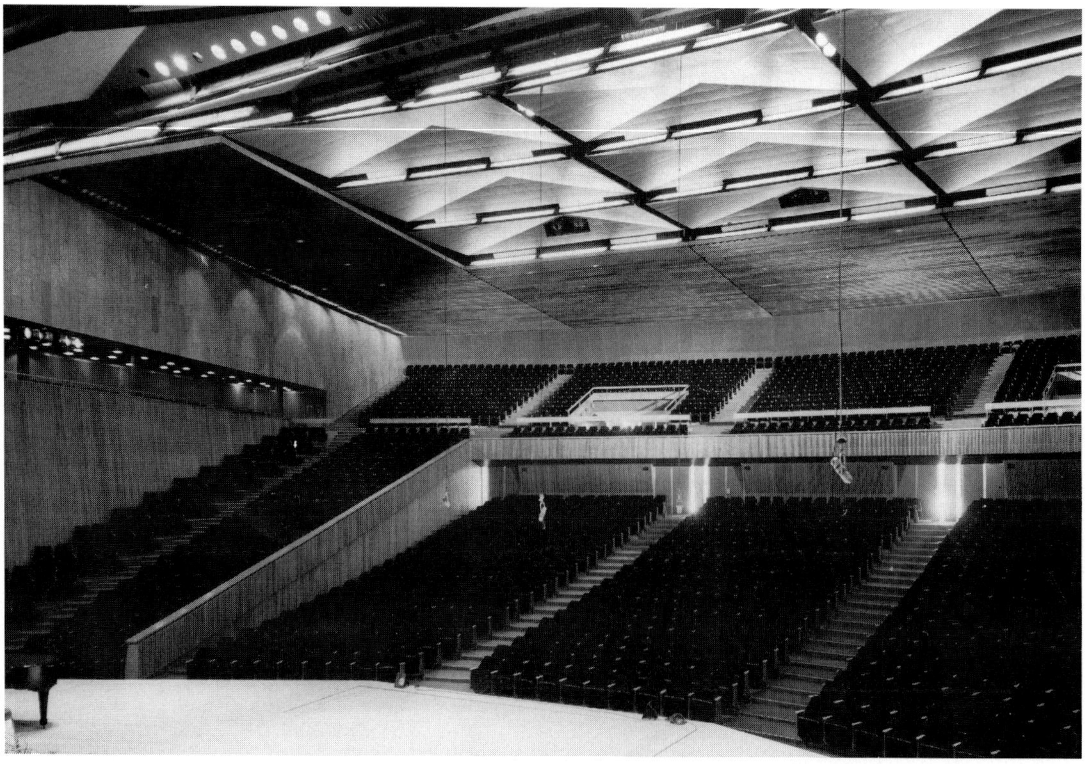

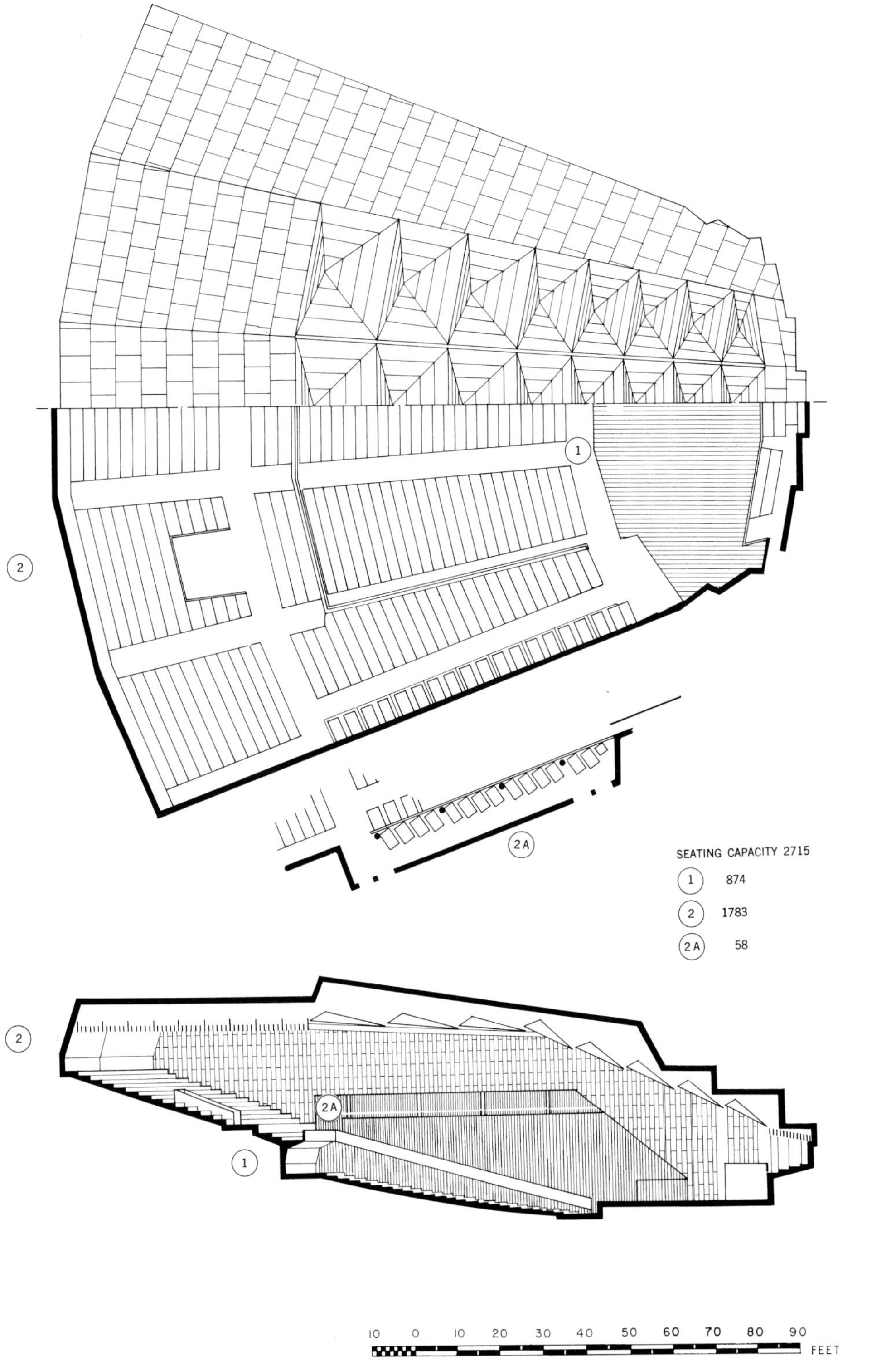
1
2
2A
SEATING CAPACITY 2715
1 874
2 1783
2A 58
10 0 10 20 30 40 50 60 70 80 90
FEET
5 0 10 20 30
METERS

Architectural and structural details

Uses: orchestra, chamber music, and soloists. *Ceiling:* solid upper ceiling, 0.75 in. (1.9 cm) plaster; hung center portion (1/3 of area) is pyramid shaped to diffuse sound, made of 0.16 in. (0.4 cm) asbestos board; visible hung portion is 6 in. (15 cm) deep wooden egg-crate sections, each 12 × 12 in. (30 × 30 cm). *Side and rear walls:* on the upper side walls are three types of panels, each 18 × 56 in. (46 × 142 cm). One-third of the panels are made of 0.25 in. (0.6 cm) ash plywood, to the back of which a 2 × 2 × 0.75 in. (5 × 5 × 1.9 cm) egg-crate structure is glued. One-third of the panels have the same egg-crate backing, but two layers of 0.25 in. plywood. The remaining one-third of the panels are a sandwich of two 0.25 in. plywood panels, with about 0.5 in (1.25 cm) of softwood filling, making a solid panel of 1 in. (2.5 cm). The lower part of the side walls is constructed of vertical slats about 2 in. (5 cm) wide, with no airspaces behind; the rear wall is made of 0.25 in. plywood panels. *Carpet:* none. *Floor:* vinyl tile on concrete. *Stage enclosure:* None. (*Note:* the drawing does not show the recent change in the stage surroundings—see photograph.) *Stage floor:* Heavy wood over airspace. *Stage height:* 30 in. (76 cm). *Seating:* rear of backrest and armrest are of wood; front of backrest and top of seat are upholstered; underseat is solid.

Architect: Z. Rechter and D. Karmi. *Associate architect:* J. Rechter. *Acoustical consultant:* Bolt Beranek and Newman. *Photographs:* courtesy of the architects. *References:* L. L. Beranek, "Acoustics of the F. R. Mann Concert Hall," Jour. Acoust. Soc. Am. **31**, 882–892 (1959), and "Audience and seat absorption in large halls," Jour. Acoust. Soc. Am. **32**, 661–670 (1960).

*Technical details**

V = 750,000 ft^3 (21,240 m^3)	S_a = 14,500 ft^2 (1,350 m^2)	S_A = 18,300 ft^2 (1,700 m^2)
S_o = 2,100 ft^2 (195 m^2)	S_T = 20,800 ft^2 (1,932 m^2)	N = 2,715
V/S_T = 36 ft (11 m)	V/S_A = 41 ft (12.5 m)	V/N = 239 ft^3 (6.76 m^3)
S_A/N = 5.82 ft^2 (0.54 m^2)	H = 40 ft (12.2 m)	W = 132 ft (40.2 m)
L = 100 ft (30.5 m)	D = 127 ft (38.7 m)	H/W = 0.30
L/W = 0.76	t_I = 30 msec	

**The terminology is explained in Appendix 1.*

Italy

60

Milan
Teatro Alla Scala

August 3, 1778, La Scala opened its doors to a future of great music, glamour, and unequaled tradition. Great opera composers, Verdi, Rossini, Puccini, Donizetti, have been intimately identified with La Scala. Its lineage of famous conductors includes Arturo Toscanini, Cleofonte Campanini, Herbert von Karajan, and Carlo Maria Giulini. Singers include Adelina Patti, Enrico Caruso, Renata Tebaldi, Maria Callas, and scores of others.

The architect of La Scala was Giuseppi Piermarini. He designed and built the largest and best equipped theater of his day. The exterior of La Scala looked in 1778 very much as it does today. Until World War II it experienced only minor changes—in 1883 it got electric lights. In 1943 La Scala was the victim of a bombing attack; the walls remained standing, but little else. In May 1946 it reopened, its appearance almost as before. Today it has 2,289 seats, including 154 unnumbered seats from which the stage is not visible. With standees the number is augmented.

La Scala is a beautiful and engaging theater. It is a horseshoe in plan with high balcony faces and a vaulted ceiling 6 ft higher at the center than at the sides. Intimacy is conveyed by its narrow main floor. Nevertheless the hall has a regal air that derives from the great height of its ceiling. The theater is lighted by a huge central chandelier of 365 lights and white glass globes in groups of five placed at intervals along the bases of the balcony faces.

The acoustics are excellent for those lucky enough to sit either at the front of the boxes, on the main floor, or in the galleries. The openings to the boxes are only 4.5 feet square (1.37 m) so that the wall they present is only about 40% acoustically absorbent. The large reflecting faces of the boxes and the resulting small cubic volume of the house achieves unexpected acoustical spaciousness, ASW. The reverberation time is a little longer than in other large opera houses. The sound is clear, warm, and brilliant. Sound is returned to the stage from the faces of the boxes with an intensity that is not reached in any other large opera house. The vaulted ceiling returns the sound of the orchestra and the singers to the conductor, clear and loud. Both singers and conductors are enthusiastic about the acoustics.

Milan, Teatro Alla Scala

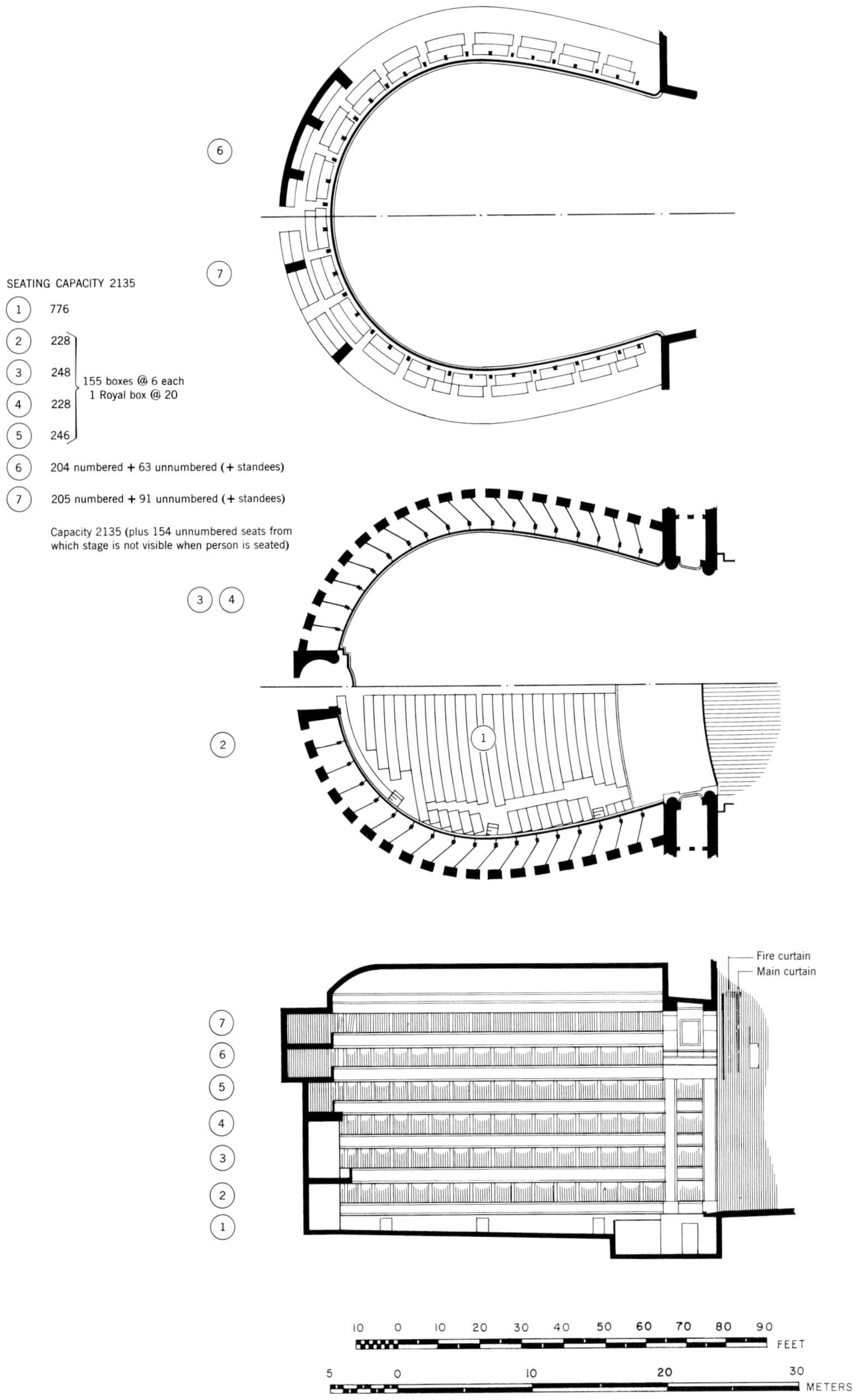
SEATING CAPACITY 2135
1 776
2 228
3 248
4 228
5 246
155 boxes @ 6 each
1 Royal box @ 20
6 204 numbered + 63 unnumbered (+ standees)
7 205 numbered + 91 unnumbered (+ standees)
Capacity 2135 (plus 154 unnumbered seats from which stage is not visible when person is seated)
6
7
3
4
2
1
Fire curtain
Main curtain
10 0 10 20 30 40 50 60 70 80 90
FEET
5 0 10 20 30
METERS

Architectural and structural details

Uses: opera and ballet. *Ceiling:* vaulted, 6 ft (1.8 m) higher at the center than the sides; plaster on lath attached to 1 × 4 in. (2.5 × 10 cm) longitudinal boards; there are no irregularities (coffers) on the ceiling. *Walls:* box faces are of plaster 42 in. (1.07 m) high; vertical columns at railings are plaster 6 in. (15.2 cm) wide; each box opening is 54 × 54 in. (1.37 × 1.37 m). *Floors:* wood over 3 ft (0.91 m) airspace over concrete. *Carpets:* on all floors. *Pit floor:* wooden floor, flat, elevator type; often located about 10 ft (3 m) below stage level. *Stage height:* 60 in. (152 cm) above floor level at first row of seats. *Seating:* on the main floor the seats are of solid wood except that the front of the backrests and the top of the seat-bottoms are upholstered; the boxes have upholstered stools (no backs).

Architect: Giuseppe Piermarini. *References:* plans, details, and photographs courtesy of the management of La Scala.

*Technical details**

Opera

V = 397,300 ft^3 (11,252 m^3)	S_o (pit) = 1,200 ft^2 (11 m^2)	S_o (pit floor) = 1,350 ft^2 (125.4m^2)
V' = 318,200 ft^3 (9,012 m^3)**	S_A = 14,000 ft^2 (1,300 m^2)	S_P = 2,400 ft^2 (223 m^2)
S_T = 17,600 ft^2 (1,635 m^2)	S_{AMF} = 7,700 ft^2 (715 m^2)***	S_{TMF} = 11,300 ft^2 (1,050 m^2)***
N = 2,289 (including unnumbered)	N_T = 2,489 (N+0.5 standees)	V/S_T = 22.6 ft (6.9 m)
V/S_A = 28.3 ft (8.65 m)	V/N = 174 ft^3 (4.92 m^3)	S_A/N = 6.1 ft^2 (0.57 m^2)
H = 63 ft (19.2 m)	W = 66 ft (20.1 m)	L = 99 ft (30.2 m)
D = 105 ft (32 m)	H/W = 0.95	L/W = 1.5
t_I = 20 msec		

**The terminology is explained in Appendix 1.*
***Volume in open space above main floor.*
****Main floor seating only.*

Osaka Symphony Hall

The Osaka Symphony Hall, which opened in 1982 on the occasion of the 30th anniversary of the Asahi Broadcasting Corporation, was the first concert-only hall built in Japan. It has a very pleasant ambiance, in large part because the most remote seat is only 98 ft (30 m) from the stage. It is used daily for classical music concerts and has a good reputation—a tribute to the care taken in acoustical design. A primary goal was to achieve an optimum reverberation time of between 1.8 and 2.0 sec, fully occupied.

For a hall that seats only 1,702 persons, it is surprisingly wide, the main floor width measuring 92 ft (28 m) and the first-balcony cross-hall width 119 ft (36.3 m). This poses some difficult acoustical problems. To produce a satisfactorily short, initial-time-delay gap, 26 suspended, convex, sound-reflecting panels are positioned over the stage. Early lateral reflections are directed to the main floor seating areas both by these suspended panels and by the downward-sloping balcony fronts. Such reflections are not provided by the lower side walls because of the presence of large-scale diffusing elements (see the photograph). Concert reverberation is provided by a high ceiling, from which are hung an array of 40 convex panels, chosen to simulate the acoustical diffusion provided in classical European halls by ceiling coffers. The stage is very wide and large in area (3,070 ft^2; 285 m^2).

I attended a concert by an 85 piece symphonic orchestra in 1993. The violins sat 2 m from the front of the stage and 4 m from each side of the stage, so that the players were using an area equal to that of the entire stage in Boston's Symphony Hall. Where I sat in the first balcony, third row, 14 seats off center, the sound was excellent. The reverberation time was satisfactory, subjectively 2 sec at mid-frequencies. The balance among sections of the orchestra was flawless and the ensemble was perfect. As expected, the orchestra seemed very close, visually and acoustically. On the main floor the various sections of the orchestra did not blend as well, probably because of the great width of the hall and insufficient early lateral reflections from the lower side walls at mid- and high frequencies.

Osaka is justly proud of this beautiful and satisfactory hall.

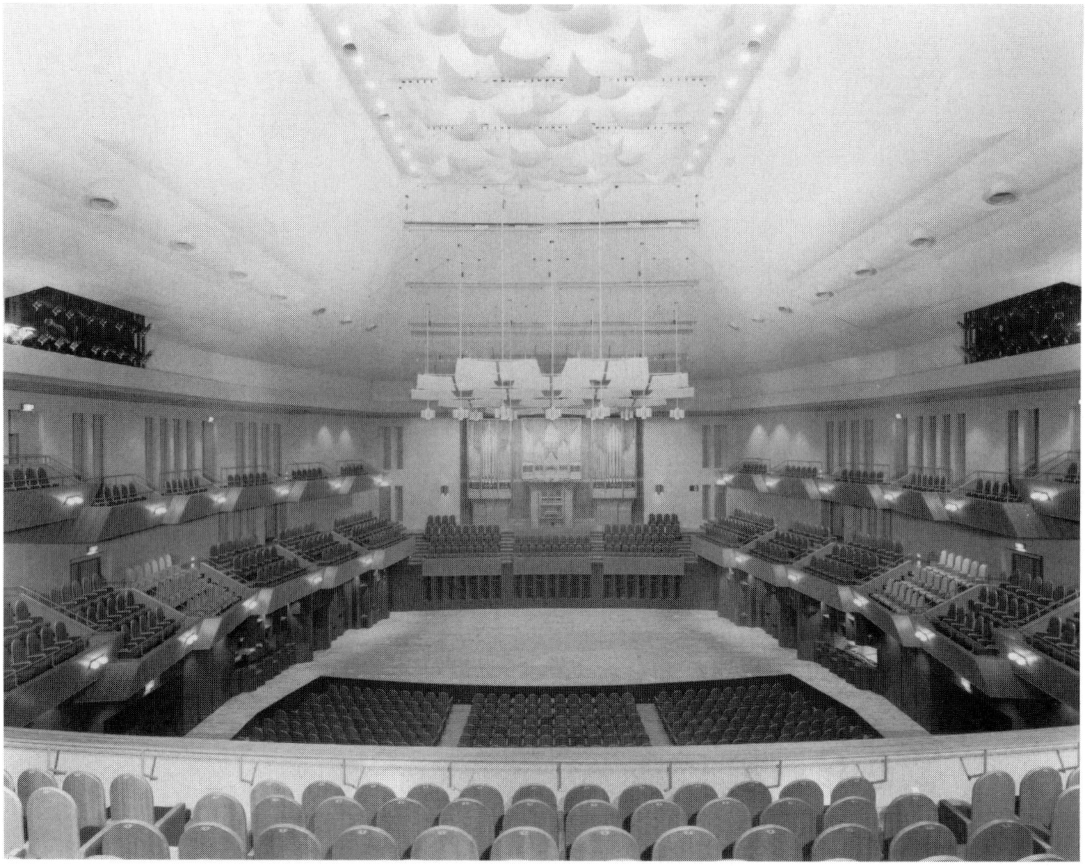

OSAKA, SYMPHONY HALL

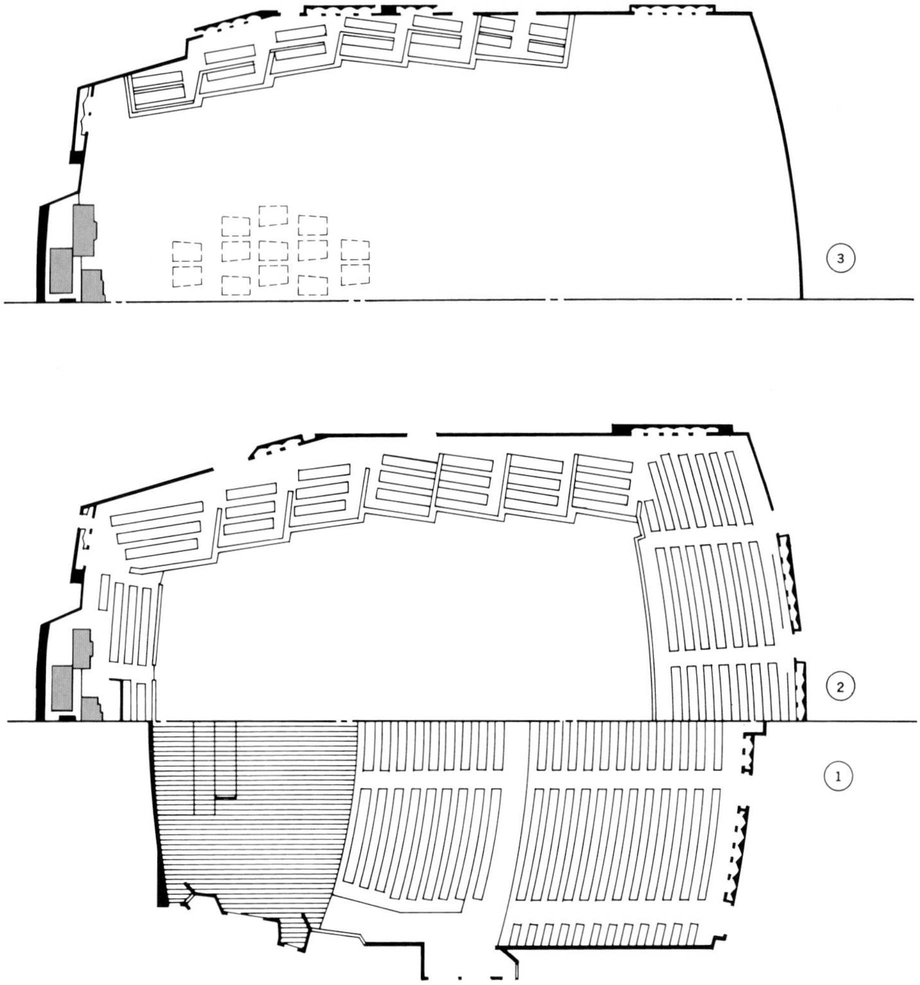

SEATING CAPACITY 1702

1	796
2	754
3	152

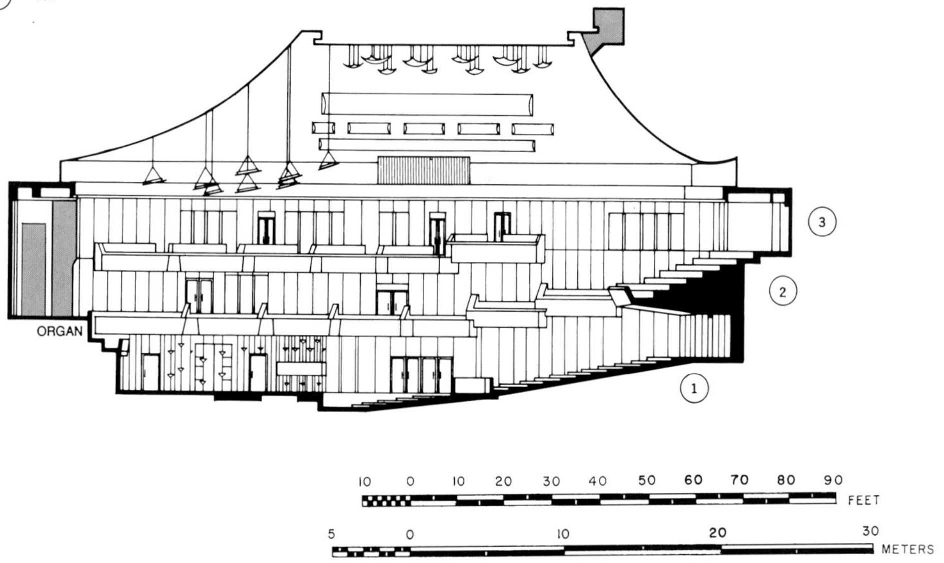

Architectural and structural details

Uses: classical music concerts. *Ceiling:* 2 layers of gypsum or calcium board, total thickness 1.5 in. (3.8 cm), some openings. *Walls:* plastered concrete, with a gypsum board layer to which is cemented artificial marble; balcony faces are plywood over concrete. *Floors:* cork tile over concrete. *Carpet:* none in hall. *Stage walls:* same as side walls. *Stage floor:* 0.75 in. tongue-and-groove hardwood on 0.75 in. plywood subfloor on sleepers. *Stage height:* 37 in. (94 cm). *Sound absorbing materials:* none. *Seating:* wooden seat back; front of seat back and seat bottom upholstered with porous fabric over polyvinyl foam; underseat, perforated wood; arms, wooden.

Architects: Taisei Corporation. *Acoustical consultants:* Kiyoteru Ishii and Hideki Tachibana. *Photographs:* courtesy of Taisei Corporation.

*Technical details**

V = 628,500 ft^3 (17,800 m^3)	S_a = 9,774 ft^2 (908 m^2)	S_A = 13,304 ft^2 (1,236 m^2)
S_o = 3,068 ft^2 (285 m^2)	S_T = 16,372 ft^2 (1,521 m^2)	N = 1,702
H = 68 ft (20.7 m)	W = 104 ft (31.7 m)	L = 93 ft (28.3 m)
D = 98 ft (30 m)	V/S_T = 38.4 ft (11.7 m)	V/S_A = 47.2 ft (14.4 m)
V/N = 369 ft^3 (10.5 m^3)	S_A/N = 7.81 ft^2 (0.725 m^2)	H/W = 0.65
L/W = 0.89	t_I = 40 msec	

**The terminology is explained in Appendix 1.*

Japan

62

Tokyo Bunka Kaikan

Prior to 1975, most of the halls of Japan used for the performance of music had been built as city halls or general-purpose public halls. Dramas, public speeches, and traditional Japanese opera (Kabuki) were their mainstay. All had stage houses and used a concert stage enclosure for symphonic, chamber, and recital music. The most enduring one for concerts is the Bunka Kaikan in Ueno Park, seating 2,327, along with several art museums and a zoo.

The hall, dedicated in 1961, is diamond shaped. The width at the proscenium is 66 ft (20 m), at the rear, 60 ft (18 m), and at the center 112 ft (34 m). Two large, very irregular walls extend from the stage into the hall along the entire sides of the main floor. The orchestra enclosure is striking in appearance. In plan, it is fan shaped. Starting at a height of about 20 ft (6 m) above the rear stage riser, the stage ceiling soars upward to double that height at the proscenium. A permanent section of the ceiling extends into the hall, reaching a height of 56 ft (17 m) above stage level. This steep sound reflecting canopy is modulated in convex, curved segments so that reflected sound spreads nearly evenly over the stage, most of the main floor, and the lower balconies. A large part of the side walls of the stage are unusual, not seen in any other hall. They consist largely of horizontal parallel slats ranging in widths from one to a few inches, spaced 4 in. (10 cm) apart (see the photograph). Behind these slats are vertically splayed surfaces.

With a reverberation time of only 1.5 sec, occupied, at mid-frequencies, one is surprised at the liveness of the hall. This is explained by the large number of early reflections that come from the canopy, the front sides of the stage, the irregular side walls, and the balcony fronts, giving an early sound decay time EDT of 1.85 sec (average throughout the hall). On the main floor, the overall impression is one of strong bass and lovely string tone. Apparently the parallel slats act to weaken the higher overtones and give the music a warm, rich patina. A solo violin is very clear and resonant, aided by the 1.85 sec EDT. The brass is in good balance with the strings. The woodwinds have an optimal sound. The public gives Bunka Kaikan high marks.

Tokyo, Bunka Kaikan

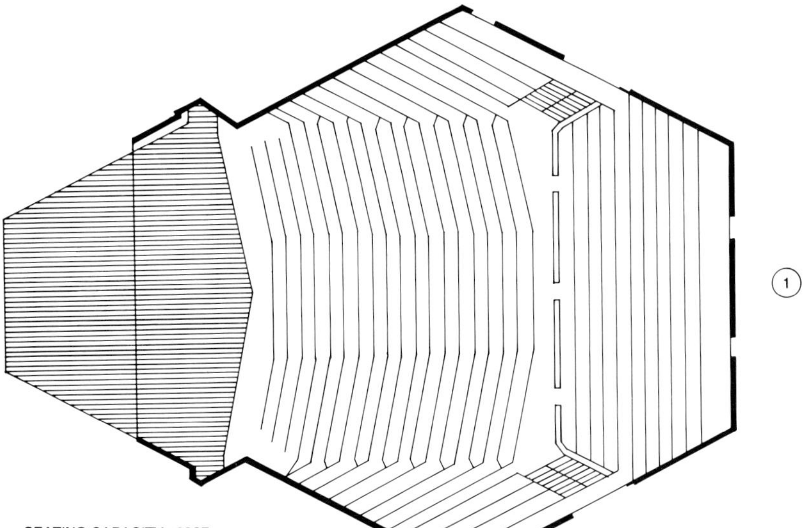

SEATING CAPACITY 2327

(1) 1306

(2) 238

(3) 355

(4) 268

(5) 160

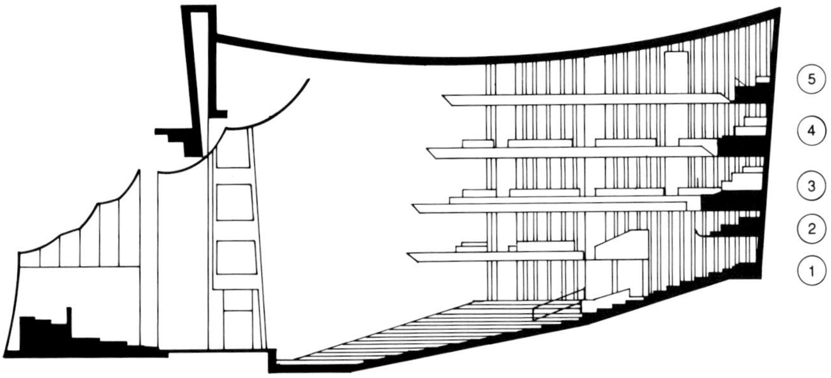

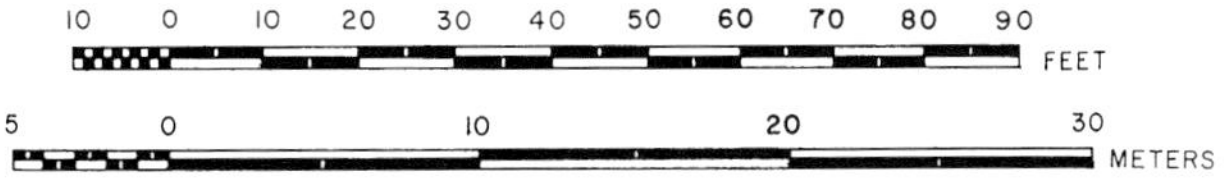

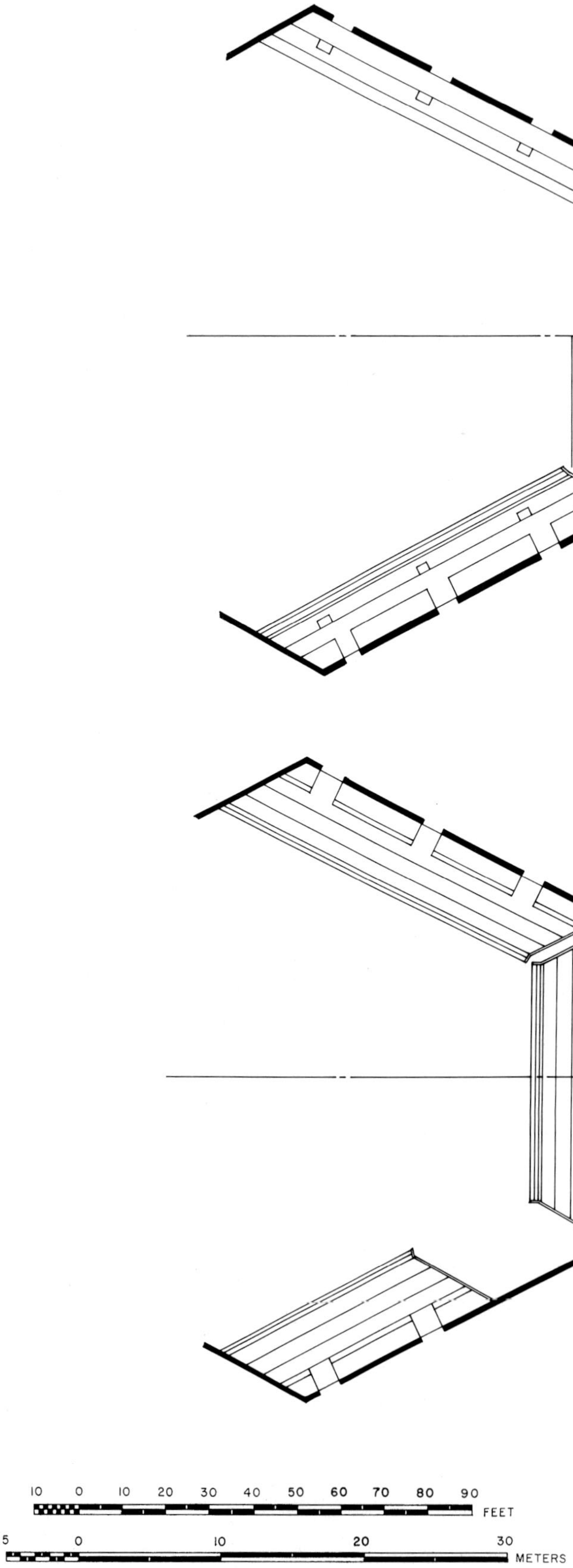
5
4
3
2
10 0 10 20 30 40 50 60 70 80 90
FEET
5 0 10 20 30
METERS

Architectural and structural details

Uses: orchestral music, drama, public functions, and recitals, *Ceiling:* 1 in. plaster on wire lath suspended beneath heavy structure. *Walls:* concrete. *Floors:* concrete. *Carpet:* in aisles only. *Stage enclosure:* walls: (see the text). *Stage height:* 19.7 in. (50 cm). *Acoustic reflectors:* the two side walls extending from the proscenium to the back of the balconies are heavily modulated to produce diffuse reflections. *Sound absorbing materials:* on rear walls. *Seating:* wooden seat back; front of seat back and top of seat bottom upholstered with porous fabric facing; underseat, wood, unperforated; arms not upholstered.

Architect: Kunio Maekawa. *Acoustical consultant:* NHK Technical Research Laboratories. *Photographs:* courtesy of NHK. *References:* Y. Makita, M. Nagata, A. Usuba, H. Tsukuda, H. Takato, T. Yamamoto, Y. Sakamoto, T. Yamaguchi, H. Nakajima, R. Nishimura, and A. Mizoguchi, "Acoustical Design of the Tokyo Metropolitan Festival Hall," Technical Journal of NHK, Vol. 15, No. 1–2 (January 1963).

*Technical details**

V = 610,900 ft^3 (17,300 m^3)	S_a = 10,581 ft^2 (983 m^2)	S_A = 14,000 ft^2 (1,301 m^2)
S_o = 2,600 ft^2 (241 m^2)	S_T = 16,600 ft^2 (1,542 m^2)	N = 2,327
H = 57 ft (17.4 m)	W = 87 ft (26.5 m)	L = 104 ft (31.7 m)
D = 118 ft (36 m)	V/S_T = 36.8 ft (11.2 m)	V/S_A = 43.6 ft (13.3 m)
V/N = 262 ft^3 (7.4 m^3)	S_A/N = 6.0 ft^2 (0.56 m^2)	H/W = 0.66
L/W = 1.2	t_I = 14;12 msec	

**The terminology is explained in Appendix 1.*

Japan
63

Tokyo
Hamarikyu Asahi Hall

The Hamarikyu Asahi Hall takes its place in Tokyo as a location for musical performance hospitable to intimate concert music. Small orchestras, chamber groups, and soloists demand a close relationship to their audiences. The solution here is a hall of intimate size, proven shape, with a properly tailored stage and attendant architectural details throughout the hall.

Seating 552 persons, the hall was dedicated in 1992. Tokyo's building code prevents the use of wood except on the stage floor. A marble-like material with a corrugated surface is used on the walls below the balcony. Elsewhere, all walls and the ceiling are either gypsum board or artificial wood. A thin wooden ply, for appearance, is cemented to the hard backing above the balcony and on the walls surrounding the stage. The random vertical corrugations on the marble-like facing were added to scatter the high frequencies above 1,500 Hz into the reverberant sound field, thus reducing the high-frequency energy in the early specular reflections and giving the early reflected sound a more mellow quality (see Chapter 10). The balcony fronts were designed by computer and model measurements to reflect early lateral energy to the seating areas. Similarly, the ceiling is coffered to scatter the first reflections and to diffuse the reverberant sound field. A tilted, corrugated panel is located around the top of the stage enclosure to provide good communication among the players. The stage depth was held to 23 ft (7 m) and the area to 786 ft^2 (73 m^2) to favor small performing groups.

Measurements in the completed hall disclosed that the seats were absorbing more low frequency energy than those tested during the design period. The result was a peak in the reverberation time of 0.2 sec between 500 and 2,000 Hz. This peak was flattened by adding a thin sheet of sound absorbing material behind an impervious face in the "white" spaces above the balcony (see the photograph).

Performers have expressed satisfaction with the stage acoustics and the sound is uniform in quality throughout the hall. The acoustical measurements show that the goal of an occupied mid-frequency reverberation time of 1.7 sec has been achieved.

Tokyo, Hamarikyu Asahi Hall

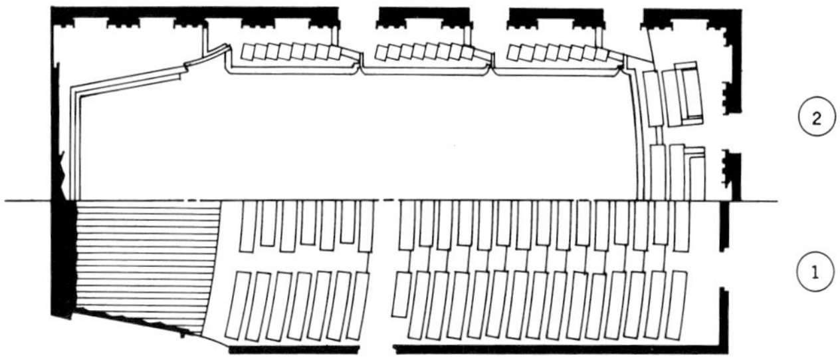

SEATING CAPACITY 552

1 448

2 104

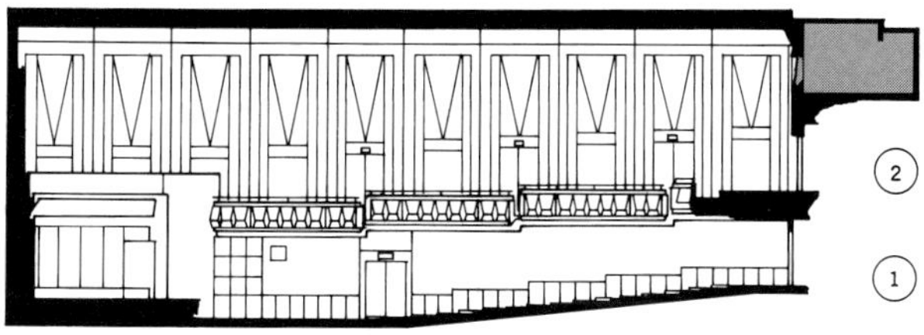

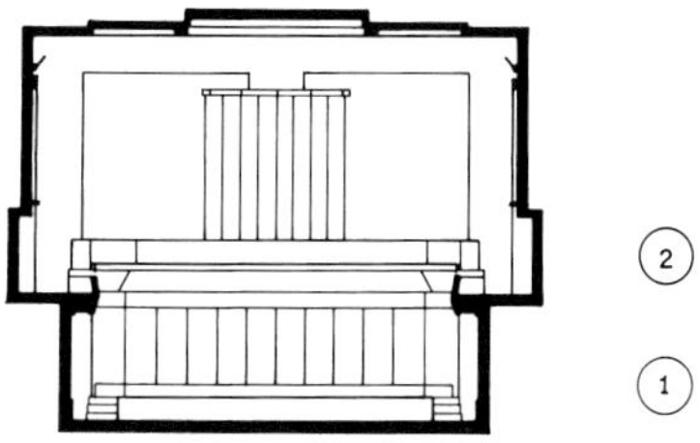

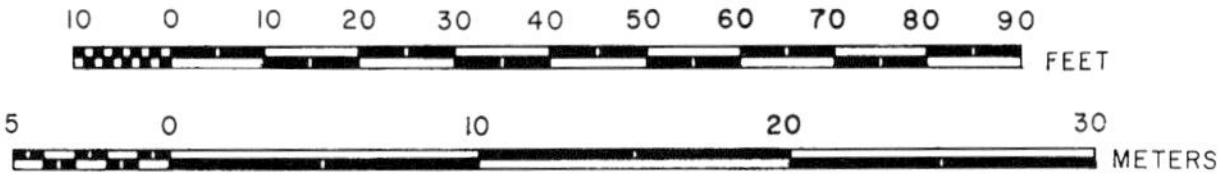

Architectural and structural details

Uses: chamber music and recitals. *Ceiling:* 0.83 in. (2.1 cm) gypsum board. *Overstage reflecting panels:* chevron shapes, artificial wood (phenol foam board mixed with glass fiber). *Walls above balcony and balcony fronts:* thin ply of maobi wood cemented to 0.31 in. (0.8 cm) artificial wood. *Walls around main floor:* corrugated marble-like urethane-coated silicate board cemented to 1.7 in. (4.2 cm) gypsum board. *Floors:* parquet cemented to solid concrete. *Carpet:* none. *Stage height:* 30 in. (0.75 m). *Seating:* upholstered both sides of seat back and seat with polyvinyl cushion covered by porous fabric; armrests wooden.

Architect: Takenaka Corporation, Tokyo. *Acoustical design consultant:* Leo L. Beranek. *Acoustical Research Laboratory:* Takenaka Research and Development Institute. *Photographs:* Taisuke Ogawa. *Reference:* T. Hidaka *et al.*, "Acoustical design and evaluation of Hamarikyu Asahi Hall," Proc. of Acoust. Soc. of Jpn., March (1993) (in Japanese).

*Technical details**

V = 204,800 ft^3 (5,800 m^3)	S_a = 3,046 ft^2 (283 m^2)	S_A = 4,252 ft^2 (395 m^2)
S_o = 785 ft^2 (73 m^2)	S_T = 5,037 ft^2 (468 m^2)	N = 552
H = 39 ft (12 m)	W = 49 ft (15 m)	L = 81 ft (24.7 m)
D = 80 ft (24.4 m)	V/S_T = 37.3 ft (11.4 m)	V/S_A = 43.8 ft (13.3 m)
V/N = 371 ft^3 (10.5 m^3)	S_A/N = 8.48 ft^2 (0.79 m^2)	H/W = 0.8
L/W = 1.65	t_I = 16 msec	

**The terminology is explained in Appendix 1.*

JAPAN

64

Tokyo Metropolitan Art Space Concert Hall

Opened in 1990, the Tokyo Metropolitan Art Space is one of the four large concert halls of Tokyo. It seats 2,017, compared to Suntory, 2,006, Bunka Kaikan, 2,327, and Orchard, 2,150. It contains four auditoriums, Concert Hall, theater, and two mini-theaters. Several of the Tokyo metropolitan symphony orchestras hold part of their abonnement concerts here. The entrance to the Art Space is by way of a huge all-glass atrium, 92 ft (28 m) high. Audiences take a single escalator to the fifth floor, and then go up another escalator or ascend a flight of stairs. Blinded by the sun and reeling from the people noise of the atrium, the quiet of the hall is soothing.

The broad design goal was to follow the general shape of the Bunka Kaikan. A much larger reverberation time was prescribed, 2.15 sec at mid-frequencies, fully occupied, compared to 1.5 sec for the Bunka Kaikan. Early reflections from many directions following the direct sound were to be provided to all parts of the seating area. The measured results are in agreement with the design concept. The reverberation time rises from 2.15 sec at 500 Hz to 2.55 sec at 125 Hz. The sound level is remarkably constant on the main floor, and drops off as normally expected in the first balcony, but regains its level in the second balcony. The clarity measure is normal for good halls. The earliest reflected sound energy is found on the main floor, the least in the second balcony, but both within normal limits.

Over the stage, a large canopy, adjustable segmentally, provides communication among the players and sends early reflections to the main floor. The balcony faces are tilted to send early sound reflections to the seating areas and large sound reflecting and diffusing elements are provided on the side walls.

Listening to a concert from the main floor center, featuring Mahler's *Second Symphony*, gave me a very different impression from that in the Bunka Kaikan. The music was very much louder—one is enveloped by the sound, almost drowned in it—and the clarity is less. Because of the rise in reverberation time at low frequencies, the bass and cello sounds are very strong, primarily on the main floor. The players have found the sound on stage quite acceptable. Of great interest will be the audiences' and orchestras' subjective comparisons of the four Tokyo concert halls over time.

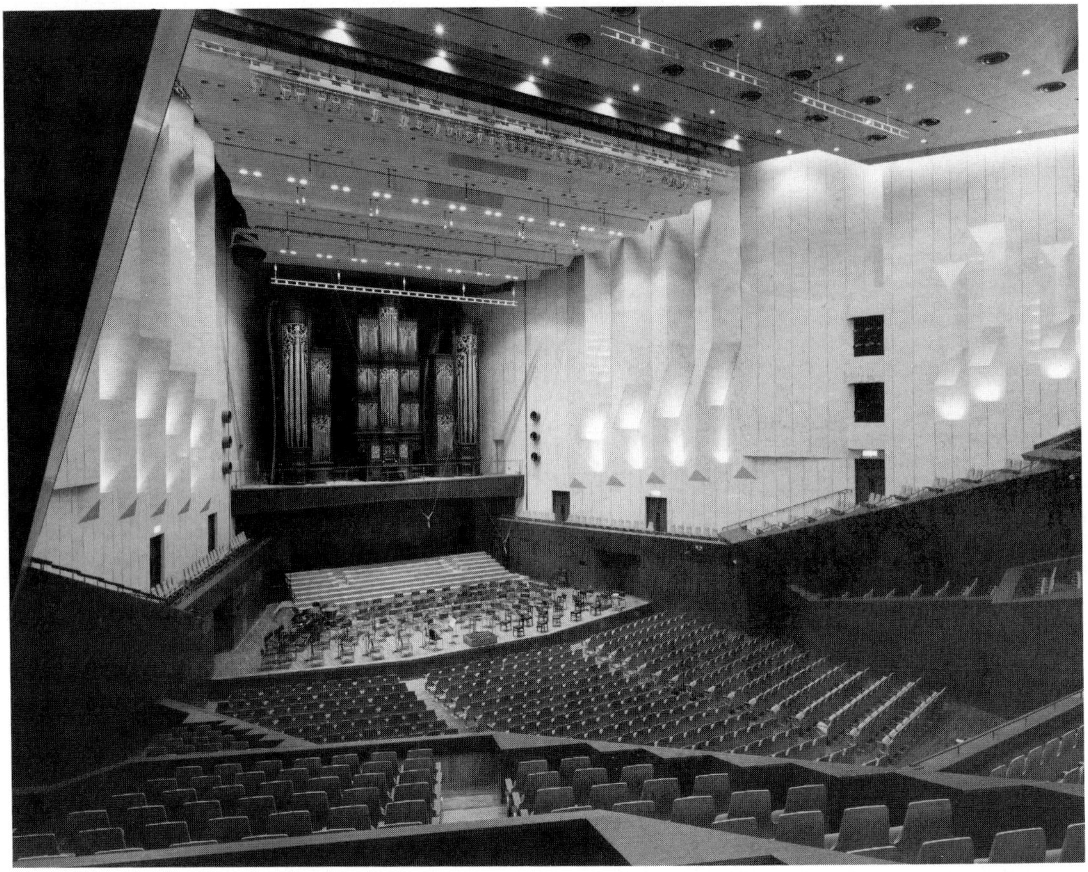

Tokyo, Metropolitan Art Space Concert Hall

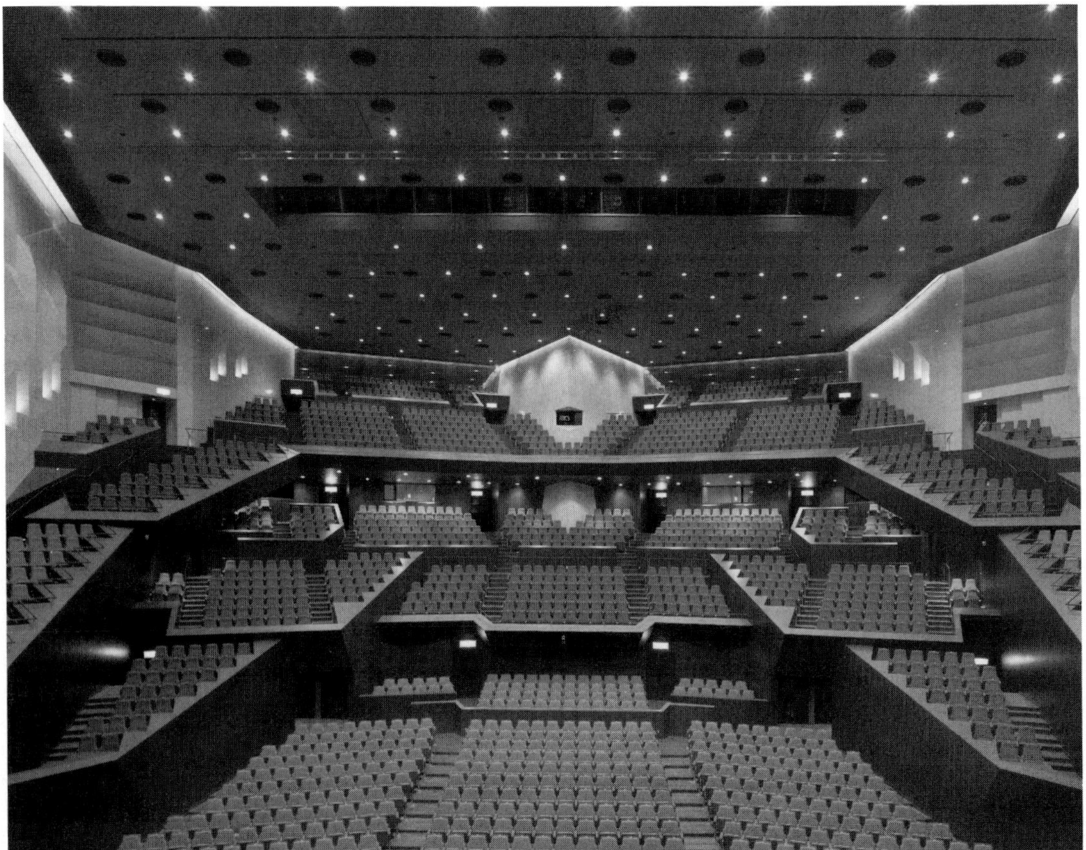

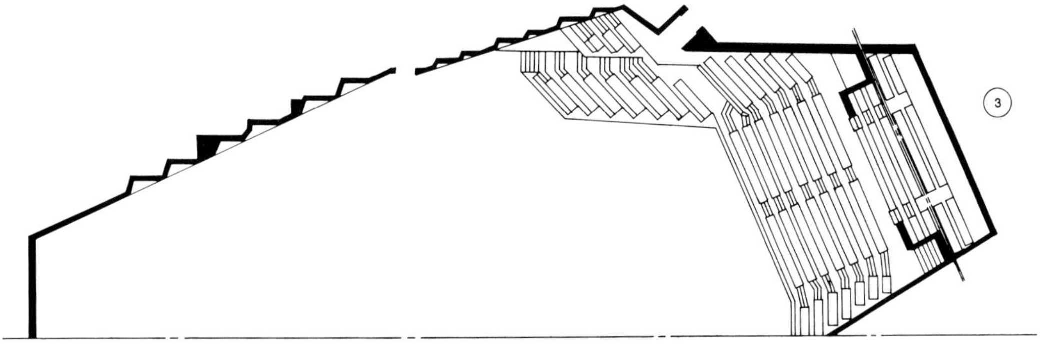

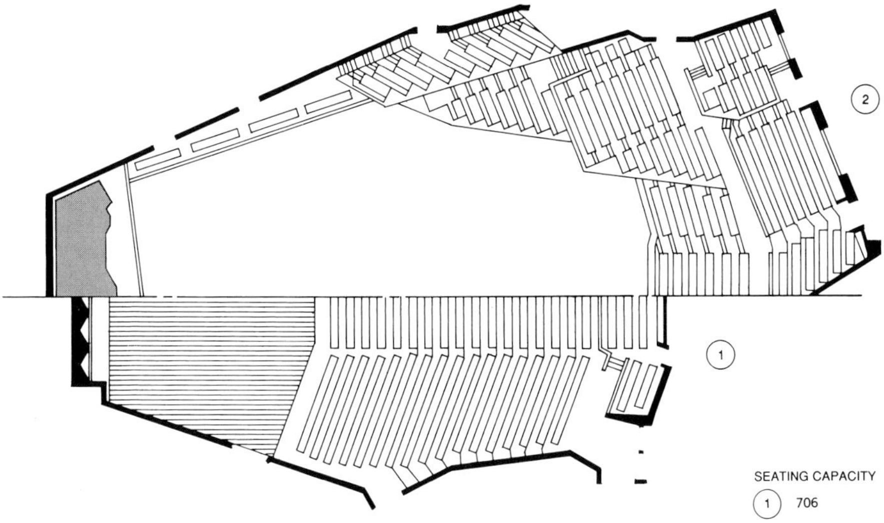

SEATING CAPACITY 2017

1	706
2	674
3	637

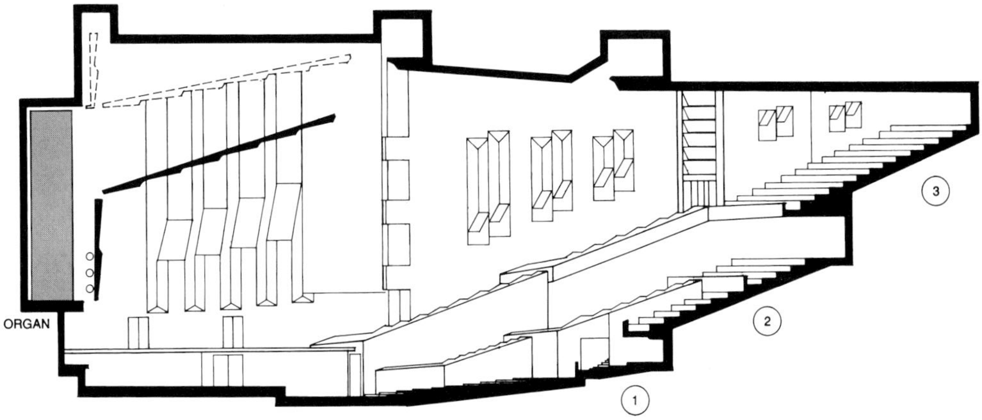

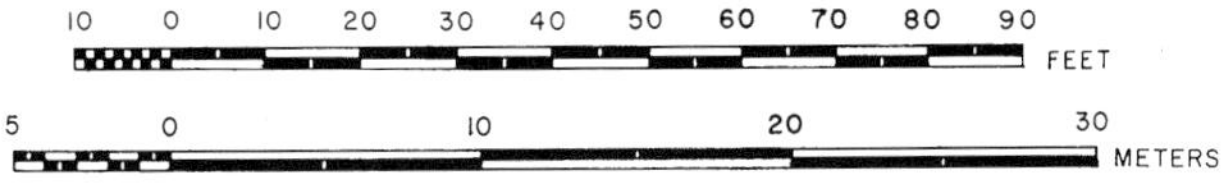

Architectural and structural details

Uses: music only. *Ceiling:* 1.4 in. (3.6 cm) plasterboard, above which is large airspace; cloth finish above seating; perforated board applied on the surrounding areas. *Walls:* sloping; lower side walls concrete, covered with 0.3 mm walnut veneer, upper side walls marble veneer (see the photographs); rear wall at first balcony level, glass wool behind perforated board; balcony fronts, plaster covered with walnut veneer. *Sound diffusers:* on side walls, marble veneer. *Floors:* Japanese oak, penetrated by ventilation mushrooms. *Carpets:* none. *Stage enclosure:* lower part, same as lower side walls; upper part marble veneer; canopy, 1.4 in. (3.6 cm) plaster board with cloth finish; canopy, adjustable for small concerts, completely concealing pipe organ; full height for organ and large concerts. *Stage floor:* 1.6 in. (4 cm) Japanese oak over 1 in. (2.4 cm) board. *Stage height:* 31.5 in. (80 cm). *Seating:* underseats and rear backs, molded plywood; porous cloth over polyurethane foam on front of backs and top of seat; armrests, solid. (*Note:* A large sliding door is installed under the pipe organ which, when opened, usually at intermission, gives the audience a view of a beautiful garden.)

Architect: Yoshinobu Ashihara & Associates. *Acoustical consultant:* Nagata Acoustics, Inc. *Photographs:* Kokyu Miwa. *Reference:* M. Nagata, S. Ikeda, and K. Oguchi, "Acoustical Design of the Tokyo Metropolitan Art and Cultural Hall," paper presented at 120th Meeting of Acoustical Society, November 1990, J. Acoust. Soc. Am., **88**, p. S112 (abstract).

*Technical details**

V = 880,000 ft^3 (25,000 m^3)	S_a = 10,000 ft^2 (929 m^2)	S_A = 14,120 ft^2 (1,312 m^2)
S_o = 2,230 ft^2 (207 m^2)	S_T = 16,350 ft^2 (1,519 m^2)	N = 2,017
H = 51 ft (15.5 m)	W = 92 ft (28 m)	L = 115 ft (35 m)
D = 155 ft (47.2 m)	V/S_T = 53.8 ft (16.5 m)	V/S_A =62.3 ft (19 m)
V/N = 436 ft^3 (12.4 m^3)	S_A/N = 7.0 ft^2 (0.65 m^2)	H/W = 0.55
L/W = 1.25	t_I = 27msec	

**The terminology is explained in Appendix 1.*

JAPAN

65

Tokyo
NHK Hall

The Japanese Broadcasting Corporation (NHK) uses this hall, seating 3,677 persons, primarily as a concert hall, but also for opera, variety shows, and popular music. Opened in 1973, it is the home of the NHK Symphony Orchestra which holds subscription concerts six days a month. Three halls in Japan were used as a basis for design, one of which was the Bunka Kaikan, described in this book. A semi-fan plan was adopted, fan at front and parallel walls in rear half. At each level, the audience is divided into three areas. NHK Hall takes its place as one of the largest concert halls in the world used by a major orchestra. The concert stage can range from 2,100 ft^2 (196 m^2) up to 3,360 ft^2 (310 m^2) in three steps, by removing up to 150 seats.

The audience on the main floor receives early reflections from the stage enclosure, from the impressive wedge-shaped balcony fronts and from the succession of overhead curved reflectors that begin at the rear wall of the stage and continue as an integral part of the ceiling over most of the audience. Shown clearly in the photographs are protruding elements attached to the surfaces of the side walls of the stage and the auditorium which spread, by diffusion, early sound reflections, of lesser magnitude, over a large percentage of the audience. The greatest distance of a listener from the non-augmented stage front is 156 ft (47.5 m), compared to Boston Symphony Hall's 133 ft (40.5 m), seating 2,625. The mid-frequency reverberation time, with full audience, is about 1.7 sec, a little on the low side for symphony concerts, but an excellent compromise for the many uses made of the hall.

I have attended two concerts in NHK Hall, one by the Boston Symphony Orchestra and the other by the NHK orchestra. I sat in three seats, one on the main floor, the second 15 seats off center in the second balcony, and the third on the aisle near an exit stair in the first balcony. I was surprised at the similarity of the sound at the three seats and at its strength, although a little weaker than in Boston. The orchestral sections were well balanced and the sound was clear and warm. The lower reverberation time and the lack of reverberant sound energy from behind, made the sound more directional than in classical, smaller; rectangular halls. The Boston players expressed no dissatisfaction.

TOKYO, NHK HALL

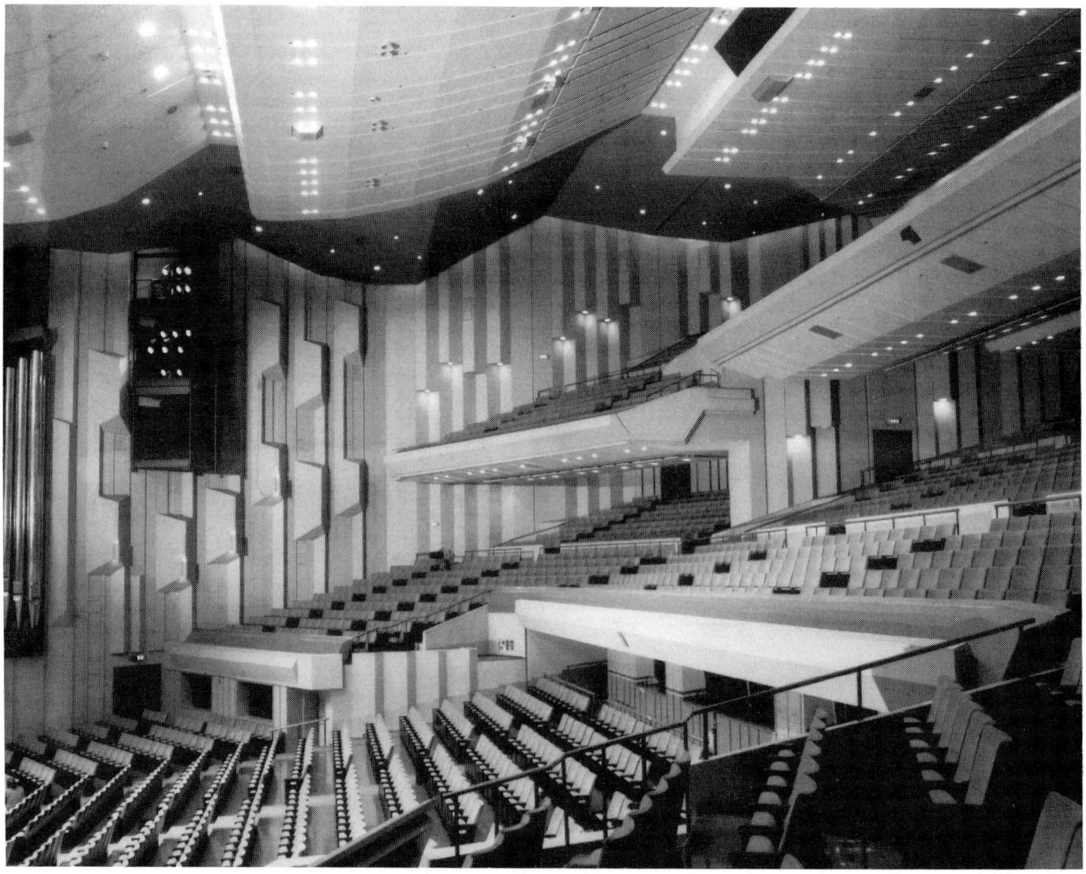

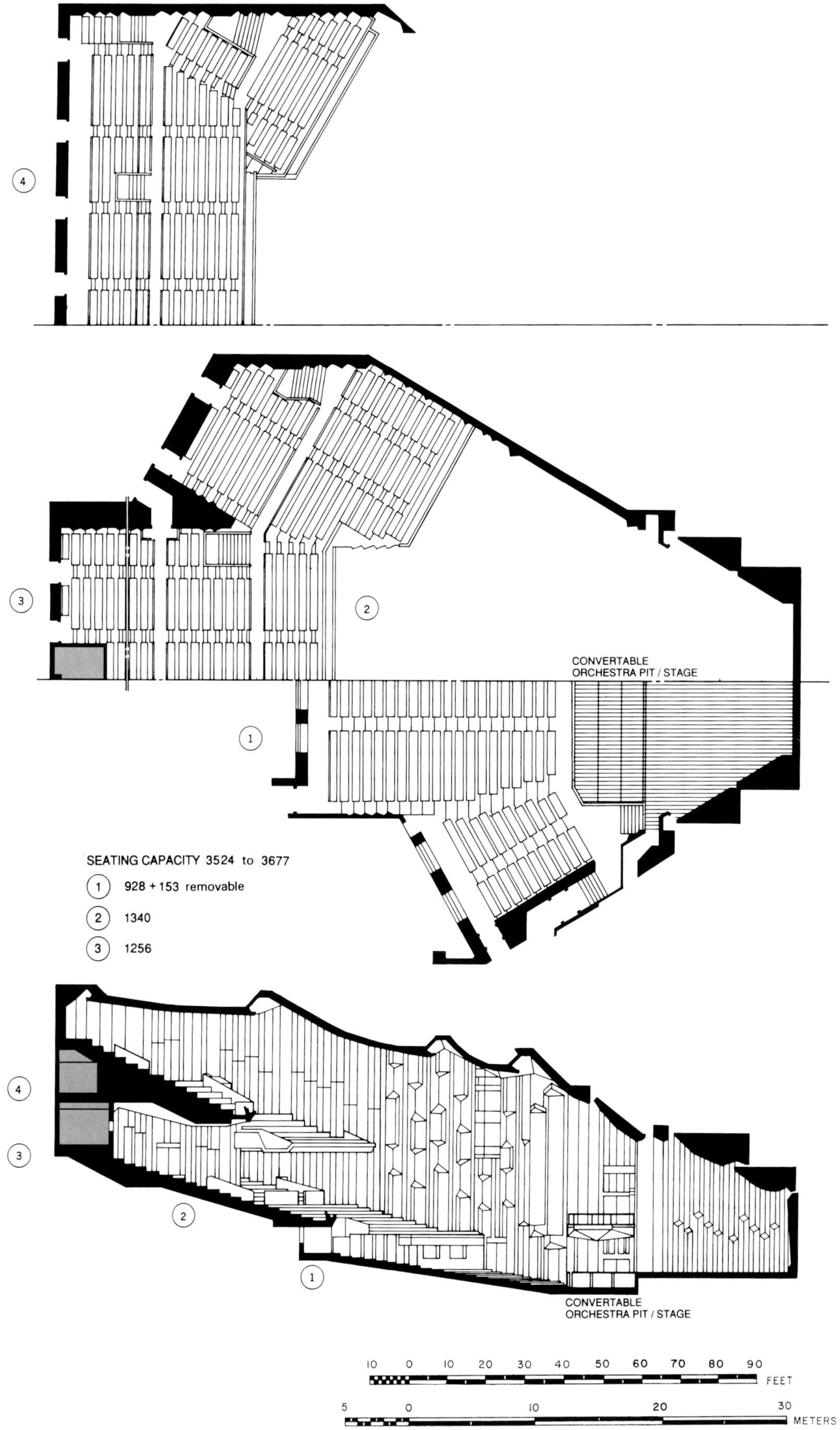
4
3
2
1
CONVERTABLE ORCHESTRA PIT / STAGE
SEATING CAPACITY 3524 to 3677
1 928 + 153 removable
2 1340
3 1256
4
3
2
1
CONVERTABLE ORCHESTRA PIT / STAGE
10 0 10 20 30 40 50 60 70 80 90
FEET
5 0 10 20 30
METERS

Architectural and structural details

Uses: primarily concerts, variety shows, musical comedies, and popular audience-participation TV productions. *Ceiling:* 0.2 in. (5 mm) asbestos board. *Stage ceiling and side walls:* 0.6 in. (1.7 cm) compound panel. *Main and balcony side walls:* 1.2 in. (3 cm) mortared, reinforced concrete and 0.8 in. (2 cm) thick asbestos board. *Sound absorption:* in rear part of ceiling, two large areas of perforated asbestos board with 1 in. (2.5 cm) glasswool and airspace behind; same for rear walls of balconies. *Stage floor:* 1.9 in. (4.8 cm) wooden strips. *Stage height:* 35 in. (89 cm). *Audience floor:* vinyl tile on concrete. *Carpet:* thin, on aisles. *Seating:* seat back, molded plywood; tops of seats and fronts of the backrests are upholstered with cushion; porous cloth covering; underseat solid; armrests, wood.

Architect: Nikken Sekkei Ltd., Tokyo. *Acoustical consultant:* Technical Research Laboratories of NHK. *Photographs:* courtesy of Takashi Nishi, NHK. *References:* T. Yamamoto, M. Nagata, and H. Tsukuda, "Acoustical Design of the New NHK Hall," NHK Technical Monograph, No. 19, 37 pages (March 1972). A. Mizoguchi, T. Yamamoto, Y. Ogawa, T. Fukunishi, and F. Suzuki, "Acoustics of the NHK Hall, report of the Architectural Acoustics Committee of the Acoustical Society of Japan, No. AA73–13, 24 pages (1973).

*Technical details**

V = 890,000 ft^3 (25,200 m^3)	S_a = 15,700 ft^2 (1,458 m^2)	S_A = 19,600 ft^2 (1,821 m^2)
S_o = 2,077 ft^2 (193 m^2)	S_o (pit) = 1,030 ft^2 (95.8 m^2)	S_T = 21,677 ft^2 (2,014 m^2)
N = 3,677	H = 49 ft (14.9 m)	W = 126 ft (38.4 m)
L = 124 ft (37.8 m)	D = 156 ft (47.6 m)	V/S_T = 41 ft (12.5 m)
V/S_A = 45.4 ft (13.8 m)	V/N = 242 ft^3 (6.85 m^3)	S_A/N = 5.33 ft^2 (0.5 m^2)
H/W = 0.39	L/W = 0.98	t_I = 23 msec

* *The terminology is explained in Appendix 1.*

Japan

66

Tokyo
Orchard Hall

Orchard Hall is the largest hall in a cultural complex called "Bunkamura" (cultural village), constructed and owned by the Tokyu Group of Companies, situated in a busy and flourishing subcenter of Tokyo. Orchard Hall has a stage house whose configuration can be tailored to suit symphonic concerts, opera, ballet, and smaller musical groups. The hall opened in 1989 with the Bayreuth Festival Company from Germany, led by Wolfgang Wagner, presenting the opera "Tannhauser" and several orchestral concerts featuring Wagner's music.

Rectangular in shape and seating 2,150, it closely approximates the width and length of Boston Symphony Hall. The hall is beautiful, with clean contemporary lines. The visual ceiling is transparent to sound; the acoustical ceiling is 10 ft (3 m) above. Various sizes of stage enclosure are accomplished with telescoping "shelters" that provide platform areas from 940 ft^2 (87 m^2) to 2,680 ft^2 (249 m^2). To vary reverberation time, areas of sound absorbing material can be exposed, or for smaller performing groups, the volume can be reduced by up to 10%, with a corresponding decrease in reverberation time. The reverberation time, with medium-size shelter, which is normally used for symphonic music, being about 1.8 sec at mid-frequencies for full occupancy. The tone quality is excellent, both on the main floor and in the balconies. There is good balance among the sections of the orchestra.

As this book has emphasized elsewhere, every hall has its own personality, even when built reasonably close to another model. Orchard hall has a clearness or transparency of sound that distinguishes it from many others, probably because it has less "baroque" ornamentation than the classical rectangular halls in which there is greater diffusion of the sound.

At one symphonic concert in May 1991 by the Berliner Rundfunk Orchestra, conducted by Vladimir Ashkenazy, I sat for the first half (*Rococo Variations* for cello and orchestra by Tchaikovsky) on the main floor and the second half (Brahms *Symphony No. 4)*, in the center of the first balcony. I preferred the somewhat fuller sound of the balcony, an observation that is true of most halls, because of the shorter initial-time-delay gaps farther back.

Tokyo, Orchard Hall

3

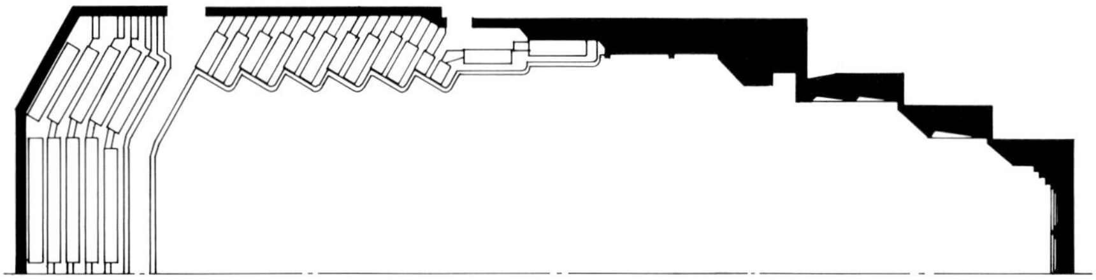

2

1

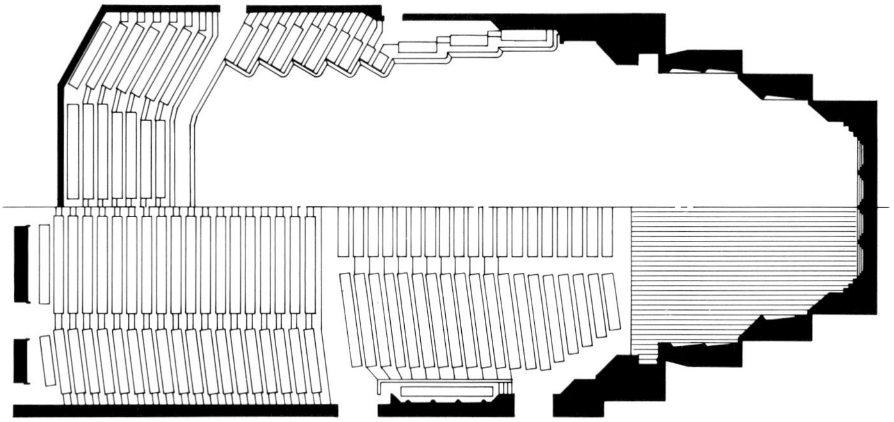

SEATING CAPACITY 2150

1 1424

2 410

3 316

3

2

1

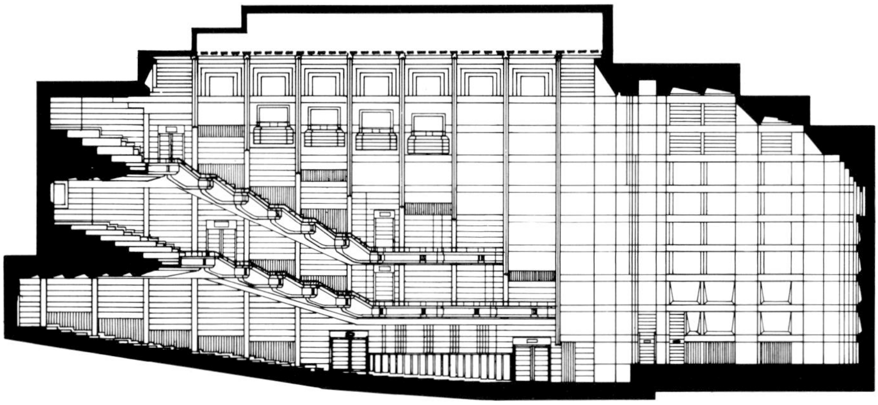

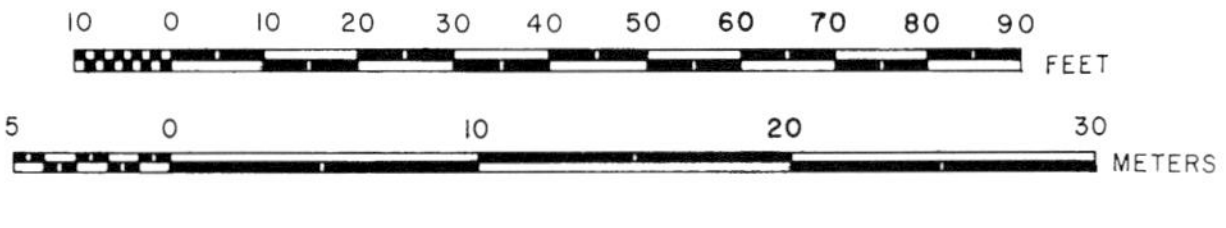

Architectural and structural details

Uses: concerts, 70%; music, small groups, 10%; opera and ballet, 20%. *Ceiling:* two layers of wood chip board, each 0.7 in. (1.8 cm). *Visual ceiling:* acoustically transparent screen. *Side walls:* same as ceiling, with sound diffusing elements. *Balcony facia:* precast gypsum affixed to concrete. *Sound absorbing surfaces:* rear wall under first balcony, absorbs low frequencies, comprised of hard thin covering with slits and sound absorbing material behind. *Floors:* 0.6 in. (1.5 cm) wood impregnated in acrylic plastic, on 0.35 in. (0.9 cm) plywood, cemented to concrete. *Carpet:* none. *Stage enclosure:* built in three pieces, which telescope into each other—for largest stage with chorus extension, the stage volume is 141,000 ft^2 (4,000 m^3); without extension, 121,800 ft^3 (3,450 m^3); for medium stage, 94,600 ft^3 (2,680 m^3); for smallest stage, 50,850 ft^3 (1,440 m^3). *Stage floor:* resilient wood, 1.2 in. (3 cm) thick, over two plywood sheets 1 in. (2.4 cm) total, over large airspace. *Stage height:* 43 in. (1.1 m). *Seating:* molded plywood back, unperforated plywood seat bottom; upholstered front of seat back and top of seat bottom with polyvinyl cushion covered by porous fabric; armrests wood.

Architect: Yuzo Mikami and MIDI Architects. *Acoustical consultant:* Kiyoteru Ishii and Kimura Laboratory of Nihon University. *Photographs:* Osamu Murai. *References:* Staff Editor, "The Orchard Hall, Bunkamura, Shibuya, Tokyo," SD [Space Design], No. 302, pp. 88–99 (October, 1989) (in Japanese); "Design philosophy of the Orchard Hall and its development," Yuzo Mikami and Kiyoteru Ishii, Architectural Acoustics and Noise Control, **19**, 61–68 (1990) (in Japanese).

*Technical details**

V (symphony) = 723,850 ft^3 (20,500 m^3)	S_a = 10,760 ft^2 (1,000 m^2)	S_A = 14,140 ft^2 (1,314 m^2)
S_o = 2,337 ft^2 (217 m^2)	S_T = 16,480 ft^2 (1,531 m^2)	N = 2,150
H = 75 ft (23 m)	W = 80 ft (24.4 m)	L = 126 ft (38.4 m)
D = 131 ft (40 m)	V/S_T = 43.9 ft (13.4 m)	V/S_A = 51.2 ft (15.6 m)
V/N = 337 ft^3 (9.53 m^3)	S_A/N = 6.58 ft^2 (0.61 m^2)	H/W = 0.94
L/W = 1.57	t_I = 26 msec	

**The terminology is explained in Appendix 1.*

Tokyo Suntory

In 1986, Suntory Hall opened on the occasion of the 60th anniversary of Suntory, Ltd., Japan's largest distillery. Located in the busiest section of Tokyo's Akasaka, one is surprised by the enclosed courtyard and the gracious lobby. Entering the hall, one is awed by the beautiful light-colored wood interior and the "vineyard" style in which the audience is arranged in blocks of various heights. Side surfaces of the individual terraces, made of smooth white marble, provide early reflections to most of the seats, simulating those that are found in the traditional rectangular concert hall. The roomy and comfortable seats, numbering 2,006, were demanded by Suntory's Chairman, Keizo Saji, a large man among fellow Japanese.

The reverberation time for Suntory, fully occupied, is 2.0 sec at mid-frequencies, equal to that of the best liked concert halls and just right for the baroque repertory especially enjoyed by the Japanese. Diffusion of the reverberant sound field is accomplished by splayed side wall surfaces and stepped sections in the convex ceiling. The stage area is 2,530 ft^2 (2,325 m^2) and the distance between side walls is 75 ft (23 m), both a little large compared to the highest rated halls. The musicians receive early sound reflections from 10 convex fiberglass panels, each with an area of 43 ft^2 (4 m^2) at a height of 39 ft (12 m). With a small orchestra, the double basses are likely to be far from a wall, thus losing the boost that their sound would otherwise receive.

The acoustical data show that some parts of Suntory Hall receive more early reflections (less than 50 ms), which is desirable, than others. The best seats, in this regard, are in the rear half of the hall.

This hall is one of the most popular in Tokyo, in large part because the world's best orchestras on tour tend to go to Suntory. It is also used heavily by five of Japan's Symphony Orchestras. Another reason for its reputation is that touring orchestras generally praise those halls with high reverberation times, whereas for concentrated rehearsals, necessary at home, a lower RT is often preferable. In all, Suntory Hall is beautiful, the acoustics are very good, and it serves the musical public very well.

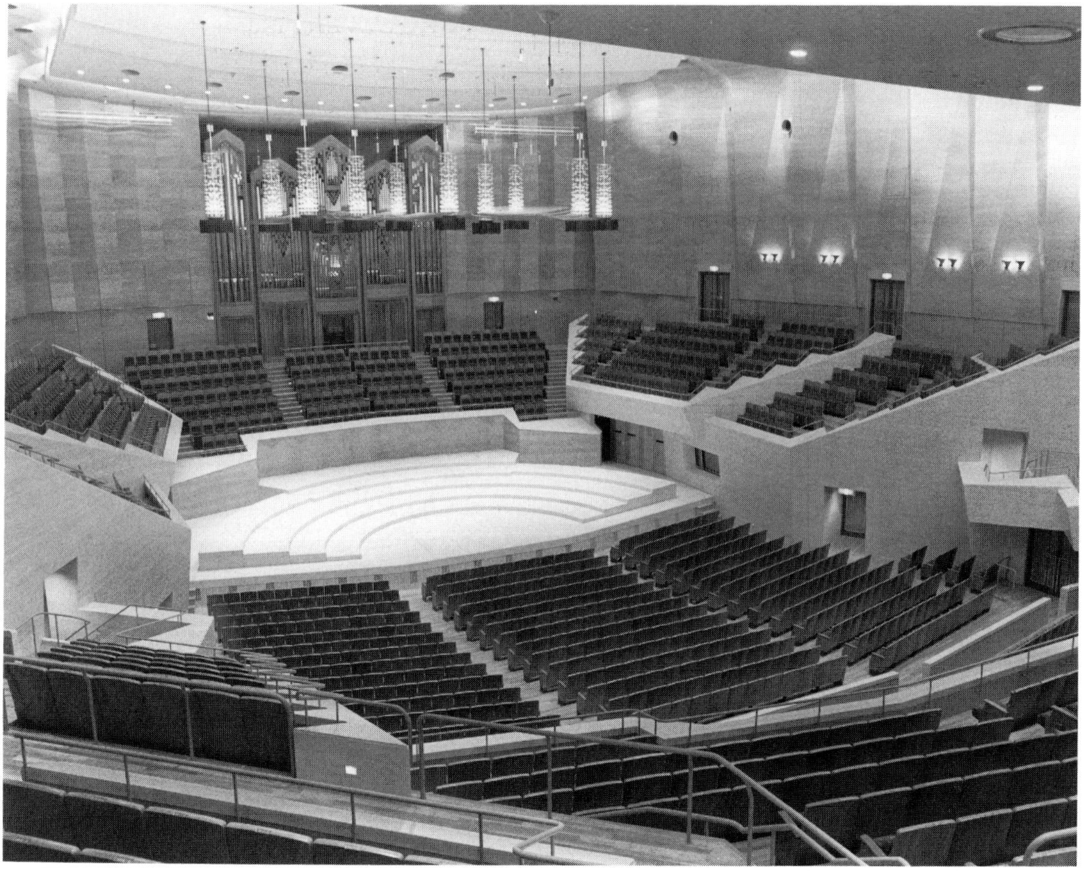

TOKYO, SUNTORY

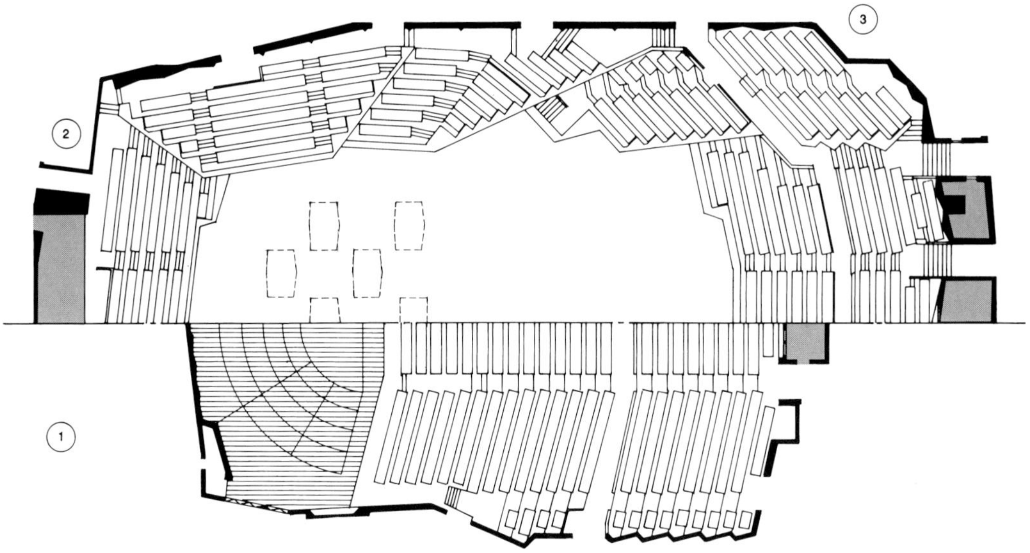

SEATING CAPACITY 2006

1	914
2	806
3	286

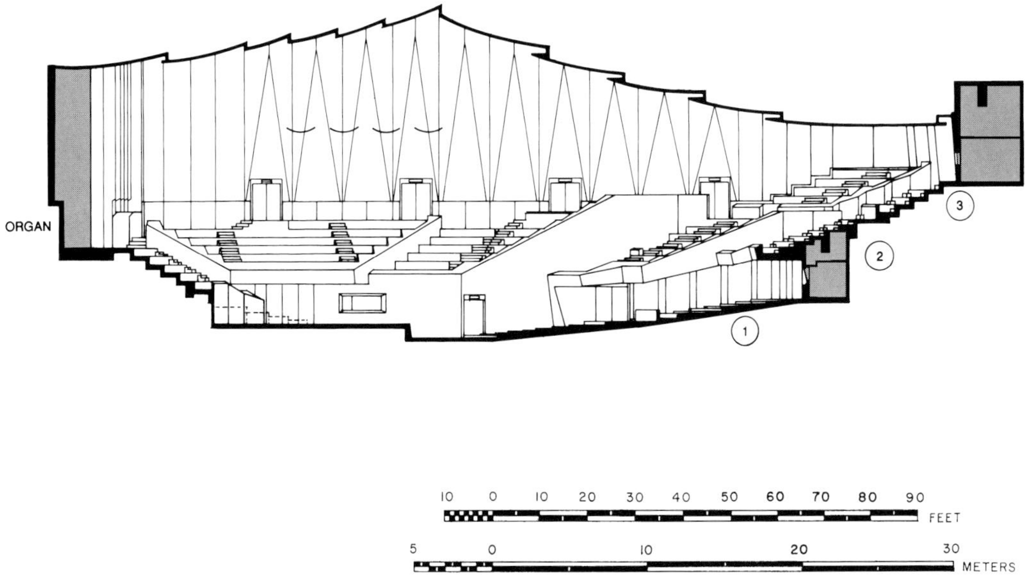

Architectural and structural details

Uses: primarily classical music. *Ceiling:* two layers of 0.5 in. (1.25 cm) gypsum board beneath airspace. *Side walls:* two principal portions, flat and splayed; flat portions are triangles with base at dado line, 2 layers 2 in. woodchip board, 0.3 in. (0.8 cm) plaster board and thin wood ply; splayed portions resemble pillars, with point at dado line, widening and deepening until widest portions touch just at the ceiling line and then continue under the ceiling; these splayed portions are 1 or 2 layers of 0.7 in. (1.8 cm) chip board, plus plaster board and wood ply; walls on sides of the organ, 1 layer of chip board; back walls splayed (see the drawing) with combination of solid and perforated board; several small areas 2 in. fiberglass blanket behind grille; sides of terraces are marble held by mortar to concrete. *Floor:* 0.5 in. hardwood, on 0.5 in. plywood, on concrete. *Stage enclosure:* marble (see the photograph). *Stage floor:* 1.6 in. (4 cm) wood on 0.5 in. plywood, on 2.5 in. × 2.5 in. (6 cm) sleepers, 1 ft (30 cm) on centers. *Stage height:* fixed portion at front is 31 in. (80 cm) high. *Stage elevators:* five elevators create risers; piano elevator, in fixed portion. *Seating:* molded oak plywood back and seat-bottoms; front of backs and seat tops, upholstered with porous cloth and polyurethane foam.

Architect: Yasui Architects. *Acoustical consultant:* Nagata Acoustics, Inc. *Photographs:* courtesy of the architect.

*Technical details**

V = 740,000 ft^3 (21,000 m^3)	S_a = 11,220 ft^2 (1,042 m^2)	S_A = 14,680 ft^2 (1,364 m^2)
S_o = 2,530 ft^2 (235 m^2)	S_T = 17,210 ft^2 (1,600 m^2)	N = 2,006
H = 54 ft (16.5 m)	W = 102 ft (31.1 m)	L = 100 ft (30.5 m)
D = 118 ft (36 m)	V/S_T = 43 ft (13.1 m)	V/S_A = 50.4 ft (15.4 m)
V/N = 369 ft^3 (10.5 m^3)	S_A/N = 7.32 ft^2 (0.68 m^2)	H/W = 0.53
L/W = 0.98	t_I = 30 msec	

**The terminology is explained in Appendix 1.*

MEXICO

68

Mexico City
Sala Nezahualcoyotl

Sala Nezahualcoyotl concert hall bears the name of one of Mexico's legendary poets and musicians. Built on the campus of the Universidad Nacional Atonoma de Mexico in 1976, seating 2,376, it is the home of one of Mexico City's professional orchestras. It boasts of being the first concert hall in North America to surround the stage with audience. The arrangement of the audience into tiers creates side-wall reflecting surfaces that emulate seating in a narrower hall. Also planned was a short gap in time between the direct sound and the first arriving reflections at each listener's position. An innovation is a large reverberant room located beneath the stage which is coupled to the hall by horizontal grilles located along the front and rear edges of the stage and by grillwork along the entire front face of the stage. This reverberant room also communicates with the hall through an open grille under the first rows of seats. The purpose is to enhance the lowest register tones, but it frequently becomes a convenient storage space.

An impressive part of the acoustical planning is the dominating arrangement of sound reflectors over the stage and the forward part of the main floor seating. In the ceiling is a reverse-pyramid structure arranged over the orchestra and the main-floor audience. Beneath it hang brown-tinted acrylic reflectors of two shapes, "watch crystals" and "prisms," each designed to reflect and diffuse the high and upper-middle tones to orchestra and audience. The watch-crystals reflect over 360°, and the prisms are directed to the audience areas to shorten the initial-time-delay gap. The low frequencies pass through the arrays and are reflected, diffusely, by the ceiling structure. Of importance acoustically are the relatively high walls around the stage, 9 ft (2.7 m), with diffusing facias and an overhanging "shelf" at the top. Finally, on the wall behind the chorus seating, a large number of organ-pipe-like diffusing elements are placed to improve the quality of the reverberant sound field.

Is the Sala Nezahualcotyl successful? With the Cleveland Symphony Orchestra, under Lorin Maazel, performing Beethoven's *Ninth Symphony*, the hall received good reviews from music critics imported from New York, Chicago, and Boston. When asked by Chancellor Peter Czirnich of Munich in 1979, Maazel wrote, "The best new hall that I know of is the one built for the University of Mexico..."

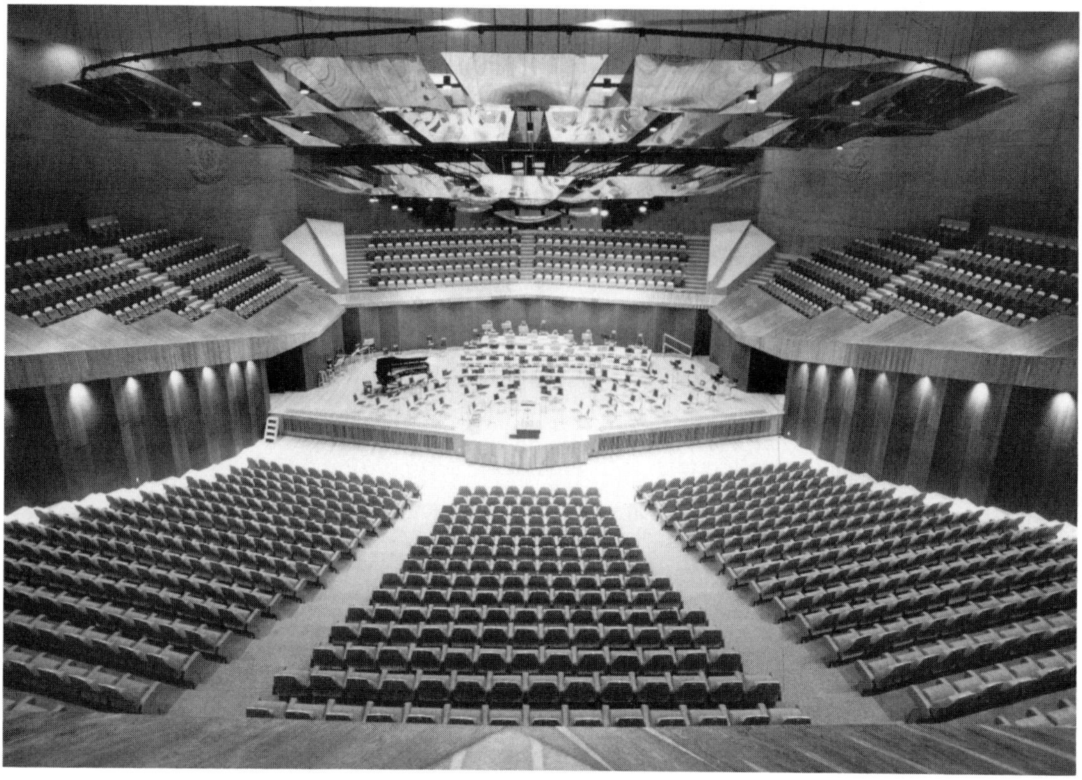

Mexico City, Sala Nezahualcoyotl

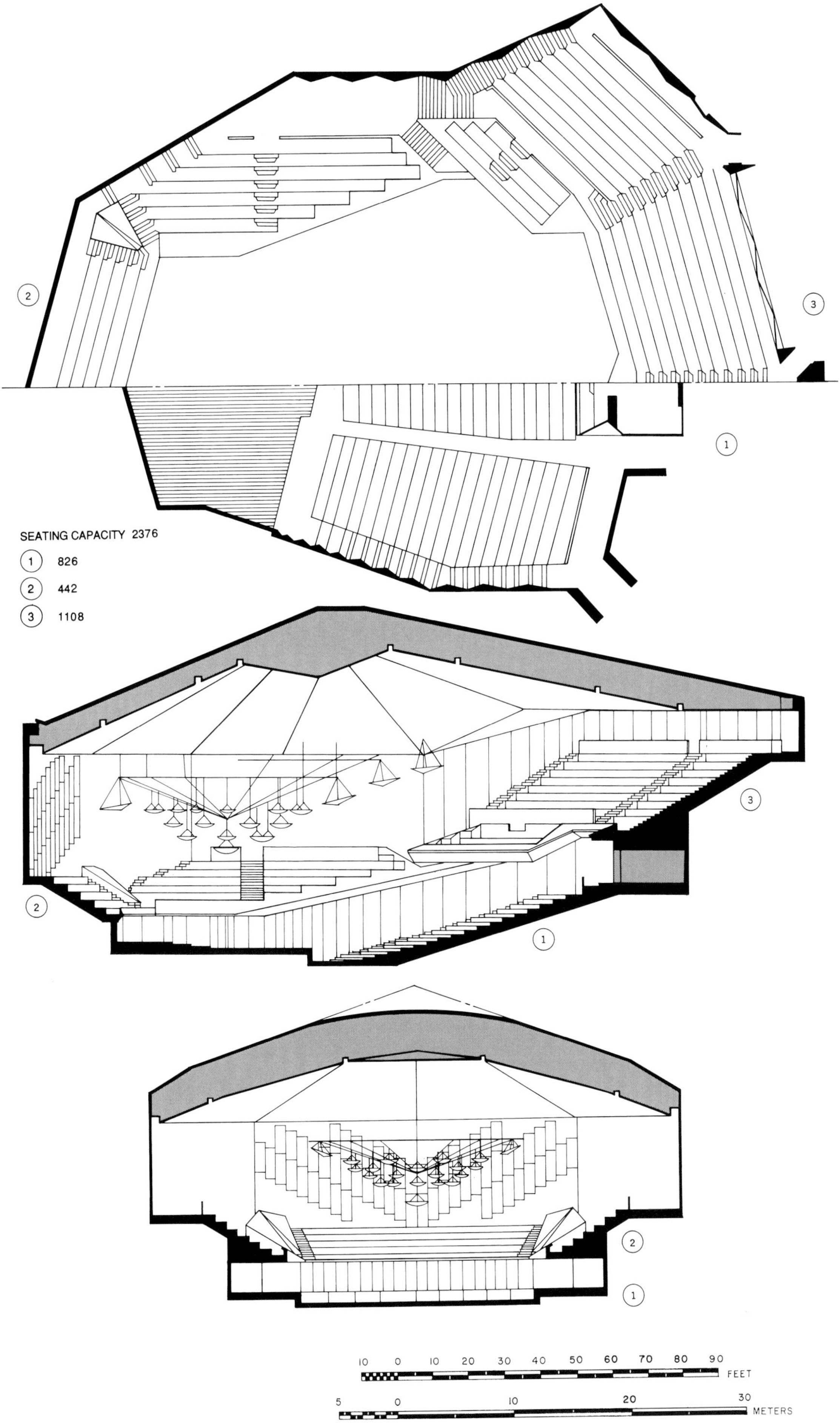

SEATING CAPACITY 2376
1 826
2 442
3 1108
1
2
3
10 0 10 20 30 40 50 60 70 80 90
FEET
5 0 10 20 30
METERS

Architectural and structural details

Uses: orchestral music and recitals. *Ceiling:* 2 layers of splayed 1 in. (2.5 cm) gypsum board, with batt insulation above. *Walls:* rear walls, 1 in. splayed wood boards with glass fiber batts behind; other walls, poured concrete with decorative splayed 1 in. wood boards. *Floors:* in main floor, 2 in. (5 cm) wood over 2 in. airspace; in balconies, concrete. *Carpet:* in aisles only. *Stage enclosure:* walls: 1 in. splayed wood boards with glass fiber behind; floor, 2 in. wood over acoustic moat with 20% grille openings under audience seating. *Stage height:* 37 in. (94 cm). *Acoustic reflectors:* all reflectors are acrylic, 0.75 to 1 in. thick; the watchglasses are 6 to 10 ft (1.8 to 3 m) in diameter, convex in shape, and located over most of stage; the prisms are splayed and located over the near parts of the audience. *Sound absorbing materials:* none. *Seating:* wooden seat back; front of seat back upholstered with some wood showing; top of seat-bottom upholstered with porous fabric; underseat, metal, perforated on main floor only.

Architects: Orso Nunez, Arcadio Artis, Manuel M. Ortiz, Arturo Trevino, and Roberto Ruiz. *Acoustical consultant:* Jaffe Holden Scarbrough. *Photographs:* courtesy of the architects. *References:* "Acoustic Devices Enhance Sound of Music in a Surround Hall," *Architectural Record,* 125–128 (January 1978); "El Placer de Una buena Acustica," *Obras* (June 1979).

*Technical details**

V = 1,082,000 ft³ (30,640 m³)	S_a = 15,877 ft² (1,476 m²)	S_A = 18,126 ft² (1,684 m²)
S_o = 2,906 ft² (270 m²)	S_T = 21,032 ft² (1,954 m²)	N = 2,376
H = 52 ft (15.8 m)	W = 134 ft (40.8 m)	L = 113 ft (34.4 m)
D = 138 ft (42 m)	V/S_T = 51.4 ft (15.7 m)	V/S_A = 59.7 ft (18.2 m)
V/N = 455 ft³ (12.9 m³)	S_A/N = 7.63 ft² (0.71 m²)	H/W = 0.39
L/W = 0.84	t_I = 16 msec	

**The terminology is explained in Appendix 1.*

69

Amsterdam Concertgebouw

The Amsterdam Concertgebouw, which opened in 1888 and seats 2,037 persons is rated by almost anyone familiar with the concert halls of the Western world as one of the three best. These include Vienna's Grosser Musikvereinssaal and Boston's Symphony Hall, all of which follow the tradition of rectangularity and a high ceiling.

Several of the physical features of the Concertgebouw are different. It is wider than those two halls, 91 ft (27.7 m) compared, respectively, to 65 and 75 ft (19.8 and 22.9 m). Twenty percent of the audience is seated on steep stadium steps behind the orchestra. The front of the stage is higher than that of any hall studied, 60 in. (153 cm).

The floor of the Concertgebouw is flat and the seats are removable. The irregular walls and deeply coffered ceiling produce excellent sound diffusion. The reverberation time at mid-frequencies, fully occupied, is about 2 sec.

Opinions of conductors of major orchestras and soloists obtained through the years include: "The Concertgebouw has marvelous acoustics. It is probably one of the best halls in the world," "I went into the audience and heard the Boston Symphony. It sounded excellent acoustically," "The reverberation in this hall gives great help to a violinist. As one slides from one note to another, the previous sound perseveres and one has the feeling that each note is surrounded by strength," "The sound is fabulous," "The Concertgebouw has marvelous acoustics and is probably one of the best in the world."

I have attended many concerts in the Concertgebouw and from my most recent notes, I glean, "The sound is well balanced, strong in bass. The reverberation sounds greater than that in other rectangular halls, a quality that generally pleases visiting conductors. The cello (in a concerto) sounds loud and luxurious. The full orchestra plays with rich tone."

For my taste, the sound in the balcony is better than on the main floor, probably because in those seats the articulation is somewhat better. But on the main floor, for those who love a full sumptuous sound with rich bass, and completely surrounded in an ocean of music, this hall has no superior.

Amsterdam, Concertgebouw

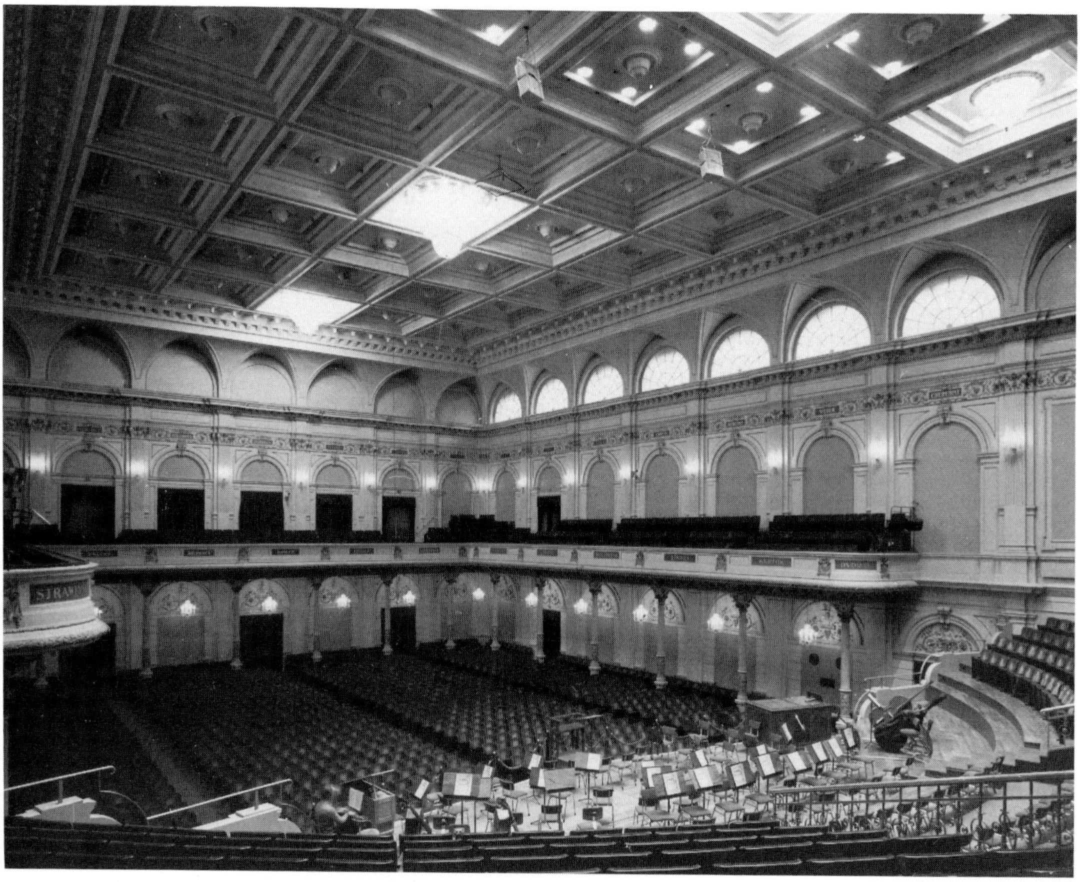

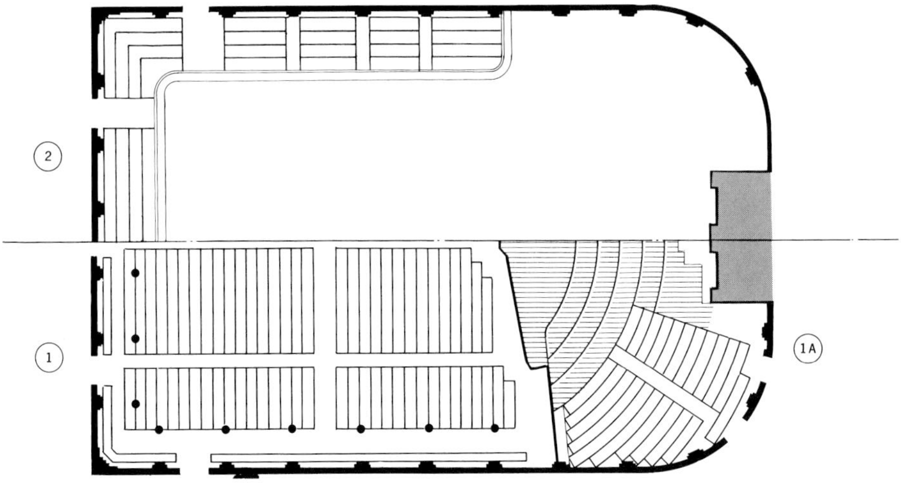

SEATING CAPACITY 2037

(1) 1305

(1A) 312

(2) 420

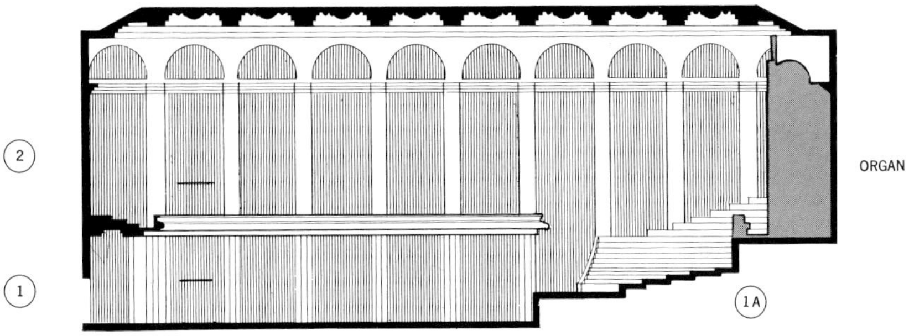

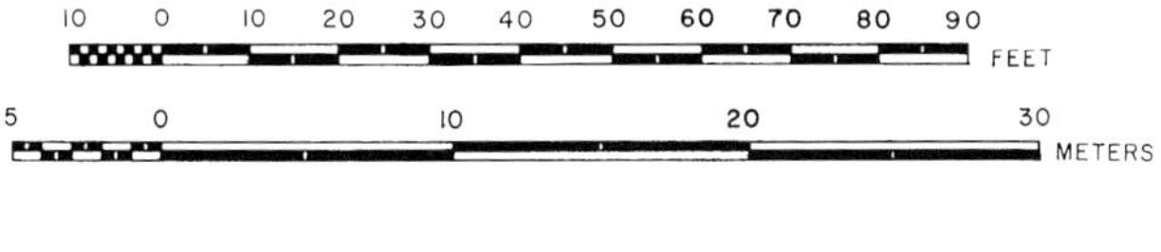

Architectural and structural details

Uses: all types of music, with emphasis on orchestra. *Ceiling:* 1.5 in. (3.8 cm) plaster on reeds, coffered and with ornamentation; there are deep "window" recesses around the top edges. *Side and rear walls:* below the balcony, plaster on brick; above the balcony, plaster on reed, which sounds dull or damped when tapped with the fingers. *Floors:* 5 in. (13 cm) concrete, on top of which hardwood boards are nailed to 2 × 3 in. (5 × 7.5 cm) wooden battens; cavity filled with 4 cm layer of sand. *Carpet:* on main floor aisles only. *Stage enclosure:* none. *Stage floor:* heavy wood over deep airspace. *Stage height:* 59 in. (150 cm). *Added absorptive material:* 700 ft^2 (65 m^2) of draperies over the front of the little room at the rear of the balcony and around the doorways. *Seating:* upholstered in thick, hard-weave material.

Architect: A. L. van Gendt. *Details:* courtesy of the Council, Concertgebouw, Amsterdam. *Photographs:* stage view: Hans Samson; seating view: Robert Schlingemann.

*Technical details**

V = 663,000 ft^3 (18,780 m^3)	S_a = 9,074 ft^2 (843 m^2)	S_A = 12,110 ft^2 (1,125 m^2)
S_o = 1,720 ft^2 (160 m^2)	S_T = 13,830 ft^2 (1,285 m^2)	N = 2,037
V/S_T = 48 ft (14.6 m)	V/S_A = 54.7 ft (16.7 m)	V/N = 325 ft^3 (9.2 m^3)
S_A/N = 5.94 ft^2 (0.552 m^2)	H = 56 ft (17.1 m)	W = 91 ft (27.7 m)
L = 86 ft (26.2 m)	D = 84 ft (25.6 m)	H/W = 0.62
L/W = 0.94	t_I = 21 msec	

**The terminology is explained in Appendix 1.*

70

Rotterdam
De Doelen Concert Hall

De Doelen Concert Hall was dedicated in 1966 at a time when acoustics was still based on visual observation of good and bad halls and on general rules-of-thumb. The reverberation time, the length of time it takes for a sound to die to inaudibility, was understood to be important and the quality of the reverberation was known to depend on large and small irregularities on the walls and ceiling, so-called sound diffusing elements. Comparison of halls of different reputations had shown that a hall had to be as narrow as possible in order to keep the gap in time between the direct sound and the first reflected sound wave as small as possible so that a large number of reflections could occur very soon after arrival of the direct sound. Yet to be discovered was that a large part of these early reflections should arrive at listeners' ears laterally—from the sides—for best sound quality. With the design adopted, these acoustical attributes were to a considerable extent achieved. A seating capacity of 2,242 was significantly more than in Vienna's Grosser Musikvereinssaal (1,680 seats) and Amsterdam's Concertgebouw (2,037 seats), two best liked of Europe's halls.

Architecturally, all known factors acoustically were taken into account in the design of De Doelen. The central part of the main floor is a walled enclosure whose top is 10 ft (3 m) above stage level and whose average width in the first two-thirds of the area is 69 ft (21 m), making the main floor equivalent to a small concert hall (594 seats). A large number of sound diffusing "boxes" and indentations line all sides of this enclosure, including the walls around the stage. These diffusers scatter the incident sound and send early lateral reflections to all seats. In the rear seats (facing the stage) outside the "inner hall" the earliest sound reflections arrive primarily by way of the sound diffusing ceiling. Later lateral reflections come from the sound diffusing side walls. As usual, seats to the sides and rear of the stage are not favored with as pleasant a sound, but seeing the orchestra and conductor up close seems to compensate. There are no echoes and the noise level from machinery is very low. The musicians report that maintaining good ensemble playing is easy.

The acoustics of De Doelen has been praised by visiting conductors and musicians, because the sound on stage and in the "inner hall" is excellent.

Rotterdam, De Doelen Concert Hall

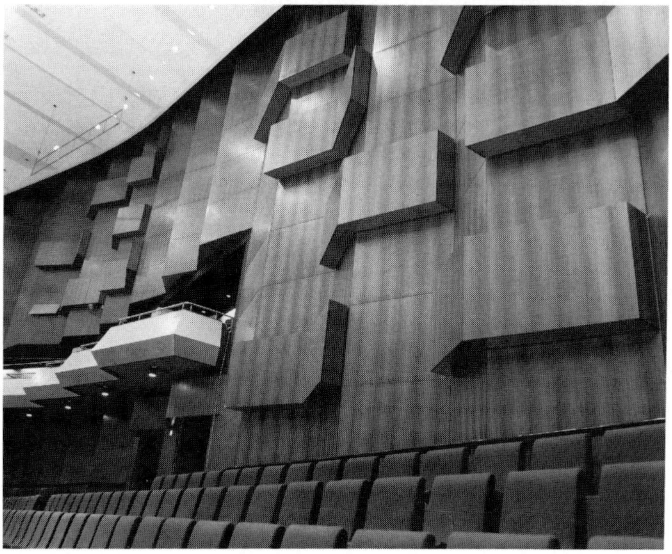

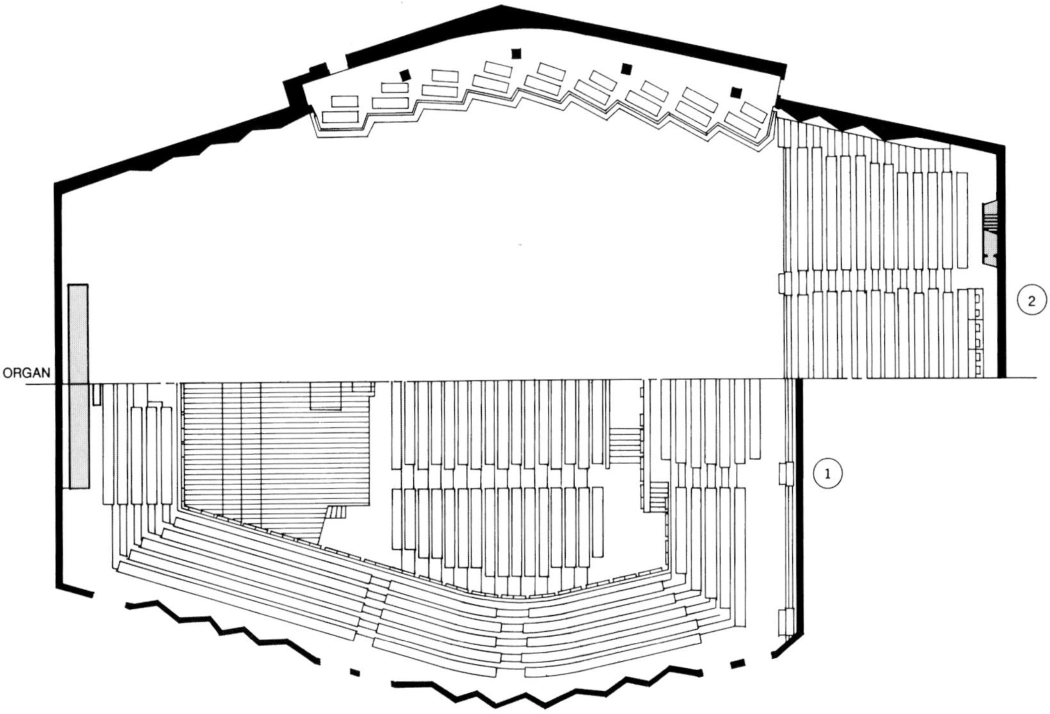

SEATING CAPACITY 2242

1 1577

2 665

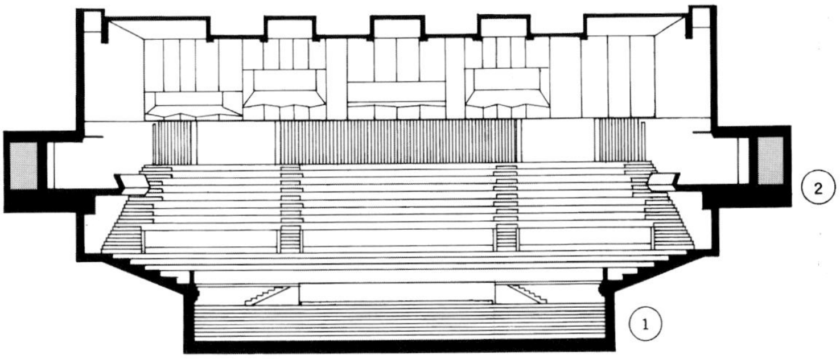

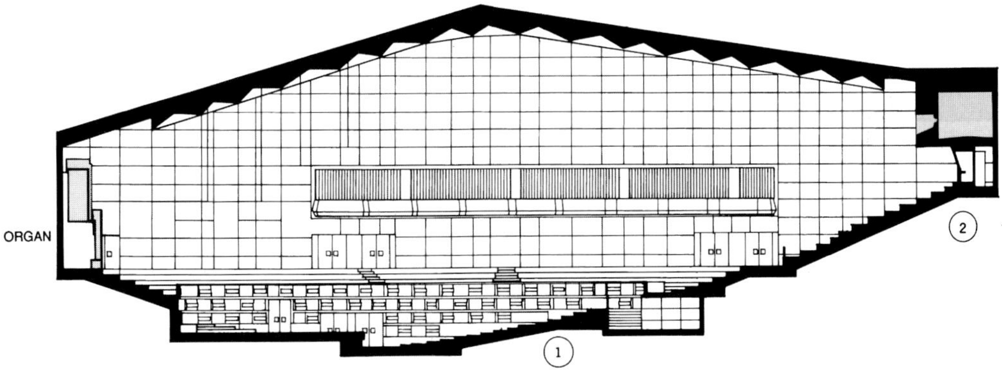

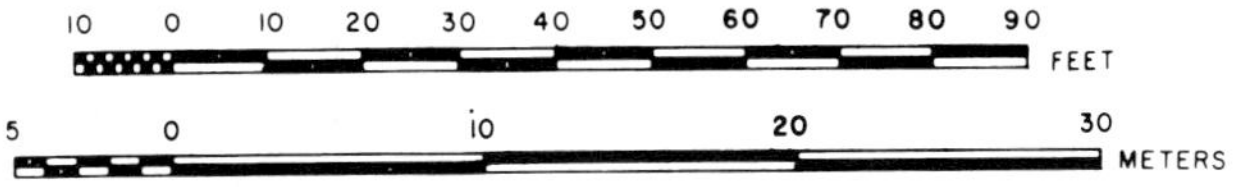

Architectural and structural details

Uses: classical music including large and small groups. *Ceiling:* heavy concrete, 1.5 in. (4.5 cm) thick of which visual layer is 0.4 in. (1 cm) plywood. *Upper walls:* dense concrete to which is attached finished walls including diffusing panels, constructed like ceiling. *Walls around "inner hall":* marble, diffuse in two dimensions. *Balcony fronts:* fibrous plaster, 1/2 in. (1.5 cm) thick. *Floors:* concrete with linoleum surface. *Carpet:* none. *Stage:* composite structure: top surface, 0.8 in. (2.4 cm) tongue-and-groove wood; three layers asphalt paper; 0.4 in. (1 cm) particle board; 0.65 in. (2 cm) elastic mounts, spaced 16 in. (40 cm) in one direction and 10 ft (3 m) other direction; airspace of about 2 ft. (61 cm). *Stage height:* 30 in. (0.75 m). *Seating:* molded plywood back and unperforated plywood seat bottom; upholstered front of seat back and top of seat bottom with polyvinyl; all surfaces covered by porous fabric; armrests wooden, covered by artificial leather.

Architect: Kraaijvanger Architekten bv. *Acoustical consultants:* C. W. Kosten and P. A. de Lange. *Photographs:* courtesy of the architects. *References:* E. H. Kraaijvanger, H. M. Kraaijvanger, and R. H. Fledderus, "De Doelen, concert- en congresgebouw," Kraaijvanger Architekten bv, Watertorenweg 336, 3063HA Rotterdam (1966). C. C. J. M. Hak and H. J. Martin, "The acoustics of the Doelen Concert Hall after 30 years," Faculty of Architecture, Eindhoven University of Technology (April 1993).

*Technical details**

V = 849,900 ft^3 (24,070 m^3)	S_a = 11,313 ft^2 (1,051 m^2)	S_A = 16,240 ft^2 (1,509 m^2)
S_o = 2,110 ft^2 (195 m^2)	S_T = 18,350 ft^2 (1,704 m^2)	N = 2,242
H = 47 ft (14.3 m)	W (lower) = 80 ft (24.4 m)	W (upper) = 106 ft (32.3 m)
L (lower) = 49 ft (14.9 m)	L (upper) =104 ft (31.7 m)	D = 126 ft (38.4 m)
V/S_T = 46.3 ft (14.2 m)	V/S_A = 52.3 ft (16 m)	V/N = 379 ft^3 (10.7 m^3)
S_A/N = 7.24 ft^2 (0.67 m^2)	H/W (lower) = 0.59	H/W (upper) = 0.44
L/W (lower) = 0.61	L/W (upper) = 0.98	t_I = 35 msec

**The terminology is explained in Appendix 1.*

New Zealand

71

Christchurch
Christchurch Town Hall

Among concert halls, Christchurch Town Hall is the most startling visually. Here acoustical requirements had full swing in the design. The Town Hall, opened in 1972, was the first hall built following introduction of the concept by Harold Marshall that laterally reflected early sound energy was necessary to create spatial impression. Spatial impression was defined as the listener feeling as though he were immersed in the sound field rather than hearing the sound as though it were coming from direct ahead through a window. Subsequent studies have shown that for good spatial impression there must be a number of reflections in about the first 80 milliseconds after arrival of the direct sound at a listener's ears and that a fair percentage of them should be lateral, but not necessarily all.

Advantages of the Town Hall are that no part of the audience of 2,662 is more than 92 ft (28 m) from the stage, there are good sight lines, and the potentially dangerous elliptical shape is prevented from creating focal spots in the hall by the overhead array of panels. A large sound-diffusing canopy is installed above the stage to provide good communication among the players.

The eighteen, very large, tilted, free-standing, reflecting panels that surround the audience are designed to spread the early sound uniformly throughout the seating areas. The balcony fronts and their soffits are shaped to provide additional early reflections. These areas accomplish their purpose—the sound is clear, the listener's impression is of running liveness and the hall seems intimate, both visually and acoustically. The ensemble and orchestral balance are good.

Different from being in Boston Symphony Hall where one feels enveloped in the later reverberant sound field, in Christchurch the listener feels enveloped in a sound that is comprised of many closely spaced early reflections that arrive early. When the music comes to a sudden stop, the later reverberation sounds weak, although the reverberation time RT is 1.8 to 2.1 sec, measured fully occupied. However, the early decay time EDT is 1.9 sec, *unoccupied.* Usually the *occupied* RT is about 0.2 sec less than EDT. This discrepancy needs further study to explain the subjective impression of little energy in the later reverberant sound.

Christchurch, New Zealand, Town Hall

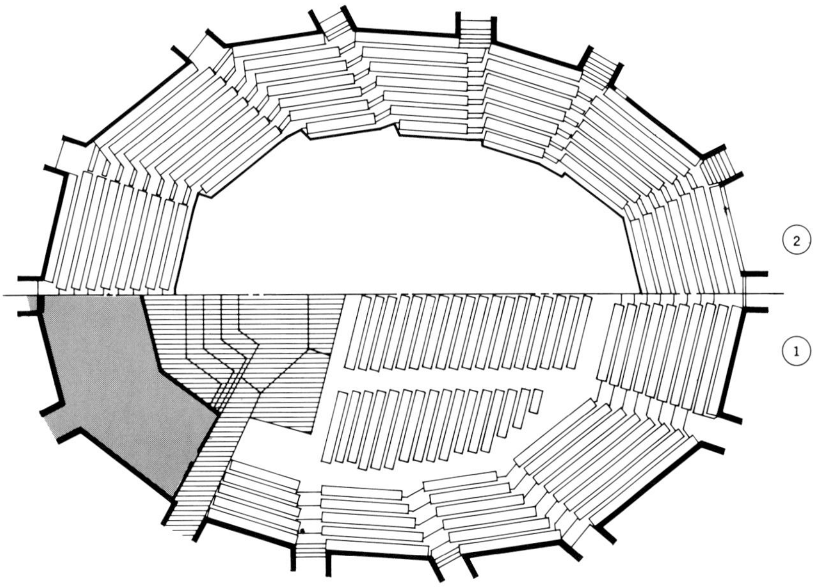

SEATING CAPACITY 2662

(1) 910 + 324 choir

(2) 1428

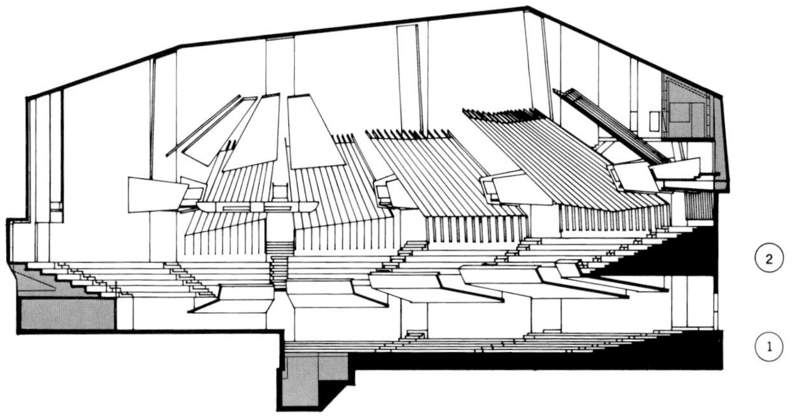

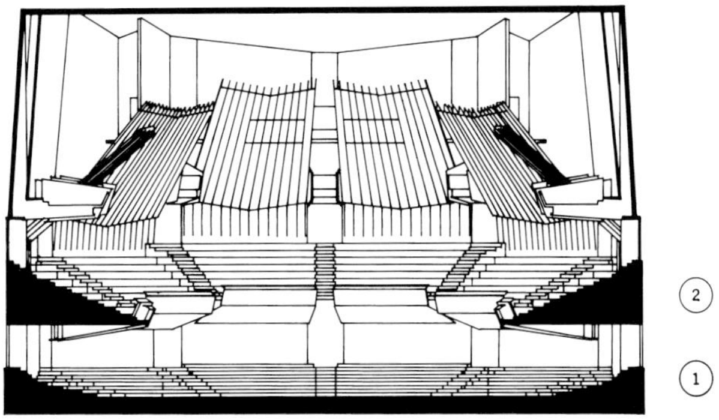

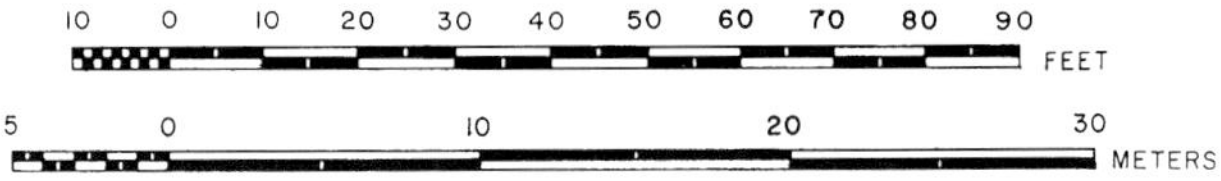

Architectural and structural details

Uses: orchestral music, recitals, choral, and speech events. *Ceiling:* concrete. *Walls:* concrete; free-standing reflectors are of wood, 1 in. (2.5 cm) thick, heavily braced. *Floors:* concrete. *Carpet:* none. *Stage enclosure:* walls: 1 in. wood; floor, 2 in. wood over airspace over concrete; 26 ft (7.9 m) irregular canopy hung 24 ft (7.3 m) above stage. *Stage height:* 52 in. (132 cm). *Sound absorbing materials:* none. *Seating:* wooden seat back; front of seat back and top of seat-bottom upholstered with porous fabric; underseat, wood, unperforated.

Architects: Warren and Mahoney. *Acoustical consultant:* A. Harold Marshall. *Photographs:* Mannering & Associates, Ltd. *References:* A. H. Marshall, "Acoustical determinants for the architectural design of concert halls," Arch. Sci. Rev., Australia **11**, 81–87 (1968); and "Acoustical design and evaluation of Christchurch Town Hall, New Zealand," J. Acoust. Soc. Am. **65**, 951–957 (1979).

*Technical details**

V = 723,855 ft^3 (20,500 m^3)	S_a = 12,130 ft^2 (1,127 m^2)	S_A = 15,240 ft^2 (1,416 m^2)
S_o = 2,090 ft^2 (194 m^2)	S_T = 17,330 ft^2 (1,610 m^2)	N = 2,662
H = 61 ft (18.6 m)	W = 96 ft (29.3 m)	L = 92 ft (28 m)
D = 93 ft (28.4 m)	V/S_T = 41.7 ft (12.7 m)	V/S_A = 47.5 ft (14.5 m)
V/N = 272 ft^3 (7.7 m^3)	S_A/N = 5.72 ft^2 (0.53 m^2)	H/W = 0.64
L/W = 0.96	t_I = 11 msec	

**The terminology is explained in Appendix 1.*

72

Gothenburg Konserthus

The Konserthus of Gothenburg, was opened in 1935 and renovated in 1985. It is finished entirely in wood. Having only 1,286 seats, it is small compared to the new halls of this period. There is no balcony, and the floor is interestingly subdivided by elevated sections of seats at the sides and rear of the hall. Some decorative organ pipes are visible above the orchestra canopy—the live ones are concealed behind.

The warm color of the wood, the lighting, the intimate contact between the audience and the stage, and the adequate reverberation time combine to make listening to music in this hall a rewarding experience.

Lest any reader jump to the questionable conclusion that wood accounts for its superiority, let me stress that the interior of the Konserthus is made of panels about 1 in. thick and 30 by 80 in. (76 by 203 cm) wide and long, heavily braced behind, that are securely held in place on heavy frames—all bolted to a 7 in. (18 cm) concrete wall. Clearly, every attempt has been made to render the wood immobile and therefore nonresonant; consequently, the walls are inactive and, like plaster walls, serve as effective reflecting surfaces to preserve the bass tones.

In 1962, Igor Markevich, Bruno Walter, Eugene Ormandy, and Isaac Stern considered the hall to be very good to outstanding, and all commented favorably on its small size.

Troubles that formerly existed with orchestral balance and ensemble, have been greatly improved by reshaping the canopy, now made convex. The stage has been enlarged to handle larger performing groups. Draperies are hung at the rear of the stage to improve the balance, particularly between the instruments in the back rows and those further forward.

The Konserthus illustrates one of the basic tenets of acoustics; in a hall for music, small size is attended by many of the desirable attributes of acoustic quality. This hall is not excessively wide and it has no balcony overhang. The reverberation time is optimum, about 1.6 sec at mid-frequencies, for orchestral and chamber music in this size of hall. When all these factors are combined with a pleasing appearance, the success of a concert hall, and this hall in particular, is assured.

Gothenburg, Konserthus

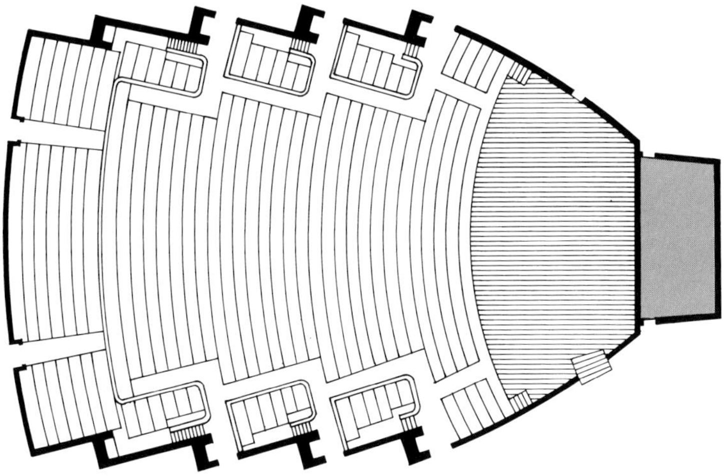
SEATING CAPACITY 1286

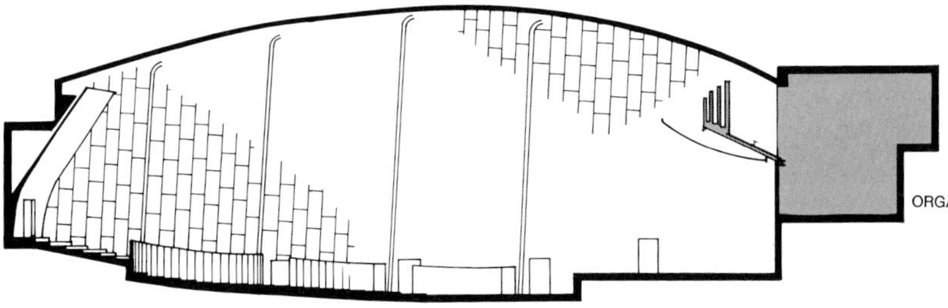
ORGAN

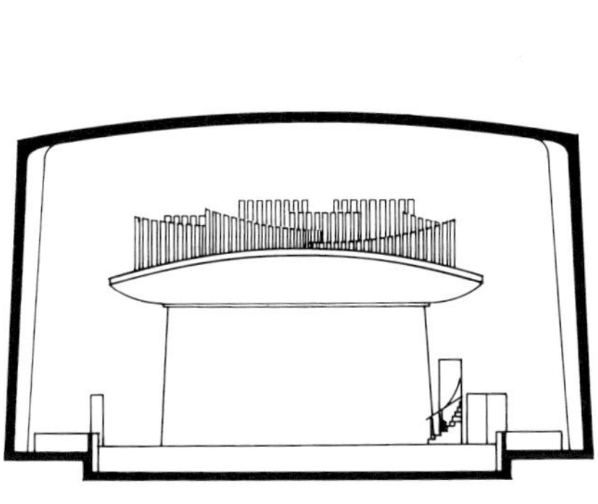

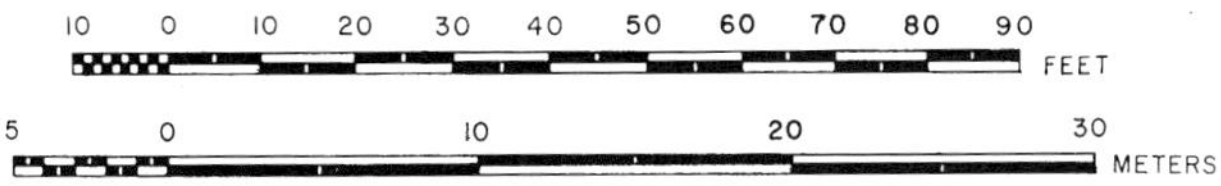
10 0 10 20 30 40 50 60 70 80 90
FEET
5 0 10 20 30
METERS

Architectural and structural details

Uses: symphonic, 80%; soloists and chamber music, 5%; popular concerts, 10%; miscellaneous, 5%. *Ceiling:* plywood affixed directly to a concrete sheet that is suspended from a steel overhead. *Side and rear walls:* see the text above. *Floors:* linoleum on concrete. *Stage enclosure:* walls same as above, canopy 0.75 in. (2 cm) plywood, curtains on rear wall. *Stage floor:* wood over large airspace with on-stage movable risers of wood. *Stage height:* 39 in. (99 cm). *Seating:* Wooden rear seat back and underseat, wooden arms, fully upholstered seat back and upper seat.

Architect: Nils Einar Eriksson. *Acoustical consultants:* (Original) H. Kreuger. (Renovations) Ingemansson Acoustics. *Photographs:* Max Plunger. *Other information:* courtesy of Tomas Odebrant

*Technical details**

V = 420,000 ft^3 (11,900 m^3)	S_a = 6,300 ft^2 (585 m^2)	S_A = 7,170 ft^2 (666 m^2)
S_o = 1,830 ft^2 (170 m^2)	S_T = 9,000 ft^2 (836 m^2)	N = 1,286
H = 45 ft (13.7 m)	W = 83 ft (25.3 m)	L = 100 ft (30.5 m)
D = 97 ft (29.6 m)	V/S_T = 46.7 ft (14.2 m)	V/S_A = 58.5 ft (17.8 m)
V/N = 326 ft^3 (9.25 m^3)	S_A/N = 5.58 ft^2 (0.52 m^2)	H/W = 0.54
L/W = 1.2	t_I = 33 msec	

**The terminology is explained in Appendix 1.*

SWITZERLAND

73

Basel
Stadt-Casino

Built in 1776, the Stadt-Casino preceded the famous Leipzig "Neues" Gewandhaus (destroyed in World War II) by ten years. Seating 1,448, smaller by 112 seats, it bears all the distinguishing hallmarks of its former northern sister. It is rectangular with a flat coffered ceiling that connects to the side walls with a sloping cornice. Both halls resemble the ballrooms of their heritage, with flat main floors and shallow balconies. The widths of both are nearly the same, 69 ft (21 m), making the Stadt-Casino very intimate, acoustically.

On entering the hall, one is struck by the large windows above the balcony, necessary then because of lack of artificial lighting and air conditioning. Four ornate chandeliers grace the ceiling. The beautiful organ stands above the highest stage riser on which the percussion or the organ console customarily sit.

The hall has been reseated since the photographs were taken, with upholstered backrests and seat bottoms. The reverberation time, about 1.8 sec at mid-frequencies, fully occupied, is nearly equal to that of Boston.

The interior is plaster so that the bass is warm and the higher registers are brilliant. The hall responds well to the music and musicians love to perform in it.

Herbert von Karajan said of the Stadt-Casino (1960): "This is a typical rectangular hall—small, with a wonderfully clear and crisp resonance. It is almost perfect for Mozart. Although one can play nearly every kind of music in it, the volume of a very large orchestra is smashing," Dimitri Mitropoulos (1960) also thought the Stadt-Casino a very good hall but too small for full orchestra.

In my judgment, the pianissimo playing of the cellos and double basses is extraordinarily beautiful. Violin and bass parts are well balanced. The percussion and brass can be too loud. But, in brief, all music that is properly scaled to the size of the Stadt-Casino sounds wonderful there. The enthusiasm of the musicians who know the hall well is fully merited.

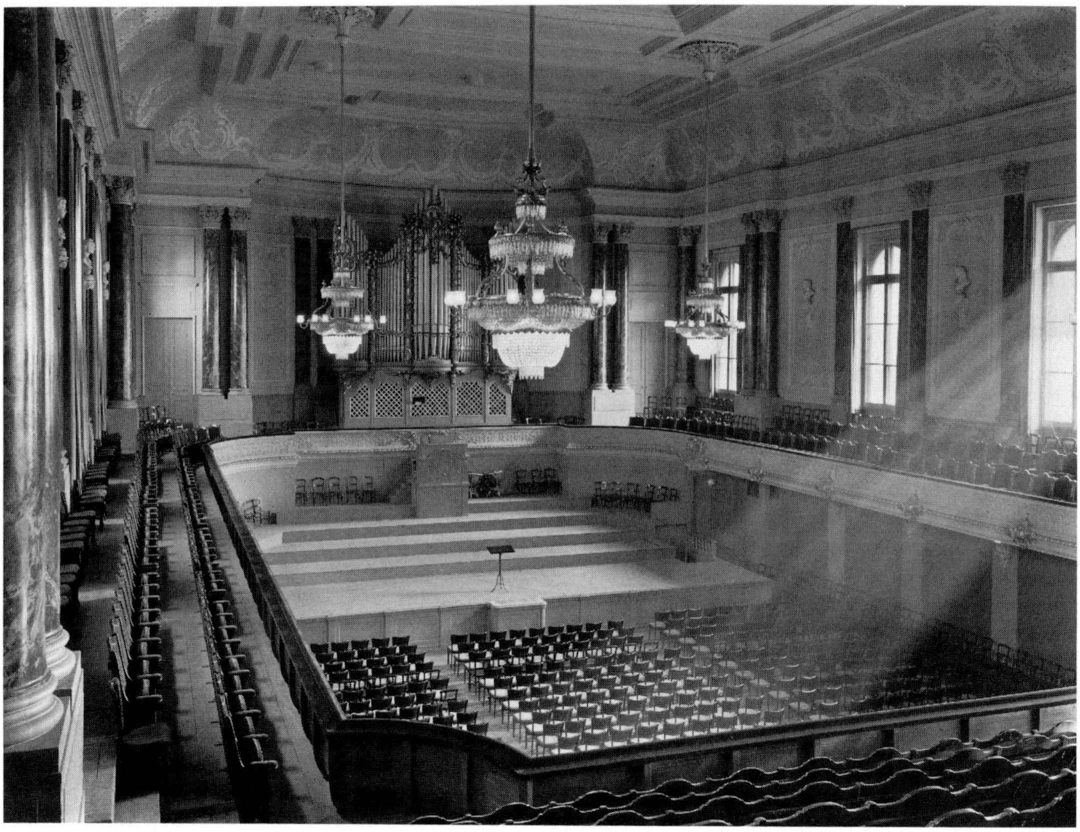

Basel, Stadt-Casino

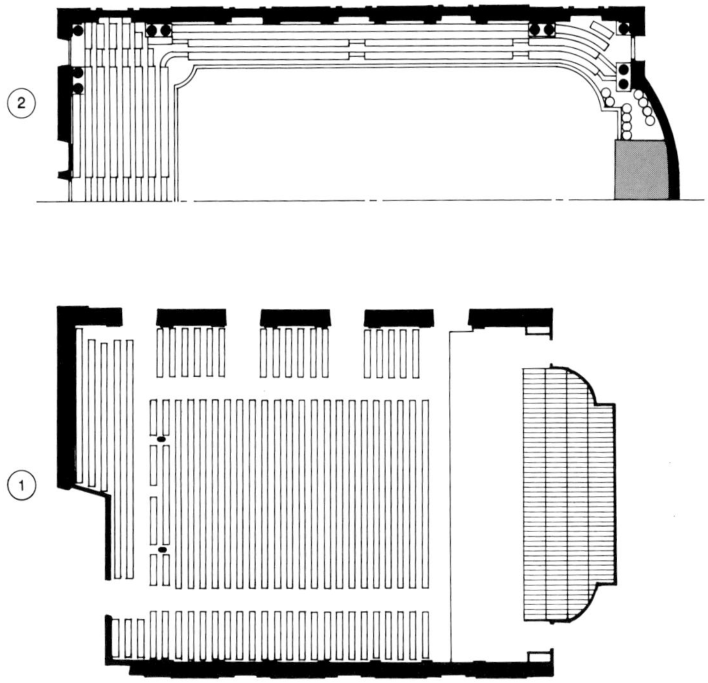

SEATING CAPACITY 1448

1 890

2 558

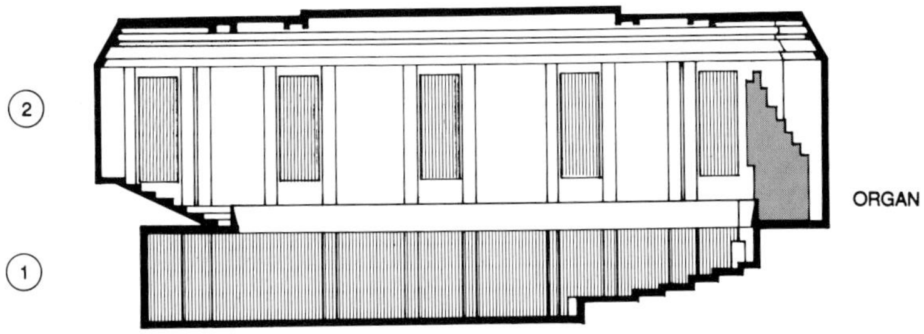

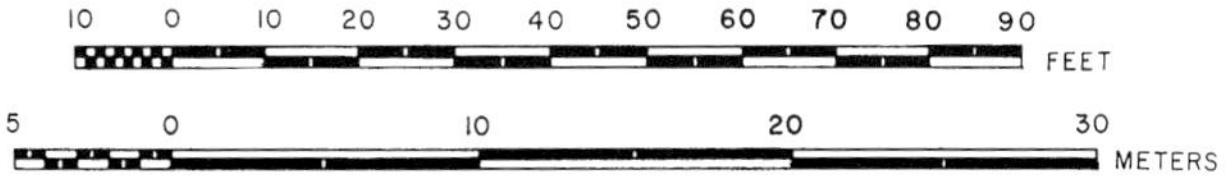

Architectural and structural details

Uses: mostly orchestra and recitals. *Ceiling:* plaster, coffered. *Side and rear walls:* plaster with a small amount of wood; baroque ornamentation, and columns. *Floors:* parquet over solid base. *Carpet:* none. *Stage floor:* heavy wood over airspace. *Stage height:* 36 in. (91 cm). *Seating:* tops of seat-bottoms and fronts of backrests upholstered; underseats solid metal.

Architect: Johann Jacob Stehlin-Burckhardt. *Photographs:* courtesy of Swiss National Tourist Office. *Reference:* W. Furrer, Raum- und Bauakustik, Larmabwehr, 2nd Edition, Birkhauser Verlag, Basel and Stuttgart (1961).

*Technical details**

V = 370,750 ft^3 (10,500 m^3)	S_a = 6,290 ft^2 (584 m^2)	S_A = 7,870 ft^2 (731 m^2)
S_o = 1,720 ft^2 (160 m^2)	S_T = 9,600 ft^2 (891 m^2)	N = 1,448
V/S_T = 38.6 ft (11.8 m)	V/S_A = 47.1 ft (14.4 m)	V/N = 256 ft^3 (7.25 m^3)
S_A/N = 5.44 ft^2 (0.50 m^2)	H = 50 ft (15.2 m)	W = 69 ft (21 m)
L = 77 ft (23.5 m)	D = 80 ft (24.4 m)	H/W = 0.72
L/W = 1.12	t_I = 16 msec	

**The terminology is explained in Appendix 1.*

74

Zurich
Grosser Tonhallesaal

The Tonhalle, completed in 1895 and renovated in 1930, accommodates an audience of 1,546 persons. Two glittering chandeliers hang beneath a series of oil paintings on the ceiling that portray Gluck, Haydn, Schubert, Brahms, Mozart, and Handel. The walls are a grayish ivory abundantly decorated with gold. Beneath the balcony, natural birch paneling gives the hall an appearance of being all wood, but this is not the case. Plaster forms more than 80% of the walls and ceiling. The floors are wood parquet. The seats are not upholstered; during rehearsals the orchestra finds it necessary to lay thin layers of cloth over the seats on the main floor to control the reverberation.

The mid-frequency reverberation time, fully occupied, is about 2.0 sec, a value that is achieved by the majority of the best liked halls in this study.

Three of the four conductors interviewed rated the Grosser Tonhallesaal as acoustically excellent. The fourth, who favors contemporary music, said, "This hall is not so good and not so bad. It is sort of in between." Music critics have generally given high praise to the acoustics.

My one musical experience with this hall was very pleasant. The program consisted of music of the Baroque and early classical periods, and the reverberation time of the hall seemed ideal. The bass was not as satisfactory in the main floor as in the galleries, possibly owing to some thin wood on the lower side walls. The violins sang forth clearly—their sound was intimate, live, and brilliant. Ensemble playing was good as was the balance among orchestral sections, with only a moderate tendency for the brass to dominate. The blend was excellent. The sound was not as good in the rear corners of the main floor and at the rear of the side balconies as on the main floor and in the rear balcony. All in all, it is an excellent hall.

Zurich, Grosser Tonhallesaal

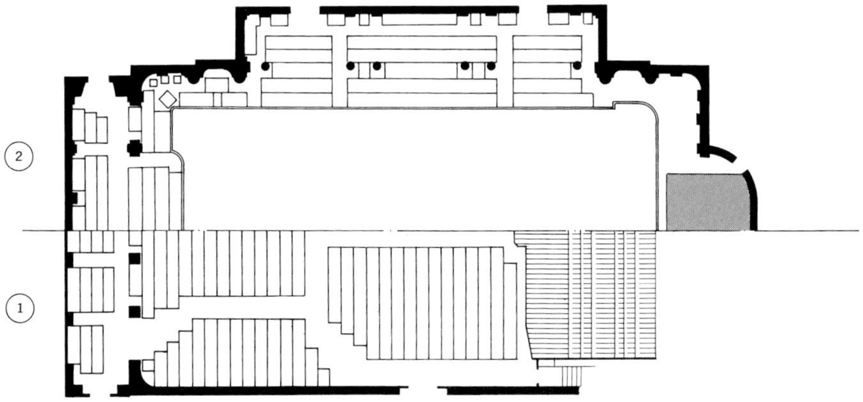

SEATING CAPACITY 1546

(1) 925

(2) 621

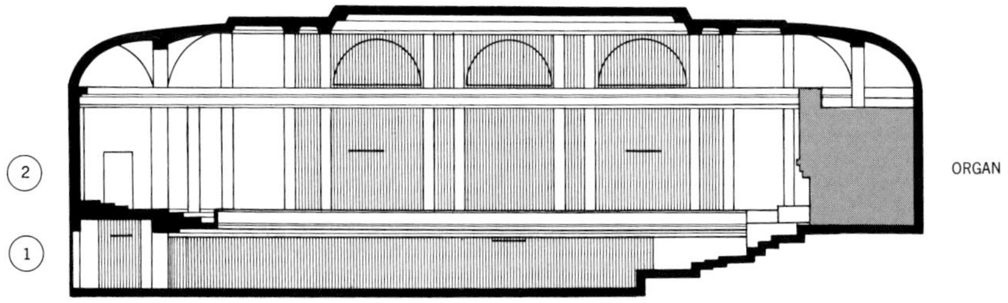

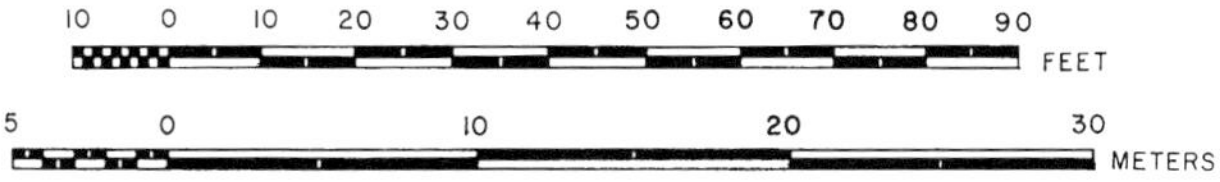

Architectural and structural details

Uses: symphony music 200 days a year, piano and violin recitals, oratorio 12 days, and occasionally organ. *Ceiling:* plaster on wire lath with deep irregularities in the ceiling and rounded cornices, interrupted by clerestory windows. *Side walls:* wood paneling beneath the balcony and on the soffit under the balcony; walls and decorations are of plaster above the balcony; balcony fronts are of plaster. *Floors:* wood parquet over solid base on the main floor and linoleum over solid base in balcony. *Carpet:* none. *Stage floor:* heavy wood over airspace. *Stage height:* 48 in. (122 cm). *Added absorptive material:* cloth curtains hang over the clerestory windows; during rehearsals large areas of cloth are placed over half the seats on the main floor. *Seating:* all wood. (*Note:* the doors at the rear of the main floor may be opened, exposing 200 additional seats in the Kleiner Tonhallesaal.)

Architect: Fellner and Helmer of Vienna. *Photographs:* courtesy of Swiss National Tourist Office. *Details and seating plan:* from the General Manager. *Reference:* drawings courtesy of W. Furrer.

*Technical details**

V = 402,500 ft^3 (11,400 m^3)	S_a = 7,550 ft^2 (702 m^2)	S_A = 9,440 ft^2 (877 m^2)
S_o = 1,560 ft^2 (145 m^2)	S_T = 11,000 ft^2 (1,022 m^2)	N = 1,546
V/S_T = 36.6 ft (11.2 m)	V/S_A = 42.6 ft (13 m)	V/N = 260 ft^3 (7.37 m^3)
S_A/N = 6.11 ft^2 (0.57 m^2)	H = 46 ft (14 m)	W = 64 ft (19.5 m)
L = 97 ft (29.6 m)	D = 98 ft (29.9 m)	H/W = 0.72
L/W = 1.5	t_I = 14 msec	

**The terminology is explained in Appendix 1.*

75

Taipei Cultural Centre Concert Hall

The Taipei Concert Hall must rank as the most stunning building in the world for music performance. Strongly reminding one of the palace buildings in the Forbidden City of Beijing, its majestic roof lines and column-enclosed veranda, make a breathtaking appearance, especially when illuminated at night. The striking three-story foyer leads one with great expectations into the hall itself. Inside, the concept is more subdued, more contemporary in design.

The concert hall is rectangular in shape with two balconies. The horizontal ceiling is deeply coffered and the side walls are irregular to promote diffusion of the sound field, essential to a good singing tone. Basically the hall resembles Boston Symphony Hall, wider with the same height to give it a longer reverberation time. The stage is very large, 270 m^2 (2,900 ft^2) which should make ensemble playing for a small orchestra somewhat difficult. The stage ceiling is a canopy designed partially to send sound to the audience and partially to return sound to the players. The side walls are planned to do likewise. A large organ covers the entire back wall of the stage. The seating capacity is 2,074, with 862 seats in the balconies. Achieved was the acoustical design goal, which called for a reverberation time of 2 sec, ideally suited to the Romantic repertoire.

To achieve the least loss of sound as it travels over the audience rows, the floor contour was sloped in the form of a logarithmic spiral. The heights of the steps increase from front to rear, ascending gradually to 10 ft (3 m). There are no sound absorbing materials in the hall. The floors are parquet without any carpet. The walls provide some bass absorption, meaning that the reverberation time does not rise at lower frequencies above that at middle frequencies. The finish is dark mahogany.

The Taipei Concert Hall opened in 1987 with the Cleveland Orchestra and Taipei's own two symphony orchestras. Isaac Stern wrote afterwards, "Yo Yo Ma, Emanuel Ax and I had the pleasure of performing in [this new hall]. We...took the trouble, with great care, to go into the auditorium and to listen to the sound of the house both empty and full...We all found the acoustics of the auditorium absolutely wonderful, clearly world class."

Taipei, Cultural Centre Concert Hall

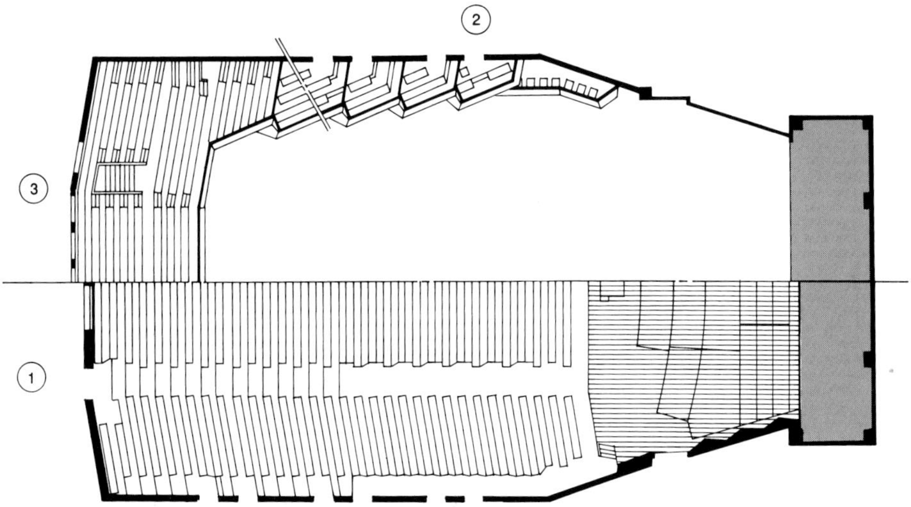

SEATING CAPACITY 2074

1 1212

2 422

3 440

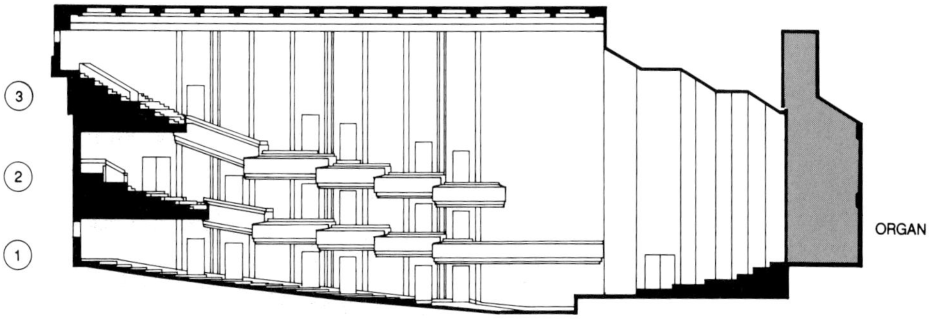

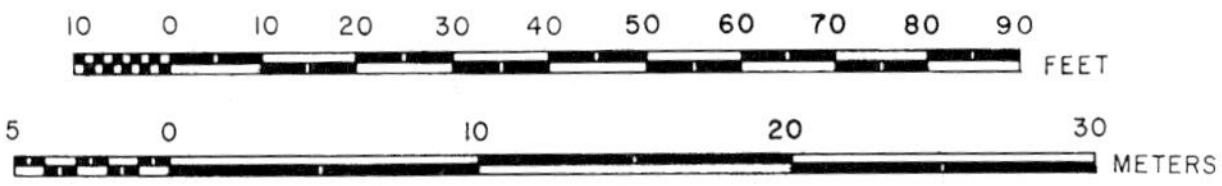

Architectural and structural details

Uses: primarily orchestra. *Ceiling:* 117 quadratic coffered spaces, each 18 in. (45 cm) deep, with upper surfaces chipboard 1 in. (2.5 cm) thick. *Side and rear walls:* 0.9 in. (2 cm) thick chipboard backed by an airspace 3 to 7 in. (8 to 18 cm) deep. *Floors:* parquet on concrete. *Carpet:* none. *Stage enclosure:* side walls and ceiling 1.7 in. (4 cm) chipboard; back wall: pipe organ which can be closed by a special organ door; the back wall beneath the organ reflects sound back to the musicians. *Stage floor:* heavy wood over air space. *Stage height:* 37.5 in. (95 cm). *Seating:* tops of seat-bottoms and fronts of backrests upholstered, with upholstering ending at a height of 33.5 in. (85 cm) above the floor to avoid sound absorption; underseats solid.

Architect: C. C. Yang. *Acoustical consultant:* K. Heinrich Kuttruff. *Photographs:* courtesy of the architect. *Reference:* H. Kuttruff, "Acoustical design of the Chiang Kai Shek Cultural Centre in Taipei," *Applied Acoustics*, 27, 27–46 (1989).

*Technical details**

V = 590,000 ft^3 (16,700 m^3)	S_a = 11,000 ft^2 (1,022 m^2)	S_A = 13,570 ft^2 (1,261 m^2)
S_o = 2,900 ft^2 (269 m^2)	S_T = 16,470 ft^2 (1,530 m^2)	N = 2,074
V/S_T = 35.8 ft (10.9 m)	V/S_A = 43.5 ft (13.2 m)	V/N = 284 ft^3 (8 m^3)
S_A/N = 6.54 ft^2 (0.61 m^2)	H =59 ft (18 m)	W = 88 ft (26.8 m)
L = 106 ft (32.3 m)	D = 116 ft (36.4 m)	H/W = 0.67
L/W = 1.2	t_I = 29 msec	

**The terminology is explained in Appendix 1.*

76

Caracas
Aula Magna

Fantastico is the word that aptly describes the Great Hall of the University of Caracas. It is the only hall anywhere in which the work of a sculptor is so much in evidence. How that came about is an interesting story.

The architect won a competition with his design for the hall. His plans called for a very broad, fan-shaped room with a domed ceiling and a rear wall that formed a sector of a circle with its center of curvature at the rear of the stage. When the preliminary drawings were complete, the acoustical firm of Bolt Beranek and Newman was consulted. The curved ceiling and the circular rear wall presented serious problems of focused echoes, dead spots, and a general lack of uniformity in sound distribution—in all, an acoustical nightmare. The acoustical consultant urged a major modification of the shape of the hall, but by that time the plans had already been fixed.

An alternative solution was then explored, and this solution must be credited to the late Robert B. Newman. He recommended that sound-reflecting panels, equal in area to about 70% of the ceiling, be hung below the ceiling and on the side walls. These panels were originally recommended to be rectangular in shape. But the designers of the Aula Magna, hoping for a more satisfying solution contacted Alexander Calder in Paris, a sculptor whose mobiles had by that time made him famous. He was invited to participate in an unusual and rewarding collaboration of sculptor with architect, engineers, and acoustical consultant. The result is beautiful—in both form and color—an exciting array of "stabiles" suspended from the ceiling and standing away from the side walls. No photograph can do justice. One must be inside the hall—inside the sculpture—to feel its rhythm and color. I was with the architect when he first entered the hall after the color was added to the stabiles, he spread his arms in an overhead "V" and shouted the word, "FANTASTICO".

The hall is a university auditorium and seats 2,660 people. It is used for lectures, convocations, music, and drama. It was dedicated in 1954 and its first use was by the International Pan-American Congress. I was present during the summer of that year when the initial acoustical tests were being conducted. There was just noticeable echo

Caracas, Aula Magna

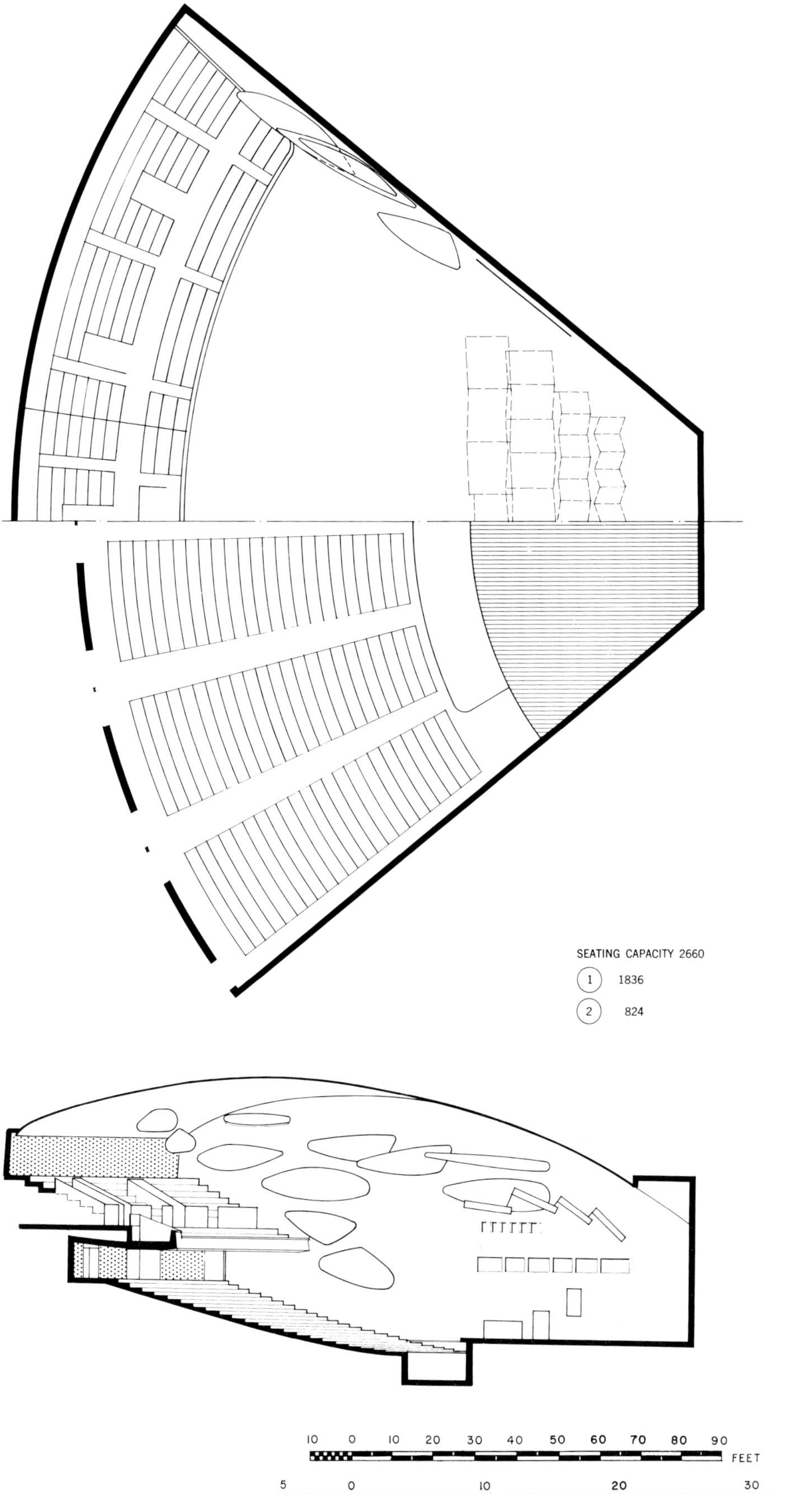
SEATING CAPACITY 2660
1 1836
2 824
10 0 10 20 30 40 50 60 70 80 90 FEET
5 0 10 20 30 METERS

in the front of the hall from the focusing rear wall above the balcony. It was necessary to add the sound absorbing material shown on the drawing to eliminate this problem. All other surfaces are plaster on a concrete backing. No other adjustment was necessary. Because of the solid walls and ceiling construction and the thick stabiles, two 0.5 in. thick layers (1.25 cm each) of plywood glued together, the reverberation time lengthens at low frequencies and gives the sound a warm character.

The Aula Magna serves many purposes for the university and though its basic shape is potentially unfavorable for music, it has received favorable comments from conductors and music critics. Music played there is clear and distinct. The string tone is brilliant. Both on stage and in the audience the bass is rich and warm. Short initial-time-delayed early reflections are provided by the hanging panels. Because the edges of the hanging panels are frames 4 to 8 in. wide, sound is reflected laterally, giving a distinct feeling that the orchestra is wider and fills the room, even with 2,660 seats. The distance from the front of the stage to the farthest listener is only 116 ft (35.4 m) compared to Boston's 133 ft (40.5 m), which also helps the feeling of intimacy.

The reverberation time of the hall was optimized for the Pan-American Congress at 1.35 sec with full occupancy, by adding 2,770 ft^2 (257 m^2) of 1 in. (2.5 cm) of glass fiber blankets above the hanging panels. When this is removed, the reverberation is about 1.7 sec which is more nearly optimum for symphonic concerts. Thus, as measured, the hall is excellent for piano, modern music, and chamber music—for all music where clarity of detail is desired. In either case, the music lacks the singing tone of the classical rectangular halls because the very wide fan shape prevents a general mixing of the sound from cross reflections between the side walls.

On stage the sound is excellent, as a result of an effective canopy over the performers. Just after a tour around South America with the New York Philharmonic Orchestra in 1957, the late Leonard Bernstein said to me, "This hall was the best in which I conducted in South America. After the concert I told reporters that on the stage the sound is excellent. I wished that I could take that part of the hall back to New York for the Philharmonic to use [in Carnegie Hall]."

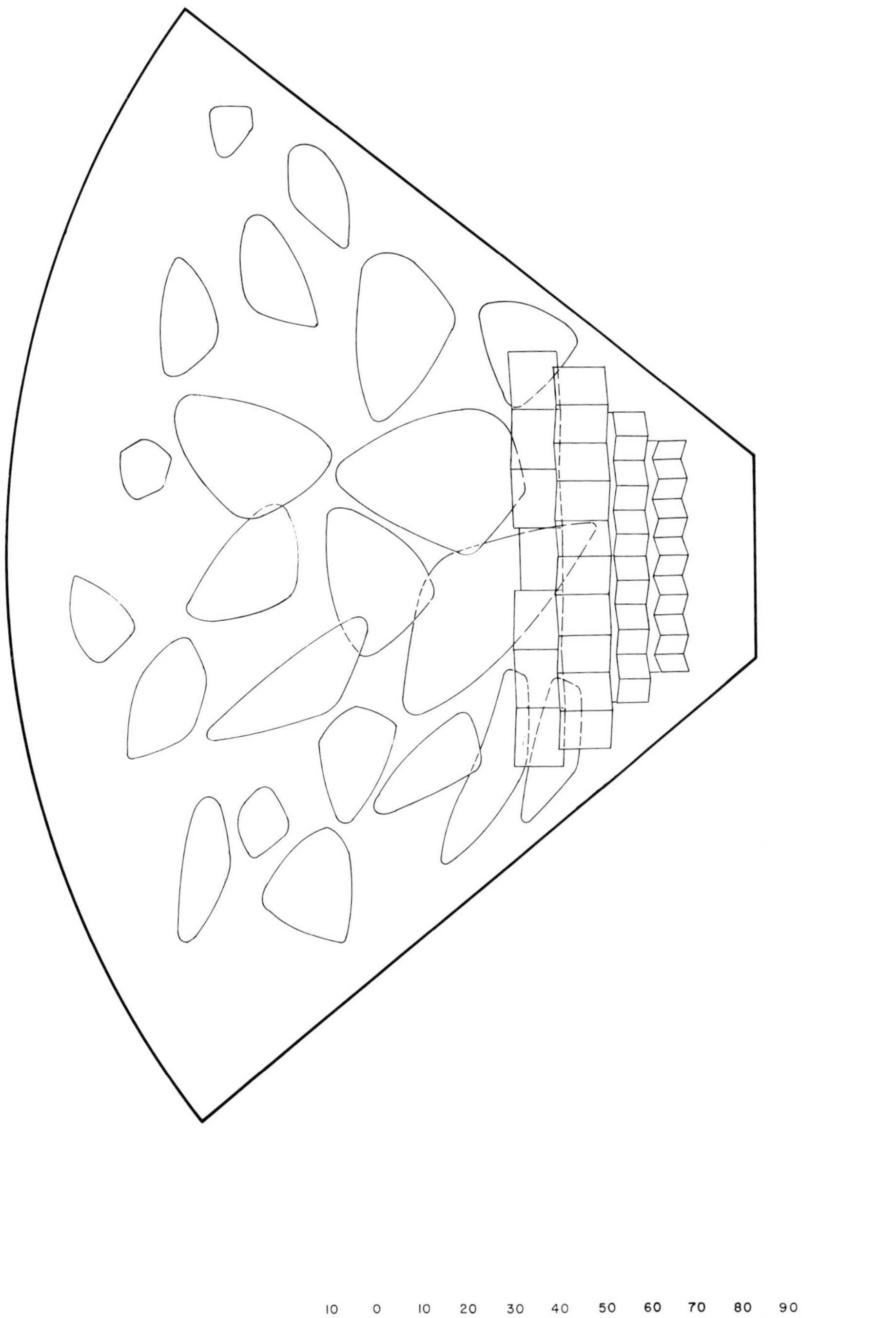
10 0 10 20 30 40 50 60 70 80 90
FEET
5 0 10 20 30
METERS

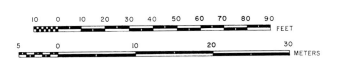

Architectural and structural details

Uses: university auditorium. *Ceiling:* plaster on metal lath. *Side walls:* plaster on concrete. *Rear walls:* highly absorbent to prevent echo. *Floors:* quarry tile. *Stage enclosure:* canopy of plywood, about 1 in. (2.5 cm) thick; rear wall of the stage and about 20 ft (6.1 m) of the two side walls contiguous to that wall are of wood on solid concrete. *Stage floor:* wood over airspace. *Stage height:* 40 in. (102 cm). *Carpets:* main aisles only. *Added absorbing material:* at the time the reverberation data were taken, 2,770 ft^2 (257 m^2) of 1 in. (2.5 cm) glass fiber blanket had been installed on top of the stabiles to make the hall optimum for the Pan-American congress; without this material, the mid-frequency reverberation time, fully occupied, will increase to about 1.7 sec, more nearly optimum for music. *Seating:* front of backrest and top of seat-bottom are upholstered; underseat is perforated with rock wool inside. *Hanging reflectors:* 30, each of which is made of two layers of 0.5 in. (1.25 cm) laminated wood, glued together, on heavy framing, 4 to 8 in. (10 to 20 cm) thick.

Architect: Carlos R. Villanueva. *Associated designers:* Santiago Briceno-Ecker and Daniel Ellenberg. *Acoustical consultant:* Bolt Beranek and Newman, now ACENTECH, Cambridge, MA. *Photographs:* courtesy of S. Briceno.

*Technical details**

V = 880,000 ft^3 (24,920 m^3)	S_a = 17,000 ft^2 (1,580 m^2)	S_A = 20,300 ft^2 (1,886 m^2)
S_o = 2,200 ft^2 (204 m^2)	S_T = 22,500 ft^2 (2,090 m^2)	N = 2,660
V/S_T = 39 ft (11.9 m)	V/S_A = 43.3 ft (13.2 m)	V/N = 331 ft^3 (9.37 m^3)
S_A/N = 7.63 ft^2 (0.71 m^2)	H = 58 ft (17.7 m)	W = 189 ft (57.6 m)
L = 102 ft (31.1 m)	D = 116 ft (35.4 m)	H/W = 0.31
L/W = 0.54	t_I = 30 msec	

**The terminology is explained in Appendix 1.*

◊7◊

Concert Halls: Age, Size, Shape, Materials, and Seating Density

The list of concert halls sorted in accordance with their acoustical quality in Table 5.2, p. 58, sparks a series of questions. Why are superior halls more than ninety-five years old? Do most excellent halls seat less than 2,000? Is a reverberation time of 1.9 to 2.0 sec crucial to a hall's long-time success? Isn't reverberation time a prime determinant of acoustical quality since a decrease in it parallels a decrease in the ratings of concert halls? Was the legendary conductor Wilhelm Furtwaengler right when he remarked to the music critic of the Chicago *Tribune*, "The hall with the best acoustics is the hall with the best performance"? Is shape a paramount ingredient of excellent concert hall acoustics? These conundrums have vexed architects since ancient times.

The Roman architect Vitruvius believed that a theater should be tuned and various architectural elements introduced that resonate with the harmonics of the voice. (Morgan, 1960). He taught that the architect had to understand canonical and mathematical theory and be able to tune strings and resonators to proper frequencies. He believed that in closed rooms, strings of twisted sinew should be stretched across near the ceiling and tuned "until they give the same correct note to the ear of the skilled workman." Also, he taught that bronze vessels, tuned in accordance with the musical intervals based on mathematical principles, should be placed in niches under seats. Whenever the voice of an actor falls in unison with any of the resonant frequencies of the vessels, the power of the voice will be increased, he said, and "reaches the ears of the audience with greater clearness and sweetness." Thus, he equated the "tuning" of a theater to the tuning of a musical instrument. He said, "by giving heed to these theories, one can easily bring a theatre to perfection, from the point of view of the nature of the voice, so as to give pleasure to the audience." He also recommended that bronze vessels be utilized in outdoor theaters. If one wished to avoid the use of bronze vessels, he asserted that the theater should be built of wood boarding, "which must be resonant," instead of marble, masonry or stone. He obviously did not realize that tuned vessels and thin wood panels absorb sound, rather than adding "resonance."

But Vitruvius was teaching from hearsay. He wrote, "If however, it is asked in what theatre these vessels have been employed, we cannot point to any in Rome itself, but only to those in the districts of Italy and in a good many Greek states. We have also the evidence of Lucius Mummius, who, after destroying the theatre in Corinth, brought its bronze vessels to Rome, and made a dedicatory offering at the temple of Luna with the money obtained from the sale of them."

Several of his convictions, however wrong, continued even into more recent times. The intractable acoustics of London's Royal Albert Hall were attacked without success in 1880 by stretching miles of wires beneath its dome. And the belief that "wood is good" in concert halls persists to this day.

Charles Garnier, designer of the Opéra Garnier in Paris, said in his book, *The Grand Opera in Paris*, that he had pursued diligently the elusive factors of good acoustics, but he confessed that he finally trusted to luck, "like the acrobat who closes his eyes and clings to the ropes of an ascending balloon." "*Eh bien!*" he concludes, "*Je suis arrivé!*" He went on, "The credit is not mine, I merely wear the marks of honor. It is not my fault that acoustics and I can never come to an understanding. I gave myself great pains to master this bizarre science, but after fifteen years of labor, I found myself hardly in advance of where I stood on the first day.... I had read diligently in my books, and conferred industriously with philosophers—nowhere did I find a positive rule of action to guide me; in the contrary, nothing but contradictory statements. For long months, I studied, questioned everything, but after this travail, finally I made this discovery. A room to have good acoustics must be either long or broad, high or low, of wood or stone, round or square, and so forth.... Chance seems as dominant in the theatrical [opera house] world as it is in the dream world in which a child enters Wonderland!"

In this chapter we shall discuss the less technical aspects of acoustical behavior. In the next chapter optimum reverberation times will be discussed, and in later chapters we shall take up the six most important acoustical attributes in detail.

AGE

All three of the halls in the A+ "superior" category were built in 1900 or before. It is quite likely that these old halls are famous because they have housed world-class orchestras whose musicians would not long have tolerated them if they had inferior acoustics. There are numerous examples where concert halls with poor acoustics have been destroyed and halls with good acoustics saved. The examples of Carnegie Hall, which was saved from the wrecking ball by those who loved its acoustics, and the destruction of several halls in New York earlier in this century because of poor acoustics stands as proof. Concert halls in three cities in Canada have been or are being abandoned in favor of new halls built with the expectation of superior acoustics. The same is true in England. Renovations of halls with unsatisfactory acoustics are also common.

Yes, there probably is truth in Maestro Furtwaengler's statement that the best halls acoustically are those with the best performances. This is probably demonstrated, at least to some degree, by the results of the self-administered rating questionnaires of Appendix 3. Over half of those concert halls placed in the "excellent" category are the homes of world renowned orchestras.

But do the acoustics of concert halls mellow with age? Logic alone says that there should be no change in the acoustics of a hall which has not been modified. A hall's acoustical characteristics depend on cubic volume, interior shape, density of materials that form the surfaces, the kind and density of the chairs, the carpets, and the size of the audience. There may be some difference in clothing worn or brought into the hall, but the customs for checking outer clothing have generally not changed in any given hall in this century.

There are only nine halls in this book that have not been modified during the past 30 years and for which comparable acoustical data exist. The comparisons are given in Table 7.1. It is apparent that over the periods indicated, there is no discernable change in reverberation times—the only acoustical quantity that could be measured 30 years ago.

In the majority of halls over 25 years old, the chairs have been changed, usually for ones that are more sound absorbent. Other common changes include enlargement of the stage, removal or addition of carpets, addition or removal of pipe organs, and the like. Some modifications worsen the acoustics.

SIZE

It is commonly believed that small halls, less than 2,000 seats, are superior to large halls that seat more than 2,500. The ratings, shown in Table 5.2, seem to confirm that this is true. The median values of those halls in categories A+, A, and B+ is 2,160 seats and those in B, C+, and C is 2,730 seats.

Table 7.1. Comparison of reverberation times in seconds in occupied or unoccupied halls measured about 30 years apart. The accuracy of measurements between the two time periods is probably about 0.2 sec.

	Frequency in Hz				
	125	250	500	1,000	2,000
Boston, Symphony Hall (occupied)					
1957	2.2	2.0	1.8	1.8	1.7
1992/93	2.0	1.85	1.85	1.85	1.65
Vienna, Musikvereinssaal (occupied)					
1956	2.4	2.2	2.1	2.0	1.9
1987	2.2	2.2	2.0	2.0	1.8
Liverpool, Philharmonic Hall (unoccupied)					
1953	1.9	1.8	1.7	1.6	1.6
1982	1.95	1.85	1.75	1.75	1.65
Amsterdam, Concertgebouw (occupied)					
1958	2.2	2.2	2.1	1.9	1.8
1986	2.2	2.2	2.0	2.0	1.8
Stuttgart, Liederhalle, Grosser Saal (unoccupied)					
1956	2.0	2.0	2.2	2.2	2.1
1987	1.8	1.8	2.0	2.2	2.1
Milan, Teatro alla Scalla (unoccupied)					
1947	1.8	1.5	1.4	1.4	1.2
1993	1.8	1.6	1.4	1.3	1.2
Tokyo, Bunka Kaikan (unoccupied)					
1961	2.7	2.0	2.0	2.0	1.8
1993	2.0	1.8	2.0	2.0	1.8
Royal Festival Hall (unoccupied, assisted resonance off)					
1959	1.4	1.4	1.6	1.8	1.8
1982	1.45	1.7	1.6	1.7	1.7
Sydney Opera House Concert Hall (unoccupied)					
1973	2.4	2.5	2.4	2.6	2.6
1992	2.2	2.4	2.3	2.6	2.6

Usually for financial reasons, halls built since World War II tend to be larger than those built previously, particularly outside Continental Europe. It is encouraging to see that in the A+, A, and B+ group, 70% of the halls seat more than 2,000 and 40% are larger than 2,500. This observation is an indication that the art and science of acoustics has developed to the point where properly designed larger halls can be built with reasonable assurance of acoustical success. Support for this statement lies in the success of concert halls in Dallas (McDermott/Meyerson Symphony Hall); Leipzig (Gewandhaus); Costa Mesa, Orange County, California (Segerstrom Hall); Salt Lake City (Utah Symphony Hall); Cardiff, Wales (St. David's Hall); New Zealand (Christchurch Town Hall);

Birmingham (Symphony Hall); Baltimore (Meyerhoff Symphony Hall); Berlin (Philharmonie and Konzerthaus Halls); Glasgow (Royal Concert Hall); Tokyo (Suntory and Orchard halls); and Rotterdam (De Doelen)—all built since WWII.

But, there are valid reasons why small halls should outrank large halls in judged acoustical quality. These include greater intimacy, more acoustic energy per listener assuming the same size of orchestra, shorter distances between the farthest listener and the stage, more energy in the lateral reflections, and larger values of the spaciousness factor ASW.

But let us look at size from another standpoint. Comparison of the cubic volumes of the nine of the best-liked concert halls in this study with those of the eight least-liked halls is made in Table 7.2. Remember that "best-liked" or "least-liked" is not a judgment by local audiences, but rather by musicians, music critics, and music lovers who travel a lot. The least-liked halls are 25% larger in volume than the top nine, but that difference, although significant, is not enough by itself to cause those questioned to rank the two groups so far apart in acoustical quality. Undoubtedly, Symphony Hall (662,000 ft^3; 18,750 m^3) in Boston and Grosser Musikvereinssaal (530,000 ft^3; 15,000 m^3) in Vienna are better halls for music than either the Royal Albert Hall (3,060,000 ft^3; 86,660 m^3) in London or the Indiana University Auditorium (950,000 ft^3; 26,900 m^3) in Bloomington. But, as we will show later, reasons exist that account for the good reputations of Segerstrom Hall (981,600 ft^3; 27,800 m^3) in Costa Mesa, California and Tanglewood Music Shed (1,500,000 ft^3; 42,480 m^3) in Lenox, Massachusetts. Because of proper design, some large halls are acoustically preferable to some small ones.

Although an overly large size is always potentially detrimental to the acoustics of a hall, many of the negative effects of great size can be neutralized by special construction and by keeping the background noise level very low. In addition, it is not always easy to separate visual from acoustical impressions. Both contribute to one's feeling of

Table 7.2. Number of seats, cubic volume and reverberation.

	Average No. of Seats	Average Cubic Volume		Average Reverberation Time, Occupied, Sec
		Cubic Feet	Cubic Meters	
8 best-liked concert halls*	1,950	614,400	17,400	1.9
8 least-liked concert halls*	2,800	768,900	21,800	1.5

* The smallest and largest halls are eliminated from these averages, one from Category A and the other from Category C.

the quality of a hall. For example, the equivalent of the close visual rapport between musicians and audience in the Stadt-Casino (370,000 ft^3; 10,500 m^3) of Basel, Switzerland, also exists in the Mann Auditorium (750,000 ft^3; 21,240 m^3) in Tel Aviv, Israel — it is achieved through clever architectural design. And decor is very important, witness the exasperation of the late Maestro George Szell when he strode on the stage for the first time at a rehearsal in New York's ill-fated Philharmonic Hall whose walls had been painted a deep blue and exclaimed loudly, "How can one make love in a blue room?"

Isaac Stern, the violinist, believes that form, placement, and loudness make a difference. He said, "The hall should bring the audience to you. The audience should sit on the edges of its chairs waiting to hear the faintest tones—and they must be loud enough or the listeners lose them and become restless. Then the magic effect is shattered."

The loudness of the sound depends on the size of the hall in several ways. The direct sound is louder if the distance between listener and performers is not too great. It is also louder, if strong reflections of early sound from walls, suspended or splayed panels, and balcony fronts augment the direct sound significantly. Finally, the strength of the reverberant sound adds considerably to the loudness.

The loudness of the reverberant sound is directly related to the length of the reverberation time RT and inversely related to the cubic volume V. This statement says that RT must be near optimum for the type of music being played, not shorter. And the room must have as small a cubic volume as is possible considering the size of the audience.

We shall show later that when you choose the loudness first, you automatically select the area over which the chairs of the audience sit. Audiences absorb sound in direct relation to their area, not according to the number of people in the area. This is not so strange when you think that a carpet absorbs sound in direct relation to its size and not to the number of tufts in it. This says that for each level of loudness you desire, the audience area must fit it—that is why small halls are likely to be better than large ones. But loudness also depends on preserving the sound. Rugs, draperies, thin wood, openings in the ceiling and walls and the like all soak up energy and must be avoided. These considerations become more crucial when the hall is to accommodate a large audience.

CONCLUSION: The acoustics are poorer in a hall with a small cubic volume than in a large hall if the reduction in volume is achieved by lowering the ceiling and, hence, shortening the reverberation time below its range of accepted values. The acoustics are also poorer if the cubic volume is made too large, because of a large audience, which means that there is too little acoustic energy per person. And all carpets, draperies, and sound-absorbing materials must be eliminated from the hall, and the audience must be seated in as small an area as possible to achieve the desired loudness if the concert hall is larger than about 2,000 seats.

SHAPE

Reference to the drawings indicates that all the halls in the A+ category and four out of six in the A category are rectangular, "shoebox," in shape. But of the 35 halls in the B+ group, only seven fall in the shoebox category. Certainly the shoebox shape, provided the hall is not too wide, is a safe acoustical design because parallel side walls assure early lateral reflections to the audience on the main floor, essential to the desired acoustical attribute ASW, the more important component of spaciousness. But, as demonstrated in a number of recent halls, spaciousness can also be achieved by some combination of suspended or splayed panels like those shown in Chapter 6 for the halls of Christchurch, New Zealand, Glasgow, Scotland, Copenhagen (Radiohuset), and San Francisco (Davies Hall, whose recent modifications are shown in the photographs and drawings of Chapter 6). The "vineyard" construction of Costa Mesa, California, is augmented by panels suspended from the side walls and by sound reflecting balcony facia that provide surfaces for creating lateral reflections. The shaping of side walls near the proscenium are specially effective in this regard.

SEATING DENSITY

The importance of keeping the area covered by the audience as small as possible has already been emphasized. In the following halls nearly the same amount of sound absorption results from the presence of quite different numbers of people: Boston, Symphony Hall, 445 people; Carnegie Hall, 438 people; and Leipzig, Gewandhaus, 369 people. That number of people in each of the halls occupies the same amount of floor area, 2,500 ft^2 (232 m^2). Small seating blocks absorb more sound than larger ones, because of the "edge" absorption—the sound that reaches the "sides" of an audience block absorbs as well as the "top." In every description of Chapter 6, the true area occupied by the audience is listed as "S_a". The acoustic area, which includes the edge effects, is called "S_A." The ratio of S_A to S_a ranges between 1.12 and 1.41 in different halls, depending on the number and length of the aisles, and the number of access points in the hall. When the area occupied by the orchestra is added, the total acoustical area is given as "S_T." To preserve loudness, this area must be controlled.

Widely spaced seats make the audience more comfortable, but usually at the expense of acoustical quality and high building costs. If the seats in a hall are too generously spaced, the architect is likely to design a wide hall in order to obtain the necessary floor area. As a result, spaciousness and intimacy as perceived by listeners will be diminished.

If, in order to accommodate the oversized seating, the architect selects the alternative of adding depth to the balconies rather than widening the hall, a large percentage of the audience may be hemmed in by balconies over their heads.

A wide hall or deep balconies—either one—will create poor acoustics for music for a significant part of the audience. These and inflated construction costs should serve as effective deterrents to owners or building codes that demand unnecessarily large row-to-row or seat-to-seat spacing, or large aisles and access areas, or, simply, an unreasonably large audience.

MATERIALS

Except around the stage, the three halls in the A+ category are constructed of plaster on wire or on wood lath for the ceiling, and stucco plaster on brick or on concrete block for the walls. In the Vienna and Boston halls, the floors are wood. In many halls, wood veneer ("wall-paper") on a solid backing is used to give the hall a warm, traditional appearance, which is suitable. But wood alone absorbs the bass and reduces the warmth of the music played in the hall. If wood is necessary, it should be thick, 1.5 in. (3.8 cm), and dense, as we shall show in Chapter 8. The stage floor is usually constructed of flexible wood so as to amplify the sound of the double basses and cellos that stand on pins on the floor.

Carpets are to be avoided, or when desired should be very thin and cemented directly to a solid base. All cracks, openings in the ceiling, large areas of ventilation grilles, and the like should be avoided to preserve the bass. In general, all surfaces, except the stage floor, should be of heavy, dense material.

This theme will be repeated many times in this book.

⋄8⋄

Reverberance, Brilliance, and Warmth (Bass Strength)

REVERBERANCE AND REVERBERATION TIME

Reverberance in a concert hall is a subjective acoustical parameter that has been an important constituent of musical composition and performance since the early eighteenth century. In Chapter 3 we demonstrated how fullness of tone and clarity (definition) of the music being performed is affected by the duration of the reverberation. In Chapter 4 we learned that psychoacoustic studies performed in several research laboratories have, in common, found that reverberation time is one of several important acoustical attributes of a concert hall. We shall carefully examine its significance in this chapter.

Two types of reverberation time have been measured for the majority of the halls in Chapter 6. One is called the *early-decay-time* (EDT), the length of time, multiplied by a factor of 6, that it takes for the sound to decay 10 dB after the instant the sound source is turned off. The second is called the *reverberation time* (RT), the length of time, multiplied by a factor of 2, that it takes for the sound to decay over the range beginning 5 dB down from turn-off to 35 dB down. The factors of 6 and 2 are necessary to make the two measurements comparable with each other and with an historical definition of RT that called for 60 dB of sound decay.

Table 5.1 (p. 55) displays the measured values of EDT and RT and other physical quantities taken from the "Technical Details" at the end of the descriptions for each of the halls in Chapter 6. The EDTs are for unoccupied halls, usually measured at 8 or more seats, and for one to three locations of the sound source on stage. The RT values are for fully occupied halls usually measured in the few seconds of quiet periods following orchestral stop-chords recorded during concerts. Such recordings are usually made at only one or two seats. There are a few cases where audiences, usually without orchestra on stage, have sat quietly through the same procedure that is customary for unoccupied halls.

In those cases in this and later chapters where RT is not available, it will be estimated using EDT (unoccupied) as a surrogate . As seen in Table 8.3, EDT for concert halls with upholstered seats is about 0.2 sec larger than RT. For seven halls in Table 5.1, this is not true because the seats are not upholstered or upholstered very lightly, so that the sound decays slowly in those halls when empty. These halls are in Amsterdam, Basel, Berlin (Konzerthaus), Boston, Vienna, and Zurich.

COMPARISONS OF REVERBERATION TIMES WITH THE RATING CATEGORIES

In this section the RTs and EDTs for the concert halls that were ranked subjectively from the interviews in different levels of acoustical quality in Table 5.2 are compared. The measurement RTs and EDTs are tendered in Table 8.1. There are 8 halls in Group (A+, A) "excellent;" 35 in Group (B+) "very good;" and 8 in Group (B, C+) "good." London's Royal Albert Hall in Category C "fair" is so unusual size and shape that it is not compared with the other halls. And the Tokyo Hamarikyu Hall is not included here because of its small size. Subjective ratings were not obtained for 13 of the 66 halls in Table 5.1.

The average values of RT for the excellent, very good, and good categories are 1.9, 1.7, and 1.5 sec, respectively. Particular notice should be taken of the range of RT

Table 8.1. Relation between the subjective rating categories of Table 5.2 and the average values of the mid-frequency (500 and 1,000 Hz averaged), occupied-hall, reverberation times RT, and, unoccupied hall, early decay times EDT, for 52 concert halls of the 66 appearing in Table 5.1.*

	Occupied, sec		Unoccupied, sec	
Rating Categories	**Mid-freq. RT**	**Range of RTs**	**Mid-Freq. EDT**	**Range of EDTs**
Group A+ , A	1.9	1.8 to 2.05†	2.45†	2.1 to 3.1
Group B+	1.7	1.2 to 2.2	2.0	1.7 to 2.6
Group B, C+	1.5	1.25 to 1.85	1.8	1.4 to 2.15
Average for all halls:	**1.7**	**1.2 to 2.2**	**2.0**	**1.4 to 3.1**

* The one small hall Tokyo Hamarikyu and the very large Hall, London Royal Albert Hall are not included. Subjective ratings were not obtained for 13 of the concert halls. In each hall, the reverberation times were measured at two to twenty positions, often with more than one source position on stage. The data for all measuring positions in each hall were averaged to obtain the values in Table 5.1.

† Smallest hall eliminated.

values in each category. In the top Group, the range is 1.8 to 2.05 sec, while in the bottom Group the range is 1.2 to 1.85 sec. Because there is almost no overlap it appears that even if all other acoustical attributes were near optimum, halls with RTs (occupied) below 1.75 sec probably could not achieve the top Group rating. unless they were small.

By contrast, the RT values for Group B+ completely overlap the other two groups. This finding suggests that the halls in this group with RTs of 1.8 and above did not achieve excellent ratings because there were deficiencies in one or more of the other important acoustical parameters, namely, loudness, spaciousness, intimacy, warmth, and envelopment. This observation will be tested when the values for all six acoustical attributes are brought together in the calculation scheme of Chapter 15.

It also is apparent from Table 8.1 that the ranges of EDT are wider than those of RT because unoccupied seats are of widely varying construction, with different sound absorptions. At frequencies above about 350 Hz, audiences tend to absorb about the same amount of sound regardless of the type of seats they are occupying (see Table A5.6, p. 626). At frequencies below 350 Hz, people absorb less sound and the RT, and thus the bass ratio BR, depends to a greater extent on the design of the chairs. It is obvious that RTs must be measured in fully occupied halls if the results are to be used for judging acoustical quality.

REVERBERATION TIMES PREFERRED BY LISTENERS

The professional musicians and music critics stated that their judgments of acoustical quality were based on listening to symphonic music during concerts. Let us review some quotations from my 1962 book, which are still valid today:

Dry Halls

Liveness (reverberance) is consistently mentioned as an important aspect of the acoustics of a concert hall. A room that is not live enough is usually described as "dry" or "dead." Table 8.2 gives the mid-frequency reverberation times of six halls known for their dryness.

Erich Leinsdorf described the sound in the Old Festspielhaus as "dead dry" or "straw dry."

Table 8.2. Mid-frequency reverberation times, with full audience, of six dry halls.

	Reverberation Time, Occupied, RT, sec
Old Festspielhaus, Salzburg*	1.0
Academy of Music, Philadelphia*	1.2
Orchestra Hall, Chicago	1.2
Kleinhans Music Hall, Buffalo	1.3
Alberta Jubilee Hall, Edmonton	1.4
Royal Festival Hall, London (Assis. Res. Off)	1.4

* The Salzburg hall, though not one of the halls discussed in this book, is included as an example of extreme dryness. The Academy of Music was designed as an opera house, but it is used today principally for concerts. It is evaluated in this book only as an opera house.

Of Orchestra Hall, Chicago, Alfred Frankenstein said, "This hall has no life when the audience is in it; it is as dead as any I know." Fritz Reiner said, "When Orchestra Hall is fully occupied, the reverberation time is too short." Roger Dettmer said, "When the hall is full, there is almost no reverberation."

Reiner called Kleinhans Hall "completely dead." William Steinberg said, "Kleinhans is dry." Tauno Hannikainen called it "a little dry."

Pierre Monteux said of the Academy of Music in Philadelphia, "This hall is too dry; the tone stops instantly." Eugene Ormandy said, during the time he was the Music Director, "The Academy is a little dry." Reiner spoke of halls with a horseshoe shape and many balcony rings, of which the Academy of Music is one, as "the dry Italian type."

Munch, Monteux, and Ormandy considered the Royal Festival Hall (without assisted resonance) too dry. Each of them has mentioned that there is no "resonance," even when the hall is empty. Alexander Gibson wrote of the Royal Festival Hall, "The dry acoustics of this hall make for a clinical effect." Sir John Barbirolli commented, "Everything is sharp and clear and there is no impact, no fullness on climaxes."

I could cite many more authorities, but suffice it to say that, for the repertoires of today's symphony orchestra, conductors and trained listeners consider a reverberation time of 1.5 sec or less to be too short, and they call its acoustics dry.

Live halls

Table 8.3 shows the reverberation times of 13 highly praised halls when fully occupied. The average RT is 2.0 sec.

Table 8.3. Mid-frequency occupied reverberation times and unoccupied early decay times for a selection of very good to excellent halls seating more than 1,400 persons.

	RT, Occupied	EDT, Unoccupied	
		Upholstered Seats	Unupholstered Seats
	RT, sec	EDT, sec	EDT, sec
Meyerson/McDermott Concert Hall, Dallas	2.8	1.9	
De Doelen Concertgebouw, Rotterdam	2.05	2.3	
Konzerthaus (Schauspielhaus), Berlin*	2.0	-	2.4
Grosser Musikvereinssaal, Vienna*	2.0	-	3.0
Gewandhaus, Leipzig	2.0	-	-
St. David's Hall, Cardiff, Wales	1.95	2.1	-
Grosser Tonhallesaal, Zurich*	2.05	-	3.1
Concertgebouw, Amsterdam*	2.0	-	2.6
Philharmonie Hall, Berlin	1.9	2.1	-
Symphony Hall, Boston	1.85	2.4	-
Carnegie Hall, New York	1.8	-	-
Stadt-Casino, Basel*	1.8	-	2.2
Segerstrom Hall, Costa Mesa	1.6	2.2	
Average	**2.0**	**2.2**	**2.7**

*Halls with unupholstered chairs

Commenting on several of these halls, Igor Markevich said, "I prefer a bit more reverberation than Symphony Hall has. The Musikvereinssaal has a longer reverberation time than the Boston hall, but I would not want a longer time than that of the Musikvereinssaal. The Concertgebouw has very good acoustics. Carnegie Hall is too muted." (See Table 5.1 for Carnegie and other halls.)

Herbert von Karajan said of the Grosser Musikvereinssaal, "The sound in this hall is so full that the technical attack of instruments—bows and lips—gets lost. Also successive notes merge into each other. I consider Symphony Hall a little better than the Musikvereinssaal."

Dimitri Mitropoulos commented, "The Musikvereinssaal rings too much. Carnegie is good; it is not overly reverberant. Symphony Hall has good acoustics."

Monteux said, "The Concertgebouw has marvelous acoustics. The Musikvereinssaal too is very good. I find Carnegie a little dead with audience. Symphony Hall I like very, very much, and Tanglewood is also extremely good."

Ormandy said, "The Musikvereinssaal is just right acoustically. Boston has one of the world's best halls. Carnegie is not as reverberant as it might be."

Charles Munch said, "The Musikvereinssaal has a beautiful quality of sound. Carnegie could use more reverberation. Symphony Hall is excellent. Tanglewood is also excellent, especially for large orchestra and violin."

George Szell observed, "The Musikvereinssaal is just right acoustically. Boston has one of the world's best halls. Carnegie is not as reverberant as it might be."

Sir Adrian Boult wrote, "Symphony Hall is our ideal."

Reiner says, "The Musikvereinssaal and Symphony Hall are the two best halls. I do not consider the Concertgebouw as good."

Herman Scherchen said, "The Musikvereinssaal is very good for Romantic music, but not for Bach. The Concertgebouw is not as good."

Isaac Stern says, "The Concertgebouw is marvelous for the violin; it rings when you sound a tone. Symphony Hall is excellent. Carnegie is better in rehearsal than with audience. Tanglewood has brilliant, warm, singing sound."

Leopold Stokowski said, "The Musikvereinssaal is excellent."

Bruno Walter said, "The Musikvereinssaal has beauty and power, and I consider it better than Carnegie. Boston is very fine, more live than Carnegie. I like the Concertgebouw; it is really a live hall."

Mitropoulos and von Karajan both spoke favorably of the Stadt-Casino, but because of its small cubic volume, they remarked that full-orchestra music played in it often is too loud.

Most of the musicians, critics, recording engineers, and experts whom I have consulted arrive at the same specification: For the average symphony orchestra's repertoire they prefer a reverberation time at mid-frequencies of 1.8 to 2.0 sec. When asked about music from the Baroque and Classical periods only, they thought a lower reverberation time desirable, say, between 1.6 and 1.8 sec.

As one conductor remarked, "With such a range in reverberation time depending on the type of music, how can one say what is a good hall?" There may be some truth in this, but fortunately the building has to satisfy only today's musicians, today's audiences, and today's musical repertoire. This means choosing 1.8 to 2.0 sec as the ideal, or if we use EDT as a surrogate, 2.0 to 2.3 sec. Tomorrow's musicians and listeners may choose to listen differently, but how could we try to predict their taste?

Throughout the interviews, Boston Symphony Hall is rated as being more reverberant than Carnegie Hall. The RT data do not adequately support that consensus, the values being 1.85 sec in comparison to 1.80 sec. Unfortunately, I was unable to obtain modern data pertinent to the other acoustical factors in Carnegie. But it is clearly observable that the reverberation is more obvious in Symphony Hall than in Carnegie. Comparison of the two halls indicates one important difference. The initial-time-delay gap is about twice as large in Carnegie as in Boston, which would shorten EDT and, hence, the running liveness.

As illustrations of the differences in EDT and RT it is informative to examine two newer design concepts that are receiving critical praise. These are the Segerstrom Hall (2,903 seats) in Costa Mesa and the McDermott/Meyerson Hall (2,065 seats) in Dallas. Both halls have upholstered seats. The Dallas hall has a high RT (occupied) and a low EDT. The Costa Mesa Hall has just the opposite. Both are judged "very good to excellent" halls. Each has its own special sound, just as do Boston Symphony Hall and Berlin Philharmonie Hall. Just as for all halls in this book the occupied RTs were derived from analyses of orchestral stop chords recorded during regular concerts, with an eye on the orchestral scores to make certain that the after-rings of tympani were not determining the RT.

For Segerstrom Hall, its 2,903 seats make a conventional shoebox hall out of the question because of the great length that would ensue if the width and balcony overhangs were kept within acceptable limits. The "vineyard" plan was chosen, with four audience terraces, each giving listeners the feeling of being in a smaller hall. To obtain the necessary "fullness of tone" (discussed in Chapter 3), sufficient clarity (C_{80}), and a short initial-time-delay gap to render intimacy, large panels, suspended from the side walls, were installed to direct much of the early energy from the stage onto the audience, while at the same time allowing a reverberant upper volume.

This solution gives the unoccupied hall an EDT of 2.2 sec, the same as for the other excellent halls with upholstered chairs. But, in Segerstrom Hall, *this EDT remains at 2.2 sec with full audience*, more than the occupied EDTs in Berlin, Cardiff, and Dallas. Thus, it exhibits strong "running liveness" which contributes lively support to symphonic music, although the lingering sound after a stop chord is noticeably less. Most symphonic music and solo presentations sound in this hall pretty much as they do in Amsterdam, Basel, Rotterdam, or Boston but lacking the occasional after-ring.

In Meyerson/McDermott Hall the philosophy of design was to create a narrow hall like that of Vienna and Boston, which is possible with limited audience size, but to add a long after-ring—later reverberation time—by an overhead reverberation chamber with motorized access doors. The hall has less running liveness than Costa Mesa—

in fact the architect/consultant selected a lower EDT than in any of the halls of Table 8.3—but it has a very long reverberation tail that enhances the sound of certain compositions and adds a musical dimension to all musical pieces that is not heard in any other hall in this country. Russell Johnson, the acoustician, wrote, "Meyerson's achievement is a long, long reverberant tail with more than adequate clarity, a sound quite unlike Amsterdam or Vienna. In the late 1980's, symphony [management] boards were becoming more amenable to lower seating capacities. Consequently a narrow hall with an adjustable cubic volume were feasible, permitting the performers to select the length of the RT tail according to the composition and the desired interpretation."

These two halls stride away from the conventional shoebox form common in the previous century and often used to this day. Each provides a high degree of clarity with different reverberation characteristics. Accordingly, they offer audiences two different, but pleasing, musical experiences. Time will tell whether both concepts survive, enriching our senses just as do white wines and red wines.

Table 8.3 further shows the differences between EDTs at mid-frequencies in halls with normally upholstered seats and those with unupholstered seats. The five halls that are in the latter category have EDTs that, on average, are 0.5 sec greater than the others.

Optimum reverberation times for concert halls

Several inferences follow from these observations about reverberation. As already stated, a concert hall that is to be used for symphonic concerts receives the most praise if its reverberation time, occupied, at mid-frequencies, is of the order of 1.9 to 2.0 sec. The optimum RT for a hall (without means for creating two slopes one for EDT and the other for RT), should probably be in the range of 1.8 to 2.0 sec. If the mid-frequency reverberation time in a hall is as short as 1.4 to 1.6 sec, the rating of the hall drops in judged quality. If the reverberation time lies between 1.1 and 1.4 sec the hall will receive low ratings. Reverberation times of less than about 1.1 sec add nothing to the fullness-of-tone of music played in a concert hall.

Optimum reverberation times for opera houses

We shall see from Table 16.1 that no optimum reverberation time can be inferred from the measured data. The most highly praised opera houses are La Scala in Milan and Staatsoper in Vienna. Their RTs (occupied) are 1.2 and 1.3, respectively. On the other hand, the Opera Colón in Buenos Aires also ranks among the best and has a reverberation time of 1.7 sec, consistent with the optimum value for concert halls.

It is obvious that an opera is different from a symphony. In addition to the beauty of the orchestral music, opera buffs wish to hear the words of the singers. In my interviews, I also heard praise for the Kennedy Center Opera House and the Philadelphia Academy of Music. Their reverberation times, occupied, are 1.5 sec and 1.2 sec, respectively. With such a range, one can only hazard a recommendation, namely, that the optimum RT lies between 1.3 and 1.5 sec.

BRILLIANCE

Although reverberation time at the mid-frequencies has proved to be a reliable indicator of the liveness of a hall, RT at higher frequencies has been found to have surprisingly little relation to brilliance. Let us investigate if there is any correlation between brilliance and either RT or EDT.

A comparison of the RTs and EDTs at 2,000 and 4,000 Hz to those at the mid-frequencies, 500 and 1,000 Hz (averaged), is shown in Table 8.4 for four classes of halls, those with high and low RTs and those with high and low bass ratios (BR). There is no significant difference among the numbers in any one of the columns, which means that brilliance is not related to RT or EDT. It is well known from acoustical theory and measurements that, as shown in Table 8.4, the decreased values of RT and EDT at 2,000 and 4,000 Hz, compared to the average RT and EDT at 500 and 1,000

Table 8.4. Ratios of reverberation times RTs and early-decay-times EDTs at high frequencies to those at mid-frequencies (500 and 1,000 Hz, averaged).

	Occupied in sec		Unoccupied in sec	
Classification of Halls	$T_{2,000}/T_{mid}$	$T_{4,000}/T_{mid}$	$EDT_{2,000}/EDT_{mid}$	$EDT_{4,000}/EDT_{mid}$
Short reverberation times at mid-frequencies	0.93	0.84	0.86	0.70
Long reverberation times at mid-frequencies	0.94	0.84	0.94	0.72
Halls deficient in bass	0.97	0.84	0.94	0.76
Halls with strong bass	0.90	0.81	0.83	0.70
Average	**0.93**	**0.84**	**0.90**	**0.72**

Hz, are caused by loss of energy in sound waves as they travel through the air caused by friction among the air particles and resonant interactions among the molecules.

In acoustical design, this means that to preserve brilliance at high frequencies the RTs must not be allowed to go below the ratios shown in Table 8.4.

CONCLUSION: To preserve brilliance in a concert hall or opera house, no high-frequency sound-absorptive materials should be introduced into the room, except as necessary in small quantities to avoid acoustical "glare" and echoes. This means that draperies and carpets should be strictly avoided or limited in area, except in opera houses where lower reverberation times are permissible.

WARMTH

Warmth is the subjective feeling of strength of bass. Wilkens (1975), who was one of the participants in the German studies at the Technical University of Berlin, identified "emphasized bass" as one of three orthogonal acoustical attributes and give it the title "timbre of the total sound." In my 1962 book, I felt that "emphasized bass reverberation" was a primary factor in the acoustical quality of concert halls. I used the formulation, (RT at 125 Hz + RT at 250 Hz) divided by (RT at 500 Hz + RT at 1,000 Hz) as a measure of emphasized bass and called it BR. The RTs are measured in fully occupied halls. Wilkens formulation was slightly different, similar in concept, but his measurements and judgments were made in unoccupied halls.

In an attempt to see whether BR is a major factor in the judgments of acoustical quality by those interviewed, BR was determined for 55 halls and, for part of them, tabulated in three sub-groups as shown in Table 8.5.

It is immediately apparent that BR does not correlate strongly with the rating categories that are listed in Table 5.2. For example, in the BR group of Table 8.5 from 1.45 to 1.12, we find the Buffalo hall (C+) along with Zurich and Basel (A). In the middle group, we find the London, Barbican Hall (C+) along with Vienna, Amsterdam, and Boston (A+). In the third group, from 1.00 to 0.92, we find Edmonton (B) along with Cardiff (A).

It is possible to have too high a bass ratio BR, at least in small concert halls. Two recent experiences can be cited. In one, the Berlin Konzerthaus (formerly Schauspielhaus) (1,575 seats), the BR when first opened was 1.29, with a mid-frequency reverberation time RT of 2.05 [Beranek (review paper)1992, p. 33]. The cubic volume is 530,000 ft^3

Table 8.5. Three groups of halls selected to determine whether the Bass Ratio BR is related to subjective category ratings of acoustical quality. Fifty-five halls were in the original tabulation.

	Bass Ratio BR Occupied Halls
Halls with BR from 1.45 to 1.12	
Lenox, Tanglewood Shed	1.45
Costa Mesa, Segerstrom Hall	1.32
Buffalo, Kleinhans Music Hall	1.28
Zurich, Grosser Tonhallesaal	1.23
Berlin, Konzerthaus (Schauspielhaus)	1.23
Paris, Salle Pleyel	1.23
Tokyo, Bunka Kaikan	1.20
Basel, Stadt-Casino	1.17
Edinburgh, Usher Hall	1.17
London, Royal Festival (Resonance On)	1.17
Chicago, Orchestra Hall	1.15
Mexico City, Nezahualcoyotl Hall	1.15
Cleveland, Severance Hall	1.12
Halls with BR from 1.11 to 1.01	
Berlin, Philharmonie Hall	1.01
Boston, Symphony Hall	1.03
Bristol, Colston Hall	1.05
Washington, Kennedy Concert Hall	1.06
London, Barbican, Large Concert Hall	1.07
Amsterdam, Concertgebouw	1.08
Birmingham, U.K., Symphony Hall	1.08
Gothenburg, Konserthus	1.08
Tokyo, Suntory Hall	1.08
Salzburg, Festspielhaus	1.10
Vienna, Gr. Musikvereinssaal	1.11
San Francisco, Davies Hall	1.11
Halls with BR of 1.00 or below	
Liverpool, Philharmonic Hall	1.00
Munich, Philharmonie am Gasteig	1.00
Edmonton, Alberta Jubilee Aud.	0.99
Tel Aviv, F. R. Mann Auditorium	0.98
Sydney, Opera House Concert Hall	0.98
Leipzig, Gewandhaus	0.97
Manchester, Free Trade Hall	0.97
Cardiff, Wales, St. David's Hall	0.96
Rotterdam, de Doelen	0.95
New York, Avery Fisher Hall	0.93
Royal Festival Hall (Resonance off)	0.92

(15,000 m^3). The complaints were sufficient that the RT had to be shortened at low frequencies. Bass-resonator sound absorbers were employed to reduce BR to 1.23. The other example is a recently opened hall with a cubic volume of 400,000 ft^3 (11,300 m^3), seating 1,100. Its bass ratio was 1.32, with an RT of 1.7 sec. Steps are being taken to achieve better spectral balance.

Optimum Bass Ratio (BR)

Because all three of the halls rated A+ have bass ratios ranging from 1.03 to 1.11, and because of the experiences with too much BR, at least in smaller halls, with high reverberation times, it would seem to be safe and desirable in design to aim for BR between 1.1 and 1.25, for halls with high RTs and 1.1 to 1.45 for halls with RTs of 1.8 sec or less. Interpolate for RTs between 2.2 and 1.8 sec.

STRENGTH OF THE BASS SOUNDS

It must be emphasized, that BR deals with the *ratio of the reverberation time at low-frequencies to that at mid-frequencies.* It does not deal with the *strength* of the bass, that is to say, the intensity of the music at bass frequencies (below 350 Hz) compared to that at the middle frequencies.

One intuitively knows that a rich bass is to be desired in a concert hall. There are two acoustical attributes that can contribute to bass richness; one is BR as defined above and the other is the strength of the bass-frequencies G_{low} as compared to the strength of mid-frequencies G_{mid}. Table 8.6 tabulates the values of these two quantities and their difference.

The average difference between G_{mid} and G_{low} is –0.9 dB and the range is –3.4 to +1.1, which means that very few unoccupied halls have appreciable bass gains. However, the sound absorption by occupied compared to unoccupied chairs is relatively greater at mid-frequencies than at low-frequencies. Hence the bass remains stronger than mid-tones after occupancy. This indicates that the average difference between G_{low} and G_{mid} will be a positive number for most halls when occupied. Such data will probably be available as measuring techniques for occupied halls become more simple. No conclusion can be drawn from the present G_{low} and G_{mid} because they are for unoccupied halls.

Table 8.6. Relations among EDT/*V*, G_{mid}* and G_{low}* for unoccupied halls.

City and Name of Hall or House CONCERT HALLS	EDT/V × 10^6 From Table 5.1	G_{low}* Compromise Average dB	G_{mid}* Compromise Average dB	Difference $G_{low}-G_{mid}$ dB
Amsterdam, Concertgebouw	138	5.5	6.0	–0.5
Baltimore, Meyerhoff Hall	107	3.3	4.1	–0.8
Basel, Stadt-Casino	210	8.4	7.5	0.9
Berlin, Konzerthaus (Schausplhaus)	160	7.1	6.0	1.1
Berlin, Philharmonie Hall	100	3.2	4.3	–1.1
Boston, Symphony Hall	128	2.6	4.7	–2.1
Bristol, Colston Hall	137	4.2	5.8	–1.6
Buffalo, Kleinhans Music Hall	88	3.5	2.9	0.6
Cardiff, Wales, St. David's Hall	95	1.8	3.8	–2.0
Cleveland, Severance Hall	108	3.1	3.9	–0.8
Copenhagen, Radiohuset	168	7.1	6.4	0.7
Costa Mesa, Segerstrom Hall	79	2.6	4.3	–1.7
Edinburgh, Usher Hall	134	3.7	4.6	–0.9
Edmonton, Alberta Jubilee Aud.	65	–1.7	–0.4	–1.3
Glasgow, Royal Concert Hall	75	2.1	2.2	–0.2
Lenox, Tanglewood Shed	78	0.3	4.9	–0.6
Liverpool, Philharmonic Hall	133	2.2	3.9	–1.7
London, Barbican Lrg Concert Hall	107	0.0	3.4	–3.4
London, Royal Albert Hall	30	–1.2	–0.1	–1.1
London, Royal Festival (Res. Off)	64	0.8	2.6	–1.8
Manchester, Free Trade Hall	110	2.0	4.1	–2.1
Montreal, Salle Wilfrid-Pelietier	72	–0.1	0.7	–0.8
Munich, Philharmonie, Gasteig	71	0.8	2.2	–1.4
Paris, Salle Pleyel	116	5.5	4.5	–0.2
Philadelphia, Academy of Music	76	–0.4	2.0	–2.4
Salt Lake, Utah, Symphony Hall	102	0.5	2.0	–1.5
Salzburg, Festspielhaus	116	2.8	4.0	–1.2
San Francisco, Davies Hall	87	2.2	2.8	–0.5
Stuttgart, Liederhalle	131	3.5	4.3	–0.8
Tokyo, Bunka Kaikan	107	2.8	3.7	–0.9
Tokyo, Hamarikyu	310	7.0	9.3	–2.4
Tokyo, Met. Art Space	102	3.4	3.6	–0.2
Tokyo, Suntory Hall	117	3.0	4.5	–1.5
Toronto, Roy Thompson Hall	67	3.5	3.8	–0.3
Vienna, Gr. Musikvereinssaal	200	7.1	7.0	0.1
Washington, JFK Concert	91	2.4	3.3	–0.9
Worcester, MA, Mechanics Hall	200	5.6	5.6	0.0
Zurich, Grosser Tonhallesaal	272	8.4	8.0	0.4
Average	**119**	**3.1**	**4.0**	**–0.9**

* The compromise values for G_{mid} and G_{low} were obtained by subtracting 0.6 dB from Takenaka data and adding 0.6 dB to other laboratories measurements. The procedure followed in obtaining this compromise is given in Chapter 9 in the Section, "Measured values of G_{mid}." If data were available from more than one laboratory the compromise values were averaged. All measurements were in unoccupied halls.

PRINCIPAL CAUSES OF LOSS OF BASS

Thin wood paneling

Thin wood paneling was not used in the older concert halls, probably because of the danger of fire. It is also prohibited in Japan and some other countries today. However, in the United Kingdom, the USA, and many other industrialized countries, thin wood paneling with an airspace behind found considerable use before the publication

Table 8.7. Construction materials in thirteen very good to excellent halls.

Concert Hall	Construction	$G_{low}-G_{mid}$ Unoccupied	BR Occupied
Amsterdam, Concertgebouw	Plaster	–0.5	1.08
Basel, Stadt Casino	Plaster with small amount wood	0.9	1.17
Berlin, Konzerthaus, (Schauspiel)	Plaster or thick plasterboard	1.1	1.23
Boston, Symphony Hall	Plaster, except for stage enclosure which averages more than 0.75 in. (1.9 cm) wood. All seats are on raised wooden floor.	–2.1	1.03
Cardiff, Wales, St. Davids	Heavy surfaces everywhere except on wall around stage and some other surfaces which are plywood.	–2.0	0.96
Christchurch Town Hall	Main side walls, concrete. Free-standing reflectors 2 in.(5 cm) wood. Stage enclosure 1 in. (2.5 cm) wood.	-	1.06
Cleveland, Severance Hall	Plaster	–0.8	1.12
Costa Mesa, Segerstrom Hall	Plaster	–1.7	1.32
Leipzig, Gewandhaus	Mostly 1.4 in. (3.6 cm) gypsum or plywood panels, except some areas are free to vibrate and to absorb sound between 50 and 150 Hz.	-	0.97
New York, Carnegie Hall	Walls, ceiling and stage enclosure, plaster.	-	1.14
Tokyo, Hamarikyu Asahi Hall	Ceiling: Gypsum board 0.83 in. (2.1 cm) thick. Walls 1.7 in. (4.2 cm) gypsum board, except some panels above balcony, 0.31 in. (0.8 cm) artificial wood.	–2.4	0.94
Vienna, Musikvereinssaal	Plaster except around stage where wood is of medium thickness	0.1	1.11
Zurich, Tonhallesaal	Plaster except for walls beneath the balcony which are plywood.	0.4	1.23

of my 1962 book which clearly showed the negative effects of such construction in concert halls and opera houses.

In Table 8.7 the finishing materials of 13 highly rated halls are tabulated. It is seen that in all except the Tokyo hall the interiors are of thick plaster, or equivalent. Because the Tokyo hall is small, the extra absorption of the thinner material above the balcony prevents the sound from becoming too loud.

A similar listing is made in Table 8.8 for the halls that show the greatest deficiency in bass—the measurements were made with the halls unoccupied.

Those halls with low BRs and G_{low}'s, as listed in Tables 8.7 and 8.8, have considerable amounts of wood on their surfaces. A hall lined with thin wood is expected to be deficient in bass. On the other hand, thick wood (1.5 in., 3.8 cm), plaster, or wood of any thickness, provided it is securely cemented to thick smooth plaster or concrete, is acoustically satisfactory, and the architect may choose freely among these three constructions.

Table 8.8. Examples of halls with low values of G_{low} minus G_{mid}. See discussion in the text.

Name of Hall	$G_{low}-G_{mid}$ (Unoccupied)	Probable Reason for Difference	Bass Ratio (Occupied)
London, Barbican Concert Hall*	−3.4	Large areas of 1 cm thick wood paneling on side walls. Unusual built-in seating	1.07
Philadelphia, Academy of Music	−2.4	Walls, thin wood over airspace	1.11
Boston, Symphony Hall	−2.1	All seating on raised wooden floors	1.03
Manchester, Free Trade Hall	−2.1	Wooden panels on lower walls. Large areas absorbing materials	0.97
Cardiff, St. David's Hall	−2.0	Wooden floors with airspace beneath. Balcony fronts and some other wall areas, wooden	0.96
London, Royal Festival Hall (assisted resonance off)	−1.8	Large areas of thin plywood on side and rear walls	0.92
Costa Mesa, Segestrom Hall	−1.7	Large areas of QRD sound diffusers	1.32
Liverpool, Philharmonic Hall	−1.7	404 m^2 wood paneling on lower sidewalls	1.06
Bristol, Colston Hall	−1.6	Below the balcony, the sidewalls are 1.25 cm plywood	1.05
Salt Lake, Utah Symphony Hall	−1.5	Wood paneling on all side walls	1.06
Edmonton, Alberta Jubilee Aud.	−1.3	Entire side walls are 0.6 cm thick plywood	0.99

* The thin plywood side wall panels were thickened to 7 cm in summer of 1994 after these measurements were made.

Technical data on the absorbing effect of thin wood with air space behind are readily available in books on acoustics. Some typical data are given in Fig. 8.1. The curves show that at 125 Hz 0.375 in. (0.94 cm) thick plywood with 3 to 4 in. of airspace behind it absorbs about 1/4 of the intensity from a sound wave every time the

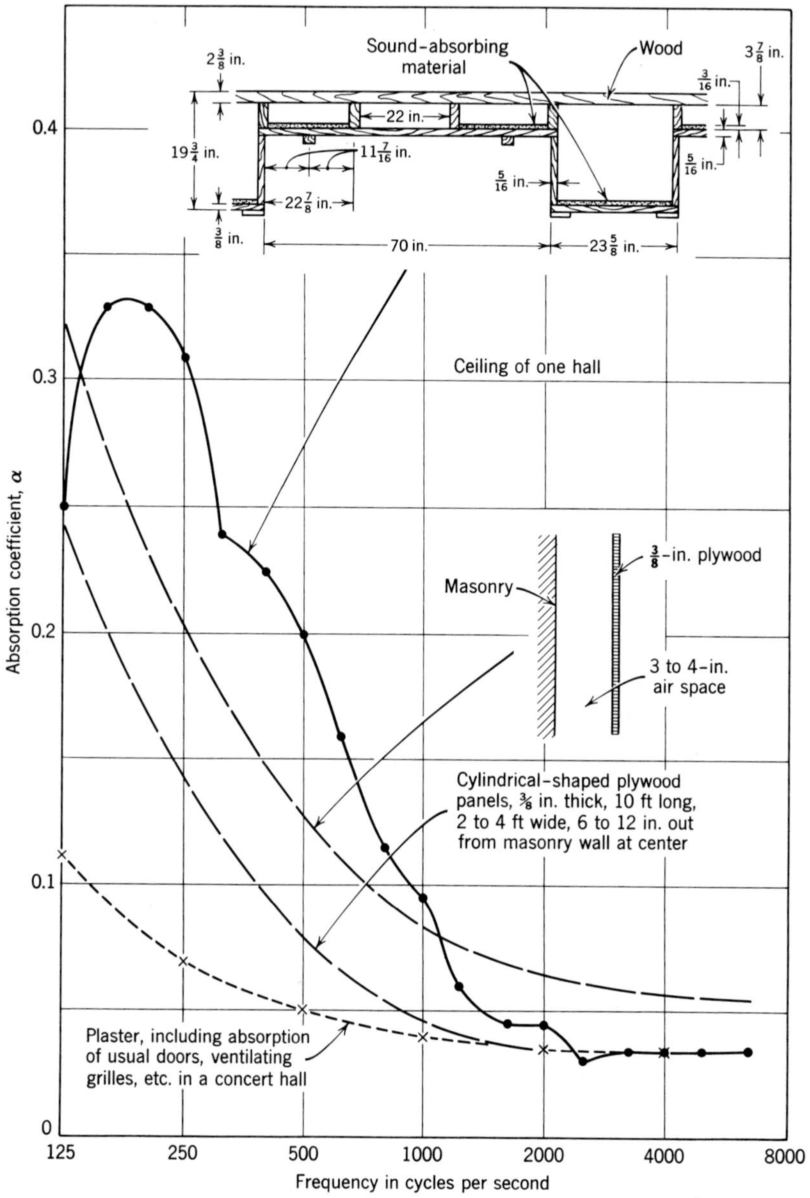

Figure 8.1. Sound absorption coefficients for walls and ceilings made of thin wood [0.25 in. (0.63 cm) to 0.63 in. (1.6 cm)], or of plaster. The upper ceiling construction was taken from the Hercules Hall in Munich.

wave reflects from it. In a concert hall whose ceiling and side walls are made of such wooden paneling, a sound wave traveling around the room at the rate of 1,130 ft per sec strikes a wall surface about 10 times each second. The sound intensity remaining in a 125 Hz wave after 10 reflections is a very small part of the original intensity.

A plaster wall, on the other hand, reduces the sound intensity of this bass note very little after 10 reflections. Thus, 1 sec after it has sounded, a low-frequency sound wave is many times more intense in a plaster hall than in a hall lined with thin wood. Above 1,000 Hz, both wood and plaster absorb sound to about the same degree. Figure 8.1 also shows the sound absorption of a kind of cylindrical-shaped plywood panels often used in broadcasting studios and on concert hall stage enclosures and of the special type of ceiling construction employed in the Herkulessaal in Munich.

Heavily upholstered audience chairs

The other common cause of bass deficiency in halls is overly absorbent chairs, particularly at frequencies below about 700 Hz. There is not space in this text to discuss the details of chair design, but suffice it to say, that the backs and underseat surface should be of molded plywood, say, 0.5 in. (1.25 cm) thick, and the upholstering on the front of the seat back should be no greater than 1 in. (2.5 cm) in thickness. The upholstering on the top of the seat bottom should be only as thick as necessary for reasonable comfort, if possible no thicker than 3 in. (7.5 cm).

The sound absorption coefficients of two types of chairs, one of conventional over-upholstered type and the other of special design to reduce low frequency sound absorption, are shown in Fig. 8.2. The data are for the chairs both occupied and unoccupied and were taken in a national, approved, test laboratory. The difference between the occupied and unoccupied absorptions of sound by these two chairs is shown in the right-hand graph. The difference is nearly the same for the two chairs and the maximum occurs at 500 Hz. The effect that this increased absorption at 250 to 500 Hz for seat A has on the quality of music in a concert hall is treated in Chapter 14 under the Section "Distortion."

The data of Fig. 8.2 are not for use in calculating the reverberation times in halls, but are intended only for inter-comparison of chairs. Instead use Table A5.7, p. 626.

As before, it is seen that after 10 reflections, the intensity of the sound absorbed by the fully upholstered chair (occupied) in the 250 Hz frequency band as compared to the specially designed chair will be 30 times as much.

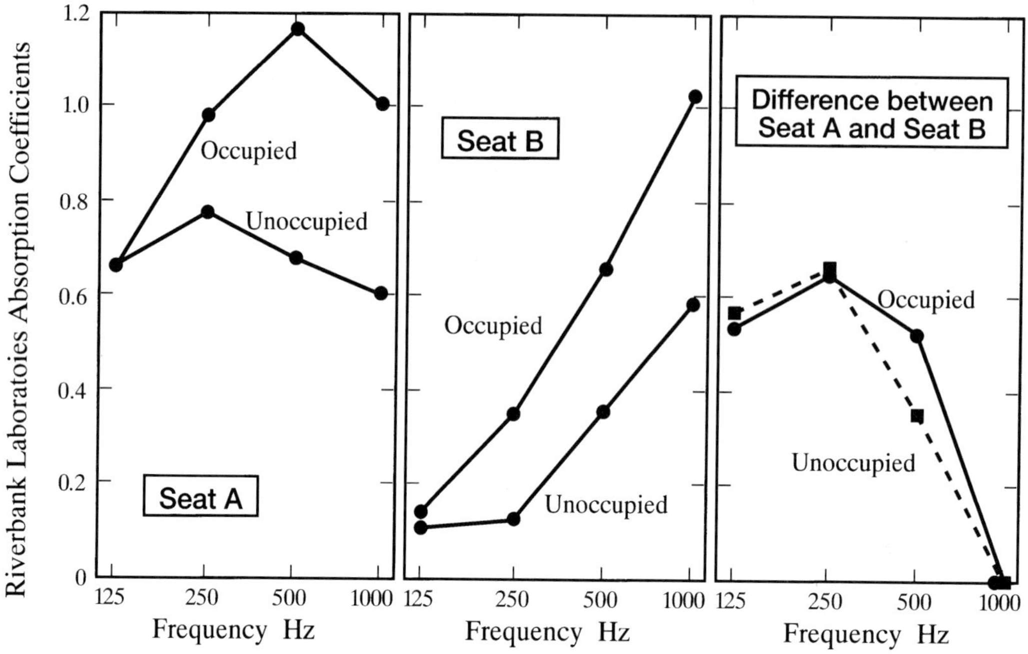

Figure. 8.2. Sound absorption coefficients for concert hall chairs measured in a national laboratory. The seats were made by one manufacturer. Seat A: Metal-pan seat-bottom with 6 in. (15 cm) seat cushion; fully upholstered seat back, both sides; arms fully upholstered. Seat B: Bucket-shaped plywood seat bottom with 3 in. (7.5 cm) seat cushion; plywood seat back with 1 in. (2.5 cm) pad on front side of seat back only; arms made of wood and unupholstered. The right-hand graph shows the difference in sound absorptions of the two chairs both occupied and unoccupied.

TECHNICAL SECTION FOR SPECIALISTS

The Sabine equation

From Sabine's equation the reverberation time, defined as the duration in seconds of 60 dB of sound decay after a source is turned off, is

$$RT = 0.16\ V/A \text{ sec} \qquad (8.1)$$

where V is the cubic volume of the room in m^3 measured as though no seats are present and A is the total sound absorption defined as:

$$A = S_T\alpha_T + S_R\alpha_R + S_N\alpha_N + \text{air absorption} \quad m^2 \qquad (8.2)$$

where S_T is the "acoustical area" in m^2 of the audience and orchestra combined (see Appendix 1 for method of determining S_T and Appendix 5 for air absorption); S_R is the remaining areas of walls, ceiling, under-balconies, and aisles not included in S_T; and S_N is the area of carpets, draperies, thin wood paneling, and added sound absorbing materials used for echo and glare control and aesthetics.

The sound absorption coefficients have different values at 125, 250, 500, 1,000, 2,000, and 4,000 Hz. Values are also sometimes given at 62.5 and 6,000 Hz. α_T is the sound absorption coefficient at each of the frequencies for the area S_T—it depends on the kind of chairs in these areas and whether they are occupied or unoccupied. At frequencies of 1,500 Hz or greater, α_T for occupied chairs is nearly independent of the type of chairs. At frequencies of 500 Hz and below, particularly at 125 and 250 Hz, α_T for occupied chairs may vary considerably with chair design (see Fig. 8.2). α_R is the average coefficient for areas S_R in all halls which have interior surfaces of either one or combinations of (a) plaster with thickness of 1.5 in. (3.8 cm) or greater, or (b) heavier materials such as plaster on concrete block, or (c) hard-wood thicknesses of 1.5 in. (3.8 cm) or greater. α_R also includes the sound absorption of usual ventilation grilles, cracks around entrance doors, and chandeliers.

Typical values of α_T, α_R, and α_N are given in Appendix 5, Table A5.7, p. 626.

Relation between RT_{mid} and V/S_T for occupied halls

In a hall where the interior surfaces meet the requirements for α_R above and there are no added acoustical materials, $S_R \alpha_R$ for an occupied hall is usually about 33% of $S_T\ \alpha_T$ at mid-frequencies. With this assumption, Eq. (8.1) becomes,

$$RT_{occup} \cong (0.16/1.33\ \alpha_{mid})(V/S_T) \quad (8.3a)$$

$$RT_{occup} \cong 0.14(V/S_T) \quad (8.3b)$$

where α_{mid} equals 0.85 (see Appendix 5).

Values for V/S_T are given in Table 5.1. To learn whether this simple formula, involving only V and S_T, predicts RT reasonably well, we plot RT_{occup} versus V/S_T in Fig. 8.3. The straight line is a plot of Eq. (8.3b).

The measured points follow the theoretical line reasonably closely up to V/S_T equal to 14. Differing amounts of residual absorption in the halls and, more important, differences in the seats certainly account for most of the scatter of the datum points.

For V/S_T between 14 and 19, the points are clustered around an RT of 1.95 sec. The likely reason for the flattening off at V/S_T = 14 is that sound absorbing materials may have been in-

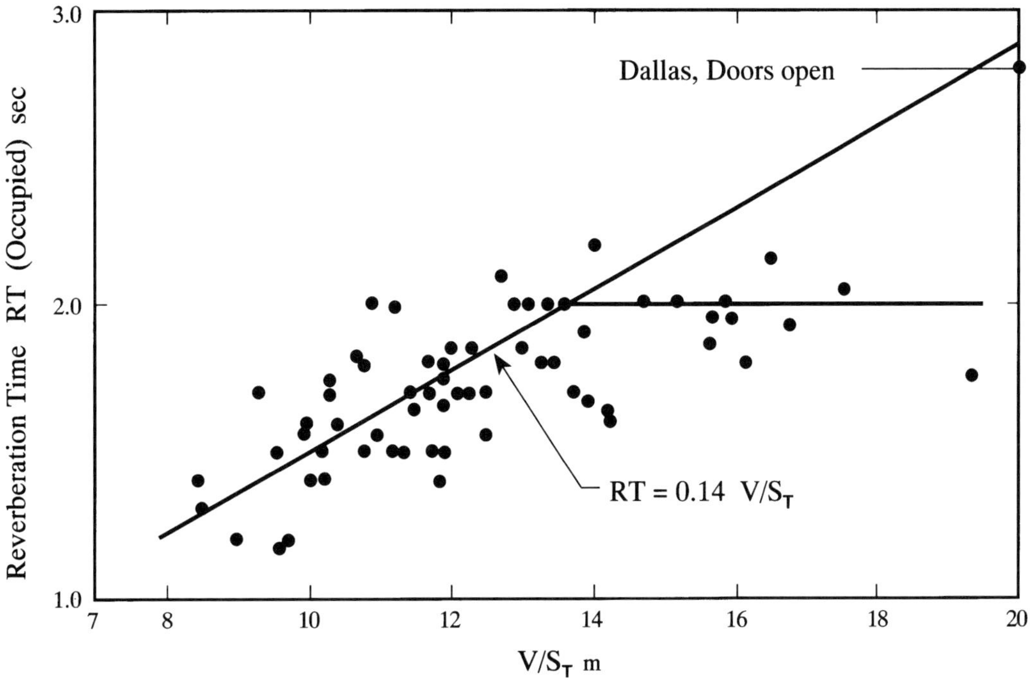

Figure 8.3. Plot of mid-frequency reverberation times in occupied concert halls versus V/S_T, where S_T is the acoustical area of a concert hall as defined in Appendix 1 and is given for each hall among the "Technical Details" that follow the descriptions of the 76 halls and opera houses in Chapter 6. V/S_T is listed for the halls in Table 5.1 The straight line is a plot of Eq. (8.3b), which assumes that the residual absorption in Sabins in a concert hall at mid-frequencies is about 25% of the audience/orchestra absorption which, in turn, is 0.93.

troduced into the halls to hold the RT near optimum or they happened that way by chance and the halls survived because of their good acoustics. The point for the Dallas hall, where the added volume is that of the reverberation chamber (no absorption exposed), yields a RT approximately equal to that of Eq. (8.3b).

Another reason the RT's do not follow the 1.4 line is that when the audience plus stage areas become a smaller part of the total volume, the values of the $S_R\alpha_R$ become larger that 33% of $S_T\alpha_T$. This is not surprising, because the residual area S_R increases with increasing volume and thus becomes more controlling in determining RT.

For greater accuracy in calculating RT, we need better data on the residual sound absorption by the walls and ceiling. For the few halls in which all surfaces were completed before seats were installed, there is enough variation in the residual absorption, particularly at frequencies of 125 and 250 Hz to make calculations hazardous (see Table A5.3, p.623).

The principal conclusion to be drawn from Fig. 8.3 is that a RT of about 2 sec can be achieved if the value of V/S_T is greater than 14 (metric units), and the residual absorption has low values.

A plot of RT versus V/N was also made to see whether the absorption of an audience is more closely related to the number of people in the audience than to the acoustical area S_T. The scatter of points was so large that any value of V/N larger than 7 would be equally likely to produce a RT between 1.6 and 2.2 sec. There were not enough halls with RTs of 1.5 sec and less, to determine whether V/N values less than 6 would predict RT better than V/S_T. This exercise removes any doubt that RT is more accurately determined from the acousitcal area S_T than the number of persons, seated over that area.

◇9◇

Loudness, Optimum Hall Size, and Design of Halls to Specification

The thrill of hearing Bach's *B-Minor Mass*, Beethoven's *Ninth Symphony*, or Mahler's *Eighth Symphony* is not only determined by the quality of the orchestra and the interpretation of the conductor, but is enhanced immeasurably by the dynamic response of the concert hall. Response means both quiet support for the pianissimo parts and majestic levels at the fortissimos. As the psychoacoustic studies of Chapter 4 disclosed, loudness may also be associated with intimacy because listeners have experienced music in small halls where the levels at climaxes may even shake the body. Owing to the need for greater box office income, halls are built larger today than a century ago. This chapter investigates the strength of the sound in current concert halls, relates those data to the interviews of professional musicians and music critics, and determines the size of concert hall that both meets the optimum RT and the optimum G_{mid}. Finally, charts are presented for enabling the designer to determine the cubic volume and number of seats in a modern hall, once the reverberation time RT and the strength factor G_{mid} have been chosen, or vice versa.

Architectural Factors Affecting Loudness

Loudness is affected by three architectural factors: The distance of the listener from the stage, the presence of surfaces for reflecting early sound energy to the audience, the area the audience sits over and the mid-frequency reverberation time.

The sound from an instrument that reaches the listener first is called the direct sound and its loudness decreases as it travels from front to rear of the hall— the greater the length of the hall, the greater the decrease.

To counteract this drop in level, special suspended panels can be installed on the side walls and the ceiling to reflect early sound energy toward the listeners. To be effective, these reflections must reach the listeners within the first 50 to 80 msec after arrival of the direct sound.

In a narrow rectangular hall, like the Musikvereinssaal in Vienna, adequate energy from early lateral reflections is achieved from the side walls alone. But in halls that must seat up to double the number of people in modern chairs, suspended panels are becoming a general solution. The 3,000 seat Segerstrom Hall of Costa Mesa, California, No. 7 in Chapter 6, is an example. It has a series of sloping panels on the upper side walls that guide sound from the orchestra to the several seating areas. The acoustical behavior of these panels is portrayed in Fig. 9.1 and by cross-hatched areas on three of the six drawings of the hall in Chapter 6.

In addition, early lateral reflections to the central seating areas come from the sides of the "trays," that is, the walls surrounding the different seating levels as shown in Fig. 9.2. This is not to say that music played in a "vineyard" type of hall will sound the same as in a small (1,500 seat) rectangular hall like the Vienna hall, but if the reflecting surfaces are properly designed the music is very beautiful.

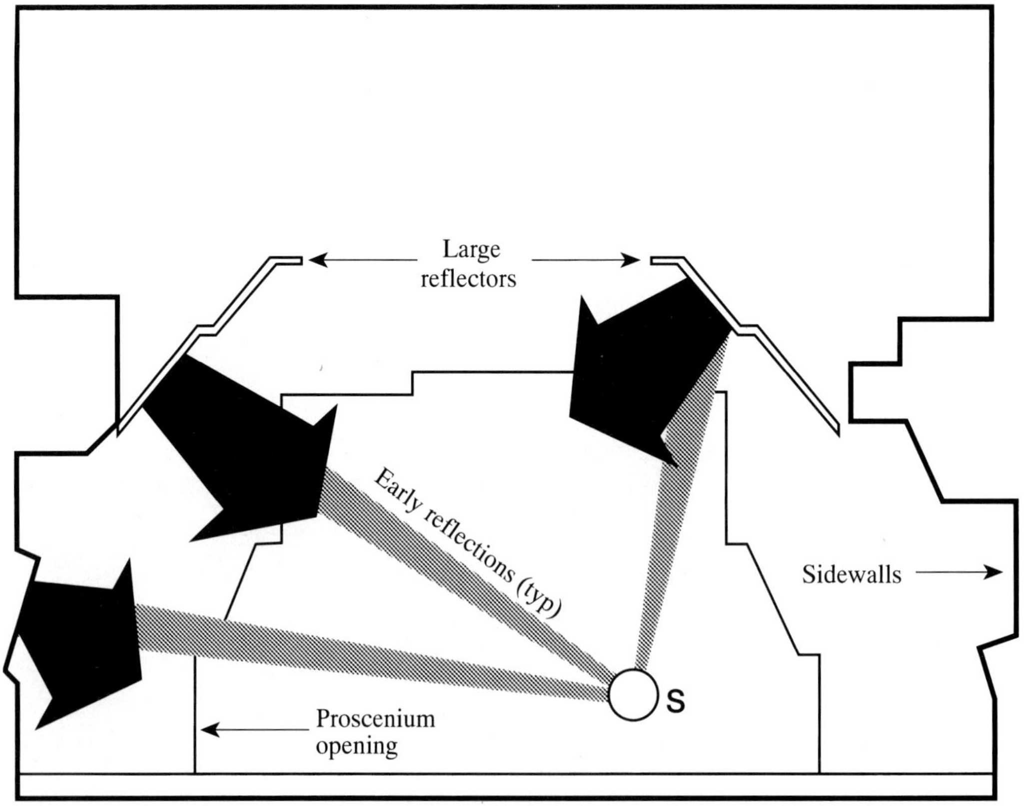

Figure 9.1. Sound radiated by the source *S* on stage in the Costa Mesa, Segerstrom Hall, travels to the tilted panels, spaced out from the wall, and is reflected to the audience areas as indicated by the black arrows.

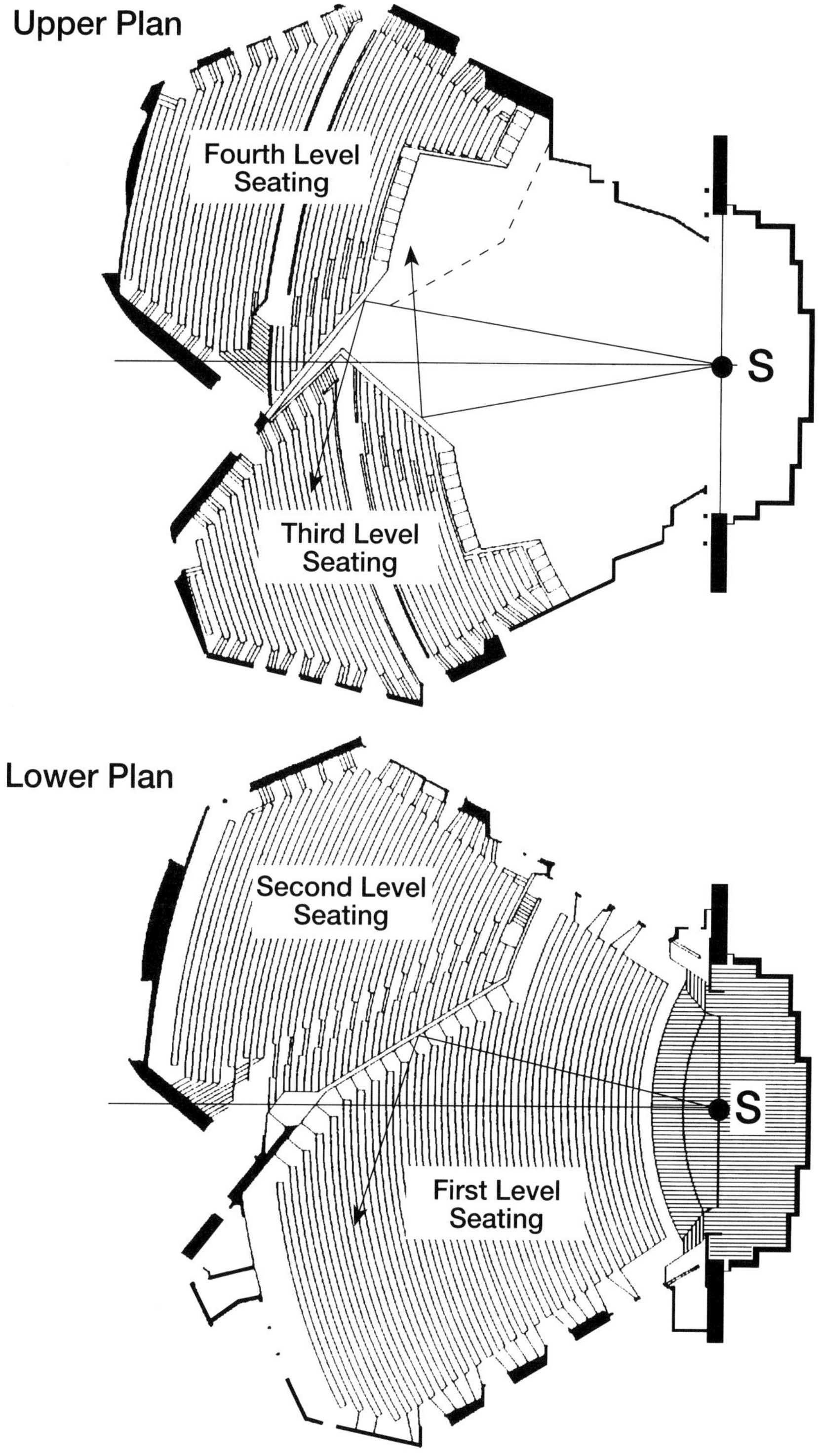

Figure 9.2. Sound reflected from the sides of the vineyard "trays" supplies early lateral reflections to the audience areas.

The third component of loudness is the ratio of reverberation time to size of the audience. The higher the reverberation time, the greater the loudness, but reverberation time must be balanced against the clarity of the music that is performed in the hall, as illustrated in Fig. 3.2, and this limits its length. Further, the larger the audience, the less musical energy is available for each person.

Figure 9.3 is a plot of the sound level as a function of the distance from the stage in the Baltimore, Meyerhoff Symphony Hall. It shows the combined effects of the decrease in level of the direct sound and its augmentation by early reflections and reverberant sound level. A decrease of 2 to 4 dB in sound level in a well designed hall of this size, 2,500 seats and RT = 2 sec, is typical.

The area occupied by the audience and the orchestra is the principal sound absorbing element in a hall and the ratio of the cubic volume of the hall to this area determines the reverberation time. The need for a large number of seats and adequate reverberation time dictates a large room volume. On the other hand, adequate loudness can only be obtained if more energy is available per person, that is if the audience size, and, hence, the volume is small. Further, only if the lateral dimensions are kept reasonably small will the early reflections be strong and will augment the loudness. The architect and the owner alone must confront this paradox. Their goal should be to limit the

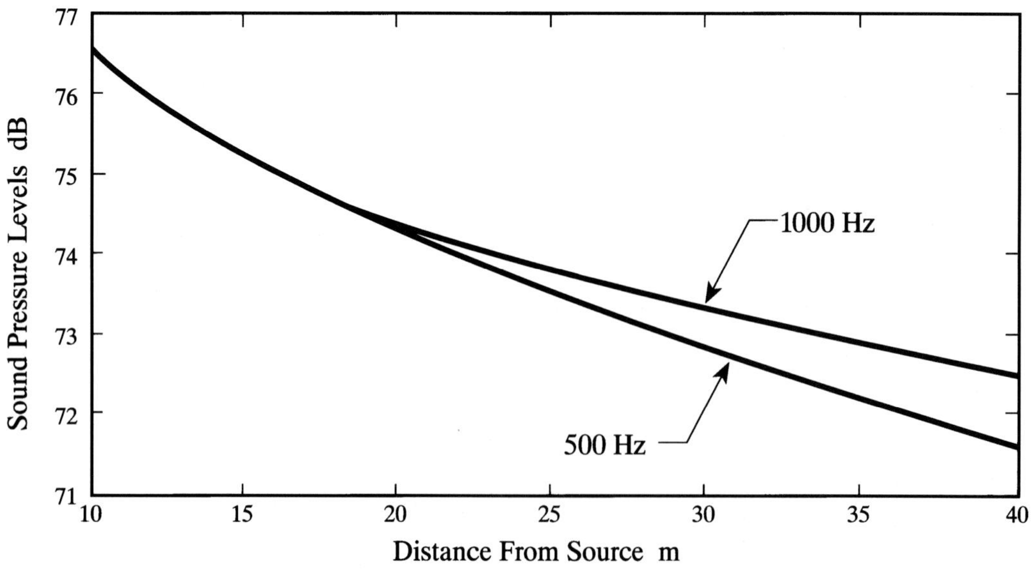

Figure 9.3. Sound pressure level measured in a typical unoccupied concert hall with upholstered seats (Meyerhoff Symphony Hall in Baltimore) as a function of the distance from the sound source on the stage to various seat positions in the audience. Under-balcony seats were avoided.

audience size as much as possible if excellent concert hall acoustics are to be achieved.

During my earlier interviews I found deep concern among conductors about the trend of acoustics in halls that had been completed in the decade before 1962. These included the Royal Festival Hall in London, Ford Auditorium in Detroit, Frederic Mann Auditorium in Tel Aviv, Queen Elizabeth Theatre in Vancouver, Liederhalle in Stuttgart, Free Trade Hall in Manchester, and the Alberta Jubilee Auditoriums in Edmonton and Calgary, Canada. Two common failings of this group were short reverberation times and large areas of thin wood on side walls. In the defense of the acoustical consultants, the literature on acoustics at that time greatly underestimated the amount of sound absorbed by an audience, particularly at low frequencies, with the result that the room volumes chosen were too small and the reverberation times came out much smaller than planned. Both the loudness and the fullness of tone suffered. This problem is not found in most halls built since 1965.

OPTIMUM VALUES OF G_{mid} IN ARCHITECTURAL DESIGN

Measured values of G_{mid}

The consensus of the various acoustic and psychoacoustic research laboratories as discussed in Chapter 4 was that the loudness of the music in a hall correlates with the measurable acoustic quantity known as the *strength factor* G *in decibels* (defined in Appendices 1 and 2). Measured values of *G* in octave bands having as their center frequencies, 125, 250, 500, 1,000, 2,000, and 4,000 Hz are available for about half of the concert halls and are given in Appendix 4. The four lowest bands are commonly split into two packages: the mid-frequency value G_{mid}, defined as the average of the measured values of *G* in the 500 and 1,000 Hz octave bands, and the low-frequency value G_{low}, defined as the average of the values of *G* in the 125 and 250 Hz bands.

The loudness is determined primarily by the value of G_{mid}. The value at low frequencies, G_{low}, is also vitally important as discussed in the previous chapter, because it affects the strength of the bass and it significantly influences the sensation of spaciousness as is discussed in the next chapter. The quantity *G* was found in the psychoacoustic studies to be among the half-dozen most important acoustical attributes of a concert hall.

The measurements of G were obtained by various laboratories in the USA, Canada, and abroad that used at least three different methods of calibrating the dodecahedran loudspeaker generally used as a sound source. It is discovered, now that the data are in hand, that the measurements of the Takenaka Research and Development Institute of Chiba, Japan, with whom I have worked closely for over six years and who have supplied much of the data for this study, differ by about 1.2 dB from those of the Western laboratories. Parenthetically, a difference of a decibel is not large as measurements of sound level go.

The method used for calibrating the Takenaka dodecahedran loudspeaker utilizes a reverberation chamber. However, in this chapter it is necessary that I make some arbitrary adjustment of the data from the various laboratories so that I can combine them to derive preferred values.

In this chapter and Chapter 8 only, the Takenaka data are lowered in magnitude by 0.6 dB and the data of the other laboratories are raised by 0.6 dB so that they can be plotted on one graph. These values are called "compromise* G*'s."

The original measured data tabulated in Appendix 4 for all laboratories are unchanged. When a world standard for calibration of the sound source used for this measurement is established, this problem will disappear and old data can be corrected accordingly.

All available measured values of compromise G_{mid} and G_{low} are recorded in Table 8.6 of the previous chapter.

An important compilation of the G_{mid}'s for 38 concert halls is presented in Fig. 9.4. The vertical scale is EDT/V (multiplied by a million), where V is the volume of the hall measured in cubic meters and EDT is the early decay time in sec, averaged for the 500 and 1,000 Hz octave bands. The horizontal axis is compromise G_{mid} in decibels.

Theory says that the value of G should be proportional to the reverberation time and inversely proportional to the cubic volume of the hall. This means that G_{mid} should rise by 3 dB for each doubling of EDT/V and indeed it does as shown by the straight line on the graph, the first time this correlation has been published. EDT was chosen rather than RT (unoccupied) because it is not as sensitive to varying sound absorptions of different types of chairs.

No reason can be given as to why the compromise G_{mid} values for the Toronto, Berlin Philharmonie, and Costa Mesa halls are about 1.5 dB higher than the theoretical line or why the two Canadian and the Salt Lake halls are about the same amount below.

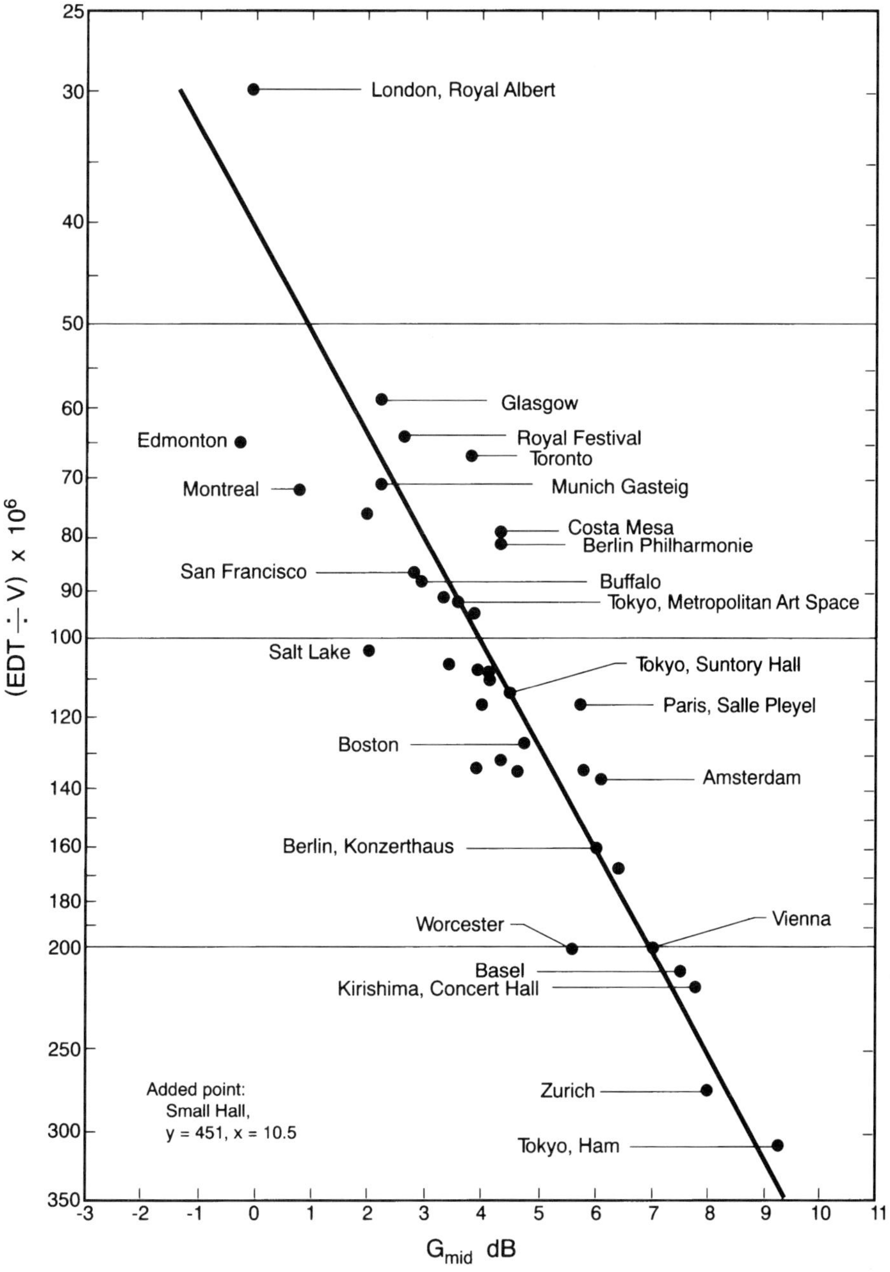

Figure 9.4. Measured mid-frequency strength factor (compromise) G_{mid} for 38 halls plotted as a function of the ratio of early decay time to the cubic volume of the hall (EDT/V) multiplied by a million. EDT is measured in seconds and V is measured in cubic meters. Data were obtained from different laboratories and are adjusted to bring differences owing to their methods of calibration of the source into agreement for this chapter only. The measurements were made at 8 to 20 positions and often for three source positions on stage and the data were averaged to distill a hall-average value for each point. Compromise G_{mid} is explained in the text.

From this graph, it appears that the bulk of the halls being built today have G_{mid} values equal to 3.5 dB plus or minus 1.5 dB (compromise numbers).

DESIGN VALUE FOR G_{mid}

A number of the professionals interviewed said that for large orchestral presentations, the music in the Basel, Zurich, Vienna, and Berlin (Konzerthaus) halls is often overpowering. For those halls, the values of compromise G_{mid} lie between 6 and 8 dB. The Tokyo (Hamarikyu) hall does not have a stage large enough for a full sized orchestra. In some listeners' opinion, Amsterdam, at 5.4 dB, just borders on the overpowering side.

The observations above suggest that for optimum loudness in a concert hall the compromise G_{mid} value should lie in the range of 4 to 5.5 dB. From Fig. 9.4 this means a range of EDT/*V* (times a million) of 100 to 145. Because, as shown in Table 8.1, on average the unoccupied EDT values in modern halls are about 1.1 times the occupied RT values, the equivalent values for RT/*V* (times a million) is 90 to 130. Translated to the particular measuring laboratories, this compromise G_{mid} = 4 to 5.5 dB is equivalent to: Canadian and European calibration of sound sources, G_{mid} = 3.5 to 5 dB; and Japanese calibration of sound source, G_{mid} = 4.5 to 6 dB.

THE OPTIMUM CONCERT HALL SIZE

If, in design, the dual specification of RT (occupied) at mid-frequencies and the strength factor G_{mid} has been chosen, then the size of audience and the cubic volume of the concert hall are automatically determined. (Formulas and examples are given in a technical section at the end of this chapter.)

For the non-technical reader, the graphs of Figs. 9.5 and 9.6 can be used to relate these specified quantities to the cubic volume of the hall, the number of persons that can be seated in the hall and the acoustical area S_T over which they and the orchestra are seated.

But let us divert for a moment to understand S_T. In Appendix 1 acoustical area S_T is defined as $S_T = S_A + S_o$, where S_A is the acoustical area of the audience and S_o is the area of the stage (unless it is so large that the orchestra does not fill it, in which case the area the orchestra sits over is used.)

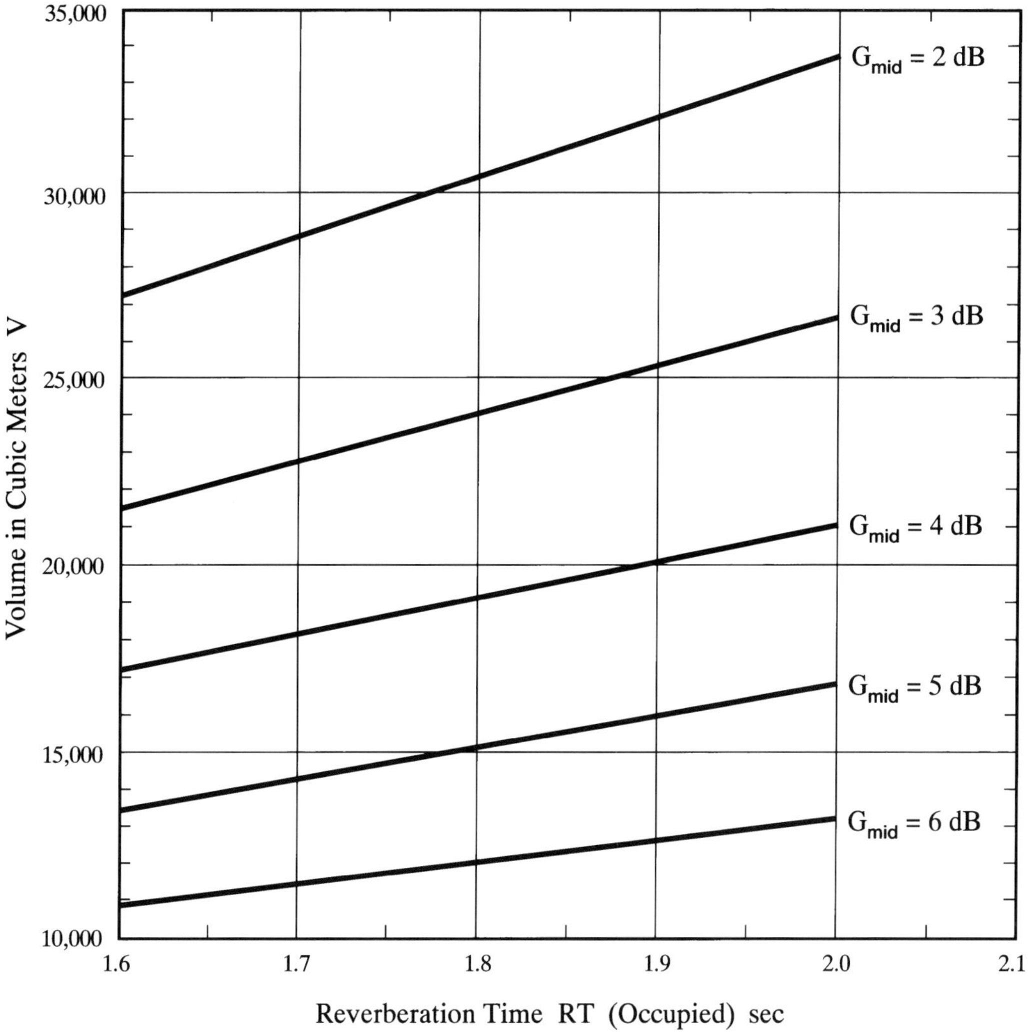

Figure 9.5. Computational chart for determining the volume of a concert hall when the (a) occupied, mid-frequency RT and (b) unoccupied, mid-frequency strength-factor compromise G_{mid} are specified. Compromise G_{mid} is explained in the text.

The acoustical area S_A is also defined in Appendix 1. Approximately, it assumes that the acoustical area of the audience is 0.5 m larger on all sides than the actual area over which it sits. For example, if the actual area S_a of the audience seated in two equal blocks in a hall is twice 20 × 25 m, equal to 1,000 m^2, the acoustical area S_A is twice 21 × 26 m or 1,092 m^2. If the orchestra stage has an area S_o equal to 190 m^2, S_T equals 1,282 m^2.

Fortunately, the last column of Table 5.1 in Chapter 5 simplifies all this by giving the ratio of seats per unit S_T, that is it gives the quantity N/S_T. So, if the design charts

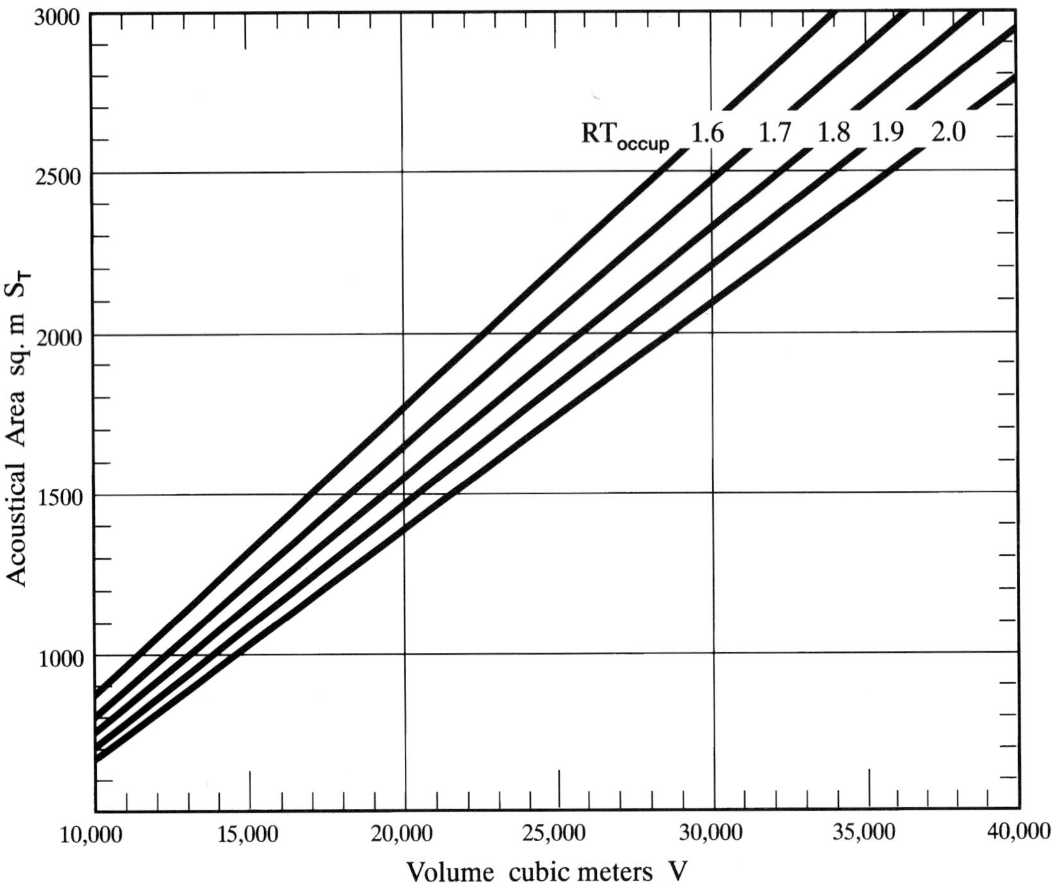

Figure 9.6. Computational chart for determining the acoustical area of a concert hall when the occupied, mid-frequency RT and the volume of the hall are known. Actually, the equations show that the acoustical area S_T can be found from knowledge of the strength factor G_{mid} alone with the intervention of Fig. 9.4.

are set up in terms of S_T directly, we can get the number of persons seated in the hall by multiplying it by N/S_T. For example, if we take from Table 5.1 a value for $N/S_T = 1.45$, typical for modern halls seating 2,000 to 2,800 persons, we would find that an area S_T = 1,282 m^2 would mean that the hall would seat about 1,860 persons.

Now, let us used the charts of Figs. 9.5 and 9.6 to determine the number of seats and the cubic volume of a hall that is being planned. [Alternatively, use Fig. 9.4 to obtain (EDT/V) $\times 10^6$ and Eq. (9.7) for S_T and Eq. (9.8) for V.] Assume that the owner asks for optimum values of RT and G_{mid}, say 2.0 sec and 5 dB. From Fig. 9.5 we find that the volume will be 16,900 m^3 and from Fig. 9.6 that S_T will equal 1,185 m^2. Multiplying this by N/S_T = 1.45 tells us that the hall will hold N = 1,718 seats, not a very large number. Yet it helps explain why some of the older halls like the Grosser Musikvereinssaal which seats 1,680 and has a reverberation time 2 sec has been so successful.

We can only increase the number of seats by specifying a lower value of G_{mid}, say 3.5 dB. And, if the owner wants to keep the volume low, let us accept a reverberation time of 1.8 sec. From Figs. 9.5 and 9.6, we get V = 22,000 m^3, S_T = 1,711 m^2, and N = 2,480. If the volume can be increased to make RT equal to 1.9 sec, it would need to be 23,220 m^3.

It must be emphasized again, that Eq. (9.7) below and the paragraph that follows, reveals that the area S_T *is determined solely by* G_{mid}. *Setting RT after choosing* G_{mid} *and, hence,* S_T *determines the volume of the hall [from Eq. (9.8)].*

TECHNICAL SECTION FOR SPECIALISTS

The development here is to show that when the reverberation time RT and the level at mid-frequencies G_{mid} are specified, the volume V and the acoustical area S_T of the hall are automatically determined. Then, when the seating density is known, the number of seats is determined.

From the technical section at the end of the previous chapter, we saw that, approximately,

$$RT_{occup} \approx 0.14(V/S_T). \tag{9.1}$$

The assumptions made there to get an equation this simple were that the average audience and orchestra absorption coefficient at mid-frequencies is 0.85 and that the total sound absorption by the audience and orchestra is 75% of the entire sound absorption for the hall.

Equation (9.1) can be recast as,

$$(RT \times 10^6/V) = (0.14/S_T) \times 10^6 \tag{9.2}$$

or,

$$(EDT\times10^6/V) = (EDT/RT)(0.14/S_T) \times 10^6 \tag{9.3}$$

and,

$$S_T = 0.14(EDT/RT)(EDT \times 10^6/V)^{-1} \times 10^6 \tag{9.4}$$

obviously,

$$N = S_T(N/S_T). \tag{9.5}$$

From Eq. (9.1),

$$V = (RT/0.14)S_T. \tag{9.6}$$

Preparation of charts:

From Table 5.1, we see that for modern halls the average ratio EDT/RT is about 1.1. Other values can be chosen as seems suitable by comparison with the halls listed. With the value of 1.1,

$$S_T = 0.154(EDT\ \ 10^6/V)^{-1} \times 10^6. \tag{9.7}$$

This equation says that once the value of G_{mid} is selected, we can go to Fig. 9.4, find the value of (EDT × 10^6/V). Division of 0.154 by it and multiplication by a million yields the acoustical audience area S_T. Note that this takes place without any mention of RT.

From Table 5.1 we can select a seating density by comparison with other halls. For modern halls, the density (N/S_T) is about 1.45. Multiplying S_T by 1.45 yields N, the number of seats.

Finally, once the reverberation time RT, occupied, is chosen, we can calculate the volume V from Eq. (9.1),

$$V = (RT_{occup} S_T)/0.14. \qquad (9.8)$$

Figures 9.5 and 9.6 are made up from Eqs. (9.6), (9.7), and (9.8) with the strength factor G_{mid} and RT_{occup} as parameters.

Design examples

Assume the optimum values of RT = 1.9 sec and G_{mid} = 5 dB (the compromise value of this chapter), (EDT/RT) = 1.1, and seating density N/S_T = 1.45. From the equations or the charts, we find,

Using Fig. 9.4,

$$EDT \times 10^6/V = 130.$$

From Eq. (9.7),

$$S_T = 1{,}185 \text{ m}^2.$$

From Eq. (9.8),

$$V = 16{,}080 \text{ m}^3.$$

From N/S_T = 1.45,

$$N = 1{,}718.$$

This is a rather low seat count, but it is for an ideal hall with modern seating.

It was stated earlier that the average G_{mid} for modern halls, from Fig. 9.4, is 3.5 dB, which gives $(EDT \times 10^6 / V)$= 90. With this one change, we obtain,

$$S_T = 1{,}711 \text{ m}^2,$$

$$V = 23{,}200 \text{ m}^3,$$

$$N = 2{,}480.$$

Reduction of the reverberation time alone does not gain audience area. Equation (9.7) shows that S_T is determined entirely from Fig. 9.4 and only G_{mid} shows on that figure. Once G_{mid}, and hence S_T, are determined, Fig. 9.6 shows that reducing RT permits reduction of the volume of the hall.

The reverberation equation (9.1) indicates that if the volume is held constant, S_T can be increased by decreasing RT. But doing this, also decreases G_{mid}, which is why only it appears in Eq. (9.7) (through the intervention of Fig. 9.4).

10

DIFFUSION AND SURFACE IRREGULARITIES

Concert music sounds better to a listener when the early sound is mellow and the origin of the reverberant sound seems to arrive from many directions—from the sides, from overhead, as well as from in front.

Many of the finest concert halls in the world—often halls built in the nineteenth century, in Amsterdam, Boston, Vienna, Berlin (Konzerthaus), Leipzig, Cleveland, Basel, and Zurich—have coffers, beams or curved surfaces on the ceiling and columns, niches, irregular boxes, and statues on the side walls. In addition, the surfaces of these halls often have fine-scale ornamentation. These irregularities and ornamentation "diffuse" the sound when reflected and give the music a mellow tone.

There are two ways in which diffusion can affect the listener's enjoyment of music—that associated with the early sound and that associated with the reverberant sound.

DIFFUSION: EARLY SOUND

If one listens to music in a rectangular hall with flat side walls, the sound takes on a brittle or hard or harsh sound, analogous to optical glare, sometimes called frequency coloration. Such a harsh sound was heard in the upper balcony of the original New York Philharmonic Hall, because the principal early lateral reflections came from smooth plaster side walls.

In an experiment conducted in the hall before it opened, a canvas cloth was hung from the ceiling above the second balcony rail facing the stage. The canvas, which weighed about 0.9 kg per m^2 (2 lbs/ft^2), did not extend the full width of the balcony front, and there was a large space between the cloth and the ceiling. It appeared to have no effect on the reverberant sound. A group of people went into the balcony and listened behind the cloth as the orchestra repeated a piece that the listeners had just judged to have acoustic glare. The music behind the cloth was unbelievably mellow and beautiful. The glare had completely disappeared.

The reason for the improvement was that the canvas "rolled off" the high frequencies, decreasing their strength gradually starting at about 1,000 Hz and continuing to higher frequencies. This roll-off decreases the levels in the higher frequencies just as they are decreased when traveling through the air, because of the natural absorption of sound by the air molecules. The reverberation times also decrease at the higher frequencies due to this phenomena (see Chapter 8, "Brilliance"). It is seen from Fig.10.1, that the early reflections behind the canvas (solid line), merged naturally into the reverberant sound (dashed line), both having the same slope.

Acoustic glare is observed in many modern halls because of their smooth walls and lack of ornamentation. The currently accepted corrections for glare on surfaces that reflect early sound are fine-scale irregularities or QRD or MLS reflectors or very thin layers of acoustical absorbing material (see Carnegie Hall, No. 13, Chapter 6).

QRD REFLECTORS

QRD reflectors are a design of irregular flat surfaces for the purpose of creating diffusion of the sound on reflection (Schroeder, 1986). The basic shape is shown in Fig. 10.2 (courtesy, RPG Diffusor Systems). It consists of a series of parallel "wells" of varying depths. These wells are strips in a panel that could, for example, be 2 ft (0.6 m)

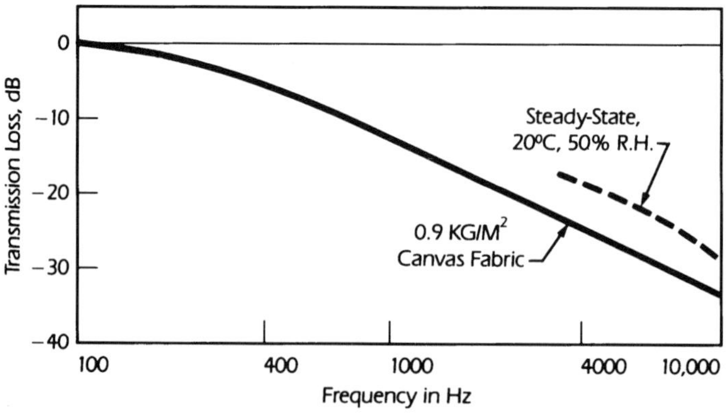

Figure 10.1. These curves demonstrate the reason that the acoustic glare caused by smooth side walls in a concert hall was eliminated by interposing a canvas fabric sheet between the listeners and the direction of the reflected sound wave. The solid curve shows the "roll-off," i.e., the decrease, in high-frequency energy (in decibels) that was transmitted through a canvas fabric sheet in comparison with the shape of the curve of energy level in the reverberant sound field. A modified form of this roll-off can be achieved by cementing a thin layer (0.25 in., 0.64 cm) of felt to a "glarey" flat surface.

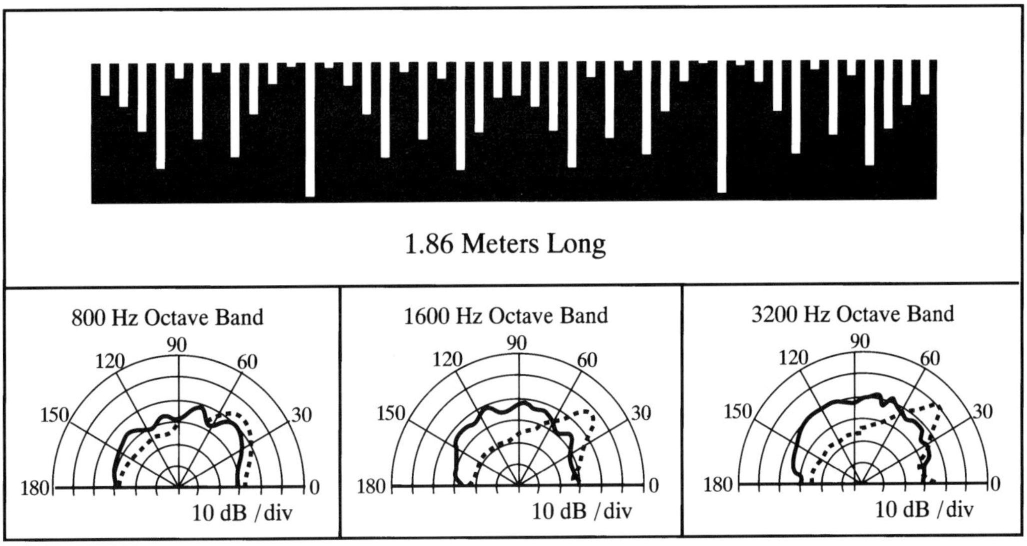

Figure 10.2. Structure and performance of a QRD diffuser. The unit is about 4.85 ft (1.48 m) wide, 5 ft long and 9 in. deep. The lower graphs show the diffusion patterns at 800, 1,600 and 3,200 Hz, as measured in octave bands. The reason for the unusual frequencies for the bands is that the measurements were made at one-fifth full scale, which requires test bands with mid-frequencies of 4,000, 8,000 and 16,000 Hz.

wide, 4 ft (1.22 m) long and 9 in. (23 cm) deep. The panel shown in the figure is about 9.4 in. (0.24 m) deep and 4.85 ft wide (two sections in width).

The diffusion pattern for this panel is also shown in Fig. 10.2. The radii of the circles on the graphs are separated 10 dB from each other. At 3,200 Hz, the right-hand graph, it is shown that when a sound wave incident at 135 degrees (arriving from the upper left) strikes the horizontal QRD surface (at the center point of the circles) the QRD reflects sound energy off, as shown by the solid curve, in almost equal intensity at all angles between 30 degrees and 150 degrees. In other words it diffuses the incident wave. The dotted curve shows that if the wave were incident instead on a smooth flat panel, also at 135 degrees, almost all the energy would be reflected at 45 degrees only (angle of reflection equal to the angle of incidence). Comparison of the dotted line with the solid line reveals that the energy reflected from the flat panel at 45 degrees would be 10 to 14 dB greater than that from the QRD panel.

The highest frequency at which diffusion can take place is determined by the width of the wells in the QRD diffuser and the lowest is determined by the depth of the cells—16 in. (41 cm) being about the greatest practical depth.

A set of QRD diffusers at the back of a concert hall stage is shown in one of the photographs of the Baltimore Meyerhoff Symphony Hall (Chapter 6, No. 1). QRD diffusers were also used at the sides and rear of the stage of the renovated Davies Hall in San Francisco. (Chapter 6, No. 18). The purpose in both cases is to spread the sound on stage so that the musicians hear each other's music better.

The negative side of the QRD diffusers is that they absorb sound at low frequencies and therefore cannot be used in large areas in a hall unless specially designed to reduce the sound absorption as much as possible. The manufacturers supply both the diffusion patterns and the sound absorption data on request.

MLS DIFFUSERS

Maximum sequence length (MLS) diffusers are a special variation on QRD diffusers. They absorb less sound at low frequencies and, hence, greater areas of them can be used in a concert hall. One design, installed in 1994 on the side walls of Salle Pléyel in Paris, is shown in Fig. 10.3. It is about 2.6 ft (0.8 m) long and 2.5 in. (6 cm) deep. Of course, the irregular piece shown would be repeated many times along a wall.

WALL IRREGULARITIES TO REDUCE ACOUSTIC GLARE AND ECHO

To reduce acoustic glare caused by flat side walls or flat suspended panels, irregularities of the order of 1 in. (2.5 cm) may be used embossed into the surface. Two

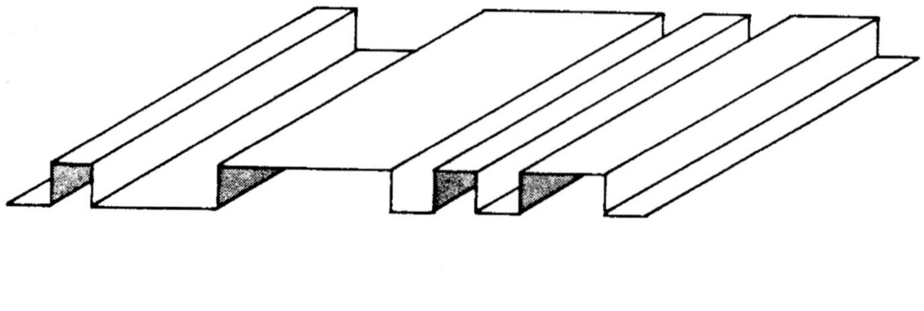

Figure 10.3. A diffuse reflecting panel designed according to the MLS theory. This panel was used on the side wall reflectors of the Salle Pléyel Hall in Paris. (See Hall No. 36 of Chapter 6.)

designs, made by the Takenaka R & D Institute, for main-floor side wall and overhead canopy treatment are shown in Figs. 10.4 and 10.5, respectively. In those cases, the diffusion starts at about 1,000 Hz and reaches a maximum of about 8 dB at about 5,000 Hz. Another application for a QRD is to reduce echo. An example is found on the rear wall of the main floor of Carnegie Hall (see the Chapter 6, No. 13). The rear wall of the main floor previously returned a disturbing echo to the musicians and the audience sitting in the front rows of the main floor. The Carnegie QRD is 38 ft (5.53 m) long, 5.8 ft (1.7 m) high, and 6 in. (15 cm) deep. Its design was tailored to reduce low frequency sound absorption. In addition, because of the wide-angle diffusion of the sound, the rear-main floor audience receives an improvement in listener envelopment (LEV), an acoustical attribute that is discussed in the next chapter.

DIFFUSION: REVERBERANT SOUND

The acoustical quality of the reverberant sound depends on the degree of diffusion imparted to the sound waves by irregularities and ornamentation on the ceiling and walls and by adequate space in the upper rear part of a hall to permit full formation of reverberation. Diffusion of the reverberant sound is sensed, in large part, by whether the reverberant sound arrives at the listener's position from all directions. No standardized test has been developed for judging reverberant diffusion even though there is general agreement that it is important.

An attempt has been made in this study to relate reverberant sound diffusion to the interaural cross-correlation coefficient $IACC_L$, determined at a listener's position for the time interval beginning 80 msec after arrival of the direct sound and ending about 1 sec after that arrival. It was averaged over the three octave bands, 500, 1,000, and 2,000 Hz, and called $IACC_{L3}$. The results of this exercise are presented in the last

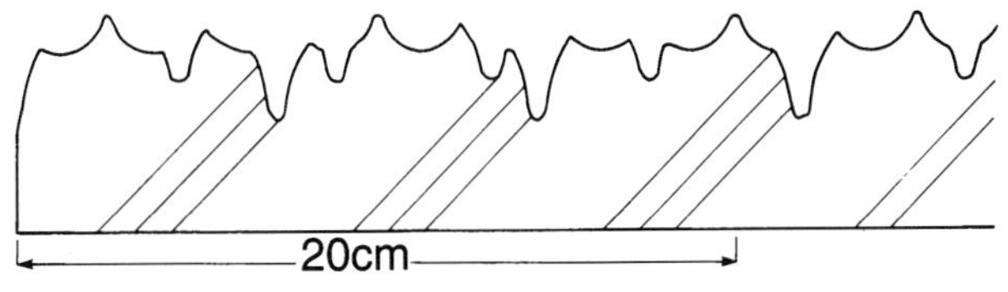

Figure 10.4. Corrugations molded into the surface of the below-balcony side walls in the Hamarikyu Asahi Hall in Tokyo. The corrugations run vertically. Diffusion begins at about 1,000 Hz and reaches a maximum at 4,000 Hz.

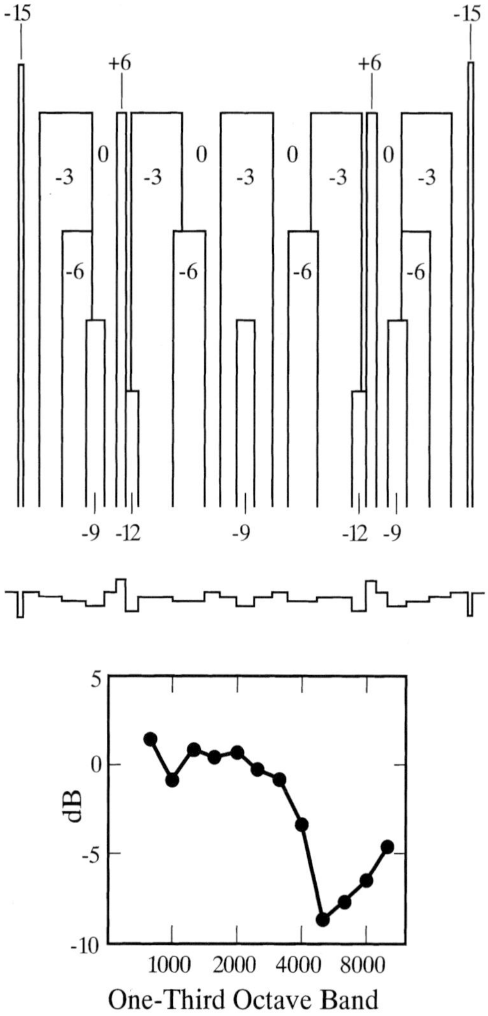

Figure 10.5. A diffusing surface designed by laboratory experiments for a concert hall in construction in Japan. The corrugations run right to left on a hung canopy, located at the top and on the audience side of the proscenium, designed to send diffuse reflections to a main-floor audience area. The diffusion is about the same as that for the corrugations of Fig. 10.3. The graph shows the attenuation in dB of the sound wave for 135° incidence and measurement at 45°.

section of Chapter 11 and Table 11.3. In summary, in all halls, *which were unoccupied when* $IACC_{L3}$ *was measured,* values of (1–$IACC_{L3}$) were between 0.84 and 0.9 (on a scale of 0 to 1.0), except for the Buffalo Kleinhans Music Hall, where it had a value of 0.72. Thus, (1–$IACC_{L3}$), *when determined in unoccupied halls,* seems only able to distinguish halls with poor diffusivity from all others. It is important that the usefulness of $IACC_{L3}$ as a measure of diffusivity be investigated in occupied halls before discarding it.

DIFFUSION: AN OVERALL VISUAL RATING

A recent study (Haan and Fricke, 1993) relates the acoustical quality of a concert hall to visual inspection, from photographs and drawings, of the degree of surface irregularities on the sidewalls and ceiling. They call the amount of surface irregularities "degree of diffusivity." They refine their method by assigning weightings to the irregularities in a hall by giving greater weightings to areas with a higher diffusivity versus those with lower diffusivity.

The criteria they used for categorization of the diffusivity of the surfaces are immediately below (names of a few halls as they rated them follow). Their classification is worded for the ceiling, but was translated to the side walls:

High Diffusivity

Coffered or checker-designed with deep recesses or deep beams
[greater than 4 in. (10 cm) in depth]
or random diffusing elements over the full area of the ceiling
(greater than 2 in. in depth)
and all of the area must not embody any sound absorbing materials.

Medium diffusivity

Angled array of broken surfaces
or ornamentally decorative treatment applied with shallow recesses
[less than 2 in. (5 cm) in depth]
or flat concrete surfaces behind a semi-acoustically transparent screen with mostly reflective materials.

Low diffusivity

Large separate paneling
or smoothly curved surface
or large flat and smooth surface
or semi-acoustically transparent mesh metal screen
or heavy absorptive treatment applied.

Examples of halls visually judged to have these three levels of diffusivity are:

1. **High diffusivity**: Vienna Grosser Musikvereinssaal and Boston Symphony Hall (coffered ceiling, statues, niches and ornamentation on sidewalls), Bonn Beethoven Hall (specially designed ceiling for random diffusion and diffusing panels on the side walls), Salzburg Festspielhaus (special geometrical construction on ceiling and walls meeting the description)

2. **Medium diffusivity**: Chicago Orchestra Hall (ceiling with shallow beams and decorative treatment and sidewalls with some niches and decorative treatment); Copenhagen Tivoli Koncertsal (angled broken surfaces of ceiling and saw-tooth walls with flat surfaces), Munich Herkulessalle (smooth upper walls and surrounding passageways on main floor), Berlin Philharmonie Hall (diffusing elements on the ceiling and seats surrounded by many smooth balcony fronts of the "vineyard" seating blocks)

3. **Low diffusivity**: Detroit Ford Auditorium (large flat surface for ceiling and walls— see Beranek 1962 for drawings and photographs as the hall no longer exists), Sender Freies Berlin Hall (acoustically semi-transparent mesh screen with high ceiling above—see Beranek 1962), Bristol Colston Hall (continuous array of separate paneling attached on sidewalls and smoothly curved ceiling with absorptive treatment).

Haan and Fricke assigned a numerical rating to each degree of diffusivity: "high" equals 1.0; "medium" equals 0.5; and "low" equals 0. They then weighted the diffusivity of each surface, for example, if a ceiling had a total area of 3,200 m^2 and 1,000 m^2 of it was smooth and the remainder deeply coffered, it would be rated "$0 \times 1{,}000 + 1 \times 2{,}200$" = 2,200 area points." This number would be added to the area points for the sidewalls (end walls neglected) and divided by the total area of the ceiling and sidewall surfaces to get a diffusivity rating for the hall. A hall like the Vienna Musikvereinssaal received an overall rating of 0.96. At the other extreme, the London Barbican Hall received a rating of only 0.23.

They then correlated their diffusivity rating with their subjective ratings of acoustical quality that were derived from self-administered questionnaires (Appendix 3). This comparison led to the surprising conclusion, "*Surface diffusivity appears to be largely responsible for the difference between halls which are rated as excellent as opposed to those rated as good or mediocre.*"

This sentence is overly inclusive. Surface diffusivity plays an important role in determining the quality of a hall, but it says nothing about early lateral reflections, reverberation time, loudness and bass response, other prime reasons why excellent halls distinguish themselves from mediocre ones.

An explanation for the conclusion that diffusivity appears so prominent may lie in the fact that acousticians from the time of Wallace Sabine (1900) have recognized that tone quality is improved by irregularities on the walls and ceiling. Thus, every carefully designed concert hall has surface irregularities, and those halls without them generally have other deficiencies, such as too low reverberation times, insufficient loudness (too low a ceiling), no lateral reflections and too short initial-time-delay gap (fan or round or oval shape without special panels to satisfy those requirements).

The Haan/Fricke study drives home the importance of sound diffusion in a concert hall even though there is as yet no satisfactory objective measurement of its effectiveness. When designing a concert hall, architects and acousticians should devote major attention to the provision of adequate irregularities, both large scale and small on walls and ceilings. Diffusivity is an architectural feature that must not be underestimated.

◇11◇ SPACIOUSNESS

INTRODUCTION

Before 1962, the only physical measure of acoustical quality in a concert hall or an opera house was determination of reverberation times at low, middle, and high frequencies. Reverberation, though unmeasured before 1900, has always played an important part in the composition of symphonic pieces, particularly in the periods when composers plied their profession with a single hall in mind. Conductors probably always adapted their interpretations to the acoustical ambience of a performing space. Recent studies, as presented in Chapter 8, have affirmed the importance of reverberation times in room acoustics, but only as one of several acoustical parameters that together determine the acoustical quality of a concert hall.

Two big acoustical surprises came to the fore in the last thirty years, one the importance of a short initial-time-delay gap and the other, the existence of spatial impression. These two acoustical parameters are defined in Chapter 3 in the section headed, "Important Indicators of Acoustical Quality," with sub-sections "Intimacy: (initial-time-delay gap t_I)" and "Spaciousness: (apparent source width ASW and listener envelopment LEV)."

It was observed in 1959 (Johnson *et al.*,1961) that an array of panels hung in the forward part of a very wide, fan-shaped hall, the Tanglewood Koussevitzky Music Shed, upgraded its acoustics rating from an unimpressive B to an exciting A. The music became more intimate, clearer and louder. The concept was tried again in the Aula Magna in Caracas, Venezuela, another wide fan-shaped hall, with acknowledged success. The purpose of these panels is to reflect early sound to the listener, greatly reducing the initial-time-delay gap t_I, and increasing the loudness without affecting the reverberation times. It appeared for a time that t_I was the most important single measure of acoustical quality in concert halls (Beranek, 1962). But there were skeptics who said that "something in addition must explain why narrow rectangular halls are so successful and fan-shaped halls often are not." This led to the concept of spaciousness.

APPARENT SOURCE WIDTH

The early development of spaciousness is covered in Chapter 4 under the section: "Marshall and Barron's Studies." The essence of their discovery was the concept of apparent source width ASW, the more important sub-parameter of spaciousness. ASW arose from the observation that in a narrow rectangular hall, the early sound reflections arrive at a listener's position from the side walls, that is, laterally. Such reflections appear to broaden the source and impart body and fullness to the music. Although spaciousness comes automatically in narrow rectangular halls, architects do not wish to be bound to that shape when designing concert halls.

Marshall had an opportunity to test the hypothesis that lateral reflections might make a non-rectangular hall almost as good acoustically as a shoebox-shaped hall, when he advised the architect for the proposed Christchurch Town Hall in New Zealand to install large panels in an elliptically shaped hall. These panels are mounted on the upper side walls and skewed to direct early sound laterally to the listeners (see Hall No. 71, Chapter 6). The hall is successful and has received international attention.

INTERAURAL CROSS-CORRELATION COEFFICIENT IACC

Mindful that people listen with two ears, Schroeder *et al.* (1974) proposed a *binaural* measure for assessing acoustical quality in a concert hall. This measure, in part, determines the relative energy in the early lateral reflections. The procedure makes use of two tiny microphones mounted at the outer ear canals of a person or a dummy head. The electrical outputs of these microphones are connected (usually by an intermediate sound recording) to a computer which determines a mathematical quantity, the *interaural cross-correlation coefficient* (IACC). (The equation is in Appendix 2.)

The IACC is a measure of the difference in the sounds arriving at the two ears at any instant. A sound wave arriving to a listener laterally will enter one ear earlier than the other, and also, because of the intervening head, the character of the sound will be somewhat different at the two ears. If the sounds at the ears were to be completely different, the value of (1–IACC) will be 1.0, meaning that the correlation between the sounds at the two ears is zero. At the other extreme, a sound wave that arrives from straight ahead will engage the two ears alike (perfect correlation) and the value of (1– IACC) will take on the value of 0.0, meaning no spatial impression. In concert halls, the values lie in between.

The concept of IACC was studied in some depth by Ando in a highly refined electronically simulated concert-hall environment. His conclusion (Ando, 1985) was that IACC is one of four orthogonal (statistically independent) measures of acoustical quality in concert halls, the other three being RT, G, and t_I. RT and G have been discussed in detail in previous chapters and t_I is treated in Chapter 12.

DEVELOPMENT OF IACC AS A SENSITIVE MEASURE OF CONCERT HALL QUALITY

In order to place emphasis on *early* lateral reflections, the measurements of IACC values are separated into two parts. The first part is the value obtained when only the sounds arriving at a listener's position within 80 msec after the direct sound are considered. It is called $IACC_E$, where "E" means early. The second part is the value obtained when the sounds in the period after 80 msec (up to 1 or 2 sec) is considered, labeled $IACC_L$, where "L" means late. The early part measures the difference between the form and intensity of early lateral reflections at the ears of a listener and the later part the difference between the reverberant sounds at the two ears. The measurement of IACC for the complete time interval from 0 to 1 or 2 sec is labeled here as $IACC_A$.

Is there a psycho-physical basis for IACC?

Potter (1993) investigated the physical parameters influencing the perceptual attributes of spaciousness (image broadening) in order to establish a relation between psycho-acoustic measures and room acoustics. His research was founded on the physiologically derived Central Spectrum theory for binaural hearing and led to a quantity called central modulation coefficient (CMC). Without going into details here, he showed a high degree of correlation between subjective judgments, made by a group of listeners, of the apparent source width ASW of binaural recordings made in the front and rear parts of eight concert halls and (1) the psycho-physical parameter (1–CMC) and (2) the objectively measured attribute (1–$IACC_A$) at the same positions. He concludes that his studies establish a link between room acoustics and psychological acoustics and provide a psycho-physical basis for the use of the IACC.

Bands of equal importance to spaciousness

The interaural cross-correlation coefficient is usually measured in six octave-frequency bands at each of eight or more positions in a hall, and often for three source positions on stage. An average of measured values for all seat locations and source positions is made. The next step toward making it a useful tool for judging the acoustical quality of a concert hall is to ascertain which of the six frequency bands are of most importance.

Okano *et al.* (1994), in a laboratory experiment, asked listeners to judge when the apparent source widths, ASWs, for individual octave bands of symphonic music, played in different simulated concert-hall environments, sounded alike. The simulated sound consisted of the direct sound and from two to eleven early reflections as well as the subsequent reverberation.

It was found that four of the six frequency bands are equally important in determinations of ASW for different concert-hall conditions, namely, the 500, 1,000, 2,000, and 4,000 Hz bands. However, the loudness of symphonic music in the 4,000 Hz band is considerably less than that in the other three bands, so that the most sensitive formulation of IACC is to eliminate that band. This leads to $IACC_{E3}$ and $IACC_{L3}$.

> $IACC_{E3}$ is defined as the average of the measured $IACC_E$'s for the three octave frequency bands with center frequencies of 500, 1,000, and 2,000 Hz. This quantity is expected to correlate with the more important component of spaciousness, the "apparent source width ASW."
>
> $IACC_{L3}$ is defined as the average of the measured $IACC_L$'s for the same three octave frequency bands. This quantity is expected to correlate with the second component of spaciousness, "listener envelopment LEV." At least it should correlate with the state of diffusion of the reverberant sound in the room.

IS IACC AN ORTHOGONAL ACOUSTICAL ATTRIBUTE?

It is important to know, before proceeding further, whether the various objective measurements, including at least, IACC, G, RT, and t_I, are orthogonal, that is to say, statistically independent of each other. Mathematically a correlation matrix among these and other common measures was set up that involved the various physical measures to determine whether they are statistically independent. It was found that for medium to high values of (1–$IACC_{E3}$), $IACC_{E3}$ and $IACC_{L3}$ are orthogonal to (low correlation with) reverberation time RT, early decay time EDT, early to reverberant sound energy ratio C_{80}, and initial-time-delay gap t_I. There is a some correlation with G because increasing the intensity of the early reflections both increases $IACC_E$ and G. However, the correlation is low enough and listeners seem able to separate loudness from spaciousness in real halls adequately, that neither can be a surrogate for the other.

Where (1–$IACC_{E3}$) is low, $IACC_{E3}$ correlates to a minor extent with all the other measures except the initial-time-delay gap. Ando (1985) also found little correlation between $IACC_A$ and these other measures.

As would be expected, $IACC_{E3}$ (0 to 80 msec, three band average) and $IACC_A$ (0 to 1 sec, and wide band) are highly correlated. Either could be used to compare with concert hall quality, except that $IACC_{E3}$ is a much more sensitive measure, with approximately double the spread of values for the range of concert halls that rank between A+ and C.

INTERAURAL CROSS-CORRELATION COEFFICIENTS AND THE CONCERT HALL RATINGS

Subjective ratings for 53 halls are given in Table 5.2 of Chapter 5. Values of $IACC_E$ in six frequency bands for 35 of these halls are given in Appendix 4. We note that data for all the different acoustical measures in Appendix 4 are for unoccupied halls except reverberation time RT and bass ratio BR which are for occupied halls.

Correction for unupholsted seating

When attempting to compare the values of $IACC_{E3}$ measured in unoccupied halls with the quality ratings of Chapter 5 that apply to occupied halls, there is a troublesome factor. All halls do not have upholstered seats. Sound traveling over rows of chairs, when unoccupied, will reach the measuring positions differently if the seats are not upholstered (or very lightly upholstered) than if fully upholstered. The direct wave from the source in an unupholstered seating area is augmented by diffracted waves from the (unoccupied) chairs surrounding the measurement position. Because the object of this chapter is to draw conclusions as to architectural design from the results, and because nearly all modern halls use some form of upholstered chairs, a correction factor is needed to make the data from halls with unupholstered chairs comparable to the others.

By comparison of measurements on upholstered and unupholstered chairs, correction of the (1–$IACC_{E3}$) values for the unupholstered halls were determined as follows: Vienna (+0.07), Amsterdam (+0.08), Basel (+0.02), Berlin (Konzerthaus) (+0.02), and Zurich (+0.07) (Hidaka *et al.*, 1995). These corrections are present in the data that follow, but not in the data tabulated in Appendix 4.

Ratings for the concert halls and associated values of (1–$IACC_{E3}$)

In Table 11.1, a comparison is made of the six categories of concert hall acoustical quality taken from Table 5.1 and the measured values of (1–$IACC_{E3}$) for 18 halls for which both ratings and these data are available.

The ratings have the following meanings: A+ means "Superior;" A means "Excellent," B+ means "Good to Excellent," B means "Good," C+ means "Fair to Good," and C means "Fair." There are no poor halls in this study. As before, the names of the halls in Category B+ are not given to avoid damaging the reputations of halls, all of which are the homes of very good orchestras and are liked by their regular audiences.

The tabulations of Table 11.1, and the measured values of (1–$IACC_{E3}$), are plotted in Figure 11.1 and a summary of the data is shown in Table 11.2.

Because of the small number of halls in all categories except B+, they are combined into three groups: Group (A+, A); Group B+; and Group (B, C+). The two very large halls, the Royal Albert Hall and the Tanglewood Koussevitzky Music Shed, are treated *sui generis*. The Tanglewood Shed is discussed in Chapter 17 in the section, "Design of stages for concert halls," and in the last section below, "Comment and caution."

Analysis of (1–$IACC_{E3}$)

Table 11.2 and Fig. 11.1 clearly demonstrate that this measure separates the measured data into three groups with no overlap, and that the separation is the same as that found from the subjective ratings. That is to say, the sequence along the bottom axis of Fig. 11.1 is in accordance with the rank orderings deduced from the interviews the author made of professional listeners.

We see that the median value of Group 1 is 0.66; that of Group 2 is 0.56; and Group 3 is 0.42. Overall, the spread of the data is large, from 0.41 to 0.71. This confirms that the steps taken to choose the most sensitive octave bands (500, 1,000, and 2,000 Hz) and to consider only the early reflections (prior to 80 msec after the

Table 11.1. Hall Averaged $IACC_{E3}$'s and LF_{E4}'s for which ratings and data exits. The values of ($1-IACC_{E3}$) for five halls are corrected as described in the text. The subjective ratings are based on interviews. The halls in the A+, A, B+ categories are the homes of excellent orchestras and the local audiences are, in general, satisfied with their sound. Takenaka Research Institute data are used where available, augumented through the courtesy of the National Research Council of Canada, A. C. Gade and Sandy Brown Associates. All LF data are from NRC, Barron and Gade. In each category the halls are listed alphabetically.

	City and Name of Hall or House	($1-IACC_{E3}$) 0.5/1/2 kHz bands With Corrections Unoccupied	LF_{E4} 0.125/0.25/0.5/1 kHz Bands Unoccupied	No. of Seats	Volume in Cubic Meters
Category A+, "Superior"					
A+	Amsterdam, Concertgebouw	0.62	0.18	2,037	18,780
A+	Boston, Symphony Hall	0.65	0.20	2,625	18,750
A+	Vienna, Gr. Musikvereinssaal	0.71	0.17	1,680	15,000
Category A "Excellent"					
A	Basel, Stadt-Casino	0.64	-	1,448	10,500
A	Berlin, Konzerthaus (Schauspiel)	0.66	-	1,575	15,000
A	Cardiff, Wales, St. David's Hall	-	0.17	1,952	22,000
A	Costa Mesa, Segerstrom Hall**	0.62	0.23	2,903	27,800
A	Tokyo, Hamarikyo Asahi Hall	0.70	-	552	5,800
A	Zurich, Grosser Tonhallesaal	0.71	-	1,546	11,400
Category B+ "Good to Excellent"		**Halls for Which ($1-IACC_{E3}$) Exist**	**Halls for Which LF_{E4} Exist**		
Number of Halls		7	15		
Range of Values		0.46 to 0.61	0.11 to 0.20		
	Median Value	0.55	0.16		
Category B "Good"					
B	Edmonton, Alberta Jubilee Aud.	-	0.13	2,678	21,500
B	Montreal, Salle Wilfrid-Pelletier*	-	0.12	2,982	26,500
B	San Francisco, Davies Hall*	0.44	-	2,743	24,070
B	Tel Aviv, F. R. Mann Auditorium	0.41	-	2,715	21,240
Category C+ "Fair to Good"					
C+	Buffalo, Kleinhans Music Hall*	0.41	0.10	2,839	18,240
C+	London, Barbican Lrg Concert Hall*	-	0.12	2,026	17,750
Category C "Fair"					
C	London, Royal Albert Hall	-	0.14	5,080	86,660

* Before renovations either recently completed, underway or in planning, designed to improve the acoustics.

** Costa Mesa Segestrom Hall is included in the A group because it was at the top of Group B+. Its only deficiency is an RT_{mid} = 1.6 sec. However, its EDT ranked equal to the other Group (A +, A) halls with upholstered seats, it had a high strength factor G_{mid} and no other deficiencies. No IACC data are available on NewYork, Carnegie Hall, which is rated "A."

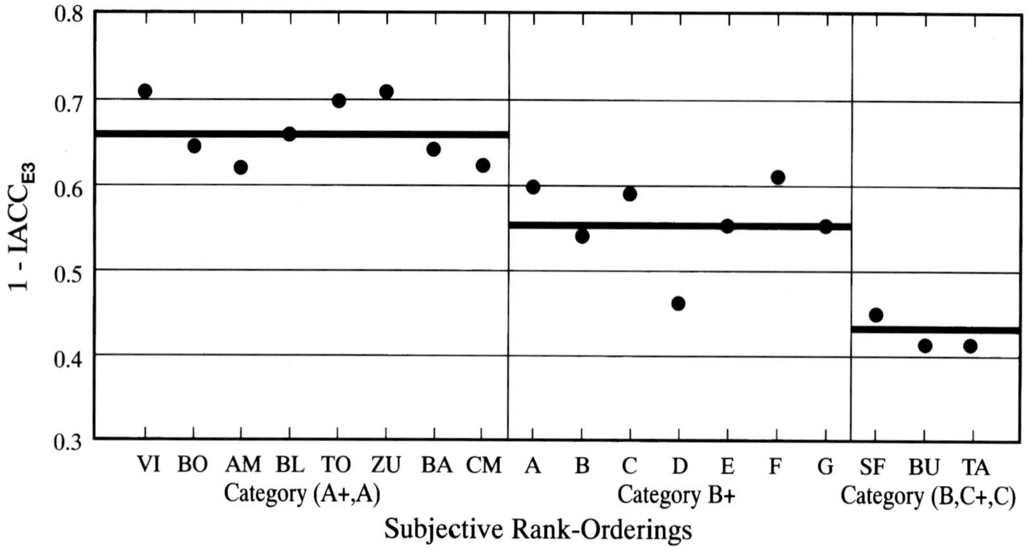

Figure 11.1. Plot of (1–$IACC_{E3}$) data from Table 11.1 against subjective rank ordering of all halls for which such data are available. The initials on the x-axis go with the names of the cities listed for the (1–$IACC_{E3}$) ratings in Table11.1, except that the halls in Category B+ are not identified.

direct sound arrives at a measuring position) were choices that provide clear separation of the three categories of subjective ratings.

In a separate study, shown in Fig. 11.2, $IACC_{E3}$ data taken by the Takenaka R & D Institute in 13 halls were used to determine statistically whether they, at the 95% confidence level, fall into one measurement category. Data from one laboratory only were chosen in order to eliminate possible differences in calibration or measurement procedures. We see that the $IACC_{E3}$ values for the 13 halls shown are well separated and fall

Table 11.2. Relation between the subjective rating categories of Table 5.1 and the medians and ranges of the unoccupied-hall values of the quantities listed in Table 11.1 for 34 concert halls for which IACC and LF data are available.

	(1–$IACC_{E3}$)	LF_{E4}
Groups A+, A	**0.66**	**0.18**
Range	0.62 to 0.71	0.17 to 0.23
Group B+	**0.55**	**0.16**
Range	0.46 to 0.61	0.11 to 0.20
Groups B, C+	**0.41**	**0.12**
Range	0.41 to 0.44	0.10 to 0.14

Note: Costa Mesa is counted in Group B+.

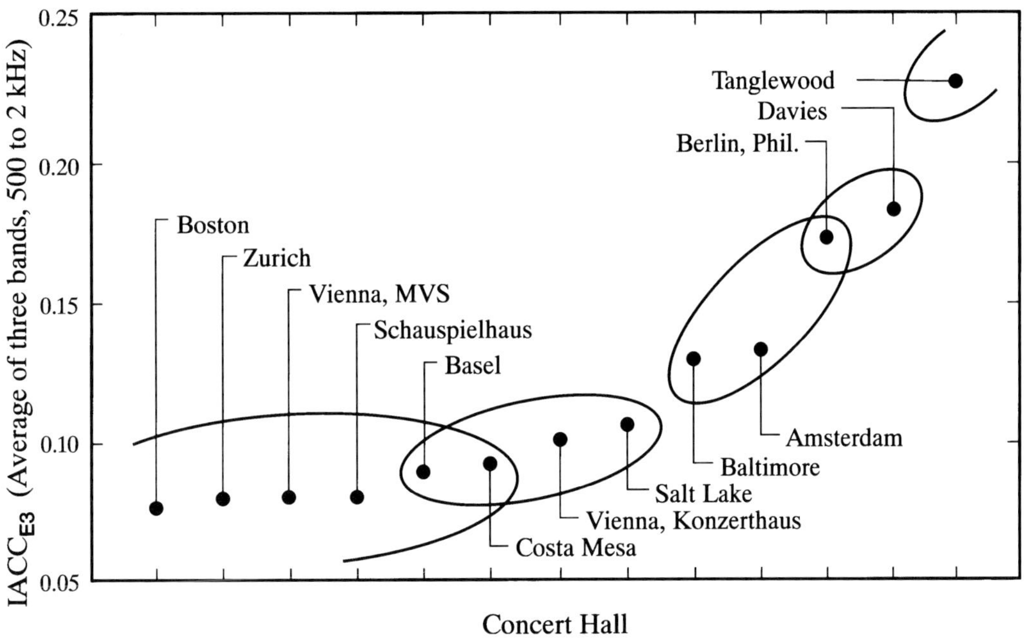

Figure 11.2. Ovals showing 95% statistical confidence that the halls fall within the ovals shown for the 9 to 20 measurements of $IACC_{E3}$ made in each hall. All data were taken by the Tachenaka R & D Institute to avoid mixing measurement techniques and calibrations. All halls within one oval statistically fall into one measurement category. As seen, of the 13 halls, only three overlap.

into five groups. All halls within one oval should statistically fall into one measurement category. Even though the groupings on this graph bear no intended relation to the subjective rating groups of Table 11.2, they follow closely, except in the case of Amsterdam (no corrections for unupholstered seats were made in Fig. 11.3, which explains, at least in part, why Amsterdam does not fall in the first or second loop). As stated above, the Tanglewood Shed is discussed in Chapter 17.

The conclusion to be drawn is that ($1-IACC_{E3}$), even when determined from measurements made in unoccupied halls, is a good measurement tool to use along with other acoustical measures to evaluate the musical quality of concert halls at regular concerts when occupied.

LATERAL FRACTION AND THE CONCERT HALL RATINGS

To measure ASW objectively, Barron and Marshall (1981) devised a two microphone method to determine the relative strength of the energy in the lateral reflections.

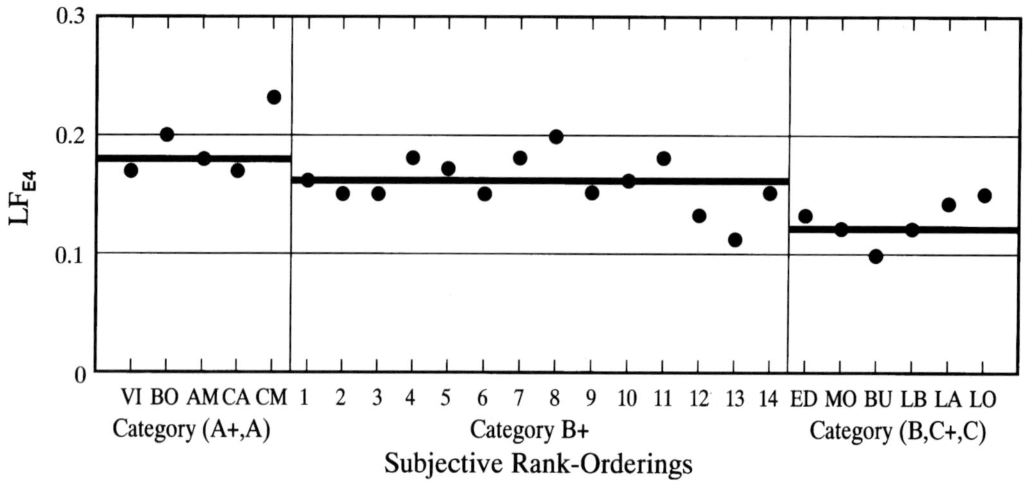

Figure 11.3. Plot of LF_{E2} data from Table 11.1 against subjective rank ordering of all halls for which data are available. The initials on the x-axis go with the names of the cities listed for the LF ratings in Table 11.1, except that the halls in Category B+ are not identified.

The lateral part of the energy is measured by a figure-eight microphone, which does not respond to sound traveling from the direction of the source. The overall energy is measured by an ordinary non-directional microphone. The ratio of the output of the former to that of the latter is call the lateral fraction (LF). It must be noted that it is a *monoraural* measure.

Measurements of LF_{E4} measured and averaged in the four frequency bands 125, 250, 500, and 1000 Hz, exist for 25 of the 53 halls for which subjective ratings are given in Table 5.1 of Chapter 5, based on interviews. These data were taken almost entirely by Bradley (1994) and Barron (1993).

As seen from Fig. 11.3 and Table 11.2, LF_{E4} is a different story from $(1–IACC_{E3})$. The median values of LF_{E4} for the first two rating categories are almost the same, 0.18 and 0.16. Because the values of LF_{E4} spread over a narrow range and the standard deviation is about half the mean value, it appears that it is not a suitable mechanism for dividing a set of concert halls into several groups, regardless of what the groups might correlate with.

This statement is further bolstered by the statistical analysis of Fig. 11.4. Using only LF_{E4} data measured by one laboratory, the NRC of Canada, the same statistical test of separability of 13 concert halls was made as in Fig. 11.2 and is shown in Fig. 11.4. From a 95% statistical confidence level, 10 of the 13 halls listed fall into one measurement category and there is massive overlap.

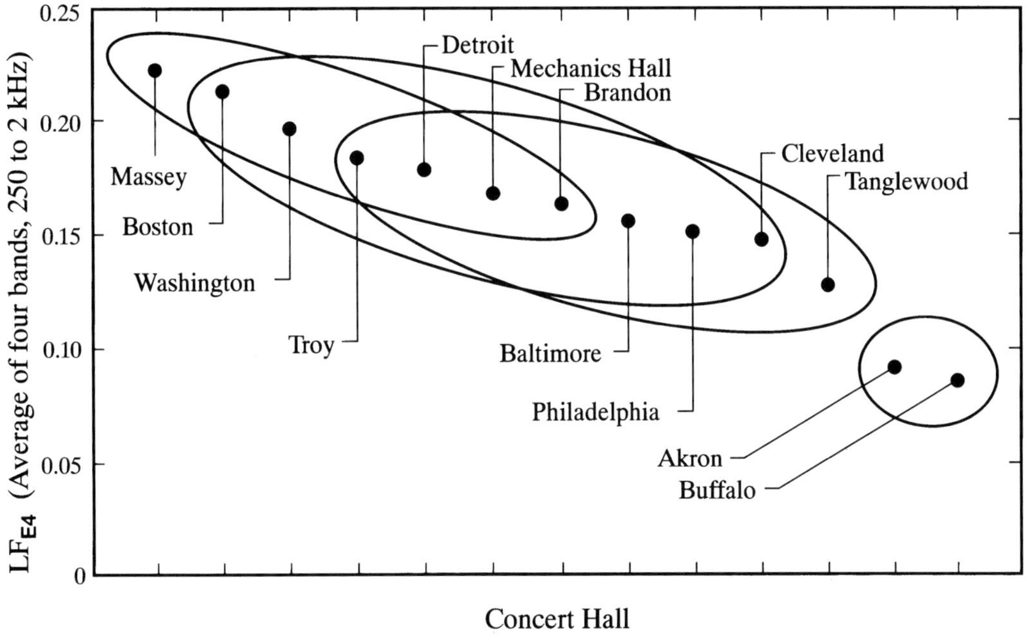

Figure 11.4. Ovals showing 95% statistical confidence that the halls fall within the ovals shown for the 8 to 20 measurements of LF_{E4} made in each hall. All data were taken by the National Research Council of Canada, Acoustics Division, to avoid mixing measurement techniques and calibrations. All halls within one oval statistically fall into one measurement category. Of the 13 halls shown, only two do not overlap and the values for those two indicate very little energy in the early lateral reflections.

There is an acceptable separation between the first group (Excellent) and the third group (Fair to Good). The range of values for those two groups do not overlap, even though the complete set of data for the two groups extends only over a range of 0.10 to 0.23, as compared to the range for $(1–IACC_{E3})$ of 0.41 to 0.71. The LF_{E4} data for Group B+ almost completely overlap the data for both Groups (A+, A) and (B, C+).

Analysis of LF_{E4}

The data of Table 11.2 and Fig. 11.2 clearly show that LF_{E4} is not a suitable measure for separating unoccupied concert halls into levels of acoustical quality as judged for halls at regular concerts. The loops of Fig. 11.4 indicate that the halls effectively fall into one grouping and thus have no relation to the rating categories or any other subdivision into groups except for two halls out of the 13. However, before discounting LF_{E4}'s effectiveness completely, the same kind of data as for these unoccupied halls should be taken in a range of halls of varying acoustical quality at regular concerts and determine whether it is better at separating them into rating groups when the halls are fully occupied.

$IACC_{L3}$ AS A MEASURE OF LISTENER ENVELOPMENT

In Chapters 2 and 3 *listener envelopment* was defined as the subjective impression of being enveloped by the reverberant sound in a hall or opera house (reverberant sound being considered as that sound arriving at a listener's ears 80 or more msec after arrival of the direct sound). We shall now investigate whether $IACC_{L3}$ is able at least to identify the degree of sound diffusion that exists in a concert hall. Diffusion in a sound field means that the sound waves arrive simultaneously from all directions at the position of the listener.

We were not able to derive a scale of subjective judgments of envelopment from the interviews, so $IACC_{L3}$ as a measurement must be evaluated only on whether it tends to separate the halls into different groups in the manner of $IACC_{E3}$.

Table 11.3 is a tabulation of $IACC_{L3}$ for the average of the 500, 1,000, and 2,000 Hz bands as was measured in 18 concert halls all for which such data exist.

Table 11.3. Tabulation of all available $IACC_{L3}$ data in the 250 through 2,000 Hz bands for the concert halls in the acoustical-quality, category groups (A+, A); (B+); (B, C+).

	Number of Seats	Cubic Volume m^3	$IACC_{L3}$ Unoccupied 0.5/1/2 kHz	$(1–IACC_{L3})$ Unoccupied 0.5/1/2 kHz
Group (A+, A) "Excellent"				
Amsterdam, Concertgebouw	2,037	18,780	0.12	0.88
Basel, Stadt-Casino	1,448	10,500	0.11	0.89
Berlin, Konzerthaus (Schauspielhaus)	1,575	15,000	0.13	0.87
Boston, Symphony Hall	2,625	18,750	0.14	0.86
Costa Mesa, Segerstrom Hall	2,903	27,800	0.13	0.87
Tokyo, Hamarikyu Asahi	552	5,800	0.16	0.84
Vienna, Grosser Musikvereinssaal	1,680	15,000	0.11	0.89
Zurich, Grosser Tonhallesaal	1,546	11,400	0.10	0.90
Median $IACC_{L3}$			0.12	0.88
Group B+ "Very Good to Excellent"				
Number of Halls:		7		
Range of $IACC_{L3}$, Avg. of 0.5,1,2 kHz			0.12 to 0.22	0.88 to 0.78
Median $IACC_{L3}$			0.13	0.87
Group B, C+ "Good"				
Buffalo, Kleinhans Music Hall*	2,839	18,240	0.28	0.72
San Francisco, Davies Hall*	2,743	24,070	0.12	0.88
Tel Aviv, Mann Auditorium	2,715	21,240	0.15	0.85
Median $IACC_{L3}$			0.15	0.85

For Group (A+, A) the median value of (1–$IACC_{L3}$) is 0.88, for Group B+ (7 halls), 0.87 and for Group (B,C+), 0.85. These median values are very little different. Also, the spread in values in all three groups overlap.

One hall stands out from the others, the Buffalo, Kleinhans Hall. For it, (1–$IACC_{L3}$) at 500/1,000/2,000 Hz is 0.72. The latter value is much lower than that for any other hall, indicating a low value of diffusion of the sound field. Kleinhans is the only hall with a minimum of irregularities on the walls or ceiling and the reverberation time is short, both factors that influence negatively the diffusion of the sound field.

One must conclude from this small sampling that (1–$IACC_{L3}$) as a measure of sound diffusion and, hence, envelopment, is not sensitive to the level of differences found in the rather good concert halls of this study, although it can separate a hall with poor diffusion from the others. As stated in Chapter 10, it is important that the usefulness of (1–$IACC_{L3}$) as a measure of diffusivity be investigated in occupied halls before discarding it.

CONTRIBUTION OF LOW FREQUENCY SOUND STRENGTH TO ASW

The interaural cross-correlation coefficient is not a measure of changes in ASW at low frequencies. Though there is considerable discussion about the nature of binaural hearing at low frequencies, particularly as related to concert hall music, it seems obvious that when the wavelengths of sound are long compared to the distance between the human ears, the sounds at the two eardrums will be almost identical. Tests show that (1–IACC), which is a measure of that difference, becomes very small at frequencies below about 300 Hz. Further, using only that part of the sound spectrum above 300 Hz, it correlates well with subjective evaluations of concert hall quality.

The obvious question is, "In what way do low frequency sounds contribute to apparent source width ASW, if at all, and how should that contribution be measured?" Keet was first to show that ASW increases when the overall level of music increases. He did not determine whether level changes at any particular part of the frequency spectrum was responsible for most of the ASW change.

Okano *et al.* (1994) set up an experiment, using symphonic music as the source for the subjective judgments, designed to determine how changes in levels of different parts of the spectrum affect ASW. In the experiment, the levels were increased or decreased at frequencies below 355 Hz, while holding the levels constant at frequencies above and ASW was judged. Also, the reverse situation was investigated, how is ASW affected by changes in levels at frequencies above that cut-off, holding the levels constant at lower frequencies.

The experiments showed that ASW widens by about 2 degrees for each decibel change in low frequency level (below 355 Hz)—the level at higher frequencies held constant. The change in ASW when the levels at high frequencies was varied, holding the low-frequency level constant, was 0.6 degree for each decibel change.

Unfortunately, the differences from one hall to another of G_{low} minus G_{mid}, as reported in Table 8.6 of Chapter 8, amount to only a few decibels, the average difference among the 35 halls for which data were available is only 0.9 dB. An ASW change of a couple degrees caused by low frequency sound level differences is miniscule in comparison with the variation in ASW at higher frequencies as measured by $(1–IACC_{E3})$. The spread in $(1–IACC_{E3})$ from the least liked concert halls to the best liked, is from 0.4 to 0.7. That difference corresponds to a change in ASW of about 15 degrees.

More puzzling is the evidence of Tables 8.7 and 8.8 that among those halls with the largest differences between G_{low} and G_{mid} are several halls that are rated in the interviews as "very good to superior" acoustically. Conversely, the lowest rated halls exhibited no greater differences between G_{low} and G_{mid} than those rated in the higher rating categories.

It appears at this writing that G_{low} minus G_{mid} is not a satisfactory measure of acoustical quality. The bass ratio BR remains the only known acoustical attribute concerned with low frequencies that correlates reasonably well with concert hall quality. Parenthetically, sound strength at mid frequencies, G_{mid}, is an important acoustical attribute as was shown in Chapter 9.

COMMENT AND CAUTION

The study reported here shows that the direction set by Schroeder and Ando, who chose IACC as one of several orthogonal objective parameters that might correlate with the quality of orchestral music heard in concert halls, was correct. Because $(1–IACC_{E3})$ so clearly separates the 18 halls of Fig. 11.1 into three groups which coincide with the subjective ratings from intervies, it qualifies as one of the most significant physical attributes for judging the acoustical quality of occupied concert halls. However, its relative importance will be better assessed when it is combined in Chapter 15 with the five other acoustical attributes for predicting the category rankings of those halls for which full data are available.

But a strong word of caution—although it alone of the known six satistically independent acoustical attributes has clearly separated the halls of Fig. 11.1 in the same groups as the interview ratings, it fails to predict the subjective ratings of two halls. These halls are the Lenox, Tanglewood Music Shed, and the Berlin Philharmonie Hall. For the Tanglewood Music Shed the value of $(1–IACC_{E3})$ is 0.37 and for the Berlin Philharmonie it is 0.46—sufficiently low to put them both in rating Group (B, C+, C) if one were to believe only Fig. 11.1

In the front 60% of Tanglewood (which seats over 5,000 and in which the rear and a large part of the side walls are open to the outdoors), there is no doubt that the sound is in the A class. In fact, I sat recently with one internationally famous musician whose opinion I respect who said that, although a little different, the front part of Tanglewood is equal to Boston Symphony Hall in acoustical quality. This is partly due to the reverberation time which at mid-frequencis is 1.9 sec and at 500 Hz is 2.1 sec; the strength factor G_{mid} which in that part of the hall is 4.9 dB and the Bass Ratio BR which is 1.45, or compared to 500 Hz is 1.29. Also, its Surface Diffusivity Factor is 0.8 and the initial-time-delay gap is 19 msec. In the calculation scheme that follows in Chapter 15, these six numbers 0.46, 2.1 sec, 4.9 dB, 1.45, 0.8, and 19 msec, place it in the B+ group, but not in the A group. In the Berlin Philharmonie, these six numbers are 0.56, 1.95 sec, 4.6 dB, 1.0, 0.8, and 21 msec also place it in the B+ group. In Chapter 15, the values are chosen for the first 2/3 of the hall's seating. With these numbers the Berlin Philharmonic is calculated as A and Tanglewood as the highest hall in category B^+.

In both cases, if one limits his subjective appraisal to the seats in the front half of the hall facing the normal front of the stage, the halls subjectively are very good. This would indicate that the calculation scheme of Chapter 15 is not as good at estimating the acoustical rating of wide-spread halls (wide fan shape or vineyard surround) as it is in estimating the quality of more conventional halls. Certainly ratings for them derived from Fig. 11.1 alone would be faulty.

◇12◇

Clarity, Intimacy, and Texture

The three subjective parameters clarity, intimacy, and texture are difficult to define and more difficult to relate to physical measurements.

The easiest one to discuss is clarity because it is related in an inverse way to reverberation time in all but a few halls, for example, Costa Mesa, Dallas, and Birmingham. We have already introduced clarity (definition) and its relation to different types of music in Chapter 3. Here, we will treat its measurement and how it varies from one class of hall to another.

Intimacy means different things to different listeners. One definition arises from the observation that a blind person can tell the size of a room from its sound. The hope of every acoustical designer is that the music in a new concert hall will sound as though it were being played in a smaller room. Recording engineers speak of the sound in a room as having "presence," a feeling that the listener is closely related to the performance.

The hardest parameter to define is texture, because it is not a dominant attribute. It involves the number and nature of the early sound reflections, those that arrive at a listener soon after the direct sound. Even when all other parameters are acceptably near optimum, unsatisfactory texture may create remarks such as "the music is missing something," or "the music has an edge," or it is "a bit off."

In regard to intimacy and texture, Ando (1985) states, "All independent objective parameters of acoustic information, which must be contained in the sound pressures present at the two ears, may be reduced to the following...(ii) the second objective parameter is...the initial-time-delay gap between the direct sound and the first reflection, as well as the structure of the early reflections..."

CLARITY

The usual physical measurement of clarity is the ratio of the energy in the early sound to that in the reverberant sound, a ratio that is designated by C_{80} and is expressed in decibels (dB). Early sound is that which is heard in the first 80 msec after the arrival of the direct sound, and the reverberant sound is that which is heard afterwards.

The measurement of C_{80} requires two pieces of equipment, one to produce an impulse sound, such as the bursting of a balloon, a pistol shot, or a short electrical beep, and the other, a tape recorder that is moved about the hall to record successive impulses at a number of seats. Using a computer, two energies are taken from the recording: (a) the energy of the sound that arrives directly from the loudspeaker plus all reflections from surfaces in the hall that occur within 80 msec thereafter, and (b) the energy of the sound that arrives after 80 msec, usually within 1 or 2 sec. The ratio of (a) to (b) is C_{80}, in dB.

Obviously, if there is no reverberation—that is to say, the room is very dead—the music will be very clear and C_{80} will have a large *positive* value (in decibels). If the reverberation is large—such as exists in a huge cathedral—the music will be unclear and C_{80} will take on a large *negative* value. C_{80} equals 0 dB when the early and reverberant sound energies are equal.

To maximize C_{80}'s sensitivity to the judgment of acoustical quality, the measured values in the 500, 1,000, and 2,000 Hz bands are averaged and the symbol $C_{80}(3)$ is used to designate it. In Appendix 4, C_{80} is a generic expression for the values in each of eight bands taken individually and *all apply to unoccupied rooms*. Values of $C_{80}(3)$ are given in Table 12.1.

A peculiar thing about clarity is that different amounts of it are desirable in different situations. During rehearsals, a conductor will often express satisfaction with a hall that has a $C_{80}(3)$ of 1 to 5 dB (measured with the hall unoccupied), so that all the details of the music can be heard. But at a concert, whether conducting or in the audience, the same person will usually prefer a more reverberant space, $C_{80}(3)$ equal to –1 to –4 dB, also measured with the hall unoccupied.

In the interviews that were conducted for this study, the persons were asked to judge the halls as an audience would. As expected, the halls with less clarity were judged the best. However, in no situation would a hall for symphonic music be acceptable if it had cathedral-like reverberation.

A plot of the $C_{80}(3)$ values for the halls in the three subjective groupings is shown in Fig. 12.1. They lie in the range of ±4 dB. Also, the values of $C_{80}(3)$ in the three groups overlap greatly, indicating that other acoustical attributes more strongly influence acoustical quality. Further, the fact that these data were taken only in unoccupied halls introduces variation because the variety of seats absorb sound differently.

Table 12.1. Basic material for RT, C_{80}, and t_I for 68 concert halls, for which the data are available.

CONCERT HALLS	No. of Seats	RT Occup. mid-freq. (sec)	$C_{80}(3)$ Unoccup. 0.5/1/2 kHz (dB)	ITDG t_I msec
Amsterdam, Concertgebouw	2,037	2.0	–3.3	21
Baltimore, Meyerhoff Hall*	2,467	2.0	–1.6	13
Basel, Stadt-Casino	1,448	1.8	–2.3	16
Berlin, Kammermusiksaal	1,138	1.8	–1.7	20
Berlin, Konzerthaus (Schauspielhaus)	1,575	2.0	–2.5	25
Berlin, Philharmonie	2,335	1.9	–0.5	21
Birmingham, Symphony Hall	2,211	1.85	–3.0	27
Bloomington, Ind. Univ. Aud.	3,760	1.4		40
Bonn, Beethovenhalle	1,407	1.65		27
Boston, Symphony Hall	2,625	1.85	–2.7	15
Bristol, Colston Hall	2,121	1.7	0.5	21
Brussels, Palais des Beaux-Arts	2,150	1.4		23
Budapest, Patria	1,750	1.7		44
Buffalo, Kleinhans Music Hall*	2,839	1.3	3.1	32
Caracas, Aula Magna	2,660	1.3		30
Cardiff, Wales, St. David's Hall	1,952	1.95	–0.9	25
Chicago, Orchestra Hall*	2,582	1.2		36
Christchurch, N. Z., Town Hall	2,662	1.8	–2.8	11
Cleveland, Severance Hall	2,101	1.5	0.4	20
Copenhagen, Radiohuset	1,081	1.5	–0.7	29
Copenhagen, Tivoli Koncertsal	1,789	1.3		16
Costa Mesa, Segerstrom Hall	2,903	1.6	–0.4	31
Dallas, McDermott Concert Hall	2,065	2.8		21
Edinburgh, Usher Hall	2,564	1.5	–1.2	33
Edmonton, Alberta Jubilee Hall	2,678	1.4	4.1	31
Glasgow, Royal Concert Hall	2,459	1.75	0.6	20
Gothenburg, Konserthus	1,286	1.65	0.3	33
Helsinki, Kulttuuritalo	1,500	1.05		26
Jerusalem, Binyanei Ha'Oomah	3,142	1.75	0.2	26
Leipzig, Gewandhaus	1,900	2.0		27
Lenox, Seiji Ozawa Hall	1,180	1.7		23
Lenox, Tanglewood Music Shed	5,121	1.9	–3.1	19
Liverpool, Philharmonic Hall*	1,824	1.5	1.2	25
London, Barbican Concert Hall*	2,026	1.6	–1.6	27
London, Royal Albert Hall	5,080	2.4	0.5	15
London, Royal Festival Hall "ON"	2,901	1.5	0.5	34
Manchester, Free Trade Hall	2,351	1.6	1.0	25
Mexico, Salla Nezahualcoyotl	2,376	1.95		16
Minneapolis, Minn. Orchestra Hall	2,450	1.85		33
Montreal, Salle Wilfrid-Pelletier*	2,982	1.65	–0.3	20
Munich, Herkulessalle	1,287	1.8		24

Table 12.1 Continued

CONCERT HALLS	No. of Seats	RT Occup. mid-freq. (sec)	$C_{80}(3)$ Unoccup. 0.5/1/2 kHz (dB)	ITDG t_I msec
Munich, Philharmonie-Gasteig	2,487	1.95	–0.7	29
New York, Avery Fisher Hall	2,742	1.75	–1.5	30
New York, Carnegie Hall	2,804	1.8		23
Osaka, Symphony Hall	1,702	1.8	–1.2	35
Paris, Salle Pleyel	2,386	1.5	1.7	35
Philadelphia, Academy of Music	2,921	1.2	2.2	19
Rochester, Eastman Theatre	3,347	1.65		2
Rotterdam, De Doelen Cncrt Hall	2,242	2.05	–2.8	35
Salt Lake, Utah, Symphony Hall	2,812	1.7	–1.8	30
Salzburg, Festspielhaus	2,158	1.5	–0.3	27
San Francisco, Davies Hall*	2,743	1.85	–0.9	12
Stuttgart, Liederhalle	2,000	1.6	–0.2	29
Sydney, Opr. Hse. Concert Hall	2,679	2.2		36
Taipei, Concert Hall Auditorium	2,074	2.0	–0.3	29
Tel Aviv, Mann Auditorium	2,715	1.5	–0.4	30
Tokyo, Bunka Kaikan, Ueno	2,327	1.5	–1.0	14
Tokyo, Hamarikyu Asahi	552	1.7	–0.2	16
Tokyo, Metropolitan Art Space	2,017	2.15	–1.1	27
Tokyo, NHK Hall	3,677	1.7	0.0	23
Tokyo, Orchard Hall, Bunkamura	2,150	1.8	–2.0	26
Tokyo, Suntory Hall	2,006	2.0	–1.1	30
Toronto, Roy Thompson Hall	2,812	1.8	0.6	35
Vienna, Musikvereinssaal	1,680	2.0	–3.7	12
Vienna, Staatsoper	1,709	1.3	2.7	15
Washington, Kennedy Cncrt Hall	2,759	1.85	–0.3	25
Worcester, Mechanics Hall	1,343	1.55	–1.0	28
Zurich, Grosser Tonhallesaal	1,546	2.05	–3.6	14
Average	**2,311**	**1.7**	**–0.7**	**25**

For example, if the four halls with unupholstered seats were removed from Group (A+, A), Amsterdam, Boston, Vienna, and Zurich, the median of the remaining halls would be little different from the median for the other two groups.

Figure 12.2 is a plot of $C_{80}(3)$ (unoccupied) versus reverberation time (occupied halls) in sec. This graph confirms that $C_{80}(3)$ is not statistically independent; it is highly correlated with RT and EDT.

A good feature of $C_{80}(3)$ is that it can be judged qualitatively by an experienced listener. It is easy to hear whether the music is too clear, or the reverberant energy is too strong, or the balance between the reverberant and the early sound is not optimal.

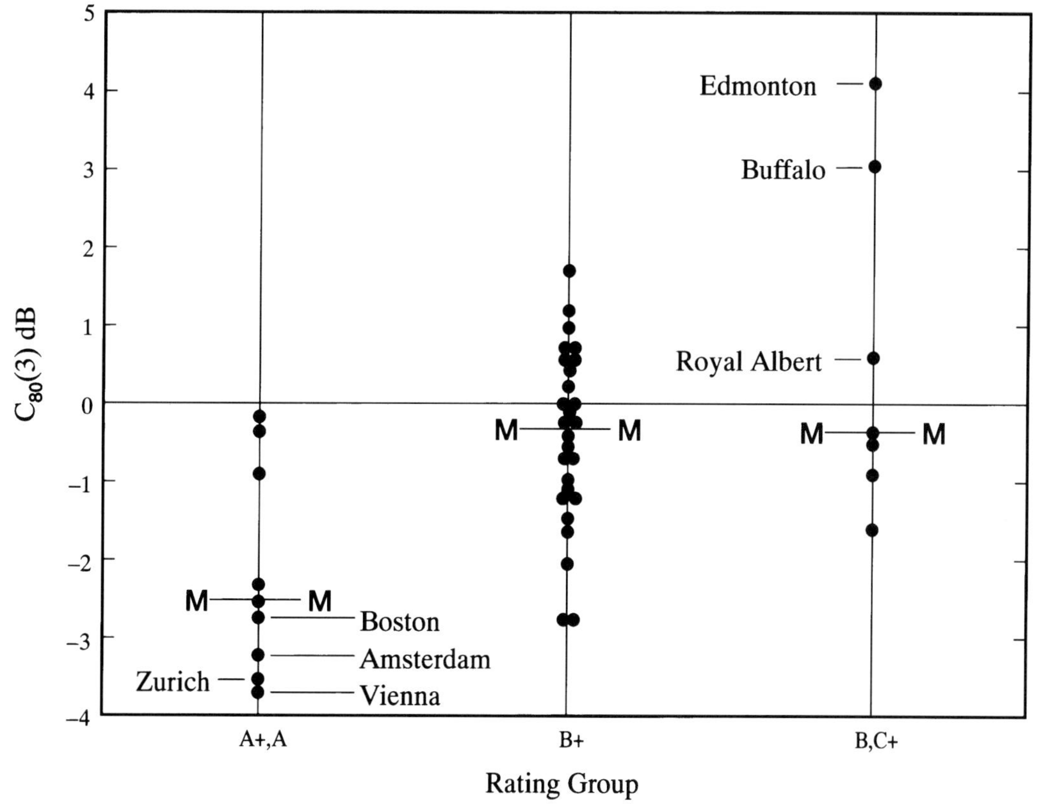

Figure 12.1. Plot of $C_{80}(3)$, three band average, in decibels, for 35 halls in the three rating groups, (A+, A), B+, and (B, C+). The median values for each group are shown by "*M—M*". The two halls with very high values of $C_{80}(3)$ have low reverberation times, 1.3 and 1.4 sec, fully occupied. $C_{80}(3)$ was measured with the halls unoccupied.

Nevertheless, it must be concluded that $C_{80}(3)$ is not a useful acoustical attribute for calculating occupied concert hall quality.

INTIMACY

There are several acoustical measures related to intimacy, one of which has been established as an important acoustical attribute, the initial-time-delay gap (t_I), measured in milliseconds (msec).

The subjective impression of listening to music in a large room and its sounding as though the room were small is one definition of intimacy. Barron (1988 and 1993, p. 115) coined a definition: "Intimacy refers to the degree of identification between the listener and the performance, whether the listener feels acoustically involved or detached from the music."

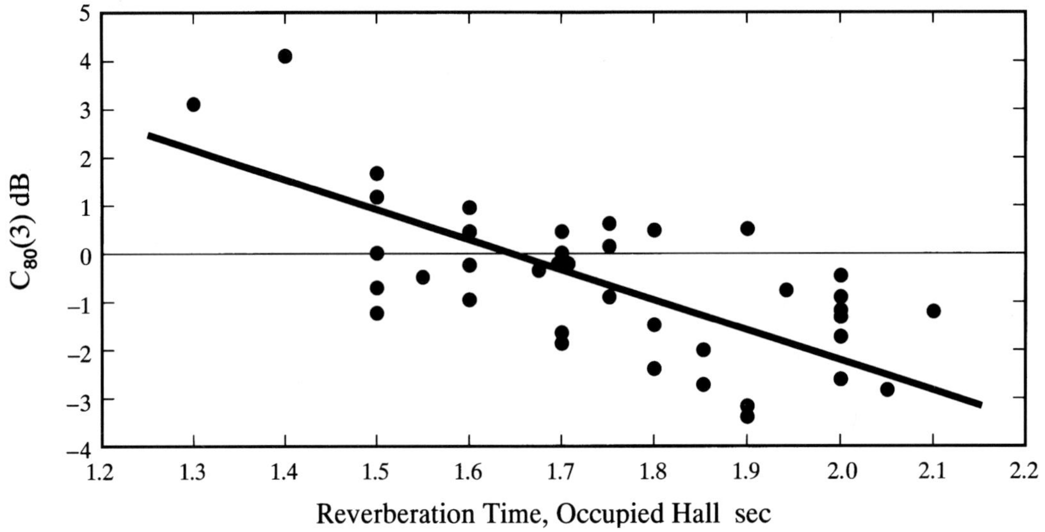

Figure 12.2. Plot of $C_{80}(3)$ in decibels for 44 halls as a function of their occupied reverberation times in sec. $C_{80}(3)$ was measured in unoccupied halls.

Beranek (1992) used the initial-time-delay gap t_I as a measure of intimacy—primarily because in two very large halls, the Tanglewood, Koussevitzky Music Shed, and the Caracas, Aula Magna, the musical quality was greatly improved by the addition of horizontal suspended panels put there to shorten t_I. After their introduction into the 5,000 seat Tanglewood Music Shed, the music suddenly seemed to engage the listeners and the result was and remains highly praised by musicians, music critics, and audience.

In this text t_I is only given for a position at the center of the main floor, about half-way between the stage and the first balcony front. Near to walls and balcony fronts, t_I becomes very short and meaningless as a measure of the general acoustics. A major reason for the mid-floor position is that a blind person can judge the size of a large room accurately only when standing near the center.

The subjects in Barron's listening experiment (see Chapter 4), who were judging the acoustics of twelve concert halls in England, indicated that there is a correlation between intimacy and loudness, the latter being measured by the strength factor *G*. Obviously, the music in a small hall is louder than in a large hall, and Barron's subjects were apparently accustomed to the increase in loudness that occurs in a smaller more intimate hall.

Barron also reported that the questionnaires executed by the British subjects showed that there was little correlation between the initial-time-delay gap and intimacy. One observes, however, that in the seven of his twelve halls for which data on t_I are available in this text, the average value of t_I is 27 msec and the range is ± 6 msec, which is not a great enough difference to move halls from one rating category to another, so that loudness, at least in that group of seven halls, was the only acoustical quantity that the listeners could relate to intimacy.

In Fig. 12.3, the range and median values of t_I for 44 concert halls are shown for the three rating groups. The median values in the two Groups (A+, A) and (B+) are widely separated, 16 msec and 28 msec, respectively. The A+ halls have initial-time-delay gaps of 12 to 25 msec. In my 1962 book, this range of t_I's would place these same halls in the then A+ group. The fact that several halls in the B+ group have relatively low t_I's indicates that one or more of the other primary acoustical attributes in those halls is deficient. The median for Group (C+, C) would have been much higher if more halls in this study were very large, say, public auditoriums seating over 3,000. No effort was made to take data on halls poor for symphonic music.

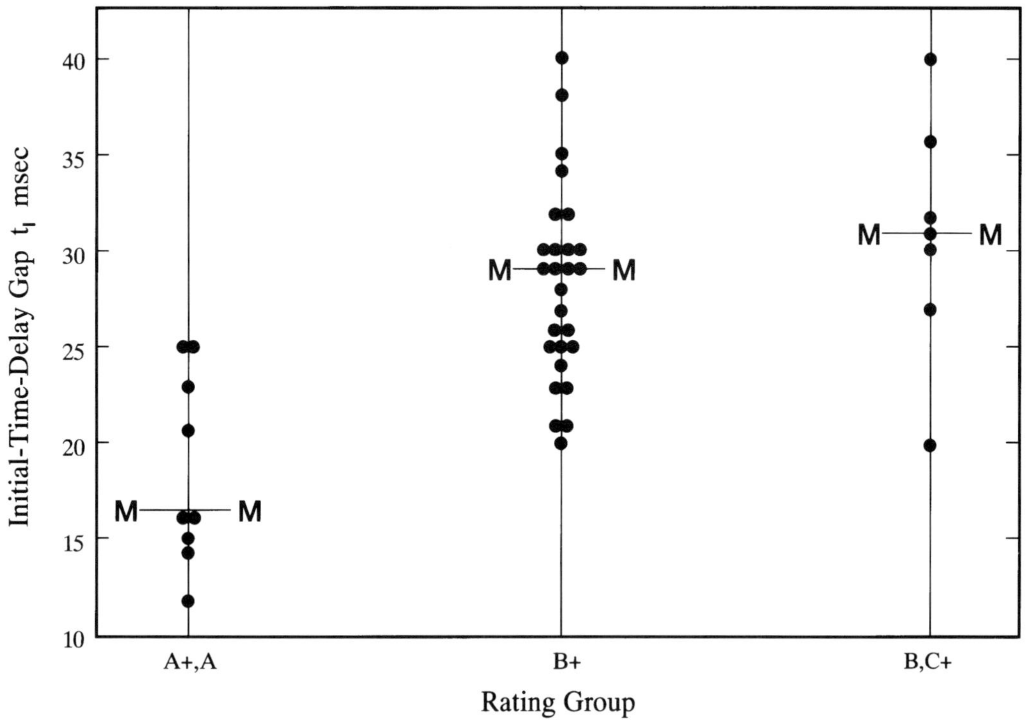

Figure 12.3. Plot of the initial-time-delay gap in millisec for 44 halls in the three rating groups (A+, A), (B+) and (B, C+). The median values in each category are shown by "*M—M*".

The conclusion to be drawn, is that the initial-time-delay gap t_I is important in determining acoustic intimacy in a concert hall. From the wide difference in the median values for the first two groups shown in Fig. 12.3, it is right to call it one of the half-dozen important acoustical parameters for judging the acoustical quality of a concert hall at regular concerts.

TEXTURE

There is no measure of texture, except visual inspection of time patterns of the types shown in Fig. 12.4. To produce a time pattern, a sound source which can emit a short "beep" is located on the stage. For the two halls for which patterns are shown in Fig. 12.3, the microphone that recorded the beep was in a seat about 60% of the way back from the stage to the rear wall. The upper pattern is for one of the B+ halls and the lower one is for one of the A+ halls.

The long vertical line at the left end of a pattern indicates the direct sound, the first sound to reach the microphone. The second long vertical line is the 80 msec division between the region of early sound and the region of reverberant sound. The peaks in the pattern indicate reflections of the sound "beep" from side walls, ceiling, balcony fronts, rear wall, etc.

The time separation of the first reflection from the direct sound is the initial-time-delay gap t_I. For the upper graph, the B+ hall, the first strong reflection, which determines t_I, occurs 40 msec after the direct wave. In the lower graph, for the A+ hall, t_I equals 21 msec.

It is obvious that there are a larger number of substantial early reflections in the first 80 msec for the A+ hall and that they have approximately the same height (sound level) and are approximately evenly spaced. This combination is a visual measure of good texture. It should be added that the upper hall has a cubic volume that is 40% larger than the A+ hall, which partially accounts for the average lower level of the reflections, but the more important reason is that in the A+ hall the sidewalls are parallel and closer together.

From comparisons like this, one can say that texture is related to the number, the strength and the spacing of the reflections in the first 80 msec after the arrival of the direct sound and that the initial-time-delay gap must be short enough to allow time for a considerable number of such reflections.

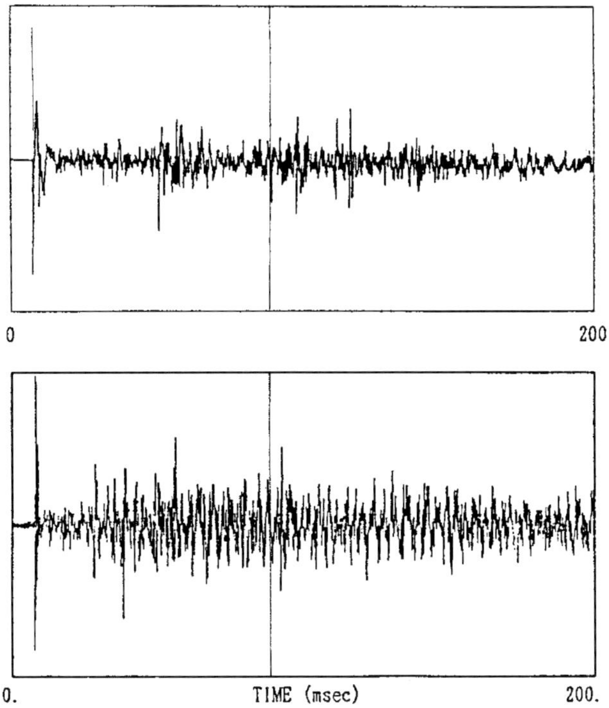

Figure 12.4. Time patterns for observing texture for two halls measured at a seat 60% of the way back from the stage to the rear wall. The vertical scale is the magnitude of the sound pressure (in Newton's per m^2) and the horizontal scale is time in msec. The first, long, vertical line is the direct sound, and the second long vertical line indicates a time span of 80 msec after the direct sound. The upper hall lies in rating group (B+) and the lower in rating group (A+, A). The sound from the source, indicated by the first line is a little weaker in the upper graph than in the lower one.

ASW AND TEXTURE & SPACIOUSNESS

One of the most important acoustical attributes, ASW, is measured by ($1-IACC_{E3}$). In order for its value to be large, a number of the early reflections must arrive at the listener's ears from *lateral* directions and t_I must be reasonably short. Not all early reflections need be lateral, because additional non-lateral reflections also add to the subjective impression "texture" and increase G_{mid}.

13

Balance, Blend, Ensemble, and Attack

The players in a symphony orchestra are aware of the principle attributes that determine the quality of acoustics for listeners in the audience. But there are other acoustical attributes that directly affect their playing, which, for the most part, are brought together under the phrase, "sending end of the hall." The sending end includes the platform, the sound-reflecting surfaces above and at the sides, and the surface at the rear of the stage. It also includes portions of the ceiling and sidewalls of the hall at the front part of the audience. In an opera house the pit must also be considered.

The sending end of the hall should mix or blend the sounds from the various performers in such a way that they are heard harmoniously by the listeners. It must also contribute to the balance among the various sections of the orchestra or between the soloists and the orchestra or in an opera house, between the singers and the pit orchestra.

Deficiencies in the stage environment can be overcome in varying degrees by the skills of the conductor. But imagine the joy of a conductor and players whose home is a concert stage that is supportive and makes playing only a matter of interpretation of the composition.

The word "balance" in this chapter means that quality of the stage acoustics that treats the sections of an orchestra more or less equally—where no instrumental group seems to dominate or be overpowered by another, nor does the stage make it difficult for soloists and orchestra to perform together. "Blend" means that the different instruments are perceived as being tightly coupled, sounding as one body, not as several sections trying to play together. "Ensemble" means that the players can hear each other and play in unison without watching every movement of the conductor to learn their exact tempo and the instants of sounding notes. "Attack" means immediacy of response of the hall, which is related to the manner in which the first reflections from surfaces in the hall arrive back at the musicians' ears.

Let us discuss first these aspects of player performance in terms of the stage surroundings present in the three "superior" halls of Boston; Vienna; and Amsterdam; and then take up the stage provisions in some of the newer halls, San Francisco, Davies Hall (after recent revisions as shown on drawings and photographs); New York, Avery Fisher Hall; Dallas, McDermott Hall; Birmingham, Symphony Hall; Lenox, Tanglewood Shed; and Costa Mesa, Segerstrom Hall. Quick inspection of the drawings and photographs of the first three halls shows striking dissimilarity among their sending ends, which indicates that we must probe deeper to fathom their popularity.

Boston, Symphony Hall (No. 3 in Chapter 6)

It, alone among the three, has a separate stage house. The platform of the stage is small by current standards, 1,600 ft^2 (149 m^2), which can be extended into the hall by 5 ft (1.52 m) for choral or large symphonies. The side walls of the stage each spread at an angle of 20 degrees and their average separation is about 50 ft (15.2 m). The average ceiling height above the stage is 43 ft (13 m) and slopes at an angle of 15 degrees. It is interrupted by openings for ventilation and lighting and has two wooden hanging pieces, about 1 in. thick and 3 ft in vertical height, that shield the lights from audience view. The side walls are wood paneling in sections about 3 ft (0.91 m) square; the frames are about 1 in. thick and 6 in. high (2.5 and 15 cm) the centers are about 0.5 in. (1.25 cm) thick, except that from the stage floor up to a height of about 14 ft (4.3 m) the paneling is about 1 in. thick.

Especially important, is the diffusing soffit below the pipe organ, which is about 1 m deep in the middle one-third of the stage width and about half a meter deep to either side. It reflects sound energy across the players. Similarly, the back one-third of the stage ceiling provides early sound reflections to the players on the front half of the stage.

Although there is no reasonable way to measure it, the pipe organ, which covers nearly all of the upper rear wall area, absorbs some portion of the sound of the orchestra, but probably uniformly with frequency.

I had the opportunity to conduct Sousa's "Stars and Stripes Forever," with the Boston Symphony Pops Orchestra (regular orchestra minus the principal player from each orchestral section) and a full audience. During the piece, I purposely changed tempo, loudness, and sectional balance. The composition contains parts that range from piccolo solos to full orchestra and is an useful base for exploring stage acoustics.

Surprising to me, the acoustical support seemed to come from the stage enclosure alone—the hall's acoustics were almost unnoticeable, that is to say, they were in the background, not heard as dead sound. Every instrumental section sounded in good balance with the others. Also, the bass/treble balance was ideal to my ear. Most noticeably, the orchestra seemed small, partly due to the small stage area and its shape, which meant that no instrument was more than 30 ft (9.2 m) distant from the podium. Although the hall has a lower reverberation time and a larger cubic volume than the Vienna and Amsterdam's halls, the sound level on the stage is higher by 1 or 2 dB, owing to the reverberation in the orchestra enclosure (Bradley, 1991).

Vienna (No. 25 in Chapter 6)

Vienna's Grosser Musikvereinssaal lacks a stage enclosure, but the orchestra is surrounded on three sides by an overhanging balcony that sends strong reflections across the orchestra. The stage is steeply raked and some listeners are seated around the outer edges of the orchestra in front of the stage side walls. The average height of the ceiling above the players is about 50 ft (15.2 m). As in Symphony Hall, an organ at the rear upper part of the rear wall absorbs some of the sound. Beneath the balcony, the walls around the stage are wooden, but their thickness is not known to the author. By comparison, one would expect that the players in the orchestra in the Vereinssaal would be more aware of the acoustics of the hall as a whole because of the lack of a confining stage enclosure. But otherwise there are similarities to Boston. The stage area is 1,754 ft^2 (163 m^2). The most distant player is only about 30 ft from the podium. The side walls of the stage are only about 3 ft (1 m) more distant from the center line of the stage than the average stage width in Symphony Hall. The strong early reflections from the balcony overhangs around the stage make up for the greater height of the ceiling.

Acoustical measurements (Gade, 1989b and Bradley, 1994) show that the sound returned from the walls to a player in the center of the orchestra by a player seated 1 m to his/her side is about 1 dB higher than that returned in Boston. These comparisons would indicate that the acoustical conditions on stage are very similar in the Vienna and Boston halls both to the conductor and the players.

Amsterdam (No. 25 in Chapter 6)

The sending end of Amsterdam's Concertgebouw is greatly different. As in Vienna, there is no stage house and there is an organ at the rear which absorbs some sound. Although the platform area is about the same as in the other two halls (160 m^2), meaning that the distance from the conductor to the farthest player is also about 30 ft. The average ceiling height above the players is about 55 ft (16.8 m) and the distance to the side walls from the stage centerline is about 48 ft (14.6 m). In Symphony Hall, the average ceiling height above the stage is 43 ft (13 m) and the distance between side walls is about half as great.

There is no balcony overhang, as in Vienna, to provide early strong reflections—indeed the large area of seated audience around the three sides of the orchestra would seem almost to eliminate early reflections from the side walls, leaving only the scattered reflections from the organ facade as a source of cross-orchestra reflections. The sound returned by the hall to a player at the center of the orchestra originating from a player one meter to his/her side has been measured and is about 5 dB less than that in the Vereinssaal, and 4 dB less than in Symphony Hall, very significant differences.

The sound heard by the conductor is less clear than that in either Boston or Vienna's halls because of the lack of strong early reflections, although it has the same small size of the stage. The late Maestro Eugene Ormandy, after months of conducting in the hall, stated to me, "The ceiling over the stage seems too high. There is a jumble of sound and poor orchestral balance." Other conductors have praised the hall, saying that it has marvelous acoustics or, at worst, is not as good as the Musikvereinssaal but is one of the best halls in the world.

San Francisco, Davies Hall (No. 18 in Chapter 6)

The players in the SF Symphony complained from the beginning about their inability to hear each other on stage—to play in unison. During major remodeling in 1991–92, the side walls on either side of the stage were brought in at the top, creating a large reflecting surface above the orchestra for spreading the sounds across the stage. In addition, a computer-controlled array of 59, 6 ft (1.83 m) square, convex panels at a height of 30 to 35 ft (9 to 10 m) were installed above the stage and the first row of seats. The spaces between the panels are about 50% of the total area of the array.

These panels improve communication on stage and provide early reflections to the main floor and early balcony. The sides and corners of the stage embody QRD reflecting panels which spread the sound more evenly among the players. The players have responded favorably to the changes.

Dallas and Birmingham (Nos. 8 and 46 in Chapter 6)

In both halls a multi-part, but solid, canopy is hung over the stage and the first rows of the audience. These canopies are designed to improve communication among the players and to enhance attack. In addition, reflecting "shelves" above the stages send early reflections back to the players, and enhance ensemble and attack.

Lenox, Tanglewood Koussevitzky Music Shed (No. 9 in Chapter 6)

To provide better communication among the players and to give clarity and intimacy to the music in the hall as a whole, a large, 50% open, canopy and sloping, sound-diffusing stage sidewalls were built in a 1959 revision. The results have been startlingly better. A definite advantage is that the trumpets and trombones never dominate the strings as heard in any part of the shed.

Costa Mesa, Segerstrom Hall (No. 7 in Chapter 6)

To provide better stage communication an orchestra enclosure is provided in this multi-purpose hall that embodies sloped QRD reflectors on the upper sides of the stage, diffusing surfaces on the lower levels and suspended ensemble panels over the stage. Stage communication and attack are judged excellent. (See artists sketch by John Szeliski in No. 7.)

Attack

Immediacy of response, created by early reflections not as early as those from the boundaries of the stage, is provided in Vienna, Amsterdam, San Francisco, Dallas, Birmingham, and Costa Mesa by reflections from the ceiling, the edges, and surfaces above and around the stage. In Boston, the early reflections come primarily from the stage ceiling and the coffers in the ceiling above the front of the audience. All six halls have good reputations for the attribute "attack."

The saving feature of the Amsterdam Concertgebouw's sending end from the orchestra's viewpoint, must be the orderly response of the reflections from the coffers in the ceiling, the irregularities in the walls around the stage, and, although more distant, the curved front edges of the balcony. In other words, the "texture" as heard by the orchestra must be ideal.

Conclusions

From this evidence, it can be concluded from an acoustical standpoint that when the average width of the stage is greater than about 60 ft and the area is greater than about 2,000 ft^2 (18.3 m and 185 m^2, respectively), special means must be provided to create early reflections to the players so that they can hear each other during performances. Some combination of reflecting soffits, stage ceiling, suspended panels, canopies, shelves, and diffusing irregularities must be incorporated into the architectural design of the sending end of the hall. Whichever stage enclosure design is contemplated, it also must be integrated acoustically into the overall architecture of the hall to be sure of its ability to project the sound with proper blend and balance to the audience. Stage and orchestra pit design will be discussed further in Chapters 16 and 17.

14
ECHO, NOISE, DISTORTION, AND NONUNIFORMITY

A motion picture artfully conceived and movingly acted would never be submitted to the Cannes Festival if the film were overexposed. Nor would the most noble gastronomic effort of the chef at the Tour d'Argent surmount the addition of an extra spoonful of salt. The whitened scene and the briny taste of acoustics are echoes, noise, tonal distortion, and non-uniformity of hearing conditions. These attributes can only detract from the beauty of the music; they add nothing.

ECHO

In a concert hall or opera house, there are many reflections that arrive at a listener's ears after the arrival of the direct sound. These reflections are specially beneficial if they arrive within about 35 milliseconds (msec) after the direct sound. After 35 msec, they are beneficial if they arrive in sequence, each one succeeding the previous one with decreasing intensity. It is such a decreasing sequence that gives the important attributes of EDT and RT. But any one of those reflections can become an echo if its intensity is greater than the reflections immediately surrounding it. An echo is defined as a long-delayed reflection, sufficiently loud to become annoying to a listener.

In a non-reverberant space, such as outdoors, an echo is usually perceived after a time delay of 50 msec, but only if the reflecting surface is focused enough (or electronically amplified) that the sound returned to the ears of the listener is equal or greater in level than the outgoing sound. At 60 msec delay, the reflected sound will be heard as an echo if its level is not as much as 4 dB below the outgoing signal. For example, if the round trip time of travel of the sound of a handclap is 60 msec, it will be heard as an echo if its level is, say, only 3 dB weaker than the outgoing signal but not if its level is, say, as much as 6 dB weaker. At 80 msec delay, an echo is heard if the return level is less than 11 dB below; at 100 msec, if it is less than 15 dB below; at 200 msec, if it is less than 20 dB below; and at 300 msec or more if its level is less than 30 dB below the outgoing sound.

In a reverberant space, a reflected signal will definitely not be heard as an echo if its level is less (weaker) than the limits given above, that is, if it meets the same requirements as in a non-reverberant space. However, with reverberation the reflected level can be higher (stronger) provided it does not stand out from the reverberant sound field surrounding it. In technical terms, at 200 msec the return level may be higher (less negative) than –20 dB if the reverberation levels measured in one-third octave bands on either side of it are less than –21 dB below the outgoing signal.

The musical instrument that most often produces an echo in a concert hall is the trumpet, because of its piercing staccato tones and because its bell directs its sound onto whatever surface is available to return the echo. An usual solution to a trumpet echo is to reseat the brass section so that the bells of the trumpets do not point toward the offending surface.

The prediction of whether a reflection will be audible as an echo is not simple. The refined localization abilities of the ear can be tuned to detecting echoes or to suppressing them. At first, one might not hear an echo, but once heard, one may not be able to ignore it. On the other hand, I have sat in seats where, to me, an echo was disturbing, but, on questioning regular subscribers to the concerts in the adjoining seats, they seemed oblivious of it.

The rear wall of a narrow rectangular hall, with sufficient reverberant sound energy, seldom causes an echo if there are balconies, even shallow ones, in front of it. The echo from a high, bare rear wall can be avoided by providing sound diffusing surfaces on the side walls so that the sound is scattered and not all of its energy reaches the rear of the hall or by providing diffusing panels on the rear wall. One type of panel is called "QRD diffuser". These panels are technically known as "quadratic residue diffusers" and are discussed in Chapter 10. The success of these panels depends on the amount and tilt and on the dimensions and shape of the hall, the rake of the main-floor seating, and other factors.

Echoes resound from focusing domes, semi-circular walls, and other acoustically difficult shapes, and great care must be taken to avoid them in design.

An echo that is difficult to suppress occurs in a wide fan-shaped hall whose rear wall is a sector of a circle with its center of curvature on the stage. Two such halls are the Aula Magna in Caracas and the Music Shed at Tanglewood. In the Aula Magna, the echo was suppressed by applying highly absorbent materials to the rear wall and doors and by splaying the doors so they would not return sound directly to the front of the hall.

In Tanglewood, echoes were avoided by tilting the top half of the rear wall forward so that the sound energy is reflected downward into the audience and absorbed before it becomes an echo. The lower half of the wall at Tanglewood is already highly absorbent since it opens to the outdoors.

In New York's Carnegie Hall (No. 13 in Chapter 6), after the 1986 renovation of the sending end, the audience at the front of the main floor and the players on stage were troubled by echoes from the rear wall of the main floor. To eliminate the high frequency components of the reflections from that rear wall, QRD sound-diffusing panels were installed just below the soffit of the balcony above. They spread the impinging sound energy sideways, thus returning less sound energy to the front of the hall.

The Salle Pléyel in Paris (No. 36 in Chapter 6) stands historically as an example of how echoes may occur if the sidewalls and ceiling are smooth, if the reverberation time is low and if the length of the hall (from the center of the stage) is great. Further, it has a parabolic longitudinal section, and the side walls flare outward. The sounds from the trumpets and percussion, as reflected back to the stage from the far rear wall, travel over 200 ft and are delayed in time by about 200 msec, an obvious candidate for an echo. In a hall built like this, with a relatively short reverberation time of 1.6 sec, the musicians can hear the hall's response, instead of an echo, only if there are elements (e.g., niches, projecting panels, and coffers) on the walls and ceiling that partially reflect their sounds back to the stage. If there are no such elements, the first reflection heard on stage, which obviously comes from the more distant rear wall or balcony fronts, stands out like a black spot on a white surface.

At an earlier renovation of Salle Pléyel, this echo was reduced by partially tilting the rear walls and adding sound absorbing materials to them.

In the renovations of 1994, this echo was further reduced by the addition of projecting, sound-diffusing, elements on the side walls which deflect sound energy away from the rear walls. These elements also serve the dual purpose of providing strong lateral reflections to the main-floor audience and to return energy to the orchestra.

NOISE

Noise is a serious nuisance in a hall. It may arise from ventilation openings, machinery, subways, trains, aircraft, and auto traffic. Vibrations are also troublesome, whether their source is machinery beneath the main floor or above in the attic or if there are subways running near or beneath the hall. In Symphony Hall, Boston, the rumble of heavy trucks on the street alongside the hall can be felt in the seats of the cantilevered balconies.

In order for a concert hall or an opera house to be adequately quiet, its noise level, measured without audience with an American Standard sound level meter and octave level analyzer, should lie below the lower curve in Fig. 14.1. In no circumstances should the noise levels be permitted to exceed the levels of the upper curve. Further precautions are given in the caption.

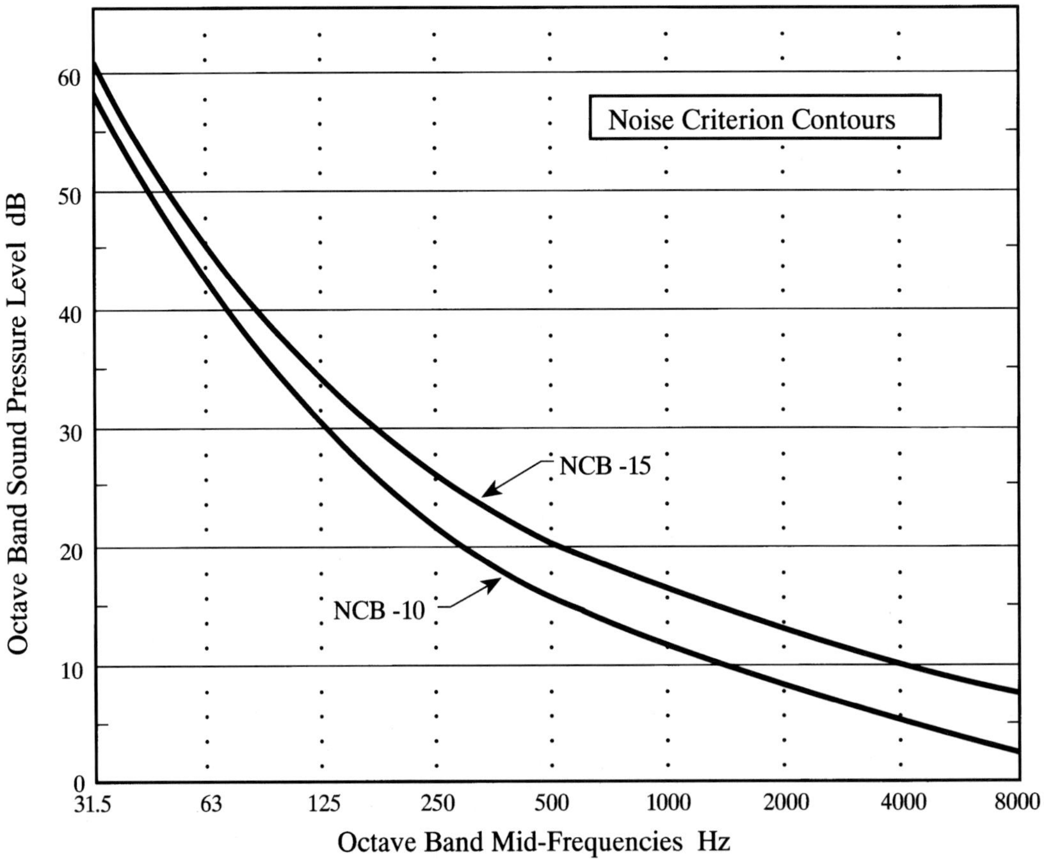

Figure 14.1. The range of acceptable noise levels in concert halls and opera houses. The lower curve NCB-10 is the recommended limit for the noise. The upper curve NCB-15 represents the limit above which noise levels would be seriously disturbing. For either of the curves chosen, the level in the 125 Hz octave band should not exceed the average of the levels in the four octave frequency bands from 500 to 4,000 Hz by more than 23 dB; the level in the 250 Hz band should not exceed the average of those four bands by more than 14 dB; and the level at 500 Hz should not be more than 8 dB above. If the number in any one of those three bands is greater than indicated, the noise will take on an unpleasant "rumbly" sound. These curves have been established for measurements made with an American Standard sound level meter and octave band analyzer in a hall without audience.

Air-conditioning machinery and fans should be placed in a separate, remote, room, floated on vibration mounts, that is to say, completely isolated from the concert hall. A most desirable acoustical condition results if the spans of acoustically lined ducts are long and there are discontinuities in the paths over which the noise and vibrations travel.

No standards exist for permissible vibration levels in concert halls and opera houses. The architect or acoustical designer would do well to reduce single-frequency vibration levels of the floors, on which the musicians and audience are seated, to below an acceleration of 1 cm per sec per sec.

The reduction of noise and vibration is a subject too vast to be covered here. Technical treatments of these matters can be found in such texts as: L. L. Beranek, Editor, *Noise and Vibration Control, Revised Edition,* Institute of Noise Control Engineering, P. O. Box 3206 Arlington Branch, Poughkeepsie, NY 12603, 1988; L. L. Beranek and I. L. Ver, *Noise and Vibration Control Engineering, Principles and Applications*, John Wiley & Sons, New York, Chichester and Singapore, 1992; and C. M. Harris, Editor, *Handbook of Acoustical Measurements and Noise Control,* Third Edition, McGraw-Hill, New York, 1991.

DISTORTION

Tonal distortion is a special kind of acoustical fault that may take many forms. Distortion in the hall may inject into the music sounds that have not been played, or it may suppress tones that the musicians have sounded. Proper initial acoustical design can eliminate these problems on the drafting board, but they are difficult to solve in the completed hall.

Selective sound absorption

Of the 76 halls in this study, 15 exhibit excessive sound absorption at frequencies near 250 Hz. In Fig. 14.2, the ratio of the median reverberation times at 125, 250, 2,000, and 4,000 Hz to the average of the reverberation times at 500 and 1,000 Hz are plotted for those 15 halls. A decreased reverberation time in a narrow frequency range means that some of the surfaces in a hall are selectively absorbing the musical sound. Of the halls shown, about half have wooden walls, or ceilings, or large areas of hung wooden panels, that may resonate at 250 Hz. For the others, and perhaps for most of them, the chairs appear to be the most important source of resonant sound absorption.

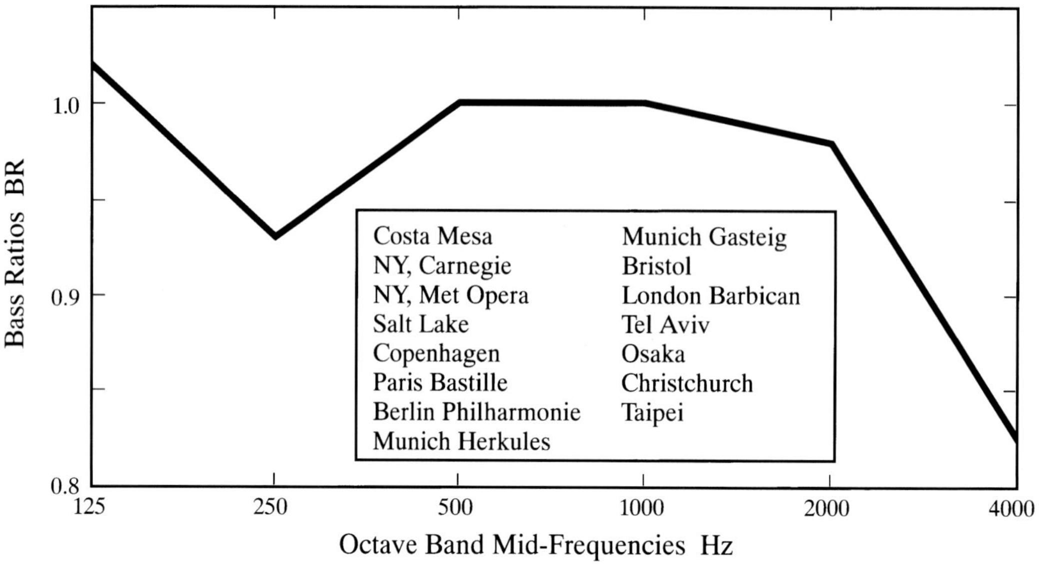

Figure 14.2. Ratios of (a) RTs at low frequencies (in unoccupied halls) to (b) the 500/1,000 Hz average reverberation time. The halls selected all had seriously decreased reverberation times at 250 Hz; the other halls in this book did not. The drop at high frequencies is caused by energy losses in the air itself. Sound absorption at 250 Hz; by the audience chairs, whether occupied or not, can cause this dip (see Fig. 8.2 of Chapter 8). Large thin plywood surfaces may also.

In regard to sound absorption by thin plywood surfaces, this subject was covered in Chapter 8 (see Fig. 8.1). Additional sound absorption data are given in Appendix 5. The absorption of thickly upholstered seats both occupied and unoccupied is discussed in Chapter 8 (see Fig. 8.2) and Table A5.6, p. 626.

All that is known about the seating in these 15 halls is that all seats are heavily upholstered. It can be speculated that the excess seat absorption in some of the halls is caused by a "bubble" resonance, meaning that the seat and rear support cushions are encased in an airtight covering such as would be produced by a back-sprayed or front-sprayed upholstering fabric. The excess absorption is not caused by the seat-dip effect, which is discussed shortly, because that is a wave cancellation phenomenon and is not caused by high sound absorption. Besides, the seat-dip effect occurs in nearly all of the halls in this book, usually at about 125 Hz (see below), but only these fifteen halls show selective sound absorption of this magnitude at 250 Hz.

In order to avoid the possibility of bubble resonance, the seats should be tested before purchasing in an authorized test-reverberation chamber *with the same materials and upholstering fabric, including chemical treatments* as will be installed in the completed hall. The tests should be made with the seats unoccupied and occupied and compared with the absorptions of lightly upholstered chairs. If about 20 seats are tested as a group, selective sound absorption of this type should be found. The seats must then be redesigned to eliminate the resonance, or seats purchased from a different supplier.

Seat-dip effect

When musical sounds are propagated over rows of seats, before they reach a listener, they are attenuated at low frequencies by both the seats and the audience (Schultz and Watters, 1964; Sessler and West, 1964; and Barron, 1995). In a conventional concert hall this loss of intensity occurs at frequencies between about 50 and 500 Hz, usually reaching a maximum loss in the frequency range between 100 and 150 Hz where the sound may be about 10 dB weaker than at 1,000 Hz. The frequency at which the dip is greatest decreases as the height of the stage or the rake of the audience seating is increased. Reflections from a low ceiling or hanging panels can mitigate the effect of the seat-dip phenomenon, the attenuation decreasing to only a few dB. Bradley (1991) found that the maximum attenuations range between 8 and 11 dB at about 125 Hz in the rectangular, high-ceilinged unoccupied halls of Vienna, Amsterdam, and Boston, in all of which the main floor is only modestly raked. As was mentioned above, the seat-dip effect is usually at 125 Hz, instead of at 250 Hz, so it is not believed to be the cause of the dip in the reverberation time shown in Fig. 14.2.

The seat-dip effect is the result of cancellation of sound waves by destructive interference. Thus it does not seem to have an effect on the loudness of the music. Strangely, the seat-dip effect is not apparent to listeners in the three rectangular halls just mentioned. In fact, in Boston, the string basses sound stronger on the main floor than in the front row of the first balcony opposite the stage where obviously there are no intervening rows of seats.

This subject is not fully understood and does not seem to have played a part in the results of the subjective questioning of musicians and music critics. There seems to be no practical way of eliminating the seat dip effect except by providing some strong early reflections from overhead (Barron, 1993).

Sympathetic ringing tones

I have known of only two halls in which ringing tones can be heard following the sharp cut-off of a musical chord. The offending tone has a frequency equal to the resonance frequency of whatever is set into sympathetic vibration. In one of these halls, the organ grill is made of hollow, square metal bars, each about 10 ft long, that ring loudly in sympathetic vibration (resonance) whenever a tone of 580 Hz—about the D an octave above middle C—is sounded. The response of these bars is so unusual as to be disturbing to any critical listener, and the ringing makes it impossible to record music properly there on disk or tape. The solution required to kill such a resonance is to apply a vibration-deadening material to each metal bar.

In the second hall the singing tone is heard as part of the reverberation, and is not as disturbing to the audience. The tone is produced by an acoustical resonance between the uniformly spaced beams of the exposed structure of the ceiling and occurs at about 250 Hz. The remedy could be to enclose the exposed beams with a heavy, hung, irregularly thick, coffered, plaster ceiling. Of course any such uniform spacing of sound reflecting entities should be avoided in the original design.

Acoustical diffraction grating

In a hall where the side walls are covered with a decorative series of uniformly spaced vertical projecting slats (see Fig. 14.3) up to a height of 10 ft (3 m) or more above the main-floor level, the music reflected from it takes on a rasping sound as heard by the audience on the main floor. This series of vertical projections constitutes what is known as an acoustic diffraction grating. It has the power during reflection to amplify a single tone, and in doing so it imparts an odd tonal distortion to music containing that tone. Such an uniform structure must be avoided, although benefits result if the depth and spacing of the projecting members are varied in a random manner (see Chapter 10).

Flutter echo

A flutter echo occurs between any two parallel flat walls. If you stand in the center of a 20 ft (6 m)-wide corridor and clap your hands once, you will hear immediately afterwards a succession of claps in very rapid sequence, creating a sound described as "flutter." It sounds like a "buzz," and in a concert hall, distorts the music. It is usually

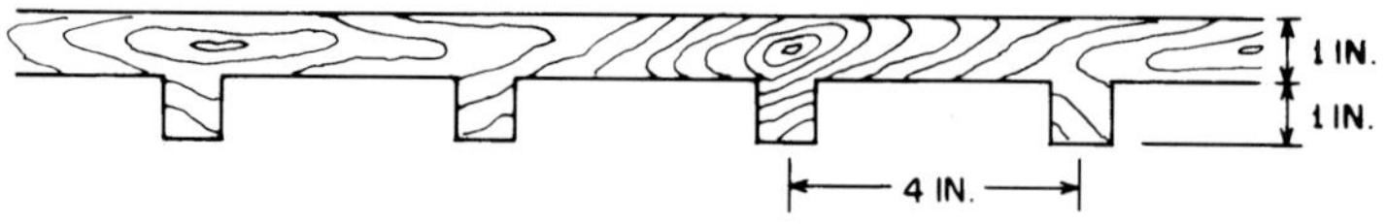

Figure 14.3. A side wall construction that creates an acoustic diffraction grating.

heard when staccato notes are being played. The obvious remedy is to avoid opposing large parallel surfaces anywhere in the hall. Even a slight splay between opposing surfaces usually prevents the problem.

NON-UNIFORMITY IN HALLS

One of the most unfortunate acoustical flaws in a hall is non-uniformity of the sound. There are a number of ways in which the music may be distributed unevenly to the various sections of a hall; each one wears away one's expectation of an evening of pleasant entertainment. Almost every hall has some poor seats; these poor locations are known to the architect and owner, but pecuniary realities necessitate the use of every possible space.

Balcony overhangs

Balconies are used in large halls to reduce the distance between the stage and the farthest row of seats. The architect must choose between one large balcony or a number of smaller ones. Whichever he selects, he is faced with the problem that people seated underneath a deep overhang do not receive sound reflected from the upper part of the hall and there the hall sounds non-reverberant. If the balcony is deep and the mouth of the opening is not very high, even the sound that travels directly from the stage will be muffled.

Figure 14.4 shows three relatively satisfactory designs for balconies. The overhang in the Mann Auditorium in Tel Aviv (upper sketch) covers only one row of seats, which is an ideal arrangement. The well-designed overhang in the Northern Jubilee Auditorium in Edmonton, Alberta, Canada, covers only three rows of seats. In addition, the openings are high and the soffits are shaped to direct the sound toward the listeners' heads. Sound from the upper ceiling is reflected into the last row. The third example, Symphony Hall in Boston, does not provide the listeners beneath the lower balcony with very good sound, although listeners beneath the upper balcony near the center of the hall have relatively good conditions. However, sound that is reflected from the ceiling does not penetrate very far under either overhang, and the extreme back corners of the hall under the two balconies have less than perfect acoustics.

Figure 14.5 shows three very deep balcony overhangs. Deep overhangs are more damaging to symphonic music than to opera, since many styles of symphonic music

(a)

(b)

(c)

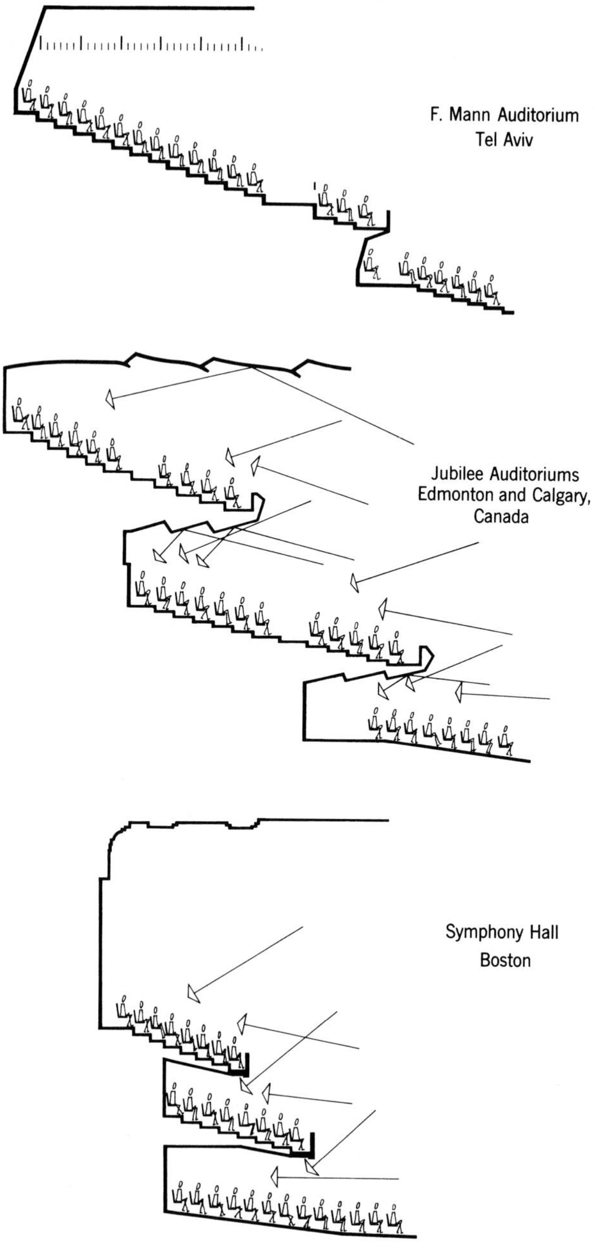

Figure 14.4. Three relatively satisfactory balcony designs: (a) excellent design, no overhang; (b) very good, little overhang and wide openings; (c) center balcony is good acoustically except for last three rows, which do not receive sound from the upper part of the hall. The last five rows of seats in the lower balcony are also less good.

require the overhead reverberation of the hall to convey the full meaning of the composer. The balcony overhang in the Indiana University Auditorium in Bloomington has a relatively high mouth, and the forward part of the soffit helps to direct sound to the

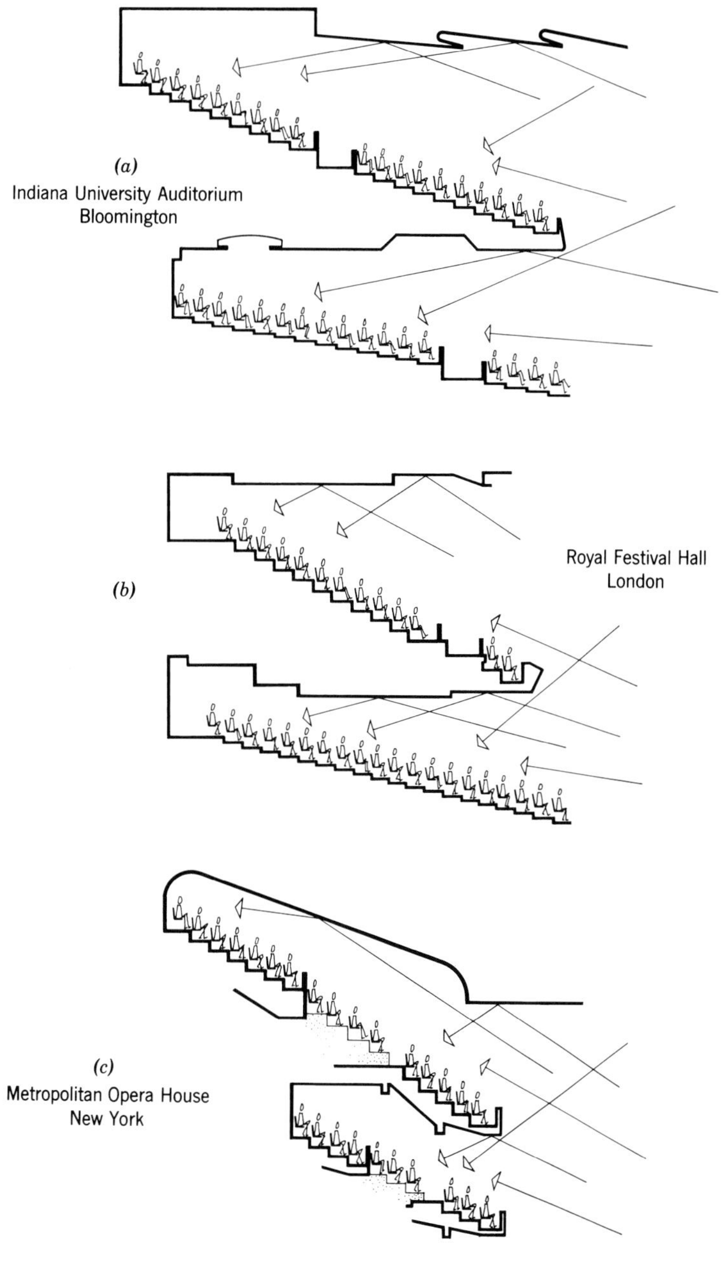

Figure 14.5. Three balcony designs of lesser quality: (a) fair acoustics, large overhang; (b) fair, large overhang and small opening; (c) lower balcony is poor, receives little sound from upper hall and opening is small. [Note: The (c) design was taken from the demolished Metropolitan Opera House in New York.]

heads of the listeners. Sound reflected from the ceiling penetrates nearly halfway back under the overhang. The rear part of the Royal Festival Hall is much the same as the Bloomington hall, except that the height of the mouth is lower at Royal Festival. The back rows hear only the direct sound. The lower of the two balconies shown for the (former) Metropolitan Opera House was not satisfactory for symphonic music, although the direct sound from the opera stage could be heard quite well. The soffit did nothing toward reflecting the direct sound to the rear, and the overhang cut off the ceiling reflections from six of the eleven rows. The upper balcony was much better; the sound in the front five and the back five rows was excellent.

Barron (1995) measured RT, EDT, C_{80}, G and LF under balconies in six large British halls, including Colston, Royal Festival Hall, Manchester, and Edinburgh. He found that the most sensitive measure of acoustical quality under balcony overhangs is EDT (at mid-frequencies). He relates EDT to the vertical angle θ shown in Fig. 14.6.

The degradation in acoustical quality, as determined by Barron, is shown in Fig.

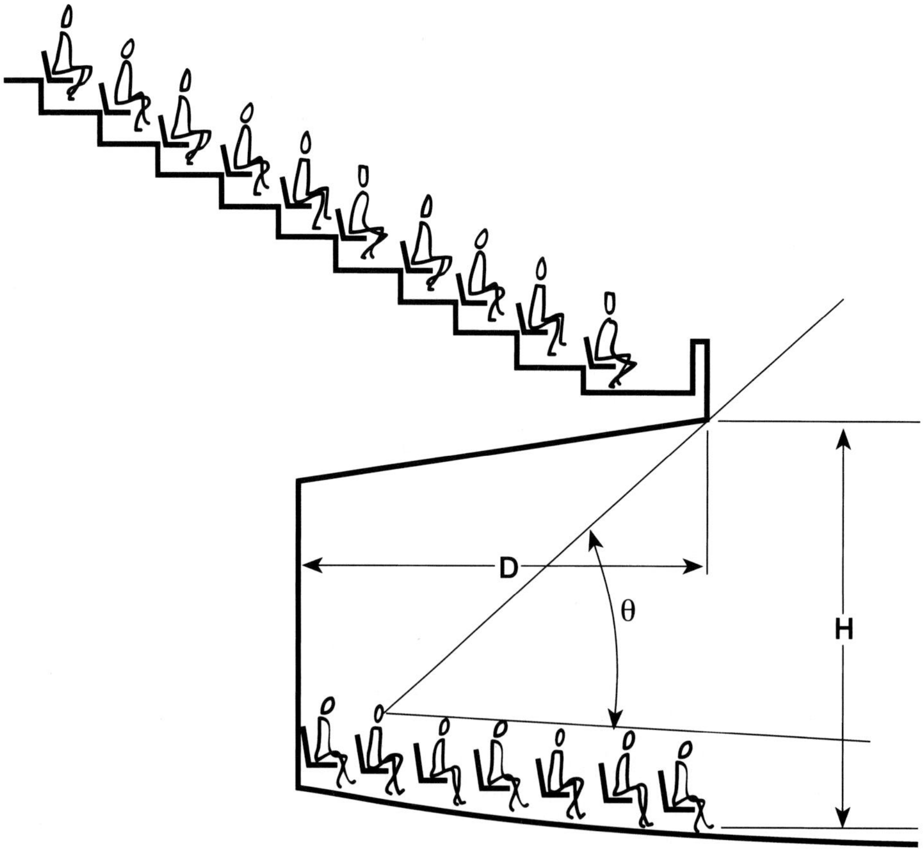

Figure 14.6. Recommended designs for excellent balcony overhangs in concert halls As a general principle, D should not exceed H. Angle θ is a better measure and should not be less than 45°. The under-balcony soffit and the rear wall should be shaped to reflect the direct sound toward the heads of the listeners. Shaping is specific to each hall and depends on the location of the stage and the rake of the floor beneath the seats.

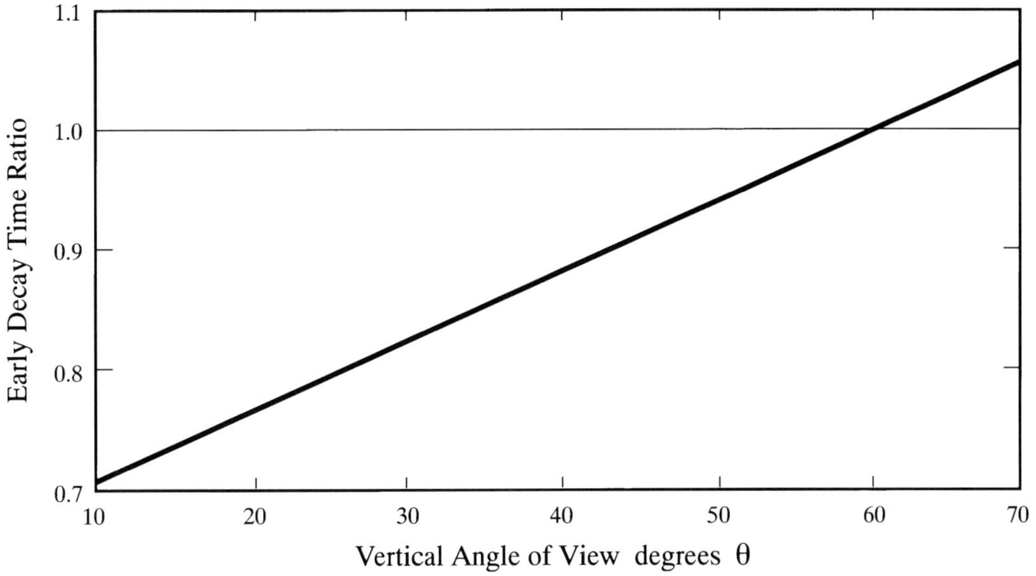

Figure 14.7. Decrease in the early decay time EDT as determined by the vertical anagle of view θ under a balcony overhang. See Fig. 14.6 for the definition of angle θ. Ideally, θ should not be less than 45°.

14.7 as the ratio of EDT at an underbalcony seat to the EDT at the same seat but with no balcony overhang, plotted against the angle θ.

Recommendation for balcony designs in concert halls:

A study of balcony overhangs suggests two general recommendations, which are illustrated in Fig. 14.6.

1. As a general rule, the distance *D* should not exceed the height *H*. In addition, the soffit and the rear and side walls should be shaped to reflect the direct sound to the heads of the listeners.

2. As a more sensitive measure, the angle θ should be greater than 45°.

It must be noted, however, that the effects of a balcony overhang can be mitigated to a some extent by a substantial number of lateral reflections that penetrate into the far reaches of the overhang. This will increase the early decay time EDT, which will add liveness to the music, even though the general reverberant sound field is weak. An example of a side wall design beneath a balcony overhang which improves the acoustics can be seen in the main-floor drawing for the Manchester, Free Trade Hall (No. 56 in Chapter 5). Barron (1993) writes, "A further positive of the design is the use of the reverse-splay form at the rear of each seating level. This enhances reflections, particularly lateral ones, so that the sound does not deteriorate seriously at remote seats."

◇15◇
An Objective Rating Method

The studies of the preceding chapters, which had as their beginnings the psychoacoustic experiments of the past third of a century, have led to the isolation of six statistically independent acoustical attributes that are related to the quality of the acoustics in occupied concert and opera halls.

Some of the attributes have been obvious from ancient times—reverberation, loudness and clarity found their place in Vitruvius' writings of the first century BC (Morgan translation, 1960). Wallace Clement Sabine, the father of modern architectural acoustics, was the first to quantify reverberation time and to measure it in many halls. The Bell Telephone Laboratories and foreign PTT companies developed instruments for measuring sound pressure and relating it to the subjective parameter of loudness. Intimacy and warmth were given space in Beranek's *Music, Acoustics, and Architecture* (1962). But spaciousness, the apparent broadening of a sound source in a hall owing to lateral sound reflections ASW and the surrounding of a listener by the reverberant sound field (LEV), were developments of a series of investigators' works, starting with a group of researchers at Goettingen University (Schroeder *et al.*, 1974), and enunciated by Marshall (1967 and 1968), Barron and Marshall (1981), and Ando (1985), and continuing until today through the works of many others (see Beranek review paper, 1992) and Hidaka *et al.* (1995).

In this chapter the findings, recommendations and comments of the previous chapters are brought together and used in a computational scheme to develop a single number that is related to the acoustical quality of concert halls at regular concerts. This is not the first attempt to meld accumulated acoustical knowledge into a method that may assist in the design of halls. Sabine (1900), Beranek (1962 and 1992), Cremer and Mueller (1982), Ando (1985), and Barron (1993) are among those who have made previous attempts. Lacking in most previous studies has been extensive data for any of the acoustical attributes except reverberation time. Such acoustical data for many halls are available for the first time in Appendix 4.

One must issue a caveat. Because of the lack of acoustical data for occupied halls with orchestra on stage or in the pit, and further because one expects new findings in the field, the efforts of this chapter may also look inadequate in future eras. Nevertheless, the attempt to bring existing knowledge together to develop an indicator of acoustical quality in occupied concert halls appears worthwhile.

THE ACOUSTICAL ATTRIBUTES AND THEIR PREFERRED VALUES

The method for transforming the independent measured attributes to a scale of acoustical quality in occupied concert halls, requires a summary of the findings in the previous chapters. These include measures pertinent to the acoustical parameters: liveness and fullness of tone; spaciousness (including both ASW and LEV); loudness; intimacy; and warmth.

Except for RT and BR which were measured in occupied halls, almost all other data were measured only in unoccupied halls. The calculation scheme, about to be presented, requires that all of the acoustical attributes be either obtained or converted to equivalent conditions. Where necessary, conversion is made by studying the statistical differences for other halls where both were available. The bases for the conversions are stated.

Reverberation time (RT), early decay time (EDT) and early/reverberant energy ratio (C_{80})

EDT changes less with occupancy than RT, at least in larger halls (occupancy above 1,500 persons). In larger halls, sound waves undergo fewer reflections from the audience surfaces within the first 10 dB of decay (about 200 msec), than in smaller ones. Also, in halls with upholstered seats, the difference in sound absorption whether the hall is occupied or unoccupied does not make a large change in EDT at middle frequencies (average of EDT at 500 and 1,000 Hz). There are only three concert halls with upholstered seats in this book in which EDT was measured both with and without an audience, Costa Mesa Segestrom Hall, Tokyo Hamarikyu Hall, and Sydney Opera House Concert Hall. The differences in EDT at mid-frequencies did not exceed 0.1 sec.

The clarity factor C_{80} will not be used as an independent measure of acoustical quality in the calculations that follow. Reference to Table 12.1 and Fig. 12.2 in Chapter

12 shows that its medians differ little from one rating group to another provided the Amsterdam, Basel, Berlin (Konzerthaus), Worcester, Zurich, and Vienna halls, with unupholstered seats, are eliminated. Further, Fig. 12.2 shows that C_{80} is highly correlated (inversely) with RT, so that it adds no new information to the calculation scheme.

PREFERRED REVERBERATION TIME FOR *OCCUPIED* CONCERT HALLS: The range of preferred RT is 1.8 to 2.0 sec (Chapter 8). Table 8.3 gives data for RT and EDT measured in 13 very good to excellent halls. The average RT is 2.0 sec and ranges from 1.6 sec (one hall with emphasis on early reflections) to 2.8 sec (one hall with added reverberant chambers). Table 8.3 also shows that for halls with upholstered chairs EDT has an average value of 2.2 sec with a range only from 1.9 to 2.4 sec. Because of this much narrower spread, EDT is chosen instead of RT for the calculations.

The difference between RT (occupied) and EDT (unoccupied) for the halls of Table 8.3 with upholstered seats is 0.2 dB. In halls with unupholstered seats, the EDT (unoccupied) is abnormally high. The procedure followed for them to obtain the EDT needed for the calculations is to *add 0.2 dB to the occupied-hall RTs*. For example, EDT (unoccupied) for Vienna becomes 2.2 sec, for Berlin (Konzerthaus) 2.2 sec, for Zurich 2.2 sec, and for Basel 2.0 sec. instead of the values measured. *The EDTs in Table 5.1 of Chapter 5, in the various tables of Chapter 8, and in Appendix 4 are unchanged from their measured values.*

In Chapter 17 two halls were singled out for special discussion. The Dallas McDermott/Meyerson Hall has a measured EDT of 1.9 sec and a RT (occupied) of 2.8 sec when the doors to the reverberation chamber are open. The Costa Mesa, Segerstrom Hall has a measured EDT of 2.2 sec and a RT (occupied) of 1.6 sec. Both are receiving excellent reviews. The Costa Mesa hall being older was included in the interview survey, but the Dallas hall was not. From this evidence, which is to be chosen, EDT or RT, in the calculation method? EDT seems the better choice because it is little different for the two halls, while RT is widely different. Since both halls are being well accepted, the quantity that more closely corresponds to this fact is EDT.

Spaciousness—apparent source width ASW

Two measures are used for ASW, $(1\text{–}IACC_{E3})$ and LF_{E4}. It is shown in Table 11.2 and Figs. 11.1 and 11.3 of Chapter 11 that $(1\text{–}IACC_{E3})$ clearly separates the halls in this study into three groups that are coincident with the subjective rating groups, while LF_{E4} is statistically less reliable. Unfortunately, there are only 21 halls for which $IACC_{E3}$'s have been measured because its importance was not recognized until recently. LF_{E4}'s have been measured in 31 halls. In only 14 halls of these halls have both measurements been made. Because of the greater reliability of $IACC_{E3}$, it will be used in the calculations that follow. However, to get better statistics more halls are needed in the calculations. This problem mandates a conversion chart—a rosetta stone for ASW.

The two measures of ASW, $(1–IACC_{E3})$ and LF_{E4}, are plotted against each other in Fig. 15.1. Eight of the points adhere to the line fairly closely—six deviate. The correlation appears sufficient to permit reasonable conversion of LF_{E4} data to $(1–IACC_{E3})$values.

Unupholstered/upholstered seat correction

The $(1–IACC_{E3})$ data in halls with unupholstered seats must be converted to the equivalent for upholstered seats. The corrections are treated in Chapter 11 and, in greater detail, in Hidaka *et al.* (1995). For five halls with unupholstered seats, the following additions to $IACC_{E3}$ are made: Vienna (–0.07), Amsterdam (–0.08), Basel (–0.02), Berlin Konzerthaus (–0.02), and Zurich (–0.07).

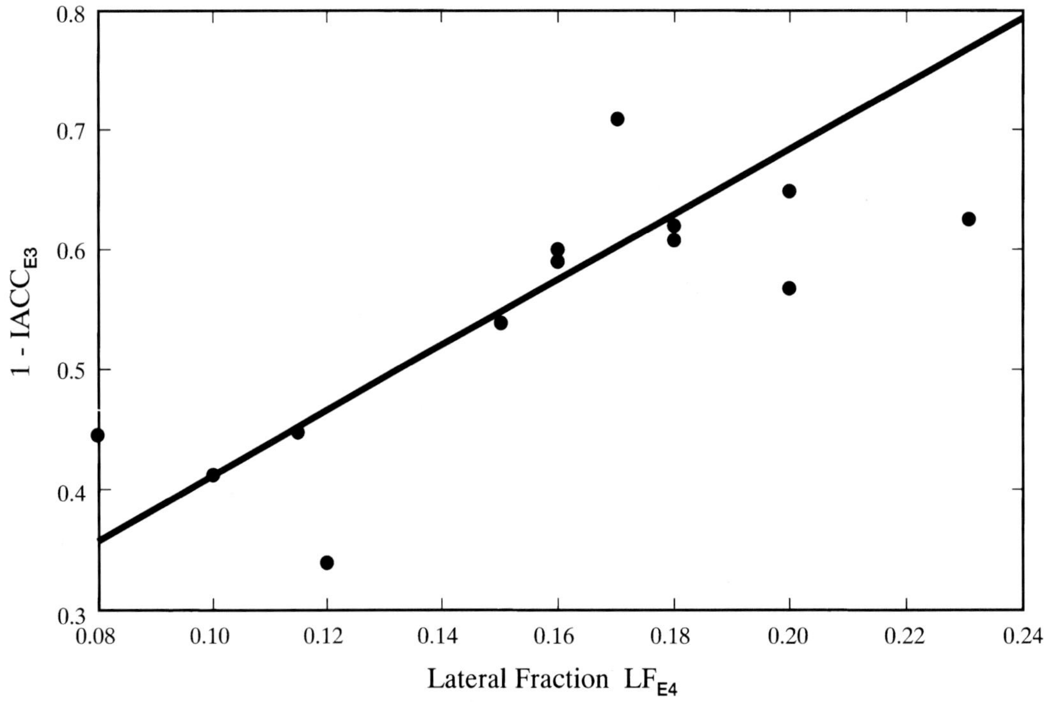

Figure 15.1. Graph for conversion of Lateral fraction LF_{E4} into $(1–IACC_{E3})$.

Rotterdam, De Doelen

Available data for Rotterdam are RT, EDT, C_{80}, and t_I, but missing are G_{mid} and (1–IACC_{E3}). Potter (1993) published measured values of IACC_A determined for the frequency band of 250–2,000 Hz at two positions in both the De Doelen Concert Hall and the Amsterdam, Concertgebouw. One position was in row 9 in the front and slightly left from the center-axis of the hall and the other at row 20 at the right side. The integration time was long enough to measure the total pulse energy and the delay range was -1 msec$<\tau<+1$msec. In this text this measure is called IACC_A.

The values of IACC_A measured by Potter for De Doelen were 0.54 front and 0.30 back, averaging 0.42. For the Concertgebouw, they were 0.35 front and 0.20 back, averaging 0.28. The ratio is 1.5, with the greater value for ASW in Amsterdam.

Measurements of IACC_{E3} were also made in the Amsterdam Concertgebouw by the Takenaka Research Institute. Generally, IACC_{E3} is about double IACC_A. For nearly the same two positions in Amsterdam as used by Potter, IACC_{E3} was 0.65 front and 0.48 back, averaging 0.56, just double that of Potter's IACC_A. The Takenaka hall-average value for Amsterdam was 0.46. The ratio of hall average to two-seat average is 0.46 ÷ 0.56 = 0.82.

To deduce IACC_{E3} for De Doelen, the Potter two-seat IACC_A average of 0.42 is multiplied by 0.82 to get the expected De Doelen hall average, 0.34. If this number is multiplied by 1.5, IACC_{E3} for De Doelen becomes 0.51, or $(1\text{–IACC}_{E3}) = 0.49$. This number seems a little low for a hall of this type so we shall arbitrarily raise it to 0.55, because the conversion from two seats to whole hall may not be the same for both halls.

G_{mid} for Rotterdam is determined from Fig. 9.4. With $(\text{EDT}/V) = 85$, G_{mid} is equal to 3.2 dB.

PREFERRED VALUES OF ASW: There is no preferred value for (1–IACC_{E3}). It, apparently, should approach 0.7, indicating fairly low correlation between the sounds at the two ears. The median value for the halls that fall in the "excellent" class of Table 11.2 is 0.66 with a range of 0.62 to 0.71. For "very good" halls, the median value is 0.55; for "fair" to "good" halls, 0.41.

Initial-time-delay gap t_I

The initial-time-delay gaps for the halls are only given in this text for the center of the main floor, approximately halfway between the first balcony front, if any, and the stage or proscenium front. Obviously, t_I can take on any value depending on whether it is measured near a wall, back of the hall or in front. This mid-hall location is chosen here because it is where a blind person is best able to judge the size of a hall, or its intimacy. Another justification is that in most countries the most expensive seats are in the middle of the main floor.

PREFERRED VALUES OF t_I: The preferred values of the initial-time-delay gap at this position are 20 msec or less. A number this low is possible in the classical shoebox halls that have widths of less than about 30 m (90 ft). In halls with large seating capacities, special reflecting surfaces must be introduced to reduce the time gap. Values of t_I in excess of 35 msec generally mean a significant reduction in acoustical quality of a hall.

The strength factor G_{mid}

G_{mid} is a measure of the strength of the sound at seats in a hall from a loudspeaker source that has a known power output. It is expressed here as the average of the measured values at 500 and 1,000 Hz and as the average of these values measured at 8 to 20 positions in a hall.

As was said before, five of the halls have unupholstered seats and, when unoccupied, the values of G_{mid} are higher than in equivalent halls with upholstered seats. To use those data the procedure tabulated in Table 15.1 is employed. The measured values of RT (occupied) and EDT (unoccupied) are shown in the first two numerical columns. In Column 3, 0.2 dB has been added to RT to get the "upholstered" EDT. EDT/V (times a million) for the five halls is tabulated in Column 5 and G_{mid} from Fig. 9.4 of Chapter 9 is given in Column 6.

There are seven halls (Table 15.2) for which EDT and V are known but for which

Table 15.1 Determination of G_{mid} for halls with unupholstered seats, but with G_{mid} corrected as though seats were upholstered.

Hall	RT(Occup.) as Measured sec	EDT (Unoccup.) as Measured sec	EDT (Unoccup.) Corrected = RT (Occup.) + 0.2 sec	Volume V cu m	EDT(corr)/ V× million	G_{mid} from Fig. 9.4 dB
Zurich	2.0	3.1	2.2	11,400	193	6.7
Vienna	2.0	3.0	2.2	15,000	147	5.5
Amsterdam	2.0	2.6	2.2	18,780	117	4.3
Berlin (Konz.)	2.0	2.4	2.2	15,000	147	5.5
Basel	1.8	2.2	2.0	10,500	190	6.6

Table 15.2. Determination of G_{mid} for halls with upholstered seats but for which G_{mid} was not measured.

Hall	EDT(Unoccup.) as Measured sec	Volume cu m	EDT/V × million dB	G_{mid} from Fig. 9.4
Rotterdam	2.3	24,070	96	3.2
Christchurch	2.0	20,500	98	3.8
NY Avery				
Fisher	2.0	20,400	98	3.8
Jerusalem	1.9	24,700	75	2.6
Gothenburg	1.8	11,900	151	5.8
Osaka	2.1	17,800	118	4.6
Tel Aviv	1.7	21,240	80	2.9

G_{mid} was not measured. With the ratios EDT/V the values of G_{mid} were determined from Fig. 9.4 and are listed in the last column.

PREFERRED VALUES OF G_{mid}: The preferred value of G_{mid} is 5 dB with a range of 4 to 5.5 dB. These numbers are the "compromise" between the values that would be measured in by Takenaka and in the Western Countries. The Takenaka values would be 0.6 dB higher and the Canadian, European, and USA values would be 0.6 dB lower.

Bass ratio BR

BR is the ratio of two reverberation times for an occupied hall. The denominator is the average of the RTs at 500 and 1,000 Hz and the numerator is the average of the RTs at 125 and 250 Hz. Since the reverberation times for all the halls, occupied, are available no manipulation is necessary.

PREFERRED VALUES OF BR: The preferred values of the bass ratio used in these calculations are between 1.1 and 1.25 for halls with high RT's, and 1.1 to 1.45 for halls with RT's of 1.8 sec or less. Between, interpolation is possible. These numbers are not firm, and the lack of accuracy of RT measurements at low frequencies makes it impossible to be more definite.

Surface Diffusivity Index SDI

This quantity is the hardest to determine with a desired degree of accuracy. The procedure was developed by Haan and Fricke (1993) and is described in Chapter 14. It amounts to a visual inspection of the ceiling and side walls (neglecting end walls). The degrees of diffusivity are area weighted.

OPTIMUM VALUES OF SDI: The optimum value of SDI is 1.0. Halls in the "excellent" categories have SDIs in the range of 0.8 to 1.0.

THE CALCULATION SCHEME

A study of methods for obtaining a calculated rating number for concert hall acoustical quality reveals that the method presented by Ando shows the most promise. Encapsulated in a tiny text loaded with mathematics, Ando's *Concert Hall Acoustics (1985)* is a challenge that few architects and acoustical consultants have braved, especially the computational method described in his Chapter 5, "Theory of Subjective Preference." In that treatise he coupled the theory of hearing with four independent subjective acoustical parameters that came from the succession of psychoacoustic experiments described in his Chapter 4.

Ando's description of the hearing process starts with the sound that arrives at the outer ear, continues through the small bones to the basilar membrane, then by nerve paths to the superior olivary complex, the lateral lemniscus, the medial geniculate body, and ends at the auditory cortex of the right and left hemispheres in the human brain. He believes that the acoustical phenomena reverberation, echo, coloration, and initial-time-delay gap are processed in the left hemisphere of the brain, and that loudness and interaural dissimilarity measured by IACC are processed in the right hemisphere.

Ando's "Theory of subjective preference"

Ando's method, as modified for use here, is given in the "Technical Section for Specialists," which follows. Without further elaboration, the course followed here is to:

(1) use the basics of his procedure;

(2) identify the orthogonal (statistically independent) acoustical parameters that are needed to judge the acoustical quality of a hall;

(3) select optimum values for each parameter; and

(4) determine whether the procedure rank-orders the concert halls of this study in substantially the same ranking groups as was forged from the subjective interviews reported in Chapter 5.

An important decision to be made is how to choose the constants in his equations so that each of the acoustical attributes is given the proper weighting relative to each other in the computation. From these studies, the relative weightings that have evolved are approximately as follows:

$(1-\mathrm{IACC}_{E3})$	25%
EDT	25%
SDI	15%
G_{mid}	15%
t_I	10%
BR	10%

To avoid using the formulas of Ando for the calculation, they have been reduced to a series of six charts presented in Fig. 15.2. They enable determination of the contributions of each of six acoustical attributes to the total calculated rating.

THE BASIC DATA AND THE CALCULATIONS

The adjusted basic data for 37 concert halls are given in Table 15.3. Because neither the rank orderings that resulted from the interviews, nor the sequence that results from the computational method are precise, the best comparison between both is to determine whether the computational scheme separates the 37 halls into three rating groups (A+, A), (B+), and (B, C+, C) in reasonable conformance with the subjective ratings of Chapter 5 (see Table 5.2). The actual computed numbers are not presented here in order to avoid the detailed rank ordering that would have no meaning.

The results of the calculations appear in the left-hand column of Table 15.4. Comparison of the Group (A+, A) halls in Column 1 with those of Column 2, shows satisfactory agreement. This conclusion eliminates Glasgow and Worcester which were not subjectively rated because they were not known by enough of those interviewed. New York (Carnegie) was not calculated because insufficient data are available. Thus, the only difference is that the calculations place Baltimore, Berlin (Philarmonie) and Costa Mesa in Group (A+, A). Two of those halls fell just below the dividing line in the interviews. Actually, in an earlier paper, Baltimore and Costa Mesa had been used as examples among "Four Recent Successful Halls" (Beranek, 1994), the other two being Berlin (Konzerthaus) and Dallas.

At the other end of the rating scale, Group (B, C+, C) comparisons of Columns 1 and 2 reveal that the calculations fail to place only two halls, San Francisco's Davies Hall and Montreal (in this lower group both halls rated and calculated before recent modi-

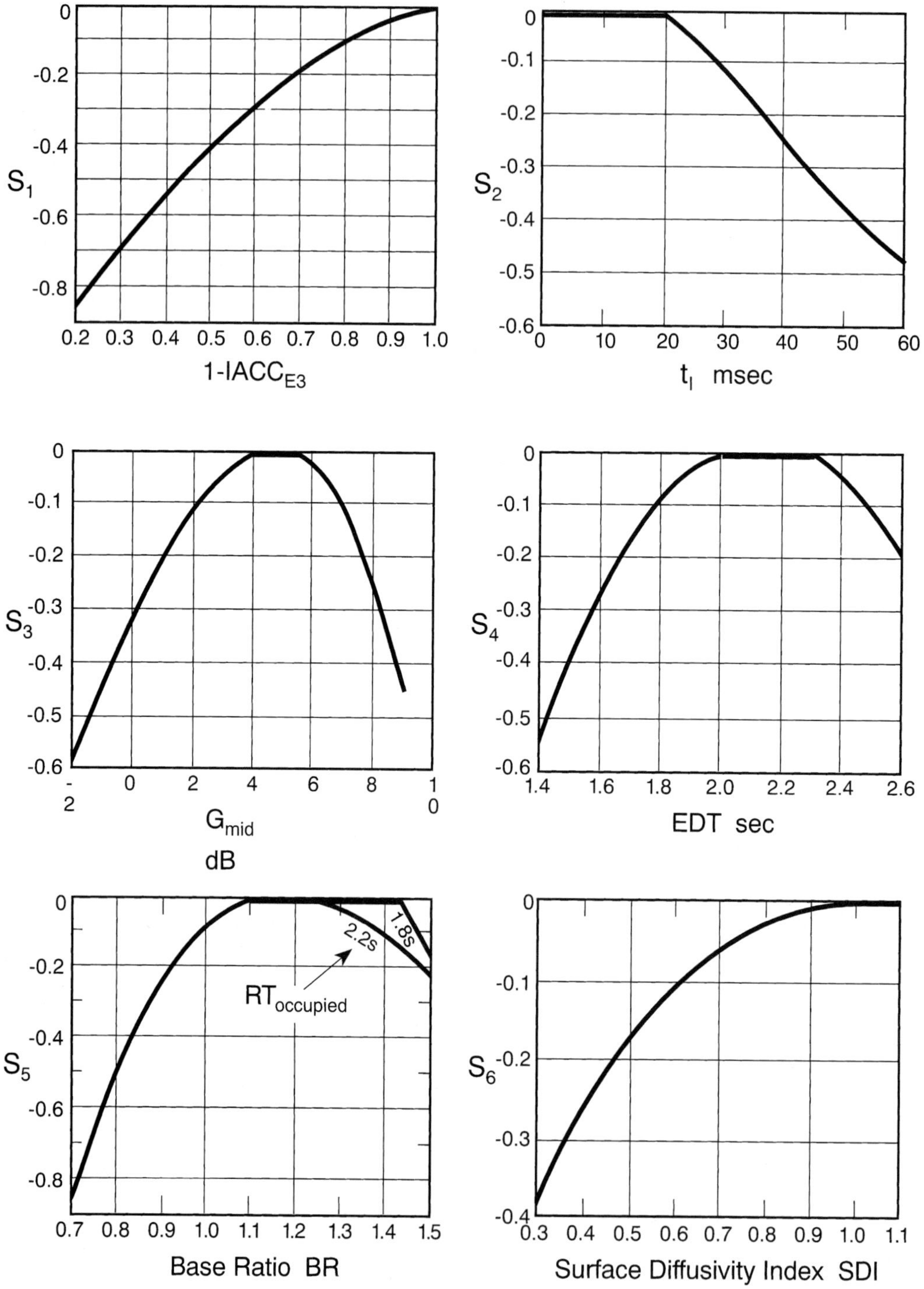

Figure 15.2. Charts for determining scale factors for the six orthogonal acoustical attributes that relate to the acoustical quality of concert halls.

Table 15.3. Basic data for 36 halls to be used in calculations of acoustical quality. All quantities were measured in unoccupied halls except BR.

City and Name of Hall	(1–IACC_{E3})**	t_I	G_{mid}**	EDT	BR	SDI
Amsterdam, Concertgebouw	0.62	21	4.3	2.2	1.08	1.0
Baltimore, Meyerhoff Hall	0.54	13	4.1	2.3	1.10	0.8
Basel, Stadt-Casino	0.64	16	6.6	2.0	1.17	0.8
Berlin, Konzerthaus (Schauspielhaus)	0.66	25	5.5	2.2	1.23	1.0
Berlin, Philharmonie Hall	0.46	21	4.3	2.1	1.01	0.8
Boston, Symphony Hall	0.65	15	4.7	2.1	1.03	1.0
Bristol, Colston Hall	0.63	21	5.8	1.85	1.05	0.3
Buffalo, Kleinhans Music Hall*	0.41	32	2.9	1.6	1.28	0.3
Cardiff, Wales, St. David's Hall	0.60	25	3.8	2.1	0.96	0.6
Christchurch, Town Hall	0.55	11	3.8	2.0	1.06	0.6
Cleveland, Severance Hall	0.59	20	3.9	1.7	1.14	0.8
Copenhagen, Radiohuset	0.58	29	6.4	2.0	1.07	0.5
Costa Mesa, Segerstrom Hall	0.62	31	4.4	2.2	1.32	0.9
Edmonton, Alberta Jubilee Aud.	0.49	31	0.4	1.4	0.99	0.3
Glasgow, Royal Concert Hall	0.77	20	2.2	1.7	1.12	0.8
Jerusalem, Binyanei Ha'Oohmah	0.55	26	2.6	1.85	1.05	0.4
Lenox, Tanglewood Music Shed***	0.46	19	4.9	2.1	1.45	0.8
Liverpool, Philharmonic Hall*	0.60	25	3.9	1.8	1.00	0.4
London, Barbican Large Concert Hall*	0.46	27	3.4	1.9	1.07	0.3
London, Royal Albert Hall	0.52	15	-0.1	2.6	1.13	0.5
London, Royal Festival (Res on)	0.63	34	2.6	1.7	1.17	0.6
Montreal, Salle Wilfrid-Pelietier	0.46	20	0.8	1.9	1.21	0.6
Munich, Philharmonie,Gasteig	0.49	29	2.2	2.1	1.00	0.8
New York, Avery Fisher	0.54	30	3.8	1.95	0.93	0.7
Osaka, Symphony Hall	0.56	35	4.6	2.1	1.00	0.8
Paris, Salle Pleyel*	0.54	35	4.5	1.8	1.23	0.5
Rotterdam, De Doelen Concertgebouw	0.55	35	3.2	2.3	0.95	0.9
Salt Lake, Utah Symphony Hall	0.59	30	2.0	2.1	1.06	0.6
Salzburg, Festspielhaus	0.54	27	4.0	1.85	1.10	0.9
San Francisco, Davies Hall*	0.44	12	2.8	2.15	1.11	0.7
Stuttgart, Liederhalle	0.44	29	4.3	2.1	1.00	0.5
Tel Aviv, Fredric Mann Auditorium	0.41	30	2.9	1.7	0.98	0.5
Toronto, Roy Thompson Hall	0.54	35	3.8	1.9	1.10	0.5
Vienna, Gr. Musikvereinssaal	0.71	12	5.5	2.2	1.11	1.0
Washington, JFK Concert Hall	0.61	25	3.3	1.75	1.06	0.6
Worcester, MA, Mechanics Hall	0.57	28	5.6	2.15	1.16	0.8
Zurich, Grosser Tonhallesaal	0.71	14	6.7	2.2	1.23	0.9

* Before renovations recently completed, underway, or in planning, designed to improve the acoustics.

** For those halls with unupholstered seats, G_{mid} and (1–IACC_{E3}) are converted to values that would obtain for upholstered seats (see Table 15.1 and Chaper 5, p. 6) and G_{mid} for them is the compromise value of Chapter 9, p. 6.

*** Semi-outdoor facility.

Table 15.4. Comparison of calulated rank orders in Groups (A+, A), B+ and (B, C+, C) with subjective judgments of Chapter 5.

CALCULATED	INTERVIEW JUDGMENTS
Calculated Group (A+, A) Halls, Listed Alphabetically, Using the Methods of This Chapter.	Halls in Group (A+,A) from Table 5.2 in Chapter 5, Listed Alphabetically. These are interview appraisals.
Amsterdam, Concertgebouw **Baltimore, Meyerhoff Hall Basel, Stadt-Casino **Berlin, Philharmonie Berlin, Konzerthaus (Schauspielhaus) Boston, Symphony Hall **Costa Mesa, Segerstrom Hall (Glasgow, Royal Concert Hall) Vienna, Gr. Musikvereinssaal (Worcester, MA, Mechanics Hall) Zurich, Grosser Tonhallesaal	Amsterdam, Concertgebouw Basel, Stadt-Casino Berlin, Konzerthaus (Schauspielhaus) Boston, Symphony Hall Cardiff, Wales, St. David's Hall (New York, Carnegie Hall) (Vienna, Gr. Musikvereinssaal) Zurich, Grosser Tonhallesaal
Notes: 1. (New York, Carnegie), was not calculated because data were not available. 2. Tokyo (Hamarikyo) is not listed because it will not accommodate a full orchestra and thus cannot be compared.	Notes: 1. (Glasgow) and (Worcester) were not rated in this column because of unfamiliarity by those interviewed.
Calculated Group B+ Halls. Nineteen of the 20 halls that the calculations place in Group B+ were also rated B+ by the interviews. The Tanglewood Shed calculated at the top of the B+ group, but was rated A by the interviews.	
Calculated Group (B, C+, C) Halls Listed Alphabetically, Using the Methods of This Chapter	Halls in Group (B, C+, C) From Table 5.2 in Chapter 5, Listed Alphabetically.
Buffalo, Kleinhans Music Hall* Edmonton, Alberta Jubilee Aud. London, Barbican Large Concert Hall* London, Royal Albert Hall **Paris, Salle Pléyel* Tel Aviv, Mann Auditorium	(Bloomington, Univ. Auditorium) Buffalo, Kleinhans Music Hall* (Chicago, Orchestra Hall*) Edmonton, Alberta Jubilee Hall London, Barbican Concert Hall* London, Royal Albert Hall **Montreal, Salle Wilfrid–Pelletier* **San Francisco, Davies Hall* Tel Aviv, Mann Auditorium
Notes: (Bloomington) and (Chicago), were not calculated because data were not available.	

* Before renovations either recently completed, underway or in planning, designed to improve the acoustics

**Halls where calculations and judgments are different.

fications.) Note that Chicago and Bloomington could not be calculated because of insufficient data.

In regard to the Group (B, C+, C) rankings in Appendix 3, there are some surprising differences. We have already noted in Chapter 5 that the interviews praised Brussels' Palais des Beaux Arts, placing it almost on the same level as the three "superior" halls. Bonn's Beethoven Hall, after destruction by fire, was rebuilt as an exact duplication of the original because it was felt that its acoustics were and are very good to excellent.

The Group (A+, A) halls in Appendix 3, also have several surprises. First, Chicago and New York (Carnegie) could not be calculated because there is insufficient data. From the interviews I also placed Carnegie in the (A+, A) group. It would seem that Chicago hardly belongs in the top group in the light of the Trustee's decision to undertake major renovations in the hall to improve its acoustics. The plan is, by 1997, to raise the roof and lengthen the hall, a callosal undertaking.

The Chicago, Berlin (Philharmonie) and Cleveland halls are the homes of three world renowned orchestras, and it is possible that Furtwaengler's statement in Chapter 7 was a reason for their being included in Group (A+, A) in the self-administered questionnaires. It must be noted also, that the music critics who responded to the questionnaire were drawn from USA Music Critics Association, and their loyalties and experience were likely mostly with American halls.

I wish to emphasize that rank orderings within rating categories based on the interviews was not possible. Thus, any numerical calculations cannot be compared one-on-one with subjective ratings.

CONCLUSION

The satisfactory agreement between the interviews and the calculation scheme of this Chapter would seem to indicate that the method is a useful aid for estimating the acoustical quality of a concert hall when fully occupied.

It must not be concluded from this study that even if the calculation scheme should place a concert hall in the top categories that the hall will be judged excellent by the musicians who use it. The method regards halls only from a listener's standpoint. It does not include the degree to which musicians can hear each other and themselves onstage. It takes no account of the acoustical factors discussed in Chapters 13 and 14, which include balance among the sections of an orchestra, stage blend, ensemble and attack. It disregards the negative effects of echo, non-uniformity, distortion and noise. And, there may be other measurable parameters as yet unidentified that might also play some part in the acoustical quality of a concert hall when its design deviates from the types of halls for which data existed for this study.

A concert hall is a musical instrument. Makers of violins try to copy precisely the successful instruments of the past. This practice is not followed by architects in the design of concert halls, and because every hall has its own sound some innovations are certain to be better liked than others. It is hoped that this study will prevent major mistakes in design, and that the need for subsequent modifications be part of the construction budget when a radically different design is proposed. In Chapter 17 that follows, some architectural factors are discussed that will, it is hoped, help the architect in applying the findings of this book.

TECHNICAL SECTION FOR SPECIALISTS

Ando's theory of subjective preference

Based upon a synthesized room-acoustic sound field in an anechoic chamber, Ando determined from paired-comparison tests that scale values of preference in a concert hall were possible. In fact, he found that his subjective results could be predicted by a single formula. Necessary are orthogonal objective (physically measurable) attributes that will include all signals arriving at both ears.

The N-dimensional significant objective attributes are given by $x_1, x_2, \ldots x_n$. The scale value of a one-dimensional subjective response is expressed by,

$$S = g\,(x_1, x_2, \ldots x_n). \qquad (15.1)$$

The psychoacoustic studies confirmed that the total scale of subjective preference could be expressed by

$$S = \Sigma g\,(x_i) = \Sigma S_i. \qquad (15.2)$$

This equation is analogous to the principle of superposition in a linear electronic system. Ando then assumes for convenience that the preferred value for each objective attribute should be zero, i.e., $[g\,(x_i)]_{pref} = 0$, whether $i = 1, 2, \ldots n$, and thus $S_{max} = 0$, thus demanding logarithmic transformations.

In these studies we have identified six independent acoustical attributes, which have been shown by correlation tests to be orthogonal. These are given in Table 15.3 and are defined in Appendices 1 and 2. Each, from Ando's experiments, are given by,

$$S_i = -a_i\,|x_i|^{3/2}, \qquad (15.3)$$

where,

x_i is a function of one of six significant acoustical attributes, four of which were derived from Ando's experiments and two, BR and SDI were identified in this book.

The subscript i is a numerical tag for each attribute, i.e.,

No. 1 is interaural cross-correlation coefficient $IACC_{E3}$

No. 2 is initial-time-delay gap t_I

No. 3 is signal strength at mid-frequencies G_{mid}

No. 4 is early decay time EDT

No. 5 is bass ratio BR

No. 6 is surface diffusivity index SDI

Thus, the total subjective preference for an acoustical environment, in other words, the quality of the acoustics of a concert hall, is given by the summation,

$$S = S_1 + S_2 + S_3 + S_4 + S_5 + S_6. \qquad (15.4)$$

Let us now define the quantities $x_1, x_2, \ldots x_6$ that go with the S's.

$$x_1 = \text{IACC}_{E3} \qquad (15.5)$$

$$x_2 = \log\,[t_I/(t_I)_{\text{pref}}] \qquad (15.6)$$

$$x_3 = G_{\text{mid}} - (G_{\text{mid}})_{\text{pref}}\ \text{dB} \qquad (15.7)$$

$$x_4 = \log\,[\text{EDT}/(\text{EDT})_{\text{pref}}] \qquad (15.8)$$

$$x_5 = \log\,[\text{BR}/(\text{BR})_{\text{pref}}] \qquad (15.9)$$

$$x_6 = \log\,[\text{SDI}/(\text{SDI})_{\text{pref}}] \qquad (15.10)$$

a_i is a numerical constant that determines the relative importance of each of the parameters. It sometimes has two values, one below the range of preferred values of an attribute and the other above the range of preferred values.

The values for the a_i's developed in this book are:

$a_1 = 1.2$

$a_2 = 1.42$

$a_3 = 0.04$ for $G_{\text{mid}} < 4.0$

$ = 0.07$ for $G_{\text{mid}} > 5.5$

$a_4 = 9$ for EDT < 2.0

$ = 12$ for EDT > 2.3

$a_5 = 10$ for 2.2 sec

$a_6 = 1$

Finally, the preferred values of the four objective parameters, for substitution in Eqs. (15.6–15.11), as determined from the earlier chapters in this book are:

IACC_{E3} = (There is no preferred value. It should be low. From Chapter 11 we see that the lowest values in excellent halls are about 0.3.)

$(t_I)_{\text{pref}} = 20$ msec or less

$(G_{\text{mid}})_{\text{pref}} = 4$ to 5.5 dB

$(\text{EDT})_{\text{pref}} = 2$ to 2.3 sec

$(\text{BR})_{\text{pref}} = 1.1$ to 1.25 for RT = 2.2 sec

$(\text{BR})_{\text{pref}} = 1.1$ to 1.45 for RT = 1.8 sec

$(\text{SDI})_{\text{pref}} = 1.0$

The formulas, functions, constants and preferred values are combined into the six graphs, of Fig. 15.2.

◇16◇ Architectural Design of Opera Halls

SIZE AND TYPE

In a theater for opera, an important consequence of small size is the advantages to the singers. Harold C. Schoenberg wrote in *The New York Times*, September 3, 1961:

> The big, revolutionary conclusion that I have arrived at may be very small stuff, but at least it is my own....It is easier to sing in a small house than a large one.
>
> For some three decades our ears have been conditioned to hearing opera singers in one of the largest houses in the world. Acoustics of the Metropolitan Opera are altogether different from the acoustics at Bayreuth, or the Altes Festspielhaus in Salzburg, or the Prinzregententheater in Munich. Singers who sound one way at the Metropolitan Opera tend to sound different in smaller European theaters. They are less inclined to push, for one thing. They give the impression that they are more comfortable, as indeed they are. All this makes for more relaxed listening.

Fredric Dannen, writing in The New Yorker, October 3, 1994, speaks of the Metropolitan Opera House, the largest of the major opera houses in the world—3,816 seats versus Vienna's 1,709:

> It can also be argued that the Met's most profound artistic problem is beyond [the Artistic Director, James] Levine's control: the sheer size of the theatre. The house at Lincoln Center has thirty-eight hundred seats and one of the largest stages in the United States. It is virtually too big to accommodate operas such as Mozart's "Cosi Fan Tutte" and "La Clemenza di Tito," and even Rossini's "Il Barbiere di Siviglia." Ironically, these are the operas that can be better cast today than in [Rudolf] Bing's time,

> while the opposite is true of the larger-scale Wagner, Verdi, and Puccini works, around which the new house was designed. During Bing's last season at the old Met, in 1965–66, he presented four different Toscas—Renata Tebaldi, Birgit Nilsson, Dorothy Kirsten, and Régine Crespin. Now Tosca is a difficult role to cast at all."

Finally, music is louder in a small house than in a large one. Although the size of an orchestra can be adjusted somewhat to the cubic volume of a hall, a soloist does not have the same range.

Architectural choices for opera halls

In recent years, the architects for two halls for opera in major cities, Paris and New York, have faced the challenge of choosing the style of architecture. Both were assigned the task of creating halls of size, 2,700 seats in Paris and 3,800 in New York, large by comparison with Vienna's Staatsoper, 1,700, and London's Royal Opera House, 2,120. Should they copy the Romantic style of Milan, Philadelphia, Buenos Aires or Paris' Garnier? Or choose a hall more friendly to concerts like the Festspielhaus in Salzburg? The Romantic style is characterized by a horseshoe shape with many boxes, more atuned to the social aspects of opera than to the music. The modern concert hall generally provides good sightlines and open space around the listeners.

The architects in both cities compromised. New York has eschewed the horseshoe, but retained the boxes (No. 14, Chapter 6). Paris has abandoned both in the Opera Bastille (No. 34, Chapter 6). It is not our intention to dissect these designs, but rather to dwell on what the acoustics must be in an hall to make listening to opera as enjoyable as possible.

The elements of good acoustics for opera

Opera is a combination of singers and an orchestra. In a concert hall, the orchestra is the center attraction, visible and with no obstacles between it's sound and the listeners. For several reasons this is not the *modus operandi* in an opera theater. The singers, the drama and the sets are central to the operatic performance. Both the vocalists and the orchestra must see the conductor. The orchestra with its greater power needs some acoustic suppression. The logical solution, perhaps the only one short of electronic presentation, is to depress it in a pit in its customary position. The architectural design must embody a structure that projects the full power of the voices uniformly over the audience while preserving the beauty of the orchestral music rising from the pit.

Barron (1993) in his chapter, "Acoustics for Opera" has ably broken down the elements: Design in plan, ceiling design, balcony design, long-section design, and the stage and pit design. Most essential is limitation in size of the audience. In a country without government support, the United States of America being the example, opera on a grand style is possible only if the theater is large enough to generate sizeable box-office revenue—hence, 3,800 seats. But such a colossus makes great demands on the singers and limits the number who can perform successfully hours at a time.

TWO CONTEMPORARY DESIGNS

The Deutsche Oper in Berlin

One of the successful opera theaters built in the post World War II period is Berlin's Deutsche Oper. Seating 1,900, it embodies most of the recent acoustical advances. (See Barron 1993, p. 317–318 for drawings.) It comprises two large balconies with extensions down the side walls that are segmented to create boxes in which the occupants face the stage—that is to say, each box resembles a miniature balcony. The ceiling is the most conspicuous acoustical element—each of eighteen segments modulated to give even coverage of the reflected sound energy over the entire audience area. The main floor has a rake of 10 degrees, providing good vision from every seat. The balcony overhangs meet the strict design requirements of the next section. The vertical surfaces at the sides of the proscenium provide lateral reflections to the main floor. The stage overhangs the orchestra by about 6 ft (2 m). A feature not common to other opera houses, is a horizontal panel inside the upper edge of the proscenium, approximately 12 ft (3.7 m) in width and the length of the proscenium opening. Its purpose is to reflect sound between the stage and the pit.

The reverberation time at mid-frequencies with full occupancy is 1.35 sec and the bass ratio is about 1.15, both in the optimum range. With its open, theater-type seating design, audience envelopment by the reverberant sound is assured. (*Architect:* F. Bornemann. *Acoustical consultant:* L. Cremer and Mueller-BBM of Munich.)

The Japan Arts Council, center for the performing arts

The Japan Arts Council and several Japanese corporations are in the process of constructing a center for the performing arts in Tokyo, in the Shibuya district of Tokyo, several miles west of the Imperial Palace grounds and very near the sky-scrapers of the municipal government. The architect is TAK Associated Architects. Scheduled for opening in 1997, the center will contain, along with other theaters and a concert hall, the New National Theatre, the first to be built in Japan exclusively for Western opera and ballet. Wisely, the audience size for the theater is limited to 1,800. In plan, the hall will be of moderate fan shape. It will have three balconies that extend down the sides of the auditorium. Great effort has been taken to make every surface work acoustically. To either side and above the proscenium, shaped surfaces with planned irregularities are oriented to project the singers voices uniformly over the seating areas and to suppress acoustic glare. Early lateral sound reflections will be distributed over the audience from the face of each balcony and from the side wall surfaces above and below, as well as from the areas at the sides of the proscenium. The ceiling is shaped and covered with irregularities both to distribute the sound to the balconies and to give the sound a mellow patina. The orchestra pit is constructed like that in the Staatsoper in Vienna. With a moving rear wall it can be extended under the stage to hold up to 110 musicians and it will be adjustable in width.

Particular attention has been paid to the chairs in the audience. Lack of bass, as discussed in Chapter 8, is often associated with poorly designed upholstered chairs. The prototype is the chair of Vienna's Grosser Musikvereinssaal, only with a thicker cushion to provide greater comfort during long operas. Because there are no boxes resembling those in the classical houses like La Scala, the sightlines are excellent for all seats and each person will feel enveloped by the reverberant sound. At the rear, the under-balcony overhangs are only a row deeper than the height of the opening at the front and the overhangs on the sides are minimal. Provision has also been made to adjust the strength of the reflection from the rear wall so as to provide beneficial feedback to the singers at levels that meet with their approval.

The mid-frequency reverberation time is planned to be 1.4 sec, a value that will give a sense of liveness to the house, especially with the rich number of early reflections, and yet will preserve the intelligibility of the words.

ORCHESTRA PITS

For non-Wagnerian opera, the acoustical requirements of an orchestra pit are for clear, undistorted projection of the music into the hall, in good balance and blend, without tonal distortion. In order to sing in good ensemble with the orchestra, the vocalists must be able to hear a clear and balanced orchestral sound, so that they can adjust their voice levels properly. The musicians in the pit should be able to hear other sections of the orchestra without the undesirably long time-delays that result from too long a pit, and the musicians also need to hear the singers in order to maintain good ensemble. As for visual requirements, it is necessary for the singers and players to be able to see the conductor easily. It is more important that the orchestra players and the singers hear each other than see each other and this favors the open pit .

For Wagnerian opera, on the other hand, the creation of a "mystical" sound by an "invisible" orchestra was an important element in the composer's dramatic conception, at least for his later works. This requirement led Wagner to develop the sunken, covered pit whose acoustical behavior is quite different from the open pit (Chapter 6, No. 37). Some pits combine features of both of these plans, but generally with only moderate success.

Types of Orchestra Pits

For purpose of discussion, orchestra pits are classified in three ways:

1. Open pit (e.g., Vienna Staatsoper).
2. Sunken pit, covered (e.g., Bayreuth Festspielhaus).
3. Sunken pit, open (e.g., Eastman Theatre in Rochester).

Open pit

The first objection to an entirely open pit is the disturbing visual effect on the audience of the lights from the conductor's and orchestra's music stands. A second objection is that, in order to accommodate a large orchestra of 80 to 110 pieces, a fully open pit must be 22 to 30 ft (6.7 to 9.1 m) wide, measured from the stage to the railing on the audience side, at the centerline. A sizable gulf is thereby created between the singers and the audience. The pit depth is usually between 8 and 11.5 ft (2.5 to 3.5 m). Some conductors prefer a shallow pit so that they can be seen easily by the audience.

A slight overhang of the pit by the forestage is not objectionable acoustically and has the advantage of increasing the reflecting area of the stage between the singers and the audience, a very desirable feature in a large hall. An overhang of about 3 ft (1 m) is found in many of the German opera theaters built since World War II and in the present Metropolitan Opera House. The overhang in Deutsche Oper in Berlin is twice as large. La Scala in Milan has a sliding forestage with a minimum overhang of about

3.5 ft (1.1 m) and a maximum overhang of about 12 ft (3.7 m). Several of the conductors who were interviewed expressed themselves strongly against adjusting the overhang at La Scala to more than 3.5 ft.

In 1962, Bolt Beranek and Newman, Inc. (their architectural acoustics division is now a separate company, ACENTECH) designed an open pit as part of a study done for the new Metropolitan Opera House in New York (shown in Fig. 16.1). It's average width was planned to be 21.6 ft (6.6 m), accommodating about 80 musicians. The floor of the pit was to consist of three elevators whose height could be adjusted individually.

In the present Metropolitan Opera House the pit width is 25 ft (7.6 m), accommodating up to 95 musicians. Planned for the Japanese opera house is a pit whose rear wall, beneath the stage, can be moved back to create a total width of up to 29.5 ft (9 m), with a maximum stage overhang of 9.5 ft (2.9 m), seating up to 110 musicians.

In the BBN pit of Fig. 16.1, there is no stage overhang and the open area is 1,420 ft^2 (132 m^2), providing about 17.7 ft^2 (1.65 m^2) for each of 80 musicians. Barron suggests 16 ft^2 (1.5 m^2) as acceptable. The elevators shown at the two ends could be raised to form end walls, thereby reducing the pit area to 1,220 ft^2 (113 m^2).

A special feature of the pit in Fig. 16.1 is the overhangs at each end, which form small rooms. These rooms are planned to lie behind the French horns at one end and the percussion instruments at the other. Sound-absorbing materials can be included on some of the surfaces of these small rooms to prevent them from ringing like empty barrels when the pit is not occupied by a full orchestra. For a large orchestra—for Wagner, say, or Berg—these spaces can serve more musicians. If desired, solid panels can cover the sound-absorbing materials when a full orchestra performs. Or, the panels in the end rooms can be made rotatable, one side being absorbent.

The wall at the stage side of the pit is vertical and hard so as not to absorb sound. It is intended that the double basses be placed against this wall to provide strong support for bass tones.

The strength levels from a source of sound in the orchestra pit have been measured only in two opera houses, Opéra Garnier in Paris and the Staatsoper in Vienna. In Paris, G_{mid} is 0.6 dB higher for a sound source on the stage than for one in the pit. In Vienna, the opposite is true, G_{mid} is 1.2 dB higher for a source in the pit than for one on the stage. The only explanation is that the pit extends further under the stage and more of the forestage is available for reflecting singers' voices. One might have expected them to be more alike, because the stage house is more reverberant in Vienna than in Paris.

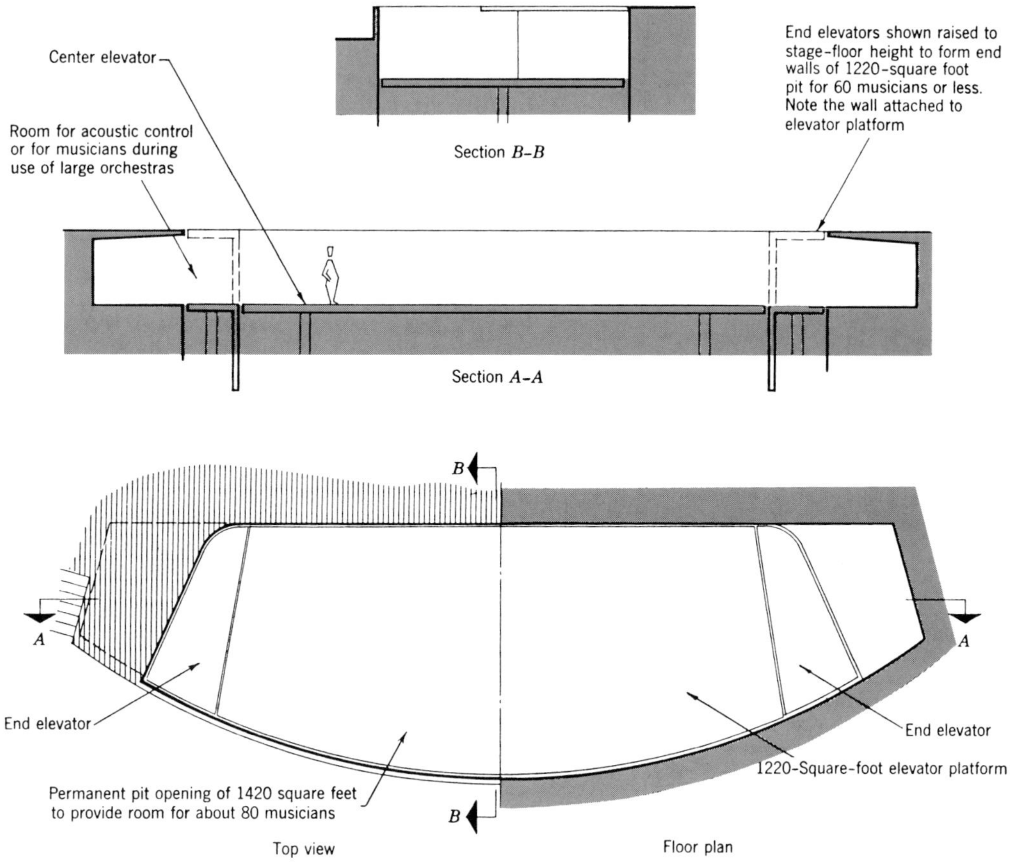

Figure 16.1. Design study for the pit of the (new) Metropolitan Opera House. The design built is shown in No. 14, Chapter 6. (Courtesy of ACENTECH of Cambridge, MA.)

Sunken pit, covered

The antithesis of the open pit is the covered pit designed by Wagner for the Festspielhaus in Bayreuth, Germany. It is partly buried beneath the stage and the remaining portion is nearly completely covered by an overhang. The Bayreuth pit is used with a very large orchestra in a hall that has a relatively long reverberation time, 1.55 sec.

Except for Wagner's music, the Bayreuth pit is not considered satisfactory because the string tones are muffled and the orchestra takes on an eerie sound.

Sunken pit, open

In a sunken pit, the floor area is usually at least twice as great as the open area. To the best of my knowledge, no existing pit that is in large part buried under a platform gives the orchestra the natural kind of sound heard in the opera houses of Vienna, Milan, Paris, or London, all of which have open pits.

BOXES AND BALCONIES

Boxes

Since the early days of opera, as illustrated in the Teatro alla Scala in Milan, Italy (see Fig. 16.2), boxes have been common in opera halls. It was said that they were designed to show off their inhabitants, particularly the jewelery and dress of the female attendees, while the men sat in the seats behind the opening or retreated to the bars. A photograph taken during a gala performance shows better attendance by men than indicated, but it is true that the balcony openings at the lower levels mostly frame women. The architectural arrangement of Fig. 16.2, shows that the La Scala balconies have two characteristics. On the good side, the box openings constitute only 43% of the surface of the sidewalls, thus reflecting considerable sound to the center cubic volume and producing more lively acoustics for those seated on the main floor and for those at the front rails of the boxes. On the bad side, such a small opening makes the sound weak and muffled at the rear of the box. In the side boxes, in particular, those high up would receive better sound at home on the TV.

The boxes in London's Royal Opera House (Fig. 16.3) are more hospitable to the music. The openings of the boxes consitute about 65% of the side walls and the sides between the boxes are set back, so that sound can reach the back seats much more easily. True, this returns much less sound to the main floor, but it distributes it more evenly to the attendees.

In Philadelphia's Academy of Music (No. 15 in Chapter 6), which is treated in this book as an opera house, the dividers between the boxes have been completely removed, so that everyone in the opera house receives nearly the same share of the sound energy that eminates from the stage. Also, the box openings occupy aout 75% of the sidewall area. From an acoustical standpoint, the Philadelphia's architecture is superior to that in the other two halls.

Balconies

As reviewed in Chapter 14 in the section on "Non-Uniformity: Balcony Overhangs," a balcony serves to reduce the distance from the rearmost auditor to the stage

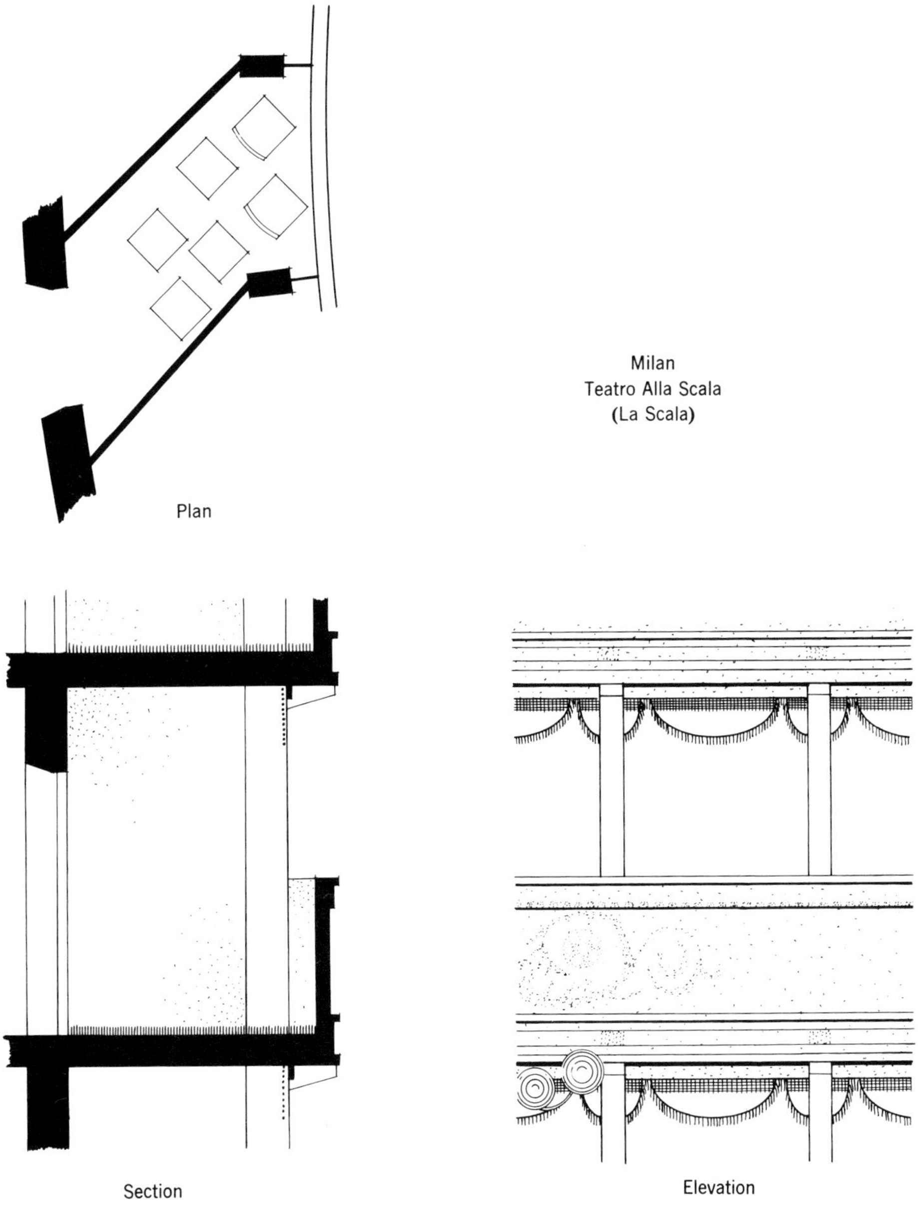

Figure 16.2. Sketches of a typical box in La Scala in Milan. Note the small opening at the front of the box to the house.

and in doing so overhangs rows of audience beneath. Deep overhangs are less damaging to opera music than to concert music, because in opera houses, the overhang eclipses reverberation originating from the upper part of the hall and thus gives greater clarity to the instrumental music and voices. Nevertheless, even the direct sound will suffer if

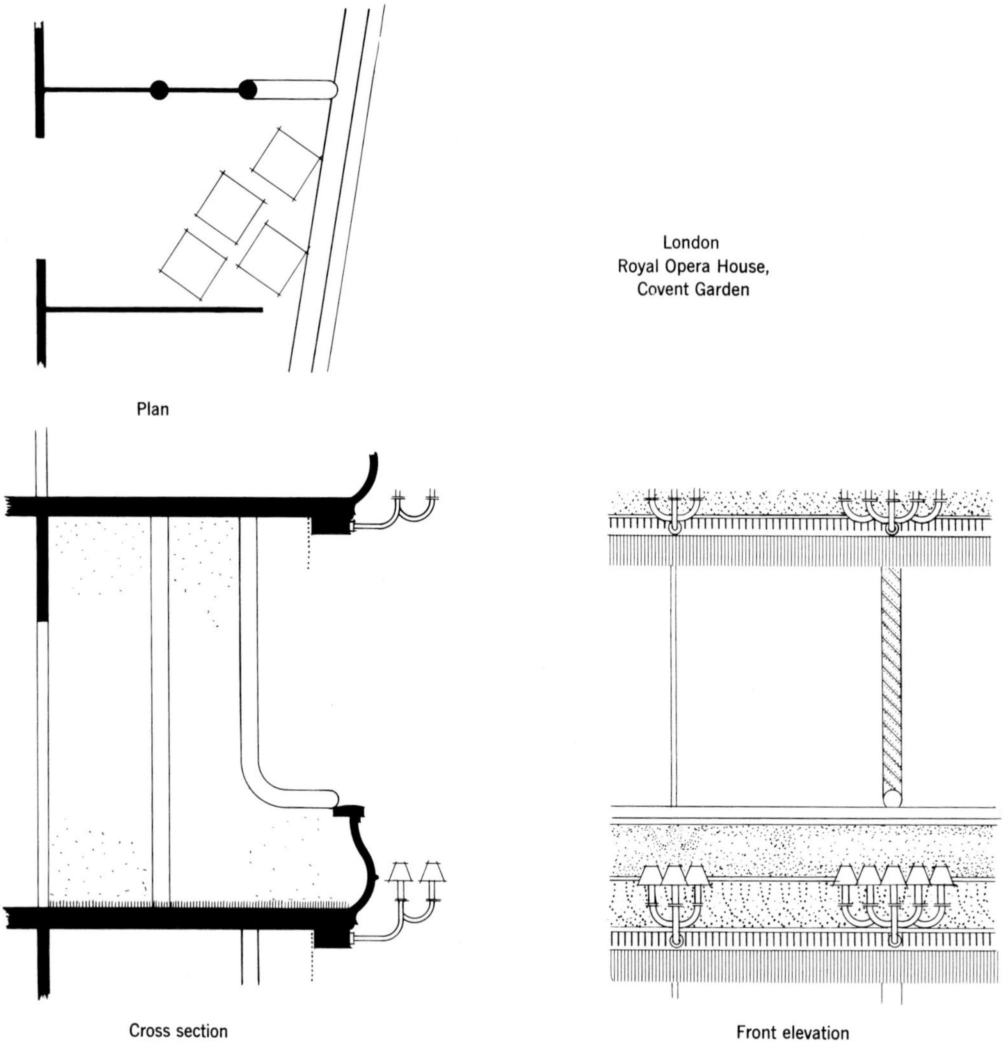

Figure 16.3. Sketches of a typical box in the Royal Opera House of London. Note the relatively large opening at the front of the box to the house.

the overhang is too great. Examples are shown in Figs. 14.4 and 14.5 of good and bad overhangs. The upper balcony of the (old) Metropolitan Opera House, Fig. 14.5(c) stands as the poorest of designs, while the lower overhang of Fig. 14.4(c) is reasonably satisfactory for opera.

Recommendations for balcony designs in opera halls

Two general recommendations for balcony overhangs in opera halls are illustrated in Fig. 16.4.

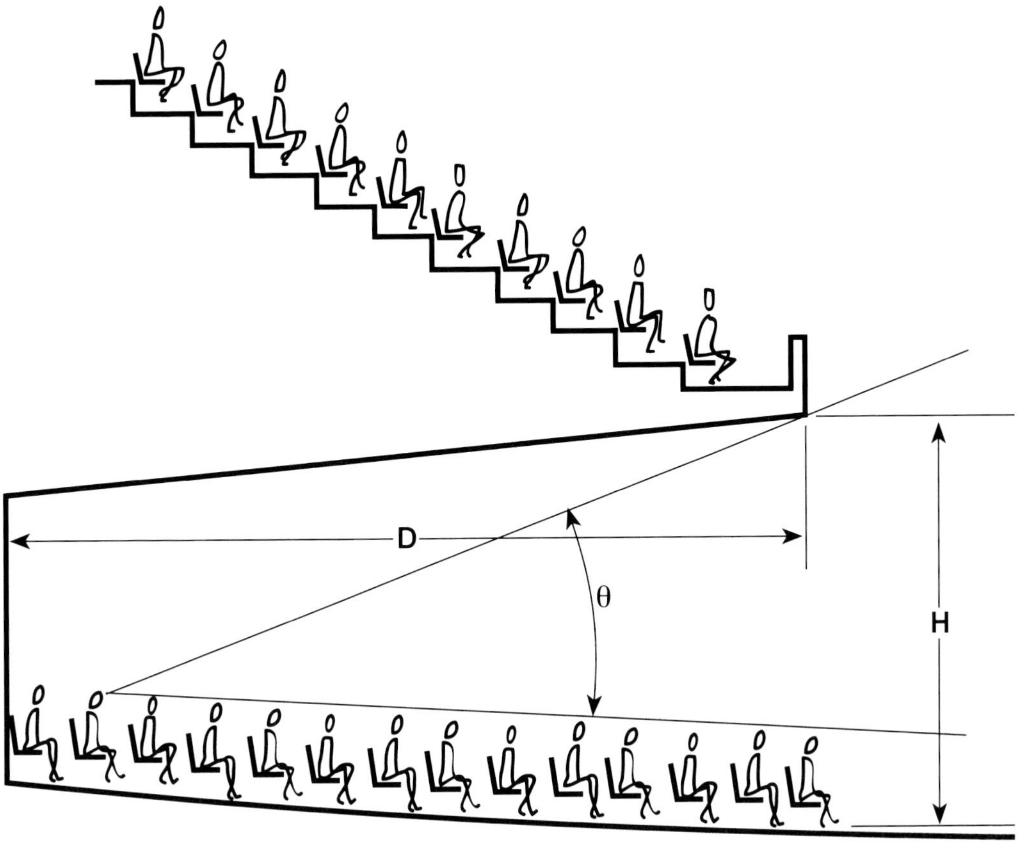

Figure 16.4. Recommended designs for satisfactory balcony overhangs in opera houses. As a general principal, D should not exceed $2H$. The angle θ is a more stringent measure based on audience acceptance (Barron, 1993) and should not be less than 25°. The under-balcony soffit and the rear wall should be shaped to reflect the direct sound toward the heads of the listeners. Shaping is specific to each hall and depends on the location of the stage and the rake of the floor beneath the seats.

1. As a general rule, the distance D should not exceed twice the height H. In addition, the soffit and the rear and side walls should be shaped to reflect the direct sound to the heads of the listeners.
2. As a more sensitive measure than the D over H ratio, the angle · should preferrably be greater than 25°.

The other recommendations of Chapter 14 are applicable both to concert hall and to opera house balcony design.

REVERBERANCE AND WARMTH

From Table 16.1 it is seen that the average reverberation time RT for sixteen opera houses is 1.5 sec. Six of the larger houses, Costa Mesa, New York, Tokyo, Paris Bastille,

Rochester, and San Francisco have the higher reverberation times, between 1.55 to 1.8 sec. This is balanced by four of the smaller houses, London, Milan, Paris Garnier, and Vienna, where the reverberation times are between 1.1 and 1.3 sec. Low reverberation times favor Italian opera where both the music and the singing words are highly articulated. For this reason, La Scala with a reverberation time of 1.2 sec is often held up as a model. But it seems that higher reverberation times are not held against the six houses named above, so that one might ask whether understanding the singing words is as important as a higher reverberance for the orchestral music?

Warmth is created in a hall by higher values for the bass ratio BR (for occupied hall), the ratio of the RT's at low frequencies to those as mid-frequencies. In concert halls with average reverberation times of 1.7 sec (occupied), BR averages 1.10. Table 16.1 shows that for opera, the average BR is higher, 1.18. This difference seems to have no meaning except that it gives more suport to male voices.

In the best opera halls, the initial-time-delay gap t_I is 26 msec or less. Only in two halls, the largest, Rochester and San Francisco, do the t_I's exceed 42 msec. In my previous study, I found that the optimum range of t_I's for opera houses may extend as high as 24 msec, in place of 20 msec for concert halls. Hence, any t_I up to about 40 msec is acceptable.

LOUDNESS

Loudness has been related to the strength factor G at middle frequencies. In Table 16.1, values of G_{mid} for seven opera houses are shown. It was derived in Chapter 9 that G_{mid} is related to EDT/V which is also tabulated in Table 16.1. If the EDT/V numbers are plotted on Fig. 9.4, it appears that G_{mid} for opera theaters is, on average, about 1.5 dB lower than that for concert halls, the largest differences being for those theaters with very low mid-frequency RT's of 1.1 sec. This difference is significant, and it adds weight to the need for higher reverberation times. The optimum reverberation time for an opera hall is about 1.4 sec. It must be noted, however, that the huge New York Metropolitan Opera House has a mid-frequency RT of 1.7 sec, which explains, at least in part, why the loudness attained in it by vocalists is sufficient to make it acceptable to critical audiences.

ASW

The important acoustical parameter, apparent source width ASW, is not as large as in the best of concert halls because of the paucity in most opera houses of side wall and

TABLE 16.1. Basic properties of opera houses, or halls used for opera.

OPERA HOUSES	No. of Seats	Cubic Volume cu m	RT Occup. sec	EDT Unoccup. sec	BR Occup.	G_{mid} (Compromise) Source on Stage dB	t_I msec	(1–$IACC_{E3}$)	LF_{E4}	EDT/V times a million sec/m³
Bayreuth, Festspielhaus	1,800	10,308	1.55	-	1.11	-	14			
Bloomington, Univ. Auditorium	3,718	25,545	1.4	-	1.12	-	40			
Buenos Aires, Teatro Colón	2,487	20,570	1.8*	-	-	-	19			
Costa Mesa, Segerstrom Hall	2,994	27,800	1.6	2.15	1.32	4.4	31	0.62	0.23	77
London, Royal Opera House	2,120	12,250	1.1	1.05	1.07	1.2	18		0.24	86
Milan, Teatro Alla Scala	2,289	11,252	1.2	1.2	1.21		20	0.48		
New York, Met. Opera House	3,816	24,724	1.8	2.25	1.20	-	34			91
Paris, Opéra Bastille	2,700	21,000	1.55	1.6	1.05	2.0	41			76
Paris, Opéra Garnier	2,131	10,000	1.15*	1.2	-	1.2	17	0.50		120
Philadelphia, Academy of Music	2,827	15,100	1.2	1.2	1.12	2.0	19	0.47	0.16	79
Rochester, Eastman Theatre	3,347	23,970	1.65	-	1.26	-	55			
Salzburg, Festspielhaus	2,158	14,020	1.5	1.9	1.10	4.0	23		0.16	136
San Francisco Opera House	3,252	20,900	1.5*	-	-	-	51			
Tokyo, Orchard Hall	1,928	17,050	1.8	-	1.12	-	26			
Vienna, Staatsoper	1,709	10,665	1.3	1.4	1.10	2.2	15	0.60		131
Washington, Kennedy Opera Hse	2,142	13,027	1.5	-	1.30	-				
AVERAGE	**2,603**	**17,446**	**1.5**	**1.55**	**1.18**	-	**29**			

*Estimated

side proscenium surfaces for sending strong lateral reflections to the audience areas. The best of the seven halls for which data are available in this regard are the London Royal Opera House, the Vienna Staatsoper and the Costa Mesa Segerstrom Hall. (Nos. 7, 26, and 55 of Chapter 6).

INTIMACY

All of the highly respected opera houses have initial-time-delay gaps t_I's less than 30 msec, near optimum. When the late Maestro Eric Leinsdorf was asked to rank in order by acoustical quality the seven opera halls in which he had performed during the past two years, his ranking was directly coordinated with the shortness of the distance between the side walls or the side balcony fronts. It is well known that t_I is determined either by side balcony fronts, suspended panels, or sidewalls, whichever returns the first strong reflections to the center of the main floor. From Table 16.1, the truth of Leinsdorf's implication is apparent—in the best houses t_I is short.

ECHO AND DISTORTION

Opera house "echo"

The subject of echoes in concert halls was discussed at some length in Chapter 14. In an opera house an echo may not be an echo—in fact, this may also be true in a concert hall, but no data are known to support it. Singers in an opera house desire acoustic feedback, if it is at the right level, because their voices are more directional than stringed instruments and they stand near the front of the stage where they get little support from surfaces around or behind the proscenium.

It has been stated (Beranek, 1992) that an opera house might best be designed with some degree of variability in the amount of sound that is reflected back to the stage by the rear wall on the main floor and the balcony fronts. Areas of the rear wall, which would otherwise return too strong a reflection, can be "toned down," made sound absorbing, by selectively adding a sound-absorptive material, 0.5 to 1.0 in. (2 to 5 cm) in thickness, which absorbs sound at frequencies of 500 Hz and higher. If the distance the sound travels and returns is as much as 2 × 100 ft =200 ft (60 m), it will result in a time delay of 180 msec. Soloists particularly want to hear that they are "filling the hall" at a comfortable singing level. How much sound energy should be returned to the stage to accomplish this without becoming an annoying echo? Since no means has been devised to predict this amount accurately, sound absorbing material should be added incrementally until the correct amount of "toning down" has been accomplished.

Nakamura *et al.* (1991) determined from extensive experiments that for a delay time of 140 msec (reflection from a surface about 80 ft, 48 m, distant), the level of the frontal reflection should lie 25 to 35 dB below the level of the direct sound (both measured with a microphone 1 m in front of the singer). Okano (1994) performed somewhat the same experiment with a group of soprano singers and asked them for their judgment of the tolerance level of the wall reflection. For delay times of 120, 170, and 220 msesc (reflecting surface at 68, 95, and 124 ft distant, respectively) the most sensitive of the vocalists reported tolerance levels (measured 1 m in front of the singer) of, respectively, 36, 38 and 42 dB below the direct sound.

Beranek (1962, p. 89–92), writes that the Indiana University Auditorium in Bloomington, Indiana (No. 2, Chapter 6), often used for opera, confirms these observations, "Near the front and on the stage [of this 3,760-seat hall] there is a special kind of liveness due to reflections from the rear wall of the main floor, the balcony front, the solid surfaces projecting back from the edges of the large grilles on the side walls, and the lighting coves in the ceiling. Singers say that this auditorium supports their voices well." It was stated to the author that large areas of sound-absorbing material were installed gradually to "tone down" the echoes until they were "just not echoes."

DISTORTION, NOISE AND NON-UNIFORMITY

Distortion, noise and non-uniformity have been discussed extensively in Chapter 14 and will not be repeated here.

◇17◇

Architectural Factors in the Design of Concert Halls

INTRODUCTION

Acoustics and architecture are inseparable. When commissioned to produce a space for music, the architect wishes to create both a memorable visual environment and a sound that satisfies the psychoacoustic peculiarities of listeners and the basic laws of physics. The acoustician serves as the interpreter of these complex subjects. But both the architect and the consultant function in a world of enormous complexity.

Conductors, musicians, and music critics are often quick to criticize a new hall with a slightly different sound. Each brings to the table his own memory of impressive performances that he has created or heard—often on modern CD's where the recording procedures may be more important than the characteristics of the acoustical space. And the public's acclaim may rest on the visual impression.

Furthermore, the quality of the orchestral music performed in a new hall frequently improves with time as the musicians adapt their playing to the individual characteristics of the space. Such is the example of the Berlin Philharmonie Hall, where a radical new design burst on the musical world in 1963. In spite of a unique performing environment and variability of the acoustics from one part of the hall to another, the musicians have adapted their style to the acoustics and the public has become accustomed to the sounds of different locations. The hall is highly estimated today.

Fortunately, the studies of this book have verified that there is no single architectural solution to the acoustical challenge. Successful acoustics for music have been achieved with rectangular, fan, vineyard, spread, horseshoe, and asymmetrical plans. Of the halls rated "excellent" and "good to excellent" in this study, each shape is represented. For each successful hall many attributes of musical-architectural acoustics are closely interrelated and the architect must deal with them simultaneously. For symphonic music, acoustical quality comes almost automatically in narrow, rectangular halls of low seating capacity, a fact that accounts for many of the successes of the nineteenth century. For opera, the horseshoe plan has been prevalent because it supplies good, but not excellent, acoustics with the social desire to see and be seen. But these successful designs are not binding today.

In the eighteenth and early nineteenth centuries, the models for new halls were often the very halls for which the music of their era was composed. How different now—halls must not only accommodate a musical repertoire dating over several centuries composed for various types of environments, or the radio alone, and generally must seat an audience so large that they constitute an entirely different acoustic venue. The multi-purpose character of many of today's halls introduces further complexities. If a hall must house concerts, drama, ballet, lectures, and other non-musical uses, the design of the stage and its integration with the hall itself can tax the ingenuity of even the most clever of architects and acousticians.

EARLY PERIOD IN A HALL'S DESIGN

The acoustician ought to be consulted during the selection and development of the site for a new hall, so that the potential effects of exterior noises are evaluated. If there is a subway, a highway, or a busy airport nearby, an additional budget allotment for vibration and noise control in the hall may be needed.

Acoustical planning for the interior of the hall should begin at the time that the pattern of use, the audience size, the desired level of acoustical quality, and the available budget are being discussed. Optimum reverberation times and loudness of the music in the hall dictate not only the permissible size of the audience but the cubic volume. If audience count is large, the choice of balconies may dictate the height and foot-print of the hall. Necessary compromises among uses, optimum acoustical attributes, and audience size must be recognized early and communicated to the user and the public to avoid later censure. Each element of a hall has its effect on the ultimate acoustical result, and many attributes cannot be corrected once the basic shape, size, and location are set.

After these preliminaries, the design requires the combined talents of architect, acoustical consultant, lighting and electronic sound engineers, structural specialists, and costing experts. The building owner and the performing groups should also be involved in the planning stages if the acoustics of the hall are to satisfy their needs.

Because of the myriad of architectural possibilities for design, this chapter cannot hope to present specific recommendations, but the more important generic parameters and pitfalls are reviewed.

HIERARCHIES IN CONCERT AND OPERA HALL DESIGN

A process as complex as the design of a concert or an opera hall should only be approached in terms of its "whole." The hierarchy of the "whole" involves four major levels, Puissance, Art/Craft, Engineering, and Science, as suggested by Marshall (1990) and shown in Table 17.1.

In many cases of acoustical failures, Puissance has taken precedence over the objective needs to the point where neither the desired acoustics nor the architect's artistic concepts were achieved. Severe problems in New York's Philharmonic Hall resulted, in part, because the Building Committee, in the interest of saving money, cancelled two vital components—namely, sound-diffusing irregularities on the walls, balcony fronts, and ceiling and the motorized winches necessary for adjusting the hanging panels.

Each of the other levels in the hierarchy can contribute to acoustical failure. The hall may be designed for lectures, but end up being used primarily for symphonic concerts. Substitution of light weight wall and ceiling materials for heavier construction may cause loss of bass. From the technical side, the acoustical consultant may not have been given the resources to use available CAD (computer assisted design) programs or to construct real models in which to establish the efficacy of a new design

TABLE 17.1

Subjective	
Puissance:	Owner aspirations, public's needs and expectations, music critics, media, donor's restrictions, politics, architect's imagination, management structure, budget and control of costs.
Art/Craft:	Musical repertoire, performance expectations (symphonic, choral, soloist), audience and critics conception of acoustical quality, architectural design skills, crafts.
Objective	
Engineering:	Engineering (acoustical, mechanical, interior, lighting, air processing, sound systems), psychophysics, construction process, product suitability.
Science:	Laws of physics (acoustics), computer software, mathematics.

concept and to refine details. Vitally important, the architect's design staff must become acquainted with the acoustic and noise control essentials so that important factors are not overlooked when making the construction drawings and supervising the construction.

STRATEGY FOR CONCERT HALL DESIGN

Marshall also postulated a design strategy that led to the successful completion of Segerstrom Hall, in Costa Mesa, California, a 3,000 seat, multipurpose hall, that has excellent acoustics. Nearly the same strategy was followed in the 1959 renovations of the Tanglewood's Koussevitzky Music Shed and in the McDermott/Meyerson Concert Hall in Dallas. The design process was carried out in the following steps:

(1) The owner and the manager of the complex, responding to a public and cultural need, wrote a preliminary set of specifications—containing alternate locations of the building, the seating capacity that they felt would best fit the public's need, the probable range of uses for the hall, the estimated budget availability, and the musicians' and management's requirements for rehearsal, dressing room, recording, TV and radio, library, office, and public spaces.

(2) In the Tanglewood case, where improvement of existing acoustics was the goal, the acoustical consultant was selected many months prior to the architect and told the owner's desires. These included elimination of the "muddiness" of the sound in the front half of the hall, design of a greatly enlarged stage, improvement of communication among musicians, elimination of echoes, increased loudness, and maintenance of the same level of reverberation as already existed. The consultant was asked to determine whether these requests could be executed without rebuilding the hall and to suggest solutions. When these initial acoustical studies were completed, the architect was commissioned and the two worked together to produce a highly successful result.

If the requirement had been for a new hall in a city, the preliminary recommendations by the acoustical consultant would have included discussions of the site and orientation of the hall, ways of meeting the acoustical needs of multiple users, compromises in acoustical quality related to seating capacity and building budget, the probable cubic volume of the hall, and possible role-model halls to be visited and understood. These broad considerations would enable the owner to firm up the goals for the hall and to make a clearer presentation to the architect and the users.

(3) After the owner has redefined the goals following these studies and recommendations the architect is given approval to begin the design and assemble the principal members of the design team—the structural engineers, planners, interior designers, lighting engineers, building code experts, and cost estimators. The architect then prepares a preliminary design, working with the acoustical consultant. This process may be interleaved with visits to role model halls.

(4) The revised specifications, the architect's preliminary design and the acoustician's first report are given by the architect to the members of the design team in preparation for a grand design conference.

(5) The design conference is held. In the Segerstrom Hall case, this was a multi-week meeting of the assemblage. Its purpose was to hammer out a preliminary design that began to take on the shape of the eventual hall and that included the essentials of size, acoustics, lighting, air handling, and materials. This and other experiences have shown that nearly every major concept eventually built had been developed during this kind of conference.

(6) The architect, in close consultation with the acoustical consultant, then prepares and renders his design concept in drawings that are adequate for the acoustical consultant to use in computer modeling.

(7) A three-dimensional computer model is programmed that includes all major surfaces of the interior of the hall. A simulated source "radiates sound waves" into the "hall." At each listener's position chosen, the direct and reflected "sounds" are recorded.

As an example, in Fig. 17.1 a plan (a) and a crossection (b) plot of the progress of sound waves in a three-dimensional computer model of a 2,000 seat concert hall is shown. At the left in (a), *S* is the beginning of a group of emerging lines that represent outgoing sound waves from a source on the stage. After reflection, these waves arrive at the listener's position *L* on the main floor. In the longitudinal crosssection (b), reflections from the ceiling, the balcony fronts and their soffits are evident.

In Fig. 17.2, the early reflections as found from the computer model are shown in (b) and (d) for two listeners' positions, with (b) corresponding to the listener's position of Fig. 17.1 and (d) to a position farther forward in the hall. With the computer model the room surfaces can be adjusted easily to bring about a more uniform distribution of sound waves over the audience and a better sound texture. A report on the findings with recommendations for alternative designs is then prepared by the acoustical consultant and presented to the architect.

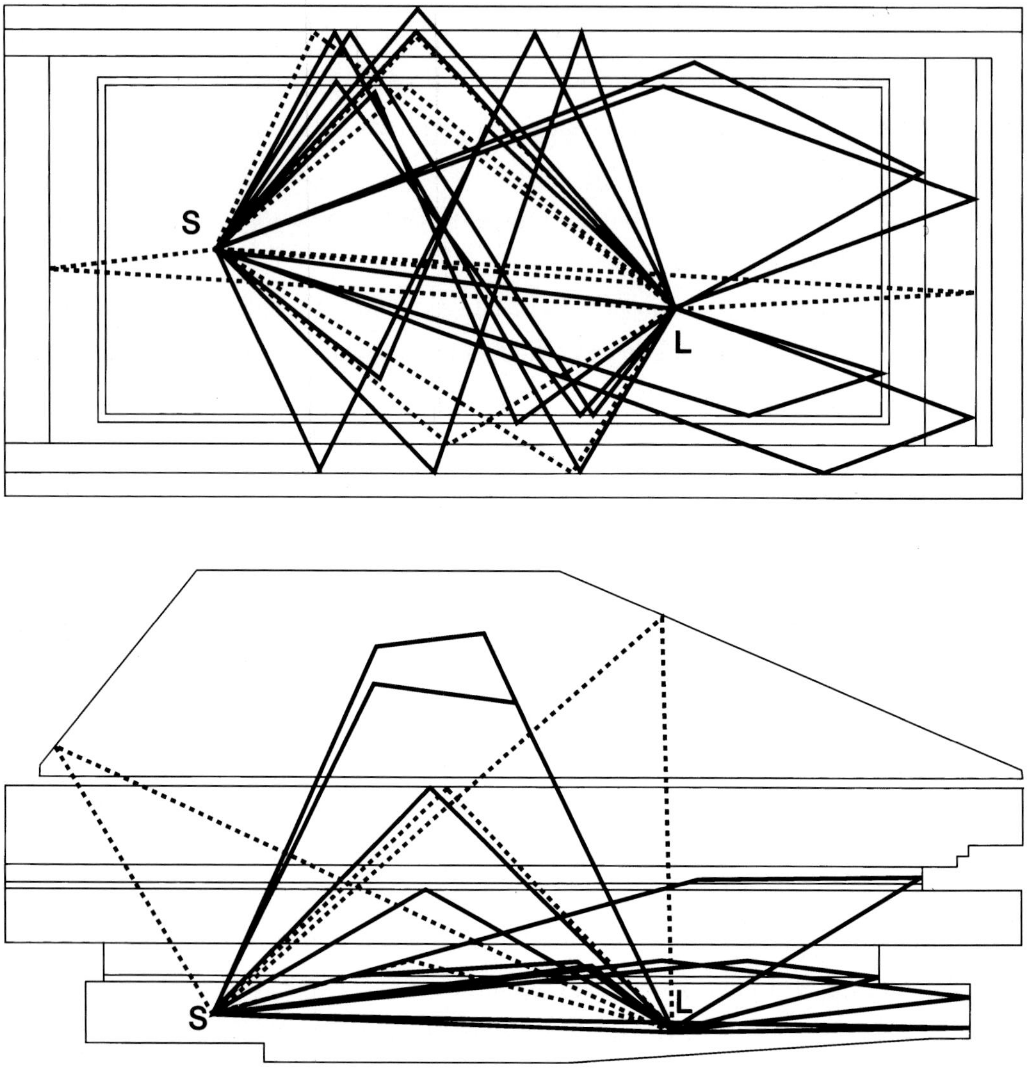

Figure 17.1. CAD produced reflection patterns of the first and second order reflections between a source S and a listener L in a study for a proposed design of a concert hall. The results of the study are shown in (b) and (d) of Fig. 17.2.

(8) The architect receives these findings and evolves a more detailed design in coordination with his engineers and consultants. He then prepares a set of drawings that are detailed enough to be used for the construction of a real model of the hall.

(9) A real model has much to recommend it. If time, money and space permit, a 1:10 or 1:20 scale model is best, because it is easy to include details of wall and ceiling irregularities, modify balcony fronts, add items such as cornice reflectors, QRD diffusers, and sound absorbing materials. In such a model, fairly accurate acoustical simula-

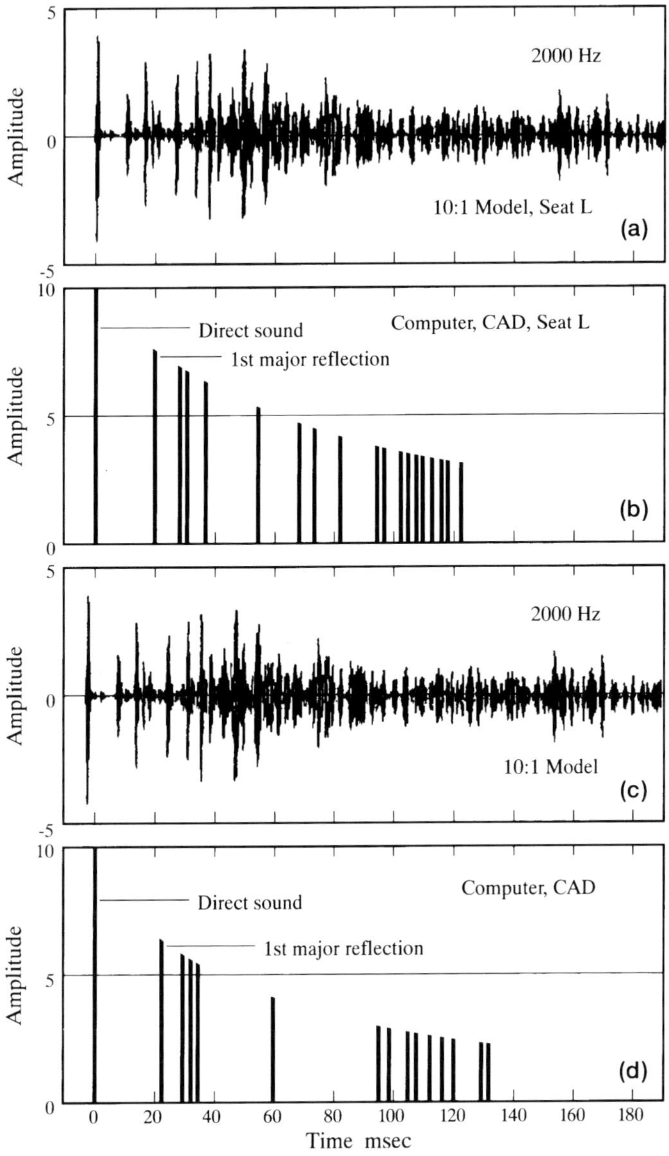

Figure 17.2. Reflectograms obtained in a 10:1 physical model of the proposed concert hall for which the earlier CAD study of Fig. 17.1 was made. The listener is designated L as in Fig. 17.1. (a) and (b) are for the same location of L as in Fig. 17.1 and (b) and (d) are for L farther forward in the hall. The CAD and 10:1 patterns do not match because the detailed design of the hall was changed between the two records.

tion of the audience and the manner in which it scatters and absorbs sound is possible. Especially important, a source of music, a tiny loudspeaker, can be placed on the stage and a "dummy head," one to two-centimeters in diameter, with two tiny microphones for ears can be placed anywhere in the audience for binaural evaluation.

The vital acoustical attributes discussed in Chapters 8 to 12 can be measured in the model; reverberation time RT, bass ratio BR, early-decay-time EDT, energy level G, interaural cross-correlation coefficient IACC, initial-time-delay gap t_I, clarity ratio C_{80} and the presence or absence of echo. Especially important is determination of the uniformity of distribution and the maintaining of quality of the on-stage sound throughout the audience areas.

In Fig. 17.2 (a) and (c) "reflectograms" made in a 1:10 real model are shown for comparison with the earlier computer model results of (b) and (d). Reflectogram (a) is for the seat L on the main floor as for Fig. 17.1, while (c) is for a seat nearer the front. A reflectogram is made by sending out a short pulse (like a strong, sharp handclap) from the source. At the listener's position the binaural microphones send a signal to a computer screen which shows the direct wave and the succession of reflected waves that follows. These comprise the sound texture.

As can be seen from Fig. 17.2, the 1:10 real model shows more detail than the computer model. For example, it indicates a reflection, of lesser magnitude, occurring before the first reflection shown on the computer model.

If a 1:10 or 1:20 model is not practical, models of varying efficacy can be built with scale ratios of up to 1:50. A 1:50 model can be built from "foam-core" board, with QRD reflectors made from a machined acrylic sheet, in as little as a few days. The acoustical data can be available in report form within less than a month, although it will not be as complete or as accurate as that from a larger model.

(10) When the date of opening of the hall is apparent, the construction time must be planned so that the interior will be completed three months in advance. A test concert is arranged for that time which, if possible, should involve the symphony orchestra that is to use the hall. Acoustical measurements can then be made both in the unoccupied hall and in the hall occupied with a captive audience and orchestra. In the three-months following the test concert, adjustments can be made in the sound reflecting surfaces. If, for instance, the balance between high and low frequencies needs correction or if there is an unexpected echo, carefully-placed sound absorbing materials can be added to control it. In this period, the other building trades can correct problems in lighting, air handling, and audience conveniences.

(11) A few final words of advice are directed to the owner/manager. The user should be urged to limit the opening night performance to the regular-sized orchestra, seated on the regular-sized stage (as contrasted with an extended stage), and to playing compositions that are known to the audience rather than to feature one that premiers a composer's new symphony. At one disastrous opening night concert, a 300 member choral group, a 200 piece orchestra and a new composition that was excruciatingly loud and raucous sent everybody home with a headache. A favorable review could hardly be expected.

In the material that follows, a logical process that can be followed starting from the owners' statements of their needs in a concert hall to a successful design is presented by example.

CRUCIAL EARLY DESIGN DECISIONS

Audience area and seat count

The architects and acoustical consultants of Western Europe usually have been commissioned to design relatively small halls because the states and cities subsidize orchestra and opera so that their costs are borne only partly by the sale of tickets. As listed in Table 17.2 the halls in those countries generally accommodate audiences of only 1,100 to 2,500 with an average volume of about 16,500 m^3 (585,000 ft^3). Non-European halls (Table 17.3) seat between 1,700 and 3,700 with an average volume of 25,667 m^3 (906,300 ft^3). In a hall as large as 24,000 m^3 the side walls, balcony fronts and the ceiling are so far away from the main floor audience that the acoustical attributes of spaciousness ASW and intimacy t_I are not satisfied except by the addition of reflecting panels.

In a recently introduced design concept, a relatively narrow hall with seating capacity of under 2,100 is augmented by a coupled reverberant chamber. Acoustical access to the chamber can be varied by operable doors. This design combines the acoustical attributes of clarity associated with narrow halls plus a selection of longer reverberation tails usually associated with much larger spaces. This concept allows the conductor and musicians selectively to add acoustical variety to their performances. Examples are Dallas, McDermott/Meyerson Concert Hall and Birmingham, Symphony Hall. This concept has been well received.

The architect's and acoustical consultant's first concern in the design of a new hall should be the total seating capacity, since this is the factor that fixes the size and complexity of the hall. He should make certain that the number of seats called for by the owner is actually what is needed. A hall should not be built to accommodate the largest anticipated audience. No musical group performs its best in a half-filled house, and half the acoustical battle is won if the hall is small.

TABLE 17.2. Number of seats and cubic volumes for typical European concert halls.

	Seats	Volume cu m
AUSTRIA		
Vienna, Grosser Musikvereinssaal	1,680	15,000
Salzburg, Festspielhaus	2,158	15,500
BELGIUM		
Brussels, Palais des Beaux-Arts	2,150	12,520
DENMARK		
Copenhagen, Radiohuset, Studio 1	1,081	11,900
FRANCE		
Paris, Salle Pléyel	2,386	15,500
GERMANY		
Berlin, Konzerthaus (Schauspielhaus)	1,575	15,000
Leipzig, Gewandhaus	1,900	21,000
Berlin, Philharmonie	2,335	21,000
Bonn, Beethovenhalle	1,407	15,730
Munich, Herkulessalle	1,287	13,590
Munich, Philharmonie Am Gasteig	2,487	29,700
Stuttgart, Liederhalle, Grosser Salle	2,000	16,000
NETHERLANDS		
Amsterdam, Concertgebouw	2,037	18,780
Rotterdam, De Doelen Concert Hall	2,242	24,070
SWITZERLAND		
Basel, Stadt-Casino	1,448	10,500
Zurich, Grosser Tonhallesaal	1,546	11,400
Average	**1,851**	**16,505 m^3**

EXAMPLE

Assume that the owner wants a seating capacity of about 2,500. After discussion with the user it is decided to try for a strength factor G_{mid} equal to 4.0 dB (compromise value discussed in Chapter 15) and an RT of 1.9 sec. Assume EDT to be 0.2 sec higher, 2.1 sec. From Fig. 9.4, we obtain $(\text{EDT}/V) \times$ million = 100. From Eq. (9.4), the total acoustical area S_T = $(0.14 \times 1.105 \div 100) \times$ million = 1,547 m^2. From this, subtract the area of the stage, 200 m^2, giving S_A = 1,347 m^2. From Table 17.4, we find, on

TABLE 17.3. Number of seats and cubic volumes of typical non-European concert halls.

	Seats	Volume cu m
UNITED STATES		
Baltimore, Meyerhoff Hall*	2,467	21,520
Bloomington, Indiana U. Auditorium	3,760	26,900
Boston, Symphony Hall	2,625	18,750
Buffalo, Kleinhans Music Hall*	2,839	18,240
Chicago, Orchestra Hall*	2,582	18,000
Cleveland, Severance Hall	2,101	15,690
Costa Mesa, Segerstrom Hall	2,903	27,800
Dallas, McDermott/Meyerson	2,065	23,900
Lenox, Tanglewood Music Shed	5,121	42,480
Lenox, Seiji Ozawa Hall	1,180	11,610
New York, Avery Fisher Hall	2,742	22,600
New York, Carnegie Hall	2,804	24,270
Rochester, N Y, Eastman Theater	3,347	25,470
Salt Lake, Utah, Symphony Hall	2,812	19,500
San Francisco, Davies Hall*	2,743	24,070
Washington, Kennedy Concert Hall	2,759	19,300
Worcester, MA Mechanics Hall	1,343	10,760
AUSTRALIA		
Sydney Opera House, Concert Hall	2,679	24,600
CANADA		
Toronto, Roy Thompson Hall	2,812	28,300
Edmonton, Alberta Jubilee Hall	2,678	21,500
Montreal, Salle Wilfrid-Pelletier*	2,982	25,000
GREAT BRITAIN		
Birmingham, Symphony Hall	2,211	25,000
Bristol, Colston Hall	2,121	13,450
Cardiff, Wales, St. David's Hall	1,952	22,000
Edinburgh, Usher Hall	2,547	15,700
Glasgow, Royal Concert Hall	2,459	22,700
Liverpool, Philharmonic Hall*	1,824	13,560
London, Barbican Concert Hall*	2,026	17,750
London, Royal Albert Hall	5,080	86,660
London, Royal Festival Hall	2,901	21,950
Manchester, Free Trade Hall	2,351	15,430
HUNGARY		
Pátria Saal	1,750	13,400
ISRAEL		
Jerusalem, Binyanei Ha'Oomah	3,142	24,700
Tel Aviv, Mann Auditorium	2,715	21,240

Table 17.3. *Continued*

	Seats	Volume cu m
JAPAN		
Osaka, Symphony Hall	1,702	17,800
Tokyo, Bunka Kaikan, Ueno	2,327	17,300
Tokyo, Metropolitan Art Space	2,017	25,000
Tokyo, NHK Hall	3,677	25,200
Tokyo, Orchard Hall, Bunkamura	2,150	20,500
Tokyo, Suntory Hall	2,006	21,000
MEXICO		
Mexico City, Salla Nezahualcotyl	2,376	30,640
NEW ZEALAND		
Christchurch, N. Z., Town Hall	2,662	20,500
TAIWAN		
Taipei, Concert Hall Auditorium	2,074	16,700
VENEZUELA		
Caracas, Aula Magna	2,660	24,920
Average	**2,610**	**25,667 m³**

* Acoustical improvements in process or completed.

average, $S_A/S_a = 1.22$. The area the seats will sit over is $S_a = 1{,}347/1.22 = 1{,}104$ m^2. And with $S_a/N = 0.51$, $N = 2{,}164$ seats. If we had used Figs. 9.5 and 9.6 and $S_T/N = 1.45$ instead of the more exact formulas, we would have obtained 2,200 seats. To obtain 2,500 seats, recalculations show that we would have to sacrifice about 0.6 dB of sound strength, i.e., $G_{\text{mid}} = 4.4$ dB and S_T would be 1,750 m^2. The volume of the room is determined from Eq. 9.6. Thus, $V = (1.9/0.14) \times S_T = 23{,}750$ m^3. These numbers are similar to those for Glasgow, Royal Concert Hall.

Balconies

Most halls require two or more balconies. If there are several balconies, the number of aisles and access ways has to be increased, and part of this area adds to the total sound-absorbing area of the hall S_T. It is a difficult problem for an architect to accommodate his design to the conflicting requirements of reasonable cubic volume, satisfactory apparent source width ASW and reasonable intimacy t_I. As discussed in Chapters 14 and 15, deep balcony overhangs must be avoided.

APPARENT SOURCE WIDTH ASW (SPACIOUSNESS)

Every surface in a hall is capable of being used to provide early lateral sound reflections to some part of the audience area. Particularly important are surfaces near the front of the hall. Experiments have shown (Ando, 1985, p. 52), that the most important lateral reflections arrive at a listener's ears from angles between 35° and 75°

TABLE 17.4. Stage and audience areas for halls built after 1962, and for three halls built 1900 and earlier.

	S_o Stage Area sq m	S_a Chairs Area sq m	S_A Acoustic Area sq m	S_T Total Acoustic Area sq m	Ratio S_A/S_a	N	S_a/N sq m per seat
CONCERT HALLS AFTER 1962							
Baltimore MEYERHOFF HALL	186	1,196	1,486	1,672	1.24	2,467	0.48
Berlin KAMMERMUSIKSAAL	78	618	829	907	1.34	1,138	0.54
Berlin, KONZERTHAUS (SCHAUSPIELHAUS)	158	784	943	1,101	1.20	1,575	0.50
Berlin PHILHARMONIE	172	1,057	1,385	1,557	1.31	2,325	0.45
Birmingham SYMPHONY HALL	279	1,031	1,320	1,599	1.28	2,211	0.65
Budapest PÁTRIA HALL	156	1,140	1,286	1,442	1.13	1,750	0.65
Cardiff, Wales ST. DAVID'S HALL	186	1,000	1,235	1,421	1.24	1,952	0.51
Christchurch, N.Z. TOWN HALL	194	1,127	1,416	1,610	1.26	2,662	0.42
Costa Mesa SEGERSTROM HALL	223	1,504	1,742	1,965	1.16	2,903	0.52
Dallas, MEYERSON CONCERT HALL	250	980	1,210	1,460	1.23	2,065	0.47
Glasgow ROYAL CONCERT HALL	218	1,147	1,365	1,583	1.19	2,459	0.44
Leipzig GEWANDHAUS	181	1,036	1,197	1,378	1.16	1,900	0.55
London, BARBICAN CONCERT HALL	160	1,123	1,326	1,486	1.18	2,026	0.55
Mexico City, SALLA NEZAHUALCOYOTL	270	1,476	1,684	1,954	1.14	2,450	0.60

Table 17.4. *Continued*

	S_o Stage Area sq m	S_a Chairs Area sq m	S_A Acoustic Area sq m	S_T Total Acoustic Area sq m	Ratio S_A/S_a	N	S_a/N sq m per seat
Minneapolis MINN. ORCH. HALL	203	1,266	1,574	1,777	1.24	2,450	0.52
Montreal SALLE WILFRID-PELLETIER	172	1,550	1,767	1,939	1.14	2,982	0.52
Munich PHILHARMONIE-GASTEIG	230	1,329	1,639	1,869	1.23	2,487	0.53
New York AVERY FISHER HALL	203	1,189	1,480	1,683	1.24	2,742	0.43
Rotterdam, DE DOELEN CONCERT HALL	195	1,178	1,509	1,704	1.28	2,242	0.53
Salt Lake, Utah SYMPHONY HALL	218	1,486	1,669	1,887	1.12	2,812	0.53
San Francisco DAVIES HALL	200	1,214	1,562	1,762	1.29	2,743	0.44
Sydney Opera House CONCERT HALL	181	1,362	1,563	1,744	1.15	2,679	0.51
Taipei, CONCERT HALL AUDITORIUM	269	1,022	1,261	1,530	1.23	2,074	0.49
Toronto ROY THOMPSON HALL	222	1,401	1,681	1,903	1.20	2,812	0.50
Averages	**203**	**1,157**	**1,405**	**1,608**	**1.22**	**2,304**	**0.51**
SUPERIOR HALLS BEFORE 1901							
Amsterdam CONCERTGEBOUW	160	843	1,125	1,285	1.14	2,037	0.41
Boston SYMPHONY HALL	152	1,056	1,370	1,522	1.11	2,625	0.40
Vienna MUSIKVEREINSSAAL	163	690	955	1,118	1.17	1,680	0.41
Averages	**158**	**863**	**1,150**	**1,308**	**1.14**	**2,114**	**0.41**
JAPANESE HALLS AFTER 1962							
Osaka SYMPHONY HALL	285	908	1,236	1,521	1.36	1,702	0.53
Tokyo METROPOLITAN ART SPACE	207	929	1,312	1,519	1.41	2,017	0.46
Tokyo, ORCHARD HALL, BUNKAMURA	217	1,000	1,314	1,531	1.31	2,150	0.47
Tokyo SUNTORY HALL	235	1,042	1,364	1,599	1.31	2,006	0.52
Averages	**220**	**990**	**1,330**	**1,550**	**1.35**	**2,058**	**0.48**

measured from the vertical plane passing through the listener and the center of the performing group. Balcony front reflections, produced by proper shaping of the balcony surfaces, the side walls of a shoebox shaped hall, or specially hung sidewall reflectors, are important sources of early lateral reflections. But overhead reflections must not be neglected; they add to the texture of the sound and become more important as the number of lateral reflections decreases.

Four types of solutions are available today for assuring an audience's feeling of acoustical spaciousness, ASW, which is measured best by one minus the interaural cross-correlation coefficient (1–$IACC_{E3}$). The first solution is the classical narrow rectangular hall.

The next solution appears in three halls in this book—the New Zealand, Christchurch Town Hall; the Paris, Salle Pleyel; and the U.S.A., Costa Mesa, Segerstrom Hall. The construction consists of slanted, large, reflecting panels spaced out from the sidewalls that serve to reflect early sound energy to all parts of the seating areas. For maximum effectiveness, the surfaces of these reflectors are covered with properly designed QRD sound reflectors.

Another solution to the need for adequate ASW, is an architectural concept called "vineyard" design, which embodies several audience "trays" or tiers located at different heights. The side walls of each tier act to reflect early sound energy laterally to the audiences seated in adjacent tiers. This principle was first tried with success in the Berlin, Philharmonie Hall and later in the Tokyo, Suntory Hall and the Kammermusiksaal of the Philharmonie (see Chapter 6). It is also used in combination with the large sloping panels in Costa Mesa, Segerstrom Hall which seats 3,000.

The fourth solution is used in the Tanglewood, Koussevitzky Music Shed; the Mexico City, Salla Nezahualcoyotl; and the Cardiff, Wales, St. David's Hall, in all of which many overhead surfaces are used to produce a feeling of spaciousness and intimacy, without necessarily achieving a large (1–$IACC_{E3}$). The reasons for the success of this design is given for the Tanglewood Music Shed in the sections entitled Comment and Caution, p. 475 and Lenox, pp. 559 and 560.

The hanging panel solution is somewhat critical in design, because a good balance between the reverberant sound field and the early sound reflections provided by the suspended panels must be achieved. If the suspended panels are too dense, the space above the panels will sound like a second room coupled through a door to the first. If they are too small in area, they will have little noticeable effect. The proper ratio of the area of the panels in an array to the area within the circumference of the array is around 0.5, but this number has not yet been set definitely.

ENVELOPMENT (DIFFUSION)

Envelopment, a listener's subjective impression that the sound field surrounds him, was discussed in Chapter 11. From the standpoint of architectural design, the rule for providing good envelopment is to provide surface irregularities everywhere and to have no focusing areas. These requirements came naturally in the period of Baroque architecture. Today, they are acoustical necessities.

The principal component of envelopment is diffuseness of the sound field, that is to say, the reflections should come from everywhere. This is achieved quite naturally in halls where the seats are not steeply raked so that the sound can reach all walls, where there are no deep balconies, and where the ceiling and sidewalls incorporate major irregularities. Also, the balcony fronts and the under-balcony soffits should not be plain.

Where this does not happen is at seats in the forward part of a long, steeply sloped, rear balcony. Reverberant sound cannot come from behind because the audience behind the listener absorbs it.

A deep balcony overhang may kill off the impression of reverberant sound envelopment completely for those sitting beneath it, unless its mouth is very high and the under-balcony soffit is designed to spread the incoming sound evenly over the audience seated there. Examples of halls with various qualities of balcony overhangs are given in Chapters 14 and 16.

CLARITY

The clarity of the sound in a concert hall is usually measured by the quantity C_{80}, the ratio of the energy in the early sound, i.e., direct plus early reflections, to the energy in the later reverberant sound. It is easily perceived by an experienced listener.

A short initial-time-delay gap usually means that more early reflections are present in the first 80 msec after arrival of the direct sound wave, which indicates more energy in the early sound. Also, a desired low value of $IACC_{E3}$ is associated with adequate sound energy in the early, before 80 msec, time period.

Looking at the C_{80} data plotted in Fig. 12.1, one concludes that a design goal should be to achieve a value for it of 0 to −4 dB and should avoid values of +1 and higher for symphonic concert halls.

LOUDNESS OF DIRECT AND REVERBERANT SOUND

DIRECT SOUND STRENGTH: Although the energy in the direct sound drops off rapidly with distance, the same as outdoors, at a rate of about 6 dB for each doubling of distance, it is still the first sound that reaches a listener and thus is perceptible. A rule to go by is that no listener on the main floor should be seated farther from the concertmaster than about 100 ft (30 m). In the balcony, the distance may be greater, say as much as 130 ft (40 m) if the walls and ceiling guide part of the sound (very early reflections) into the balcony. This distance in Boston Symphony Hall is about 133 feet (40.5 m).

REVERBERANT SOUND STRENGTH: As we have already discussed in Chapter 9, the (compromise) strength factor at mid-frequencies G_{mid}, which is a measure of the loudness of the reverberant sound, should optimally be in the range of +3 to +5 dB averaged throughout the hall. In terms of other measurable quantities this corresponds to a value between 70 and 130 for the ratio of early-decay-time (EDT) in the unoccupied hall to the cubic volume in meters multiplied by a million. If V is in cubic feet, the range of EDT/V (times a million) would be 2 to 3.7.

WARMTH AND BASS STRENGTH FACTOR

Warmth and the bass strength factor together determine a concert goer's perception of the strength of the bass. Warmth is ratio of the reverberation times at low frequencies (average of the RT's at 125 and 250 Hz) to the reverberation times at mid-frequencies (average of the RT's at 500 and 1,000 Hz) The bass strength factor G_L is the energy in the total sound field surrounding the listener at low frequencies. The former is discussed in Chapter 8 and the latter in Chapter 9. The two are compared in Table 8.8 for those halls in which the values of G_L are more than one decibel less than G_M, the strength factor at mid-frequencies.

Although warmth was found by the Berlin group (Cremer and Mueller, 1982 and Beranek, 1992), to be a significant factor in the subjective ratings of concert halls, it appears (from comparison of the interviews in this study with the measurements of reverberation times) to be of lesser importance than four of the other measures. Nevertheless, a proper strength of the bass is a one indication of a good hall, although Boston Symphony Hall is split—it has a satisfactorily bass ratio BR, but the strength factor G_L is a little less than that of the majority of the halls.

To avoid troubles caused by lack of perceived bass, the architect should follow these rules:

(a) Avoid the use of thin wood (under 1 in., 2.5 cm, but preferreably use 1.5 in., 3.8 cm) in the sidewalls and ceiling of a concert hall, except in very limited areas.

(b) Use 1 in. or more of plaster, well painted concrete block, or poured concrete for sidewall construction if possible. If a wood appearance is desired, use a wooden veneer cemented directly to plaster.

(c) Choose chairs that do not absorb the bass excessively. Comparisons between different types of chairs in regard to sound absorption is made in Appendix 5. Occupied, one chair has a sound absorption coefficient of 0.76 at 125 Hz and the other 0.54. Use of the first chair instead of the second could yield a subjective rating for the completed hall of "fair to good" whereas with the second chair it might have been "very good to excellent."

(d) There is some danger of too little sound absorption by the walls and chairs at low frequencies. In the Berlin Konzerthaus (formerly known at the Schauspielhaus) non-upholstered chairs are used and all walls and the ceiling are made of heavy materials, so that overall the absorption in the hall is very low at low frequencies. The hall, when opened, had a bass ratio of about 1.30, with a mid-frequency reverberation time of 2.05 seconds. The reverberant sound was so excessive that special low-frequency sound-absorbing resonators were installed in the ceiling to reduce the RT's at low frequencies. This resulted in a decrease of the bass ratio to 1.15, which is ideal for a hall with high reverberation time and with a satisfactory value for $(1–IACC_{E3})$.

Careful calculations must be made of the reverberation times in advance of purchase of chairs so that the bass ratio comes out as near to 1.15 as possible, but the bass strength factor must not be weaker than the mid-frequency strength factor.

(e) Avoid the use of thick carpets with underpads. If carpets are desired, they should be limited to the aisles, be thin, and be cemented directly against a solid base.

(f) If there are coat rooms at the rear of boxes, such as are found in Orchestra Hall in Chicago, these rooms should be closed off with automatic closing doors to prevent the clothing, chairs and other absorbing material in them from affecting the bass ratio and bass strength.

(g) Care must be used in the selection of QRD diffusers if any appreciable areas of them are used because they tend to absorb sound excessively at the lower frequencies if they are very thick (deep). The manufacturers publish the sound absorption for each type of diffuser. For deep units (in excess of 4 in., 10 cm, in thickness), they may absorb considerable sound at low frequencies.

DESIGN OF STAGES FOR CONCERT HALLS: BALANCE, BLEND, AND ENSEMBLE

Before 1980, very little appeared in the acoustical literature about the acoustical needs of musicians on the stages of concert halls. At this writing, more is known on this subject and an objective acoustical measurement is regularly made to quantify the ability of one musician to hear the music of fellow players and to sense the response of the stage to his music.

The sound field on a stage is extremely complex because of the directivity of the instruments (Meyer, 1978), the orchestration of each piece, the arrangement of the orchestra on stage, the use of risers or not on the stage, and the acoustics of the sound reflecting surfaces surrounding the players—either with or without a stage enclosure.

Area of concert stage

Recent studies (Barron, 1993) indicate the desirability of providing the following net areas per player for different groups of instruments:

13.5 ft^2 (1.25 m^2) for upper string and wind instruments
21.6 ft^2 (2 m^2) for cello and larger wind instruments
19.5 ft^2 (1.8 m^2) for double bass
10.8 ft^2 (1.0 m^2) for each tympani and double that for other percussion instruments.

For a 100-piece symphony orchestra, these requirements set a stage area of about 1,615 ft^2 (150 m^2). The stage at Boston Symphony Hall has 1,600 ft^2. If the platform is built at 180 m^2, (1,940 ft^2) this leaves ample extra space for soloists, space to compensate for losses due to risers, and for access routes. Barron adds, "For seated choirs, 0.5 m^2 (5.4 ft^2) per person is needed, so that a 100 person choir requires a further 50 m^2

(540 ft^2) of space....[in the Royal Festival Hall] choir seating is in a separate elevated choir balcony...when not required as choir seating, these seats are sold to concertgoers..."

The Boston Symphony Orchestra regularly adds a 5 ft (1.5 m) strip to the front of the stage, with an area of about 323 ft^2 (30 m^2) when a chorus is on stage. Serious discussions are underway to expand the stage permanently to this area (1,923 ft^2) and to add risers on the stage. The negative arguments are that the players will be farther apart—thus, possibly, making ensemble less easy—and the brass will be higher making their sound louder and unbalancing the orchestra's overall sound. Further, the front two rows of the main floor will be lost, reducing the capacity of the hall from 2,625 to 2,567.

The stage areas in the older halls have an average area of 1,700 ft^2 (158 m^2) and in the newer halls 2,185 ft^2 (203 m^2) (see Table 17.4). The older halls with high ceilings over the stage are usually characterized by a relatively shallow stage; the median depth is 35 ft (10.7 m). In more recent halls, the median depth is 42 ft (12.8 m), ranging from 35 to 50 ft (10.7 to 15.2 m).

Stage shape

Very wide or very deep stages have serious disadvantages. When the stage is too wide, a listener seated on either side of the hall hears the instruments near him before he hears the sound from the other side of the stage. This difference in time may be great enough to affect the blend adversely. When the stage is very deep, the sound from the instruments at the back of the stage will arrive at the listener's ears a detectable instant after sound from the front of the stage, with similar adverse effects. In addition, a very wide stage makes it difficult for the conductor to hold the sections of the orchestra in good ensemble. To avoid these troubles, all parts of a stage should fit within a rectangle of about 55 ft (16.8 m) in width and about 40 ft (12.2 m) in depth. The stage area should be guided by the figures of the previous sub-section.

Stage surroundings

Orchestral players speak of two considerations: ability to hear each other (making better ensemble possible) and response from the hall. The stage surroundings for a number of halls were discussed in Chapter 13. The options include a stage house, reflecting surfaces at the side walls of the stage, overhead canopies, overhead arrays of panels, and various combinations of the foregoing.

There are at least five options for design of the areas surrounding the stage: (Beranek, 1992):

(1) Use a complete stage enclosure like that in Boston, New York (Avery Fisher), Cleveland, Salzburg, and Tokyo (Bunka Kaikan).

(2) Have no stage enclosure except for side walls like Amsterdam, Vienna, and Leipzig.

(3) Have side walls and a multi-panel canopy relatively high overhead like Tokyo (Suntory), Berlin (Philharmonie and Kammermusiksaal), and Mexico City.

(4) Same as (3), except that a multi-panel canopy is lower, like San Francisco (Davies), Baltimore, and Lenox (Tanglewood Shed).

(5) Have no stage enclosure, but employ a solid stage canopy, like those in Dallas, Christchurch, and Birmingham.

The choice among the five possibilities depends on an integration of the dimensions and nature of the side wall and ceiling surfaces of the rest of the hall. The object is to achieve good values for the six primary acoustical attributes of Chapter 15, a satisfactory value for the support factor ST1 (see *Objective measurements of stage acoustics*, p. 561) and adequate cross-communication among musicians.

If the stage of a concert hall must be very wide, there are two considerations. First, in a hall that is wide at the front, special, spaced out, tilted panels like those in the upper side-walls of the Costa Mesa, Segerstrom Hall should be used to reflect early lateral sound reflections, particularly to the main floor audience areas.

Lenox, Tanglewood, Koussevitzky Music Shed

The Tanglewood Music Shed has a very wide stage, measuring 86 ft (26 m) at the front. The hall has a wide fan shape, so that early reflections to the main floor seating are only possible by the use of a suspended array of panels, whose open area is chosen to give a proper balance between early sound and later reverberation. In spite of the lack of strong *lateral* early sound reflections in such a broad fan-shaped structure, the hall's excellent acoustical reputation is due to a long reverberation time (2.1 sec at 500 Hz), a short initial-time-delay gap (19 msec), a large negative value of $C_{80}(3)$ (–3.5 dB, equal to that of Vienna, Amsterdam, and Zurich), a very high bass ratio (BR = 1.45), and, in the front half of the main hall, a strength factor G_{mid} equal to 4.9 dB, (equal to that of Boston and Amsterdam). A respectable value of ASW is achieved by this strength factor (Okano *et al.*, 1994). Finally, the surface diffusivity factor is 0.8.

An important feature of the Tanglewood design is the carefully crafted surround for the players. The walls are highly modulated and they slope inwards (see Chapter 6, No. 9) and have a correspondingly modulated cornice around the top. These two features, with the important help of the 50% open suspended ceiling, assure that the sound from one orchestral section is propagated across the stage to other sections. As will be shown shortly, the musicians have strong support (ST1) from the stage, which also helps the shed's reputation.

Stage overhang

In my experience a valuable addition to a symphonic stage is the equivalent of a cornice, or a 3 ft (1 m) deep overhanging balcony surrounding the platform, at a height of ca 13 ft (4 m). This construction may also be the under-edge of a wide pipe organ case. Examples are seen in Baltimore, Boston, Dallas, New York (Avery Fisher), Tanglewood Shed, San Francisco (Davies), Leipzig, Vienna, Munich (Gasteig), Tokyo (Metropolitan Art Space), and Mexico City.

Demountable orchestra shells

Orchestra "shells," usually demountable, are found in every multi-purpose auditorium because the acoustics of a stage house are unfriendly to symphonic music. Examples abound: Philadelphia, Cleveland, Costa Mesa, Rochester, Buenos Aires, Salzburg, Montreal, Budapest, Tokyo (NHK, Orchard, and Bunka Kaikan). Several of these seem particularly successful for the type of hall with which they are used, for example, Philadelphia, Cleveland, Salzburg (as shown in the photograph of Chapter 5), Tokyo (Bunka Kaikan), and Costa Mesa (see sketch in No. 7, Chapter 6).

Nakamura *et al.* (1991) asked the players in four orchestras (the Boston Symphony Orchestra, the Chicago Symphony Orchestra, the Leipzig Gewandhaus Orchestra, and the Japanese Symphony Orchestra) to fill out questionnaires on the acoustics of the stages as they experienced them during concerts. The orchestras played in a total of 23 Japanese halls nearly all of which had demountable orchestra shells that resembled each other. The findings were: (1) the stages that the foreign orchestras preferred provided the players with ample early reflected sound—sound that was associated with the degree of diffusion created by large irregularities on the walls surrounding the platform, and (2) in the four best-liked stages, the rear walls were considerably narrower than the proscenium openings, and the ceilings sloped upward fairly steeply and had three or four "waves" on them that extended the full width of the stage ceiling (for example, Tokyo, Bunka Kaikan).

Contemporary multi-use sending-end design

Jaffe (1995) reports that in the United States new multi-use theaters are built with large stage houses which have sufficient spare volume to permit an increase in cubic volume over the stage platform. The extra volume augments the liveness and eliminates harshness of the sound in the hall as a whole. This over-stage volume must be accompanied by an open canopy hung 15 to 25 ft (4.6 to 7.6 m) above the players in order to give them early sound reflections (25 to 40 msec) and to improve inter-player hearing conditions and sectional balance.

Scenery is often stored in the upper part of the stage house which, if not isolated, deadens the space in the stage house. To accommodate both needs, a removable "floor" that cuts off the upper portion is installed as shown in Fig. 17.3. This "shaper floor" slides into position creating a reverberant volume beneath it of 200,000 to 250,000 ft^3 (5,660 to 7,080 m^3). It is constructed of wood reinforced with steel weighing in total about 3.5 lb/ft^2 (17 kg/m^2).

Objective measurements of stage acoustics

Gade (1989b) has suggested an objective acoustical measure, called ST1, for determining the degree of support the concert hall gives to the musicians on stage. The mathematical definition is given in Appendix 2.

ST1 is measured with no musicians on stage, but with chairs, music racks and percussion in place. For the measurement, an impulsive sound (like a loud, sharp hand clap) is emitted from a non-directional loudspeaker. A microphone is located 1 m (3.28 ft) away on stage. The energy that is reflected from the immediate surroundings of the stage (within about 55 ft, 16.8 m) is measured in decibels by the microphone and compared with the energy that was sent out. The difference (in decibels) of the two readings is ST1.

In Table 17.5, values for ST1 are shown for 26 of the halls in this book for which such data are available. Indicated are those halls for which subjective rank-orderings are available in the categories of A+, A, B, and C+, as taken from Table 5.2. We see that five of the eight (A+, A) halls have relatively favorable values for ST1, but the other three are almost at the other end of the column. The B and C+ values are along the middle.

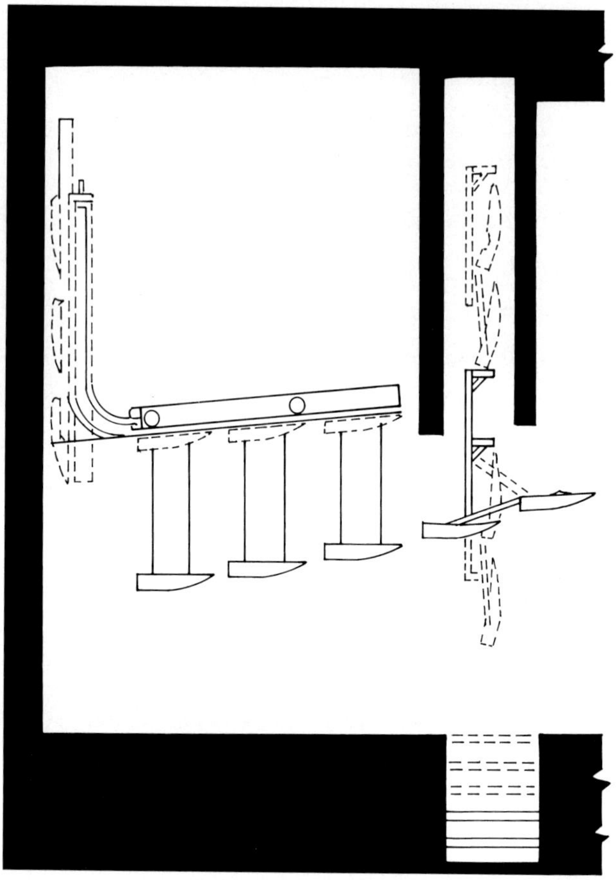

Figure 17.3. "Concert Hall Shaper," a movable floor that cuts off the upper portion of the stage house and that introduces suspended panels above the players to improve on-stage hearing and to achieve better sectional balance. Additional panels drop down from a slot to provide early reflections to the main floor listeners and to improve communication among the sections (Courtesy of C. Jaffe, 1995).

This may simply mean that judgments of the quality of music in the audience part of the hall (Table 5.2) are not strongly related to measures of the support that musicians receive for their music on stage.

Particularly interesting is the 4-dB less support that the players receive on the stage of the Concertgebouw in Amsterdam, as compared to that in the other A+ halls. Inspection of the photographs and drawings indicates that there should be a lower degree of support as measured by ST1. The ceiling and side walls are about 50 ft (15.2 m) away from the surface and edges of the stage. Also the presence of audience behind and to the sides of the musicians means that they receive no support from the rear and side walls.

TABLE 17.5. Tabulations of ST1 for halls for which data are available. ST1 is measured in first 100 ms and is average of 250 to 2,000 Hz octave bands.

Location and Name of Hall	ST1 Average Decibels	Table 5.1 Ratings in A+, A, B, C+ Categories
Baltimore, Joseph Meyerhoff Hall*	–12.2	
San Francisco, Davies Hall*	–12.4	B
Zurich, Grosser Tonhallesaal	–12.6	A
Lenox, Tanglewood Shed (front)	–12.8	A
Salt Lake, Utah, Symphony Hall	–12.9	
London, Barbican Large Concert Hall*	–13.2	C+
Basel, Stadt-Casino	–13.7	A
Boston, Symphony Hall	–13.7	A+
Vienna, Gr. Musikvereinssaal	–13.9	A+
Costa Mesa, Segerstrom Hall`	–14.3	B+
Goteborgs, Koncerthaus	–14.3	
Philadelphia, Academy of Music	–14.3	
Copenhagen, Radiohuset, Studio 1	–14.5	
Stuttgart, Liederhalle, Grosser Saal	–14.5	
Cleveland, Severance Hall	–14.8	
Buffalo, Kleinhans Music Hall	–14.8	C+
Salzburg, Festspielhaus	–15.8	
London, Royal Festival (Res. Off.)	–16.0	
Worcester, MA, Mechanics Hall	–16.1	
Edinburgh, Usher	–16.3	
Cardiff, Wales, St. David's Hall	–16.6	A
Berlin, Konzerthaus (Schauspiel)	–16.8	A
Berlin, Philharmonie Hall	–16.8	
Amsterdam, Concertgebouw	–17.8	A+
Munich, Philharmonie am Gasteig	–18.0	
Washington, Kennedy Concert Hall	–18.1	

*Before recent renovations.

Apparently the lack of support in the Concertgebouw is not disturbing to most conductors, with the exception of the late Eugene Ormandy, who said to me during an interview, "There is a jumble of sound and poor orchestral balance. The ceiling over the stage seems too high." Ormandy as conductor of the Philadelphia Orchestra was accustomed to a hall with low reverberation time (1.2 sec occupied) and with an orchestra "shell" that gives large support to the orchestra.

Regardless of Table 17.5, the musicians today are demanding better acoustical support from the hall and from the sound reflecting surfaces around the stage. Examples of designs that receive praise can be seen in Chapter 6 for New York, Avery Fisher Hall (the recent revision shown in the drawings and photographs), San Francisco, Davies Hall (the drawings and photograph show the hall since the 1993 renovations), Costa Mesa, Segerstrom Hall (see the stage sketch), and Baltimore, Joseph Meyerhoff Hall (the recent renovations are shown on the drawings and the photographs).

Barron, referring to Gade, in his comprehensive book, *Auditorium Acoustics and Architectural Design* (1993), arrives at an important conclusion, "The most effective surface for providing early reflections on the platform is the ceiling. In halls with exposed platforms and high ceilings, it will often be necessary to suspend an array of reflectors over the platform. Depending on the fractional area of the reflectors compared to the floor area beneath (the degree of perforation), the average height of the reflectors should, if possible, not exceed 6 to 8 m (20 to 26 ft) above the stage for them to be fully effective...Recent investigations seem to indicate that more small elements are preferable to fewer larger ones [see San Francisco (Davies) and Copenhagen in Chapter 6]. This arrangement provides more uniform coverage... It is probably wise to provide for reflections from a number of surfaces surrounding the platform, such that it is not necessary to rely on or to exaggerate the contribution from one particular surface or direction."

CONCLUDING REMARK

It is hoped that this book enlightens the reader, aids the architect, and provides new data for the acoustical consultant. There is no doubt that the science and art of acoustics has progressed since the immediate post World War II period when the only measurable acoustical attribute was reverberation time. In 1995 alone no less than five international conferences and several regional meetings have been held, each featuring concert and opera hall acoustics, illustrating the intense international interest in the subject of this book.

Exactly 100 years ago the first efforts were begun to conquer the problem of Architectural Acoustics which had "defied scientific investigators from the beginning of time."(Orcutt, 1933, from which the remainder of this paragraph is also taken.) At that time, a 27-year old Assistant Professor, Wallace Clement Sabine, accepted a request from the President of Harvard University to do something about a new lecture hall, in the then Fogg Art Museum, which had to be abandoned because of disastrous acoustics. The only person in America who had tried to solve a similar project, Professor Thomas Mendenhall, warned Sabine that he was "undertaking a problem that fairly bristles with difficulties, the extreme complexity of which seems to indicate that a complete solution is hopeless," and Sabine's colleagues in the Department of Physics looked upon his new assignment as a grim joke.

Sabine spent the next five years on this problem, during which he discovered and published his seminal research which inaugurated the famous equation for calculating reverberation time, Eq. (8.1) in Chapter 8. Very little progress beyond Sabin's equation was made until major research projects were established in the early 1970's. This progress is summarized in my review paper (Beranek, 1992).

Between 1895 and 1975 the path of concert hall acoustics was strewn with disappointments—except for those halls that copied the acknowledged successes in the world, which were largely extensions of the ballrooms of the European palaces of the 19th Century.

In 1778 opera was blessed with the opening of Teatro alla Scala in Milan, Italy, designed by Architect Giuseppi Piermarini. Proclaimed a success, it was copied everywhere. But as a science, aside from Wallace Sabine's contributions, concert and opera hall acoustics was dormant until awakened in 1962, in part, by my book, *Music, Acoustics, and Architecture*, and immediately followed by the fruitful projects of Goettingen and Berlin Universities. Today, acoustical research on Concert Halls is everywhere, and important discoveries are being made and lie ahead. This book and that by Barron (1993) serve as milestones marking progress up to this moment.

Appendix 1
Terminology and Conversion Factors

DIMENSIONAL QUANTITIES IN CHAPTER 6 DESCRIPTIONS

N = number of seats in the hall (usually wheelchair space is not counted). If significant, one-half the number of standees is included. Standees are usually only considered in opera houses where the number is often large.

V = volume of the hall in cubic feet (cubic meters).

In *concert halls* V includes the volume of air in the main hall and in the orchestra enclosure. If there is a stagehouse, the volume V does not include that volume of the stagehouse that lies outside the orchestra enclosure unless the construction is like that of Fig. 17.3 in Chapter 17. V is measured as though there were no seats in the hall. The volume occupied by the solid balcony structures is excluded.

In *opera houses*, V includes the volume of air contained in the house forward of the main curtain. It does not include the volume of air in the stagehouse or the volume occupied by the solid balcony structures.

NOTE: It is assumed that all areas following are in square feet (square meters).

S_a = area of floor space over which the audience chairs are located. The seating areas presented in this book are the projected areas. That is to say, in sloped (raked) floors, as in balconies, the slant area is not measured.

S_A = acoustical audience area. It includes the sum of: (a) the area S_a (see above) and (b) the areas of strips 0.5 m (20 in.) wide around the separated blocks of the seating area, except that such strips are neither included at the front edge of a balcony where the audience is seated against a balcony rail nor where the seats abut a wall. In this book, the range of $S_A \div S_a$ is 1.11 to 1.41, with the average equal to 1.22. The largest ratios are found in Japanese halls and the lowest ones in the famous old halls built before 1901. If significant, the areas of standing room spaces are included.

In boxes, the same rule applies, unless the seats are far apart or the box is much larger than the seating area S_a. In that case, use S_A (per chair) = 7.5 ft² (0.7 m²). However, the number of seats in the box times 7.5 (or 0.7) must not exceed the area of the floor of the box.

S_c = area occupied by the chorus, or by the audience if seated in the chorus area. It is not considered if closed off during non-choral performances.

S_o = area of stage, unless it is very large, then S_o is the area actually occupied by the orchestra. No side strips are added.

S_{pit} = area of the open surface of the pit.

S_P = area of the proscenium curtain. It is assumed that the fire curtain is pulled up.

$S_T = S_A + S_o + S_c$ (for concert halls)

$S_T = S_A + S_{pit} + S_P$ (for opera houses)

NOTE: It is assumed that all lengths following are measured in feet (meters).

H = average room height, measured from main floor to ceiling in that part of the main-floor audience area not covered by balconies.

W = average width, measured between side walls in the audience area on the main floor, disregarding any balcony overhang.

L = average room length, measured from the platform front to the average of the back wall positions at all levels.

D = distance from the front of the stage to the most remote listener, measured on the centerline, unless the rear wall is not flat or curved outward, in which case an alternate location on the rear wall must be chosen.

SD = average stage depth.

SW = average stage width.

SH = mean ceiling height above the stage area, measured relative to the front of the stage.

ACOUSTICAL ATTRIBUTES OF APPENDIX 4

RT = reverberation time in sec. It is defined as the time, multiplied by a factor of 2, that it takes for the sound in a hall to decay from –5 to –35 dB below its steady-state value. The factor of 2 is necessary, because RT must conform to the original definition of sound decay which was from 0 to –60 dB. Roughly speaking, RT is the time it takes for a loud sound to decay to inaudibility after its source is cut off. RT is usually measured in octave or one-third octave bands. The source of sound may be a pink noise or a sound impulse. Originally, RT was determined from a plot of sound pressure level vs. time as recorded on the moving paper of a graphic level recorder. Today it is determined by the Schroeder (1965) method which involves computer integration of a backward-played tape-recording of the decaying signal. The mid-frequency RT is the average of the RT's at 500 and 1,000 Hz. The measurement is generally made in both occupied and unoccupied halls, at two positions when occupied or at 8 to 24 positions when unoccupied. The data in each frequency band at the various positions are averaged. A least-squares fit to the –5 to –35 dB portion of the decay curve is used in setting the value of RT for each band and position.

EDT = early-decay-time in sec. It is measured in the same fashion as RT except that EDT is the time it takes for a signal to decay from 0 to –10 dB relative to its steady state value. A multiplying factor of 6 is necessary to make the EDT time comparable to RT.

$IACC_A$ = measure of the difference in the sounds arriving at the two ears of a listener facing the performing entity in a hall. It is called the "interaural cross-correlation coefficient." For the data reported in this book the source of sound is an omnidirectional (dodecahedron) loudspeaker fed by an impluse sound. IACC is usually measured by recording on a digital tape recorder the outputs of two tiny microphones located at the entrances to the ear canals of a person or a dummy head, and quantifying the two ear differences with a computer program that performs the operations of Eqs. (A2.1) and (A2.2) of Appendix 2. $IACC_A$ is determined with a frequency band width of about 100 to 8,000 Hz and for a time period of 0 to about 1 sec. No frequency weighting is used.

IACC(bands) = the same as above except determined in each of the six frequency bands with mid-frequencies of 125, 250, 500, 1,000, 2,000, and 4,000 Hz. The time periods considered are selected as follows:

$IACC_{E3}$ = the interaural cross-correlation coefficient determined for a time period of 0 to 80 msec. It is the average of the values measured in the three octave bands with mid-frequencies of 500, 1,000, and 2,000 Hz. It has been shown to be a sensitive measure for determining the apparent source width ASW of a performing entity as heard by a person seated in the audience.

$IACC_{L3}$ = the interaural cross-correlation coefficient determined for a time period of 80 to 750 msec and is the average of the values measured in the three frequency bands with mid-frequencies of 500, 1,000, and 2,000 Hz. It correlates approximately to the state of sound diffusion in the hall.

$C_{80}(3)$ = the clarity factor. It is the ratio, expressed in decibels, of the energy in the first 80 msec of an impulse sound arriving at a listener's position divided by the energy in the sound after 80 msec. The divisor is approximately the total energy of the reverberant sound. The symbol (3) indicates the average of the C_{80} values in the 500, 1,000, and 2,000 Hz bands. C_{80} is given by Eq. (A2.3).

LF_{E4} = the lateral energy fraction determined by the ratio of the output of a figure-8 microphone with its null axis pointed to the source of the sound, divided by the output of a non-directional microphone at the same position. LF_{E4} is determined for the time period of 0 to 80 msec and is the average of the LF's in the four frequency bands, 125, 250, 500, and 1,000 Hz. It is equal to the ratio of the weighted energy in the sound that does not come from the direction of the source to that which comes from all directions including that of the source. LF_{E4} also correlates with the apparent source width ASW. It is given by Eq. (A2.4).

G = the "strength factor." It is the ratio, expressed in decibels, of the sound energy at a seat in a hall that comes from a non-directional source (usually located successively at one to three different positions on the stage) to the sound energy from the same source when measured in an anechoic room at a distance of 10 m. G is measured in the usual six octave frequency bands. It is given by Eq. (A2.5).

G_{mid} = the mid-frequency strength factor. This means that the decibel levels are the average of the G's measured in the 500 and 1,000 Hz frequency bands.

G_{low} = the low-frequency strength fractor. This means that the decibel levels are the average of the G's measured in the 125 and 250 Hz bands.

BR = the "bass ratio" equal to the ratio of the average of the RT's at 125 and 250 Hz to the average of the RT's at 500 and 1,000 Hz. It is determined only for a hall when fully occupied. It is given by Eq. (A2.6)

t_I = ITDG = the initial-time-delay gap, the time interval in msec between the arrival at a seat in the hall of the direct sound from a source on stage to the arrival of the first reflection (see Fig 3.3 of Chapter 3). In this book, its value is generally given only for a position near the center of the main floor. It correlates with the subjective impression of "intimacy."

ST1 = the degree of support that the hall, including the walls and ceiling of the hall and of the enclosure immediately surrounding the players, give to the players on stage. It is the difference, in decibels, between the impulse sound energy from an omnidirectional sound source that arrives at a player's position within the first 10 msec, measured at a distance of 1 m from the sound source, and that which arrives in the time interval between 20 and 100 msec at the same position. The sound arriving in the later interval has been reflected from one or more surfaces surrounding the player's position on the stage and its strength, minus the strength of the sound in the first 10 msec, is a measure of the support received by the musicians from the hall. The measurements are made with the chairs, music stands, and percussion in place, except that those near the source and receiver are set aside. The measurements are made at several positions and the data are averaged. ST 1 is given by Eq. (A2.7).

CONVERSION FACTORS

To Convert	Into	Multiply by	Conversely Multiply by
inches (in.)	centimeters (cm)	2.54	0.394
	feet (ft)	0.0833	12
	meters (m)	0.0254	39.4
feet (ft)	centimeters (cm)	30.5	3.28 times 10^{-2}
	meters (m)	0.305	3.28
square feet (ft^2)	square centimeters (cm^2)	929	1.076 times 10^{-3}
	square meters (m^2)	0.0929	10.76
cubic feet (ft^3)	cubic centimeters (cm^3)	2.83 times 10^4	3.53 times 10^{-5}
	cubic meters (m^3)	0.0283	35.3
pounds (lb)	ounces (oz)	16	0.0625
	kilograms (kg)	0.454	2.205
yards (yd)	inches (in.)	36	0.0278
	meters (m)	0.914	1.094
pounds per square foot (lb/ft^2)	kilograms per square meter (kg/m^2)	4.88	0.2048
pounds per cubic foot (lb/ft^3)	kilograms per cubic meter (kg/m^3)	16.0	6.24 times 10^{-2}

Note: $10^{-2} = 0.01$; $10^{-3} = 0.001$; $10^{-4} = 0.0001$; $10^{-5} = 0.00001$; $10^2 = 100$; $10^3 = 1,000$; $10^4 = 10,000$

APPENDIX 2
EQUATIONS FOR ACOUSTICAL ATTRIBUTES

The Interaural Cross-Correlation Family, IACF, $IACC_A$, $IACC_E$, and $IACC_L$

A binaural measure of the difference in the sounds at the two ears produced by a sound source on the stage is the interaural cross-correlation function $\mathrm{IACF}_t(t)$:

$$\mathrm{IACF}_t(\tau) = \frac{\int_{t_1}^{t_2} p_L(t)\, p_R(t+\tau)\, dt}{\left(\int_{t_1}^{t_2} p_L^2 dt \int_{t_1}^{t_2} p_R^2 dt\right)^{1/2}}, \qquad \text{(A2.1)}$$

where L and R designate the entrances to the left and right ears, respectively. The maximum possible value of Eq. (A2.1) is unity. Time "0" is the time of arrival of the direct sound from the impulse radiated by the source. Integration from 0 to t_2 msec includes the energy of the direct sound and whatever early reflections and reverberant sounds fall within the t_2 time period.

Because the time it takes for a sound wave impinging perpendicular to one side of the head to travel to the other side is about 1 msec, it is customary to vary τ over the range of -1 to $+1$ msec. Further, to obtain a single number that measures the maximum similarity of all waves arriving at the two ears within the time integration limits and the range of τ, it is customary to select the maximum value of Eq. (A2.1) which is then called the interaural cross-correlation coeficient (IACC):

$$\mathrm{IACC}_t = \left|\mathrm{IACF}_t(\tau)\right| \max \qquad \text{for } -1 < \tau < +1. \qquad \text{(A2.2)}$$

With different integration periods we have IACC_A ($t_1 = 0$ to $t_2 = 1{,}000$ msec); $\mathrm{IACC}_{E(\mathrm{arly})}$ (0 to 80 msec); and $\mathrm{IACC}_{L(\mathrm{ate})}$ (80 to 1,000 msec). The *E*(arly) IACC is a measure of the apparent source width ASW and the *L*(ate) IACC is a measure of the listener envelopment LEV.

The Clarity Factor, C_{80}

The clarity factor C_{80}, expressed in decibels, is the ratio of the early energy (0 to 80 msec) to the late (reverberant) energy (80 to 3,000 msec):

$$C_{80} = 10 \log \frac{\int_0^{.08} p^2(t)dt}{\int_{.08}^{\infty} p^2(t)dt} \text{ dB.} \tag{A2.3}$$

The Lateral Energy Fraction, LF

The lateral energy fraction LF is the ratio of the output of a figure-8 microphone (with its null direction aimed at the source) to the output of a non-directional microphone. The figure-8 microphone weights the non-direct energy by $\cos^2 \theta$, where θ = 90° is in the direction of the sound. LF is given by:

$$\text{LF} = \frac{\int_{.005}^{.08} p_8^2(t)dt}{\int_0^{.08} p^2(t)dt}. \tag{A2.4}$$

As shown, the time integration is usually performed over the interval of 5 to 80 msec for the figure-8 microphone and 0 to 80 msec for the omnidirectional microphone. The 5 msec value is introduced to make certain that the direct sound is eliminated.

The Strength Factor, G

The strength factor *G is a measure of the sound pressure level at a point in a hall, with an omni-directional source on stage, minus the sound pressure level that would be measured at a distance of* 10 m *from the same sound source operating at the same power level and located in an anechoic chamber. The equation is:*

$$G = 10 \log \frac{\int_0^{t_2} p^2(t)dt}{\int_0^{t_2} p_A^2(t)dt} \text{ dB,} \tag{A2.5}$$

where $P_A(t)$ is the free-field sound pressure level at a distance of 10 m.

The Bass Ratio, RT

Bass ratio RT is the ratio of the low to mid-frequency reverberation times, given by:

$$\mathrm{BR} = \frac{\mathrm{RT}_{125} + \mathrm{RT}_{250}}{\mathrm{RT}_{500} + \mathrm{RT}_{1{,}000}}, \tag{A2.6}$$

where the RT's are the reverberation times at the frequencies shown in the subscripts.

The Support Factor, ST1

The support factor ST1 is the difference in decibels between two measurements of sound pressure level made on a stage or in a pit where the orchestra members play. A sound source (loudspeaker) emits an impulse and the microphone receives it at a point 1 m removed from the center of the source, which is omnidirectional. The first measurement is of the energy in the time interval from 0 to 10 msec and the second measurement is of the energy in the time interval from 20 to 100 msec. It is given by the equation:

$$\mathrm{ST1} = 10 \log \left[\frac{\int_{.02}^{0.1} p_8^2(t)dt}{\int_{0}^{.01} p^2(t)dt} \right]. \tag{A2.7}$$

APPENDIX 3
SURVEYS OF ACOUSTICAL QUALITY OF CONCERT HALLS

Contributed by Fergus R. Fricke

INTRODUCTION

The importance of subjective data in the evaluation of concert halls as a means for selecting and weighting acoustic parameters has been demonstrated in this text. Experience shows that it is extremely difficult to obtain subjective comparisons of different auditoriums. This is partly because people have limited knowledge of halls, partly because people tend to prefer the halls they know, and partly owing to a host of other factors such as the music and performers heard and the seat(s) occupied.

Ideally a group of performers and listeners should be taken blindfolded to many halls around the world and they should play and listen to the same music in each hall and in different seats in each hall. Even this ideal scenario is unlikely to produce fully useful information because of the difficulty in remembering the different halls and performances and becoming accustomed to the music. Unfortunately there is no musical equivalent of existing tests for determining the intelligibility of speech in rooms. The creation of "virtual acoustics" offers the possibility of better comparisons in the future.

A number of studies have been carried out using different procedures for evaluating the acoustic quality of rooms for music. Several surveys have used direct inquiry of people who are in the best position to know (called the Delphi technique). The respondents have usually been musicians, music critics, academics, acoustic experts, or knowledgeable listeners who have listened to music extensively in different parts of the world.

Somerville (1953) argued that the best group of subjects for surveys on the acoustical quality of halls are music critics because they gave more concordant answers than performing musicians, consultants, and the general public. But, unless critics travel a lot, they may know only a few halls, so that they are likely to have preconceived ideas about the halls.

Others have insisted that the artists tend to evaluate the halls only from their experience on the stage where the acoustical conditions could be quite different from those at the seats of the listeners. There does not appear to have been an attempt prior to now to correlate the judgments of musicians and music critics about existing concert halls to test this contention.

If the acoustical evaluation of concert halls is to be extended beyond national borders to maximize the range of designs studied and minimize prejudices, some of the best people to make these evaluations are internationally acclaimed conductors and soloists because they have the knowledge of halls, the expertise to evaluate them, many opportunities to visit halls owing to regular concert engagements, and the need to consider what the audience hears rather than just the stage acoustics.

Beranek (1962) interviewed outstanding musicians as a first source of reliable information in his study of 54 halls for music. Likewise, in the present (Fricke) study, it was decided to ask musicians to evaluate the acoustics of halls using a self-administrated questionnaire.

The present survey was designed, in part, to serve as a comparison with the evaluations of acoustical quality that appear in this book (Chapter 5). In addition, more halls are included with as many different shapes as possible in order to investigate the effects of hall geometry.

Most of the questionnaire respondents were conductors and soloists from Australia, Europe, Japan, and North America, who have performed as guest artists with many different orchestras in many auditoriums in many countries. One of the added advantages of using this cohort of musicians is that the results should not be influenced by local cultural factors.

Later in this study, the questionnaire was sent to members of the Music Critics Association of the USA. Despite the limitations of a single country, there appears to be a strong correlation between the opinions of musicians and music critics.

PREVIOUS SUBJECTIVE SURVEYS ON QUALITY OF ACOUSTICS IN HALLS

It was decided at the outset of this study that the reliability of opinions of people is increased if the respondents have made notes of their impressions in a diary or a letter. For this reason we believed that written questionnaires were preferable because they retain their validity even after a number of years (Cremer, 1978). Questionnaires are also probably more reliable because they tend to evoke more considered responses.

Beranek suggests that interviews are effective because the interviewees can be asked as to what lies behind their statements. But the cost of obtaining and conducting interviews with renowned conductors throughout the world makes this approach all but impossible.

Parkin *et al.* (1952) made the first known use of questionnaires to rate the general acoustic quality of halls numerically. His investigation covered ten British concert halls. The questionnaires were sent to music critics, music academics, and composers. Of the 170 questionnaires mailed 75 were returned and 42 were found useful.

The evaluation of the British halls were made using a three point scale (good, fair, and bad) to rate the acoustic quality of halls. Only six percent of the responses gave "bad" judgments to any of the halls and there were few "fair" judgments. Perhaps the respondents rated halls as "bad" only if they had obvious acoustic defects (echoes, noise) and, perhaps, the majority of the ten British halls were of nearly the same quality. In any event, only the number of "good" responses were used for the evaluation.

Other questionnaire studies have been of two types: one favoring preference comparisons, the other semantic differential ratings. Hawkes and Douglas (1971) evaluated 16 subjective attributes, taken from Beranek's (1962) study, by means of questionnaires administered to persons who were asked to rate their acoustical impressions on a one-dimensional scale whose end-points were given names with opposite extremes, such as "Cold...Warm;" "Clear...Muddy;" "Reverberant...Unreverberant;" etc.

Gade (1981) interviewed 32 musicians to obtain ideas about room acoustical quality from the musician's viewpoint on stage. He collected 12 attributes of which the most important were hearing-each-other, reverberation, support, timbre, dynamics, time delay, and change of pitch. The most important parameter proposed by the musicians was "hearing each other" which is related to "balance, blend, ensemble, and attack" in Chapter 13.

Barron (1988) used continuous semantic differential scales to determine which parameters were related to the acoustical quality of halls. He included 11 British concert halls in the survey and asked expert listeners, mostly acousticians, to make subjective judgments using seven scales (see Fig. 4.1 in Chapter 4). A summary of the results is given in Chapter 4.

THE PRESENT QUESTIONNAIRE

The present study appears to be the first international one undertaken since Beranek's in 1962. The questionnaire used employs a three point scale (like Parkin, but avoiding the "bad" category) and included concert halls only.

Questions

Using a self-administered questionnaire, musicians and conductors were asked to express their opinions on the acoustics of up to 74 concert halls. Particularly, the respondents were asked to make judgments about the acoustics of halls for classical symphonic music. The questionnaire included questions about preferences for music and concert halls. Next, a list of the halls was included and respondents were asked to rate them acoustically, based on their experience, as either "excellent," "good," or "mediocre." The terminologies used for the three levels of acoustical quality were suggested by Lawrence (1983).

As all the listed halls in the present survey are well known and are regularly used for concerts the acoustics of these halls are not likely to be bad. Thus the ordering scale was designed to start from "mediocre."

Each respondent was also asked to indicate two concert halls which, in his/her opinion, had "excellent" and which had "poor" acoustics.

Selection of halls

Most of the halls listed in the questionnaire were located in Europe and North America because information about them was readily available in the literature.

The list includes halls with four different shapes: rectangular, fan, horseshoe, and geometric. They are given in Table A3.1, in the alphabetical order of first the country, and next the city where they are located.

MUSICIANS AND MUSIC CRITICS SURVEYED

The subjects for this survey were mainly musicians who had performed in Australia during the 1990, 1991, and 1992 concert seasons and the members of the Music Critics Association of the USA.

A total of 110 questionnaires were mailed to musicians and 33 were returned (32% response). Those returned came from 12 countries and included 16 conductors,

Table A3.1. The concert halls listed in the questionnaire.

Country, City, and Name of hall	Type	Country, City, and Name of hall	Type
AMERICA, UNITED STATES OF		Munich, Philharmonie am Gasteig	FAN
Baltimore, Lyric Theatre	REC	Stuttgart, Liederhalle, Grosser Saal	GEO
Baltimore, Meyerhoff Hall	GEO	GREAT BRITAIN	
Boston, Symphony Hall	REC	Birmingham, Symphony Hall	GEO
Buffalo, Kleinhans Music Hall	FAN	Bolton, Town Hall, Albert Hall	REC
Cambridge, Kresge Auditorium	GEO	Bristol, Colston Hall	REC
Chicago, Orchestra Hall	HSU	Cardiff, St. David's Hall	GEO
Cleveland, Severance Hall	HSU	Croydon, Fairfield Hall	REC
Costa Mesa, Segestrom Hall	GEO	Edinburgh, Usher Hall	HSU
Dallas, McDermott Concert Hall	GEO	Glasgow, St. Andrew's Hall	REC
Denver, Boettcher Concert Hall	GEO	Liverpool, Philharmonic Hall	FAN
New York, Avery Fisher Hall	REC	London, Barbican Concert hall	GEO
New York, Carnegie Hall	HSU	London, Royal Albert Hall	GEO
Philadelphia, Academy of Music	HSU	London, Royal Festival Hall	REC
Rochester, Eastman Theatre	FAN	London, Wigmore Hall	REC
San Francisco, Davies Hall	GEO	Manchester, Free Trade Hall	REC
Washington, D.C., JFK Cnct. Hall	REC	Northampton, Derngate Center	REC
Worcester, MA, Mechanics Hall	REC	Nottingham, Royal Concert Hall	GEO
AUSTRALIA		IRELAND	
Sydney, Op. Hse. Concert Hall	GEO	Dublin, National Concert Hall	REC
Melbourne, Vic. Arts Ctr. Cnct. Hall	GEO	ISRAEL	
Adalaide, Town Hall	REC	Tel Aviv, Frederic R. Mann Aud.	FAN
AUSTRIA		JAPAN	
Vienna, Grosser Musikvereinssaal	REC	Osaka, Symphony Hall	REC
Salzburg, Festspielhaus	FAN	Tokyo, NHK Hall	FAN
BELGIUM		Tokyo, Suntory Hall	REC
Brussels, Palais des Beaux-Arts	HSU	NETHERLANDS	
CANADA		Amsterdam, Concertgebouw	REC
Calgary, Jack Singer Hall	GEO	Groningen, De Oosterpoort, Cnct. Hl.	FAN
Toronto, Roy Thompson Hall	GEO	Haarlem, Concert Hall	REC
Vancouver, Queen Elizabeth Thtr.	GEO	Rotterdam, De Doelen Concert Hl.	GEO
DENMARK		Utrecht, Music Ctr. Vredenburg, Hl.	GEO
Copenhagen, Radiohuset Studio 1	FAN	NORWAY	
Copenhagen, Tivoli Koncertsal	FAN	Oslo, Concert Hall	FAN
Odense, Cnct. Hse., Carl Nielsen Hl.	REC	RUSSIA	
FRANCE		St. Petersburg, Philharmonic Hall	REC
Paris, Radio France, Grand Aud. 104	FAN	SPAIN	
Paris Salle Pléyel	FAN	Granada, Centre Manuel de Falla	GEO
Strasbourg, Pal. deLa Mus., Erasme	GEO	SWEDEN	
GERMANY		Gothenburg, Konserthus	GEO
Berlin, Philharmonie Hall	GEO	Stockholm, Berwald Hall	GEO
Berlin, Sender Freies, Gr. Sendessaal	FAN	Stockholm, Concert Hall	GEO
Berlin, Konzerthaus (Schauspielhaus)	REC	SWITZERLAND	
Bonn, Beethovenhalle	GEO	Basel, Stadt-Casino	REC
Leipzig, Gewandhaus	GEO	Zurich, Grosser Tonhallesaal	REC
Munich, Herkulessaal	REC		

13 soloists, and 3 other musicians. All musicians were professionals who performed regularly in many auditoriums. Among the 32 musicians, 21 performed more than once a week and the rest performed at least once a month. They are listed in Table A3.2.

Responses from 40 music critics were obtained, comprising 10% of the membership of the Music Critics Association of the USA. Those who wished to be acknowledged are listed in Table A3.3.

ACOUSTICAL QUALITY INDEX OF HALLS

The respondents commented on 60 of the halls listed in the questionnaire, eight were excluded from the analysis for various reasons, the main one being that at least five responses were required for the evaluation of acoustical quality. Thus, 52 halls are analyzed. The average number of ratings for each hall was 15, with a maximum of 30 for the Sydney Opera House Concert Hall.

A numerical value of "1" was assigned to "excellent," "0.5" to "good," and "0" to "mediocre." An acoustic quality index (AQI) for each hall was calculated by normalizing all the rated values by the number of responses. For the musicians, the AQI values of the halls were distributed in the range 0.22 (Henry and Edsel Ford Auditorium,

Table A3.2. The respondents to the questionnaire: musicians.

Richard Mills	Conductor	Tadaaki Otaka	Conductor
Patrick Thomas	Conductor	Kaori Kimura	Pianist
David Pereira	Cellist	Hans Vonk	Conductor
Goeffrey Parsons	Pianist	Kees Bakels	Conductor
Vittoro Sangiorgio	Pianist	Michael Houston	Pianist
Alice Giles	Harpist	Frans Helmerson	Cellist
Joan Carden	Soprano	Matthias Bamert	Conductor
Damian Whiteley	Bass	Sir Charles Mackerras	Conductor
Albert Rosen	Conductor	John Hopkins	Conductor
Michael Gielen	Conductor	Evelyn Glennie	Percussionist
Ernst Kovacic	Violinist	Jorge Mester	Conductor
Jiri Belohlavek	Conductor	Sergiu Comissiona	Conductor
Raphael Oleg	Violinist	Joseph Kalichstein	Pianist
Mark Elder	Conductor	Anonymous	Soloist
Bruno Weil	Conductor	Anonymous	Soloist
Muhai Tang	Conductor	Anonymous	Soloist
Hiroyuki Iwaki	Conductor		

Table A3.3. The respondents to the questionnaire: music critics who agreed to identification.

Michael Ajzenstadt	Dr. Gary Lemco
William Aguiar, Jr.	Nancy Lang
Carroll Bottino	Robert Markow
Clarke Bustard	David McKee
Charles Carroll	Boris E. Nelson
John Charles	Byron Nelson
Albert Cohen	Nancy Raabe
Mark Conrad	Yoshihisa Sasaki
Mary Jane Doerr	Samuel Singer
Dimitry Drobatschewsky	Tom Strini
Scott Duncan	James Taylor
Pauline Finch-Durichen	James A. van Sant
John Fleming	Donald Vroon
Gilbert French	Michael Walsh
Richard Ginell	William Zakariasen
Paul Hertelendy	

Detroit, recently demolished) to 0.98 (Grosser Musikvereinssaal, Vienna). The critics AQI values ranged from 0.19 to 0.94.

The results of this study are in broad agreement with the categories adopted in Chapter 5 if the following equivalences are used:

Category A+—"Superior," AQI: 1.0 to 0.90
Category A—"Excellent," AQI: 0.90 to 0.63
Category B+—"Good to Excellent," AQI: 0.63 to 0.40
Category B—"Good," AQI: 0.40 to 0.25
Category C+—"Fair," AQI: less than 0.25

Further, in regard to this listing, a problem became apparent when Beranek discussed the ratings with a number of the officials of halls who contributed information to this book. Although science might be served by identification of those in Category B+, both art and commerce plead for circumspection. Hence, no names are given in connection with the 12 halls in the B+ category.

It is important to note that all halls in the B+ category are used regularly by very good to excellent orchestras and the local concert-goers believe them to have completely satisfactory acoustics.

LISTING OF THE CONCERT HALLS INTO CATEGORIES OF ACOUSTICAL QUALITY BY MUSICIANS AND CRITICS COMBINED

Using the table of equivalences above, the AQI values are used to place the halls in the five categories of acoustical quality.

Note: The list is restricted to those halls that were both covered in these surveys and are included in Chapter 6, totaling 30 halls. Within categories, the halls are not rank-ordered. They are listed alphabetically, first by country, then by city. USA is indexed as America.

Category A+: Not rank-ordered

Boston, Symphony Hall
Vienna, Grosser Musikvereinssaal
Amsterdam, Concertgebouw

Category A: Not rank-ordered

Chicago, Orchestra Hall
Cleveland, Severance Hall
New York, Carnegie Hall
Worcester, MA, Mechanics Hall
Berlin, Philharmonie
Munich, Herkulessaal
Cardiff, St. David's Hall
Rotterdam, De Doelen
Zurich, Grosser Tonhallesaal

Category B+

Note: 12 halls not named.

Category B: Not rank-ordered

Brussels, Palais des Beaux-Arts
Copenhagen, Radiohuset Std #1*
Bonn, Beethovenhalle
London, Royal Festival Hall**

Category C:

London, Barbican Concert Hall*

*Many of the ratings may apply to the halls before renovations designed to improve the acoustics were completed.

**It is not known how many of the ratings were made with or without the assisted resonance system in operation.

COMPARISON WITH RATINGS IN CHAPTER 6

In the A+, "Superior" category, the same three halls appear as in Chapter 5, with the Vienna hall ranking highest.

In the A, "Excellent" category, Cardiff (St. David's) and Zurich (Grosser Tonhallesaal) appear in Chapter 6 with the same ratings. Rated higher in this study than in the interviews' study of Chapter 5, are Cleveland (Severance Hall); Chicago (Orchestra Hall); Berlin (Philharmonie); Munich (Herkulessaal); and Rotterdam (De Doelen). In the interview study of Chapter 5, too few knew Worcester (Mechanics Hall) to yield a rating.

One cannot help but feel that part of the rating of a concert hall is the quality of its home orchestra. To begin with, the Berlin and Cleveland orchestras are ranked as among the world's best.

A more striking example is Orchestra Hall in Chicago. The Chicago Symphony Orchestra (with George Solti as conductor until 1993) is also recognized as one of the world's great orchestras. The AQI rating for Orchestra Hall is "A." Yet, Chicagoans are so dissatisfied with the acoustics of Orchestra Hall that plans have been drawn for a major renovation that will raise the roof and ceiling to increase the reverberation times and extend the length of the hall to provide better hall and stage acoustics. This example points out the difficulties of accurate rank orderings of concert halls that are the homes of orchestras with top reputations.

At the other end, a surprise is Brussels' Palais des Beaux-Arts, which was so highly spoken of in Beranek's interviews of conductors.

Another interesting point is that of the halls listed, nine of the A-rated halls are over 50 years old; only three are less than 50 years old. Of all halls below A-rating, 16 out of 19 are less than 50 years old. (Age and acoustics are discussed in Chapter 7.)

COMMENTS ON PARTICULAR HALLS BY MUSIC CRITICS

The music critics' ratings were in close agreement with those of musicians ($r^2 = 0.86$), especially on conventionally shaped halls (rectangular and horseshoe) and less so in fan and geometrically shaped halls (see also Haan and Fricke, 1995).

The music critics' comments on five halls ranging over the rating spectrum are presented in brief here.

Vienna, Grosser Musikvereinssaal

"Marvelous acoustics;" "From Bruckner to Mozart, the hall is the perfect host;" "Wonderfully alive, full and detailed;" "Too bright and live for my taste. Sound is almost garish at high volume levels;" "Responsive hall, sound carries well and warmly."

Boston, Symphony Hall

"Marvelous acoustics. I feel enveloped in a garment of music;" "Rich, full, balanced and very mellow;" "Excellent—a model to be followed;" "Over bright;" "Clear and natural;" "Probably the best hall in the US;" "Warm, clear and embrasive."

Berlin, Philharmonie Hall

"It has clear resonance, especially suited for contemporary music;" "Great acoustics, great sight lines;" "Terrible sound. Mozart sounds lost while Beethoven is at home;" "Not as good as it should be. Still the best 'surround' hall I know."

New York, Avery Fisher Hall

"Rich middle range with good focus and clarity;" "It was bad before, but after modification in 1992, it became a pretty good hall;" "Fine since latest overhaul. Good sound, good tonal response up and down scale; 'resonance';" "Acoustics fair;" "Warm, reverberant acoustic. Still intimate, refined;" "Not very good—no blend, no warmth;" "Gets my vote as the best of those I know. Excellent resonance;" "Dreadful. Sound not well blended."

London, Royal Festival Hall

"On the dry side;" "Big, bright and crisp;" "Very resonant, cool sound;" "Terrible—dry, reverberant, unresonant;" "Good."

Halls mentioned (not simply checked on the questionnaire) by the music critics as "Excellent" Halls (excluding the three "superior" halls about which nearly all critics agree), in order of number of mentions:

New York, Carnegie Hall (13)
Cleveland, Severance Hall (5)
New York, Avery Fisher Hall (3)
Philadelphia, Academy of Music (3)
Chicago, Orchestra Hall (3)

Halls mentioned by the critics as "Poor" Halls, in order of number of mentions:

San Francisco, Davies Hall
(before renovation) (10)
New York, Avery Fisher Hall
(probably before renovation) (8)
Toronto, Roy Thompson Hall (5)
Philadelphia, Academy of Music (2)
Chicago, Orchestra Hall (2)

Conclusion

From the above view by critics, Philadelphia Academy of Music and Chicago would seem to belong in the B+ group and not above as shown, while Carnegie and Severance would seem, by their judgments, to belong in the A group.

The biggest difference between musicians and music critics were for Chicago (Orchestra Hall), Berlin (Philharmonie), Munich (Herkulessaal), and New York (Carnegie). This spread helps explain the difference in ratings by the AQI method and the interview method of Chapter 5.

RELATION OF HALL GEOMETRICAL FACTORS TO SUBJECTIVE PREFERENCE RATINGS, AQI'S

The degree of sound quality in a room is likely to depend on the room shape as well as the volume and surface finishes. In this section the dependence of acoustic quality judgments on room type is investigated.

Musicians opinions

Twenty eight of the 32 musicians who responded said they had a particular preference for hall shape for symphonic music. Twenty-one of these (75%) preferred rectangular concert halls. This is in accordance with the finding of Gade (1981) that musicians preferred shoebox type halls as an ideal room shape. Six of the thirteen halls in the A+, A groups are rectangular (46%), while only 19 of the 52 halls surveyed were rectangular (36%). The second most common preference was for horseshoe type halls.

Geometrical factors

Geometrical data on the 53 concert halls was assembled together with the subjective evaluation. The parameters used were:

Hall depth *D* is defined as the distance between proscenium wall and the rear wall, or if there is no proscenium, the front of the stage. Hall width *W* is the horizontal distance between the side walls in rectangular halls. In the case of non-rectangular halls, the hall width is the average width of the plan which is converted to a rectangle of the same area, and *W* is the width of the rectangle. The hall height *H* is the mean distance between the floor and the ceiling. The angle of the side walls ASW is twice the average angle that a single side wall makes with the centerline of the hall.

Unexpectedly, the highest correlation between geometric factors and AQI was found between the degree of surface irregularities DSI and the AQI ($r^2 = 0.63$). The DSI's were judged *visually* from photographs and drawings (see pp. 457–459).

The second highest correlation was with the angle of the side walls ASW. The next highest was with the ratio of hall width to hall height *W* / *H*. This was followed, with decreasing correlations, by the mean rake angle MRA, and the ratio of the hall depth to hall width *D* / *W*. For further information in relation to this study, see Haan and Fricke (1993).

These architectural factors are discussed in the Chapters of the last half of this book.

ACKNOWLEDGMENTS

The author wishes to acknowledge the collaboration of his doctoral student C. H. Haan in the execution of the AQI procedure.

REFERENCES

Barron, M. (1988). "Subjective study of British symphony concert halls," Acustica **66**, pp. 1–14.

Beranek, L. L. (1962). *Music, Acoustics, and Architecture* (Wiley, New York). In Japanese (1972) translated with modifications and added Appendix 4 by M. Nagatomo (Kajima Institute, Tokyo).

Cremer, L. and Mueller, H. (1978 and 1982). *Principles and Applications of Room Acoustics, Vol. 1*, English translation with additions by T. J. Schultz (Applied Science Publishers, Essex, England) and in USA and Canada (Elsevier, New York, 1982). Originally published in German (1978) by Hirzel, Stuttgart.

Gade, A. C. (1981). "Musicians' ideas about room acoustical qualities," Report No. 31, The Acoustics Lab. Technical University of Denmark, p. 55.

Haan, C. H., and Fricke, F. R. (1993). "Surface diffusivity as a measure of the acoustic quality of concert halls," Proceedings of Conference of the Australia and New Zealand Architectural Science Association, Sydney, pp. 81–90.

Haan, C. H. and Fricke, F. R. (1995). "Musician and music critic responses to concert hall acoustics," Proceedings of 15th International Congress on Acoustics, Trondheim, Norway, June 1995.

Hawkes, R. J., and Douglas, H. (1971). "Subjective acoustic experience in concert auditoria," Acustica **24**, p. 235.

Lawrence, A. "Sightlines and soundlines—the design of audience seating area," Applied Acoustics **16**, pp. 427–440.

Parkin, P. H., Scholes, W. E. and Derbyshire, A.G. (1952), "The reverberation times of ten British concert halls," Acustica **2**, p. 97.

Somerville, T. (1953). "An empirical acoustical criterion," Acustica **2**, p. 365.

Professor Fergus R. Fricke
Faculty of Architecture
Department of Architectural and Design Science
University of Sydney
NSW 2006 Australia

Appendix 4
Acoustical Data for Halls

SEQUENTIAL INDEX

(*continued*)

(Sequential Index, continued)

MEASURED ACOUSTICAL ATTRIBUTES OF CONCERT AND OPERA HALLS

Attribute	Measured by	Year of data	125	250	500	1,000	2,000	4,000
			Center frequencies of filter bands					
1. BALTIMORE, JOSEPH MEYERHOFF SYMPHONY HALL (Opened 1982, 2,467 Seats)								
RT, unoccupied	Takenaka	1991	2.67	2.36	2.31	2.31	2.12	1.82
	Bradley	1992	2.85	2.44	2.40	2.37	1.95	1.54
	Gade	1992	2.83	2.44	2.36	2.32	1.98	1.58
	Average		2.78	2.41	2.36	2.33	2.02	1.65
RT, occupied	Extrapolated		2.20	2.20	2.00	2.00	1.86	1.68
EDT, unoccupied	Takenaka	1991	2.61	2.41	2.38	2.31	2.07	1.71
	Bradley	1992	2.55	2.35	2.28	2.27	1.84	1.39
	Gade	1992	2.63	2.38	2.30	2.31	1.95	1.46
	Average		2.60	2.38	2.32	2.30	1.95	1.52
$IACC_A$, unoccupied	Takenaka	1991	0.93	0.76	0.27	0.19	0.20	0.16
	Bradley	1992	0.94	0.73	0.26	0.21	0.22	0.16
	Average		0.94	0.75	0.27	0.20	0.21	0.16
$IACC_E$, unoccupied	Takenaka	1991	0.95	0.84	0.53	0.44	0.40	0.26
	Bradley	1992	0.96	0.83	0.51	0.45	0.38	0.28
	Average		0.96	0.84	0.52	0.45	0.39	0.27
$IACC_L$, unoccupied	Takenaka	1991	0.91	0.70	0.18	0.10	0.07	0.06
	Bradley	1992	0.93	0.70	0.18	0.09	0.11	0.09
	Average		0.92	0.70	0.18	0.10	0.09	0.08
LF, unoccupied	Bradley	1992	0.18	0.15	0.13	0.15	0.18	0.13
	Gade	1992	0.16	0.20	0.20	0.18	0.18	0.18
	Average		0.17	0.18	0.17	0.17	0.18	0.16
C_{80}, dB, unoccupied	Takenaka	1991	–4.10	–3.90	–2.80	–1.90	–1.30	–0.10
	Bradley	1992	–3.90	–3.20	–2.00	–1.30	–0.20	0.80
	Gade	1992	–2.05	–2.83	–2.13	–1.88	–1.17	0.36
	Average		–3.35	–3.31	–2.31	–1.69	–0.89	0.35
G, dB, unoccupied	Takenaka	1991	4.30	3.60	4.60	4.80	4.90	4.80
	Bradley	1992	2.71	2.77	3.73	3.22	1.43	–0.95
	(See Chapter 9 for Compromise Average of *G*.)							
2. BLOOMINGTON, INDIANA UNIVERSITY AUDITORIUM (Opened 1941, 3,760 Seats)								
RT, unoccupied	M.A.A.	1959	2.00	1.55	1.50	1.40	1.40	1.40
RT, occupied	M.A.A.	1959	1.70	1.50	1.45	1.40	1.30	1.30
3. BOSTON, SYMPHONY HALL (Opened 1900, 2,625 Seats)								
RT, unoccupied	M.A.A.	1958	2.50	2.80	2.70	2.85	2.85	2.10
	Schultz	1963	2.70	2.70	2.60	2.50	2.30	1.95
	Mastracco	1981	2.60	2.40	2.70	3.00	2.80	
	Average before 1982		2.60	2.63	2.67	2.78	2.65	2.03
	Takenaka	1991	2.11	2.19	2.33	2.69	2.80	2.47
	Bradley	1992	2.17	2.38	2.56	2.70	2.67	2.38
	Gade	1992	2.12	2.30	2.39	2.56	2.59	2.26
	Selected average after 1988		2.13	2.29	2.40	2.63	2.66	2.38

Attribute	Measured by	Year of data	125	250	500	1,000	2,000	4,000
3. BOSTON, SYMPHONY HALL, *continued*								
RT, occupied	Hidaka/Beranek	1992	1.80	1.90	1.80	1.80	1.70	1.40
	Griesinger/Kirkegaard	1993	2.10	1.80	1.90	1.90	1.60	1.20
	Average		1.95	1.85	1.85	1.85	1.65	1.30
EDT, unoccupied	Takenaka	1991	2.13	2.23	2.28	2.68	2.85	2.41
	Bradley	1992	2.00	2.08	2.19	2.38	2.43	2.14
	Gade	1992	2.00	2.12	2.26	2.45	2.57	2.14
	Average		2.04	2.14	2.24	2.50	2.62	2.23
$IACC_A$, unoccupied	Bradley	1992	0.94	0.76	0.27	0.24	0.21	0.22
	Takenaka	1991	0.91	0.73	0.29	0.14	0.11	0.11
	Average		0.91	0.74	0.28	0.19	0.16	0.17
$IACC_E$, unoccupied	Bradley	1992	0.93	0.82	0.40	0.41	0.43	0.43
	Takenaka	1991	0.95	0.82	0.49	0.30	0.27	0.23
	Average		0.94	0.82	0.45	0.36	0.35	0.33
$IACC_L$, unoccupied	Takenaka	1991	0.89	0.70	0.23	0.11	0.07	0.06
	Bradley	1992	0.93	0.74	0.25	0.14	0.07	0.07
LF, unoccupied	Bradley	1992	0.23	0.19	0.17	0.22	0.25	0.18
	Gade	1992	0.15	0.25	0.28	0.25	0.24	0.25
	Average		0.19	0.22	0.23	0.24	0.25	0.22
C_{80}, dB, unoccupied	Takenaka	1991	−2.90	−3.50	−3.10	−3.40	−3.80	−2.90
	Bradley	1992	−2.87	−2.46	−2.25	−1.98	−1.91	−2.00
	Gade	1992	−1.50	−1.92	−2.94	−2.18	−3.21	−2.04
	Average		−2.42	−2.63	−2.76	−2.52	−2.97	−2.31
G, dB, unoccupied	Takenaka	1991	2.90	3.60	5.00	5.80	6.50	6.50
	Bradley	1992	1.43	2.61	3.70	4.27	3.70	2.34
	(See Chapter 9 for Compromise Average of *G*.)							
4. BUFFALO, KLEINHANS MUSIC HALL (Opened 1940, 2,839 Seats)								
RT, unoccupied	M.A.A. (BBN)	1959	2.30	2.00	1.80	1.60	1.50	1.35
	Bradley	1992	2.60	2.01	1.95	1.70	1.60	1.49
	Gade	1992	2.46	2.02	1.91	1.68	1.63	1.50
	Average of Bradley & Gade		2.53	2.02	1.93	1.69	1.62	1.50
RT, occupied	M.A.A.	1959	1.70	1.65	1.35	1.30	1.25	1.10
EDT, unoccupied	Bradley	1992	1.92	1.78	1.72	1.39	1.26	1.00
	Gade	1992	1.97	1.78	1.85	1.42	1.37	1.06
	Average		1.95	1.78	1.79	1.41	1.32	1.03
$IACC_A$, unoccupied	Bradley	1992	0.96	0.85	0.60	0.51	0.27	0.30
$IACC_E$, unoccupied	Bradley	1992	0.97	0.90	0.79	0.61	0.37	0.38
$IACC_L$, unoccupied	Bradley	1992	0.95	0.80	0.40	0.30	0.12	0.12
LF, unoccupied	Bradley	1992	0.12	0.09	0.08	0.10	0.12	0.07
	Gade	1992	0.10	0.11	0.10	0.09	0.09	0.08
	Average		0.11	0.10	0.09	0.10	0.11	0.08
C_{80}, dB, unoccupied	Bradley	1992	−0.91	1.10	1.99	3.59	3.73	4.73
	Gade	1992	0.49	1.60	1.62	3.85	3.57	4.67
	Average		−0.21	1.35	1.81	3.72	3.65	4.70

Center frequencies of filter bands: 125, 250, 500, 1,000, 2,000, 4,000

Attribute	Measured by	Year of data	125	250	500	1,000	2,000	4,000
			Center frequencies of filter bands					
4. BUFFALO, KLEINHANS MUSIC HALL, *continued*								
G, dB, unoccupied	Bradley	1992	3.34	2.44	2.72	1.83	0.45	–1.08
	Gade	1992	4.83	3.39	2.49	2.78	2.58	–0.23
	(See Chapter 9 for Compromise Average of *G*.)							
5. CHICAGO, ORCHESTRA HALL (Opened 1904, 2,582 Seats)								
RT, unoccupied	Kirkegaard	1994	1.73	1.63	1.46	1.45	1.32	1.01
RT, occupied	Kirkegaard	1994	1.44	1.29	1.21	1.16	1.10	0.98
6. CLEVELAND, SEVERANCE HALL (Opened 1931, 2,101 Seats)								
RT, unoccupied	Bradley	1992	2.02	1.90	1.85	1.78	1.66	1.54
	Gade	1992	1.90	1.84	1.78	1.74	1.66	1.49
	Griesinger	1995	2.00	1.70	1.70	1.70	1.50	1.40
	Average		1.97	1.81	1.78	1.74	1.61	1.48
RT, occupied	Griesinger	1995	1.70	1.60	1.50	1.45	1.35	1.30
EDT, unoccupied	Bradley	1992	1.66	1.70	1.67	1.68	1.61	1.45
	Gade	1992	1.70	1.71	1.74	1.72	1.68	1.45
	Average		1.68	1.71	1.71	1.70	1.65	1.45
$IACC_A$, unoccupied	Bradley	1992	0.93	0.81	0.36	0.26	0.18	0.20
$IACC_E$, unoccupied	Bradley	1992	0.95	0.87	0.51	0.41	0.30	0.32
$IACC_L$, unoccupied	Bradley	1992	0.91	0.77	0.27	0.15	0.12	0.07
LF, unoccupied	Bradley	1992	0.20	0.14	0.13	0.15	0.18	0.13
C_{80}, dB, unoccupied	Bradley	1992	–0.85	0.19	0.18	0.42	0.68	0.98
	Gade	1992	–0.37	–0.02	–0.47	–0.29	–0.07	0.73
	Average		–0.61	0.09	–0.15	0.07	0.31	0.86
G, dB, unoccupied	Bradley	1992	1.78	3.24	3.51	3.10	1.95	0.85
	Gade	1992	1.86	4.12	3.46	2.08	2.93	0.82
	(See Chapter 9 for Compromise Average of *G*.)							
7. COSTA MESA, SEGERSTROM HALL, ORANGE COUNTY PERFORMING ARTS CENTER (Opened 1986, 2,903 Seats)								
RT, unoccupied	Takenaka	1991	2.27	2.14	2.14	2.27	2.10	1.81
	Hyde	1993	2.52	2.25	2.27	2.46	2.26	1.97
	Barron	1986	2.43	2.37	2.41	2.47	2.27	-
	Average, Barron and Hyde		2.48	2.31	2.34	2.47	2.27	1.97
RT, occupied	Takenaka & Hyde	1995	2.23	1.89	1.62	1.57	1.44	1.16
EDT, unoccupied	Takenaka, all seats	1991	2.16	2.02	2.01	2.01	1.90	1.56
	Hyde, all seats	1993–4	2.50	2.20	2.30	2.40	2.20	1.90
	Takenaka, w/o under balc. seats	1991	2.19	2.09	2.07	2.06	1.95	1.59
	Hyde, w/o underbalcony seats	1993–4	2.32	2.14	2.14	2.28	2.05	1.66
	Average, all measurements		2.29	2.11	2.13	2.19	2.03	1.68
EDT, occupied	Takenaka & Hyde	1995	2.67	2.43	2.25	2.12	1.86	1.84
$IACC_A$, unoccupied	Takenaka	1991	0.90	0.17	0.26	0.20	0.16	0.19
$IACC_E$, unoccupied	Takenaka	1991	0.92	0.80	0.47	0.37	0.31	0.30

Attribute	Measured by	Year of data	125	250	500	1,000	2,000	4,000
			Center frequencies of filter bands					
7. COSTA MESA, SEGERSTROM HALL, *continued*								
IACC$_L$, unoccupied	Takenaka	1991	0.88	0.64	0.19	0.10	0.09	0.07
LF, unoccupied	Barron	1986	0.27	0.19	0.23	0.22	-	-
C_{80}, dB, unoccupied	Barron	1986	−3.70	−1.90	−0.70	−0.40	1.20	-
	Takenaka	1991	−3.10	−1.60	−0.90	−0.50	−0.20	0.60
	Hyde	1993	−3.20	−1.35	−1.05	−0.50	0.00	1.00
	Average		−3.15	−1.48	−0.98	−0.50	−0.10	0.80
G, dB, unoccupied	Barron	1986	0.80	3.30	3.70	4.10	3.70	-
	Takenaka	1991	2.90	3.50	4.70	5.10	4.70	4.70
	Hyde	1993	1.80	2.40	3.80	3.95	3.80	2.30
	(See Chapter 9 for Compromise Average of G.)							
8. DALLAS, McDERMOTT CONCERT HALL IN MEYERSON SYMPHONY CENTER								
							(Opened 1989, 2,065 Seats)	
RT, unoccupied	(1992) ARTEC:Canopy-mid; Rev. open		3.44	3.16	2.93	2.87	2.58	2.08
	(1992) ARTEC:Canopy-low; Rev.closed		3.22	2.94	2.70	2.50	2.37	1.97
RT, occupied	(1994) Anon.–I:Canopy high; Rev.open		3.53	3.21	2.85	2.92	2.46	2.22
	(1995) Anon.–2:Canopy high;Rev.open		-	3.15	2.73	2.68	2.27	1.71
	Average: Canopy high, reverberation doors open		3.50	3.18	2.79	2.80	2.37	1.97
EDT, unoccup.	(1992) ARTEC:Canopy-mid; Rev. open		2.00	2.00	1.80	2.00	1.80	1.60
	(1992) ARTEC:Canopy-low; Rev.closed		2.20	2.10	1.80	2.00	1.90	1.60
EDT, occupied	(1995) Anon:–2:Canopy-high; Rev. open		-	3.16	2.31	2.07	1.96	1.81
C_{80}, dB, unoccup.	(1992) ARTEC:Canopy-mid; Rev. open		−0.90	−4.20	0.70	−0.70	0.20	0.40
	(1992) ARTEC:Canopy-low; Rev.closed		−4.40	−5.30	−0.60	−1.40	−0.20	1.10
C_{80}, dB, occup.	(1995) Anon.–2:Canopy-high; Rev.open		-	−3.90	−2.60	0.30	−2.10	−1.70
9. LENOX, MASSACHUSETTS, TANGLEWOOD, KOUSSEVITZKY MUSIC SHED								
							(Opened 1938, 5,121 Seats)	
RT, unoccupied	Takenaka/Beranek	1993	4.29	4.06	3.86	3.09	2.68	2.32
	Bradley	1993	4.13	4.00	3.65	3.09	2.65	2.29
	Average		4.21	4.03	3.76	3.09	2.67	2.31
RT, occupied	Takenaka/Beranek	1994	2.85	2.63	2.09	1.69	1.50	1.42
EDT, unoccupied	Takenaka/Beranek	1993	4.02	3.81	3.77	2.98	2.51	2.22
	Bradley	1993	3.42	3.87	3.60	2.98	2.49	2.16
	Average		3.72	3.84	3.69	2.98	2.50	2.19
ICCA$_A$, unoccupied	Takenaka/Beranek	1993	0.94	0.79	0.50	0.33	0.29	0.22
	Bradley	1993	0.97	0.80	0.39	0.30	0.22	0.19
	Average		0.96	0.80	0.45	0.32	0.26	0.21
IACC$_E$, unoccupied	Takenaka/Beranek	1993	0.96	0.89	0.76	0.65	0.57	0.44
	Bradley	1993	0.97	0.89	0.73	0.58	0.47	0.38
	Average		0.97	0.89	0.75	0.62	0.52	0.41
IACC$_L$, unoccupied	Takenaka/Beranek	1993	0.92	0.75	0.40	0.15	0.09	0.06
	Bradley	1993	0.95	0.76	0.27	0.13	0.07	0.06
	Average		0.94	0.76	0.34	0.14	0.08	0.06
LF, unoccupied	Bradley	1993	0.10	0.14	0.10	0.12	0.15	0.12

Attribute	Measured by	Year of data	125	250	500	1,000	2,000	4,000
			Center frequencies of filter bands					
9. LENOX, TANGLEWOOD SHED, *continued*								
C_{80}, dB, unoccupied	Takenaka/Beranek	1993	−3.99	−4.83	−5.03	−3.44	−2.14	−1.32
	Bradley	1993	−0.62	−3.92	−3.85	−2.76	−1.29	−0.65
	Average		−2.31	−4.38	−4.44	−3.10	−1.72	−0.99
G, dB, unoccup.	Taka/Ber Hall Average		0.00	1.10	3.10	3.10	−1.70	−2.50
(1993)	Bradley Hall Average		0.18	−0.16	−0.90	−1.92	−3.21	−5.29
	Taka/Ber 10th row, off center line		2.9	4.6	6.5	6.5	2.7	2.4
	Taka/Ber 20th row, off center line		1.1	2.3	4.2	5.0	0.2	−0.3
	(See Chapter 9 for Compromise Average of *G*.)							
10, LENOX, MASSACHUSETTS, SEIJI OZAWA HALL (Opened 1994, 1,180 Seats)								
RT, unoccupied (rear wall closed)	Kirkegaard	1995	2.34	2.36	2.21	2.28	2.16	1.70
RT, occupied (rear wall open)	Takenaka/Beranek	1994	2.24	2.16	1.82	1.50	1.35	1.28
11. MINNEAPOLIS, MINNESOTA ORCHESTRA HALL (Opened 1974, 2,450 Seats)								
RT, unoccupied	Schultz	1979	2.35	2.30	2.35	2.20	2.15	1.90
RT, occupied	Harris	1974	2.10	1.95	1.90	1.80	1.70	1.50
12. NEW YORK, AVERY FISHER HALL (Opened 1976, 2,742 Seats)								
RT, unoccupied	Takenaka	1986	-	2.24	2.26	2.20	2.03	1.48
	Beranek (orchestra there)	1994	1.93	1.98	2.15	2.18	2.06	1.80
RT, occupied	Beranek	1994	1.60	1.76	1.78	1.74	1.74	1.80
EDT, unoccupied	Takenaka	1986	-	2.00	2.01	1.90	1.64	1.24
$IACC_A$	Takenaka	1986	-	0.70	0.22	0.17	0.32	0.21
LF, unoccupied	Takenaka	1986	-	-	0.13	0.11	0.12	-
C_{80}, dB, unoccupied	Takenaka	1986	-	−2.80	−2.30	−2.00	−0.20	0.80
13. NEW YORK, CARNEGIE HALL (Opened 1891, 2,804 Seats)								
RT, unoccupied	Annon.	1968	2.20	1.85	2.10	2.20	1.80	1.40
RT, occupied	M.A.A. (BBN)	1958	2.30	1.80	1.80	1.80	1.60	1.60
14. NEW YORK, METROPOLITAN OPERA HOUSE (Opened 1966, 3,816 Seats)								
RT, unoccupied	V. L. Jordan	1966	2.30	2.10	2.30	2.25	2.05	1.50
	Takenaka (20 dB curve)	1986	1.90	1.62	1.75	1.80	1.65	1.15
RT, occupied	V. L. Jordan (80% full)	1966	2.25	2.00	1.75	1.80	1.65	1.15
EDT, unoccupied	V. L. Jordan	1966	2.10	2.10	2.25	2.25	2.00	1.55
EDT, occupied	V. L. Jordan (80% full)	1966	2.10	2.10	1.70	1.80	1.70	1.30
	(Note that Jordan EDT and Takenaka RT are similar indicating stagehouse influence on other data.)							
15. PHILADELPHIA, ACADEMY OF MUSIC (Opened 1857 , 2,827 Seats for Opera)								
RT, unoccupied	M.A.A. (BBN & Potwin)	1959	2.00	1.80	1.60	1.50	1.40	1.30
	(There were changes in the hall after 1959, including new seats and added carpets.)							

Attribute	Measured by	Year of data	125	250	500	1,000	2,000	4,000
			Center frequencies of filter bands					
15. PHILADELPHIA, ACADEMY OF MUSIC, *continued*								
	Kirkegaard	1992	1.50	1.30	1.30	1.20	1.20	1.10
	Bradley	1992	1.50	1.32	1.35	1.30	1.21	1.02
	Marshall	1992	1.40	1.40	1.40	1.30	1.30	1.10
	Average		1.47	1.34	1.35	1.27	1.24	1.07
RT, occupied	(M.A.A.)	1958	1.40	1.70	1.45	1.35	1.25	1.15
(Note the changes after 1959 as above.)								
	Kirkegaard	1992	1.40	1.30	1.20	1.20	1.10	1.00
EDT, unoccupied	Marshall	1992	1.30	1.20	1.20	1.20	1.20	1.10
	Bradley	1992	1.23	1.11	1.20	1.21	1.13	0.89
	Average		1.21	1.16	1.20	1.21	1.17	1.00
$IACC_A$, unoccupied	Bradley	1992	0.94	0.79	0.44	0.41	0.35	0.30
$IACC_E$, unoccupied	Bradley	1992	0.94	0.81	0.58	0.54	0.48	0.41
$IACC_L$, unoccupied	Bradley	1992	0.90	0.73	0.25	0.18	0.12	0.12
LF, unoccupied	Bradley	1992	0.19	0.16	0.14	0.17	0.19	0.12
C_{80}, dB, unoccupied	Marshall	1992	−1.20	−0.20	2.00	0.30	2.30	2.10
	Bradley	1992	1.70	2.34	1.97	2.31	2.45	4.09
	Average		0.25	1.07	1.99	1.31	2.38	3.10
G, dB, unoccupied	Bradley	1992	−1.87	−0.12	1.77	1.13	−0.53	−2.35
(See Chapter 9 for Compromise Average of *G*.)								
16. ROCHESTER, NY, EASTMAN THEATRE (Opened 1923, 3,347 Seats)								
RT, unoccupied	M.A.A. (BBN)	1959	3.10	2.50	1.90	1.75	1.70	1.55
RT, occupied	M.A.A. (BBN)	1959	2.30	1.85	1.75	1.55	1.45	1.30
17. SALT LAKE CITY, ABRAVANEL SYMPHONY HALL (Opened 1979, 2,812 Seats)								
RT, unoccupied	Takenaka	1991	2.08	1.92	2.03	2.03	1.92	1.72
RT, occupied	Estimated		1.80	1.80	1.70	1.70	1.60	1.50
EDT, unoccupied	Takenaka	1991	2.05	1.99	2.09	2.07	1.94	1.70
$IACC_A$, unoccupied	Takenaka	1991	0.91	0.73	0.28	0.19	0.17	0.14
$IACC_E$, unoccupied	Takenaka	1991	0.93	0.81	0.48	0.40	0.35	0.26
$IACC_L$, unoccupied	Takenaka	1991	0.90	0.69	0.22	0.10	0.08	0.07
C_{80}, dB, unoccupied	Takenaka	1991	−4.60	−3.90	−2.10	−1.80	−1.40	−0.90
G, dB, unoccupied	Takenaka	1991	1.90	0.30	2.40	2.70	2.50	1.60
(See Chapter 9 for Compromise Average of *G*.)								
18. SAN FRANCISCO, DAVIES SYMPHONY HALL (Opened 1980, 2,743 Seats)								
(All data taken before 1993–94 renovations.)								
RT, unoccupied	Takenaka	1991	2.58	2.41	2.29	2.24	1.96	1.63
(Since 1993, the volume is 5% less. Estimated RT, unocc.)			2.45	2.29	2.18	2.13	1.86	1.55
RT, occupied	Kirkegaard	1992	-	1.90	1.90	1.80	1.70	1.40
EDT, unoccupied	Takenaka	1991	2.69	2.51	2.26	2.04	1.72	1.38
$IACC_A$, unoccupied	Takenaka	1991	0.93	0.77	0.39	0.30	0.29	0.27
$IACC_E$, unoccupied	Takenaka	1991	0.95	0.87	0.65	0.54	0.50	0.40

		Year	Center frequencies of filter bands					
Attribute	**Measured by**	**of data**	**125**	**250**	**500**	**1,000**	**2,000**	**4,000**
18. SAN FRANCISCO, DAVIES SYMPHONY HALL, ***continued***								
IACC$_L$, unoccupied	Takenaka	1991	0.92	0.72	0.23	0.09	0.09	0.08
C_{80}, dB, unoccupied	Takenaka	1991	–5.10	–3.90	–2.30	–0.60	0.10	1.30
G, dB, unoccupied	Takenaka	1991	2.50	3.00	3.30	3.40	2.90	2.90
(See Chapter 9 for Compromise Average of *G*.)								
19. SAN FRANCISCO, WAR MEMORIAL OPERA HOUSE (Opened 1932, 3,252 Seats)								
(No measured data. Estimated RT, occupied, mid-frequencies 1.7 sec.)								
20. J. F. KENNEDY CENTER FOR THE PERFORMING ARTS, OPERA HOUSE (Opened 1971, 2,142 Seats)								
RT, unoccupied, asbestos curtain down	Harris	1971	2.20	2.00	1.80	1.60	1.50	1.40
RT, occupied, during opera, chords	Harris	1971	2.00	1.90	1.60	1.40	1.20	1.20
21. WORCESTER, MASSACHUSETTS, THE GRAND HALL, MECHANICS HALL (Opened 1857, 1,343 Seats)								
RT, unoccupied	Bradley	1993	2.10	2.40	2.30	2.00	1.60	1.40
RT, occupied	Bradley	1993	1.70	1.90	1.60	1.50	1.40	1.30
EDT, unoccupied	Bradley	1993	2.10	2.30	2.30	2.00	1.70	1.40
EDT, occupied	Bradley	1993	1.80	1.90	1.70	1.50	1.40	1.30
IACC$_A$, unoccupied	Bradley	1993	0.90	0.70	0.20	0.20	0.20	0.20
IACC$_E$, unoccupied	Bradley	1993	0.95	0.81	0.47	0.45	0.44	0.42
IACC$_L$, unoccupied	Bradley	1993	0.92	0.70	0.22	0.21	0.22	0.24
LF, occupied	Bradley	1993	0.20	0.20	0.20	0.20	0.20	0.30
LF, unoccupied	Bradley	1993	0.30	0.20	0.20	0.20	0.20	0.30
C_{80}, dB, unoccupied	Bradley	1993	–1.00	–2.00	–2.00	–1.00	0.00	1.00
G, dB, unoccupied	Bradley	1993	4.00	6.00	5.50	4.50	2.00	–1.50
(See Chapter 9 for Compromise Average of *G*.)								
22. BUENOS AIRES, OPERA COLÓN (Opened 1908, 2,487 Seats)								
(No measured data. Estimated RT, occupied, mid-frequencies, 1.8 sec.)								
23. SYDNEY OPERA HOUSE, CONCERT HALL (Opened 1973, 2,679 Seats)								
RT, unoccupied	Jordan	1973	2.45	2.46	2.45	2.55	2.60	2.56
	Yamasaki	1992	2.25	2.40	2.30	2.65	2.60	2.20
	Average		2.35	2.43	2.38	2.60	2.60	2.38
RT, occupied	Jordan	1973	2.10	2.20	2.10	2.30	2.20	2.00
EDT, unoccupied	Jordan	1973	2.18	2.28	2.16	2.22	2.18	2.10
EDT, occupied	Jordan	1973	2.05	2.13	1.98	2.16	2.12	2.02
24. SALZBURG, FESTSPIELHAUS (Opened 1960, 2,158 Seats)								
RT, unoccupied	M.A.A. (Schwaiger)	1960	1.90	2.30	2.25	2.10	2.10	1.80
	Gade	1987	1.70	2.00	2.00	2.00	1.80	1.60
	Bradley	1987	1.69	1.93	1.91	1.82	1.74	1.50
	Gade/BradleyAverage		1.70	1.97	1.96	1.91	1.77	1.55

Attribute	Measured by	Year of data	125	250	500	1,000	2,000	4,000
			Center frequencies of filter bands					
24. SALZBURG, FESTSPIELHAUS, *continued*								
RT, Occupied	M.A.A. (Schwaiger, BBN)	1960	1.70	1.60	1.50	1.50	1.40	1.30
EDT, unocupied	Bradley	1987	1.65	1.89	1.88	1.78	1.71	1.40
	Gade	1987	1.61	1.98	2.04	1.78	1.85	1.59
	Average		1.63	1.94	1.96	1.78	1.78	1.50
LF, unoccupied	Bradley	1987	0.17	0.16	0.14	0.12	0.11	0.19
	Gade	1987	0.18	0.16	0.15	0.16	-	-
	Average		0.18	0.16	0.15	0.14	-	-
C_{80}, dB, unoccupied	Bradley	1987	−1.61	−1.32	−0.50	0.65	−0.04	1.45
	Gade	1987	−2.66	−2.10	−1.29	0.28	−0.79	0.16
	Average		−2.14	−1.71	−0.90	0.47	−0.42	0.81
G, dB, unoccupied	Bradley	1987	1.57	2.89	3.24	3.63	3.15	2.16
	Gade	1987	2.02	4.18	4.53	3.88	1.86	1.36
	(See Chapter 9 for Compromise Average of *G*.)							
25. VIENNA, GROSSER MUSIKVEREINSSAAL (Opened 1870, 1,680 Seats)								
RT, unoccupied	various agencies	1958	3.10	3.30	3.60	3.50	3.10	2.20
	(There were changes in the seats between 1960 and 1980.)							
RT, unoccupied	Gade	1987	3.00	3.20	3.20	3.20	2.60	2.10
	Tachibana	1987	2.85	2.85	2.90	2.95	2.70	2.00
	Takenaka	1993	2.97	2.95	3.04	2.99	2.67	2.21
	Bradley	1987	3.05	3.11	3.11	3.04	2.72	2.09
	Average		2.97	3.03	3.06	3.05	2.67	2.10
	Matsuzawa (rehearsal)	1992	2.61	2.62	2.56	2.42	2.22	1.91
RT, occupied	M.A.A. (various)	1959	2.40	2.20	2.10	2.00	1.90	1.60
	Tachibana	1987	2.20	2.20	2.00	1.95	1.80	1.70
	Matsuzawa	1992	2.14	2.15	2.01	1.94	1.71	1.55
	Average		2.25	2.18	2.04	1.96	1.80	1.62
EDT, unoccupied	Gade	1987	2.93	3.37	3.31	3.18	2.77	2.08
	Bradley	1987	2.93	3.06	3.06	3.03	2.70	2.00
	Takenaka	1993	2.98	3.01	3.03	2.99	2.71	2.17
	Average of Taka & Brad		2.96	3.04	3.05	3.01	2.71	2.09
$IACC_A$, unoccupied	Takenaka	1993	0.89	0.68	0.20	0.11	0.17	0.26
$IACC_E$, unoccupied	Takenaka	1993	0.92	0.76	0.42	0.32	0.34	0.40
$IACC_L$, unoccupied	Takenaka	1993	0.88	0.66	0.17	0.09	0.07	0.07
LF, unoccupied	Bradley	1987	0.14	0.17	0.19	0.16	0.12	0.21
	Gade	1988	0.12	0.16	0.19	0.17	-	-
	Average		0.13	0.17	0.19	0.17	-	-
C_{80}, dB, unoccupied	Bradley	1987	−5.71	−4.74	−4.00	−3.18	−2.98	−1.18
	Takenaka	1993	−5.10	−5.10	−4.70	−4.00	−3.10	−1.60
	Gade	1987	−5.02	−6.56	−5.45	−4.68	−3.88	−1.93
	Average		−5.28	−5.47	−4.72	−3.95	−3.32	−1.57
G, dB, unoccupied	Takenaka	1993	8.10	7.40	7.80	7.90	6.80	6.10
	Bradley	1987	6.10	6.04	5.97	6.57	6.04	4.51
	(See Chapter 9 for Compromise Average of *G*.)							

Attribute	Measured by	Year of data	125	250	500	1,000	2,000	4,000
			Center frequencies of filter bands					
26. VIENNA, STAATSOPER (Opened 1869, 1,709 Seats)								
RT, unoccupied	M.A.A. (Bruchmeyer)	1955	2.00	1.90	1.80	1.80	1.70	1.50
	TAK (Source So)	1988	1.84	1.61	1.55	1.54	1.44	1.28
	TAK (Source pit)		1.67	1.52	1.53	1.54	1.44	1.27
RT, occupied	M.A.A (various agencies)	1960	1.40	1.45	1.40	1.20	1.20	1.15
EDT, unoccupied	TAK (Source So)	1988	1.56	1.43	1.38	1.47	1.34	1.07
	TAK (Source pit)		1.51	1.31	1.35	1.43	1.39	1.13
$IACC_A$, unoccupied	TAK (Source So)	1988	0.90	0.72	0.36	0.28	0.24	0.20
	TAK (Source pit)		0.93	0.77	0.34	0.18	0.15	0.13
$IACC_E$, unoccupied	TAK (Source So)	1988	0.92	0.80	0.49	0.38	0.32	0.24
	TAK (Source pit)		0.94	0.82	0.47	0.31	0.26	0.19
$IACC_L$, unoccupied	TAK (Source So)	1988	0.89	0.65	0.23	0.15	0.13	0.09
	TAK (Source pit)		0.91	0.74	0.27	0.13	0.11	0.09
C_{80}, dB, unoccupied	TAK (Source So)	1988	–0.20	1.50	2.50	2.80	2.70	4.30
	TAK (Source pit)		–2.10	–0.70	–0.70	–0.60	–0.20	1.20
G, dB, unoccupied	TAK (Source So)	1988	–1.40	0.70	3.10	2.50	1.30	–1.80
	TAK (Source pit)		0.20	2.70	4.30	3.60	2.50	–0.90
	(See Chapter 9 for Compromise Average of *G*.)							
27. BRUSSELS, PALAIS DES BEAUX-ARTS (Opened 1929, 2,150 Seats)								
RT, unoccupied	M.A.A. (Raes and RTB)	1961	2.20	2.40	2.00	1.90	1.75	1.60
RT, occupied	M.A.A. (Raes and BBN)	1961	1.90	1.75	1.50	1.35	1.25	1.10
28. EDMONTON, NORTHERN ALBERTA JUBILEE AUDITORIUM (Opened 1957, 2,678 Seats)								
RT, unoccupied	M.A.A. (Northwood)	1957	1.50	1.70	1.80	1.80	1.70	1.50
	Bradley	1992	1.80	1.70	1.67	1.65	1.43	1.21
RT, occupied	M.A.A. (Northwood)	1957	1.30	1.45	1.45	1.40	1.35	1.20
EDT, unoccupied	Bradley	1992	1.51	1.52	1.50	1.36	1.11	0.96
LF, unoccupied	Bradley	1992	0.14	0.10	0.13	0.16	0.17	0.14
C_{80}, dB, unoccupied	Bradley	1992	1.86	2.53	3.56	3.88	4.73	5.22
G, dB, unoccupied	Bradley	1992	–2.55	–2.08	–0.25	–0.22	–1.72	–3.90
	(See Chapter 9 for compromise average of *G*.)							
29. MONTREAL, SALLE WILFRID–PELLETIER (Opened 1963, 2,982 Seats)								
RT, unoccupied	Bradley	1989	2.49	2.10	1.98	1.87	1.69	1.29
	Acentech	1989	-	2.47	2.25	1.95	1.68	1.30
RT, occupied	Schultz	1963	2.20	1.85	1.73	1.60	1.50	1.20
EDT, unoccupied	Bradley	1989	2.47	2.18	1.98	1.88	1.61	1.19
LF, unoccupied	Bradley	1989	0.09	0.12	0.15	0.12	0.09	0.16
C_{80}, dB, unoccupied	Bradley	1989	–6.50	–2.44	–1.04	0.39	–0.37	1.60
G, dB, unoccupied	Bradley	1989	–0.41	–0.94	–0.37	0.53	–0.47	–3.22
	(See Chapter 9 for compromise average of *G*.)							

Attribute	Measured by	Year of data	125	250	500	1,000	2,000	4,000
			Center frequencies of filter bands					
30. TORONTO, ROY THOMPSON HALL (Opened 1982, 2,812 Seats)								
RT, unoccupied	Bradley	1988	2.37	2.22	2.21	2.11	1.94	1.49
RT, occupied	Schultz, extrapolated	1982	1.97	1.86	1.83	1.78	1.60	1.38
EDT, unoccupied	Bradley	1988	2.23	2.01	1.97	1.84	1.56	1.18
LF, unoccupied	Bradley	1988	0.10	0.16	0.16	0.16	0.13	0.19
C_{80}, dB, unoccupied	Bradley	1988	−4.48	−1.58	0.01	0.95	0.74	2.92
G, dB, unoccupied	Bradley	1988	2.84	2.93	3.20	3.29	3.28	2.44
(See Chapter 9 for compromise average of *G*.)								
31. COPENHAGEN, RADIOHUSET, STUDIO 1 (Opened 1945, 1,081 Seats)								
RT, unoccupied	Jordan, V. L.	1945	1.60	1.70	2.00	2.00	1.90	1.20
	Gade	1993	1.75	1.74	1.86	1.99	2.15	1.95
	Average		1.68	1.72	1.93	2.00	2.03	1.58
RT, occupied	Jordan, V. L.	1945	1.60	1.60	1.50	1.50	1.50	1.20
EDT, unoccupied	Gade	1993	1.59	1.72	1.91	2.02	2.19	1.86
LF, unoccupied	Gade	1993	0.11	0.17	0.17	0.17	0.15	0.19
C_{80}, dB, unoccupied	Gade	1993	0.83	−0.36	−0.35	−0.26	−1.53	−0.52
G, dB, unoccupied	Gade	1993	8.26	4.76	5.40	6.24	6.17	5.38
(See Chapter 9 for compromise average of *G*.)								
32. COPENHAGEN, TIVOLI KONCERTSAL (Opened 1956, 1,789 Seats)								
RT, unoccupied	M.A.A. (Jordan)	1956	2.10	2.10	2.20	2.30	2.40	2.10
RT, occupied	M.A.A. (Jordan)	1956	1.50	1.35	1.30	1.30	1.35	1.30
33. HELSINKI, KULTTURITALO (Opened 1957, 1,500 Seats)								
RT, occupied	M.A.A. (Arni)	1960	1.20	1.25	1.10	1.00	0.90	0.90
34. PARIS, OPÉRA BASTILLE (Opened 1989, 2,700 Seats)								
RT, unoccupied	CSTB	1992	1.80	1.70	1.70	1.70	1.70	1.50
	Commins	1992	1.55	1.55	1.70	1.70	1.65	1.40
	Commins (stage set)	1992	1.59	1.60	1.69	1.74	1.66	1.33
	Average		1.65	1.62	1.70	1.71	1.67	1.41
RT, occupied	CSTB	1992	1.70	1.60	1.55	1.60	1.40	1.25
	Commins (calculated)	1992	1.45	1.45	1.50	1.50	1.45	1.30
EDT, unoccupied	CSTB	1992	1.75	1.65	1.55	1.65	1.55	1.20
	Commins	1992	1.56	1.59	1.52	1.52	1.37	1.20
EDT, occupied	CSTB	1992	1.60	1.40	1.30	1.35	1.20	1.00
C_{80}, dB, unoccupied	CSTB	1992	−0.50	2.00	3.50	3.30	4.40	7.00
	Commins	1992	−0.85	0.63	1.25	2.24	2.59	2.29
G, dB, unoccupied	CSTB	1992	−30.00	−30.00	−28.00	−26.50	−27.00	−28.00
G, dB, occupied	CSTB	1992	−32.00	−31.00	−29.00	−27.50	−27.50	−29.50
(See Chapter 9 for compromise average of *G*.)								

Attribute	Measured by	Year of data	125	Center frequencies of filter bands 250	500	1,000	2,000	4,000
35. PARIS, OPÉRA GARNIER (Opened 1875, 2,131 Seats)								
RT, unoccupied	TAK (Source So)	1988	1.84	1.40	1.26	1.18	1.14	1.02
	TAK (Source pit)	1988	1.48	1.32	1.20	1.15	1.11	1.01
RT, occupied	Estimated			1.1 sec. mid-frequencies				
EDT, unoccupied	TAK (Source So)	1988	1.43	1.30	1.20	1.12	1.12	1.04
	TAK (Source pit)	1988	1.21	1.39	1.33	1.12	1.04	0.93
$IACC_A$, unoccupied	TAK (Source So)	1988	0.94	0.80	0.46	0.37	0.32	0.30
	TAK (Source pit)	1988	0.93	0.79	0.34	0.23	0.19	0.15
$IACC_E$, unoccupied	TAK (Source So)	1988	0.96	0.86	0.58	0.48	0.43	0.40
	TAK (Source pit)	1988	0.93	0.86	0.45	0.32	0.28	0.24
$IACC_L$, unoccupied	TAK (Source So)	1988	0.91	0.74	0.30	0.13	0.13	0.12
	TAK (Source pit)	1988	0.91	0.74	0.30	0.17	0.15	0.10
C_{80}, dB, unoccupied	TAK (Source So)	1988	1.40	1.50	3.60	5.10	5.00	5.50
	TAK (Source pit)	1988	−0.80	−1.30	−1.10	0.20	1.80	2.50
G, dB, unoccupied	TAK (Source So)	1988	−2.40	0.20	1.10	0.30	−1.50	−3.40
	TAK (Source pit)	1988	−3.50	0.20	0.50	−0.40	−2.20	−4.00
	(See Chapter 9 for compromise average of *G*.)							
36. PARIS, SALLE PLÉYEL (Opened 1927, 2,386 Seats)								
	(All data taken before revisions of 1994.)							
RT, unoccupied	Bradley	1987	3.11	2.49	2.05	1.83	1.61	-
	Barron	1981	3.10	2.50	2.10	1.80	1.60	-
	CSTB, Paris		3.10	2.40	2.20	2.00	1.95	1.70
	Average		3.10	2.46	2.12	1.88	1.72	0.57
RT, occupied	CSTB		2.10	1.60	1.55	1.40	1.30	1.20
EDT, unoccupied	CSTB		2.40	2.00	1.90	1.80	1.75	1.50
	Bradley	1981	2.81	1.97	1.86	1.60	1.57	1.34
	Average		2.61	1.99	1.88	1.70	1.66	ERR
LF, unoccupied	Bradley	1987	0.10	0.15	0.19	0.15	0.11	0.18
	Barron	1981	0.23	0.11	0.16	0.17	-	-
	Average		0.17	0.13	0.18	0.16	-	-
C_{80}, dB, unoccupied	Barron, w/o overhung seats	1981	−5.90	−0.40	0.00	1.40	2.30	-
	Barron, all seats	1981	−5.90	0.10	0.50	2.00	2.90	-
	CSTB		−7.00	−2.00	2.00	4.50	2.50	2.00
	Bradley	1987	−2.84	−0.83	−0.72	0.95	0.43	1.11
	Average		−5.41	−0.78	0.45	2.21	2.03	0.78
G, dB, unoccupied	CSTB		5.00	2.50	1.00	0.05	0.00	−1.00
	Bradley	1987	5.96	3.88	3.94	4.25	3.99	3.34
	Barron	1981	5.00	2.50	3.60	3.80	3.30	-
	(See Chapter 9 for compromise average of *G*.)							
37. BAYREUTH, FESTSPIELHAUS (Opened 1876, 1,800 Seats)								
RT, occupied	various agencies	1960	1.75	1.70	1.60	1.50	1.40	1.30

Attribute	Measured by	Year of data	125	250	500	1,000	2,000	4,000
38. BERLIN, KAMMERMUSIKSAAL DER PHILHARMONIE (Opened 1987, 1,138 Seats)								
RT, unoccupied	BeSB, Berlin	1987	2.18	2.00	2.07	2.20	2.11	2.19
RT, occupied	BeSB (2 positions)	1987	1.70	1.55	1.74	1.89	1.72	-
EDT, unoccupied	BeSB, Berlin	1987	2.04	2.01	1.99	2.21	2.11	1.64
EDT, occupied	BeSB (2 positions)	1987	1.40	1.55	1.48	1.88	1.65	-
C_{80}, dB, unoccupied	BeSB, Berlin	1987	-	-	−1.17	−2.37	-	-
39. BERLIN, KONZERTHAUS (SCHAUSPIELHAUS) (Opened 1986, 1,575 Seats)								
RT, unoccupied	Takenaka	1993	2.85	2.79	2.51	2.43	2.24	1.92
(Bass resonators added 1990.)	Fasold, w/90 piece orchestra	1990	2.12	2.30	2.16	2.10	2.00	1.75
	Matsuzawa, rehearsal	1992	2.75	2.53	2.30	2.18	2.04	1.76
RT, occupied	Fasold, before resonators	1986	2.60	2.50	2.15	2.00	1.90	1.60
	Fasold after resonators	1990	2.20	2.10	2.00	2.00	1.90	1.60
	Kimura, after resonators	1992	2.65	2.35	2.10	2.00	1.85	1.60
	Matsuzawa	1992	2.53	2.34	2.05	1.87	1.74	1.59
	Selected average		2.20	2.10	2.00	2.00	1.80	1.60
EDT, unoccupied	Takenaka	1993	2.87	2.71	2.47	2.39	2.19	1.83
$IACC_A$, unoccupied	Takenaka	1993	0.88	0.69	0.20	0.13	0.20	0.20
$IACC_E$, unoccupied	Takenaka	1993	0.92	0.80	0.37	0.29	0.42	0.36
$IACC_L$, unoccupied	Takenaka	1993	0.87	0.65	0.20	0.10	0.08	0.06
C_{80}, dB, unoccupied	Takenaka	1993	−4.20	−4.30	−3.90	−2.30	−1.30	−0.50
G, dB, unoccupied	Takenaka	1993	8.30	7.10	6.70	7.00	5.90	5.40
	(See Chapter 9 for compromise average of G.)							
40. BERLIN, PHILHARMONIE (Opened 1963, 2,325 Seats)								
RT, unoccupied	BeSB, Berlin	1990	2.20	1.90	2.10	2.20	2.10	1.70
	BeSB	1992	2.40	1.90	2.20	2.10	2.10	1.80
	Takenaka	1993	2.06	1.94	2.20	2.24	2.20	1.94
RT, occupied	Cremer, 300 mus. & chorus	1964	2.40	2.00	1.90	2.00	1.95	1.70
	Tachibana	1986	1.90	2.00	1.85	1.95	1.90	1.80
	Matsuzawa	1989	2.20	1.81	1.79	1.71	1.71	1.61
	BeSB, 80% occupancy	1992	2.20	1.90	1.90	2.00	1.80	1.50
	Selected average		2.10	1.85	1.85	1.95	1.80	1.60
EDT, unoccupied	BeSB	1990	2.00	1.70	1.90	2.00	1.90	1.30
	BeSB	1992	2.10	1.60	1.80	1.90	1.90	1.60
	Takenaka	1993	2.05	1.92	2.09	2.14	2.09	1.82
$IACC_A$, unoccupied	Takenaka	1993	0.93	0.76	0.31	0.22	0.27	0.27
$IACC_E$, unoccupied	Takenaka	1993	0.96	0.88	0.60	0.50	0.53	0.45
$IACC_L$, unoccupied	Takenaka	1993	0.90	0.68	0.18	0.11	0.10	0.08

Column heads 125–4,000: Center frequencies of filter bands

Attribute	Measured by	Year of data	125	250	500	1,000	2,000	4,000
			Center frequencies of filter bands					
40. BERLIN, PHILHARMONIE, *continued*								
C_{80}, dB, unoccupied	BeSB	1990	-	-	0.70	0.70	0.70	-
	Takenaka	1993	–2.20	–0.70	–0.70	–0.40	–0.50	0.00
G, dB, unoccupied	Takenaka	1993	4.20	3.40	4.90	4.90	4.10	3.70
	(See Chapter 9 for compromise average of *G*.)							
41. BONN, BEETHOVENHALLE (Opened 1959, 1,407 Seats)								
RT, unoccupied	M.A.A. (Meyer & Kuttruff)	1959	2.20	2.10	2.00	1.90	2.10	1.80
	(After a fire, new seats and some sound absorbing material were installed.)							
	Kuttruff	1984	1.80	1.80	1.80	1.80	1.80	1.50
RT, occupied	M.A.A. (Meyer & Kuttruff)	1959	2.00	1.65	1.70	1.70	1.75	1.65
	Estimate after revisions	1995	1.80	1.70	1.65	1.65	1.60	1.55
42. LEIPZIG, GEWANDHAUS (Opened 1981, 1,900 Seats)								
RT, unoccupied	Fasold	1982	1.95	2.00	2.20	2.20	2.00	1.70
RT, occupied	Fasold	1982	1.95	2.00	2.00	2.05	1.90	1.70
43. MUNICH, HERKULESSAAL (Opened 1953, 1,287 Seats)								
RT, unoccupied	M.A.A. (various agencies)	1956	2.60	2.00	2.20	2.40	2.30	1.90
RT, occupied	M.A.A. (Mueller & BBN)	1960	2.00	1.75	1.85	1.85	1.80	1.65
	Matsuzawa	1985	2.04	2.01	1.88	1.63	1.76	1.37
44. MUNICH, PHILHARMONIE AM GASTEIG (Opened 1985, 2,487 Seats)								
RT, unoccupied	Mueller	1986	2.35	2.10	2.30	2.35	2.40	2.10
	Bradley	1987	2.28	2.10	2.18	2.16	2.18	1.88
	Gade	1987	2.40	2.15	2.20	2.20	2.20	1.90
	Tachibana	1986	2.45	2.25	2.20	2.25	2.35	2.00
	Average		2.37	2.15	2.22	2.24	2.28	1.97
RT, occupied	Mueller	1986	2.00	2.00	2.10	2.10	1.90	1.20
	Tachibana	1986	1.90	2.00	1.85	1.95	1.90	1.80
	Matsuzawa	1989	1.93	1.94	1.87	1.84	1.92	1.94
	Average		1.95	2.00	1.95	2.00	1.90	1.65
EDT, unoccupied	Bradley	1987	2.32	2.03	2.16	2.13	2.14	1.74
	Gade	1987	2.28	2.26	2.09	2.08	2.12	1.80
	Average		2.30	2.15	2.13	2.11	2.13	1.77
LF, unoccupied	Bradley	1987	0.13	0.13	0.14	0.12	0.10	0.18
	Gade	1987	0.12	0.13	0.11	0.08	-	-
C_{80}, dB, unoccupied	Bradley	1987	–4.51	–1.11	–0.44	0.38	–0.71	0.61
	Gade	1987	–5.02	–2.80	–0.51	–0.82	–1.95	–0.30
	Average		–4.77	–1.96	–0.48	–0.22	–1.33	0.16

Attribute	Measured by	Year of data	125	250	500	1,000	2,000	4,000
44. MUNICH, PHILHARMONIE AM GASTEIG, ***continued***								
G, dB, unoccupied	Bradley	1987	0.04	0.42	1.28	1.85	1.65	0.51
	Gade	1987	1.16	1.48	2.72	1.81	3.33	1.72
	Average		0.60	0.95	2.00	1.83	2.49	1.12
	(See Chapter 9 for compromise average of *G*.)							
45. STUTTGART, LIEDERHALLE, GROSSER SAAL (Opened 1956, 2,000 Seats)								
RT, unoccupied	M.A.A. (ITA)	1956	2.00	2.00	2.20	2.20	2.10	1.80
	Gade	1987	1.80	1.70	2.00	2.20	2.10	2.00
	Bradley	1987	1.73	1.80	2.05	2.13	2.13	1.88
	Average (Gade, Bradley)		1.77	1.75	2.03	2.17	2.12	1.94
RT, occupied	M.A.A. (ITA, large chorus)	1960	1.60	1.60	1.60	1.65	1.60	1.40
EDT, unoccupied	Gade	1987	1.65	1.65	2.09	2.21	2.18	1.78
	Bradley	1987	1.55	1.76	2.06	2.20	2.17	1.83
	Average		1.60	1.71	2.08	2.21	2.18	1.81
LF, unoccupied	Gade	1987	0.19	0.13	0.13	0.13	-	-
	Bradley	1987	0.08	0.12	0.13	0.12	0.09	0.16
	Average		0.14	0.13	0.13	0.13	-	-
C_{80}, dB, unoccupied	Gade	1987	−2.72	−0.36	2.09	2.01	−3.10	−0.54
	Bradley	1987	−1.85	−0.99	−1.04	−1.03	−1.15	−0.34
	Average		−2.29	−0.68	0.53	0.49	−2.13	−0.44
G, dB, unoccupied	Gade	1987	2.85	2.91	3.80	4.11	3.55	2.77
	Bradley	1987	2.63	3.34	3.63	3.08	1.10	−0.40
	Average		2.74	3.13	3.72	3.60	2.33	1.19
	(See Chapter 9 for compromise average of *G*.)							
46. BIRMINGHAM, SYMPHONY HALL (Opened 1991, 2,211 Seats)								
RT, unoccupied	ARTEC, Rev. doors open	1992	2.42	2.81	2.56	2.45	2.63	1.85
	ARTEC, Rev. doors closed		2.35	2.40	2.40	1.94	1.91	-
RT, occupied	Kimura	1992	2.05	1.95	1.80	1.90	1.85	1.65
EDT, unoccupied	ARTEC, Rev. doors open	1992	2.20	2.20	2.00	1.80	1.70	1.40
	ARTEC, Rev. doors closed		2.40	2.20	2.20	1.80	2.10	-
C_{80}, dB, unocc.	ARTEC, Rev. doors open	1992	−4.80	−1.30	−0.60	1.10	0.90	1.90
	ARTEC, Rev. doors closed	1992	−3.70	−1.30	−1.40	−1.00	−0.20	-
47. BRISTOL, COLSTON HALL (Opened 1951, 2,121 Seats)								
RT, unoccupied	M.A.A. (Somerville)	1953	2.40	2.10	2.10	2.20	2.25	1.85
	Barron	1982	2.17	1.85	2.00	2.01	1.93	-

Attribute	Measured by	Year of data	125	250	500	1,000	2,000	4,000
47. BRISTOL, COLSTON HALL, *continued*								
RT, occupied	M.A.A. (Parkin)	1951	1.85	1.70	1.70	1.70	1.60	1.35
EDT, unoccupied	Barron	1982	2.08	1.96	1.81	1.87	1.78	-
LF, unoccupied	Barron	1982	0.12	0.19	0.19	0.20	-	-
C_{80}, dB, unoccupied	Barron	1982	−2.50	−1.20	−0.10	0.40	1.10	-
G, dB, unoccupied	Barron	1982	4.40	2.80	4.70	5.60	4.40	-
(See Chapter 9 for compromise average of *G*.)								
48. CARDIFF, WALES, ST. DAVID'S HALL (Opened 1982, 1,952 Seats)								
RT, unoccupied	Barron	1982	1.83	1.98	2.07	2.15	2.10	-
	Gade	1986	1.95	2.00	2.10	2.25	2.15	1.75
	Average		1.89	1.99	2.09	2.20	2.13	1.75
RT, occupied	Sandy Brown Associates	1983	1.88	1.97	1.96	1.96	1.80	1.56
EDT, unoccupied	Barron	1982	1.90	2.13	2.11	2.14	2.11	-
	Gade	1986	1.93	2.10	2.01	2.03	2.01	1.68
	Average		1.91	2.12	2.06	2.08	2.06	1.68
LF, unoccupied	Barron	1982	0.17	0.14	0.19	0.16	-	-
	Gade	1986	0.15	0.19	0.18	0.15	-	-
	Average		0.16	0.17	0.19	0.16	-	-
C_{80}, dB, unoccupied	Barron	1982	−4.20	−1.50	−0.70	−0.50	−0.90	-
	Gade	1986	−2.31	−2.17	−1.04	−0.73	−0.88	−0.08
	Average		−3.26	−1.84	−0.87	−0.62	−0.89	-
G, dB, unoccupied	Barron	1982	2.00	0.40	2.80	3.60	3.00	-
	Gade	1986	2.34	1.92	3.92	3.26	2.37	-
(See Chapter 9 for compromise average of *G*.)								
49. EDINBURGH, USHER HALL (Opened 1914, 2,547 Seats)								
RT, unoccupied	M.A.A. (various agencies)	1958	2.50	2.55	2.60	2.45	2.30	1.90
(Seats were changed after 1958.)								
	Sandy Brown Assoc.	1991	1.83	1.97	2.06	2.31	2.15	1.71
	Barron	1982	1.96	2.00	2.00	2.09	1.95	-
	Gade	1986	1.97	2.00	2.00	2.08	1.95	-
	Average, Barron & Gade		1.97	2.00	2.00	2.09	1.95	-
RT, occupied	M.A.A. (Sommerville & Parkin)	1950	1.90	1.85	1.70	1.60	1.45	1.35
	Sandy Brown Assoc.	1991	1.73	1.77	1.40	1.13	1.02	0.87
EDT, unoccupied	Barron	1982	2.01	1.97	2.08	2.22	2.12	-
	Gade	1986	1.96	2.15	2.00	2.17	2.20	1.67
	Average		1.99	2.06	2.04	2.20	2.16	-
LF, unoccupied	Barron	1982	0.32	0.27	0.31	0.28	-	-
	Gade	1986	0.25	0.27	0.21	0.22	-	-
	Average		0.29	0.27	0.26	0.25	-	-

Attribute	Measured by	Year of data	125	250	500	1,000	2,000	4,000
			Center frequencies of filter bands					
49. EDINBURGH, USHER HALL, *continued*								
C_{80}, dB, unocc.	Barron	1982	−4.00	−2.30	−1.00	−1.50	−0.20	-
	Gade	1986	−1.34	−1.34	−1.58	−1.18	−1.92	−1.59
	Average		−2.67	−1.82	−1.29	−1.34	−1.06	−0.80
G, dB, unocc.	Gade	1986	3.33	2.89	4.24	3.85	2.68	0.18
	(See Chapter 9 for compromise average of G.)							
50. GLASGOW, SCOTLAND, ROYAL CONCERT HALL (Opened 1990, 2,459 Seats)								
RT, unoccupied	Barron	1990	2.32	2.15	1.99	1.87	1.71	-
	Sandy Brown Assoc.	1990	2.35	2.21	2.00	1.94	1.71	1.46
RT, occupied	Sandy Brown Assoc.	1990	2.04	1.88	1.76	1.74	1.67	1.44
EDT, unocc.	Barron	1990	2.27	1.97	1.78	1.67	1.53	-
LF, unocc.	Barron	1990	0.20	0.28	0.24	0.19	-	-
C_{80}, dB, unocc.	Barron	1990	−1.60	1.30	0.70	1.10	1.40	-
G, dB, unocc.	Barron	1990	1.30	1.60	2.40	0.80	1.70	-
	(See Chapter 9 for compromise average of G.)							
51. LIVERPOOL, PHILHARMONIC HALL (Opened 1939, 1,824 Seats)								
RT, unoccupied	M.A.A. (Somerville & Parkin)	1953	1.90	1.80	1.70	1.60	1.55	1.45
	Barron	1982	1.94	1.87	1.77	1.77	1.66	-
	Average		1.92	1.84	1.74	1.69	1.61	1.45
RT, occupied	M.A.A. (Parkin & BBN)	1950	1.50	1.50	1.50	1.50	1.40	1.25
EDT, unoccupied	Barron	1982	1.89	1.78	1.80	1.78	1.59	-
LF, unoccupied	Barron	1982	0.08	0.22	0.17	0.21	-	-
C_{80}, dB, unoccupied	Barron	1982	−2.90	−0.50	0.60	1.30	1.80	-
G, dB, unoccupied	Barron	1982	1.20	2.00	2.80	3.80	3.50	-
	(See Chapter 9 for compromise average of G.)							
52. LONDON, BARBICAN, LARGE CONCERT HALL (Opened 1982, 2,026 Seats)								
RT, unoccupied	Barron	1984	1.80	1.60	1.76	1.95	2.02	-
	Gade	1986	1.95	1.65	1.87	2.10	2.08	1.75
	Tachibana	1986	-	1.65	1.80	1.95	1.95	1.75
	Average		1.88	1.63	1.81	2.00	2.02	1.75
RT, occupied	ARUP Acoustics	1983	1.75	1.55	1.55	1.70	1.75	1.55
	Kimura	1992	1.75	2.20	1.75	1.70	1.55	1.40
	Average of pre-1994 data		1.75	1.88	1.65	1.70	1.65	1.48
	(Acoustical changes were made in summer 1994.)							
	Anonymous	1994	1.70	1.70	1.60	1.60	1.60	1.40
EDT, unoccupied	Gade	1986	1.84	1.66	1.86	1.97	2.07	1.81
	Barron	1984	1.92	1.82	1.84	1.96	2.04	-
			1.88	1.74	1.85	1.97	2.06	0.91
LF, unoccupied	Barron	1984	0.11	0.10	0.14	0.13	-	-
	Gade	1986	0.18	0.24	0.19	0.12	-	-
			0.15	0.17	0.17	0.13	-	-

Attribute	Measured by	Year of data	125	250	500	1,000	2,000	4,000
52. LONDON, BARBICAN, LARGE CONCERT HALL, *continued*								
C_{80}, dB, unoccupied	Barron	1984	−3.30	−0.90	−0.80	−1.00	−1.50	-
	Gade	1986	−2.34	−1.32	−1.28	−1.81	−2.21	−1.46
			−2.82	−1.11	−1.04	−1.41	−1.86	-
G, dB, unoccupied	Gade	1986	2.14	1.64	3.84	3.29	2.71	-
	Barron	1984	−0.40	−0.90	2.20	3.50	-	-
	(See Chapter 9 for compromise average of *G*.)							
53. LONDON, ROYAL ALBERT HALL (Opened 1871, 5,080 Seats)								
RT, unoccupied	Barron	1982	2.92	2.85	3.03	2.99	2.96	-
	Tachibana	1986	2.75	3.20	3.15	3.15	3.30	2.50
	Average		2.84	3.03	3.09	3.07	3.13	-
RT, occupied	Barron	1982	2.80	2.64	2.42	2.40	2.27	1.81
EDT, unoccupied	Barron	1982	2.53	2.54	2.67	2.63	2.62	-
LF, unoccupied	Barron	1982	0.13	0.16	0.14	0.13	0.14	-
C_{80}, dB, unoccupied	Barron	1982	−1.30	−1.10	0.00	1.00	0.60	-
G, dB, unoccupied	Barron	1982	−1.70	−1.90	−0.50	−0.90	−0.80	-
	(See Chapter 9 for compromise average of *G*.)							
54. LONDON, ROYAL FESTIVAL HALL (Opened 1951, 2,901 Seats)								
RT, unoccupied	Barron, Assist. Res. off	1982	1.43	1.44	1.62	1.76	1.80	1.70
	Gade, Assist. Res. off	1986	1.35	1.45	1.55	1.60	1.60	1.53
	BDP Acoustics, A. R. off	1994	1.60	1.50	1.60	1.70	1.70	1.50
	Average, assisted resonance off		1.46	1.46	1.59	1.69	1.70	1.58
	Barron, Assist. Res. on	1982	2.55	2.00	1.96	1.79	1.87	1.70
	BDP Acoustics, A. R. on	1994	2.40	2.00	1.80	1.70	1.70	1.60
	Average, assisted resonance on		2.48	2.00	1.88	1.75	1.79	1.65
RT, occupied	M.A.A., Assist. Res. Off	1959	1.35	1.35	1.45	1.50	1.40	1.30
	BRS, Assist. Res. Off	1970	1.35	1.35	1.36	1.51	1.46	1.32
	Average, assisted resonance off		1.35	1.35	1.41	1.51	1.43	1.31
	Kimura, Assist. Res. on	1992	1.95	1.60	1.50	1.50	1.40	1.25
	BDP Acoustics. A. R. on	1994	1.75	1.70	1.50	1.45	1.45	1.30
	Average, assisted resonance on		1.85	1.65	1.50	1.48	1.43	1.28
EDT, unoccupied	Barron, Assist. Res. off	1982	1.33	1.37	1.43	1.57	1.66	-
	Gade, Assist. Res. off	1986	1.15	1.41	1.37	1.32	1.42	1.37
	Barron, Assis. Res. on	1982	1.92	1.92	1.75	1.57	1.70	-

Attribute	Measured by	Year of data	125	250	500	1,000	2,000	4,000
			Center frequencies of filter bands					
LONDON, ROYAL FESTIVAL HALL, *continued*								
LF, unoccupied	Barron, Assist. Res. on	1982	0.18	0.14	0.19	0.20	-	-
C_{80}, dB, unoccup.	Barron, Assist. Res. off	1982	−0.70	−0.30	0.80	1.10	0.60	-
	Gade, Assist. Res. off	1986	−0.33	−0.11	0.40	1.64	0.76	0.51
	Barron, Assist. Res. on	1982	−3.90	−0.60	0.60	0.90	0.20	-
G, dB, unoccup.	Barron, Assis. Res. on	1982	−0.50	0.00	1.90	2.20	3.00	-
	Gade, Assist. Res. off	1986	0.18	0.96	2.10	1.79	1.59	-
	(See Chapter 9 for compromise average of *G*.)							
55. LONDON, ROYAL OPERA HOUSE (Opened 1958, 2,120 Seats)								
RT, unoccupied	M.A.A. (Parkin)	1952	1.40	1.40	1.40	1.40	1.40	1.40
	Barron	1982	1.30	1.26	1.19	1.23	1.16	1.05
RT, occupied	M.A.A. (Parkin)	1950	1.20	1.15	1.10	1.10	1.00	1.00
EDT, unoccupied	Barron, no overhung seats	1982	1.33	1.19	1.03	1.05	1.06	-
LF, unoccupied	Barron	1982	0.36	0.19	0.21	0.20	-	-
C_{80}, dB, unoccupied	Barron	1982	0.90	4.10	4.80	4.70	4.00	-
G, dB, unoccupied	Barron	1982	0.90	−3.10	0.40	0.90	−1.30	-
	(See Chapter 9 for compromise average of *G*.)							
56. MANCHESTER, FREE TRADE HALL (Opened 1951, 2,351 Seats)								
RT, unoccupied	M.A.A. (Somerville)	1952	2.25	2.00	2.20	2.20	2.20	1.80
	Barron	1982	1.38	1.53	1.70	1.84	1.64	-
RT, occupied	M.A.A. (Somerville)	1951	1.50	1.60	1.60	1.60	1.75	1.40
	Barron	1982	1.40	1.50	1.50	1.60	1.60	1.50
EDT, unoccupied	Barron	1992	1.47	1.47	1.65	1.77	1.62	-
LF, unoccupied	Barron	1992	0.33	0.25	0.25	0.24	-	-
C_{80}, dB, unoccupied	Barron	1992	−2.90	0.50	0.90	1.30	1.00	-
G, dB, unoccupied	Barron	1992	1.30	1.40	3.20	3.80	3.20	-
	(See Chapter 9 for compromise average of *G*.)							
57. BUDAPEST, PÁTRIA HALL IN CONVENTION CENTER (Opened 1985, 1,750 Seats)								
RT, unoccupied	Fasold	1985	2.10	2.39	1.81	1.81	1.67	1.47
RT, occupied	Fasold	1985	2.10	1.90	1.80	1.60	1.45	1.30
58. JERUSALEM, BINYANEI HA'OOMAH (Opened 1960, 3,142 Seats)								
RT, unoccupied	M.A.A. (BBN)	1960	2.70	2.40	2.30	2.20	2.00	1.80
	Klepper/Beranek	1994	2.36	1.83	1.88	1.71	1.32	1.18
RT, occupied	M.A.A. (BBN)	1960	2.20	2.00	1.75	1.75	1.65	1.50
	Klepper/Beranek	1995	2.20	2.10	1.75	1.75	1.50	1.40

Attribute	Measured by	Year of data	125	250	500	1,000	2,000	4,000
			Center frequencies of filter bands					
58. JERUSALEM, BINYANEI HA'OOMAH, ***continued***								
EDT, unoccupied	Klepper/Beranek	1994	2.30	1.93	1.89	1.80	1.40	1.12
$IACC_A$, unoccupied	Klepper/Beranek	1994	-	-	0.34	0.22	0.24	0.34
$IACC_E$, unoccupied	Klepper/Beranek	1994	-	-	0.55	0.40	0.40	0.48
$IACC_L$, unoccupied	Klepper/Beranek	1994	-	-	0.22	0.11	0.11	0.16
C_{80}, dB, unoccupied	Klepper/Beranek	1994	−0.80	−2.20	−1.10	0.30	1.50	3.00
59. TEL AVIV, FREDRIC R. MANN AUDITORIUM (Opened 1957, 2,715 Seats)								
RT, unoccupied	M.A.A. (BBN)	1957	1.80	1.65	1.95	2.00	1.85	1.60
	Klepper/Beranek	1994	1.62	1.56	1.67	1.67	1.56	1.35
RT, occupied	M.A.A. (BBN)	1957	1.55	1.50	1.55	1.55	1.50	1.30
	Klepper	1995	1.70	1.50	1.50	1.50	1.30	-
EDT, unoccupied	Klepper/Beranek	1994	1.54	1.60	1.66	1.73	1.57	1.36
$IACC_A$, unoccupied	Klepper/Beranek	1994	-	-	0.46	0.31	0.32	0.22
$IACC_E$, unoccupied	Klepper/Beranek	1994	-	-	0.71	0.55	0.50	0.36
$IACC_L$, unoccupied	Klepper/Beranek	1994	-	-	0.25	0.11	0.09	0.08
C_{80}, dB, unoccupied	Klepper/Beranek	1994	0.20	−0.50	−1.30	−0.50	0.50	0.60
60. MILAN, TEATRO ALLA SCALA (Opened 1778, 2,289 Seats)								
RT, unoccupied	M.A.A. (Paolini)	1947	1.85	1.50	1.35	1.35	1.20	1.15
	Takenaka	1993	1.81	1.57	1.40	1.31	1.22	1.11
RT, occupied	M.A.A. (BBN, Furrer & Reichardt)	1959	1.50	1.40	1.25	1.15	1.10	1.00
EDT, unoccupied	Takenaka	1993	1.47	1.22	1.20	1.17	1.15	1.05
$IACC_A$, unoccupied	Takenaka	1993	0.94	0.79	0.42	0.35	0.41	0.41
$IACC_E$, unoccupied	Takenaka	1993	0.96	0.84	0.54	0.49	0.53	0.48
$IACC_L$, unoccupied	Takenaka	1993	0.92	0.73	0.36	0.16	0.13	0.10
C_{80}, dB, unoccupied	Takenaka	1993	1.00	1.40	2.00	3.80	4.70	4.40
G, dB, unoccupied	Takenaka	1993	−1.30	−1.80	−1.70	−1.10	−1.50	−3.00
	(See Chapter 9 for compromise average of *G*.)							
61. OSAKA, SYMPHONY HALL (Opened 1982, 1,702 Seats)								
RT, unoccupied	Tachibana	1986	2.05	1.95	2.20	2.20	2.15	1.85
RT, occupied	Anonymous	1990		500 Hz to 1,000 Hz = 1.8 sec				
EDT, unoccupied	Tachibana	1986		300 Hz to 1,400 Hz = 2.1 sec				
C_{80}, dB, unoccupied	Tachibana	1986		300 Hz to 1,400 Hz = −1.18 dB				
$IACC_A$, unoccupied	Tachibana	1986		300 Hz to 1,400 Hz = 0.22				
62. TOKYO, BUNKA KAIKAN (Opened 1961, 2,327 Seats)								
RT, unoccupied	NHK	1961	2.70	2.00	2.00	2.00	1.80	1.50
	Nagata	1984	2.50	2.00	1.90	1.90	1.60	1.20
	Nagata	1993	2.20	1.90	2.00	2.00	2.00	1.80
	TAK (no stage enclosure)	1989	2.15	1.85	1.75	1.87	1.75	1.35
	Takenaka	1995	1.92	1.79	1.89	1.99	1.95	1.78
Best estimate with hall in concert configuration			2.1	1.85	1.95	2.00	2.00	1.80

Attribute	Measured by	Year of data	Center frequencies of filter bands 125	250	500	1,000	2,000	4,000
62. TOKYO, BUNKA KAIKAN, *continued*								
RT, occupied	Nagata	1993	1.90	1.50	1.50	1.50	1.40	1.30
	Anonymous	1994	2.05	1.81	1.58	1.48	1.37	1.30
	Average		1.98	1.66	1.54	1.49	1.39	1.30
$IACC_A$, unoccupied	Takenaka	1995	-	-	0.30	0.20	0.18	0.18
$IACC_E$, unoccupied	Takenaka	1995	-	-	0.51	0.38	0.34	0.30
$IACC_L$, unoccupied	Takenaka	1995	-	-	0.20	0.10	0.09	0.08
LF, unoccupied	Takenaka	1995	0.17	0.17	0.19	0.19	0.22	0.25
C_{80}, dB, unoccupied	Nagata	1993	–2.90	–1.24	–0.08	–1.72	–1.23	–0.08
	Takenaka	1995	–1.30	–0.80	–0.30	–1.00	–0.80	0.00
G, dB, unoccupied	Takenaka	1995	3.30	3.40	4.20	4.30	4.40	5.50
(See Chapter 9 for compromise average of *G*.)								
63. TOKYO, HAMARIKYU ASAHI HALL (Opened 1992, 552 Seats)								
RT, unoccupied	Takenaka	1992	1.63	1.68	1.83	1.93	1.90	1.71
RT, occupied	Takenaka	1992	1.63	1.57	1.65	1.80	1.74	1.58
EDT, unoccupied	Takenaka	1992	1.53	1.72	1.82	1.80	1.75	1.62
EDT, occupied	Takenaka	1992	1.51	1.63	1.64	1.76	1.65	1.50
$IACC_A$, unoccupied	Takenaka	1992	-	-	0.22	0.15	0.12	0.11
$IACC_A$, occupied	Takenaka	1992	-	-	0.25	0.09	0.12	0.14
$IACC_E$, unoccupied	Takenaka	1992	-	-	0.40	0.29	0.21	0.17
$IACC_E$, occupied	Takenaka	1992	-	-	0.34	0.18	0.22	0.22
$IACC_L$, unoccupied	Takenaka	1992	-	-	0.17	0.14	0.09	0.07
$IACC_L$, occupied	Takenaka	1992	-	-	0.23	0.07	0.07	0.07
C_{80}, dB, unoccupied	Takenaka	1992	–0.30	–1.90	–1.20	0.00	0.60	0.30
C_{80}, dB, occupied	Takenaka	1992	–1.70	–1.10	–0.80	0.10	0.60	1.10
G, dB, unoccupied	Takenaka	1992	7.50	7.60	9.80	10.00	10.80	11.30
G, dB, occupied	Takenaka	1992	4.30	4.40	6.00	7.20	8.70	11.40
(See Chapter 9 for compromise average of *G*.)								
64. TOKYO, METROPOLITAN ART SPACE (Opened 1990, 2,017 Seats)								
RT, unoccupied	Nagata	1993	2.80	2.60	2.60	2.60	2.40	2.10
RT, occupied	Nagata, calculated	1993	2.60	2.30	2.10	2.10	2.00	1.70
	Matsuzawa	1993	2.50	2.23	2.17	2.19	2.08	1.91
EDT, unoccupied	Nagata	1993	2.80	2.70	2.60	2.50	2.40	2.00
$IACC_A$, unoccupied	Takenaka	1995	-	-	0.29	0.19	0.21	0.22
$IACC_E$, unoccupied	Takenaka	1995	-	-	0.48	0.37	0.37	0.35
$IACC_L$, unoccupied	Takenaka	1995	-	-	0.19	0.10	0.09	0.07
C_{80}, dB, unoccupied	Nagata	1993	–5.88	–3.55	–0.85	–1.50	–1.07	–0.30
G, dB, unoccupied	Takenaka	1995	4.50	4.20	3.90	4.50	4.50	4.90
(See Chapter 9 for compromise average of *G*.)								
65. TOKYO, NHK HALL (Opened 1973, 3,677 Seats)								
RT, unoccupied	NHK Laboratories	1973	2.30	1.90	1.90	2.00	1.90	1.60
	NHK Laboratories	1988	2.50	2.00	1.90	2.10	2.10	1.70
	Average		2.40	1.95	1.90	2.05	2.00	1.65
RT, occupied	Anonymous	1994	1.77	1.64	1.63	1.72	1.75	1.52
C_{80}, dB, unoccupied	NHK Laboratories	1973	–2.10	–0.10	0.00	0.00	0.00	0.00

Attribute	Measured by	Year of data	Center frequencies of filter bands					
			125	250	500	1,000	2,000	4,000
66. TOKYO, ORCHARD HALL, BUNKAMURA (Opened 1989, 2,150 Seats)								
RT, unoccupied	Ishi (22,500 m^3, large orchestra)	1989	2.29	2.25	2.22	2.27	2.28	2.04
	Ishi (18,490 m^3, chamber orch.)	1989	2.25	2.17	2.08	2.13	2.09	1.88
RT, occupied	Ishi (22,500 m^3 w/65 orch.)	1989	1.90	2.01	1.88	1.92	1.91	1.69
	Matsuzawa (Symph. concert)	1990	-	1.85	1.73	1.70	1.55	1.44
	Anonymous-1 (concert)	1992	2.11	2.04	1.87	1.78	1.70	1.40
	Anonymous-2 (concert)	1994	1.96	1.95	1.83	1.77	1.64	1.42
	Average 1992–1994		2.04	2.00	1.85	1.78	1.67	1.41
C_{80}, dB, unoccupied	Ishi (largest stage)	1989	-	-	−2.85	-	−1.58	-
	Ishi (smallest stage)	1989	-	-	0.05	-	0.74	-
67. TOKYO, SUNTORY HALL (Opened 1986, 2,006 Seats)								
RT, unoccupied	Tachibana	1986	2.35	2.40	2.50	2.60	2.60	2.15
	Nagata	1986	2.40	2.60	2.60	2.60	2.60	2.40
RT, occupied	Tachibana	1986	2.20	2.10	2.00	2.00	1.90	1.75
	Matsuzawa	1990/93	2.26	2.11	1.93	1.99	1.97	1.77
	Anonymous	1994	2.14	2.08	1.95	2.03	2.00	1.77
	Average		2.20	2.10	1.96	2.01	1.96	1.76
EDT, unoccupied	Nagata	1986	2.30	2.40	2.30	2.60	2.50	1.90
IACC$_A$, unoccupied	Takenaka	1995	-	-	0.30	0.20	0.21	0.22
IACC$_E$, unoccupied	Takenaka	1995	-	-	0.53	0.45	0.42	0.39
IACC$_L$, unoccupied	Takenaka	1995	-	-	0.22	0.11	0.07	0.05
LF, unoccupied	Takenaka	1995	0.16	0.15	0.17	0.16	0.18	0.19
C_{80}, dB, unoccupied	Nagata	1986	−3.81	−2.68	−0.85	−0.91	−1.00	−0.31
G, dB, unoccupied	Takenaka	1995	3.30	3.80	4.60	5.30	5.40	5.60
	(See Chapter 9 for compromise average of G.)							
68. MEXICO CITY, SALLA NEZAHUALCOYOTL (Opened 1976, 2,376 Seats)								
RT, unoccupied	Jaffe	1994	2.80	2.50	2.20	2.20	2.00	1.60
RT, occupied	Jaffe	1994	2.20	2.30	2.00	1.90	1.80	1.70
69. AMSTERDAM, CONCERTGEBOUW (Opened 1888, 2,037 Seats)								
RT, unoccupied	Takenaka	1993	2.68	2.53	2.59	2.63	2.43	2.05
	Bradley	1987	2.60	2.40	2.50	2.53	2.35	1.97
	Tachibana	1986	2.80	2.65	2.65	2.75	2.45	1.85
	Gade	1987	2.62	2.47	2.45	2.55	2.33	1.97
	Average		2.68	2.51	2.55	2.62	2.39	1.96
RT, occupied	Tachibana	1986	2.20	2.15	2.05	1.95	1.80	1.55

Attribute	Measured by	Year of data	125	250	500	1,000	2,000	4,000
			Center frequencies of filter bands					
69. AMSTERDAM, CONCERTGEBOUW, *continued*								
EDT, unoccupied	Takenaka	1993	2.51	2.47	2.58	2.64	2.44	1.98
	Bradley	1987	2.51	2.39	2.54	2.57	2.36	1.93
	Gade	1987	2.82	2.65	2.64	2.78	2.47	2.10
	Average		2.61	2.50	2.59	2.66	2.42	-
$IACC_A$	Takenaka	1993	0.91	0.69	0.21	0.17	0.27	0.28
$IACC_E$	Takenaka	1993	0.94	0.78	0.46	0.42	0.51	0.44
$IACC_L$	Takenaka	1993	0.90	0.66	0.15	0.10	0.07	0.06
LF, unoccupied	Bradley	1987	0.16	0.17	0.20	0.17	0.14	0.23
	Gade	1987	0.21	0.12	0.18	0.17	-	-
	Average		0.19	0.15	0.19	0.17	0.14	0.23
C_{80}, dB, unoccupied	Takenaka	1993	−5.20	−4.40	−3.90	−2.60	−1.70	−0.80
	Bradley	1987	−5.09	−4.80	−3.91	−2.60	−2.42	−1.38
	Gade	1987	−5.91	−4.80	−4.75	−4.02	−3.84	−2.22
	Average		−5.40	−4.67	−4.19	−3.07	−2.65	−1.47
G, dB, unoccupied	Takenaka	1993	5.80	5.90	6.20	6.50	5.80	4.90
	Bradley	1987	5.46	4.99	5.37	5.71	5.23	4.20
	Gade	1987	3.88	4.72	5.87	5.07	6.13	-
	(See Chapter 9 for compromise average of *G*.)							
70. ROTTERDAM, DE DOELEN, CONCERTGEBOUW (Opened 1966, 2,242 Seats)								
RT, unoccupied	Hak & Martin	1992	2.00	2.00	2.40	2.30	2.30	1.90
RT, occupied	Kimura	1992	1.90	2.00	2.00	2.10	2.00	1.85
EDT, unoccupied	Hak & Martin	1992	2.30	2.20	2.30	2.30	2.10	1.60
C_{80}, dB, unoccupied	Hak & Martin	1992	−6.50	−3.60	−2.90	−2.80	−2.70	−1.00
71. CHRISTCHURCH, TOWN HALL (Opened 1972, 2,662 Seats)								
RT, unoccupied	Marshall	1972	2.90	2.57	2.74	2.75	2.58	1.94
	[In 1977 a large reflector was hung over the orchestra (see text).]							
	Yamasaki	1992	2.60	2.20	2.35	2.35	2.20	1.70
	Marshall	1994	2.54	2.39	2.50	2.40	2.29	1.88
RT, occupied	Marshall	1972	2.46	2.27	2.42	2.27	2.10	1.64
	[In 1977 a large reflector was hung over the orchestra (see text).]							
	Marshall (Estimated)	1994	2.15	2.11	2.21	1.98	1.86	1.59
	Estimated (EDT–0.1 sec)	1994	2.10	1.70	1.80	1.80	1.70	1.40
EDT, unoccupied	Marshall	1972	2.65	2.20	2.40	2.57	2.45	1.80
	[In 1977 a large reflector was hung over the orchestra (see text).]							
	Barron (w/o overhung seats)	1983	1.97	1.77	2.03	2.14	2.11	-
	Barron (w/overhung seats)	1983	1.88	1.72	1.94	2.07	2.06	-
	Marshall	1994	2.17	1.77	1.90	1.88	1.81	1.53
LF, unoccupied	Barron	1983	0.16	0.15	0.14	0.14	-	-
C_{80}, dB, unoccupied	Marshall	1972	−1.10	−1.20	−3.20	−4.00	-	-
	[In 1977 a large reflector was hung over the orchestra (see text).]							
	Marshall	1994	−2.50	0.20	1.30	1.90	1.30	2.00

Attribute	Measured by	Year of data	125	250	500	1,000	2,000	4,000
72. GOTHENBURG, KONSERTHUS (Opened 1935, 1,286 Seats)								
RT, unoccupied	M.A.A. (Brand & Jordan)	1958	2.50	2.00	1.90	2.10	1.90	1.60
(New seats and other changes made after 1960.)								
	Gade	1988	2.12	1.86	1.76	1.65	1.58	1.52
RT, occupied	M.A.A. (Kuhl & Ingemansson)	1960	1.90	1.70	1.70	1.70	1.55	1.45
	Estimated	1994	1.80	1.70	1.65	1.60	1.50	1.40
EDT, unoccupied	Gade	1988	1.99	1.83	1.78	1.71	1.63	1.49
LF, unoccupied	Gade	1988	0.11	0.07	0.09	0.11	-	-
C_{80}, dB, unoccupied	Gade	1988	−3.13	−0.92	−0.05	0.18	0.90	1.02
G, dB, unoccupied	Gade	1988	5.78	6.24	4.87	4.54	3.13	1.59
(See Chapter 9 for compromise average of *G*.)								
73. BASEL, STADT–CASINO (Opened 1876, 1,448 Seats)								
RT, unoccupied	Takenaka	1993	2.78	2.74	2.31	2.31	2.23	1.90
RT, occupied	Beranek	1965	2.20	2.00	1.80	1.75	1.60	1.50
EDT, unoccupied	Takenaka	1993	2.55	2.62	2.19	2.20	2.13	1.79
$IACC_A$, unoccupied	Takenaka	1993	0.90	0.72	0.22	0.13	0.17	0.18
$IACC_E$, unoccupied	Takenaka	1993	0.89	0.78	0.46	0.34	0.33	0.29
$IACC_L$, unoccupied	Takenaka	1993	0.90	0.69	0.17	0.09	0.07	0.06
C_{80}, dB, unoccupied	Takenaka	1993	−4.10	−4.50	−3.20	−2.00	−1.70	−0.70
G, dB, unoccupied	Takenaka	1993	9.10	8.90	7.90	8.30	7.70	7.20
(See Chapter 9 for compromise average of *G*.)								
74. ZURICH, GROSSER TONHALLESAAL (Opened 1895, 1,546 Seats)								
RT, unoccupied	Takaneka	1991	3.59	3.60	3.27	3.09	2.59	2.12
RT, occupied	Beranek	1965	2.50	2.40	2.15	1.95	1.75	1.62
EDT, unoccupied	Takenaka	1991	3.58	3.77	3.21	3.02	2.58	2.01
$IACC_A$, unoccupied	Takenaka	1991	0.89	0.68	0.21	0.11	0.15	0.15
$IACC_E$, unoccupied	Takenaka	1991	0.93	0.79	0.48	0.27	0.33	0.28
$IACC_L$, unoccupied	Takenaka	1991	0.89	0.66	0.16	0.09	0.09	0.06
C_{80}, dB, unoccupied	Takenaka	1991	−5.80	−6.80	−4.40	−3.60	−2.80	−1.50
G, dB, unoccupied	Takenaka	1991	9.00	8.90	8.90	8.20	8.30	7.90
(See Chapter 9 for compromise average of *G*.)								
75. TAIPEI, CULTURAL CENTRE, CONCERT HALL (Opened 1987, 2,074 Seats)								
RT, unoccupied	Kuttruff	1987	2.45	2.35	2.4	2.4	2.35	2.15
RT, occupied	Kuttruff	1987	1.95	1.97	2.05	2.00	1.95	1.80
76. CARACAS, AULA MAGNA (Opened 1954, 2660 Seats)								
RT, unoccupied	M.A.A. (BBN)	1954	2.50	2.25	1.85	1.75	1.90	1.70
RT, occupied	M.A.A. (BBN)	1954	1.90	1.40	1.30	1.20	1.00	0.90

Attribute	Measured by	Year of data	125	250	500	1,000	2,000	4,000
CONCERT HALLS FOR WHICH ACOUSTICAL DATA ONLY ARE AVAILABLE								
77. AMERICA: AKRON, E. J. THOMAS PERFORMING ARTS HALL								
RT, unoccupied	Bradley	1992	2.59	2.10	1.99	1.79	1.52	1.32
EDT, unoccupied	Bradley	1992	2.15	1.98	1.81	1.67	1.47	1.24
$IACC_A$, unoccupied	Bradley	1992	0.95	0.84	0.44	0.40	0.23	0.24
$IACC_E$, unoccupied	Bradley	1992	0.96	0.91	0.67	0.62	0.38	0.38
$IACC_L$, unoccupied	Bradley	1992	0.92	0.79	0.28	0.18	0.10	0.10
LF, unoccupied	Bradley	1992	0.09	0.07	0.07	0.09	0.13	0.08
C_{80}, dB, unoccupied	Bradley	1992	−2.07	−1.33	0.13	0.82	0.82	1.81
G, dB, unoccupied	Bradley	1992	−0.41	0.84	2.29	1.69	−0.67	−2.60
	(See Chapter 9 for compromise average of G.)							
78. AMERICA: DETROIT, ORCHESTRA HALL								
RT, unoccupied	Bradley	1992	2.92	2.36	2.01	1.94	1.76	1.57
EDT, unoccupied	Bradley	1992	2.60	2.10	1.80	1.80	1.78	1.61
$IACC_A$, unoccupied	Bradley	1992	0.93	0.77	0.29	0.23	0.19	0.17
$IACC_E$, unoccupied	Bradley	1992	0.94	0.82	0.48	0.42	0.31	0.29
$IACC_L$, unoccupied	Bradley	1992	0.93	0.75	0.21	0.11	0.11	0.07
LF, unoccupied	Bradley	1992	0.18	0.16	0.14	0.17	0.21	0.14
C_{80}, dB, unoccupied	Bradley	1992	−2.72	−1.87	−0.75	0.00	0.48	1.11
G, dB, unoccupied	Bradley	1992	4.20	3.32	3.40	3.65	2.36	1.07
	(See Chapter 9 for compromise average of G.)							
79. AMERICA: WAHINGINGTON, D.C., J. F. KENNEDY CENTER FOR THE PERFORMING ARTS, CONCERT HALL (Opened 1971, 2,759 Seats)								
RT, unoccupied	Bradley	1992	1.90	1.95	2.07	1.99	1.83	1.65
	Gade	1992	1.89	1.86	1.90	1.88	1.78	1.56
	Average		1.90	1.91	1.99	1.94	1.81	1.61
RT, occupied	Harris, modified by unoccup. data	1992	1.80	1.80	1.90	1.80	1.60	1.40
EDT, unoccupied	Bradley	1992	1.61	1.61	1.81	1.81	1.67	1.46
	Gade	1992	1.72	1.65	1.70	1.74	1.66	1.44
$IACC_A$, unoccupied	Bradley	1992	0.94	0.73	0.25	0.23	0.20	0.16
$IACC_E$, unoccupied	Bradley	1992	0.94	0.74	0.42	0.40	0.36	0.30
$IACC_L$, unoccupied	Bradley	1992	0.93	0.73	0.19	0.10	0.09	0.10
LF, unoccupied	Bradley	1992	0.18	0.17	0.17	0.20	0.24	0.17
	Gade	1992	0.19	0.28	0.24	0.27	0.26	0.11
C_{80}, dB, unoccupied	Bradley	1992	−1.87	−0.81	−0.69	−0.12	0.25	0.17
	Gade	1992	−1.03	−0.60	−0.32	−0.51	−0.39	0.13
	Average	1992	−1.45	−0.71	−0.51	−0.32	−0.07	0.15
G, dB, unoccupied	Bradley	1992	1.79	1.78	2.73	2.71	1.75	0.01
	Gade	1992	2.44	2.97	2.98	1.66	2.76	−0.06
	(See Chapter 9 for compromise average of G.)							

Attribute	Measured by	Year of data	125	Center frequencies of filter bands 250	500	1,000	2,000	4,000
80. CANADA: BRANDON, MANITOBA, WESTERN MANITOBA CENTENNIAL AUDITORIUM								
RT, unoccupied	Bradley	1992	2.85	1.91	1.37	1.16	1.04	0.93
EDT, unoccupied	Bradley	1992	2.38	1.65	1.30	1.15	1.02	0.93
$IACC_A$, unoccupied	Bradley	1992	0.94	0.80	0.36	0.45	0.31	0.30
$IACC_E$, unoccupied	Bradley	1992	0.95	0.88	0.59	0.62	0.45	0.39
$IACC_L$, unoccupied	Bradley	1992	0.93	0.74	0.16	0.17	0.11	0.09
LF, unoccupied	Bradley	1992	0.19	0.12	0.08	0.07	0.06	0.06
C_{80}, dB, unoccupied	Bradley	1992	–2.32	0.57	2.90	3.55	4.32	4.14
G, dB, unoccupied	Bradley	1992	3.20	2.88	2.48	0.87	–0.64	–1.82
(See Chapter 9 for compromise average of G.)								

Appendix 5
Sound Absorption Data for Seats, Both Occupied and Unoccupied, and for Materials of Inner Surfaces

INTRODUCTION

Sound absorption by different types of chairs, by audiences seated in these chairs, and by materials of the interior surfaces of halls, has been treated by a number of authors (Kath and Kuhl, 1965; Bradley, 1992, 1994; Davies and Orlowski, 1990; Kosten, 1965; and Beranek, 1969). These studies, for the most part, report on comparisons of absorption coefficients measured in laboratory test chambers with those made in large halls. The principal difficulty with laboratory tests is that the diffusion of sound in a reverberation chamber is different from that in a hall for music. To complicate matters, measurements made to determine how much sound the overall surfaces of large halls absorb are few in number because they must be performed after all interior finishes have been completed, but before the seats are installed—a condition generally not encountered.

The first part of this study was devoted to the determination of sound absorption coefficients for the surfaces in each of five halls in which acoustical measurements had been carried out before installation of the chairs. Next, using an unusual technique, average sound absorption coefficients for the non-seated areas in 15 typical halls were determined and compared with those for the five halls just mentioned. Finally, also with this technique, the sound absorption coefficients for the seating areas, both fully occupied and unoccupied, were derived. These data are vastly different from previously published audience and unoccupied chair data and fill a troublesome void.

When investigating the sound absorbing properties of surfaces and seating areas in actual halls, the choice of reverberation equation (Sabine vs. Eyring) is important.

Table A5.1. Air Attenuation Coefficient multiplied by 4, yielding $4m$ in units of m^{-1} for an ambient temperature of about 20°C for four relative humidities (ISO, 1990).

	$4m$			
	Frequency, Hz			
Relative Humidity	**500**	**1,000**	**2,000**	**4,000**
50%	0.0024	0.0042	0.0089	0.0262
60%	0.0025	0.0044	0.0085	0.0234
70%	0.0025	0.0045	0.0081	0.0208
80%	0.0025	0.0046	0.0082	0.0194

The generic reverberation equation is,

$$\mathrm{RT} = 0.163\ V / (A + 4mV)\ , \tag{A5.1}$$

where V is the volume of the room in m^3; A is the total sound absorption in the room comprised of the absorption by the seats (occupied or unoccupied), interior surfaces, added absorbing materials, chandeliers, statues, etc., in units of m^2; m is the energy attenuation constant for sound traveling through air in units of m^{-1} as taken from ISO (1990). Values of $4m$ are tabulated in Table A5.1 for normal room temperature.

If the total surface area S (in m^2) of a room and its subcomponents are known, the Sabine and Eyring sound absorption coefficients are related to the total sound absorption A through the equations,

Sabine: $$A = S\,[\alpha_{\mathrm{Sab}}]\ , \tag{A5.2}$$

Eyring: $$A = S\,[-2.30 \log_{10} (1 - \alpha_{\mathrm{Eyr}})]\ . \tag{A5.3}$$

Thus, the two coefficients are related by,

$$\alpha_{\mathrm{Sab}} = -2.3 \log_{10} (1 - \alpha_{\mathrm{Eyr}})\ . \tag{A5.4}$$

α_{Sab} is always larger than α_{Eyr}, and conversion can be made with Table A5.2. For simplicity, the Sabine equation is adopted in this book with no sacrifice in accuracy.

Table A5.2. Relation between Sabine and Eyring sound absorption coefficients.

α_{Sab}	0.10	0.20	0.30	0.40	0.50	0.60	0.70	0.80	0.90
α_{Eyr}	0.10	0.18	0.26	0.33	0.39	0.45	0.50	0.55	0.59

The total Sabine absorption can be subdivided,

$$S\,[\alpha_{Sab}] = S_T\alpha_T + S_R\,\alpha_R + S_M\,\alpha_M + \text{----}, \tag{A5.5}$$

where S_T is the "acoustical area" over which the audience chairs sit, occupied or unoccupied, plus the stage area when the orchestra is present (see Appendix 1 for a detailed definition of S_T); S_R is the actual area of all other surfaces in the room except the areas over which the audience and orchestra sit, including underbalcony soffits and all of the aisle areas; and S_{M1}, S_{M2}, S_{M3}, etc., are areas of special absorbing materials like rugs, draperies and acoustical tiles. Each of the types of absorbing area S_T, S_R, and S_M has its associated absorption coefficient.

It is essential, when computing reverberation times using the values of α that are given in this book, to employ Sabine equations (A5.1), (A5.2), and (A5.5).

It has been established that in a large hall for musical performances the absorbing power of a seated audience, chorus and orchestra, or empty upholstered seats, increases in direct proportion to the floor area they occupy, almost independent of the number of seated persons or chairs in that area, provided the seats are nearly 100% occupied or unoccupied (Beranek, 1969 and Kosten, 1965). This hypothesis is valid for seating densities in the range of 0.45 to 0.79 m of floor space per person and for halls with normally diffuse sound fields. No attempt has been made to extend the applicability of these data to small auditoriums, classrooms, or churches, where the state of sound diffusion or the seating density may be substantially different.

It will be shown that the sound absorption by an audience is strongly influenced by the type of chair in which it is seated, a result that is also found in reverberation chamber measurements.

EQUIVALENT SOUND ABSORPTION COEFFICIENTS

In Chapter 8, a simple relation between the reverberation times at mid-frequencies (average of RT's at 500 and 1,000 Hz) of concert halls and V/S_T was shown to be given by the following equation and depicted in Fig. 8.3.

$$\text{RT} = 0.14\ V/S_T. \tag{A5.6}$$

Basically, this equation assumes that the mid-frequency occupied sound absorption by an audience in upholstered chairs is 0.85, and that about 75% of the total sound absorption in a hall is contributed by the audience and orchestra and the remaining 25%

by the surfaces of the hall, including walls, ceiling, doors, ventilation openings, chandeliers, statues, glass, and small areas of acoustical materials to control echoes.

In the early stages of design, this equation gives the acoustical consultant and the architect a simple way of determining the volume of a hall once the desired reverberation time, the number of seats, the row-to-row spacing, and the seat-to-seat dimensions are decided upon. It must be remembered that S_T also includes the area the orchestra occupies.

Let us now define an equivalent sound absorption coefficient α_{eq} (Kosten, 1965),

$$RT = 0.163\ V / (\alpha_{eq} S_T)\ , \tag{A5.7}$$

where *all the absorption in the room* is assigned to the seating and orchestra area, S_T. Combining this equation with Eqs. (A5.1), (A5.2), and (A5.5),

$$\alpha_{eq} = [\ \alpha_T + 4m(\ V/S_T)] +\ \alpha_R (S_R/S_T)\ , \tag{A5.8}$$

If the α_{eq}'s for the individual halls in a group of halls, either occupied or unoccupied, are plotted against (S_R/S_T) at each frequency and a straight line is drawn through the points, the intercept of this line at $(S_R/S_T) = 0$ yields $[\ \alpha_T + 4m(V/S_T)]$ and the slope of the line determines α_R. Of course, the α_T's and α_R's determined by this procedure are averages for the group of halls plotted.

RESIDUAL ABSORPTION: COMPLETED HALLS, NO CHAIRS

Only five halls used for music could be located where construction and interior finishing had been completed and acoustical measurements made before chairs were installed. Using Eqs. (A5.1), (A5.2), and (A5.5), the residual absorption coefficients α_R for these halls were directly determined and are shown in Table A5.3.

As already stated, the absorption of usual doors, ventilating grilles, statues, glass, chandeliers, and small areas of sound-absorbing material used for echo control were averaged into the residual absorption α_R as though they were part of the surfaces S_R of the interior. The areas of under-balcony soffits were included. Any special areas of sound absorbing materials, usually carpets, were given the absorption coefficients of Table A5.7 and their total absorption removed from the analysis.

The residual absorption coefficients determined for these five halls are presented in Table A5.3. Descriptions of the five individual halls are also made at the end of the table for aid in applying the data.

Table A5.3. Residual absorption coefficients α_R measured in five concert halls, measured before installation of seats, and α_R derived from the studies of this Appendix. The five actual hall types are listed in ascending order of α_R's. The derived α_R of this Appendix is listed as Type A. Special combinations may be made by comparison.

Frequency	125	250	500	1,000	2,000	4,000
Type 1	0.09	0.07	0.05	0.04	0.04	0.04
Type 2	0.13	0.10	0.08	0.08	0.07	0.06
Type 3	0.14	0.10	0.08	0.08	0.08	0.07
Type 4	0.16	0.13	0.10	0.09	0.08	0.07
Type 5	0.20	0.15	0.10	0.09	0.08	0.07
Type A	0.14	0.12	0.10	0.09	0.08	0.07

Definitions: *Type 1*: All surfaces at least 1.5 in. (3.8 cm) plaster, or plaster on concrete block; no added sound absorbing materials; aisles covered with vinyl tile or linoleum; stage floor of thick wood. *Type 2:* Side walls of the stage a mixture of 1.5 in. (3.8 cm) and 0.5 in. wood; floor of stage of thinner wood than most stages; balcony floors are 0.5 in. (1.25 cm) wood over airspace; aisles with 0.3 in. thick carpet cemented to concrete, no underpad; numerous and large ventilator openings in ceiling; tops of balcony railings are padded velour. *Type 3:* Similar to Types 1 and 2 combined except for numerous lighting fixtures in coves of ceiling and more openings for lines and light fixtures. *Type 4:* Same as Type 1, except at least 25% of the side wall surfaces are 0.5 in. gypsum board; floor of stage of wood; floors parquet; some sound absorbing materials used to control echoes; ceiling 0.75 in. (1.8 cm) plaster. *Type 5:* Side walls of auditorium of 0.39 in. (1 cm) plywood; side walls and ceiling of stage are of thin wood; ceiling 1 in. (2.5 cm) plaster; carpet with underlining on aisles; back walls covered with carpet to control echoes. Type A: Described in Appendix 5 text.

NOTE: Carpet *under* the seats is considered as part of the sound absorption coefficient α_T of the seating areas. Draperies, aisle carpets and QRD reflectors are included as separate areas S_M with their own absorption coefficients α_M.

Fifteen halls in this book were selected for the studies that follow. The choice was made in part by plotting V/S_T against S_R/S_T for all the halls and selecting only those halls where the values fell within a narrow range, indicating that there are negligible areas of special sound absorbing surfaces in the room. Also, the halls chosen were only those for which the acoustical data were obtained by actual measurements and not from calculations, estimates, or extrapolations, and where particular measured quantities did not look unreasonable. Finally, the halls were selected to give three levels of chair upholstering.

For these halls the average α_R's were derived by the slope method of Eq. (A5.8). At mid-frequencies (500/1,000 Hz), the procedure was reasonably accurate. However, at 125 and 4,000 Hz the straight line had to be drawn through a scatter of points. The range of α_R's so obtained was later narrowed by application to specific halls. The final coefficients are listed as Type A in Table A5.3. They are reasonably close to the Type 1 to 4 coefficients for four of the five halls.

SEAT ABSORPTION: HALLS, WITH CHAIRS INSTALLED

The absorption coefficients for chairs in unoccupied seating areas, with three levels of upholstering, were derived by utilizing the Type A residual absorption data of Table A5.3 and the measured unoccupied reverberation times for the selected 15 halls in Eqs. (A5.1), (A5.2), and (A5.5). The outcome is presented in Table A5.4. Parenthically, four of the 15 halls exhibit excess absorption at 250 Hz: Rotterdam, Berlin (Philharmonie), Stuttgart, and Bristol (see Fig. 14.2).

Table A5.4. Chair absorption coefficients α_T derived from the acoustical reverberation times presented in Appendix 4 and the use of Eqs. (A5.7) and (A5.8). The 15 halls listed represent unoccupied chairs with three degrees of upholstering and were selected because the data were judged reliable and were not extrapolated, computed, or estimated, and no significant amounts of added acoustical materials are known to exist in the halls for which adjustments could not be made.

	Frequency					
Halls	125	250	500	1,000	2,000	4,000
Heavily Upholstered Chairs						
Cleveland, Severance Hall	0.57	0.74	0.83	0.89	0.91	0.85
Rotterdam, De Doelen	0.88	0.94	0.79	0.86	0.75	0.76
Edmonton, Jubilee Hall	0.60	0.72	0.79	0.83	0.93	0.89
Salzburg, Festspielhaus	0.76	0.66	0.71	0.76	0.75	0.74
Berlin, Philharmonie	0.80	0.93	0.84	0.85	0.75	0.69
Average	0.72	0.80	0.79	0.84	0.82	0.79
Average from smoothed curve	**0.72**	**0.79**	**0.83**	**0.84**	**0.83**	**0.79**
Medium Upholstered Chairs						
Buffalo, Kleinhans Hall	0.31	0.50	0.58	0.71	0.68	0.63
Stuttgart, Liederhalle	0.73	0.80	0.70	0.66	0.60	0.52
New York, Avery Fisher	0.64	0.67	0.65	0.66	0.63	0.60
Bristol, Colston Hall	0.52	0.77	0.75	0.78	0.74	-
Liverpool, Philharmonic Hall	0.56	0.64	0.74	0.80	0.77	0.75
Average	0.55	0.68	0.68	0.72	0.68	0.62
Average from smoothed curve	**0.56**	**0.64**	**0.70**	**0.72**	**0.68**	**0.62**
Lightly Upholstered Chairs						
Boston, Symphony Hall	0.60	0.59	0.61	0.56	0.46	0.37
Basel, Stadt-Casino	0.33	0.41	0.65	0.68	0.62	0.61
Berlin, Konzerthaus	0.36	0.46	0.64	0.72	0.70	0.67
Vienna, Gr. Musikvereinssaal	0.33	0.39	0.46	0.50	0.51	0.56
Amsterdam, Concertgebouw	0.40	0.54	0.60	0.61	0.60	0.62
Average	0.36	0.45	0.59	0.61	0.58	0.57
Average from smoothed curve	**0.35**	**0.45**	**0.57**	**0.61**	**0.59**	**0.55**

NOTE: The seats in Boston, Symphony Hall, are mounted on 0.75 in. boards over large airspace. Hence, 125–250 Hz are disregarded.

These seat absorption curves differ markedly from those developed in earlier studies (Beranek, 1969 and 1992), which gave values for "upholstered seats, unoccupied" at 125 to 4000 Hz, as 0.19, 0.37, 0.56, 0.67, 0.61, and 0.59, respectively.

AUDIENCE AND ORCHESTRA ABSORPTION: 100% OCCUPANCY

The same procedure as detailed in the two previous sections was used to determine the audience and orchestra absorption coefficients for the selected 15 halls, fully

Table A5.5. Audience absorption coefficients α_T derived from the acoustical reverberation times presented in Appendix 4 with the use of Eqs. (A5.7) and (A5.8). The 15 halls listed represent three degrees of upholstering and were selected because the data were judged reliable and were not extrapolated, computed, or estimated, and no significant amounts of added acoustical materials are known to exist in the halls for which adjustments could not be made.

	Frequency					
Halls	125	250	500	1,000	2,000	4,000
Heavily Upholstered Chairs						
Cleveland, Severence Hall	0.65	0.78	0.92	0.99	1.02	0.96
Rotterdam, De Doelen	0.85	0.84	0.89	0.86	0.83	0.77
Edmonton, Jubilee Hall	0.91	0.83	0.88	0.95	0.93	0.98
Salzburg, Festspielhaus	0.69	0.78	0.89	0.91	0.92	0.90
Berlin, Philharmonie	0.70	0.81	0.88	0.85	0.86	0.87
Average	0.76	0.81	0.89	0.91	0.91	0.89
Average from smoothed curve	**0.76**	**0.83**	**0.88**	**0.91**	**0.91**	**0.89**
Medium Upholstered Chairs						
Buffalo, Kleinhans Hall	0.56	0.62	0.85	0.90	0.89	0.95
Stuttgart, Liederhalle	0.73	0.78	0.83	0.82	0.79	0.83
New York, Avery Fisher	0.86	0.80	0.84	0.89	0.82	0.65
Bristol, Colston Hall	0.62	0.71	0.77	0.81	0.82	0.92
Liverpool, Philharmonic Hall	0.74	0.78	0.82	0.85	0.86	0.90
Average	0.70	0.73	0.82	0.85	0.84	0.85
Average from smoothed curve	**0.68**	**0.75**	**0.82**	**0.85**	**0.86**	**0.86**
Lightly Upholstered Chairs						
Boston, Symphony Hall	0.64	0.75	0.81	0.83	0.89	0.88
Basel, Stadt-Casino	0.45	0.60	0.77	0.83	0.87	0.82
Berlin, Konzerthaus	0.56	0.67	0.79	0.82	0.87	0.88
Vienna, Gr. Musikvereinssaal	0.53	0.63	0.76	0.83	0.86	0.85
Amsterdam, Concertgebouw	0.60	0.69	0.81	0.91	0.93	0.99
Average	0.56	0.67	0.79	0.83	0.87	0.86
Average from smoothed curve	**0.56**	**0.68**	**0.79**	**0.83**	**0.86**	**0.86**

NOTE: The Amsterdam data at 1,000–4,000 Hz seem unreasonably high and are disregarded. There are high-frequency absorbing materials that were not separately calculated.

Table A5.6. Difference between the sound absorption coefficients of an audience (chairs 100% occupied) and the same chairs unoccupied.

Type of Chairs	Frequency Region		
	Low Frequencies	Middle Frequencies	High Frequencies
Heavily Upholstered	0.04	0.06	0.09
Medium Upholstered	0.11	0.13	0.16
Lightly Upholstered	0.22	0.22	0.29

Table A5.7. Absorption coefficients for: (1) occupied audience, orchestra, and chorus areas with total "acoustical" area S_T (see Appendix 1 for definition); (2) unoccupied chairs in large hall with "acoustical" area as in (1); (3) total residual absorption coefficient α_R as derived from reverberation data on 15 halls (see Appendix 1 for definition); (4) to (16) absorption coefficients taken from the literature. All absorption coefficients must be used in Sabine's equation.

Description (see caption above)	Absorption coefficients at indicated frequencies					
	125 Hz	250 Hz	500 Hz	1,000 Hz	2,000 Hz	4,000 Hz
(1) Audience,						
Heavily upholstered	0.76	0.83	0.88	0.91	0.91	0.89
Medium upholstered	0.68	0.75	0.82	0.85	0.86	0.86
Lightly upholstered	0.56	0.68	0.79	0.83	0.86	0.86
(2) Seats, unoccupied						
Heavily upholstered	0.72	0.79	0.83	0.84	0.83	0.79
Medium upholstered	0.56	0.64	0.70	0.72	0.68	0.62
Lightly upholstered	0.35	0.45	0.57	0.61	0.59	0.55
(3) Average total residual absorption for 15 halls	0.14	0.12	0.10	0.09	0.08	0.07
(4) Plaster, 1.2 in. (3 cm) on metal lath	0.14	0.10	0.06	0.05	0.04	0.03
(5) Gypsum Board, 2 layers, total 1.25 in. (3.2 cm)	0.28	0.12	0.10	0.17	0.13	0.09
(6) Wood, 1 in. (2.5 cm) with airspace	0.19	0.14	0.09	0.06	0.06	0.05
(7) Thin plywood paneling	0.42	0.21	0.10	0.08	0.06	0.06
(8) Concrete Block, with or w/o plaster, painted	0.11	0.08	0.07	0.06	0.05	0.05
(9) Glass, heavy	0.18	0.06	0.04	0.03	0.02	0.02
(10) Concrete floor	0.01	0.01	0.02	0.02	0.02	0.02
(11) Linoleum on concrete	0.02	0.03	0.03	0.03	0.03	0.03
(12) Wood parquet on concrete	0.04	0.04	0.07	0.06	0.06	0.07
(13) Board on joist floor	0.15	0.20	0.10	0.10	0.10	0.10
(14) Carpet, heavy, cemented to concrete	0.02	0.06	0.14	0.37	0.60	0.65
(15) Carpet, heavy, over foam rubber	0.08	0.24	0.57	0.69	0.71	0.73
(16) Carpet, thin, cemented to concrete	0.02	0.04	0.08	0.20	0.35	0.40

occupied. The outcome is tendered in Table A5.5. The differences between the average values before and after occupancy at low, mid, and high frequencies are given in Table A5.6.

No experiments have been conducted with and without an orchestra seated on the stage of an otherwise fully occupied concert hall. Thus, the two are assumed to have the same sound absorption coefficients per unit area, except that for the orchestra no area addition is made at the edges of the seating area.

ABSORPTION COEFFICIENTS FOR COMMON ARCHITECTURAL MATERIALS: HISTORICAL VALUES

Sound absorption coefficients for common architectural materials are contained in Fry (1988), Harris (1991), and Beranek (1992). Average values from those sources are offered in Table A5.7. It is assumed that these coefficients are valid for use in the Sabine equation, although the literature makes no mention of their applicability to calculations of reverberation times in large halls. Because the absorption by an audience plus orchestra constitutes about 75% of the total absorption in a room, any Sabine/Eyring differences in the residual absorption coefficients for these surfaces will not noticeably affect the calculated reverberation times.

Smoothed values of the absorption coefficients for chairs, occupied and unoccupied, taken from Tables A5.4 and A5.5, are also included in Table A5.7 for convenience.

References

Ando, Y. (1985). *Concert Hall Acoustics*, (Springer–Verlag, Berlin).

Barron, M. (1971). "The subjective effects of first reflections in concert halls—The need for lateral reflections," J. Sound Vib. **15**, 475–494.

Barron, M. (1988). "Subjective study of British symphony concert halls," Acustica **66**, 1–14.

Barron, M. and Marshall, A. H. (1981). "Spatial impression due to early lateral reflections in concert halls," J. Sound Vib. 77, 211–232.

Barron, M. (1993). *Auditorium Acoustics and Architectural Design*, (E & FN Spon), Chapman & Hall, London & New York.

Barron, M. (1995). "Balconies in concert halls," Proceedings of the 15th International Congress on Acoustics, Trondheim, Norway, June.

Beranek, L. L. (1962). *Music, Acoustics, and Architecture* (Wiley, New York). In Japanese (1972) translated with modifications and added Appendix 4 by M. Nagatomo (Kajima Institute, Tokyo).

Beranek, L. L. (1969). "Audience and chair absorption in large halls: II", J. Acoust. Soc. Am. **45**, 13–19.

Beranek, L. L. (1992). "Concert Hall Acoustics—1992," J. Acoust. Soc. Am. **92**, 1–39.

Beranek, L. L. (1994). "The acoustical design of concert halls," J. of Building Acoustics **1**, 3–25.

Bradley, J. S. (1991). "A comparison of three classical concert halls," J. Acoust. Soc. Am. **89**, 1176–1192.

Bradley, J. S. (1992). "Predicting theatre chair absorption from reverberation chamber measurements, " J. Acoust. Soc. Am. **91**, 1514–1524.

Bradley, J. S. (1994). "Reply to reports on [Bradley, 1992]", J. Acoust. Soc. Am. 1155–1157.

Bradley, J. S. (1994). "Comparison of concert hall measurements of spatial impression," J. Acoust. Soc. Am. **96**, 3525–35.

Bradley, J. S. (1994). *Data from 13 North American Concert Halls*, Internal Report No. 668, National Research Council of Canada, Ottawa K1A OR6, July. (Partially funded by the Concert Hall Research Group.)

Cremer, L. and Mueller, H. (1982). *Principles and Applications of Room Acoustics, Vol. 1*, English translation with additions by T. J. Schultz (Applied Science Publishers, Essex, England) and in USA and Canada (Elsevier, New York). Originally published in German (1978) by Hirzel, Stuttgart.

Davies, W. J. and Orlowski, R. J. (1990). "Methods of measuring acoustic absorption of auditorium seating," Proc. Institute of Acoustics (U.K.) **12**, 299–306.

Egan, M. D. (1988). *Architectural Acoustics*, McGraw Hill, N.Y.

Forsyth, M. (1985). *Buildings for Music*, MIT Press, Cambridge, MA, USA.

Fry, A. (1988). *Noise Control*, Pergamon Press, Oxford & N.Y.

Gade, A. C. (1985). "Objective measurements in Danish concert halls," Proc. Inst. Acoust. 7, 9–16.

Gade, A. C. (1989a). "Acoustical survey of eleven European concert halls," Report No. 44, The Acoustics Laboratory, Technical University of Denmark, Copenhagen.

Gade, A. C. (1989b). "Investigations of musicians' room acoustic conditions in concert halls," Acustica **69**, 193–203 and 249–262.

Gade, A. C. (1991). "Prediction of room acoustical parameters," J. Acoust. Soc. Am. **89**, 1857(A).

Haan, C. H. and Fricke, F. R. (1993). "Surface diffusivity as a measure of the acoustic quality of concert halls," Proceedings of Conference of the Australia and New Zealand Architectural Science Association, Sydney, 81–90.

Haan, C. H. and Fricke, F. R. (1995). "Musician and music critic responses to concert hall acoustics," Proceedings of 15th International Congress on Acoustics, Trondheim, Norway, June.

Harris, C. (1991). *Handbook of Acoustical Measurements & Noise Control*, McGraw-Hill, N.Y.

Hidaka, T., Beranek, L., and Okano, T. (1995). "Interaural cross-correlation (IACC), lateral fraction (LF) and sound energy level (G) as partial measures of acoustical quality in concert halls," J. Acoust. Soc. Am. **98**, 988–1007, June.

ISO (1990). "Attenuation of sound during propagation outdoors, Part 1," ISO/DIS 9613-1. International organization for Standardization, CH-1211 Geneva 20, Switzerland.

Johnson, F.R., Beranek, L. L., Newman, R. B., Bolt, R. H., and Klepper, D. L. (1961). "Orchestra enclosure and canopy for the Tanglewood Music Shed," J. Acoust. Soc. Am. **33**, 475–481.

Kath, U. and Kuhl, W. (1965). "Messungen zur Schallabsorption von Polsterstühlen mit und ohne Personen," Acustica **15**, 127–131.

Kimura, S. and Sekiguchi, K. (1976). "Study on criteria for acoustical design of rooms by subjective evaluation of room acoustics," (in Japanese), J. Acoust. Soc. Jpn. **32**, 606–614.

Kosten, C. W. (1965). "New method for the calculation of the reverberation time of halls for public assembly," Acustica **16**, 325–330.

McAdams, S. (1982). "Spectral fusion and the creation of auditory images," in *Music, Mind and Brain: the Neuropsychology of Music* (Plenum, New York), Chap. XV.

Marshall, A. H. (1967). "A note on the importance of room cross-section in concert halls," J. Sound Vib. **5**, 100–112.

Marshall, A. H. (1968). "Acoustical determinants for the architectural design of concert halls," Arch. Sci. Rev., Australia **11**, 81–87.

Marshall, A. H. (1979). "Acoustical design and evaluation of Christchurch Town Hall, New Zealand," J. Acoust. Soc. Am. **65**, 951–957.

Marshall, A. H. (1990). "Recent developments in acoustical design process," Applied Acoustics **31**, 7–28.

Meyer, J. (1994). *Akustik und Musicalische Auffuerung-practice.* (E. Bochinsky, Frankfurt am Main, 3rd Ed.; and (1993), "The sound of the orchestra," J. Audio Eng. Soc. **41**, 203–213.

Morgan, M. H. (1960). *Vitruvius—the Ten Books on Architecture,* Dover Publications (1960).

Nakamura, S., Kan, S., and Nagatomo, M. (1991). "Subjective evaluation of acoustics of hall stages by players of symphonic orchestras." (Personal communication.)

Okano, T., Hidaka, T., and Beranek, L., (1994). "Relations between the apparent source width (ASW) of the sound field in a concert hall and its sound pressure level at low frequencies (GL) and its interaural cross-correlation coefficient (IACC), Presented at the 128th Meeting of the Acoustical Society of America, Austin, Texas, 30 November 1994. (Submitted to ASA for possible publication.)

Orcutt, W. D. (1933). *Wallace Clement Sabine, A Biography* (out of print), Plympton Press, Norwood, MA.

Potter, J. M. (1993). *On the binaural modelling of spaciousness in room acoustics,* doctoral thesis at the Technical University of Delft, 27 April, 132 pages. (In press)

Sabine, W. C. (1922). *Collected Papers on Acoustics,* (Harvard U. Press), reprinted in 1992 by Peninsula Publishing, P.O. Box 867, Los Altos, CA 94023-9912.

Schroeder, M. R. (1965). "New method of measuring reverberation time," J. Acoust. Soc. Am. **37**, 409–412.

Schroeder, M. R. (1986). *Number Theory in Science and Communications,* 2nd Ed., Springer, Berlin [Original work on QRD diffusers in J. Acoust. Soc. Am. **65**, 958–963 (1979)].

Schroeder, M. R., Gottlob, D., and Siebrasse, K. F. (1974). "Comparative study of European concert halls: Correlation of subjective preference with geometric and acoustic parameters," J. Acoust. Soc. Am. **56**, 1195ff.

Schultz, T. J. and Watters, B. G. (1964). "Propagation of sound across audience seating," J. Acoust. Soc. Am. **36**, 885–896.

Sessler, G. M. and West, J. E. (1964). "Sound transmission over theatre seats," J. Acoust. Soc. Am. **36**, 1725–1732.

Tachibana, H., Yamasaki, Y., Morimoto, M., Hirasawa, Y., Maekawa, Z., and Poesselt, C. (1989). "Acoustic survey of auditoriums in Europe and Japan," J. Acoust. Soc. Jpn. **10**, 73–85.

Vian, J. P. and Pelorsen, X. (1991). "Auditorium acoustics: What should we measure? What do we measure and what does it mean?" J. Acoust. Soc. Am. **89**, 1856 (A).

Wilkens, H. (1975). "Mehrdunebsuibake Beschreibung subjektiver Beurteilungen der Akustik von Konzertsaelen," Dissertation, Technical Univ., Berlin.

Yamamoto, T. and Suzuki, F. (1976). "Multivariate analysis of subjective measures for sound in rooms and the physical values of room acoustics" (in Japanese), J. Acoust. Soc. Jpn. **32**, 599–605.

NAME INDEX

SUBJECT INDEX

Index to Tables and Formulas Useful in Calculations:

General Index:

A

D

E

M

S

ACOUSTICAL SOCIETY OF AMERICA

Publications, CDs, and Videos on Music, Acoustics, and Architecture

For current prices and ordering information call or write to the Acoustical Society of America, 500 Sunnyside Blvd., Woodbury, NY 11797, Tel. 516-576-2360; Fax: 516-576-2377; E-mail: asa@aip.org.

Acoustical Design of Music Education Facilities, Edward R. McCue and Richard H. Talaske, Eds. Plans, photographs, and descriptions of fifty music education facilities from around the world, with supplementary explanatory text and essays on the design process. 236 pp. paperback 1990

Acoustical Designing in Architecture, Vern O. Knudsen and Cyril M. Harris. A comprehensive, non-mathematical treatment of architectural acoustics, this volume covers general principles of acoustical designing with specific applications. 408 pp. paperback 1980 (originally published in 1950).

Acoustical Measurements, Leo Beranek. Completely revised edition of a classic text with more than half the pages and chapters revised or completely rewritten to cover new developments in acoustical instruments and measurement procedures. 841 pp. hardcover 1989 (originally published 1948).

Acoustics, Leo Beranek. An indispensable source of practical acoustical concepts and theory, with new information on microphones, loudspeakers and speaker enclosures, room acoustics, and acoustical applications of electro-mechanical circuit theory. 491 pp. hardcover 1986 (originally published 1954).

Acoustics—An Introduction to Its Physical Principles and Applications, Allan D. Pierce. A textbook introducing the physical principles and theoretical basis of acoustics, concentrating on concepts and points of view that have proven useful in applications such as noise control, architectural acoustics, and audio engineering. 678 pp. hardcover 1989 (originally published 1981).

Acoustics of Auditoriums in Public Buildings, Leonid I. Makrinenko, John S. Bradley, Ed. Developments resulting from studies of building physics are presented in this book which attempts to elucidate problems related to acoustical quality in halls of public buildings in terms of the current state of the art in architectural acoustics. 172 pp. hardcover 1994 (originally published 1986).

Acoustics of Worship Spaces, David Lubman and Ewart A. Wetherill, Eds. Drawings, photographs, and accompanying data of existing worship houses provide vital information on problems and answers concerning the acoustical design of chapels, churches, mosques, temples and synagogues. 91 pp. paperback 1985.

ASA Edition of Speech and Hearing in Communication, Harvey Fletcher; Jont B. Allen, Ed. Summary of Harvey Fletcher's 33 years of acoustics work at Bell Labs. A new introduction, index and complete bibliography of Fletcher's work are important additions to this classic volume. 487 pp. hardcover 1995 (originally published in 1953).

Collected Papers on Acoustics, Wallace Clement Sabine. Classic work on acoustics for architects and acousticians. 304 pp. hardcover 1993 (originally published 1921).

Concert and Opera Halls—How They Sound, Leo Beranek. Gives answers to the questions: How do concert halls compare? Which ones are rated the world's best? What are the acoustical and architectural features of the world's most famous halls? Illustrated with 203 architectural drawings of 76 halls of music and 152 photographs of these halls and 47 other illustrations. 643 pp. hardcover 1996.

Electroacoustics: The Analysis of Transduction and Its Historical Background, Frederick V. Hunt. A comprehensive analysis of the conceptual development of electroacoustics including the origins of echo ranging, the crystal oscillator, the evolution of the dynamic loudspeaker, and electromechanical coupling. 260 pp. paperback 1982 (originally published 1954).

Experiments in Hearing, George von Békésy. A classic in the literature on hearing containing some of the vital roots of contemporary auditory knowledge. 760 pp. paperback 1989 (originally published 1960).

Halls for Music Performance: Two Decades of Experience, 1962–1982, Richard H. Talaske, Ewart A. Wetherill and William J. Cavanaugh, Eds. With drawings, photographs, and technical and physical data on 80 halls, this volume examines standards of quality and technical capabilities of performing arts facilities. 192 pp. paperback 1982.

Hearing: Its Psychology and Physiology, Stanley Smith Stevens and Hallowell Davis. This volume leads readers from the fundamentals of the psychophysiology of hearing to a complete understanding of the anatomy and physiology of the ear, including the relationship between stimulus and sensation. 512 pp. paperback 1983 (originally published 1938).

Origins in Acoustics, Frederick V. Hunt. A history of acoustics from antiquity to the time of Isaac Newton, this volume surveys sources beginning with the ancient Greeks and Romans, and documents experiments and observations by scholars from the Arab world during the Dark Ages and by pre-Newtonian scientists in Europe. 224 pp. hardcover 1992 (originally published 1978).

Papers in Speech Communication. Three-volume series containing reprint papers charting four decades of progress in understanding the nature of human speech production and perception, and in applying this knowledge to problems of speech processing. Contains important papers from a wide range of journals from such fields as engineering, linguistics, physics, psychology, and speech and hearing science. Sold in three-volume set or individually.

Speech Production, Raymond D. Kent, Bishnu S. Atal, Joanne L. Miller, Eds. 880 pp. hardcover 1991.

Speech Perception, Joanne L. Miller, Raymond D. Kent, Bishnu S. Atal, Eds. 874 pp. hardcover 1991.

Speech Processing, Bishnu S. Atal, Raymond D. Kent, Joanne L. Miller, Eds. 672 pp. hardcover 1991.

Proceedings of the Wallace Clement Sabine Centennial Symposium, J. David Quirt, Ed. Papers presented at the symposium held 5–7 June 1994. 393 pp. paperback 1994.

Research Papers in Violin Acoustics, Carleen M. Hutchins, Ed. Two-volume set relates the development of the violin to the scientific advances as well as the musical climate of each era from the early 15th Century to the present. Includes over 120 papers with an annotated bibliography of over 400 references on subjects such as the bowed string, the bow, wood, varnish, and psychoacoustic research. 1600 pages approx., hardcover, to be published March 1996.

Theaters for Drama Performance: Recent Experience in Acoustical Design, Richard H. Talaske and Richard E. Boner, Eds. Plans, photographs, and descriptions of theater designs by acoustical consultants from North America and abroad, supplemented by essays on theater design and an extensive bibliography. 167 pp. paperback 1987.

Vibration and Sound, Philip M. Morse. This publication provides students and professionals with the broad spectrum of acoustics theory, including wave motion, radiation problems, the propagation of sound waves, and transient phenomena. 468 pp. hardcover 1981 (originally published 1936).

Auditory Demonstrations on Compact Disc, A. J. M. Houtsma, T. D. Rossing and W. M. Wagenaars, Eds. This classic collection contains interesting auditory demonstrations which are educational for the scientist as well as the lay person interested in how the human ear perceives sounds. Included on the 39 tracks are demonstrations on frequency analysis, the decibel, loudness, masking, pitch, critical bands, timbre, beats and binaural effects. A text booklet is provided which contains an introduction to each of the topics and bibliographies to obtain more detailed information. Issued in 1989.

Video on Measuring Speech Production, Maureen Stone, producer. A three-tape collection of demonstrations for use in teaching courses on speech acoustics, physiology and instrumentation. A text booklet describing the demonstrations and bibliographies for obtaining additional information is included. Issued in 1993.